MW01253799

Decided for You Cookbook

365 Dinners including your Grocery List

YOU NEVER HAVE TO COOK THE SAME THING TWICE FOR ONE ENTIRE YEAR

by Betty Hughes

© 2005 Betty Hughes. All Rights Reserved.

No part of this book may be reproduced, stored in a retrieval system, or transmitted by any means without the written permission of the author.

First published by AuthorHouse 03/12/05

ISBN: 1-4208-2431-7 (sc)

Printed in the United States of America
Bloomington, Indiana

This book is printed on acid-free paper.

authorHOUSE™

1663 LIBERTY DRIVE, SUITE 200
BLOOMINGTON, INDIANA 47403
(800) 839-8640
WWW.AUTHORHOUSE.COM

About the Author

Just wanted to let you know that the author, Betty Hughes, is a retired, working mother who learned that it was much easier in her 49 years of marriage to write down a weekly menu before going grocery shopping. This prevented stopping at the store several times a week to pick up a few non-related, unplanned items. Also, the posted menu on her refrigerator allowed her husband and two children to know in advance what was for dinner in case they didn't want to eat a particular scheduled item. Having a planned meal, versus impromptu, also cut down on precious minutes each day because it was known what food preparation had to be started first.

Because she was a working mother most of the weekday meals, depicted in this cookbook, can be created in less than 35 minutes. This allows all of you who use the cookbook more free time.

The author has also said, "She's not a Gourmet Cook, or a Dietician," just an organized mother of two who planned on cooking what her average family "<u>WANTED TO EAT</u>" versus what was "<u>ONLY GOOD FOR THEM TO EAT!</u>"

DECIDED FOR YOU COOK BOOK
-365 DINNERS -

By Betty Hughes – Initially Created October 1980 for Michelle, Revised 2004

Author's Note: This **COLLECTION OF 365 Recipes** - one year's supply of menus, one for every day so **YOU WILL NEVER COOK THE SAME THING TWICE**, unless you want too. It **includes a weekly grocery/marketing list** and some hints **DEVELOPED for the BEGINNER**, shortcuts using package mixes for **the WORKING PERSON** to create quicker meals, or ideas for **the one STAY-AT-HOME PERSON** who's bored with what he/she has been cooking, but has the time and the desire to make the recipe from scratch into "Little Masterpieces" at lower costs.

Even if you use only portions of this cookbook, I feel, you will also develop a pattern of planning which will save you time, food, and money. Many times through lack of planning we waste all of these. By projecting your menus, you can **utilize left-overs as plan-overs**; you won't buy foods, which will never be used (losing their value), and you will be sure you have everything in your kitchen necessary to complete your meals. If you begin using the menus on the correct fiscal week, your Thanksgiving Turkey recipe will fall into that special week of celebration, other Holidays are not taken into consideration.

Expense of acquiring required spices may add to your initial expenditure, but one container will last several meals. In preparing your grocery list, **check your stock and size needed against the grocery list and recipes in the book** to be sure what, if any, will be necessary to purchase. **If an item is used in more than one recipe, a number** (2) and (R) **will appear** (2R) indicating the ingredient is required in recipes twice this week. **Salt and Pepper is an understood necessity and "not listed in the grocery list"** unless it is a specially required type. For quick and handy seasoning while cooking, keep on hand a large shaker containing six parts of salt and one of pepper. Reference to **Green Salad** in the menu is shown on the grocery list to **include Iceberg Lettuce, Radishes, Onions and Tomatoes**, unless otherwise noted. The green salad can be replaced by purchasing prepared mixed salads (modern convenience) instead of using just the Iceberg Lettuce. **Salad Dressing for salads is also "understood as your choice" and not listed on the grocery list**, unless otherwise specified. Vegetable Oil is shown, but it's your choice if you want to change this out for an Olive Oil or another oil of choice.

Write up your grocery list in the **same order as** your **grocery store aisles are laid out** to **SAVE SHOPPING TIME,** and it is **"absolutely essential"** to go to the store **with a written list**.

The **menus/recipes are annotated to the left with abbreviations** so it will be **easier to find the recipe** as the **cookbook is indexed by groupings** (BF) Beef or Veal, (BRD) Bread Items, (CH) Chicken, (CRNBF) Corned Beef, (LAMB) Lamb, (MISC) Miscellaneous (meatless, or more than two meats), (PAS) Pasta, (PK) Pork or Ham, (SALAD) Salads, (SAUCES) Sauces, (SEA) Seafood, (SOUP) Soup (TUR) Turkey, (VEG) Vegetables, (WNR) Wieners. This group name will help you when you try to find if you have a particular supply of certain kind of meat, or lack of meat, and want to find out how many different ways you can use it.

There are also a few "extra" recipes especially in some of the sections that new cooks will need to know about. I wanted to offer some extra recipes in case you need to substitute one for the other assigned menu choices that your family might not be willing to eat.

I hope you **ENJOY** the use of **this cookbook** made **for the BASIC, SIMPLE, AND HOMEY, "ORDINARY FAMILY TASTES" on an everyday budget.**

Acknowledgment

DEDICATED TO MY DAUGHTER

Michelle Lavay

**Who inspired the need for the completion of this
collection of recipes. Without her encouragement,
it could not have been done.**

ALL MY LOVE,

ETERNALLY,

**Mom
October 1980/2004 Rev 1**

Words of Wisdom for Cooking

- **ACCIDENTAL LEFT-OVERS SHOULD BE ON PURPOSE** to **save shopping or cooking time**. Especially speedy solutions for the days when you know your schedule's going to be a particularly heavy one. **ALL LEFT-OVERS CAN BECOME PLAN-OVERS** or even **given a new identity** if you just take time to think about how they can be reused or the flavor can be enhanced, i.e., <u>overcooked vegetables can be turned into creamed soups, or used as a topping for a casserole, left-over mashed potatoes can be made into potato pancakes or potato salad</u>. **Plan-overs** can be **every bit as exciting and delicious on their return appearance as** they **were** at **their premier performance**. **Reprocessed meals** can **sometimes become superior to** the **original**, so if you are "just" re-warming the vegetables, at least perk them up with some Cayenne Pepper, Paprika or Hot Sauces etc.

- Another way to **SAVE MONEY** is to **GO SHOPPING WITH A FRIEND** and the two of you **exchange your list** at the entrance and **MEET UP AT THE CHECKOUT AISLE; TRADING CARTS.** If you are selecting items for another person you will not do additional or random buying which will also save you money. Remember to **MAKE YOUR LIST IN THE SAME ORDER AS THE GROCERY AISLES ARE LAID OUT** to save you shopping time.

- Every **kitchen** should **HAVE A WELL-STOCKED EMERGENCY MEAL SHELF**. Used for unexpected company or you didn't get home in time to fix what was planned. Pick a meal which can be made out of a packaged mix or canned food items and keep it in stock for those "**LAST MINUTE LIFESAVER**" times.

- **HOW TO OUTWIT TIME?** Thinking about **PREPARING YOUR MEAL BACKWARDS** will help you with timing. Begin with the time you want to serve the food, estimate the time each dish will take to cook, and count backwards so you know at what time to start cooking each dish. Then look at your recipe and estimate the amount of preparation time necessary before cooking can begin, start with the food that takes the longest to cook. Plan your menu and the proper utilization of your kitchen equipment! You cannot cook two items at the same time at different temperatures unless you have an alternate piece of equipment. The real trick is learning how to make everything come out at the same time through careful menu planning and by analyzing what can be cooked ahead of time, if any.

- Be sure to **START COOKING WITH AN "EMPTY"** or "almost empty" **DISHWASHER** to expedite cleaning up, or even consider washing a load of utensils before the meal. Utensils etc., should be added to the dishwasher as soon as they are no longer in use.

- Be sure to **PUT AWAY ALL FOOD PACKAGES** as soon as they have been used, **don't leave out on the counter**.

- Be sure to **WIPE UP ANY SPILLS** on the floor or counters as you work.

- If entertaining a large group **PHYSICALLY LAY OUT YOUR TABLE** early in the day or the night before: **Tablecloth, napkins, plates, and silverware**. **WRITE** on scraps of **paper** the **NAMES OF THE FOODS** that are being prepared: Salad, potatoes, meat, vegetable, bread, butter, etc. **PLACE THE NAME** of the food **INSIDE THE SERVING CONTAINER** with the serving utensils, and **put the container in place at the** table or buffet to make sure you have **enough serving area**. <u>This is also helpful for when someone offers to help you get your meal served</u>. They know exactly **where to put each food** and in what container.

- You should **IMPLEMENT A STAR RATING SYSTEM** for the meals you have prepared from this book. **Three stars** if the family "**will eat it again**," Two stars "**for it being easy to produce, One Star "maybe try again**," etc. With a rating system you can **REWORK THE ORIGINAL MENUS TO FIT YOUR FAMILIES' LIKES AND DISLIKES** and **WITH ALL THE COMBINATIONS YOU NOW HAVE AVAILABLE**, you will find that **YOU CAN FEED YOUR FAMILY A GOOD VARIETY FOR YEARS TO COME!**

Ideal is not always easy to achieve, but it's worth the try!

SOME HELPFUL SUBSTITUTIONS

DON'T HAVE:	CAN USE INSTEAD:
Allspice - 1 tsp	½ tsp Cinnamon + 1/8 tsp Ground Cloves
Baking Powder - 1 tsp	½ tsp Cream of Tartar plus ½ tsp Baking Soda
Breadcrumbs (Plain) 1 cup	¾ fine Cracker Crumbs or 1 slice Bread = ¼ cup dry crumbs
Butter – 1 cup	7/8 Oil or 14 Tbsp Shortening with ½ tsp Salt
Buttermilk – 1 cup	1 cup Milk + 1 Tbsp Vinegar or Lemon Juice (let stand 5 minutes) or
	1 cup Milk + 1-3/4 tsp Cream of Tartar
Cayenne – 1/8 tsp	4 drops Hot Pepper Sauce
Chives - 1 Tbsp Fresh diced	1 tsp frozen chopped Chives
Chocolate – 1 oz	3 Tbsp Cocoa plus 2 tsp Shortening
Cream (Heavy) 1 cup	¾ cup Milk plus 1/3 cup Melted Butter (Won't whip)
Cream (Light) 1 cup	¾ cup Milk plus ¼ cup Melted Butter
Flour – 1 Tbsp	1-1/2 tsp Cornstarch or Arrowroot or 1 Tbsp Potato Flour
Flour Self Rising – 1 cup	1 cup All-Purpose Flour + ¼ tsp Baking Powder & 1 tsp Salt
Herbs – 1 Tbsp fresh	1 tsp dried Herbs
Honey – 1 cup	1-1/4 cups Sugar plus ¼ cup Water
Lemon Juice – 1 tsp	½ tsp Vinegar
Milk, (Whole) 1 cup	½ cup Evaporated Milk plus ½ cup water or 1 cup skim milk plus 2 Tbsp
Melted	Butter
Mustard (Dry) – 1 tsp	2-1/2 tsp Yellow Prepared Mustard
Sour Cream – 1 cup	1/3 cup Melted Butter plus ¾ cup Sour Milk (to sour milk use ¾ cup whole
	milk + 2-1/4 tsp Lemon Juice or 2-1/3 tsp White Vinegar. (Let mixture
stand 10 minutes	before using)
Soy Sauce – ¼ cup	3 Tbsp Worcestershire + 1 Tbsp Water
Sugar – 1 cup Granulated	1-3/4 cups Powdered (do not substitute in baking)
Tomato Paste – 1 Tbsp	1 Tbsp Ketchup
Tomato Purée – 1 cup	½ cup Tomato Paste + 1-1/2 cups Water
Tomato Sauce – 1 cup	1 (6 oz) can Tomato Paste + 1-1/2 cups Water
Worcestershire Sauce – 1 tsp	1 Tbsp Soy Sauce + dash of Hot Pepper Sauce
Vanilla Extract	Flavor your batter with lemon or orange peel + lemon juice. Also can add ¼
	tsp \Nutmeg for each Tsp Vanilla or dust batter with Cinnamon
Yogurt (Plain) - 1 cup	1 cup Buttermilk

HELPFUL EQUIVALENTS

HAVE:	EQUALS:
Apples – 1 Pound	3 medium Whole
Cabbage – 1 Pound	4 cups shredded raw, or 2 cups cooked
Cheese – 1 Pound	4 – 5 cups grated
Crackers – 22 Saltine	1 cup Cracker Crumbs
Egg Yolks – 2 Yolks	1 Egg
Flour – 1 pound All-Purpose unsifted	4 cups, unsifted
Garlic – Fresh Clove	¼ tsp Garlic Powder
Gelatin – 1 envelope unflavored	1 Tbsp which will set 2 cups liquid
Ginger – 1 Tbsp Fresh	1 tsp Powdered
Lemon – Medium	About 2-1/2 Tbsp Lemon Juice
Lime – Medium	About 1 Tbsp Lime Juice
Marshmallows – 1 cup	10 miniatures
Marshmallows – 1 cup	11 – 12 Large
Meat – 1 Pound Boneless	2 cups ground meat
Mushrooms – 1 Pound fresh	5 cups sliced or 18 to 20 medium-size Whole
Noodles – Dry – 1 cup	1-3/4 cup Cooked
Nuts – ¼ Pound Shelled	1 cup chopped
Onions – 1 medium	1 cup chopped
Orange – Medium	About 7 Tbsp Orange Juice
Potatoes – 1 Pound	3 medium-size Whole, 2 cups cooked and mashed or 3-3/4 cups sliced
Shrimp – 1 pound Small	About 50
Shrimp/Prawns – 1 Pound Medium	About 20
Spaghetti – Dry – 8 oz	3-1/2 cups cooked

LEFT-OVER IDEAS

Left-overs are a basic fact that can plague or please you, depending on how cleverly you can handle them and turn them into plan-overs. Some meals, of course, will produce none and others provide plenty. Sometimes you should even cook an oversized quantity and freeze it to save you future time. Two simple rules apply, 1) Skip a day before serving them again unless you can turn them into a brand new identity and, 2) Don't wait too long to use them because they will get soggy or lose their flavor.

New flavors can be added with curry, minced French Fried onions, chopped parsley, new herbs or adding in new vegetables, i.e., mushrooms, carrots or bell peppers. Binding the ingredients together with mashed potatoes, canned potatoes, cooked rice, noodles, or eggs is good. Exchange out some of the Ground Beef if you have left-over sliced beef, pork or chicken available. You can use creamed soups, gravies, sauces and/or canned tomatoes to add moisture and eye appeal.

Some meat and vegetable left-overs are more useful than others but **"almost all" of the major ones in this cookbook, using a little bit of your imagination, can be revitalized into other recipes:**

EXAMPLES

Ala King recipes
Beans (Baked, Chili)
Bar-B-Q Sauces on a Bun
Burritos
Canapés – Hors d' Oeuvres
Casseroles – Plain and Biscuit Topped
Cheese Spreads
Chop Suey
Chowders
Creamed Soups and served over potatoes, noodles, or rice
Crepes
Croquettes
Curry recipes
Empanadas
Enchiladas
Fajitas
Frittatas
Gnocchi's
Hash
Hot Beef, Turkey Sandwiches
Monte Cristo Sandwiches
Mornay recipes

Newburg recipes
Omelet's
Pasta (w/Cream Sauces, Marinara Sauces
Stuffed, Lasagna, Mac and Cheese, Spaghetti
Pastry/Patty Shells filled
Pesto Sauce Dishes
Pita Sandwiches
Pizza
Potato Remakes (Pancakes, Hash Browns)
Quesadillas – Meat, Cheese and Vegetables
Quiches
Raviolis
Salads (Meats marinated in a Vinaigrette, Ranch Dressing, Taco Salads, Chef's etc.)
Sloppy Joes
Stew
Stroganoff
Stuffings/Dressings
Sweet and Sour Dishes
Tacos, Tostados
Tetrazzini recipes
Teriyaki recipes
Turnovers

TERMINOLOGY & MEASURMENTS

ABBREVIATIONS

~	=	approximately	Pkg	=	Package
Doz	=	Dozen	tsp	=	Teaspoon(s)
Hr	=	Hour	Tbsp	=	Tablespoon(s)
oz	=	Ounce	w/	=	with

MEASUREMENTS

Dry Ingredients			Liquid Ingredients		
A few grains equal/or less than 1/8 tsp			1 Tbsp	=	½ oz
3 tsp	=	1 Tablespoon	2 Tbsp	=	1 oz
2 Tbsp	=	1/8 cup	Jigger	=	1 oz
4 Tbsp	=	¼ cup	¼ cup/4 Tbsp	=	2 oz
5 Tbsp +1 tsp	=	⅓ cup	⅓ cup	=	2-2/3 oz
8 Tbsp	=	½ cup	½ cup	=	4 oz
10 Tbsp +2 tsp	=	2/3 cup	1 cup	=	8 oz
12 Tbsp	=	¾ cup	½ pint	=	8 oz
16 Tbsp	=	1 cup	1 Lb (Pound)	=	16 oz
2 cups	=	1 pint	1 pint	=	16 oz
4 cups	=	1 quart	1 Quart/1 Liter	=	32 oz
2 pints	=	1 quart	Fifth	=	25.6 oz
4 quarts	=	1 gallon	½ gallon	=	64 oz
8 quarts	=	1 peck	1 gallon/4 Quarts	=	128 oz
4 pecks	=	1 bushel			

TERMS/INFORMATION

Allspice – Mix together ½ tsp Cinnamon with 1/8 tsp Cloves.

Bouquet Garni – Combination of Bay Leaf, Parsley, and Thyme.

Brown – Means to sauté until it turns brown (or golden brown) on all sides. This seals the surface of the meat so that it retains its natural juices during the cooking time.

Deglaze – To scrape up residue from the bottom of a pan and add liquid to remove any cooking residue to use for gravies and sauces.

Demi-Glace – (See – SAUCE Demi-Glace - Heavy Beef Stock) = Port Wine and Reduced Veal Stock.

Done – Means tender; ready to eat; that is at the point of tenderness for maximum goodness. Cooked foods are considered tender when they can be pierced easily with a fork.

Herbs – 1 Tbsp dried equals 1 tsp Fresh

Herbes de Provence – Combination of 2 Tbsp of Each - Basil, Fennel, Savory, Rosemary. Thyme and Marjoram (optional) Lavender

Onions – 1 Tbsp dried is equivalent to ¼ cup chopped fresh Onions.

Pinch (less than 1 tsp), **Smidgen** (half of a pinch), **Dash** (Liquid splash) – Any of these will change your formula for ingredients, "just a little" so if exact duplication is your motto, don't use them. Same with measuring cups: metal vs. glass, plastic vs. glass etc – Just "always" use the same measuring cup.

Sauté –To cook food quickly in a small amount of melted fat over medium to high heat in a heavy skillet or saucepan.

Shortening Info: Cut the shortening into - With a manual three-bladed hand blender smash with short strokes, the shortening into the flour mixture until it becomes somewhat granulated in its look.

Measuring Shortening: Use a regular size ice cream scooper = ¼ cup Shortening

Steam – Cooking vegetables over a small amount of boiling, salted water in a tightly covered saucepan so that the steam, not the water, does the cooking.

MENUS

TAKE NOTES SO YOU CAN REMEMBER:

Decided for You Cookbook – 365 Dinners

Week #1

SUNDAY
(CH) Stuffed Chicken Breasts
(VEG) Asparagus – Buttered
(VEG) Potatoes – Potato Puffs

MONDAY
(BF) Beef Lasagna
(SALAD) Spinach, Mushroom
Onion Ring Salad with Dressing
(VEG) Zucchini – Zucchini Bake

TUESDAY
(BF) Beef Meatballs and Gravy
(VEG) Mushrooms – Garlic Buttered
(VEG) Potatoes – Mashed Potatoes
(VEG) Beans – Canned Green Beans

WEDNESDAY
(BF) Beef Steak Sandwiches
(VEG) Potatoes – French Fries

THURSDAY
(MISC) Pizza (Linguica, Pepperoni,
Salami, etc)
(SALAD) Caesar Salad

FRIDAY
(SEA) Tuna Noodle Skillet with
Peas
(SALAD) Carrot, Celery, Nut,
and Pineapple Slaw with Dressing

SATURDAY
(MISC) Falafel with Tahini Sauce
(SALAD) Marinara Macaroni Salad

Grocery List – Salt & Pepper, Salad Dressings of Choice if not specified

MEATS
Beef – Cubed Steaks
Beef – Ground Hamburger
Chicken – Boneless Breasts
Linguica, Pepperoni, Salami
Luncheon Meat (Boiled Ham) (2R)
Pork – Ground Sausage

VEGETABLES – FRESH
Cabbage	Onions (3R)
Carrots (2R)	Onion Red
Celery	Onions Green
Garlic (3R)	Potatoes (2R)
Lettuce – Romaine	Spinach
Mushrooms (2R)	Zucchini

FROZEN FOODS
Asparagus (or fresh)	Meatballs
French Fries	Pizza Crust

SPICES/STAPLES
Flour (2R)
Garlic Powder (2R)
Mustard – Dry (2R)
Onion Salt

Oregano (2R)
Parsley Flakes
Sugar – Granulated (3R)
Worcestershire

CANNED FOODS
Gravy – Beef
Green Beans
Marinara Sauce
Milk – Evaporated (3R)
Olives – Chopped
Peas
Pineapple – Crushed
Spaghetti Sauce (2R)
Tuna
White Sauce

OTHER
Bread – Pita
Cheese – Blue
Cheese – Cottage
Cheese – Monterey Jack (2R)
Cheese – Mozzarella (3R)
Cheese – Parmesan (6R)
Cheese – Ricotta
Cheese – Swiss
Crackers – Saltine

Croutons
Eggs (2R)
Falafel Mix
Lemon Juice (2R)
Macaroni – Salad
Margarine (7R)
Mayonnaise (3R)
Milk
Milk – Half & Half
Noodles – Egg – Flat Egg
Noodles – Egg – Lasagna
Oil – Corn
Oil – Olive
Oil – Vegetable (2R)
Rolls – Steak Sandwich
Soy Sauce
Tahini Sauce
Toothpicks
Wine Vinegar (3R)
Walnuts
Waxed Paper

Week #2

SUNDAY
(PK) Ham – Baked or Canned
(SAUCE) Ham Sweet and Hot Sauce
(VEG) Potatoes – Scalloped Potatoes
(VEG) Zucchini – Buttered
(BRD) Biscuits – Cheese Garlic Dropped

MONDAY
(BF) Beef Burgers – Stuffed by Jean
Potato Chips
(SALAD) Pasta Primavera Salad
(VEG) Olives, Carrot, and Celery Sticks

TUESDAY
(CRNBF) Tacquitos
(PAS) Rice – Spanish Rice
(SALAD) Coleslaw with Dressing
(VEG) Corn – Cream Style

WEDNESDAY
(TUR) Hot Turkey Sandwiches
(VEG) Peas – Canned Peas
Creamed
(VEG) Potatoes – Mashed
Potatoes

THURSDAY
(PK) Ham and Swiss Cheese
 Sandwiches
Potato Chips/Olives
(SALAD) Potato Salad –
Leftover Mashed
(VEG) Mushrooms – Quickie
 Marinated

FRIDAY
(SEA) Tuna, Carrots, Peas and
Macaroni Casserole
(SALAD) Green Salad

SATURDAY
(CH) Chicken in a Coffin
(SALAD) Green Salad
(VEG) Cauliflower, Broccoli and Carrots

Grocery List – Salt & Pepper, Salad Dressings of Choice if not specified

MEATS
Beef – Ground Hamburger
Chicken – Boneless Breasts
Pork – Ham – Baked, Spiral,
Canned or Leftover (2R)
Pork – Prosciutto Ham
Turkey – Sliced Deli

VEGETABLES – FRESH
Broccoli	Radishes (2R)
Cabbage (2R)	Tomatoes (2R)
Carrots (2R)	Tomatoes Cherry
Celery	Zucchini (2R)
Garlic (2R)	
Lemon	
Lettuce – Iceberg (2R)	
Mushrooms (3R)	
Onions (8R)	
Parsley (3R)	
Potatoes (3R)	

SPICES/STAPLES
Cumin	Onion Salt
Flour (2R)	Sage
Garlic Powder (2R)	Sugar
Garlic Salt	Sugar – Brown
Mustard Dry	

FROZEN FOODS
Cauliflower, Broccoli & Carrots
Peas

CANNED FOODS
Carrots – Julienne
Guacamole Dip
Corn – Cream Style
Corned Beef
Macaroni & Cheese
Milk – Evaporated (3R)
Olives (2R)
Onion Rings – French Fried
Peas (2R)
Pineapple – Crushed
Soup – Cheddar Cheese
Tomato Puree/Paste/Sauce (2R)
Tuna

OTHER
Apricot Preserves
Biscuit Mix
Bouillon – Chicken
Bread – White
Buns – Steak Sandwich

Cheese – American
Cheese – Cheddar or Parmesan
Cheese – Swiss
Eggs (2R)
Foil – Aluminum
Gravy – Instant Turkey &
 Chicken
Horseradish
Lemon Juice
Margarine (7R)
Mayonnaise (4R)
Milk
Mustard – Dijon
Mustard – Yellow
Oil – Olive or Vegetable (4R)
Pasta – Shells
Pickles – Sweet
Potato Chips (2R)
 Rice – Long Grain
Rolls – Hot Roll Mix
Rolls – Steak Sandwich
Sour Cream
Tortillas – Corn
Vinegar (2R)
Vinegar–Red Wine (2R)
Whipping Cream
Wine – White

Decided for You Cookbook – 365 Dinners

Week #3

SUNDAY
(BF) Beef Steak – London Broil
(SALAD) Green Salad
(VEG) Potatoes – Canned Potatoes
(VEG) Spinach – Spinach Balls

MONDAY
(BF) Beef Chili Mac
(SALAD) Lettuce with Cucumber
Slices Salad
(VEG) Artichoke Hearts – Marinated

TUESDAY
(BF) Beef Tacos
(PAS) Rice – Spanish Rice
(SAUCE) Salsa – Red or Green
(VEG) Beans – Refried Beans

WEDNESDAY
(WNR) Hot Dogs with Bacon
and Cheese Wraps
(SALAD) Lettuce, Mayonnaise
and Onion Salad
(VEG) Potatoes – Au Gratin
Potatoes

THURSDAY
(BF) Beef Hamburger Peas and
Corn Casserole
(SALAD) Green Salad

FRIDAY
(SEA) Salmon Patties
(SALAD) Macaroni Salad
(VEG) Corn – Cream Style Corn

SATURDAY
(BF) Beef Meat Loaf
(SALAD) Green Beans French Style
with Onion Salad and Italian Dressing
(VEG) Potatoes – Cheddar Mushroom
Stuffed Potatoes

Grocery List – Salt & Pepper, Salad Dressings of Choice if not specified

MEATS
Beef – Ground Beef (4R)
Pork – Bacon (2R)
Pork – Ground Sausage
Steak – London Broil
Wieners/Frankfurters

VEGETABLES – FRESH
Cucumbers
Lettuce – Iceberg (5R)
Mushrooms
Onions (11R)
Parsley
Potatoes (3R)
Radishes (2R)
Tomatoes (4R)

FROZEN FOODS
Spinach–Chopped

SPICES/STAPLES
Baking Powder   Garlic Salt
Basil   Mustard – Dry
Chili Powder (2R) Onion Flakes
Cumin   Onion Salt
Garlic Powder (4R) Oregano (2R)

Taco Seasoning (Dry)
Worcestershire

CANNED FOODS
Artichoke Hearts – Marinated
Corn – Cream Style
Green Beans–French Style
Milk – Evaporated
Olives – Sliced
Peas
Potatoes – Sliced
Refried Beans
Salmon
Soup – Cheddar Cheese
Soup – Cream of Mushroom
Tomato Sauce (2R)

OTHER
Bouillon – Chicken
Breadcrumbs (2R)
Cheese – Cheddar (5R)
Cheese – Parmesan
Eggs (3R)

Macaroni – Salad (2R)
Margarine (5R)
Mayonnaise (2R)
Milk Half and Half
Oil – Vegetable (2R)
Pickles – Sweet
Rice – Long Grain
Salad Dressing – Tart Italian
Salsa – Red or Green
Stuffing Mix – Chicken
   Flavored
Taco Shells
Toothpicks
Whipping Cream

Decided for You Cookbook – 365 Dinners

Week #4

SUNDAY
(BF) Beef Swiss Steak – Pepper
Steak
(VEG) Corn –- Whole Kernel
(VEG) Potatoes – Mashed Potatoes

MONDAY
(BF) Beef Hamburger Mushroom
and Potato Casserole
(VEG) Peas – Canned Peas-Creamed

TUESDAY
(BF) Beef Tamale Pie – Skillet
(SALAD) Macaroni Salad

SATURDAY
(BF) Beef Stew – Red
(BRD) Corn Bread with a Little Help

WEDNESDAY
(BF) Beef Tetrazinni with Noodles
(SALAD) Green Salad
(VEG) Broccoli, Cauliflower, and
Carrots

THURSDAY
(WNR) Wieners and Pork-n-Beans
(SALAD) Lettuce, Mayonnaise and
Onion Salad
(VEG) Corn – Cream Style

FRIDAY
(SEA) Fish Sticks
(SALAD) Caesar Salad w/Croutons
(VEG) Potatoes – Scalloped

Grocery List – Salt & Pepper, Salad Dressings of Choice if not specified

MEATS
Beef – Cubed Steaks
Beef – Ground Hamburger (3R)
Beef – Stew Meat
Wieners/Frankfurters

VEGETABLES – FRESH
Bell Peppers (2R)
Carrots or Canned
Garlic
Lettuce – Iceberg (2R)
Lettuce – Romaine
Onions (10R)
Onions – Green
Mushrooms (2R)
Potatoes (4R)
Radishes
Tomatoes (2R)

FROZEN FOODS
Broccoli, Carrots & Cauliflower
Fish Sticks

SPICES/STAPLES
Baking Powder
Chili Powder
Cinnamon
Flour (2R)
Garlic Powder (2R)
Italian Seasoning
Mustard – Dry
Sugar – Brown
Worcestershire

CANNED FOODS
Carrots
Corn – Cream Style
Corn – Whole Kernel (2R)
Milk – Evaporated (2R)
Olives Black (Opt)
Peas
Pork-n-Beans
Soup – Cream of Mushroom
Tomato Sauce (3R)

OTHER
Biscuit Mix
Cheese Cheddar
Cheese – Blue
Cheese – Cottage
Cheese – Cream
Cheese – Parmesan
Corn Meal (2R)
Croutons
Eggs (2R)
Lemon Juice
Macaroni – Salad
Margarine (5R)
Mayonnaise (2R)
Milk (2R)
Noodles – Spaghetti
Noodles – Spinach (Opt)
Oil – Olive
Oil – Vegetable
Pickles - Sweet
Sour Cream

-4-

Week #5

SUNDAY
(BF) Spaghetti with Ground Beef
Sauce
(SALAD) Romaine Lettuce,
Mushroom and Avocado Salad with
Italian Salad Dressing
(VEG) Brussels Sprouts – Buttered
(MISC) Mozzarella Sticks or Fried Cheese
(BRD) Garlic French Bread Another
Way

MONDAY
(CH) Fried Chicken
(VEG) Asparagus – Buttered
Asparagus
(VEG) Potatoes – Mashed Potatoes

TUESDAY
(BF) Beef Sloppy Joes
(VEG) Potatoes – French Fries

SATURDAY
(BF&PK) Cabbage Rolls Stuffed
(SALAD) Green Salad
(VEG) Potatoes – Creamed Cheese
Potatoes

WEDNESDAY
(CH) Creamed Chicken
(PAS) Rice – Long Grain Steamed
(SALAD) Lettuce and Bean Sprout
Salad

THURSDAY
(BF) Veal – Rolled and Stuffed
(MISC) Eggs – Deviled
(SALAD) Green Salad
(VEG) Broccoli – Buttered Broccoli

FRIDAY
Chinese Food
(PK) Sweet & Sour Pork
(PK) Pork Chow Mein
(PK) Won Ton Stuffed and Fried
(MISC) Won Ton Dipping Sauce
(PAS) Rice – Fried Rice

Grocery List – Salt & Pepper, Salad Dressings of Choice if not specified

MEATS
Beef – Ground Hamburger (3R)
Chicken Cut-Up
Chicken – Boneless Breasts
Pork – Boneless Roast
Pork – Boneless Chops
Pork – Ground Sausage (2R)
Shrimp Cooked (2R)
Veal – Boneless Cutlets

VEGETABLES – FRESH
Asparagus
Avocado
Bamboo Shoots
Bean Sprouts (2R)
Bell Peppers
Cabbage
Carrots (3R)
Celery
Garlic (4R)
Lettuce – Iceberg (3R)
Lettuce–Romaine
Mushrooms
Onions (9R)
Onions Grn (3R)
Parsley (2R)
Potatoes (2R)
Radishes (2R)
Tomatoes

FROZEN FOODS
Broccoli
Brussels Sprouts
French Fries
Mozzarella Sticks
Won Ton Skins (Wrappers)

SPICES/STAPLES
Baking Powder (2R)
Baking Soda
Cayenne Pepper (2R)
Chili Powder   Sugar (2R)
Cinnamon   Sugar Brown
Cornstarch (3R)   Tabasco
Flour (3R)
Garlic Powder (2R)
Oregano
Poultry Seasoning
Sesame Oil

CANNED FOODS
Broth – Chicken & Vegetable
Milk – Evaporated (2R)
Mushrooms Sliced
Pineapple Chunks
Soup – Condensed Beef
Soup – Creamed Chicken
Spaghetti Sauce
Tomato Sauce (3R)
Tomatoes w/puree
Water Chestnuts

OTHER
Bread – French
Buns – Hamburger

Buttermilk
Cheese – Cheddar
Cheese – Monterey Jack
Cheese – Parmesan
Chili Sauce
Eggs (3R)
Ketchup
Lemon Juice
Margarine (8R)
Mayonnaise
Milk
Mustard
Noodles – Vermicelli
Noodles – Spaghettini
Oil – Vegetable (7R)
Rice – Brown
Rice – Long Grain (2R)
Salad Dressing – Italian
Shortening
Sour Cream
Soy Sauce (4R)
Toothpicks
Vinegar (2R)
Whipping Cream
Wine – White

Decided for You Cookbook – 365 Dinners

Week #6

SUNDAY
(PK) Chile Verde
(PAS) Rice – Spanish Rice
(VEG) Beans – Refried Beans

MONDAY
(BF) Beef Steak – Broiled
(VEG) Brussels Sprouts Potatoes – Buttered
(VEG) Potatoes – New Red Potato Casserole

TUESDAY
(BF) Beef Hamburgers
Dill Pickles Slices & Olives
Potato Chips

WEDNESDAY
(CH) Chicken and Broccoli
Casserole
(SALAD) Green Salad
(BRD Rolls – Crescent Rolls

THURSDAY
(WNR) Chili Dogs
(VEG) Potatoes – French Fries

FRIDAY
(PAS) Baked Macaroni with Two
Cheeses
(SALAD) Carrot Slaw Salad
  with Coleslaw Salad Dressing
(VEG) Tomatoes – Broiled

SATURDAY
(PK) Ham Hocks and White Navy Beans
(SALAD) Lettuce, Mayonnaise and Onion Salad
(VEG) Potatoes – Fried Potatoes
(BRD) Corn Bread with a Little Help

Grocery List – Salt & Pepper, Salad Dressings of Choice if not specified

MEATS
Beef – Ground Beef
Beef – Sirloin/or New York Steaks
Chicken – Breasts
Pork – Bacon
Pork – Ham Hocks
Pork – Pork Roast Boneless

VEGETABLES – FRESH
Cabbage
Carrots
Lettuce – Iceberg (2R)
Onions (7R)
Potatoes (2R)
Potatoes Red
Radishes
Tomatoes (2R)

FROZEN FOODS
Broccoli – Cuts
Brussels Sprouts
French Fries

SPICES/STAPLES
Baking Powder
Cumin
Flour (2R)

Garlic Powder (2R)
Onion Salt
Oregano
Sugar – Granulated

CANNED FOODS
Beans – Refried
Broth – Chicken
Chili without Beans
Green Chiles
Milk – Evaporated
Olives Black Pitted
Soup – Cream of Chicken
Tomato Sauce

OTHER
Bouillon– Chicken (2R)
Beans – White Navy
Biscuit Mix
Breadcrumbs (2R)
Buns – Hamburger
Buns – Hot Dog

Cheese – Cheddar (3R)
Cheese – Parmesan Romano (2R)
Cheese – Swiss
Corn Flakes
Corn Meal
Eggs (3R)
Foil – Aluminum Wieners/Frankfurters
Macaroni – Elbow
Margarine (7R)
Mayonnaise (2R)
Milk – Half & Half (2R)
Oil – Vegetable (2R)
Pickles – Dill
Potato Chips
Rice – Long Grain
Rolls – Crescent Dinner
Sour Cream
Stuffing Mix – Herb Seasoned
Vinegar

Decided for You Cookbook – 365 Dinners

Week #7

SUNDAY
(BF) Beef Steak – San Marco
(SALAD) Tomato Wedges with
Thousand Island Salad Dressing
(VEG) Potatoes – Jacket

MONDAY
(BF) Beef Oven Porcupine Balls with Rice
(SALAD) Green Salad
(VEG) Broccoli – Broccoli Buttered

TUESDAY
(BF) Beef Hamburger Casserole with Potatoes
(SALAD) Green Salad
(VEG) Peas – Peas & Mushrooms

WEDNESDAY
(BF) Chicken Fried Steak
(VEG) Potatoes – Mashed
Potatoes with Blue Cheese
(VEG) Tomatoes – Broiled

THURSDAY
(BF) Beef Italian Chop Suey
with Macaroni and Cabbage
(MISC) Mozzarella Sticks
(BRD) Bread–Garlic French Bread

FRIDAY
(SEA) Crab Seafood Turnovers
(SALAD) Tomato, Cucumber,
Onion Salad with Tart Italian
Salad Dressing
(VEG) Carrots – Sweet Carrots

SATURDAY
(BF-VEAL) Veal Tagliarini with
Noodles and Corn
(VEG) Artichoke Hearts – Marinated
(VEG) Beans – Canned Green Beans
(BRD) Biscuits – Cheese Garlic Dropped

Grocery List – Salt & Pepper, Salad Dressings of Choice if not specified

MEATS
Beef – Bacon
Beef – Ground Hamburger (3R)
Beef – Steak
Beef – Round Steak
Beef – Veal – Ground
VEGETABLES – FRESH
Bell Peppers (2R)
Cabbage
Celery
Cucumbers
Garlic (2R)
Lettuce – Iceberg (2R)
Onions (8R)
Potatoes (2R)
Radishes (2R)
Tomatoes (4R)
FROZEN FOODS
Broccoli   Mozzarella Sticks
SPICES/STAPLES
Celery Salt (2R)
Flour
Garlic Powder (3R)
Garlic Salt

Italian Seasoning
Meat Tenderizer
Onion Salt
Oregano (2R)
Paprika
Sugar – Brown
Thyme
Worcestershire (2R)

CANNED FOODS
Artichoke Hearts - Marinated
Carrots - Julienne
Corn – Whole Kernel
Green Beans
Lobster & Crabmeat
Milk – Evaporated
Mushrooms (2R)
Soup – Mushroom
Olives
Peas
Tomato Paste
Tomato Sauce (2R)
Tomatoes – Whole (2R)

OTHER
Biscuit Mix
Bread – French
Breadcrumbs
Cheese – Blue
Cheese – Cheddar (2R)
Cheese – Processed
Cracker Meal
Eggs (2R)
Foil – Aluminum
Macaroni Shells
Margarine (6R)
Mayonnaise
Milk (2R)
Noodles – Egg – Medium Flat
Oil – Vegetable (4R)
Pastry Mix (can be frozen)
Rice – Long Grain (2R)
Salad Dressing – Tart Italian
Salad Dressing – 1000 Island
Soup – Dried Onion
Sour Cream
Soy Sauce
Vinegar

Decided for You Cookbook – 365 Dinners

Week #8

SUNDAY
(PK) Stuffed Pork Roast
(SALAD) Green Salad
(VEG) Asparagus – Supreme Asparagus Casserole
(VEG) Potatoes – Mashed Potatoes

MONDAY
(BF) Beef Tomato Swiss Steak
(PAS) Fettuccine Alfredo
(VEG) Brussels Sprouts – Buttered

TUESDAY
(PK) Pork Chops and Mushroom Gravy
(SALAD) Potato Salad – Leftover Mashed
(VEG) Asparagus Spears (Cold)

WEDNESDAY
(BF) Beef Burgers with Olive/
Monterey Jack
(SALAD) Green Salad
Olives Black Pitted
Potato Chips

THURSDAY
(WNR) Hot Dogs
(SALAD) Green Salad
(VEG) Potatoes – French Fries

FRIDAY
(SALAD) Crab Louie Salad with
Dressing
(BRD) Rolls – Refrigerator

SATURDAY
(CH) Chicken and Dumplings
(VEG) Beans – Green Beans and
Baby Carrots Savory

Grocery List – Salt & Pepper, Salad Dressings of Choice if not specified

MEATS
Beef – Ground
Beef – Steak, Cubed or Round
Chicken Cut-Up
Seafood – Crab (fresh or canned)
Pork – Pork Chops
Pork – Roast Boneless
Wieners/Frankfurters

VEGETABLES – FRESH

Asparagus	Mushrooms (Opt)
Bell Peppers	Onions (6R)
Carrots – Baby	Onions – Green
Celery (2R)	Potatoes (2R)
Green Beans	Radishes (3R)
Lettuce–Iceberg (4R)	Shallots
Lettuce–Romaine	Tomatoes (4R)

FROZEN FOODS
Brussels Sprouts
French Fries

SPICES/STAPLES
Flour (2R)

Basil	Oregano	Herbes-de-Provence
Fennel	Savory	
Rosemary	Thyme	
Marjoram		

Poultry Seasoning (2R)
CANNED FOODS
Asparagus Spears (2R)
Milk – Evaporated (2R)
Mushrooms
Olives – Chopped
Olives – Black Pitted (2R)
Soup – Cream of Mushroom (2R)
Tomatoes
Tomato Paste
OTHER
Broth – Chicken (3R)
Buns – Hamburger
Buns – Hot Dog
Butcher's String – (to tie with)
Cheese – Monterey Jack
Cheese – Parmesan
Cheese – Pimento Cream

Cracker Meal Buttered
Croutons
Eggs (4R)
Foil – Aluminum
Ketchup (Optional)
Lemon Juice (Optional)
Margarine (3R)
Mayonnaise (2R) (Optional 1R)
Milk (2R)
Mustard – Yellow (2R)
Noodles – Egg – Fettuccine
Oil – Vegetable (3R)
Pickle Relish (Optional)
Pickles – Sweet
Potato Chips
Rolls - Refrigerator
Salad Dressing – 1000 Island
Sauce – Roasted Garlic &
    Parmesan
Stuffing Mix – Herb Seasoned
Vinegar

Decided for You Cookbook – 365 Dinners

Week #9

SUNDAY
(CRNBF) Corned Beef, Potatoes,
Carrots and Cabbage Dinner
(BRD) Biscuits – Canned

MONDAY
(CH) Chicken – Parmesan with Chives
(VEG) Peas – Canned Peas – Creamed
(VEG) Potatoes – Parmesan Au Gratin

TUESDAY
(BF) Beef Burritos Supreme
(PAS) Rice – Spanish Rice
(SALAD) Green Salad

WEDNESDAY
(WNR) Corn Dogs
Mustard/Ketchup
Potato Chips/Olives

THURSDAY
(PK) Ham and Noodles
(SALAD) Green Salad
(VEG) Beans – Green Bean
          Cheesy

FRIDAY
(SEA) Shrimp or Prawns
Deep Fried
(VEG) Corn – Cream Style
Corn
(VEG) Potatoes – Tater Tots

SATURDAY
(BF) Beef Chili with Beans
(SALAD) Potato Salad – New Red
Potatoes with Garlic Italian Salad Dressing
(BRD) Bread – Garlic French Bread

Grocery List – Salt & Pepper, Salad Dressings of Choice if not specified

MEATS
Beef Ground Hamburger
Chicken – Breasts
Corned Beef Brisket
Pork – Bacon
Pork – Chorizo Sausage (Opt)
Pork – Ham Slices or diced
VEGETABLES - FRESH
Avocado   Radishes (2R)
Cabbage   Tomatoes (3R)
Carrots
Chives
Garlic (3R)
Lettuce – Iceberg (2R)
Mushrooms
Onions (7R)
Potatoes (2R)
Potatoes – New Red (2R)
FROZEN FOODS
Corn Dogs
Green Beans – Cut
Prawns/Large Shrimp Breaded

Tater Tots
SPICES/STAPLES
Bay Leaf   Onion Salt
Chili Powder   Paprika
Cloves   Pepper Corns
Cumin (2R)   Rosemary
Flour
Garlic Powder (2R)
Italian Seasoning
Basil   Oregano ⎫
Fennel   Savory   ⎬ Herbes-de-
Rosemary Thyme   ⎪ Provence
Marjoram   ⎭
CANNED FOODS
Chili w/beans (or make your own)
Corn – Cream Style
Milk – Evaporated (3R)
Green Beans – Cut
Olives Black Pitted (2R)
Peas
Refried Beans
Tomato Sauce

OTHER
Biscuits – Canned
Bouillon – Chicken (2R)
Bread – French
Cheese – Cheddar (2R)
Cheese – Parmesan
Cheese – Processed Spread
Eggs
Foil - Aluminum
Ketchup
Margarine (5R)
Mustard – Yellow
Noodles – Egg – Flat
Oil – Vegetable (2R)
Potato Chips
Rice – Long Grain
Salad Dressing – Tart Italian
Sour Cream
Taco Sauce – Green
Tortillas – Flour
Waxed Paper

Week #10

SUNDAY
(PK) Pork Chops and Rice Casserole
(SALAD) Green Salad
(VEG) Broccoli – Broccoli Buttered

MONDAY
(BF) Beef Hamburger Pie with Green
Beans and Potatoes
(SALAD) Green Salad

TUESDAY
(CH) Chicken Ala King
(PAS) Rice – Long Grain Steamed
(SALAD) Green Salad

WEDNESDAY
(PK) Pork Cutlets with Apples
(SALAD) Green Salad
(VEG) Potatoes – Shoestring
Potato Casserole

THURSDAY
(BF) Joe's Favorite
(PAS) Rice – Fried Rice
(SALAD) Romaine Lettuce,
    Mushroom and Avocado Salad

FRIDAY
(SEA) Crab Buffet Mornay
(SALAD) Green Salad
(VEG) Potatoes – Parmesan Au
Gratin

SATURDAY
(VEAL) Veal Cutlets – Breaded
(VEG) Corn – Corn-on-the Cobb
(VEG) Potatoes – Mashed Potatoes

Grocery List – Salt & Pepper, Salad Dressings of Choice if not specified

MEATS
Beef – Ground Hamburger (2R)
Beef Veal Cutlets
Chicken – Boneless Breasts
Pork – Pork Chops Boneless
Pork – Pork Loin Chops
Seafood – Shrimp Cooked

VEGETABLES – FRESH
Apples G. Smith   Potatoes (3R)
Avocado   Radishes (5R)
Bell Peppers   Tomatoes (5R)
Corn-on-the-Cobb   Zucchini
Garlic
Lettuce – Iceberg (4R)
Lettuce – Romaine
Mushrooms (2R)
Onion (9R)
Onions – Green

FROZEN FOODS
Broccoli
Shoestring Potatoes

SPICES/STAPLES
Cinnamon
Flour (3R)
Garlic Powder
Onion Flakes
Paprika

CANNED FOODS
Broth – Beef
Crabmeat
Green Beans or fresh
Milk – Evaporated (3R)
Mushrooms – Crowns
Pimento
Soup – Cream of Chicken
Soup – Cream of Mushroom
Soup – Tomato
Spinach

OTHER
Cheese – Cheddar (3R)
Cheese – Parmesan (2R)
Cheese – Swiss
Cracker Meal
Eggs (7R)
Lemon Juice
Margarine (8R)
Milk (2R)
Oil – Vegetable (3R)
Rice – Long Grain (3R)
Soy Sauce (2R)
Vermouth (Optional)

-10-

Decided for You Cookbook – 365 Dinners

Week #11

SUNDAY
(PK) – Sweet & Sour Spareribs with Tomatoes
(PAS) Rice – Fried Rice
(VEG) Vegetable Medley Casserole
(Cauliflower, Broccoli and Carrots)

MONDAY
(CH) Tuscan Chicken Rollatini with Stuffing
(PAS) Rice – Long Grain Steamed
(SALAD) Green Salad
(SAUCE) Gravy – Chicken Instant

TUESDAY
(BF) Beef American Pie with Peas and
Mashed Potatoes
(SALAD) Cabbage, Carrot and Pineapple Slaw
with Sweet Dressing

WEDNESDAY
(BF) Veal Scaloppini
(PAS) Noodles – Green
Spinach with White Sauce
(SALAD) Green Salad

THURSDAY
(TUR) Turkey Mushroom Quiche
(SALAD) Caesar Salad
(VEG) Beans – Canned Green
Beans French Style

FRIDAY
(SEA) Captain's Tuna Casserole
with Rice
(SALAD) Spinach, Mushrooms,
and Onion Salad with Dressing

SATURDAY
(BF) Beef Tomato Steak
(VEG) Potatoes – Mashed with Sweet Carrots
(BRD) Bread – Garlic French Bread

Grocery List – Salt & Pepper, Salad Dressings of Choice if not specified

MEATS
Beef – Round Steak
Beef – Sirloin Steak
Beef – Veal Scaloppini
Chicken – Boneless Breasts
Pork – Ground Pork Sausage
Pork – Spareribs
Seafood – Shrimp Cooked
Turkey – Legs/Breast

VEGETABLES – FRESH
Bell Peppers	Onions (4R)
Cabbage	Onions–Green (4R)
Carrots	Parsley
Garlic (6R)	Potatoes (2R)
Lemon	Radishes (2R)
Lettuce–Iceberg (2R)	Spinach
Lettuce – Romaine	Tomatoes (2R)
Mushrooms	

FROZEN FOODS
Cauliflower, Broccoli & Carrots
Pastry Shell or Piecrust
Peas

SPICES/STAPLES
Bay Leaf, Parsley,
Thyme   } Bouquet Garni

Cornstarch (2R)
Flour (3R)
Garlic Powder
Ginger
Italian Seasoning
Monosodium Glutamate
Mustard – Dry (2R)
Nutmeg
Oregano
Paprika (2R)
Sugar – Brown
Sugar – Granulated (4R)
Tabasco
Worcestershire

CANNED FOODS
Carrots
Green Beans French Style
Milk – Evaporated (4R)
Mushrooms (3R)
Olives – Stuffed (2R)
Pineapple–Chunks w/Juice(2R)
Soup–Crm Mushroom (2R)
Soup–Crm Shrimp
Tomatoes–Whole
Tuna

OTHER
Bouillon – Chicken & Beef
Bread – French
Cheese–Blue & Processed Amer.
Cheese–Cheddar (2R)
Cheese–Parmesan (3R)
Cheese–Swiss
Cracker Meal
Croutons
Eggs (5R)
Foil–Aluminum
Gravy Instant–Chicken & Turkey

Ketchup	Rice–LongGr.
Lemon Juice (4R)	Sour Cream
Margarine (6R)	Soy Sauce (5R)
Mayonnaise	Stuffing–Herb
Milk (2R)	Toothpicks
Mustard–Yellow	Vinegar (2R)
Noodles–Spinach	Whip'g Cream
Oil–Corn	Wine–White

Oil–Olive
Oil–Vegetable (5R)
Onions–French Fried
Potato Chips
Rice–Instant/Minute

-11-

Week #12

SUNDAY
(BF) Beef Peruvian
(PAS) Rice – Long Grain Steamed
(VEG) Peas – Canned Peas-Creamed

MONDAY
(BF) Beef Tostadas
(PAS) Rice – Spanish Rice
(VEG) Zucchini – Zucchini Fritters

TUESDAY
(BF) Beef Stuffed Pocket Bread – Pita Bread
(SALAD) Macaroni Salad
Potato Chips

WEDNESDAY
(BF) Beef Kabobs
(PAS) Noodles and Broccoli
Parmesan
(SALAD) Green Salad
(BRD) Bread – Garlic French Bread

THURSDAY
(TUR) Turkey Roast w/Gravy
(SALAD) Beets – Pickled and
Sliced Onion Salad
(VEG) Mushrooms – Marinated
(VEG) Potatoes – Baked Potatoes

FRIDAY
(SEA) Fish Lemon Rollups
(VEG) Potatoes – Scalloped
Potatoes
(VEG) Brussels Sprouts – Buttered

SATURDAY
(CH) Chicken Rice Casserole – Joan's
(SALAD) Romaine Lettuce, Mushroom
and Avocado Salad
(VEG) Beans – Green Bean Casserole

Grocery List – Salt & Pepper, Salad Dressings of Choice if not specified

MEATS
Beef – Ground Hamburger
Beef – Steak, Round
Beef – Steak, Thick London Broil
Beef – Stew Meat
Chicken – Breasts
Seafood – Fish Fillets – w/Skin

VEGETABLES – FRESH
Avocado   Tomatoes – Cherry
Bell Peppers   Zucchini (2R)
Chives
Garlic (2R)
Lettuce – Iceberg (3R)
Lettuce – Romaine
Mushrooms (2R)
Onions (10R)
Parsley
Potatoes (2R)
Radishes
Tomatoes (3R)

FROZEN FOODS
Broccoli – Chopped or Cuts
Brussels Sprouts
Green Beans – French Style
Turkey Roast

SPICES/STAPLES
Baking Powder
Cayenne Pepper
Chili Powder   Paprika (2R)
Cumin (2R)   Parsley
Flour (3R)   Tabasco (3R)
Garlic Pwdr (3R)   Tarragon
Italian Seas.   Worcestershire
Onion Salt

CANNED FOODS
Beets – Pickled
Milk – Evaporated
Mushrooms
Mushrooms – Marinated (Opt)
Onions – French Fried
Peas
Potatoes – Whole
Refried Beans
Soup – Cream of Mushroom (2R)
Tomato Sauce (2R)

OTHER
Bouillon – Beef & Chicken (3R)
Bread – French
Bread – Pocket/Pita
Cheese – Cheddar (4R)
Cheese – Parmesan

Cracker Meal (Opt)
Eggs
Foil – Aluminum (2R)
Gravy–Chicken & Turkey Instant
Lemon Juice
Macaroni – Salad
Margarine (8R)
Mayonnaise (2R)
Milk (4R)
Mustard – Dijon
Noodles – Fettuccini
Oil – Olive (2R)
Oil – Vegetable (6R)
Pepper Sauce Red Hot
Pickles – Sweet
Potato Chips
Rice – Long Grain (4R)
Salad Dressing – Tart Italian
Skewers for the Kabobs
Sour Cream (2R)
Soy Sauce
Taco Sauce
Toothpicks
Tortillas – Corn
Vinegar (2R)
Waxed Paper (Optional)

Decided for You Cookbook – 365 Dinners

Week #13

SUNDAY
(BF) Beef Steak and Lobster
(VEG) Potatoes – Baked + Extra
(VEG) Peas – Peas & Carrots
Buttered

MONDAY
(CH) Chicken Supreme with Rice and
(SALAD) Green Beans
(SALAD) Green Salad

TUESDAY
(BF) Spaghetti Ring with Beef and Spinach
(SALAD) Romaine Lettuce with Red Onion
Ring Salad
(VEG) Eggplant – Breaded Eggplant

WEDNESDAY
(PK) Pork Patties and Pea Pods –
Chinese Style
(PK) Pork Egg Rolls – Chinese
(PAS) Rice – Fried Rice

THURSDAY
(BF) Beef Salisbury Steak
(SALAD) Carrot, Celery, Nut
and Pineapple Salad & Sweet
Dressing

FRIDAY
(SEA) Tuna – Buffet Macaroni
Casserole
(SALAD) Green Salad
(BRD) Bread–Garlic French
Bread

SATURDAY
(BF) Beef Short Ribs – Bar-B-Q
(BF) Beef Chili with Beans
(SALAD) Potato Salad

Grocery List – Salt & Pepper, Salad Dressings of Choice if not specified

MEATS
Beef – Bacon
Beef – Ground Hamburger (2R)
Beef – Short Ribs
Beef – Steak (NY, Sirloin etc)
Chicken Cut-Up
Pork Boneless Roast (2R)
Pork – Ground Sausage
Seafood – Lobster Tails
Seafood – Shrimp Cooked

VEGETABLES – FRESH

Bell Peppers	Mushrooms (2R)
Cabbage	Onions (9R)
Carrots	Onions–Grn (2R)
Chives	Potatoes (2R)
Celery (3R)	Radishes (2R)
Eggplant	Tomatoes (2R)
Garlic	
Lemon	
Lettuce–Iceberg (2R)	
Lettuce–Romaine	

FROZEN FOODS
Snow Pea Pods & Chinese Vegies
Spinach, Chopped
Won Ton Skins (Wrappers)

SPICES/STAPLES
Celery Salt
Celery Seed
Cornstarch
Flour (2R)
Garlic Powder (2R)
Ginger
Italian Seasoning
Paprika (2R)
Sugar – Granulated (3R)
Worcestershire (2R)

CANNED FOODS
Bamboo Shoots
Beans – Chili
Green Beans
Milk – Evaporated
Mushrooms (2R)
Olives Black Pitted
Peas and Carrots
Pimento (3R)
Pineapple Chunks
Soup – Cream of Celery
Soup – Cream of Mushroom (2R)
Spaghetti Sauce
Tuna

OTHER
Bar-B-Q Sauce
Bread – French
Breadcrumbs (2R)
Cheese – Parmesan (3R)
Eggs (5R)
Foil – Aluminum (2R)
Lemon Juice (2R)
Macaroni & Cheese Mix
Margarine (5R)
Mayonnaise (3R)
Milk (2R)
Mustard Yellow
Noodles–Spaghetti
Noodles–Vermicelli/
  Chow Mein
Oil – Olive
Oil – Vegetable (4R)
Pickles – Sweet
Rice – Long Grain (2R)
Salad Dressing – French
Sour Cream (2R)
Soy Sauce (3R)
Vinegar (2R)
Waxed Paper
Walnut Halves
Whipping Cream
Wine–Sherry (2R)

-13-

Week #14

SUNDAY
(BF) Beef Steak – Mustard
(SALAD) Green Salad
(VEG) Potatoes – Mashed Potatoes

MONDAY
(BF) Beef Meatballs Espanól with Rice and Zucchini
(SALAD) Green Salad
(VEG) Artichokes with Mayonnaise

TUESDAY
(PK) Ham and Cheese Scallop with Potatoes
Carrots
(SALAD) Green Salad

WEDNESDAY
(BF) Bar-B-Q Sliced Beef
Potato Chips
(SALAD) Macaroni Salad

THURSDAY
(BF) Beef Betty
(PAS) Rice – Long Grain
Steamed
(VEG) Beans – Canned Green
Beans

FRIDAY
(SEA) Crabmeat and Cheese and
Casserole with Rice
(SALAD) Green Salad
(VEG) Broccoli – Buttered
    Broccoli

SATURDAY
(BF) Beef Roast – Barbecued
(PAS) Noodles with White Sauce
(SALAD) Beet and Celery Salad

Grocery List – Salt & Pepper, Salad Dressings of Choice if not specified

MEATS
Beef – Chuck Roast
Beef – Ground Hamburger
Beef – Roast Beef - Thinly Sliced
Beef – Sirloin Steaks
Beef – Stew Meat
Pork – Ham Slices

VEGETABLES – FRESH
Artichokes
Bell Peppers
Carrots
Celery
Lettuce – Iceberg (4R)
Onions – Green
Onions (7R)
Parsley (2R)
Potatoes (2R)
Radishes (4R)
Tomatoes (6R)
Zucchini

FROZEN FOODS
Broccoli Cuts or fresh

SPICES/STAPLES
Flour (3R)
Garlic Salt
Meat Tenderizer
Oregano
Sugar – Brown
Thyme
 Worcestershire (2R)

CANNED FOODS
Beets - Pickled
Chiles – Green
Crabmeat or fresh
Green Beans
Milk – Evaporated (2R)
Soup – Cream of Celery
Soup – Cream of Mushroom (2R)

OTHER
Bar-B-Q Sauce
Breadcrumbs
Buns – Hamburger
Cheese – Cheddar (3R)
Cheese – Parmesan
Ketchup
Lemon Juice (2R)
Macaroni – Salad
Margarine (6R)
Mayonnaise (2R)
Milk (2R)
Mustard – Whole Grain
Noodles – Egg – Flat
Pickles – Sweet
Potato Chips
Rice – Long Grain (3R)
Sour Cream

Decided for You Cookbook – 365 Dinners

Week #15

SUNDAY
(BF) Beef Wellington
(SALAD) Corn, Pimiento, and Peas
Marinated Salad
(VEG) Potatoes – Scalloped Potatoes

MONDAY
(BF) Beef Hamburger Tater Tot Casserole
(SALAD) Green Salad
(VEG) Cauliflower and Asparagus with
Cheese Sauce

TUESDAY
(PK) Linguica Sandwiches
Olves Black Pitted
Potato Chips

WEDNESDAY
(BF) Beef Burgundy
(PAS) Noodles with White Sauce
(VEG) Beans – Canned Green
Beans French Style

THURSDAY
(BF) Beef Stuffed Bell Peppers
(SALAD) Macaroni Salad
(VEG) Corn – Cream Style Corn

FRIDAY
(SEA) Salmon – Broiled
(SALAD) Three Bean Salad
(VEG) Potatoes – Potato
Casserole Suprema

SATURDAY
(LAMB) Viennese Leg of Lamb
(VEG) Potatoes – Rosemary Potatoes
(VEG) Brussels Sprouts - Buttered

Grocery List – Salt & Pepper, Salad Dressings of Choice if not specified

MEATS
Beef – Ground Hamburger (2R)
Beef Roast – Rolled
Beef – Stew Meat
Lamb – Leg of Lamb
Pork – Ground Pork Sausage
Pork – Linguica Sausage
Seafood – Salmon Fillets

VEGETABLES – FRESH
Bell Peppers	Parsley (2R)
Carrots	Potatoes (2R)
Celery (2R)	Potatoes-Red
Garlic	Radishes
Lettuce–Iceberg (2R)	Tomatoes (2R)
Mushrooms	
Onions (9R)	

FROZEN FOODS
Asparagus	Tater Tots
Brussels Sprouts or fresh	
Cauliflower	
Pastry Shell	

SPICES/STAPLES
Bay Leaf	Thyme

Flour (3R)
Garlic Powder (2R)
Garlic Salt
Mustard – Dry
Nutmeg
Paprika
Rosemary or fresh
Sugar – Granulated

CANNED FOODS
Beans – Kidney
Beans – Garbanzo
Corn – White Whole Kernel
Corn – Cream Style
Green Beans - French Style
Milk – Evaporated (2R)
Mushrooms
Olives Black Pitted
Peas – Baby Lesueur Small
Pimento
Soup – Cream of Celery (2R)
Soup – Tomato

OTHER
Breadcrumbs (2R)
Briquettes – Bar-B-Q (Opt)
Butcher's String/Twine

Cheese – Cheddar (2R)
Cheese – Parmesan (2R)
Foil – Aluminum
Ketchup
Lemon Juice (2R)
Macaroni – Salad
Margarine (7R)
Mayonnaise
Milk (2R)
Mustard (2R)
Mustard – Dijon (2R)
Noodles – Egg – Flat
Oil – Olive (2R)
Pickles – Sweet
Potato Chips
Rice – Long Grain
Rolls – Steak Sandwich
Salad Dressing–Italian (2R)
Soup – Dry Onion (2R)
Sour Cream
Vinegar
Whipping Cream
Wine – Burgundy
Wine – White

-15-

Week #16

SUNDAY
(VEAL) Veal Chops California
(PAS) Spagettini Noodles with
White Sauce
(VEG) Carrots – Sweet Carrots

MONDAY
(BF) Beef Hamburger Peas and Carrots over
(PAS) Rice – Long Grain Steamed
(SALAD) Iceberg Lettuce Wedges with
Thousand Island Salad Dressing

TUESDAY
(PK) Spareribs in Bar-B-Q Sauce
(SALAD) Green Salad with Bell Pepper and
Onion Rings
(VEG) Beans – Butter Beans
(VEG) Potatoes – Oven Fried Potatoes

WEDNESDAY
(CH) Chicken Stroganoff
(SALAD) Green Salad
(VEG) Beans – Canned Green
Beans French Style
(VEG) Potatoes – Mashed Potatoes
(BRD) Bread–Garlic French Bread

THURSDAY
(BF) Beef Steak and Gravy
(VEG) Cauliflower & Mushrooms
(VEG) Potatoes – Mashed Potatoes

FRIDAY
(SEA) Teriyaki Fish
(PAS) Rice – Long Grain Steamed
(SALAD) Green Salad
(VEG) Asparagus – Buttered

SATURDAY
(PK) Ham and Fettuccine Noodles with Peas
(SALAD) Green Salad

Grocery List – Salt & Pepper, Salad Dressings of Choice if not specified

MEATS
Beef – Ground Hamburger
Beef – Round Steak
Beef – Boneless Veal Chops
Chicken – Boneless Breasts
Fish – Fillets of Choice
Pork – Bacon (2R)
Pork – Ham – Whole or Slices
Pork - Spareribs

VEGETABLES – FRESH
Avocado
Bell Peppers
Garlic (2R)
Lettuce – Iceberg (5R)
Mushrooms (3R)
Onions (7R)
Onions – Green
Potatoes (3R)
Radishes (3R)
Tomatoes (3R)
FROZEN FOODS
Asparagus Spears
Cauliflower
Peas

SPICES/STAPLES
Basil
Bouquet Gravy & Season'g Sauce Opt
Flour (2R)
Garlic Powder (2R)
Ginger
Italian Seasoning
Paprika
Sugar – Brown
Sugar – Granulated

CANNED FOODS
Beans – Butter (Brown Lima Beans)
Carrots or Fresh
Gravy – Beef
Green Beans – French Style
Milk Evaporated (2R)
Peas and Carrots
Tomato Sauce

OTHER
Bar-B-Q Sauce
Bread – French
Cheese – Parmesan
Foil – Aluminum
Gravy – Instant Chicken
Gravy – Instant Turkey
Ketchup
Lemon Juice
Margarine (9R)
Milk
Noodles–Egg–Fettuccine
Noodles – Spaghettini
Oil – Vegetable (3R)
Rice – Long Grain (2R)
Salad Dressing–1000 Island
Sour Cream
Soy Sauce
Stroganoff Mix
Whipping Cream (2R)
Wine – White

Decided for You Cookbook – 365 Dinners

Week #17

SUNDAY
(MISC) Italian Calzone
(SALAD) Green Salad

MONDAY
(BF) Beef Stuffed Zucchini Boats
(SALAD) Green Salad
(VEG) Potatoes – Potato Puffs

TUESDAY
(CH) Chicken Sopa Seca
(PAS) Rice – Spanish Rice
(VEG) Brussels Sprouts – Buttered

WEDNESDAY
(BF-VEAL) Veal in Cream Sauce
(SALAD) Green Salad
(VEG) Potatoes – Mashed with
Blue Cheese

THURSDAY
(BF) Beef with Broccoli & Green
Bell Peppers Stir Fry
(PAS) Rice – Long Grain Steamed
(SALAD) Spinach, Mushroom and
Onion Ring Salad with Dressing

FRIDAY
(SEA) Shrimp New Orleans with
Rice and Artichoke Hearts
(SALAD) Romaine Lettuce &
Garlic Croutons with Italian Salad
Dressing

SATURDAY
(BF) Beef Hamburger Patties with Onions
(SALAD) Green Salad
(VEG) Potatoes – Stewed Potatoes
(BRD) Corn Bread with A Little Help

Grocery List – Salt & Pepper, Salad Dressings of Choice if not specified

MEATS
Beef – Ground Hamburger (2R)
Beef – London Broil Steak
Beef – Veal Scaloppini
Chicken – Breasts or Canned Chicken
Luncheon Meats–Deli Salami, Ham
Pork – Bacon
Pork – Ground Sausage
Seafood – Prawns/Shrimp

VEGETABLES – FRESH
Bell Peppers   Radishes(4R)
Celery   Spinach
Garlic (2R)   Tomatoes
Lettuce–Iceberg (4R) Zucchini
Lettuce – Romaine
Mushrooms (3R)
Onions (13R)
Onions Green (2R)
Potatoes (3R)

FROZEN FOODS
Broccoli Cuts
Brussels Sprouts (or fresh)
Pizza Crust
Spinach – Chopped

SPICES/STAPLES
Baking Powder
Cornstarch (2R)
Cumin
Garlic Powder (2R)
Ginger
Mustard – Dry
Onion Salt (2R)
Sugar – Granulated
Thyme

CANNED FOODS
Artichoke Hearts
Broth – Beef
Broth – Chicken
Chiles – Green
Soup – Cream of Chicken
Soup – Cream of Mushroom
Spaghetti Sauce (2R)
Tomatoes (2R)
Tomato Sauce

OTHER
Biscuit Mix
Bouillon – Chicken (2R)

Breadcrumbs
Cheese–Blue Cheese
Cheese–Cheddar
Cheese–Monterey Jack
Cheese–Mozzarella
Cheese–Romano Parmesan (2R)
Corn Meal
Cracker Meal
Croutons
Eggs (4R)
Ketchup
Lemon Juice
Margarine (4R)
Milk – Half & Half
Oil – Corn
Oil – Olive
Oil – Vegetable (3R)
Rice – Long Grain (3R)
Salad Dressing – Italian (2R)
Soup – Dry Onion
Sour Cream
Soy Sauce (2R)
Spaghetti Sauce Dry
Tortillas – Flour
Vinegar
Whipping Cream
Wine–Madeira

-17-

Week #18

SUNDAY
(PK) Spaghetti Carbonara
(SALAD) Green Salad
(VEG) Carrots – Buttered Carrots

MONDAY
(CH) Chicken Enchilada Pie
(PAS) Rice – Spanish Rice
(VEG) Beans – Refried Beans

TUESDAY
(MISC) Cheese Soufflé
(PK) Ham Slices
(SALAD) Tomatoes and Onion Salad

WEDNESDAY
(CRNBF) Corned Beef Tamale Loaf
(PAS) Noodles with White Sauce
(SALAD) Romaine Lettuce with Pickled Beets Salad
(VEG) Squash and Mushrooms

THURSDAY
(BF) Beef Cheeseburgers
(VEG) Onions – French Fried

FRIDAY
(SEA) Tuna Potato Patties with Fine Herbs
(VEG) Corn – Corn-on-the Cobb
(VEG) Potatoes – Shoestring Potato Casserole
(VEG) Tomatoes – Broiled

SATURDAY
(BF) Veal Michelle
(VEG) Potatoes – Thrice Baked
(VEG) Beans – Canned Green Beans Buttered
(SALAD) Green Salad

Grocery List – Salt & Pepper, Salad Dressings of Choice if not specified

MEATS
Beef – Ground Hamburger
Beef – Veal Boneless Cutlets
Chicken Whole
Luncheon Meat–Deli Boiled Ham
Pork – Bacon
Pork – Ham Slices (2R)

VEGETABLES – FRESH
Chives
Corn-on-the Cobb
Garlic
Lettuce – Iceberg (2R)
Lettuce – Romaine
Onions (5R)
Onions – Green (4R)
Mushrooms
Parsley (2R)
Potatoes (2R)
Radishes (2R)
Squash
Tomatoes (3R)

FROZEN FOODS
Onion Rings or Make Ur Own
Potatoes – Shoestring

SPICES/STAPLES
Basil
Chili Powder

Cumin
Flour (2R)
Garlic Powder
Mustard – Dry
Onion Flakes
Onion Salt
Oregano
Pepper – White
Rosemary
Sugar – Brown
Thyme

CANNED FOODS
Beets – Pickled
Broth – Beef
Broth – Chicken (2R)
Carrots
Chiles – Green Chopped
Corned Beef
Enchilada Sauce
Evaporated Milk (2R)
Gravy – Beef
Green Beans
Refried Beans
Soup – Cream of Chicken (2R)
Soup – Cream of Mushroom (2R)
Tomato Sauce (2R)
Tuna

OTHER
Bouillon – Chicken
Bread – White
Breadcrumbs (3R)
Buns – Hamburger
Cheese – American (4R)
Cheese – Longhorn Cheddar (5R)
Cheese – Monterey Jack
Cheese – Parmesan
Cheese – Romano
Cheese – Swiss
Corn Chips
Eggs (4R)
Ketchup
Margarine (8R)
Milk (2R)
Noodles – Flat Egg
Noodles – Spaghettini
Oil – Olive (2R)
Oil – Vegetable (2R)
Rice – Long Grain
Salad Dressing – Tart Italian
Soup – Dry Onion
Sour Cream
Toothpicks
Tortillas – Flour
Waxed Paper

Decided for You Cookbook – 365 Dinners

Week #19

SUNDAY
(PK) Italian Sausage and Spanish Rice
(SALAD) Romaine Lettuce, Mushroom
and Avocado Salad
(VEG) Beans – Canned Green Beans Buttered

MONDAY
(PK) Pork and Potato Stacks
(SALAD) Tomato Wedges with
Thousand Island Dressing

TUESDAY
(MISC) Pizza – English Muffin
(SALAD) Chef Salad

WEDNESDAY
(BF) Beef Stroganoff
(PAS) Rice–Long Grain Steamed
(VEG) Peas – Canned Peas –
Creamed

THURSDAY
(WNR) Circle Hot Dogs
(SALAD) Macaroni Salad
(VEG) Potatoes – Chili Cheese
Fries

FRIDAY
(SEA) Sole in Wine Sauce with
Mushrooms
(SALAD) Green Salad
(VEG) Broccoli – Au Gratin

SATURDAY
(BF) Beef and Mushroom Saté
(PAS) Rice – Fried Rice
(SALAD) Chinese Chicken Salad
with Dressing

Grocery List – Salt & Pepper, Salad Dressings of Choice if not specified

MEATS
Beef – Round Steak
Beef – Sirloin (or Flank)
Chicken – Boneless Breasts
Luncheon Meats Deli - Salami, Ham,
Pepperoni
Pork – Boneless Cubed Steak
Sausage – Sweet Italian
Sausage – Hot Italian
Seafood – Fish Fillets – Sole
Cooked
Wieners/Frankfurters

VEGETABLES – FRESH
Avocado
Bean Sprouts
Bell Peppers (2R)
Cilantro/Chinese Parsley
Garlic
Lettuce – Iceberg (3R)
Lettuce – Romaine (2R)
Mushrooms (3R)
Onions (7R)
Onions – Green (2R)
Peas – Sugar Snap Snow (2R)
Radishes (2R)
Tomatoes (5R)

FROZEN FOODS
Broccoli Cuts

French Fries
Hash Browns
Won Ton Skins–Wrappers

SPICES/STAPLES
Bay Leaf (2R)
Chile – Red Hot Paste
Flour (2R)
Garlic Powder
Mustard – Dry (2R)
Pepper Sauce – Red Hot
Sugar – Brown
Sugar – Granulated (2R)
Worcestershire

CANNED FOODS
Asparagus Spears
Chili w/No Beans
Evaporated Milk
Green Beans
Peas
Spaghetti Sauce
Tomatoes

OTHER
Breadcrumbs
Buns – Hamburger
Cheese – American
Cheese – Cheddar (4R)
Cheese – Mozzarella
Cheese – Parmesan
Croutons

Eggs (2R)
Foil – Aluminum
Lemon Juice
Macaroni – Salad
Margarine (4R)
Mayonnaise
Milk (2R)
Milk – Half and Half
Muffins–English Seafood–Shrimp
Noodles – Crispy Chow Mein
Oil – Sesame
Oil – Vegetable (6R)
Peanut Butter (Opt)
Pickles – Sweet Slices (2R)
Rice – Long Grain (4R)
Salad Dressing – 1000 Island
Sesame Seeds
Shortening
Soup – Dry Mushroom
Sour Cream (2R)
Soy Sauce (3R)
Stroganoff – Dry Mix
Vinegar – Rice Wine
Whipping Cream
Wine – White

Decided for You Cookbook – 365 Dinners

Week #20

SUNDAY
(CH) Chicken Rollups
(SALAD) Green Salad
(VEG) Beans – Canned Green Beans
French Style
(VEG) Potatoes – Mashed Potatoes

MONDAY
(BF) Beef California Casserole with Noodles
(SALAD) Spinach, Mushroom and Onion Ring
Salad with Dressing

TUESDAY
(PK) Pork Chops – Smoked
(SALAD) Lettuce, Mayonnaise and Onion Salad
(VEG) Mustard Greens – Braised
(VEG) Peas – Black-Eyed Peas

WEDNESDAY
(BF) Beef Zucchini Scramble
(SALAD) Green Salad
(BRD) Bread – Garlic French
Bread

THURSDAY
(PK) Chorizo Casserole
(SALAD) Cole Slaw Salad with
Dressing

FRIDAY
(SEA) Tuna Quickie Time
with Rice
(SALAD) Green Salad

SATURDAY
(BF) Beef Broccoli Pie
(SALAD) Green Salad
(VEG) Corn – Cream Style

Grocery List – Salt & Pepper, Salad Dressings of Choice if not specified

MEATS
Beef – Ground Hamburger (4R)
Chicken – Boneless Breasts
Pork – Bacon (2R)
Pork – Pork Chops Smoked
Pork – Chorizo Sausage

VEGETABLES – FRESH
Avocado
Bell Peppers
Cabbage
Carrots
Garlic (2R)
Lettuce – Iceberg (5R)
Mushrooms
Mustard Greens
Onions (12R)
Onions – Green (4R)
Potatoes
Radishes (4R)
Spinach
Tomatoes (4R)
Zucchini

FROZEN FOODS
Broccoli – Chopped

SPICES/STAPLES
Chili Powder
Flour
Garlic Powder (2R)
Italian Seasoning
Mustard – Dry (2R)
Paprika (2R)
Pepper Sauce – Red Hot
Sugar - Granulated (4R)
Worcestershire
CANNED FOODS
Black-Eyed Peas
Broth – Chicken
Chiles – Green
Corn – Cream Style
Green Beans – French Style
Milk – Evaporated (2R)
Olives – Black Pitted (3R)
Pimientos (2R)
Refried Beans
Soup – Tomato
Tomato Sauce
Tuna
OTHER
Barb-B-Q Sauce
Biscuit Mix

Bread – French
Cheese – Cheddar (2R)
Cheese – Cream
Cheese – Monterey Jack (2R)
Cheese – Parmesan Cheese
Eggs (2R)
Foil – Aluminum (2R)
Ketchup (2R)
Lemon Juice
Margarine (6R)
Mayonnaise (3R)
Milk (2R)
Noodles – Egg – Flat
Oil – Corn
Oil – Vegetable
Pepper Sauce – Red Hot
Rice – Minute
Rolls – Crescent
Shortening
Soy Sauce (2R)
Sour Cream
Tortilla Chips
Toothpicks
Vinegar (4R)

Decided for You Cookbook – 365 Dinners

Week #21

SUNDAY
(BF) Beef Get-A-Husband Steak
(SALAD) Green Salad
(VEG) Potatoes – Mashed Potatoes

MONDAY
(PK) Pork Quickie Casserole with
Cream Style Corn
(SALAD) Bell Pepper and Onion Rings Salad
with Tart Italian Salad Dressing

TUESDAY
(BF) Beef Meat and Cheese Casserole
(SALAD) Green Salad
(VEG) Tomatoes – Broiled

WEDNESDAY
(BF) Beef Sloppy Joe Pie with
Green Beans
(SALAD) Cole Slaw Salad with
Dressing

THURSDAY
(PK) Ham and Cheese with Asparagus
Casserole
(PAS) Tortellini in Cream Sauce
(SALAD) Green Salad

FRIDAY
(SOUP) Enchilada Soup with Tortilla
Chips or Other Choice

SATURDAY
(CH) Lemon Chicken
(PAS) Rice – Long Grain Steamed
(VEG) Broccoli Au Gratin

Grocery List – Salt & Pepper, Salad Dressings of Choice if not specified

MEATS
Beef – Ground Hamburger (2R)
Beef – Round Steak
Chicken – Boneless Breasts
Pork – Ham (Small) or Slices
Pork – Sausage Links

VEGETABLES
Bell Peppers (2R)
Cabbage (2R)
Carrots
Celery
Garlic
Ginger
Lemons
Lettuce – Iceberg (3R)
Mushrooms
Onions (12R)
Potatoes (3R)
Radishes (3R)
Tomatoes (3R)

FROZEN FOODS
Asparagus Cuts
Broccoli Spears
Tortellini – Cheese

SPICES/STAPLES
Cornstarch
Flour (5R)
Garlic Powder

Garlic Salt
Oregano (2R)
Paprika
Pepper Oil – Hot Asian
Sugar – Granulated (2R)
Tarragon
Worcestershire (2R)

CANNED FOODS
Broth – Chicken (2R)
Chicken – Boneless
Chile's – Green
Corn – Cream Style (2R)
Enchilada Sauce
Green Beans
Milk–Evaporated (3R)
Olives – Green Stuffed
Pimento
Tomato Sauce (2R)
Tomato Soup

OTHER
Breadcrumbs (2R)
Cheese – Cheddar (2R)
Cheese – Parmesan
Cheese – Processed American
Chips – Tortilla/Taco
Custard – Instant Lemon Powder
Eggs

Foil – Aluminum
Ketchup
Lemon Juice
Macaroni – Elbow
Margarine (5R)
Mayonnaise
Milk (2R)
Milk – Half & Half
Molasses (Opt)
Mustard Dijon
Oil – Peanut
Oil – Vegetable (2R)
Paper Sack
Rice – Long Grain
Salad Dressing – Tart Italian
Sauce – Roasted Garlic &
Parmesan
Soup – Onion-Mushroom Dry
Sour Cream
Soy Sauce
Stuffing Mix Poultry Seasoned
Vinegar (2R)
Wine – Sherry
Wine – Asian Rice

-21-

Week #22

SUNDAY
(PK) Ham and Green Bean Potato Bake Casserole
(SALAD) Lettuce Wedges w/Thousand Island
(VEG) Artichoke Hearts – Marinated

MONDAY
(CH) Cashew Chicken
(PAS) Rice – Long Grain Steamed
(SALAD) Romaine Lettuce with Red
Onion Salad
(VEG) Asparagus and Cauliflower
Cheese Sauce

TUESDAY
BF) Filet of Mignon with
Mushrooms and Pinot Noir Sauce
(SALAD) Spinach, Mushroom and
Onion Ring Salad with Croutons and
Salad Dressing
(VEG) Potatoes – Creamed Cheese Potatoes

WEDNESDAY
(BF) Beef S.O.B /S.O.S
(PK) Ham Slices
(MISC) Eggs – Scrambled

THURSDAY
(WNR) Hot Dog Casserole
with Potatoes
(VEG) Beans – Canned Green
Beans
(BRD) Biscuits – Biscuit with
Mix

FRIDAY
(SEA) Salmon Loaf
(SALAD) Macaroni Salad
(VEG) Corn – Cream Style
Corn

SATURDAY
(PK) Pork Egg Rolls – Chinese
(PAS) Rice – Fried Rice
(SALAD) Chinese Chicken Salad

Grocery List – Salt & Pepper, Salad Dressings of Choice if not specified

MEATS
Beef – Ground Hamburger
Beef – Filet of Mignon Steaks
Beef – Veal (optional)
Chicken – Boneless Breasts (2R)
Pork – Bacon
Pork – Ground Sausage
Pork – Ham small or slices (3R)
Seafood – Shrimp – cooked
Wieners/Frankfurters

VEGETABLES – FRESH
Bell Peppers
Cabbage
Celery
Cilantro or Chinese Parsley
Garlic (2R)
Lettuce – Iceberg (2R)

Lettuce Romaine	Potatoes (3R)
Mushrooms (2R)	Snow Peas
Onion (7R)	Spinach
Onion Green (4R)	Tomatoes
Parsley (3R)	

FROZEN FOODS
Asparagus and Cauliflower
Green Beans (Cut)
Won Ton/Egg Roll Skins (Wrappers)

SPICES/STAPLES
Cayenne Pepper
Cornstarch (2R)
Flour (3R)
Garlic Powder
Mustard – Dry (2R)
Pepper Sauce – Red Hot
Rosemary
Sugar-Gran. (2R)

CANNED FOODS
Artichoke Hearts – Marinated
Bamboo Shoots (2R)
Bean Sprouts
Broth – Chicken
Corn – Cream Style
Green Beans (2R)
Mushrooms (2R)
Salmon
Soup – Cream of Celery
Soup – Cream of Cheddar Cheese

OTHER
Biscuit Mix (2R)

Breadcrumbs
Butcher's String
Cashew Nuts
Cheese – Cheddar (3R)
Croutons
Demi Glace (Opt) see SAUCE
Eggs (3R)
Lemon Juice
Macaroni – Salad
Margarine (6R)
Mayonnaise
Milk (4R)
Milk – Half & Half
Noodles – Crispy Chow Mein
Oil – Corn, Olive, & Vegetable
Pickles – Sweet
Rice – Long Grain (2R)
Salad Dressing – 1000 Island
Sesame Seeds
Sour Cream
Soy Sauce (4R)
Vinegar
Wine – Pinot Noir

-22-

Week #23

SUNDAY
(CH) Bar-B-Q Chicken
SALAD) Potato Salad – New Red Potatoes
with Garlic Italian Dressing
(VEG) Corn-on-the Cobb

MONDAY
(WNR) Frankfurter Hot Dog Macaroni
(SALAD) Green Salad with Pepper and
Onion Ring Salad
(VEG) Broccoli – Broccoli Buttered

TUESDAY
(CH) Chicken Enchiladas Michelle's
(VEG) Beans – Refried Beans
(PAS) Rice – Spanish Rice
(SALAD) Green Salad

WEDNESDAY
(BF) Stuffed Beef Cheesie
(SALAD) Green Salad
(VEG) Mushrooms – Garlic
Buttered
(VEG) Potatoes – Baked
Potatoes

THURSDAY
(MISC) Grilled Cheese
Sandwiches
(SALAD) Green Salad
Carrot, Celery Sticks and Radish
Roses
Bar-B-Q Potato Chips
Kosher Dill Pickles

FRIDAY
(SEA) Lobster Thermidor
(SALAD) Carrots, Celery, Nut
and Pineapple Slaw with Sweet
Dressing Salad
(PAS) Rice – Long Grain Steamed
(VEG) Asparagus – Buttered

SATURDAY
(BF) Beef Patty Melt on Rye
(SALAD) Cole Slaw with Dressing
(VEG) Potatoes – French Fries

Grocery List – Salt & Pepper, Salad Dressings of Choice if not specified

MEATS
Beef – Ground Hamburger
Beef – Round Steak or Cubed
Chicken – Boneless Breasts
Chicken Cut-Up
Luncheon Meat – Boiled Ham
Seafood – Lobster Meat
Wieners/Frankfurters

VEGETABLES – FRESH

Bell Peppers	Mushrooms
Cabbage	Onions (10R)
Carrots (3R)	Potatoes
Celery (2R)	Potatoes–New Red
Corn on Cobb	Radishes (4R)
Lemon	Tomatoes (4R)
Lettuce Iceberg (4R)	

SPICES/STAPLES
Cumin
Flour
Garlic Powder (3R)
Onion Salt
Oregano
Paprika
Rosemary
Sugar – Granulated (2R)

FROZEN FOODS
Asparagus
Broccoli Cuts
French Fries

CANNED FOODS
Broth – Chicken (2R)
Chiles – Green
Enchilada Sauce
Evaporated Milk (2R)
Gravy – Beef w/Mushrooms
Green Beans – French Style
Mushrooms
Olives – Black Chopped (2R)
Pineapple Chunks
Refried Beans
Tomato Sauce

OTHER
Bar-B-Q Sauce
Bouillon – Chicken
Bread – Rye Sliced
Bread – White
Cheese – American
Cheese – Cheddar Sharp (5R)
Cheese – Cream

Cheese – Cottage
Cheese – Monterey Jack
Cheese – Parmesan
Cheese – Swiss (2R)
Eggs (3R)
Foil – Aluminum (2R)
Lemon Juice
Macaroni – Ring Shaped
Margarine (7R)
Mayonnaise (2R)
Milk – Half & Half
Oil – Vegetable
Pickles –Kosher Dill
Potato Chips – Barbecue
Rice – Long Grain (2R)
Salad Dressing – Tart Italian
Spray – Vegetable Oil
Toothpicks
Tortillas – Corn
Oil – Vegetable (2R)
Vinegar
Walnuts, Almonds or Pecans
Waxed Paper
Whipping Cream

-23-

Week #24

SUNDAY
(PK) Pork Dinner with Cauliflower,
Brussels Sprouts and Carrots
(SALAD) Tomato Wedges with Thousand
Island Dressing
(VEG) Potatoes – Creamed Cheese

MONDAY
(BF) Beef Savory Pie with Potato Topping
(VEG) Artichoke Hearts – Marinated
(BRD) Rolls– Refrigerator Rolls

TUESDAY
(WNR) Frankfurter Mardi Gras with Grilled
Cheese Sandwiches
(SALAD) Carrots, Celery, Nut, and Pineapple
 Slaw with Sweet Dressing

WEDNESDAY
(BF) Beef Creole Steak with
Potatoes
(VEG) Beans – Canned Green
Beans French Style

THURSDAY
(CRNBF) Corned Beef Casserole
with Sauerkraut and Potatoes
(VEG) Beans – Baked Beans

FRIDAY
(SEA) Shrimp in Crab Boil
(PAS) Raviolis – Cheese with
Roasted Garlic and Parmesan
Sauce
(SALAD) Bell Pepper and
Onion Ring Salad

SATURDAY
(BF) Beef Pepper Steak Sandwiches
(SALAD) Cole Slaw with Sweet
Dressing
(VEG) Potatoes – French Fries

Grocery List – Salt & Pepper, Salad Dressings of Choice if not specified

MEATS
Beef – Ground (2R)
Beef – Round or Cubed Steaks (2R)
Pork Boneless Roast
Seafood-Shrimp/Prawns (or frozen)
Wieners/Frankfurters

VEGETABLES – Fresh
Bell Peppers (5R)
Cabbage
Carrots (4R)   Onions (5R)
Celery   Onions Grn (2R)
Lemons (2R)   Potatoes (3R)
                     Tomatoes

FROZEN FOODS
Brussels Sprouts   French Fries
Carrots   Hash Browns
Cauliflower   Raviolis, Cheese

SPICES/STAPLES
Cornstarch
Dill Seed
Flour
Garlic Powder

Mustard – Dry
Onion Salt
Pepper Sauce – Red Hot
Sugar – Granulated (4R)

CANNED FOODS
Artichoke Hearts Marinated
Beans – Baked
Corned Beef
Evaporated Milk (2R)
Green Beans – French Style
Mushrooms
Pineapple Chunks
Sauerkraut
Soup – Cream of Mushroom
Tomato Juice
Tomatoes – Whole

OTHER
Bouillon – Chicken
Bread (2R)
Breadcrumbs
Cheese – American
Cheese – Cheddar (2R)

Cheese – Parmesan
Cheese – Swiss
Cornflakes
Crab Boil
Eggs
Lemon Juice
Margarine (3R)
Mayonnaise (2R)
Milk (2R)
Potato Puffs – Instant Mashed
Rolls – Refrigerator
Rolls – Steak Sandwich
Salad Dressing – Tart Italian
Salad Dressing – 1000 Island
Sauce – Roasted Garlic
   Parmesan
Shortening
Sour Cream
Vinegar
Walnuts
Waxed Paper
Whipping Cream

Decided for You Cookbook – 365 Dinners

Week #25

SUNDAY
(BF) Beef Crunchy Steaks
(MISC) Gnocchi's – Potato Noodles with Meat Sauce
(VEG) Beans – Green Smoked Beans

MONDAY
(CH) Chicken Teriyaki
(PAS) Rice – Fried Rice
(SALAD) Green Salad
(VEG) Corn – Cream Style

TUESDAY
(BF) Beef Ravioli Casserole with Green Beans
(SALAD) Cucumber and Onions Italian Pickled Salad
(BRD) Bread – Garlic French Bread

WEDNESDAY
(BF) Beef Italian Steak and Rice
(SALAD) Carrot, Radishes, and Celery Salad with Thousand Island Dressing
(VEG) Egg Plant Breaded

THURSDAY
WNR) Frankfurter Pronto Pups
(SALAD) Macaroni Salad
Potato Chips

FRIDAY
(SEA) Shrimp Creole
(PAS) Rice – Long Grain Steamed
(SALAD) Green Salad
(VEG) Mix Vegetable – Stir Fry

SATURDAY
(BF) Beef Enchilada Pie
(SALAD) Carrots, Radish and Celery, Iceberg Lettuce Salad and Thousand Island Dressing
(VEG) Beans – Refried Beans

Grocery List – Salt & Pepper, Salad Dressings of Choice if not specified

MEATS
Beef – Ground
Beef – Round Steak – Eye of (3R)
Beef – Stew Meat
Chicken – Boneless Breasts
Seafood – Shrimp – Cooked
Seafood – Prawns – Large
Wieners/Frankfurters

VEGETABLES – FRESH
Bell Peppers
Carrots (3R)   Onions (7R)
Celery (2R)   Onions–Grn (2R)
Cucumbers   Radishes (4R)
Eggplant   Tomatoes (3R)
Garlic (3R)
Lettuce – Iceberg (3R)

FROZEN FOODS
Broccoli
Green Beans Cut

SPICES/STAPLES
Basil
Bay Leaf
Cornstarch
Cumin

Flour (2R)
Garlic Powder (2R)
Italian Seasoning
Paprika
Parsley
Sugar – Granulated (2R)
Worcestershire (2R)

CANNED FOODS
Bamboo Shoots
Broth – Beef
Corn – Cream Style
Enchilada Sauce
Green Beans
Mushrooms – Sliced (2R)
Olives – Chopped Black
Ravioli's Beef
Refried Beans
Tomatoes (2R)
Tomato Sauce

OTHER
Bacon Bits
Beef Bouillon Granules
Bread – French
Breadcrumbs
Cheese – Cheddar (2R)

Cheese – Monterey Jack
Cheese – Parmesan (3R)
Eggs (3R)
Foil – Aluminum
Gnocchi (Potato Noodles)
Ketchup
Macaroni – Salad
Margarine (4R)
Mayonnaise
Mustard – Yellow
Oil – Vegetable (6R)
Onion Soup – Dry
Paper Sack
Pickles – Sweet
Potato Chips
Rice – Long Grain (3R)
Rolls – Crescent Dinner
Salad Dressing–Tart Italian (2R)
Salad Dressing–1000 Island (2R)
Soup – Onion Dry
Soy Sauce (2R)
Stuffing Mix–Seasoned/ Granulated
Teriyaki Sauce
Tortillas – Flour
Waxed Paper

Decided for You Cookbook – 365 Dinners

Week #26

SUNDAY
(BF) Beef Roast – Chuck
(SALAD) Lettuce and Bean
Sprouts and Mushroom Salad
(VEG) Potatoes, Onions and Carrots

MONDAY
(BF) Beef Steak Skillet – Saucy with
Potatoes and Green Beans
(SALAD) Tomato Wedges with
Thousand Island Salad Dressing
TUESDAY
(BF) Beef Roast Hash – (Leftover
Fried Bread
(SALAD) Lettuce, Green Pepper
Ring Salad
(VEG) Peas – Canned Peas – Creamed
(VEG) Potatoes – Mashed Potatoes

WEDNESDAY
(BF) Cabbage – Whole Stuffed
(SALAD) Tomato, Cucumber,
and Onion Salad w/Italian Dressing
(VEG) Potatoes – Mashed Potatoes

THURSDAY
(CH) Enchilada Chicken Casserole
(PAS) Rice – Spanish Rice
(VEG) Beans – Beans Refried

FRIDAY
(SEA) Codfish – Baked with Roast) on
Broth Topping and Potatoes
(SALAD) Green Salad
(VEG) Corn – Mexican Corn
(BRD) Bread – Garlic French Bread

SATURDAY
(BF) Beef Meat Turnovers
(SALAD) Green Salad
(VEG) Potatoes – French Fries

Grocery List – Salt & Pepper, Salad Dressings of Choice if not specified

MEATS
Beef – Ground Hamburger (2R)
Beef – Round Steak
Beef – Chuck Roast + Leftovers
Chicken – Boneless Breasts
Seafood – Codfish
VEGETABLES – FRESH
Bean Sprouts
Bell Peppers (3R)
Cabbage (2R)   Potatoes (3R)
Carrots   Potatoes New Red
Cucumbers   Radishes (2R)
Garlic (2R)   Tomatoes (4R)
Lettuce – Iceberg (5R)
Mushrooms (2R)
Onions (10R)
Parsley
FROZEN FOODS
French Fries
Green Beans
Peas & Carrots
SPICES/STAPLES
Cumin (3R)
Dill

Flour (2R)
Garlic Powder (2R)
Italian Seasoning
Marjoram
Onion Salt
Paprika
Sugar – Granulated
Worcestershire
Yeast
CANNED FOODS
Chiles – Green
Corn – Mexican
Milk – Evaporated (2R)
Peas
Pimentos
Refried Beans
Soup – Cream of Chicken
Soup – Cream of Mushroom
Tomato Sauce (3R)
Tomatoes Whole

OTHER
Bouillon – Beef Instant
Bouillon – Chicken
Bouquet Browning & Seas. Sauce
Bread – French
Bread – White
Cheese – Cheddar (2R)
Cheese – Parmesan
Eggs
Foil – Aluminum (2R)
Ketchup
Margarine (6R)
Milk – Half and Half
Mustard – Yellow
Oil – Vegetable (4R)
Rice – Long Grain
Salad Dressing – Tart Italian
Salad Dressing – 1000 Island
Salsa
Stuffing Mix – Herb Seasoned
Tortillas – Corn

Decided for You Cookbook – 365 Dinners

Week #27

SUNDAY
(BF) Beef Italian Skillet Dinner
with Potatoes and Italian Green Beans
(SALAD) Green Salad

MONDAY
(BF) Beef Steak – Rollups and Peas
(SALAD) Macaroni Salad
(BRD) Biscuits – Biscuit Mix

TUESDAY
(CH) Baked Breaded Chicken
(PAS) Noodles with White Sauce
(SALAD) Green Salad

WEDNESDAY
(MISC) Poor Boy Sandwiches
Olives, Carrot Sticks etc
Potato Chips

THURSDAY
(SEA) Spaghetti with White
Clam Sauce
(SALAD) Green Salad
(VEG) Zucchini – Zucchini
Buttered

FRIDAY
(SEA) Tuna Colcannon with
Cabbage and Mashed Potatoes
(SALAD) Tomato, Peppers,
Onion and Lettuce Salad
(VEG) Corn – Cream Style

SATURDAY
(BF) Beef Hamburger Polynesian
(VEG) Potatoes – Parisienne
(VEG) Spinach – Creamed Spinach

Grocery List – Salt & Pepper, Salad Dressings of Choice if not specified

MEATS
Beef – Cube Steaks
Beef – Ground Hamburger (2R)
Chicken – (Misc. Pieces to bake)
Luncheon Meats (Deli sliced)
Pork – Italian Sausage Thyme
Seafood – Codfish
VEGETABLES – FRESH
Bell Peppers (3R)
Cabbage
Carrots
Garlic (2R)
Lettuce Iceberg (5R)
Mushrooms
Onions (8R)
Onions – Green
Parsley
Peppers – Jalapeno
Potatoes (3R)   Tomatoes (6R)
Radishes (3R)   Zucchini
FROZEN FOODS
Green Beans-Italian
Spinach
SPICES/STAPLES
Cornstarch
Flour (3R)
Ginger

Italian Seasoning (2R)
Mustard – Dry
Nutmeg
Poultry Seasoning (2R)
Rosemary

CANNED FOODS
Clams – Minced
Corn – Cream Style
Milk – Evaporated (2R)
Olives – Black Pitted
Onions – White
Peas
Pineapple – Sliced
Potatoes – Whole
Soup – Cream of Chicken
Tomato Sauce
Tomatoes Stewed
Tuna
OTHER
Biscuit Mix
Bouquet Browning & Seasoning Sauce
Cheese – American
Cheese – Parmesan (4R)
Cherries – Maraschino
Cheese – Myzithra (Opt)
Lemon Juice

Macaroni–Salad
Margarine (8R)
Mayonnaise
Milk
Noodles – Flat Egg
Noodles – Spaghetti
Oil – Vegetable (2R)
Pickles – Sweet (2R)
Potato Chips
Rice – Long Grain
Rolls – Steak Sandwich
Salad Dressing – Tart Italian
Stuffing Mix – Herb (2R)
Toothpicks
Whipping Cream (2R)

-27-

SUNDAY
(PK) Tenderloin Pork Rounds
(SALAD) Tomato Wedges with
Thousand Island Dressing
(VEG) Potatoes – Creamed Cheese
(VEG) Brussels Sprouts – Buttered

MONDAY
(BF-PK-VEAL) Creamed Mock Chicken
    in Pastry Shells
(SALAD) Green Salad
or (VEG) Mushrooms – Garlic Buttered
(VEG) Potatoes – Potato Skins

TUESDAY
(BF) Ginger Beef
(PAS) Rice – Long Grain Steamed
(SALAD) Spinach, Mushroom and
Onion Salad with Dressing
Potato Chips
(VEG) Asparagus and Cauliflower
with Cheddar Cheese Sauce

WEDNESDAY
(BF) Beef Liver and Onions
(SALAD) Romaine Lettuce and
Cucumber Salad
(VEG) Potatoes – Au Gratin

THURSDAY
(BF) Beef Chili Burgers
(VEG) Potatoes – French Fries
Potato Chips

FRIDAY
(SEA) Tuna Cheese Toasties
with Green Beans
(SALAD) Green Salad

SATURDAY
(BF) Beef Empanadas with Peas and Carrots
(SALAD) Green Salad
(VEG) Potatoes – Tater Tots

Grocery List – Salt & Pepper, Salad Dressings of Choice if not specified

MEATS
Pork – Bacon
Beef – Ground Hamburger (2R)
Beef – Liver
Beef – Round Steak
Beef – Veal Boneless Cutlets
Pork – Boneless Chops (2R)

VEGETABLES – FRESH
Bell Peppers   Radishes (3R)
Chives   Spinach
Cucumbers   Tomatoes (4R)
Garlic (2R)
Lettuce – Iceberg (3R)
Lettuce – Romaine
Mushrooms (3R)
Onions (9R)
Onions – Green (2R)
Potatoes (4R)

FROZEN FOODS
Asparagus (or fresh)   Pastry Shells
Brussels Sprouts   Tater Tots
Cauliflower
French Fries (Opt)

SPICES/STAPLES
Cayenne Pepper
Cornstarch
Flour (4R)
Garlic Powder (2R)
Ginger
Monosodium Glutamate
Mustard – Dry
Onion Flakes (2R)
Onion Powder
Paprika
Sugar (2R)

CANNED FOODS
Broth – Beef (2R)
Broth – Chicken
Chili without Beans
Green Beans
Peas & Carrots
Pimiento
Soup – Cheddar Cheese
Soup – Cream of Chicken
Soup – Cream of Mushroom (2R)
Tuna

OTHER
Buns – Hamburger (2R)

Cheese – Cheddar (4R)
Cheese – Colby
Cheese – Cream
Cheese – Processed American
Gravy–Dry Mix w/Mushrooms
Horseradish
Lemon Juice (2R)
Margarine (7R)
Mayonnaise
Milk
Milk – Half and Half (2R)
Oil – Corn
Oil – Vegetable, Corn or Peanut
Pie Crust Mix
Potato Chips (2R)
Raisins
Rice – Long Grain
Salad Dressing – 1000 Island
Shortening
Sour Cream (2R)
Soy Sauce (2R)
Toothpicks
Vinegar
Waxed Paper

Decided for You Cookbook – 365 Dinners

Week #29

SUNDAY
(BF) Beef Wrap–Ups
(SALAD) Cole Slaw with Dressing
(VEG) Corn – Cream Style Corn

MONDAY
(BF) Beef Steak with Mushrooms
(SALAD) Romaine Lettuce, Mushroom
and Avocado Salad
(VEG) Potatoes – Mashed with Sour Cream
and Chives

TUESDAY
(BF) Beef Hash – Ranch Style with Rice
(SALAD) Green Salad
(VEG) Beans – Baked Beans

WEDNESDAY
(CH) Tso's Favorite Chicken
(PAS) Rice – Long Grain Steamed
(SALAD) Green Salad
(VEG) Mixed Vegetables – Stir Fry

THURSDAY
(BF) Beef Cubed Steaks–Pizza Style
(VEG) Cauliflower – Marinated
(VEG) Potatoes – Baked + Extra

FRIDAY
(SEA) Tuna Crunchy Bake
with Green Beans
(SALAD) Lettuce, Mayonnaise and
Onion Salad
(VEG) Potatoes – Au Gratin Potatoes

SATURDAY
(BF) Beef Mooligan's Meat
(SALAD) Potato Salad
(VEG) Brussels Sprouts – Buttered

Grocery List – Salt & Pepper, Salad Dressings of Choice if not specified

MEATS
Beef – Cubed Steak (2R)
Beef – Ground Hamburger (2R)
Beef – Round Steak
Chicken – Boneless Breasts/Thighs
Pork – Pork Steaks

VEGETABLES – FRESH
Avocado
Bell Peppers (4R)
Cabbage
Carrots (2R)   Onions–Grn (3R)
Cauliflower   Peppers–Hot
Celery (2R)   Potatoes (4R)
Chives   Radishes (2R)
Garlic (3R)   Tomatoes (2R)
Lettuce – Iceberg (3R)
Lettuce – Romaine
Mushrooms
Onions (10R)

FROZEN FOODS
Broccoli Cuts   Brussels Sprouts

SPICES/STAPLES
Basil
Celery Seed
Cornstarch
Curry Powder

Flour (3R)
Garlic Salt
Lemon Pepper
Onion Flakes
Oregano
Paprika
Pepper – Red Hot Flakes
Sugar – Granulated (4R)

CANNED FOODS
Bamboo Shoots
Beans – Baked
Broth – Beef
Corn – Cream Style
Corn – Whole Kernel
Green Beans
Milk – Evaporated (2R)
Mushrooms
Olives – Black Chopped
Pimentos
Soup – Cheddar Cheese
Soup – Cream of Mushroom (2R)
Spaghetti Sauce
Tomatoes
Tuna
Water Chestnuts

OTHER
Cashew Nuts
Cheese–American
Cheese–Cheddar (2R)
Cheese–Mozzarella
Cheese–Parmesan Romano (2R)
Cheese–Processed American
Cheese–Swiss
Eggs (4R)
Foil – Aluminum
Ketchup (2R)
Margarine (4R)
Mayonnaise (4R)
Milk
Milk – Half & Half
Onions – French Fried
Oil – Vegetable (5R)
Pickles – Sweet
Rice – Long Grain (3R)
Salad Dressing - French
Salad Dressing – Tart Italian
Sour Cream
Soy Sauce (3R)
Vinegar (5R)
Wine – White (2R)

-29-

Week #30

SUNDAY
(CH) Spicy Chicken Wings (see –
CH – Chicken Wing Party)
(MISC) Pizza – Mini Shrimp
(SALAD) Green Salad

MONDAY
(CH) Chicken and Links with Green Beans
(SALAD) Green Salad
(VEG) Potatoes – Mashed Potatoes

TUESDAY
(BF) Beef Steak – Salami Rolls
(SALAD) Spinach, Mushroom and
Onion Ring Salad with Dressing
(VEG) Zucchini – Zucchini Bake

WEDNESDAY
(PK) Pork Chop Creole with Rice
(SALAD) Green Salad
(VEG) Broccoli – Broccoli
Casserole

THURSDAY
(BF) Beef Hamburgers with
Cheese Sauce in a Vegetable
Wreath (Peas, White Onions,
Brussels Sprouts)
(PAS) Noodles with White Sauce
(SALAD) Green Salad

FRIDAY
(SEA) Salmon Quiche
(VEG) Carrots – Sweet Carrots
(VEG) Potatoes – Potato Pancakes

SATURDAY
(BF) Beef Hash and Mashed Potato
Casserole
(SALAD) Green Salad
(VEG) Beets – Pickled Beets and Olives
(VEG) Corn – Whole Kernel

Grocery List – Salt & Pepper, Salad Dressings of Choice if not specified

MEATS
Beef – Ground Hamburger
Beef – Round Steak
Beef – Stew Meat
Chicken – Cut up Fryer
Chicken – Lots of Wings
Luncheon Meat – Salami
Pork – Pork Chops – Thick
Pork – Link Sausage
Seafood – Shrimp cooked

VEGETABLES – FRESH
Bell Peppers
Celery
Garlic
Lettuce – Iceberg (5R)
Mushrooms
Onions (10R)
Onions – Green (2R)
Potatoes (3R)
Radishes (5R)
Spinach
Tomatoes (6R)
Zucchini

FROZEN FOODS
Broccoli Cuts
Brussels Sprouts
Onions – White Boiling

Peas Baby
Piecrust or Mix

SPICES/STAPLES
Baking Powder (2R)
Basil
Bay Leaf   Parsley
Cayenne Pepper   Peppercorns
Flour (4R)   Sugar – Brown
Marjoram   Sugar–Gran (2R)
Monosodium Glutamate
Mustard – Dry   Thyme
Onion Salt   Worcestershire
Oregano

CANNED FOODS
Beets – Pickled
Carrots
Corn – Whole Kernel
Green Beans (2R)
Olives Black Pitted
Milk – Evaporated (4R)
Salmon
Spaghetti Sauce
Tomatoes

OTHER
Biscuits – Canned
Bouillon – Chicken (2R)

Cheese–Cheddar Sharp (2R)
Cheese–Mozzarella (2R)
Cheese–Parmesan (2R)
Cheese–Processed American
Crackers – Saltine
Eggs (4R)
Foil – Aluminum
Ketchup
Lemon Juice
Margarine (5R)
Milk
Milk – Half and Half
Noodles – Flat Egg
Oil – Corn
Oil – Olive
Oil – Vegetable (3R)
Rice – Long Grain
Soy Sauce
Stuffing Mix–Herb Seasoned
Taco Seasoning – Dry Hot
Toothpicks
Vinegar (2R)
Whipping Cream
Wine – Burgundy (2R)

-30-

Week #31

SUNDAY
(BF) Beef Parmegiana
(PAS) Stuffed Pasta Shells
(SALAD) Green Salad
(VEG) Zucchini – Zucchini Bake

MONDAY
(PK) Pork Chops – Stuffed
(SALAD) Caesar Salad
(VEG) Corn – Hominy Corn
Potatoes

TUESDAY
(MISC) Crepes Colossal
(BF) Beef Bourguignon – Glenn's
(SALAD) Green Salad

WEDNESDAY
(BF) Beef Stuff-a-Roni
(SALAD) Cucumber and Onion
Italian Pickled Salad
(VEG) Corn – Cream Style Corn

THURSDAY
(BF) Beef Rollups with Carrots
(SALAD) Green Salad
(VEG) Potatoes – Mashed

FRIDAY
(MISC) Fondue Party – Hot Oil
Cooking, and Onion Cheese
Fondue
(SALAD) Romaine Lettuce,
Mushroom and Avocado Salad
(VEG) Broccoli – Broccoli
Casserole

SATURDAY
(CH) Chicken and Vegie Dinner
with Asparagus, Carrots, and
Potatoes
(SALAD) Green Salad

Grocery List –Salt & Pepper, Salad Dressings of Choice if not specified

MEATS
Beef – Ground Hamburger
Beef – Round Steak or Cubed (2R)
Beef – Steaks of choice
Beef – Chuck Roast or Short Ribs
Chicken – Boneless Breasts
Chicken Fryer – Cut up
Pork – Bacon (2R)
Pork – Bratwurst Sausage
Pork – Pork Chops Thick
Pork – Smokie Links – Miniature

VEGETABLES – FRESH
Avocado   Parsley (2R)
Bell Peppers   Potatoes (2R)
Broccoli   Radishes (4R)
Carrots (2R)   Tomatoes (4R)
Cauliflower   Zucchini
Celery
Cucumbers
Garlic (2R)
Lettuce – Iceberg (4R)
Lettuce – Romaine (2R)
Mushrooms (3R)
Onions (10R)

FROZEN FOODS
Asparagus Spears
Broccoli Cuts
French Fries
Meatballs
Prawns – Breaded

Scallops
Spinach – Chopped

SPICES/STAPLES
Bay Leaf   Tabasco Sauce
Flour (5R)   Thyme
Marjoram   Worcestershire
Nutmeg
Paprika
Poultry Seasoning
Savory
Sugar – Granulated

CANNED FOODS
Broth – Beef
Broth – Chicken
Corn – Cream Style
Corn – Hominy
Marinara Sauce
Milk Evaporated
Soup–Cheddar Cheese
Soup–Condensed Beefy Mushroom
Tomato Paste (2R)
Tomato Sauce

OTHER
Bouillon – Beef
Bouquet Browning & Season. Sauce
Breadcrumbs (2R)
Bread – French (Lots!)
Cheese – Blue
Cheese – Cheddar (2R)
Cheese – Mozzarella (3R)

Cheese – Parmesan (5R)
Cheese – Ricotta
Crackers – Saltine
Croutons
Eggs (6R)
Foil – Aluminum
Lemon Juice
Margarine (3R)
Milk + ½ & ½ Milk
Mustard – Dijon
Mustard – Yellow
Noodles – Stuff-a-Roni
Oil – Olive
Oil – Vegetable (6R)
Onion Dip (Commercially Made)
Pancake Mix
Pasta – Large Shells
Pickles – Dill
Salad Dressing – Tart Italian (2R)
Skewers – Wooden
Sour Cream
Stuffing Mix-Herb Seasoned (2R)
Toothpicks
Waxed Paper (Opt)
Whipping Cream
Wine – Burgundy
Wine – Ruby Port

Week #32

SUNDAY
(MISC) Game Hens – Baked
(SALAD) Cabbage Salad – Red
Shredded with Vinaigrette Dressing
(VEG) Corn – Whole Kernel Corn

MONDAY
(PK) Pork Broccoli Stir Fry
(PAS) Rice – Long Grain Steamed
(SALAD) Romaine Lettuce, and
Red Onion Rings

TUESDAY
(BF) Beef Hamburgers with Onions
and Bell Peppers, the Swedish Style
(SALAD) Cucumbers and Onion
Italian Pickled Salad
(VEG) Potatoes – Parsley Potatoes

WEDNESDAY
(CH) Chicken Cacciatore with
Noodles
(SALAD) Carrot Slaw with
    French Salad Dressing

THURSDAY
(BF) Beef Zucchini Casserole
(SALAD) Spinach, Mushroom &
Onion Ring Salad and Dressing
(VEG) Potatoes–Mashed Potatoes

FRIDAY
(SEA) Prawns – Tempura
(PK) Pork Chow Mein
(PAS) Rice – Fried Rice
(SALAD) Green Salad

SATURDAY
(PK) Ham and Leek Quiche
(SALAD) Green Salad
(VEG) Carrots – Sweet Carrots

Grocery List – Salt & Pepper, Salad Dressings of Choice if not specified

MEATS
Beef – Ground Hamburger (2R)
Chicken (Cut up Fryer)
Game Hens – Cornish
Pork – Ham Slices
Pork – Boneless Pork Chops (2R)
Seafood – Prawns or Frozen
Seafood – Shrimp Cooked

VEGETABLES – FRESH
Bell Peppers   Yams
Cabbage – Red   Zucchini (2R)
Carrots (3R)
Celery (2R)
Cucumbers
Garlic (3R)
Green Beans
Leeks
Lettuce – Iceberg (2R)
Lettuce – Romaine
Mushrooms (2R)
Onions (11R)
Onions – Green (2R)
Parsley (2R)
Potatoes (3R)
Radishes (2R)
Spinach
Tomatoes (2R)

FROZEN FOODS
Broccoli – Cuts
Pastry Shell

SPICES/STAPLES
Baking Powder
Basil
Cornstarch (2R)
Flour (2R)
Garlic Powder
Ginger
Mustard – Dry (2R)
Nutmeg
Sugar – Brown
Sugar – Granulated (3R)
Thyme

CANNED FOODS
Bamboo Shoots
Bean Sprouts
Broth – Chicken
Carrots
Corn – Whole Kernel
Milk – Evaporated (2R)
Olives Black Pitted
Tomatoes
Tomato Sauce

OTHER
Butcher's String/Twine
Cheese – Mozzarella

Cheese – Monterey Jack
Chili Sauce
Eggs (4R)
Lemon Juice (2R)
Margarine (4R)
Milk
Noodles – Egg
Noodles - Vermicelli
Oil – Corn
Oil – Sesame Oil
Oil – Vegetable (6R)
Oil – Olive
Rice – Long Grain (2R)
Salad Dressing – French
Salad Dressing – Tart Italian
Salad Dressing – Vinaigrette
Soy Sauce (4R)
Stuffing Mix (or Herb Croutons)
Vinegar (3R)
Wine - Red

Decided for You Cookbook – 365 Dinners

Week #33

SUNDAY
(PK) Ham Loaf Swirl with Green Beans
(SALAD) Green Salad
(VEG) Potatoes – Mashed Potatoes

MONDAY
(CH) Waikiki Chicken
(PAS) Rice – Long Grain Rice Steamed
(SALAD) Green Salad
Buttered
(VEG) Sweet Potatoes with
Marshmallow Topping
(VEG) Brussels Sprouts – Buttered

TUESDAY
Beef Potato Hamburger Meat
Pie (Pastel de Papa)
(SALAD) Green Salad
(VEG) Corn – Cream Style

WEDNESDAY
(CH) Chicken in Foil
(SALAD) Potato Salad
(VEG) Beans – Canned Green
Beans

THURSDAY
(BF) Hot Beef Sandwiches
(SALAD) Green Salad
(VEG) Broccoli – Broccoli

FRIDAY
(SEA) Tuna Patties
(SALAD) Macaroni Salad (BF)
(VEG) Peas – Canned Peas-
Creamed
(BRD) Bread – Garlic French
Bread

SATURDAY
(BF) Beef Spanish Steak and Potato Casserole
(VEG) Asparagus and Cauliflower with Cheese Sauce
(BRD) Biscuits – Cheese Garlic Dropped

Grocery List – Salt & Pepper, Salad Dressings of Choice if not specified

MEATS
Beef – Roast Deli Sliced
Beef – Ground Hamburger
Beef – Round Steak
Chicken – Boneless Breasts
Chicken – Whole
Pork – Ground Ham
Pork – Ground Sausage

VEGETABLES – FRESH
Bananas
Bell Peppers (2R)
Celery
Garlic
Lettuce – Iceberg (4R)
Onions (10R)
Onion Green
Parsley Chinese Cilantro
Potatoes (3R)
Radishes (4R)
Tomatoes (5R)

FROZEN FOODS
Asparagus
Broccoli
Brussels Sprouts
Cauliflower

SPICES/STAPLES
Cayenne Pepper
Celery Seed

Cornstarch (2R)
Cumin
Flour
Garlic Powder
Garlic Salt
Ginger
Italian Seasoning
Monosodium Glutamate
Paprika (2R)
Sauce – Pepper Hot
Sugar – Granulated

CANNED FOODS
Corn – Cream Style
Gravy – Beef
Green Beans (2R)
Milk – Evaporated
Olives – Black Chopped
Olives – Green Stuffed (2R)
Peas
Pineapple – Sliced
Sweet Potatoes
Tomato Juice
Tuna or Salmon

OTHER
Biscuit Mix
Bouillon – Beef
Bouillon – Chicken (2R)
Bread – French

Bread Sliced – White
Breadcrumbs (2R)
Cheese–Cheddar (2R)
Cheese–Mozzarella, Amer/Swiss
Chili Sauce
Eggs (4R)
Foil – Aluminum (4R)
Gnocchi (Potato Noodles)
Macaroni – Salad
Margarine (8R)
Marshmallows – Miniature
Mayonnaise (2R)
Milk (2R)
Milk – Half & Half (2R)
Mustard
Oats – Quick Cooking
Oil – Vegetable (2R)
Pickles Sweet (2R)
Raisins
Rice – Long Grain
Salad Dressing – French
Shake and Bake Coating Mix
Soy Sauce (2R)
Vinegar (2R)

Week #34

SUNDAY
(BF) Beef Steaks with Blue Cheese
(SALAD) Green Salad
(VEG) Broccoli and Noodles Parmesan

MONDAY
(CH) Chicken Potato Oregano Pot
(VEG) Brussels Sprouts – Buttered
(BRD) Corn Bread with a Little Help

TUESDAY
(BF) Beef Hamburgers Blue Cheese Stuffed
(SALAD) Green Salad
(VEG) Potatoes – French Fries

WEDNESDAY
(PK) Ham and Asparagus Rolls
(SALAD) Tomato Wedges with
Thousand Island Dressing
(VEG) Potatoes – Mashed Potatoes

THURSDAY
(BF) Beef Croquettes
(SALAD) Green Salad
(VEG) Corn – Cream Style Corn

FRIDAY
(SEA) Fish and Chips
(SALAD) Carrot Slaw with Raisin
Salad and French Dressing

SATURDAY
(BF) Beef Chop Suey – American Chinese
(PAS) Rice – Long Grain Steamed
(SALAD) Green Salad
(VEG) Carrots – Sweet Carrots

Grocery List – Salt & Pepper, Salad Dressings of Choice if not specified

MEATS
Beef–Ground Hamburger (2R)
Beef–New York/Sirloin Steaks (2R)
Chicken – Chicken Thighs
Pork – Boneless Pork Roast
Pork – Ham Slices – ¼"- ½" Thick
Seafood – Cod Fish Fillets

VEGETABLES – FRESH
Bean Sprouts
Bell Peppers
Carrots (2R)
Celery
Garlic (3R)
Lettuce – Iceberg (4R)
Mushrooms
Onions (9R)
Onions – Green
Parsley
Potatoes (2R)
Radishes (4R)
Tomatoes (5R)

FROZEN FOODS
Asparagus Spears
Broccoli – Cuts
Brussels Sprouts
French Fries (2R)

SPICES/STAPLES
Baking Powder
Chile Paste – Red Hot
Cornstarch
Flour (3R)
Garlic Powder
Garlic Salt
Ginger
Monosodium Glutamate
Oregano
Sugar – Brown
Sugar – Granulated (2R)
Tarragon

CANNED FOODS
Carrots
Corn – Cream Style
Milk – Evaporated (2R)
Soup – Cream of Mushroom
Soup – Cream of Shrimp
Water Chestnuts

OTHER
Beer
Biscuit Mix
Breadcrumbs
Broth – Chicken
Buns – Hamburger

Cheese – Blue (2R)
Cheese – Cheddar
Corn Meal – White
Eggs (4R)
Margarine (5R)
Milk
Newspaper
Noodles – Fettuccini
Oil – Peanut
Oil – Vegetable
Oyster Sauce Asian
Potato Flakes – Instant
Raisins
Rice – Long Grain
Salad Dressing – French
Salad Dressing – 1000 Island
Sour Cream
Soy Sauce (2R)
Spray – Vegetable Oil Cooking
Toothpicks
Vinegar
Walnuts
Wine – White (2R)

Decided for You Cookbook – 365 Dinners

Week #35

SUNDAY
(PK) Pork Roast, Potatoes and Carrots
(SALAD) Green Salad
(BRD) Biscuits – Biscuit Mix

MONDAY
(WNR) Wieners and Sauerkraut
(SALAD) Potato Salad – Hot German Style

TUESDAY
(BF) Bar-B-Q Cups
(SALAD) Macaroni Salad
(VEG) Beans – Canned Green
Beans

SATURDAY
(PK) Pork Sausage Patties
(SALAD) Cole Slaw with Dressing
(VEG) Beans – Baked Beans
(VEG) Potatoes – Mashed Potatoes

WEDNESDAY
(PK) Sliced Pork – Leftover Roast
(PAS) Noodles with White Sauce
(SALAD) Spinach, Mushroom
and Onion Ring Salad with
Dressing

THURSDAY
(BF) Beef Swiss Hamburgers on
Onion Rolls
Olives Black Pitted
Potato Chips

FRIDAY
(SEA) Crab Newburg on English
Muffins
(VEG) Asparagus – Buttered
(VEG) Potatoes – Au Gratin
Potatoes

Grocery List – Salt & Pepper, Salad Dressings of Choice if not specified

MEATS
Beef – Ground Hamburger (2R)
Pork – Bacon
Pork – Ground Sausage (2R)
Pork Loin Roast + Leftovers
Seafood – Crabmeat
Wieners/Frankfurters

VEGETABLES – FRESH
Cabbage (2R)   Radishes
Carrots (3R)   Spinach
Garlic (2R)   Tomatoes (2R)
Lettuce Iceberg
Mushrooms
Onions (7R)
Onions – Green (3R)
Potatoes (4R)

FROZEN FOODS
Asparagus

SPICES/STAPLES
Flour (3R)
Mustard – Dry
Nutmeg

Onion Flakes
Onion Salt
Paprika
Sage
Sugar – Granulated (4R)

CANNED FOODS
Beans - Baked
Milk – Evaporated (5R)
Green Beans
Olives – Black Pitted
Sauerkraut
Soup – Cheddar Cheese (2R)
Soup – Cream of Mushroom

OTHER
Bar-B-Q Sauce
Biscuit Mix (2R)
Cheese – Cheddar (2R)
Cheese – Parmesan (Opt) Myzithra
Cheese – Swiss
Eggs
English Muffins
Lemon Juice

Macaroni – Salad
Margarine (6R)
Mayonnaise (3R)
Milk – Half and Half
Mustard – Whole Grain
Noodles – Eg
Oil – Corn
Oil – Vegetable (2R)
Pickles – Sweet
Potato Chips
Rolls – Hamburger Onion
Soup – Dry Onion
Soy Sauce
Vinegar (4R)

-35-

Week #36

SUNDAY
(BF-PK) Bow Ties
(PAS) Rice – Long Grain Steamed
(SALAD) Green Salad
(VEG) Broccoli – Broccoli Buttered

MONDAY
(BF) Beef Steak Chuck and Pan Fried Potatoes
(SALAD) Romaine Lettuce & Onion Ring Salad
(VEG) Corn – Whole Kernel
(VEG) Okra – Fried Okra

TUESDAY
(BF) Beef Hamburger Acapulco
(PAS) Rice – Spanish
(SALAD) Tomato Wedges w/Italian Dressing
(VEG) Beans – Refried Beans
(BRD) Tortillas – Flour

WEDNESDAY
(CH) Chicken and Noodles in Creamy Sauce
(SALAD) Cabbage, Carrot, Pineapple Slaw with Sweet Dressing
(VEG) Peas–Canned Peas-Creamed

THURSDAY
(WNR) Frankfurter Goulash
(SALAD) Romaine Lettuce and Garlic Croutons
(VEG) Potatoes – Mashed Potatoes

FRIDAY
(SEA) Fish Fillets – Pan Fried
(SALAD) Apple, Raisins, and Walnut Salad with Poppy Seed Dressing
(VEG) Potatoes–Au Gratin Potatoes
(VEG) Spinach – Creamed Spinach

SATURDAY
(CH) Chicken in Potato Boats with Potato Puffs
(SALAD) Green Salad
(VEG) Beans – Canned Green Beans

Grocery List – Salt & Pepper, Salad Dressings of Choice if not specified

MEATS
Beef – Ground Hamburger (2R)
Beef – Chuck Steak
Chicken – Boneless Breasts
Chicken – Cut Up Fryer
Pork – Ground Pork Sausage
Seafood – Sole Fish Fillets
Wieners/Frankfurters

VEGETABLES/FRUIT – FRESH
Apples	Okra
Bell Peppers	Onins (8R)
Cabbage	Onions-Green
Carrots	Parsley
Celery (2R)	Potatoes (3R)
Garlic (2R)	Radishes (2R)
Lemon	Spinach
Lettuce–Iceberg (2R)	Tomatoes (3R)
Lettuce–Romaine (2R)	

FROZEN FOODS
Broccoli (or fresh)
Won Ton Skins (Wrappers) or fresh

SPICES/STAPLES
Caraway Seeds
Cayenne Pepper
Chili Powder (2R)
Cumin
Dill
Flour (5R)
Garlic Powder (2R)
Mustard – Dry (2R)
Nutmeg
Onion Flakes   Poppy Seeds
Paprika (2R)   Sugar Gran. (2R)

CANNED FOODS
Beans (Refried or Red)
Corn – Whole Kernel
Evaporated Milk (3R)
Green Beans
Olives Black Pitted
Peas
Pimentos
Pineapple – Chunk or Crushed
Soup – Cheddar Cheese
Soup – Cream of Chicken
Soup – Cream of Mushroom
Tomato Sauce (2R)
Water Chestnuts

OTHER
Bouillon – Chicken (2R)
Breadcrumbs
Buns – Hamburger
Cheese – Cheddar (3R)
Cheese – Cream
Cheese – Monterey Jack
Chili Sauce (Opt)
Cracker Meal
Croutons
Eggs (3R)
Guacamole Dip
Lemon Juice (3R)
Vinegar
Margarine (8R)
Mayonnaise
Milk Half & Half
Noodles – Egg
Oil – Peanut
Oil – Vegetable (4R)
Onion Juice
Potatoes – Instant
Raisins
Rice – Long Grain (2R)
Salad – Dressing Italian
Shortening
Sour Cream (3R)
Tortillas – Flour
Walnuts (2R)
Whipping Cream (2R)

Decided for You Cookbook – 365 Dinners

Week #37

SUNDAY
(BF) Veal Pot Pie with Carrots,
Celery, Peas and Biscuit Topping
(SALAD) Green Salad
(VEG) Potatoes – Mashed Potatoes

MONDAY
(BF) Beef Meat Loaf with Cheese-
Topped Potato
(SALAD) Cole Slaw with Dressing
(VEG) Corn – Cream Style Corn

TUESDAY
(CH) Chicken with Mustard Sauce
(PAS) Rice – Long Grain Steamed
(VEG) Brussels Sprouts – Buttered

WEDNESDAY
(BF) Beef Stuffed Eggplant
Parmigiana
(SALAD) Romaine Lettuce and
Red Onion Ring Salad
(VEG) Beans – Canned Green
Beans French Style

THURSDAY
(BF) Beef and Broccoli
PAS) Rice–Long Grain Steamed
(SALAD) Green Salad

FRIDAY
(SEA) Shrimp and Onion Seafood
Pie
(SALAD) Cucumber and Onion
Italian Pickled Salad

SATURDAY
(PK) Mozzarella Cristo Sandwiches
(SALAD) Green Salad with Bean Sprouts
Black Pitted Olives
Cubes of Cheddar and Monterey Jack Cheese

Grocery List – Salt & Pepper, Salad Dressings of Choice if not specified

MEATS
Beef – Ground Hamburger (2R)
Beef – Sirloin Steak
Beef – Veal Scaloppini
Chicken (fryer cut up)
Luncheon Meats – Deli Ham, Turkey
Pork – Ground Sausage
Seafood – Shrimp and Crabmeat

VEGETABLES – FRESH
Cabbage	Lettuce-Iceberg (4R)
Carrots (2R)	Lettuce Romaine
Celery (2R)	Onions (9R)
Cucumbers	Potatoes (2R)
Eggplant	Radishes (3R)
Lemons	Tomatoes (3R)

FROZEN FOODS
Broccoli (2R) – or fresh
Brussels Sprouts
Pastry Shell (or make your own)
Peas

SPICES/STAPLES
Flour (2R)
Garlic Powder

Oriental Seasoning Mix-Beef/Broccoli
Oregano
Parsley Flakes
Pepper Sauce – Hot Pepper
Sugar – Granulated
Tarragon

CANNED FOODS
Bamboo Shoots
Bean Sprouts (2R)
Broth – Chicken
Corn – Cream Style
Green Beans – French Style
Milk – Evaporated (2R)
Olives – Black Pitted
Spaghetti Sauce
Tomato Sauce
Tuna

OTHER
Biscuit Mix
Bouillon – Chicken (2R)
Bread – White
Breadcrumbs (2R)
Cheese – Cheddar (3R)

Cheese – Monterey Jack
Cheese – Mozzarella (2R)
Cheese – Parmesan
Cheese – Ricotta
Eggs (2R)
Foil – Aluminum
Margarine (7R)
Mayonnaise
Milk (2R)
Milk – Half-and-Half
Mustard – Dijon
Noodles – Angel Hair
Oil – Vegetable (3R)
Onion Soup – Dry
Rice – Long Grain (3R)
Salad Dressing – Tart Italian
Soy Sauce
Steak Sauce
Vinegar

Decided for You Cookbook – 365 Dinners

Week #38

SUNDAY
(PK) Pork Chops – Pan Fried
(SALAD) Spinach, Mushroom and
Onion Salad with Dressing
(VEG) Peas – Black-Eyed Peas
(VEG) Potatoes – Mashed Potatoes
(MISC) Gravy – Pork Chop Gravy

MONDAY
CH) – Almond Chicken
(PAS) Rice – Long Grain Steamed
(SALAD) Chinese Chicken Salad
with Dressing
(VEG) Chinese Vegetables – Stir Fried

TUESDAY
(BF) Beef Hamburger Meatball Stroganoff
(PAS) Noodles – Spinach with White Sauce
(VEG) Beans – Canned Green Beans French Style
(VEG) Tomatoes – Broiled

WEDNESDAY
(WNR) Frankfurters in
Bar-B-Q Sauce
(SALAD) Green Salad
(VEG) Peas – Peas & Carrots
Buttered
(VEG) Potatoes–Parsley + Xtra

THURSDAY
(BF) Beef Meat Loaf – Stove Top
Mini's
(SALAD) Potato Salad–Leftover
Mashed Potatoes
(VEG) Corn – Cream Style Corn

FRIDAY
(SEA) Salmon Spinach Fluff
(SALAD) Green Salad
(VEG) Potatoes – Canned Potatoes

SATURDAY
(MISC) Pizza –Versatile Style (Ham,
Bacon, Scrambled Eggs, Onion and
Mushroom or other choice)
(SALAD) Green Salad

Grocery List – Salt & Pepper, Salad Dressings of Choice if not specified

MEATS
Beef – Ground Hamburger
Chicken – Boneless Breasts
Pork – Bacon (2R)
Pork – Ham Slices
Pork – Pork Chops
Wieners/Frankfurters

VEGETABLES – FRESH
Broccoli	Parsley (2R)
Cilantro	Potatoes (3R)
Garlic	Radishes (3R)
Lemon	Snow Peas
Lettuce–Iceberg (4R)	Spinach
Mushrooms (3R)	Tomatoes (5R)
Onions (7R)	
Onions – Green (3R)	

FROZEN FOODS
Green Beans	Spinach or fresh
Meatballs	Wonton Skins
Pizza Crust	

SPICES/STAPLES
Flour (3R)	Garlic Pwdr

Mustard – Dry (2R)
Oregano (2R)
Pepper – Red Flakes
Sage
Seeds – Sesame
Sugar (2R)
Thyme

CANNED FOODS
Bean Sprouts
Black-Eyed Peas
Chicken – Boned
Corn – Cream Style
Green Beans – French Style
Milk – Evaporated (3R)
Mushrooms
Peas & Carrots
Potatoes – Sliced
Salmon
Soup – Tomato
Spaghetti Sauce
Tomato Sauce
Water Chestnuts

OTHER
Almonds – Slivered Toasted
Bar-B-Q Sauce

Bouillon – Beef
Breadcrumbs (2R)
Buns – Hot Dog
Cheese – Mozzarella
Cheese – Parmesan (2R)
Eggs (5R)
Gravy – Chicken Dry
Lemon Juice
Margarine (6R)
Mayonnaise
Milk (3R)
Mustard Yellow
Noodles – Chow Mein Crispy
Noodles – Green Spinach
Oil – Corn
Oil – Vegetable (5R)
Oil – Sesame
Pickles – Sweet Dills
Rice – Long Grain
Shortening
Sour Cream
Stroganoff Sauce Mix-dry
Soy Sauce (2R)
Tartar Sauce
Vinegar (3R)

Decided for You Cookbook – 365 Dinners

Week #39

SUNDAY
(CH) Chicken Paprikash and Noodles
(SALAD) Carrot Slaw Salad with
French Dressing
(VEG) Beans – Canned Green Beans

MONDAY
(BF) Beef Fajitas
(PAS) Rice – Spanish Rice
(VEG) Peas – Canned Peas-Creamed

TUESDAY
(WNR) Frankfurter Skillet and Scalloped
Potatoes with Ham
(SALAD) Cole Slaw with Dressing
(VEG) Beans – Baked Beans

WEDNESDAY
(BF) Beef Burgers – French
(SALAD) Romaine Lettuce,
Mushroom and Avocado Onion
Salad
Potato Chips

THURSDAY
(BF) Veal Saltimbocca
(SALAD) Lettuce Wedges with
Thousand Island   Dressing
(VEG) Carrots – Sweet Carrots
(VEG) Potatoes – Mashed Potatoes

FRIDAY
(SEA) Crab Seafood Thermidor
(PAS) Noodles with Garlic, Oil
and Pepper Sauce
(SALAD) Green Salad

SATURDAY
(CH) Chicken Wing Party with
Asian Cherry, Classic Buffalo &
Soy/Dijon with Ancho Chiles
(VEG) Asparagus – Cold Asparagus
 (PAS) Noodles – Angel Hair with
White Sauce
(SALAD) Beets (Pickled) and Onion
Salad with Italian Dressing

Grocery List – Salt & Pepper, Salad Dressings of Choice if not specified

MEATS
Beef – Ground Beef
Beef – Flank or London Broil Steak
Beef – Veal Scaloppini or Medallions
Chicken – Boneless Chicken Breasts
Chicken – Chicken Wings (Lots)
Pork – Ham Slices
Pork – Prosciutto Ham
Wieners/Frankfurters

VEGETABLES - FRESH

Avocado	Lettuce–Romaine
Bell Peppers (GYR)	Mushrooms
Cabbage	Onions (8R)
Carrots (2R)	Parsley (3R)
Chiles Ancho	Pepper-Red Pods
Garlic Cloves (5R)	Potatoes (2R)
Gingerroot	Radishes
Lemon	Tomatoes
Lettuce – Iceberg (2R)	

FROZEN FOODS
Crab Meat (or Fresh)

SPICES/STAPLES

Bay Leaf	Cumin (2R)
Cayenne Pepper	Flour
Cloves Ground	

Garlic Powder
Mustard-Dry
Onion Salt
Oregano
Paprika (2R)
Pepper Sauce – Red Hot
Sage

Sugar Brown (3R)
Sugar Granulated
Thyme

CANNED FOODS
Asparagus Cuts
Beans - Baked
Beets Pickled
Broth – Chicken
Carrots
Cherries – Dark Pitted
Green Beans
Milk – Evaporated (4R)
Mushrooms (2R)
Peas
Soup–Cream of Shrimp
Soup–Tomato (2R)

OTHER
Bouillon – Chicken
Buns – Steak Sandwich
Cheese – Blue

Cheese – Cheddar
Cheese – Parmesan (3R)
Foil – Aluminum
Lemon Juice (3R)
Margarine (8R)
Mayonnaise (2R)
Milk
Mustard Dijon
Noodles-Angel Hair or
Spaghettini
Noodles – Fettuccini
Noodles – Flat Egg
Oil – Canola/Olive (3R)
Oil – Vegetable (2R)
Potato Chips
Rice – Long Grain
Salad Dressings–Frnch/Ital./1000
Salsa Red or Green
Shortening
Soup – Dry Onion
Sour Cream (2R)
Soy Sauce (2R
Tortillas–Flour
Vinegar (4R)
Wine – Red
Wine – White

Decided for You Cookbook – 365 Dinners

Week #40

SUNDAY
(CH) Chicken Eleganté with Green Beans
and (SALAD) Green Salad
(VEG) Potatoes – Baked (with 3 or 4 leftover)
and

MONDAY
(SOUP) Potato Soup - Leftover Baked
(MISC) Crackers – Saltine

TUESDAY
(BF) Beef Hamburger Continental
with Asparagus
(PAS) Rice – Long Grain Steamed
(SALAD) Cole Slaw with Dressing

WEDNESDAY
(BF) Beef Meatballs, Zucchini
Rice Casserole
(SALAD) Spinach, Mushroom
Onion Salad with Dressing

THURSDAY
(BF) Beef Gorditas
(PAS) Rice – Spanish Rice
(SALAD) Green Salad
(VEG) Beans – Refried Beans

FRIDAY
(SEA) Tuna and Broccoli Rice
Casserole
(SALAD) Carrot, Celery, Nut
and Pineapple Slaw with
Dressing
(BRD) Bread – Garlic French
Bread

SATURDAY
(PK) Glazed Smoked Sausage-Kielbasa
(PAS) Raviolis – Cheese with Roasted
Garlic & Parmesan Sauce
(VEG) Squash – Buttered Squash

Grocery List – Salt & Pepper, Salad Dressings of Choice if not specified

MEATS
Beef – Ground Hamburger (3R)
Chicken – Boneless Breasts
Seafood – Lobster, Crab or Shrimp
Pork – Sweet Italian Sausage
Pork – Smoked Kielbasa Sausage

VEGETABLES - FRESH
Cabbage   Zucchini
Carrots (2R)
Celery (3R)
Chives
Cucumbers
Garlic (2R)
Leeks
Lemons (2R)
Lettuce – Iceberg (2R)
Mushrooms
Onions (7R)
Onions – Green
Potatoes (2R)
Radishes (2R)
Spinach
Squash (any choice)
Tomatoes (2R)

FROZEN FOODS
Asparagus Spears
Broccoli – Chopped
Green Beans – Whole
Ravioli/Tortellini Cheese Filled

SPICES/STAPLES
Basil
Chili Powder
Cornstarch (2R)
Cumin
Flour
Garlic Powder
Garlic Salt
Italian Seasoning
Mustard – Dry
Onion Salt
Oregano
Paprika (2R)
Sugar – Brown
Sugar – Granulated (3R)
Worcestershire

CANNED FOODS
Broth – Beef & Chicken
Milk – Evaporated (2R)
Pineapple - Chunks
Refried Beans
Tomatoes – Stewed
Tomato Sauce
Tuna

OTHER
Bar-B-Q Sauce
Bouillon – Chicken (2R)
Bread – French

Breadcrumbs
Buttermilk
Cheese – Cheddar (3R)
Cheese – Parmesan (2R)
Crackers – Saltines
Eggs (2R)
Foil – Aluminum (2R)
Lemon Juice
Margarine (3R)
Mayonnaise (2R)
Oil – Corn
Oil – Vegetable (3R)
Rice – Long Grain (3R)
Rice – Minute Quick Cooking
Sauce – Hollandaise
Sauce–Roasted Garlic &
   Parmesan
Sour Cream
Soy Sauce
Toothpicks
Tortillas – Corn
Tuna
Vinegar (5R)
Walnuts
Waxed Paper
Wine – White

Decided for You Cookbook – 365 Dinners

Week #41

SUNDAY
(PK) Bacon and Cheese Frittata
(PAS) Rice – Fried Rice
(SALAD Tomatoes, Peppers, Onion
Salad with Italian Dressing

MONDAY
(CH) Peanut Crusted Chicken Fingers
with Dipping Sauce
(SALAD) Green Salad
(VEG) Beans – Green Bean Casserole

TUESDAY
(BF) Beef Hamburger Teriyaki with Rice
(VEG) Snow Peas (Sugar Peas)
Mushroom,

WEDNESDAY
(BF) Beef Meat Loaf – Bar-B-Q
(SALAD) Potato Salad
(VEG) Beans – Baked Beans

THURSDAY
(CH) Broiled Chicken
(SALAD) Macaroni Salad
(VEG) Broccoli – Broccoli Buttered

FRIDAY
(SEA) Lobster – Broiled or Steamed
(SALAD) Romaine Lettuce,
and Avocado Salad
(VEG) Potatoes – Baked (+ 4
leftovers)

SATURDAY
(BF) Veal Parmigano – Betty's
(SALAD) Green Salad
(VEG) Potatoes – Mashed Potatoes

Grocery List – Salt & Pepper, Salad Dressings of Choice if not specified

MEATS
Beef – Ground Hamburger (2R)
Beef – Boneless Veal Cutlets
Chicken – Boneless Breasts
Chicken – Cut Fryer or Quarters
Pork - Bacon
Seafood – Lobster Tails
Seafood – Shrimp Cooked

VEGETABLES - FRESH
Avocado
Bell Peppers
Celery   Potatoes (4R)
Lettuce–Iceberg (2R) Radishes
Lettuce–Romaine   Snow Peas
Mushrooms (2R)   Tomatoes (4R)
Onions (6R)
Onions – Green (3R)

FROZEN FOODS
Broccoli Spears
Green Beans – French Style

SPICES/STAPLES
Cayenne Pepper
Celery Seed
Flour (2R)
Garlic Powder (4R)
Onion Powder
Seeds – Sesame
Tabasco Sauce

CANNED FOODS
Baked Beans
Bamboo Shoots
Olives – Black Pitted
Evaporated Milk
Soup-Cream of Mushroom
Spaghetti Sauce
Water Chestnuts

OTHER
Bar-B-Q Sauce
Breadcrumbs (2R)
Cheese – Cheddar
Cheese – Mozzarella

Cheese – Parmesan
Crackers – Saltines
Eggs (5R)
Foil – Aluminum
Lemon Juice
Macaroni – Salad
Mayonnaise (2R)
Margarine/Butter (5R)
Milk (3R)
Mustard – Creole
Oil – Vegetable (4R)
Onion Rings – French Fried
Peanuts – Salted
Pickles – Sweet Dill or Sweet (2R)
Rice – Long Grain (2R)
Salad Dressing – Italian
Salad Dressing – French
Sour Cream (2R)
Soy Sauce (2R)
Teriyaki Sauce
Vinegar

Week #42

SUNDAY
(BF) Beef Taco Salad
Tortilla or Taco Chips

MONDAY
(PK) Pork Chops Marengo
(VEG) Brussels Sprouts – Buttered
(VEG) Potatoes – Mashed Potatoes

TUESDAY
(CH) Chicken Poulette Parisienne with
Artichoke Hearts
(PAS) Noodles with White Sauce
(SALAD) Green Salad

WEDNESDAY
(BF) Beef Meat Pie
(SALAD) Green Salad
(BRD) Corn Bread – Tex Mex

THURSDAY
(MISC) Chile Relleno
(PAS) Rice – Spanish Rice
(SALAD) Cucumber and Onion
Italian Pickled Salad
(VEG) Beans – Refried Beans

FRIDAY
(SEA) Shrimp and Sesame
Asparagus
(SALAD) Romaine Lettuce
with Red Onion Rings
(VEG) Potatoes – Thrice Baked

SATURDAY
(BF) Beef Meat Loaf – Biscuit Wrapped
(VEG) Peas – Canned Peas – Creamed
(VEG) Potatoes – Mashed Potatoes

Grocery List – Salt & Pepper, Salad Dressings of Choice if not specified

MEATS
Beef – Ground (2R)
Chicken – Cut Up Fryer
Pork - Pork Chops
Seafood – Prawns – Large

VEGETABLES - FRESH
Asparagus (or frozen)
Avocado
Bell Peppers
Cucumbers
Lettuce – Iceberg (3R)
Lettuce – Romaine
Onions – Green (2R)
Onions (6R)
Parsley
Potatoes (3R)
Radishes (2R)
Tomatoes (3R)

FROZEN FOODS
Artichoke Hearts or Canned
Brussels Sprouts
Peas
Pie Crusts

SPICES/STAPLES
Baking Powder
Basil (2R)
Cumin
Flour (2R)

Garlic Powder (2R)
Mustard – Dry
Onion – Salt
Rosemary
Seeds – Sesame
Worcestershire (2R)

CANNED FOODS
Beef Stew
Chiles – Whole Green/Chopped (3R)
Chili with Beans
Corn – Cream Style
Milk – Evaporated (4R)
Mushrooms – Sliced
Olives Black Pitted Sliced
Peas
Refried Beans
Soup – Cream of Mushroom
Spaghetti Sauce – Meatless
Tomatoes – Chopped
Tomato Sauce
Tomato Stewed

OTHER
Biscuit Mix
Bouillon – Beef
Bouillon – Chicken
Breadcrumbs
Cheese – American (2R)
Cheese – Cheddar (4R)
Cheese – Monterey Jack

Cheese – Parmesan (Opt
Myzithra)
Corn Meal – Yellow
Eggs (3R)
Foil – Aluminum
Ketchup
Margarine (6R)
Milk
Noodles – Egg
Oil – Vegetable (5R)
Rice – Long Grain (2R)
Salad Dressing – Italian
Salsa (med to hot) (2R)
Shake-n-Bake (or make your
own)
Soup – Dry Onion
Sour Cream (3R)
Soy Sauce
Taco Seasoning – Dry
Tortilla Chips

Decided for You Cookbook – 365 Dinners

Week #43

SUNDAY
(CH) Chicken Satay with Peanut Sauce
(PAS) Rice and Mushrooms
(SALAD) Carrot, Celery, Nut and
Pineapple Slaw Salad with Sweet Dressing
(VEG) Asparagus – Buttered

MONDAY
(BF) Beef Tamales
(SALAD) Macaroni Salad
(VEG) Corn – Cream Style Corn

TUESDAY
(CH) Cheddar Chicken with Broccoli
(SALAD) Lettuce and Mayonnaise
and Onion Salad
(VEG) Potatoes-Mashed w/Garlic

WEDNESDAY
(PK) Pork Sandwiches – Bar-B-Q
(SALAD) Cole Slaw – Chicken
Seller's Imitation
(VEG) Potatoes – French Fries

THURSDAY
(BF) Beef Mother's Baked Steak
and Potatoes
(SALAD) Green Salad
(VEG) Vegetable Medley
Casserole (Cauliflower, Broccoli
& Carrots)

FRIDAY
(SEA) Tuna Panella with Peas and
Rice
(SALAD) Green Salad
(VEG) Carrots – Sweet Carrots

SATURDAY
(BF) Beef Prime Rib
(SALAD) Green Salad
(VEG) Potatoes – Baked Potatoes
(VEG) Zucchini Fritters

Grocery List – Salt & Pepper, Salad Dressings of Choice if not specified

MEATS
Beef – Prime Rib Roast
Beef – Round Steak
Chicken – Boneless Breasts (2R)
Pork – Boneless Pork Roast

VEGETABLES - FRESH
Bell Peppers
Cabbage
Carrots (2R)   Lime
Celery   Mushrooms
Chives   Onions (7R)
Cilantro   Potatoes (4R)
Garlic Cloves (3R)   Radishes (3R)
Lemon   Tomatoes (4R)
Lettuce – Iceberg (5R) Zucchini

FROZEN FOODS
Asparagus Spears or fresh
Broccoli – Chopped
Cauliflower, Broccoli & Carrots
French Fries
Peas

SPICES/STAPLES
Baking Powder
Chili Paste – Red Hot
Curry Powder
Flour (2R)
Ginger Fresh, Crystals or Powder
Sugar – Brown (2R)
Sugar – Granulated (2R)

CANNED FOODS
Carrots
Corn – Cream Style
Milk – Evaporated (2R)
Pimientos
Pineapple – Chunks
Soup – Cream of Mushrooms
Tamales - Beef
Tuna

OTHER
Almonds – Sliced
Bar-B-Q Sauce
Beer
Bouillon – Chicken
Bun – Hamburger or Steak Sandwich
Buttermilk
Cheese – Cheddar (2R)
Cheese – Swiss

Clam Juice
Eggs
Foil – Aluminum (3R)
Lemon Juice (2R)
Macaroni – Salad
Margarine (4R)
Mayonnaise (4R)
Milk (2R)
Oil – Olive
Oil – Vegetable (5R)
Onions – French Fried
Peanuts
Peanut Butter – Smooth
Pickles – Sweet or Sweet Dills
Rice – Long Grain (2R)
Rock Salt (Optional)
Skewers – Wooded
Sour Cream
Soy Sauce
Vinegar – White
Yogurt – Plain
Walnuts
Waxed Paper

Decided for You Cookbook – 365 Dinners

Week #44

SUNDAY
(CH) Chicken Breast Elisabeth
(VEG) Broccoli – Buttered Broccoli
(VEG) Potatoes – Mashed Potatoes

MONDAY
(BF) Mongolian Beef
(PAS) Rice – Fried Rice
(SALAD) Green Salad
(VEG) Corn – Cream Style

TUESDAY
(BF) Beef Skillet Patties with Smothered Onions
(SALAD) Lettuce with Alfalfa Sprouts Salad
(VEG) Potatoes – Hash Browns

WEDNESDAY
(LAMB) Deviled Lamb Chops
(SALAD) Green Salad
(VEG) Mushrooms – Garlic Buttered
(VEG) Potatoes – Fried Potatoes

THURSDAY
(CH) Chicken and Ham Lasagna with Asparagus
(SALAD) Tomato Wedges w/Italian Dressing

FRIDAY
(SEA) Sweet and Sour Fish
(PAS) Rice – Steamed Long Grain
(VEG) Chinese Vegetables – Stir Fried

SATURDAY
(BF) Beef Mexican Stew
(BRD) Corn Bread – Tex-Mex

Grocery List – Salt & Pepper, Salad Dressings of Choice if not specified

MEATS
Beef – Flank Steak
Beef – Ground Hamburger
Beef – Stew Meat
Chicken Boneless Breasts (2R)
Lamb – Lamb Shoulder Chops
Luncheon Meat – Ham (or Boiled)
Pork – Bacon or Drippings
Pork – Baked Ham Slices (2R)
Seafood – Fish Fillets
Seafood – Shrimp Cooked

VEGETABLES - FRESH
Alfalfa Sprouts
Bell Peppers G/R (2R)
Lettuce – Iceberg (3R)
Mushrooms (3R)
Onions (4R)
Onions – Green (4R)
Potatoes (3R)
Radishes (2R)
Tomatoes (4R)

FROZEN FOODS
Asparagus Cuts
Broccoli Cuts
CA Mix Corn/Green Beans

Broccoli Florets
Hash Browns
SPICES/STAPLES
Baking Powder
Cornstarch (3R)
Cumin
Flour (3R)
Garlic Powder (3R)
Garlic Salt (2R)
Onion – Flakes
Pepper – Red Flakes
Sugar - Granulated (2R)
Thyme
CANNED FOODS
Broth – Beef
Broth – Chicken (3R)
Chiles – Green (2R)
Corn – Cream Style (2R)
Milk – Evaporated
Mushrooms
Onions – White
Pineapple – Chunks
Tomatoes
Water Chestnuts
OTHER
Breadcrumbs (2R)
Bread – White
Cheese – Cheddar
Cheese – Mozzarella

Cheese - Parmesan or Romano
Chili Sauce
Corn Meal Yellow
Eggs (3R)
Foil – Aluminum
Honey
Ketchup
Lemon Juice
Margarine (9R)
Milk
Mustard Yellow (2R)
Noodles – Lasagna
Oil – Corn
Oil – Peanut
Oil – Sesame
Oil – Vegetable (6R)
Oyster Sauce
Peanut Butter
Rice – Long Grain (2R)
Salad Dressing Italian
Sour Cream
Soy Sauce 4R)
Toothpicks
Vinegar
Waxed Paper
Whipping Cream
Wine – Rice

-44-

Decided for You Cookbook – 365 Dinners

Week #45

SUNDAY
(CH) Chicken Turnovers
(VEG) Broccoli – Broccoli Buttered
(VEG) Potatoes – Scalloped

MONDAY
(BF) Beef Ground Skillet
(PAS) Noodles with White Sauce
(SALAD) Green Salad
(VEG) Cauliflower and Mushrooms

TUESDAY
(MISC) Italian Cheese Boats
(VEG) Onion Rings Texas Style –
Variation

WEDNESDAY
(BF) Beef Hamburger Dressing
Bake
(SALAD) Tomato Wedges
with Thousand Island Dressing
(VEG) Beans – Canned Green
Beans
(VEG) Potatoes – Mashed Potatoes

THURSDAY
(BF) Beef Breaded Strips
SALAD) Corn, Pimiento and Peas
Marinated Salad
(VEG) Potatoes – Oven Fried Dinner
Fries

FRIDAY
(SEA) Sweet and Sour Shrimp
(PAS) Rice – Long Grain Steamed
(VEG) Asparagus – Stir Fried

SATURDAY
(BF) Indian Taco's – Pueblo
(VEG) Beans – Refried Beans
(VEG) Corn – Corn and Jalapeno
Casserole

Grocery List – Salt & Pepper, Salad Dressings of Choice if not specified

MEATS
Beef – Ground Hamburger (3R)
Beef – Round Steak
Chicken – Thighs
Luncheon Meat – Bologna, Salami
Pork – Sausage Links
Seafood – Prawns

VEGETABLES – FRESH

Asparagus	Mushrooms
Bell Peppers (2R)	Parsley
Celery (3R)	Peppers-Jalapeno
Garlic	Potatoes (3R)
Onions (8R)	Tomatoes (4R)
Onions – Green	
Lettuce – Iceberg (2R)	

FROZEN FOODS
Broccoli Cuts
Cauliflower
Fries – Dinner
SPICES/STAPLES
Baking Powder
Cornstarch
Flour (7R)
Garlic Powder (2R)
Onion Salt
Oregano
Paprika

Mustard – Dry
Pepper – Red Flakes
Rosemary
Sugar – Granulated (3R)
CANNED FOODS
Broth – Chicken (2R)
Chiles – Green or Jalapeno
Corn – Cream Style
Corn – Whole Kernel
Corn – White Whole Kernel
Green Beans
Milk – Evaporated (2R)
Olives – Pimiento Stuffed
Peas – Baby Lesueur Small
Pineapple - Chunks
Pimiento
Refried Beans
Tomato Sauce

OTHER
Almonds – Sliced
Bouillon – Chicken
Breadcrumbs (2R)
Cheese – Cheddar (4R)
Cheese – Mozzarella
Cheese – Parmesan (2R)
Eggs (4R)

Ketchup
Margarine (9R)
Mayonnaise
Milk (4R)
Milk – Dry Solids
Noodles – Egg
Oats – Quick Cooking
Oil – Olive
Oil – Vegetable (4R)
Paper Towels
Potato Chips
Rice – Long Grain (3R)
Rolls – Crescent Dinner
Rolls – French Steak Sandwich
Salad Dressing – 1000 Island
Salad Dressing – Tart Italian
Salsa – Medium/Hot
Shortening (or Lard)
Skewers – Wooden
Sour Cream
Soy Sauce
Stuffing – Herb Seasoned Mix
Toothpicks
Vinegar

Decided for You Cookbook – 365 Dinners

Week #46

SUNDAY
(BF) Beef Steak – Chuck, Marinated
(SALAD) Potato Salad
(VEG) Beans – Canned Green
Beans

MONDAY
(PK) Ham with Rice
(SALAD) Green Salad
(VEG) Peas – Canned Peas – Creamed

TUESDAY
(BF) Beef Burgers – Bacon Lettuce Tomato
Olives Black Pitted
Potato Chips

WEDNESDAY
(VEG) Eggplant in Curry –
Coconut Sauce – Vegetarian
Dish with Ghee
(SALAD) Green Salad
(VEG) Potatoes–Mashed Potatoes

THURSDAY
(MISC) Pancakes
(MISC) Chow Chow
(PK) Bacon and Eggs
(VEG) Potatoes – Hash Browns

FRIDAY
(SEA) Shrimp – Au Gratin – Garlic
(PAS) Noodles with White Sauce
(SALAD) Green Salad
(VEG) Broccoli – Buttered Broccoli

SATURDAY
(CH) Chicken Ole'
(SALAD) Green Salad
(VEG) Potatoes – Mashed Potatoes
(VEG) Corn-on-the-Cobb

Grocery List – Salt & Pepper, Salad Dressings of Choice if not specified

MEATS
Pork – Bacon (2R)
Beef – Ground Hamburger
Beef – Chuck Steak Boneless
Chicken – cut up fryer or ¼'d
Pork – Ham – Baked or Slices
Seafood – Shrimp – Med/Large

VEGETABLES - FRESH
Celery
Chile – Red Hot Dried
Corn – On-the-Cobb
Eggplants
Garlic (2R)
Lettuce – Iceberg (5R)
Onions (8R)
Parsley (2R)
Potatoes (3R)
Radishes (4R)
Tomatoes (6R)

FROZEN FOODS
Broccoli Spears
Hash Brown Potatoes
Peas

SPICES/STAPLES
Celery Seed
Cinnamon
Cloves - Whole
Curry Powder
Flour (2R)
Onion Salt
Paprika
Sugar – Granulated
Worcestershire

CANNED FOODS
Broth – Chicken
Broth – Vegetable
Green Beans
Milk – Evaporated (4R)
Mushrooms
Olives Black Pitted – Chopped (2R)
Olives – Pimento Stuffed
Peas
Potatoes – Canned Whole

OTHER
Biscuit or Pancake Mix
Breadcrumbs
Buns – Hot Dog

Butter – Unsalted
Cashews – Unsalted
Cheese – Parmesan
Coconut – Shredded
Eggs (3R)
Ketchup
Lemon Juice
Margarine (10R)
Mayonnaise
Milk – Unsweetened Coconut
Mustard – Whole Grain
Noodles – Flat Egg
Oil – Vegetable (3R)
Pickles Sweet
Picante Sauce
Potato Chips
Raisins
Relish – Sweet Pickle
Rice – Long Grain
Salad Dressing – French
Soup – Dry Onion
Toothpicks
Vinegar
Wine – Sherry (Optional)
Wine – White

Decided for You Cookbook – 365 Dinners

Week #47

SUNDAY
(TUR) Turkey and Stuffing **
(SAUCE) Gravy – Turkey
(VEG) Beans – Green Bean Casserole
(VEG) Potatoes – Mashed Potatoes

If this is really your Holiday Week, rearrange the menus according to your family event.

MONDAY
(BF) Beef Meatballs My New Way
(PAS) Rice – Long Grain Steamed
(VEG) Carrots – Buttered Carrots

TUESDAY
(CH) Chicken Marsala
(SALAD) Corn, Pimento and Peas
Marinated Salad
(VEG) Potatoes – Mashed Potatoes

WEDNESDAY
(TUR) Turkey Broccoli Casserole
(SALAD) Romaine and Butter
Lettuce Salad with Croutons

THURSDAY
(BF) Beef Tamale and Corn
Casserole
(SALAD) Macaroni Salad

FRIDAY
(SEA) Salmon with Scalloped
Potatoes and Peas
(SALAD) Green Salad
(VEG) Mushrooms – Buttered

SATURDAY
(CH) Chicken Broccola Supreme
(SALAD) Green Salad
(VEG) Potatoes – Mashed Potatoes

Grocery List – Salt & Pepper, Salad Dressings of Choice if not specified

MEATS
Beef – Ground Hamburger (2R)
Chicken – Boneless Breasts
Chicken – Whole
Turkey – Cook enough for Leftovers

VEGETABLES - FRESH
Garlic
Lettuce–Butter
Lettuce–Iceberg (2R)
Lettuce–Romaine
Onions (7R)
Parsley (3R)
Potatoes (3R)
Radishes (2R)
Tomatoes (3R)

FROZEN FOODS
Broccoli Chopped
Broccoli Spears
Green Beans – French Style

SPICES/STAPLES
Baking Powder
Chili Powder
Flour (3R)
Garlic Powder (2R)
Paprika
Sugar – Granulated or Brown

CANNED FOODS
Carrots
Corn – White Whole Kernel
Corn – Whole Kernel
Milk – Evaporated (3R)
Olives – Black Pitted Chopped
Peas
Peas – Baby Lesueur Small
Pimentos – Chopped
Salmon
Soup – Cream of Chicken
Soup – Cream of Mushroom
Soup – Cream of Vegetable
Tamales – Beef
Tomato Sauce
Wine Marsala

OTHER
Biscuit Mix
Bouillon – Chicken
Breadcrumbs (3R)
Cheese – Cheddar (2R)
Cheese – Parmesan
Cheese Spread–Neufchatel
  w/Pimento
Cheese - Swiss
Corn Meal

Croutons
Eggs (3R)
Foil – Aluminum (2R)
Lemon Juice (2R)
Macaroni – Salad
Margarine (8R)
Mayonnaise
Mayonnaise Salad Dressing
Milk (3R)
Onions – French Fried
Pickles – Sweet
Rice – Long Grain
Salad Dressing – Tart Italian
Sour Cream
Waxed Paper

-47-

Week #48

SUNDAY
(CH) Stuffed Chicken
(SALAD) Green Salad
(VEG) Mixed Vegetables
(VEG) Potatoes – Au Gratin Potatoes

MONDAY
(BF) Beef Flank Steak and Pan Fried Potatoes
(SALAD) Green Salad

TUESDAY
(SALAD) Chicken Salad Stuffed Tomatoes
(SOUP) Onion Soup – French
(BRD) Croutons

WEDNESDAY
(BF) Beef Burger Bake–Open Faced
(SALAD) Macaroni Salad
(VEG) Broccoli – Buttered

THURSDAY
(BF) Beef Green Chilies Taco Cheese Pie
(PAS) Rice – Spanish Rice
(SALAD) Avocado and Lettuce Salad
(VEG) Beans – Refried Beans

FRIDAY
(SEAFOOD) Tuna Casserole with Cheese Biscuit Swirls and Peas
(SALAD) Tomato Wedges w/Thousand Island Dressing
(VEG) Mushrooms–Stuffed Mushrooms

SATURDAY
(MISC) Hi-Roller Sandwiches
(SALAD) Green Salad w/Mushrooms and Bell Pepper Rings
Potato Chips

Grocery List – Salt & Pepper, Salad Dressings of Choice if not specified

MEATS
Beef – Flank Steak
Beef – Ground Hamburger (2R)
Chicken – Whole to Stuff
Luncheon Meats (Bologna, Ham, & Salami)
Pork – Smokie Links

VEGETABLES - FRESH
Bell Peppers (3R)
Garlic Cloves (3R)
Lettuce – Iceberg (3R)
Mushrooms (2R)
Onions (8R)
Potatoes (2R)
Radishes (3R)
Tomatoes (6R)

FROZEN FOODS
Broccoli Cuts
SPICES/STAPLES
Cumin
Flour
Garlic Powder
Mustard – Dry
Onion Flakes

Onion Salt
Poultry Seasoning
CANNED FOODS
Artichoke Hearts – Marinated
Asparagus
Chicken – Boned
Chiles – Green Diced
Olives Black Chopped (2R)
Peas
Refried Beans
Soup – Cheddar Cheese
Soup – Cream of Mushroom (2R)
Soup – French Onion
Tomato Sauce
Tuna
Vegetables – Mixed

OTHER
Biscuit Mix (2R)
Bouillon Chicken
Breadcrumbs
Cheese – American
Cheese – Cheddar (3R)
Cheese – Monterey Jack
Cheese – Processed
Croutons (2R)

Eggs
Lemon Juice (2R)
Macaroni – Salad
Margarine (3R)
Mayonnaise (3R)
Mayonnaise Salad Dress'g
Milk
Milk Half and Half
Mustard – Dijon
Oil – Vegetable (2R)
Pickles – Sweet
Piecrust Mix
Plastic Wrap
Potato Chips
Rice – Long Grain
Roll/Sheet – Hi Roller Cracker Meal
Salad Dressing – 1000 Island
Shortening
Sour Cream
Soy Sauce
Stuffing Mix – Herb Seasoned
Taco Dry Seasoning Mix
Waxed Paper

Week #49

SUNDAY
(PK) Pork Roast Polynesian
(PAS) Rice – Long Grain Steamed
(SALAD) Cucumber and Onion Italian
Pickled Salad
(VEG) Sweet Potatoes with Marshmallow
Topping

MONDAY
(BF) Baked Ziti
(SALAD) Green Salad
(VEG) Spinach – Buttered Spinach

TUESDAY
(CH) Tandori Chicken with Yogurt
(SALAD) Macaroni Salad
(VEG) Beans – Canned Green
Beans

WEDNESDAY
(BF) Beef and Bean Yakima
(SALAD) Lettuce, Mayonnaise and
Onion Salad
(VEG) Corn – Cream Style

THURSDAY
(BF) Beef Burgers by the Yard
Olives Black Pitted
Potato Chips

FRIDAY
(SEA) Shrimp Scampi and Fettuccini
Noodles
(VEG) Asparagus – Buttered
(BRD) Bread – Garlic French

SATURDAY
(BF) Braised Beef Rolls
(SALAD) Green Salad
(VEG) Broccoli – Broccoli Buttered
(VEG) Potatoes – Mashed Potatoes

Grocery List – Salt & Pepper, Salad Dressings of Choice if not specified

MEATS
Beef – Ground Hamburger (3R)
Beef – Round Steak
Chicken – Cut up fryer
Pork – Bacon
Pork – Loin Roast
Pork – Link Sausage
Sausage – Italian Hot
Seafood – Prawns

VEGETABLES - FRESH
Bananas
Bell Peppers
Cucumbers
Garlic – Cloves (5R)
Lemon (2R)
Lettuce – Iceberg (3R)
Onions (12R)
Onions – Green
Oranges
Parsley
Potatoes
Radishes (3R)
Spinach
Tomatoes (4R)

FROZEN FOODS
Asparagus Cuts
Broccoli Cuts or fresh
Pineapple/Orange Concentrate

SPICES/STAPLES
Basil
Cardamom
Cayenne Pepper
Coriander
Cumin
Ginger
Italian Seasoning (2R)

Oregano
Paprika
Sugar – Brown
Sugar – Granulated
Turmeric

CANNED FOODS
Corn – Cream Style
Green Beans
Milk – Evaporated
Olives – Black Pitted
Pork and Beans
Soup – Tomato
Spaghetti Sauce
Tomato Paste
Tomatoes – Stewed
Yams or Sweet Potatoes

OTHER
Biscuit Mix
Bread – French (2R)
Cheese – Cheddar (2R)
Cheese – Parmesan
Foil – Aluminum (2R)

Liquid Smoke
Macaroni – Salad
Macaroni – Ziti
Margarine (7R)
Marshmallows Miniature
Mayonnaise (2R)
Milk – Half and Half
Noodles – Fettuccini (2R)
Oil – Olive
Oil – Vegetable (2R)
Pickles – Sweet or Sweet Dill
Potato Chips
Rice – Long Grain
Salad Dressing – Tart Italian
Soup – Dry Onion
Sour Cream
Soy Sauce
Toothpicks
Vinegar
Wine – White
Whipping Cream
Yogurt – Plain

Week #50

SUNDAY
(TUR) Turkey in Puff Pastry
(SALAD) Waldorf Salad w/Sweet Dressing
(VEG) Peas & Onions with Creamed Sauce
(VEG) Potatoes – Mashed Potatoes

MONDAY
(PK) Peking Pork Spareribs (King Tu Style)
with (PK) Pork Chow Mein
(PAS) Rice – Fried Rice
(SALAD) Cole Slaw with Dressing

TUESDAY
(CH) Chicken and Easy Carrot and
Biscuit Pie
(SALAD) Potato Salad

SATURDAY
(BF) Beef Short Ribs – Saucy Onion
(SALAD) Green Salad
(VEG) Mushrooms – Garlic Buttered
Mushrooms
(VEG) Potatoes – Mashed with Garlic

WEDNESDAY
(PK) Pork Chops, Rice and
Gravy
(SALAD) Green Salad
(VEG) Beans – Canned Green
Beans French Style

THURSDAY
(BF) Beef Burgers – Doubled
Surprise Inside
(SALAD) Green Salad
Potato Chips

FRIDAY
(SEA) Raviolis – Cheese with
Salmon Pesto Cream Sauce
(SALAD) Green Salad
(VEG) Peas – Canned Peas –
Creamed

Grocery List – Salt & Pepper, Salad Dressings of Choice if not specified

MEATS
Beef – Ground Hamburger
Beef – Short Ribs
Pork – Bacon
Pork – Boneless Roast
Pork – Boneless Pork Chops
Pork – Pork Chops
Seafood – Shrimp Cooked

VEGETABLES - FRESH
Apples-Red/Grn	Onions (11R)
Cabbage	Onions Green (2R)
Carrots (4R)	Parsley (2R)
Celery (3R)	Potatoes (5R)
Chives	Radishes (5R)
Garlic	Tomatoes (6R)
Lemon	Tomatoes (5R)
Lettuce – Iceberg (5R)	
Mushrooms (3R)	

FROZEN FOODS
Onions w/Cream Sauce
Pastry Crust/Patty Shells
Peas (or Peas & Onion in sauce)
Raviolis – Cheese
Turkey Roast

SPICES/STAPLES
Baking Soda	Sugar (3R)
Basil (or fresh)	Sugar – Brown
Celery Seed	Thyme
Cornstarch (2R)	Worcestershire

Flour (2R)
Garlic Powder (3R)
Meat Tenderizer
Pepper – Red Hot Flakes (Opt)

CANNED FOODS
Bamboo Shoots
Bean Sprouts
Broth – Chicken (2R)
Carrots – Whole
Chicken – Deboned
Gravy – Beef (2R)
Green Beans – French Style
Milk – Evaporated (4R)
Mushrooms
Olives Black Pitted Chopped
Pate – Liver (Opt)
Peas (2R)
Pineapple Slices
Salmon or Tuna
Sauerkraut

OTHER
Biscuits – Refrigerator
Buns – Hamburger
Cheese – Cheddar
Cheese – Parmesan
Cheese – Swiss
Eggs (3R)
Foil – Alum (2R)

Ketchup
Lemon Juice
Margarine (8R)
Mayonnaise (3R)
Noodles – Vermicelli
Oil – Olive
Oil – Peanut
Oil – Sesame
Oil – Vegetable (4R)
Pesto Sauce – Basil
Pickles – Sweet (2R)
Pine Nuts or Sliced Almonds
Potato Chips
Raisins – Golden
Rice – Long Grain (2R)
Salad Dressing – French
Soup – Dry Onion
Sour Cream (2R)
Soy Sauce (3R
Steak Sauce
Vinegar (3R)
Walnuts

Decided for You Cookbook – 365 Dinners

Week #51

SUNDAY
(BF) Beef Pot Roast with Carrots and Potatoes
SALAD) Green Salad
(BRD) Biscuits – Biscuit Mix

MONDAY
(BF) Beef Burgers Wellington
(PAS) Fettuccini Alfredo
(SALAD) Green Salad
 (VEG) Beans – Canned Green Beans Smoked

TUESDAY
(BF) Beef Cubed Steaks – Stuffed Oscar
(SALAD) Green Salad
(VEG) Potatoes – Mashed Potatoes

WEDNESDAY
(CH) Chicken Company Cakes
(SALAD) Romaine Lettuce, Pickled
Beets and Onion Salad
(VEG) Peas – Canned Peas –
Creamed

THURSDAY
(MISC) Chile Relleno Casserole with
Salsa
(PAS) Rice – Spanish Rice
(VEG) Beans – Refried Beans

FRIDAY
(SEA) Tuna Rice Rolls
(SALAD) Avocado, Tomato and
Egg Salad
(VEG) Asparagus – Cold

SATURDAY
(BF) Beef Raviolis - Stuffed with Meat Loaf &
Roasted Garlic & Parmesan Sauce
(SALAD) Green Salad
(VEG) Corn – Whole Kernel

Grocery List – Salt & Pepper, Salad Dressings of Choice if not specified

MEATS
Beef – Ground Hamburger (2R)
Beef – Cube Steaks
Beef – Pot Roast
Chicken – Ground or Boneless
Breasts
Beef – Round Steak
Pork – Ground Sausage
Pork – Proscuitto Ham (Opt)
VEGETABLES - FRESH
Avocado
Bell Peppers
Carrots (2R)
Lettuce – Iceberg (5R)
Lettuce – Romaine
Mushrooms (2R)
Onions (9R)
Potatoes (2R)
Radishes (4R)
Tomatoes (5R)
FROZEN FOODS
Asparagus Cuts
Pasta – Ravioli Sheets
Pastry Crusts/Patty Shells

SPICES/STAPLES
Cayenne Pepper
Cumin (2R)
Flour (6R)
Garlic Powder (3R)
Onion Salt
Tarragon (2R)
CANNED FOODS
Asparagus
Beets – Pickled
Chiles – Green
Corn – Whole Kernel
Gravy – Beef w/Mushrooms
Green Beans
Liver Pate (Optional)
Milk – Evaporated (3R)
Mushrooms
Peas
Refried Beans
Soup – Cream of Celery
Tomato Sauce (2R)
Tuna

OTHER
Bacon Bits
Biscuit Mix
Bouillon – Chicken
Breadcrumbs (2R)
Cheese – Cheddar (3R)
Cheese – Monterey Jack (2R)
Cheese – Parmesan
Cheese – Swiss
Eggs (6R)
Margarine (4R)
Noodles – Fettuccini
Oil – Vegetable or Olive (2R)
Pie Crust Mix or frozen
Rice – Chicken Flavored Mix
Rice – Long Grain
Salsa
Sauce–Roasted Garlic & Parmesan
Sour Cream
Toothpicks
Vinegar
Waxed Paper
Whipping Cream

Decided for You Cookbook – 365 Dinners

Week #52

SUNDAY
(PK) Pork Crown Roast with Apple Stuffing
(SALAD) Green Salad
(VEG) Carrots – Buttered Carrots
(VEG) Potatoes – Baked

MONDAY
(PAS) Macaroni and Cheese
(SALAD) Green Salad
(VEG) Beans – Canned Green Beans

TUESDAY
(BF) Beef Steak – Oriental
(SALAD) Potato Salad
(VEG) Corn – Cream Style Corn

SATURDAY
(CH) Chicken Flautas
(PAS) Rice – Spanish Rice
(SALAD) Spinach, Mushroom, and Onion Ring Salad with Dressing
(VEG) Beans – Refried Beans

WEDNESDAY
(CH) Chicken Quick Casserole
(PAS) Rice – Long Grain Steamed
(SALAD) Green Salad

THURSDAY
(PAS) Spaghetti - Baked
(SALAD) Green Salad
(VEG) Zucchini – Zucchini Bake
(BRD) Bread - Garlic French Bread

FRIDAY
(SEA) Shrimp in Puff Pastry Shells
(PAS) Noodles with White Sauce
(SALAD) Green Salad
(VEG) Peas – Canned Peas – Creamed

Grocery List – Salt & Pepper, Salad Dressings of Choice if not specified

MEATS
Beef – Sirloin Steak
Chicken – Cut up fryer
Pork – Crown Roast + leftover
Pork – Prosciutto Ham (Opt)
VEGETABLES - FRESH
Apples–Green Pippin
Bell Peppers (2R)
Celery (3R)
Garlic Cloves (2R)
Lettuce–Iceberg (5R) Potatoes (2R)
Mushrooms (2R) Radishes (5R)
Onions (13R) Spinach
Onions Green (2R) Tomatoes (5R)
Parsley Zucchini
FROZEN FOODS
Pastry Shells Prawns
SPICES/STAPLES
Celery Seed
Cornstarch
Cumin
Dill
Flour (3R)
Garlic Powder
Italian Seasoning
Mustard - Dry
Nutmeg
Onion Salt

Paprika
Sage (2R)
Sugar – Granulated
Sugar – Brown
Thyme
CANNED FOODS
Broth – Chicken
Carrots
Chicken – Boned
Chiles – Green
Corn – Cream Style
Green Beans
Milk – Evaporated (3R)
Olives Black Pitted Chopped
Peas
Pimientos (2R)
Refried Beans
Soup – Cream of Chicken
Spaghetti Sauce
Tomato Sauce
OTHER
Alfredo Sauce (Optional)
Apple Juice or Orange Juice
Bouillon – Chicken (3R)
Bread – French
Bread – Whole Wheat
Cheese – Cheddar (3R)
Cheese – Mozzarella (2R)

Cheese – Parmesan (2R)
Crackers – Saltine
Eggs (3R)
Foil – Aluminum (5R)
Lemon Juice (2R)
Macaroni – Elbow
Margarine (10R)
Mayonnaise
Milk
Molasses
Noodles – Angel Hair
Noodles – Egg Flat & Spaghettini
Oil – Corn
Oil – Sesame
Oil – Vegetable (3R)
Pickles – Sweet
Rice – Long Grain (2R)
Salad Dressing – Italian & French
Shortening
Sour Cream (2R)
Soy Sauce (2R)
Tortillas – Corn
Vinegar

RECIPES

BEFORE YOU FORGET, WRITE IT DOWN!

Decided for You Cookbook – 365 Dinners

BF – (Baked Zita)

2 Pounds Ground Beef	1/2 Pound Hot Italian Sausage, sliced
1-1/2 cups chopped Onion	2 large cloves of Garlic, minced
1 Tbsp Italian Seasoning, crushed	4 cans (10-3/4 oz ea) Tomato Soup
3 soup cans of Water	1 Tbsp Vinegar
2 tsp Salt	Grated Parmesan Cheese
1 Pound Ziti Macaroni (long hollow) or spaghetti, cooked and drained	

In a large heavy skillet, brown beef and sausage the onion with garlic and the Italian Seasoning until done. Stir to separate meat. Drain most of the fats from the meat. Stir in the soup, water, vinegar, and salt. Simmer 15 minutes; stirring occasionally. Add the macaroni. Transfer all of this into a very large baking dish or split into two dishes. Bake at 400°F for 30 minutes or until hot; stir. Top with cheese. Makes about 15 cups, plenty for leftover warm ups or you can freeze balance for another time.

Serves 4-8
MENU WEEK#49

BF – (Bar-B-Q Cups)

Mix 2 cups Biscuit mix and 1/2 cup cold water, until dough can be handled. Spoon the dough about half-full into 12-hole non-greased muffin pan. Press dough down on the bottom and up the side of each cup with your floured hands so it creates a crust to hold the ingredients.

Mix together:

1 Pound Ground Beef	1/2 cup chopped Onion
1 clove Garlic, crushed, (garlic is optional)	1/2 cup Barbecue Sauce
1/2 cup Shredded Cheddar Cheese (~2 oz)	

Heat oven to 400°F. Cook and stir the Ground Beef, Onion and Garlic in a 10" skillet over medium heat until the beef is browned. Drain the drippings. Stir in the Bar-B-Q Sauce; mix thoroughly with the meat. Spoon the beef & sauce mixture into the biscuit dough lined cups; sprinkle with the cheese. Bake until the crust is golden brown around the edge, about 15 minutes. Average two Bar-B-Q Cups per person.   Serves 6
MENU WEEK#35

BF – (Bar-B-Q Sliced Beef)

12 thin slices leftover Roast Beef or turkey slices (can use Deli sliced Beef)

1-1/2 cups chopped Onion	1-1/3 Tbsp Margarine or Butter
1-1/2 cups Ketchup	1/4 cup Brown Sugar
1/4 cup Lemon Juice	1 Tbsp Worcestershire Sauce
1-1/2 tsp Salt	1/4 tsp Pepper
6 Hamburger Buns	

Sauté onions in margarine/butter until golden, add all other ingredients except the beef. Simmer 30 minutes. Add in slices of Beef. Simmer 10-15 minutes longer. Serve on warmed buns **-OR -** Use frozen packages (or jars) of Chipped Beef and add in a Bar-B-Q sauce.   Serves 4
MENU WEEK#14

HINT: Brown sugar should be stored in an airtight container. Soak a chip of a clay pot in water and once soaked, drop inside the container to keep the brown sugar granulated. If it does dry out, use a cheese grater to remove what you need from the sugar brick –OR – Put a piece bread in the container with your sugar and it will soften in a couple hours – OR - Place sugar on a shallow baking sheet and bake at 250°F for 10 minutes and stir into a granulated state again for use.

BF – (Beef American Pie with Peas and Mashed Potatoes)

1 Pound Sirloin Steak, cut into strips
3/4 cup Water
2 tsp granulated Beef Bouillon
1/4 tsp Ginger
1 (4 oz) can non-drained Button Mushrooms
1-1/2 tsp Cornstarch
Bowl of Mashed Potatoes (can be leftovers and re-warmed in the microwave)

2/3 cup chopped Green Onions
1 Pkg (16 oz) Frozen Peas (~2 cups)
1/2 tsp Soy Sauce
2 Tbsp Margarine or Butter
1 tsp Salt
Dash of Pepper

Cut the steak into strips about 2 inches wide x 5" long. Combine the bouillon, soy sauce and ginger into a marinade. Pour over the beef and mix well. Cover and marinate in the refrigerator at least 30 minutes or more. Drain the meat but save the marinade. Melt butter in a skillet; add in the beef and brown well. Remove the meat. Cook the onions and add in the mushrooms, peas and cover and cook 'till peas are tender. Combine the cornstarch and water in a cup and stir in the salt, pepper and remaining marinade. Stir until smooth. Add this to the pea mixture, add the meat and cover the skillet. Cook slowly till sauce has thickened. Serve on top of the mashed potatoes.

6 Servings
MENU WEEK#11

BF – (Beef and Bean Yakima)

1 (14 oz) can Pork-n-Beans
1 Large Onion, sliced thin
2 medium cans of Stewed Tomatoes with celery and green Bell Peppers

2 lbs Ground Beef
3/4 cup Brown Sugar

Place layer of each of the beans, beef and onion in a greased casserole; spoon the tomatoes over as the third layer. Repeat the layers until all have been used. Spread brown sugar over the top of the casserole. Bake for 1 hour at 350°F

6 Servings
MENU WEEK#49

BF – (Beef and Broccoli)

1 Pkg Beef & Broccoli Oriental Seasoning Mix*
3/4 cup Water
2 Tbsp Vegetable Oil
2 cups Small Broccoli Florets or cuts, can be
  frozen
1 (8 oz) can Bamboo Shoots, drained

3 Tbsp Soy Sauce
1 small Onion, peeled, halved and sliced
**Hot cooked Rice or a 12 oz Pkg Chinese Rice
Noodles
1 cup Chicken Broth

3/4 Pound thinly sliced Beef (Sirloin, Flank, Round, or Deli) - If desperate you can use one Pound of Ground Beef in a pinch

In a small bowl, combine the seasoning mix, water and soy sauce; set aside. Heat oil in a large skillet. Add beef and onion; stir-fry until beef is cooked and onion is soft, about 7 or 8 minutes (if using deli beef, cook onion and add beef stirring until warm). Add broccoli and bamboo shoots; cook and stir until the broccoli is crisp tender. Add seasoning mixture, chicken broth and cook, stirring frequently until thickened. Serve over hot, steamed rice.

4 Servings
MENU WEEK#37

*   If not available add in 1 tsp Ginger, 1 tsp Sugar, Salt and Pepper, 1 Tbsp Cornstarch and 1 tsp Sesame Oil
**   You can use a Cup of Instant Noodles if you cannot find Chinese Style Noodles

BF – (Beef and Mushroom Saté)

1 Pound Boneless Beef Sirloin Steak or Flank Steak, cut into 1" thick bite-sized pieces

1/4 cup chopped Onion	1/4 cup Soy Sauce
2 Tbsp Vegetable Oil for Marinade	1 Large Green Bell Pepper cut into chunks
+ 2 Tbsp for frying	1 Pound sliced Mushrooms (can be canned)
2 Tbsp Brown Sugar	3 cloves Garlic, minced
1/2 tsp Red Pepper Sauce	3 Tbsp Lemon Juice

Slice your meat into bit-sized pieces. In a large bowl, combine the onion, soy sauce, lemon juice, oil, sugar, garlic and red pepper sauce. Add in the meat and toss to coat well. Cover and marinate for at least 2 hours, stirring occasionally. In a skillet or wok, heat 2 Tbsps of the vegetable oil and sauté the meat until lightly browned, push to the side. Cook the bell pepper slices next, basting with spoonfuls of the marinade as needed; move to the side. Add in the rest of the marinade and then add in the sliced mushrooms turning often and cook these for 2-3 minutes or until soften. Mix all ingredients together and serve.   Serves 4
MENU WEEK #19

BF – (Beef Betty)

3 or 4 lbs of Beef Stew Meat	2 cans (10-3/4 oz ea) Cream of Mushroom Soup
1 can (10-3/4 oz) Cream of Celery Soup	Salt and Pepper to taste
Onions, sliced	1/2 cup Water

Salt and pepper the meat. Place meat in a Crock Pot with the sliced onions, and 1/2 cup of water. Cook on Low for 8-12 hours until very tender. Add undiluted soups, about an hour before serving. To darken soup/gravy mixture, add a few drops of Bouquet Browning & Seasoning Sauce.   **-OR –**
Using a heavy Dutch Oven pan, flour the beef and brown in hot oil. Add one cup of water and bring to a boil. Add onions and reduce the heat to low, cover, and cook until meat is tender. Add undiluted soups and brown coloring. Serve over steamed rice, or cooked noodles. A good re-heatable leftover, **also good served inside Crepes with Sour Cream Topping**.   4-6 Servings
MENU WEEK#14

SPECIAL INTEREST ITEM: (HOME FOOD STORAGE GUIDE)

Guide:
COOLED SHELF STORAGE

Canned Fruits	12 mths		
Canned Fruit Juices	12 mths		
Canned Vegetables	8 mths		
FREEZER STORAGE			
Cakes (wrapped in plastic-wrap, stored in a sealed Container)	12 mths	Ice Cream	1 mth
Cakes – Angel Food	2 mths	Lamb Roasts	9 mths
Danish Pastry	3 mths	Meat Dinners	3 mths
Doughnuts	3 mths	Pies (unbaked)	8 mths
Meats etc.		Pork Roasts	8 mths
Beef - Hamburger, Thin Steaks	4 mths	Pork Steaks, Sausage	4 mths
Beef Roasts, Thick Steaks	12 mths	Turkey (whole)	12 mths
Chicken (cut up)	9 mths		
Chicken (whole)	12 mths		
Fish	2-3 mths		

Decided for You Cookbook – 365 Dinners

BF – (Beef Bourguignon – Glenn's)

Used inside Crepes MENU WEEK #31 - This Bourguignon dish can be made the day before and refrigerated and reheated and served inside a Crepe.

2-1/2 Pounds Beef Chuck Roast cut into 1-1/2 inch cubes or Beef Stew Meat
1 Medium Sliced Onion
2 to 2-1/2 tsp Beef Bouillon
1/2 Pound Mushrooms
1 Bay Leaf
Sour Cream
Margarine or Butter
1-1/2 cups Burgundy Wine (can be Water or Beef Broth if you don't drink Wine)
3/4 cup Ruby Port Wine (can be Water or Beef Broth if you don't drink Wine).

2-1/2 Tbsp Flour
2 Tbsp Tomato Paste
1/8 tsp Pepper
1 can (10-3/4 oz) Condensed Beef Broth undiluted

This can be cooked for a long period in a Crock pot, on the stovetop or even in the oven. Melt the margarine in a medium stewing kettle. Brown the onions until clear and tender. Salt the meat and dredge it in flour and brown it in the hot margarine on all sides. (If you are using a Crock pot, do this process in a skillet and return the browned meat to the Crock pot, rinse the cooking container with the wine or water to remove tasty drippings). Add in the bouillon, tomato paste, wines, beef broth, pepper and the bay leaf. Bring to a rolling boil and reduce the heat to a simmer. Cover the pot and cooking until the juices have reduced by over half and the meat is super tender. Add in the mushrooms and return to a simmer for an additional 8-10 minutes until they are tender. If you are using an oven, preheat to 350°F and bake for 1-1/2 hours of until the beef is super tender. **HINT: If the sauce becomes too thick you can add additional, wine or water or beef broth as needed. If your juice is not thickened you can remove some of the juices and whisk in two tablespoons of flour per cup of liquid or a tablespoon of cornstarch per two cups of liquid. Whisk both of these thickening agents into the liquid then return that mixture back into your ingredients and mix well allowing for the juices to thicken to a gravy consistency. If you use cornstarch rather than flour your gravy will have more of a translucent appearance. All gravies should be thick enough to flow from a spoon and be smooth and well flavored. Taste and adjust seasonings accordingly. You can add in a "Bouquet Browning & Seasoning Sauce" if it is not dark enough in color.** Place this beef mixture inside a cooked crepe, top with sour cream and fold over, sprinkle top with chopped green onion for a garnish **–OR-** serve over cooked, drained noodles or rice.   Serves 6 – 8
MENU WEEK #31

BF – (Beef Breaded Strips)

1 Pound Beef Round Steak, 1/2 inch thick, and cut into 3" strips
2 Tbsp Margarine or Butter
1 tsp Water
2 Tbsp Parmesan Cheese
1/4 tsp Onion Salt

1 Egg, slightly beaten
1/3 cup Fine Dry Breadcrumbs
1/2 tsp Salt
2 Tbsp Flour

Heat oven to 400°F. Melt butter in a 9 x 13 baking pan in the oven and remove. Mix the egg and water together. Mix breadcrumbs, cheese, salt and onion salt. Dip beef strips into the flour, then in the egg mixture, then in the bread crumb mixture and place in the baking pan. Bake uncovered 15 to 20 minutes; turning once and bake 10-15 minutes longer.   4 Servings
MENU WEEK #45

HINT: Save yourself time by grating all of your hard cheeses and put into sealable containers so it doesn't take time at the last minute to get it ready for your recipe.

(BF)-58

Decided for You Cookbook – 365 Dinners

BF – (Beef Broccoli Pie)

1 Pound Ground Beef
2 Tbsp All-Purpose Flour
1/3 tsp Garlic Powder
1 – 3 oz Pkg Cream Cheese, softened
2 Pkgs Refrigerator Crescent Rolls (16 rolls)
Extra Milk for Topping
1 (10 oz) Pkg of frozen Chopped Broccoli, cooked and well drained

1/4 cup chopped Onion
3/4 tsp Salt
1-1/4 cups Milk
1 beaten Egg
4 oz Monterey Jack Cheese

In a skillet, brown the ground beef and onion; drain off fat. Stir in flour, salt and garlic powder. Add milk and cream cheese; cook and stir till thickened and smooth. Add a moderate amount of hot mixture to the beaten egg (**not too much, don't want to scramble the eggs**), return this mixture back into the skillet. Cook and stir over medium heat for 1-2 minutes or until thick. Stir in the well-drained broccoli.

Unroll one package of the crescent rolls. On a floured surface, unroll the four sections of the rolls forming a 7" x 12" rectangular, sprinkle lightly with flour. Press or roll out to a 12" square and then pick up the rectangle and place into a 9" pie plate; trim edges. Spoon the mixture into the shell. Cut cheese into slices and arrange on top of the meat mixture. Roll a second package of rolls into another 12" square as before and place on top of the filling (making a double-crusted pie). Trim and crimp edges with a fork tine (press fork on top shell edge which crimps it to the bottom shell, put tine in flour if it sticks). This will seal the shells together. Cut some slits for steam to escape around the middle of your pie. **Brush the top of the pie with a little bit of milk (causes it to brown more evenly).** Bake 350°F for 40 minutes. If it browns too quickly, cover with foil during the last twenty minutes of baking time. Let it stand 10 minutes before serving.

6 Servings
MENU WEEK#20

BF – (Beef Burgers – Bacon Lettuce and Tomato)

1 package Onion Soup or other dry soups if desired
3/4 cup Warm Water
1/4 cup Ketchup
8 slices Bacon
Lettuce, chopped
Toothpicks

1 Pound Ground Beef
1 Tbsp Worcestershire Sauce
Hot Dog Buns
Tomatoes, sliced

In a large bowl combine all the ingredients except lettuce and tomatoes. Shape this into 8 oblong burgers looking like a hot dog, wrap with bacon and secure it with a toothpick. Grill, Broil or bake at 500°F turning occasionally, until brown and done. Serve with Lettuce and Tomatoes on warmed Hot Dog Buns.

8 Servings
MENU WEEK#46

(Dry Onion Soup Mix)

MAKE YOUR OWN – (Ingredients not on grocery list)

3/4 cup Dried Onions
1/4 tsp Celery Seed
4 tsp Onion Powder

1/3 cup Beef Broth Granules (not cubes)
1/4 tsp Sugar

Mix all ingredients and store in an airtight container. Five Tablespoons equals 1 package of Onion Soup mix.

(BF)-59

BF – (Beef Burger Bake – Open Faced)

1 Pound Ground Beef
2/3 cup Salad Dressing or Mayonnaise
2 Tbsp chopped Onion
2-3 medium Tomatoes, thinly sliced

1 cup (8 oz) Sour Cream
1 cup shredded Sharp Cheddar Cheese (about 4 oz)
2 cups Biscuit Baking Mix
3/4 cup chopped Green Bell Peppers

Heat the oven to 375°F. Grease an oblong baking pan 9x 13. Cook and stir the ground beef until lightly brown; drain fats and set aside. Mix the sour cream, salad dressing, cheese and onion; set aside. Stir the Biscuit baking mix and water together into a soft dough with a fork. Then mix vigorously for about 20 strokes with your hands. Pat the dough into the bottom of your casserole dish. Press the dough up the sides about 1/2-inch. Layer the beef, tomatoes and green bell pepper on top of the dough. Spoon the sour cream mixture over the top. If desired you can sprinkle the top with Paprika. Bake 25 – 30 minutes at 375°F until the edges of the dough is lightly brown.

8-10 servings
MENU WEEK#48

**HINT: If cheese edges become hardened – Rub edges of cheese with a tiny bit of butter or margarine to prevent drying and wrap in plastic wrap.
ALSO, Baking in a glass vs metal pan. Glass pan foods will brown faster, therefore, you can slightly lower the temperature and use less time.**

BF – (Beef Burgers by the Yard)

1 cup shredded Cheddar, Mozzarella, or American Cheese
1 Pound Ground Beef
1 Pkg Dry Onion Soup
1 can (6 oz) Tomato Paste
Aluminum Foil

Tomato slices, Green Bell Peppers, Onion Rings
3/4 cup Water
1 Loaf (1 lb) French Bread, split lengthwise

In a large bowl, combine the onion soup with the water. Add the beef; mix thoroughly. In a skillet, brown the mixture and drain off the fat. Stir in the tomato paste. Spread the mixture on both bread halves. Top with the tomato slices, green peppers and onion; then sprinkle with your choice of cheese. Make an Aluminum Foil Boat for the bread to rest in leaving just the top edge exposed to keep the bread from drying out. Put in the oven (375°F) for 10 minutes.

Makes 2-Long open-faced Sandwiches, which should feed 6-8 people.

MENU WEEK#49

(Dry Onion Soup Mix)

MAKE YOUR OWN – (Ingredients not on the grocery list)
3/4 cup Dried Onions
1/3 cup Beef Broth Granules (not cubes)
1/4 tsp Celery Seed
1/4 tsp Sugar
4 tsp Onion Powder

Mix all ingredients and store in an airtight container. Five Tablespoons equals 1 package of Onion Soup mix.

Decided for You Cookbook – 365 Dinners

BF – (Beef Burgers – Doubled with Surprise Inside)

Basic:	**Other Choices:**
1 – 2 Pounds of Ground Beef	Sliced Pickles, Mushrooms, Onions
Cheddar Cheese	Chopped Potatoes, Carrots & Onions
Lettuce and Sliced Tomatoes	Sauerkraut, Swiss Cheese, Onions
1 tsp Garlic Powder	Salt and Pepper to Taste
4-8 Hamburger Buns (see Make Your Own	Sliced Onions
Buns under BRD (Buns – Hamburger)	

1) Mix the ground beef, salt, pepper and garlic powder together. Make 8 thin patties. On top of one of the patties place Cheddar cheese, chopped onions. Place another patty on top and pinch the edges together. 2) On the second set of patties, place pickles, chopped mushrooms, onions. Again, top with another patty pinching the edges together. 3) On the third one put chopped potatoes, and carrots with or without the onions and place the other patty on top and seal the edges. 4) On the fourth patty, place on some sauerkraut, Swiss cheese, onions or your choice. Sealing the fourth burger – **NOTE: 2nd thru 4th choices do not appear on the grocery list and must be added if used).** Cover and brown these patties on both sides in a skillet or grill outdoors on a barbecue; cook until done. Your family will have a real surprise when they bite into them as each will have a different surprise inside. Or, you can make all four double hamburgers with the same surprise inside. Garnish with lettuce, tomatoes and place on warmed Hamburger buns and serve with your favorite side dish.

Serves 4
MENU WEEK#50

BF – (Beef Burgers – French)

1 – 2 Pounds of Ground Beef
1 Pkg Dry Onion Soup
6 French Sandwich Buns or Steak Sandwich Buns

Mix the ground beef and onion soup together then form mixture into oblong patties. Place on a grill, or in a hot skillet and brown. Place on toasted French Sandwich buns and garnish as desired.

Serves 4-6
MENU WEEK#39

Dry Onion Soup Mix

MAKE YOUR OWN – (Ingredients not on grocery list)

3/4 cup Dried Onions	1/3 cup Beef Broth Granules (not cubes)
1/4 tsp Celery Seed	1/4 tsp Sugar
4 tsp Onion Powder	

Mix all ingredients and store in an airtight container. Five Tablespoons equals 1 package of Onion Soup mix.

BF – (Beef Burgers – Pizza Style)

6 Steak Sandwich Buns	1-1/2 Pounds Ground Beef
1 jar or 26.5 oz can Pizza Sauce/Spaghetti Sauce	1/2 Pound shredded Cheddar Cheese
1/2 Pound shredded Swiss Cheese	1/2 Pound shredded Mozzarella Cheese
1/4 cup shredded or grated Parmesan Cheese	Minced Onion, Green Bell Peppers
Oregano, Salt and Pepper to Taste	Garlic Powder

Brown the onion and ground beef after adding the seasonings (salt, pepper, garlic powder). Stir mixture until done; drain off fats. Add in the Pizza/ Spaghetti Sauce sprinkle on additional oregano if desired. Spoon the mixture onto 1/2 of a steak sandwich roll. Sprinkle the top with a combination of all the cheeses, top with green bell pepper slices and olives as desired. Broil 4-5 minutes until the cheese is bubbly. Spread other half of bun and broil 2-3 minutes under the broiler until toasted. Put the Sandwich together and serve. (Extra Recipe)   Serves 4-6

HINT: Bell Pepper is one of the vegetables that are the easiest to freeze, they do not need to be blanched before freezing. After washing, cut into rings, slice or chop then package and freeze. They can be frozen for 6-9 months. They might lose their crispness when frozen and thawed, so they are best used in cooked dishes (i.e., Beef Swiss Steak). If you plan on stuffing them, then they are best blanched for 2 minutes in boiling water before chilling in the refrigerator or freezer.

BF – (Beef Burgers – Stuffed by Jean)

1-1/2 Pounds Ground Beef	1/2 tsp Garlic Powder
1 tsp ea Salt & Pepper	1 cup Cabbage, shredded fine
8 Slices American Cheese, torn into small pieces	Hot Roll Mix (or make your own)
1 cup Tomato Puree Paste or Ketchup	Margarine/Butter

Preheat your oven to 350°F. Brown the meat, drain excessive fats and add in the cabbage, garlic powder, salt, pepper, tomato puree, and the cheese. Mix these ingredients until well mixed. On a floured or greased work surface, roll out your yeast dough until it is 1/4" thick and cut into 5" squares. Place a scoop of the cooled filling in the center of each square. Fold the ends on the squares around the filling and pinch edges together; should resemble a ball. Place the seam side down on a greased baking sheet pan. Brush tops with melted margarine/butter and bake for 25 minutes.

Yeast Rolls

MAKE YOUR OWN – (Ingredients not on grocery list)

2 Eggs	1/4 cup Margarine/Butter
2 cups Warm Water	2 Tbsp Yeast
2 Tbsp Sugar (sprinkled over yeast and water)	1/2 cup Powdered Milk
5 cups+ of All-Purpose Flour	1 Tbsp Salt

Mix the water, margarine, yeast and sugar together. Let it stand 10 minutes. Mix the other ingredients (eggs, powdered milk, flour and salt). Knead together and place into a greased bowl, turning the greased side from the bottom to the top, cover with plastic wrap, set in a warm spot in the kitchen and allow this to double in size.   Serves 8 –10

MENU WEEK#2

BF – (Beef Burgers Wellington)

1-1/2 lbs Ground Round or Cut up Round Steak
1 Pkg Pastry Shells (frozen)
1 can (4 oz) chopped Mushrooms
2 Tbsp minced Onion
1/2 tsp crushed Tarragon
1 can (2-1/4 oz) Liver Pâté (optional)

2 Eggs lightly beaten
2 cups soft Breadcrumbs
1 tsp Salt
1/8 tsp Pepper
Béarnaise Cream Sauce (recipe below)

Thaw Patty Shells. Combine beef, egg, mushrooms, Breadcrumbs, onion, salt, tarragon and pepper, mix thoroughly. Shape ground round steak into 6 patties about 4" in diameter. Broil or pan fry these for 3 minutes on each side. Remove and chill. Roll out thawed patty shells, one at a time on a lightly floured board to make 8" circles. Spread the liver pâté top of each patty, placing it in the center of your pastry circle. Fold pastry over and pinch together to enclose patty. Place folded side down in a greased baking pan side-by-side, like you would place biscuits together, repeat to wrap each patty. Brush each pastry with beaten egg wash (1 egg beaten with 1 Tbsp water). Bake in a 450°F oven 15 minutes. Serve with **Béarnaise Cream Sauce**. These can also be made into a loaf rather than individual servings. Bake a loaf at 450°F for 40 minutes then chill. Cover with a pastry shell and bake again at 450°F an additional 25 minutes.   6 Servings

MENU WEEK#51

HINT: <u>1 cup soft Breadcrumbs = 2 slices Bread</u>

Béarnaise Cream Sauce

2 Tbsp minced Onion or Shallots
1 tsp Dried Tarragon
1/4 Pound sliced Mushrooms
3 Egg yolks, slightly beaten in a cup

3 Tbsp Vinegar
1/2 Pound (2 sticks) Margarine or Butter
1 cup Whipping Cream
Salt and Pepper to taste

In a small saucepan combine the onions, vinegar, and tarragon. Boil over medium heat until the liquid has evaporated. Add in the margarine and mushrooms, cook until the mushrooms are browned. Add in the cream, and bring to a boil. **Stir some of this hot mixture into the egg yolks, (this will avoid them becoming cooked scrambled eggs).** Return this diluted egg mixture to the sauce. Cook on simmer, stirring until slightly thickened. Serve in a heated gravy boat over meat or fish.

BF – (Beef Burgers with Olive/Monterey Jack)

1 Pound Ground Beef
1/2 Pound Sliced Monterey Jack Cheese
Salt and Pepper to taste

2 cans chopped Black Olives
Toasted Hamburger Buns **–OR–** Sourdough
or Rye Bread

Form into 4 patties. Brown patties on both sides and drain off the fats. Place a patty on the bottom of a toasted bun and top with Monterey Jack Cheese and then more olives. Broil 3-4 minutes or until the cheese is bubbly. Add garnishes.

Serves 4
MENU WEEK#47

BF – (Beef Burgundy)

2-1/2 to 3 lbs of Beef Stew Meat   1 cup Red Burgundy Wine
1 Pkg Dry Onion Soup   Flour
1 can (10-3/4 oz) Cream of Celery Soup diluted per can instructions
1 can (10-3/4 oz) Cream of Mushroom Soup diluted per can instructions

Coat beef with flour and brown in a lightly oiled skillet. Drain fats. Add all other ingredients, cover and reduce burner to low and cook for 1-1/2 hours until tender.
OR – Bake in a covered baking dish for 2-1/2 hrs at 325°F, or until tender.
OR – Cook in a Crock Pot for 5-6 hours on low.

Serve with cooked egg noodles or steamed rice or inside Crepes

Serves 4-6
MENU WEEK#15

Dry Onion Soup Mix

MAKE YOUR OWN – (Ingredients not on grocery list)
3/4 cup Dried Onions   1/3 cup granulated (not cubes) Beef Broth
1/4 tsp Celery Seed   1/4 tsp Sugar
4 tsp Onion Powder

Mix all ingredients and store in an airtight container. Five tablespoons of this recipe equals 1 commercial package of Onion Soup.

BF – (Beef Burritos Supreme)

1 Pound Ground Beef   1 Onion, minced
1 can (16 oz) Refried Beans   3 cloves Garlic, crushed
1 Tomato chopped   1 tsp Salt
Sour Cream   1/2 tsp Cumin
1 cup grated Cheddar Cheese   1 tsp Chili Powder
2 Tbsp Green Taco Sauce   12 Flour Tortillas
1 Avocado, sliced or Guacamole Dip

Brown beef, garlic and onion; drain off fat. Add cumin, salt and chili powder – **OR- you can substitute a package of dry Burrito Mix for these spices**. Add beans and taco sauce. Heat, stirring until blended. Place a large spoonful in the center of each tortilla. Top with cheese, tomato, sour cream and avocado. Fold sides in to enclose filling; folding over both the top and bottom. Place in a shallow baking dish and Bake 350°F 5 to 8 minutes.   Serves 6-8
Variation – use 1 can Green Chiles and/or Chorizo Sausage

MENU WEEK#9

HINT: <u>Chop your garlic and store in a little oil in the refrigerator so it is ready to be use. This will store indefinitely and always be available.</u>

BF – (Beef California Casserole with Noodles)

1 Pound Ground Beef	1 cup shredded Cheddar Cheese
1 (8 oz) Pkg Noodles – Egg Flat	3/4 cup Onion
3/4 cup Green Bell Peppers	1/4 cup Shortening
1 (8 oz) can Tomato Sauce	1 (10-3/4 oz) can Tomato Soup
1 (8 oz) can pitted Black Olives	1 (4 oz) can Pimiento
1-1/2 tsp Salt	1/2 tsp Chili Powder
1/8 tsp dry Mustard	Aluminum Foil

Cook Ground Beef over medium heat in a skillet, drain excess fat. Add the tomato soup and tomato sauce. Cook noodles per package direction. Place a layer of cooked, salted noodles and then a layer of meat sauce in a 2-quart casserole dish. Place on top of this layer all other ingredients, then another layer of noodles and meat sauce until all has been used, top with Cheddar Cheese and cover casserole with Aluminum Foil. Bake at 350°F for 45 minutes.

Serves 4-6
MENU WEEK#20

HINT: <u>1 cup Dry Noodles = 1-3/4 cups cooked.</u>

BF – (Beef Cheeseburgers)

1 Pound Ground Beef
1 Pkg dry Onion Soup (this is salty so wait and taste before re-salting)
Salt and Pepper to taste
4 slices of American or Mild Cheddar Cheese
Buns - Hamburger

Mix the ground beef and onion soup. Make this into 4 large patties and pan fry or broil (can be put on a Bar-B-Q grill if available). Cook 3 to 5 minutes on each side, then drain the fats. Place the cheese on top of the cooked patty and warm your buns thus allowing time for the cheese to melt. Serve with chips, salad of whatever you choose

OPTIONAL VARIATIONS: (see Hamburgers)
Chili-Cheeseburgers – After cooking patties, place these on top of the bottom Hamburger Bun, add the patty and top with chili, chopped onion and grated Cheddar Cheese.

4 Servings
MENU WEEK#18

HINT: <u>If your meat taste bland, next time you can perk the meat or casserole up with a dash of Worcestershire Sauce, Hot Pepper Sauce or Dry Onion Soup Mix</u>.

BF – (Beef Chili Burgers)

1 Pound Ground Beef	Sliced Onions
Shredded Cheddar Cheese (Optional)	4 Hamburger Buns – toasted
Margarine/Butter soft	
1 can Chili without Beans (Some may like it with the beans)	

Heat the chili in a saucepan and put aside. Form 4 patties and brown in a skillet, drain off the fats. Spread Margarine/Butter on four hamburger buns and grill these or toast under a broiler. Turn toasted sides up and place hamburger patty on the center of the buns; place slices of onion on top, spoon chili over these.
Optional: Sprinkle Cheddar Cheese on the top and serve.

Serves 4
MENU WEEK#28

BF – (Beef Chili Mac)

1 Pound Ground Beef
1 small chopped Onion (1/2 cup)
1/2 Pound Salad Macaroni

2 Tbsp Chili Powder
2 cans (8 oz ea) Tomato Sauce
Salt and Pepper to taste

Boil the macaroni per package directions, drain. Brown the meat, salt, pepper and onion. Drain off most of the fat. Add chili powder and stir in the tomato sauce; simmer another 5 minutes. Pour over drained salted cooked macaroni. Stir well and serve.   Serves 4-6
MENU WEEK#3

BF – (Beef Chili with Beans)

2 (15 oz ea) Chili with Beans or use leftover beans and begin with Step 3.   **–OR-**

Chili Beans
MAKE YOUR OWN FROM Step 1

1 Pound Ground Beef
1/2 Pound Chorizo (remove from casing)
1/2 cup Chopped Onion
Salt and Pepper to taste
1 tsp Garlic Powder

1 Pound Pkg Dry Pinto Beans
5 or 6 Slices Bacon, cut in half
2 to 3 Tbsp Chili Powder
1 (15 oz) Tomato Sauce

1) Wash your pinto beans, drain. Run enough clean water until it covers the beans and let soak overnight (this makes the beans more tender, removes potential for stomach gases and takes less time to cook, if soaked).
2) Rinse the beans, after they have soaked overnight, filling with new water up about two knuckles higher than the beans (touch the end of your middle finger to the beans and check the water level with your knuckles). Add the bacon, salt and cook these covered at a rolling boil until the beans
   can be smashed easily with a fork (approximately 1-3 hours, adding more hot water as needed (adding cold water will make the beans tough).
3) In a skillet brown the beef, chorizo, onion, garlic powder and salt. Drain the fat, add in the chili powder and stir into the beef mixture. Pour this mixture into the beans. Can remove the bacon if desired.
-OR: Purchase a commercially prepared brick of Chili found in the frozen food or meat section of the grocery store (Use this chili brick instead of Step 3).   Serves 6- 8
MENU WEEK#9

BEEF – MICROWAVE INFORMATION:

HINT: To assure that the meat browns, place ingredients in a browning pan or place a pan inside a large brown shopping bag. Fold the bag's opening edge back underneath container, so fats won't escape. Be sure bag doesn't touch ceiling of Microwave Oven might spark unit (check often)

Corned Beef = Simmer 90 – 120 min – Add 1 cup Water per Lb – Turn over at 1/2 time.	**Meat Loaf** = 17 – 19 min/Loaf – Let stand 10 minutes before cutting.
Ground Beef = 4 – 6 min/Lb – In a casserole Container.	**Patties** = 4 Patties/Lb = 4 to 6 min – Can add a brushed on Browning sauce
Meatballs = 9 – 12 min/Lb – Arrange 3/4" apart in a circle in dish.	Brush with Browning sauce, add 1/2 cup water for 3-5 Lb Roast.

BF – (Beef Chop Suey – American Chinese)

1 Sirloin Beef Steak – Sliced thinly in pieces **and/or***
1 Pound Boneless Pork Roast – sliced thinly in pcs*
2 tsp Chinese White Cooking Wine
1 Tbsp Soy Sauce
2 Tbsp Oyster Sauce
1 tsp Granulated Sugar
1/4 tsp Cornstarch
1 cup each Onions, Bell Peppers, Celery,
   Mushrooms all sliced thinly

1 (5 oz) can sliced Water Chestnuts
Peanut Oil for frying
1/2 tsp Chinese Hot Chili Paste
1 bunch thinly sliced Green Onions
4 oz Bean Sprouts, washed and drained
1/2 cup Chicken Broth
4 tsps chopped Garlic
Cooked Steamed Long Grain Rice, or Egg
   Noodles, drained and salted

In a large bowl combine 1 Tbsp of oyster sauce, soy sauce, 1 tsp of cooking wine, sugar, pepper flakes and 1 tsp of the cornstarch. Whisk to dissolve the cornstarch. Add in the beef and/or sliced pork, then toss to coat and marinate for 15–30 minutes. In another bowl, make a sauce of 1 Tbsp Oyster Sauce, 1 tsp wine, 1 tsp cornstarch, and Chicken broth. Whisk to dissolve the cornstarch. Place peanut oil in a hot wok over high heat, coating the sides. Add the garlic and cook for a few seconds. Add in the marinated meats and stir-fry until lightly browned (~2 minutes). Add the onions and peppers and stir-fry for 1 minute. Add the celery and the mushrooms for another minute. Add in the bean sprouts and water chestnuts, stir well and cook until crisp-tender. Make a well in the center and add the sauce and the chili paste. Cook, stirring until the sauce boils and thickens and the pork is cooked thoroughly for 1-2 minutes. Serve over the salted, drained hot noodles or long grain steam rice. *This is and/or for the Beef and Pork, can be either or with both meats.

4-6 Servings
MENU WEEK#34

BF – (Beef Creole Steak with Potatoes)

2 Pounds 1/2 inch thick Beef Round Steak
1/2 tsp Dry Mustard
1/4 tsp Pepper
1/2 cup chopped Onion
1 or 2 Bay Leaves
1 Tbsp Sugar

2 Tbsp All-Purpose Flour
1 tsp Salt
2 Tbsp Shortening or Vegetable Oil/Fats
1 medium Green Bell Pepper - sliced
1-1/2 cups Tomato Juice
6 medium Potatoes

Wipe the steak with paper toweling. Mix the flour, mustard, salt and pepper together; rub into the steak (can use the edge of a saucer to cut the mixture into the steak). Brown the meat in hot oil in a large pot or Dutch oven. Add in the onions, green bell peppers, bay leaves, tomato juice, sugar and cover. Cook 1 hour over low heat. If using a Dutch oven, add the potatoes and cook an additional 30 minutes. Thicken the tomato sauce with the flour and pour over the steak. Arrange the steak and potatoes on a hot serving platter. (All ingredients can be placed in a Crock pot and cooked all day on low). **HINT: <u>Be sure to always layer the vegetables as the first item on the "bottom" in a Crock-pot, below the meat.</u>**

Serves 4-6
MENU WEEK#24

BF – (Beef Croquettes)

1 Pound Ground Chuck
1 small Carrot, finely chopped
1 Tbsp Sugar (granulated)
1/2 tsp Ginger Powder
1 tsp Soy Sauce
2 cups Potato Flakes (instant)
2 Tbsp Water
Breadcrumbs

1/2 Onion, minced
1 tsp Garlic Salt
1 tsp Monosodium Glutamate (enhances flavors)
1 tsp Salt
1 Egg, well beaten
All-Purpose Flour
Vegetable Oil for frying
4 hard-boiled Eggs, finely chopped

Gently brown the meat in a large skillet. Drain off the fats. Add chopped eggs, carrot, onion, sugar, garlic salt, ginger, glutamate, soy sauce and salt. Cover and simmer for 15 minutes. Measure potato flakes into a large bowl. Stir in the boiling water (or per package directions). Add the meat mixture to the mashed potatoes and mix thoroughly. Form into small logs (1 x 3" each). Blend the egg with the water and roll the logs into the flour, then dip into the egg mixture, and then roll them in the Breadcrumbs. Deep fry in hot oil (370°F) until they turn golden brown, drain on paper towels.

Serves 4
MENU WEEK#34

BF – (Beef Crunchy Steaks)

4 – 6 Eye of Beef Round Steak
1/4 Pkg Seasoned Stuffing Mix (crushed)
2 Eggs + small amount of Water
All-Purpose Flour
Salt and Pepper to taste
Waxed Paper
Paper Sack
Vegetable Oil for frying

If you don't purchase stuffing mix that is already granulated, **place the cubes into a paper sack or plastic bag and smash with a meat mallet or a rolling pin.** Salt and pepper the steak on both sides. Roll in flour. Beat the eggs and water with a fork inside a shallow, flat dish. Place your dressing mix crumbs onto a piece of waxed paper. Dip your meat again into the flour, and then into the egg mixture, then roll into your dry crumb mixture. Heat oil to medium-hot and cook the coated meat on both sides for 10-15 minutes or until evenly browned.

Serves 4-6
MENU WEEK#25

EXTRA RECIPES:

BF – (Beef Cubed Steaks – Pizza Style)

1 (26.5 oz) can of Spaghetti Sauce
4 Cubed Steaks or 1-1/2 Pounds Lean Ground Beef
1 Tbsp Vegetable Oil   1 medium Onion, chopped
1/2 Pound shredded Cheddar Cheese   1/2 Pound shredded Swiss Cheese
1/2 Pound shredded Mozzarella Cheese   1/4 cup shredded or grated Parmesan Cheese

Brown the onion in the hot vegetable oil, add in the cubed steaks and brown on both sides. Add in store bought sauce and reduce the heat to a simmer. Cover and cook cube steaks 10-15 minutes or until the meat is super tender, stirring or turning occasionally; drain fats. Sprinkle the top of the meat with a combination of the pizza cheeses and return for another 5 to 10 minutes to melt all of the cheese toppings.

Spaghetti Sauce
MAKE YOUR OWN - (Ingredients not on grocery list)
1 can (16 oz) Tomatoes, chopped
2 cloves Garlic, minced
1-1/2 tsp Oregano   } SAUCE
1 tsp Salt
1/4 tsp Pepper

Serves 4
MENU WEEK#29

BF – (Beef Cubed Steaks – Stuffed Oscar)

4-6 Cube Beef Steaks   1 can (14.5 oz) Brown Gravy with Mushrooms*
Shredded Swiss Cheese   Shredded Monterey Jack
Shredded Sharp Cheddar Cheese   Toothpicks and Waxed Paper
Salt and Pepper to taste   Garlic Powder
1/2 Pkg cut frozen Asparagus cuts or 6-8 fresh Asparagus Stalks

Cook the asparagus per package directions and drain. Place the cubed steaks between 2 pieces of waxed paper or plastic wrap. Working from the center out, pound lightly with a meat mallet or rolling pin. Remove, and salt and pepper and lightly sprinkle with garlic powder on both sides. Place in the center of each steak a small portion of the Jack & Cheddar Cheese and pieces of cooked asparagus. Fold the edges over the ingredients and seal together with toothpicks. Either broil at (500°F) on the top rack of the oven, or bake in a 325°F oven for 30 minutes. You can top this with a can of warmed brown gravy with mushrooms and serve.   4-6 Servings
MENU WEEK#51

Gravy Brown*
MAKE YOUR OWN – See recipes **MISC – (Gravy – Brown)**

(BF)-69

BF – (Beef Empanadas with Peas and Carrots)

1 Pound Ground Beef
small chopped Onion (about 1/4 cup)
1 Pkg Mushroom Gravy Mix (about 1 oz dry)
1 can (15 oz) Peas and Carrots, drained (reserve the liquid)

1/4 cup Raisins, Paprika, Margarine or Butter, melted 1
1 medium Potato, finely chopped (about 1/2 cup)
1 Pkg Pie Crust Mix (22 oz) or Pastry Shells

Cook and stir ground beef and onion in a 10" skillet until the beef is light brown and onion is tender; drain. Stir in the potato, drained peas and carrots, raisins, and gravy mix. Add enough water to the reserved vegetable liquid to measure 1 cup; stir water into beef mixture in the skillet. Heat to boiling; then reduce the heat. Simmer uncovered, stirring occasionally (~ 1 minute). Cool. Heat oven to 400°F. Prepare pastry for 2-Two Crust pies as directed on piecrust mix (or **MAKE YOUR OWN**, or use frozen pastry shells). Roll out and cut into 3" round circles. Place these rounds on a non-greased baking sheet. Spoon a scant tablespoon of beef mixture onto half of each circle. (If you'd like a better seal, brush inside edges with an egg wash (1 beaten egg + 1 Tbsp Water.) Fold pastry over filling in half forcing out any air, seal edge with fork tine by pressing the two edges together sealing with a crimping action. Brush with melted butter and sprinkle with paprika. Bake until light brown, about 15 minutes (These can be baked ahead and frozen up to three weeks). Fifteen minutes before serving, place frozen Empanadas on a greased baking sheet and heat in a 400°F oven for 15 minutes.   Yields 5 Doz

MENU WEEK#28

Pie Crust - MAKE YOUR OWN see recipe BRD – (Pie Crust)

BF – (Beef Enchilada Pie)

1-1/2 Pounds Ground Beef
Salt and Pepper
1 cup shredded Monterey Jack Cheese
Chopped Black Olives

1/4 cup Chopped Onion
1 cup shredded Cheddar Cheese
8 Flour Tortillas*
1 (10 oz) can of Enchilada Sauce or make your own**

Brown the beef and onion and drain off the fats. Place a small amount of the sauce** in a greased shallow baking dish. (Can make your own sauce as seen below or can use a store bought can of Enchilada Sauce). Place a layer of the tortillas, then the beef mixture, add in the shredded cheese and spoon sauce on top.   Spread with the rest of the cheese and the chopped olives.

Serves 4-8
MENU WEEK#25

Flour Tortillas*

MAKE YOUR OWN - (Ingredients not on grocery list)
3 cups All-Purpose Flour
1/3 cup Shortening or Lard

1 tsp Salt
3/4 - 7/8 cup lukewarm Water (test it on your wrist like you do a baby's milk)

Sift the flour and salt together. Work in the shortening with a fork (or a pastry blender). Add in the water until the dough forms a ball that comes away cleanly from the side of the bowl. Knead dough in a floured bowl until smooth. Cover with a moist cloth and let it rest 15 minutes at room temperature. Divide the dough into 12 equal parts. On a floured board roll out the dough to a 7" thin circle. Place between two towels to keep moist. When you have rolled out all of the dough, cook each tortilla on a lightly greased griddle over medium heat for two minutes on each side, slightly browned.

Enchilada Sauce **

MAKE YOUR OWN – (Ingredients not on grocery list**)
3 cans (8 oz ea) Tomato Sauce
2 to 3 tsp chili powder
Blend together in a medium saucepan and cook for around 5 minutes.

1 cup water
1/2 tsp Oregano

1/4 tsp Cumin
1 clove Garlic, finely chopped

Decided for You Cookbook – 365 Dinners

BF – (Beef Fajitas)

1-1/2 Pounds Beef London Broil or Flank Steak (slightly frozen so you can cut strips thinner)
4 Garlic Cloves, minced and mixed to a paste with 1 tsp Salt

1/4 cup Lemon Juice	1-1/2 tsp Ground Cumin
2 Tbsp Olive Oil	1 Tbsp Vegetable Oil
2 assorted colored Bell Peppers, sliced thin	1 Large Red Onion, sliced thin
2 Garlic Cloves, minced	8 – 12 (7 to 8-inch) Flour Tortillas
Guacamole Dip (or Make Your Own recipe below)	Salsa, Red or Green (see SAUCE – Salsa)

In bowl whisk together for a marinade the garlic paste, lemon juice, cumin, and the olive oil. Slice the meat across the grain, on the diagonal into small, thin strips about 2" lengths. Add in the steak strips to marinate for at least 1 hour or overnight, turning occasionally to coat evenly. Grill, broil at (500°F) or pan fry the drained, steak strips for at least 3-5 minutes on each side. Transfer the meat to a warmed pan, cover with foil. While the steak is standing for about 8 minutes heat the oil in your skillet until hot, but not smoking, add in the bell peppers, onion; stirring well. Add in the balance of 2 cloves of minced garlic and cook the vegetables and garlic for 5 minutes or until the bell peppers are softened. **WARMING TORTILLAS**: Stack 4 tortilla packets at a time and wrap with aluminum foil. Warm these in a 325°F oven for 10-15 minutes. If the tortillas are very dry to begin with, pat each tortilla between dampened hands before stacking them. Or you can microwave by wrapping each stack in microwave-safe bags on high power for 30 seconds to 1 minute. **SERVING**: Spread guacamole dip on the one side of the tortilla. Fold the tortilla to enclose the filling, top guacamole with a few slices of the steak, some of the pepper mixture, and followed by salsa.

Guacamole Dip

MAKE YOUR OWN – (Ingredients not on grocery list)

2 ripe Avocados	1/2 small Onion, minced
4 tsp Lime Juice	1/2 tsp Ground Cumin
2 Tbsp chopped Cilantro, if desired	

1 Garlic clove, minced and mashed to a paste with 1/2 tsp Salt
1 fresh or picked Jalapeno Chile (wearing gloves, seed and mince)

Halve and pit the avocados and scoop the flesh out of the skin and place into a bowl. Mash the avocado pulp with a fork and stir in the onion, garlic paste, lime juice, cumin, chile, and cilantro. The guacamole should be made 2 hours in advance and chilled.   Serves 6-8
MENU WEEK#39

BF – (Beef Flank Steak and Pan-Fried Potatoes)

1 Pound Beef Flank Steak, partially frozen makes it easier to cut diagonally very thinly
4 medium Potatoes, peeled if desired, and sliced thin lengthwise

1 tsp dry Mustard	1 large clove Garlic, crushed
4 or 5 Tbsp Vegetable Oil, added at different times	Salt and Pepper to taste
2 Tbsp Soy Sauce	

In a bowl mix the soy sauce, mustard and garlic; add in the strips of steak and stir until coated. Marinate at room temperature while slicing the potatoes. Heat 3 Tbsps of the oil in a large heavy skillet. Add the potatoes in a single layer and fry until fork tender, about three minutes on each side. Remove these with a slotted spoon, drain on paper towels and keep them warm. Add the remaining 1 or 2 Tbsps of the oil to the skillet; sauté the steak strips on medium high frying a few at a time quickly, about two minutes. Season the meat with salt and pepper. Serve together with the potatoes.   **-OR- use VEG**
– (Parisienne Potato) for different effect.   Serves 4-6
MENU WEEK#48

(BF)-71

BF – (Beef Get a Husband Steak)

1 large Beef Round Steak – 2 or 3" thick would be great
1 small bottle of Stuffed Green Olives   1 (10-3/4 oz) can Tomato Soup
1 small Onion, chopped   Strips of Pimiento
Button Mushrooms   All-Purpose Flour
Vegetable Oil or Leftover Bacon Drippings   Aluminum Foil
Chopped Celery & Green Bell Peppers (Optional)

Spread on top of your meat about 1/2 cup of flour. With the edge of a saucer, cut this flour into the meat, if it needs more flour; add. Repeat for the other side and heat vegetable oil in your skillet and quickly brown the floured meat on both sides. Place the meat in a shallow baking pan and add in the olives, soup, onion, celery & green bell peppers. Cover with foil and bake this at 250°F oven for at least 3 hours. Meat should be mahogany in color, if not remove foil to brown. Make some lattice cuts in the meat and lay the pimiento in the grooves, then put the button mushrooms in the center of each square. Dribble the pan juices over the top and return the meat to the oven to reheat the meat, and cook the mushrooms for approximately 5 – 10 minutes.

4 Servings
MENU WEEK#21

HINT: 1 Pound fresh Mushrooms = 5 cups sliced or 18 to 20 medium-size Whole

BF – (Beef Gorditas)

Meat Mixture:

1 Pound Ground Beef   1 small chopped Onion
1 tsp Garlic Salt   1/2 tsp Salt
1/4 tsp Pepper   1/4 tsp Chili Powder
8 Corn Tortillas or Make Your Own Shells   2 cups shredded Longhorn Cheddar Cheese

In a skillet brown the beef, onion and seasonings for 5 to 10 minutes. While the meat is cooking, warm the Tortillas [or mix all of the ingredients for the shells, divide the dough into 6 equal parts. With a patting motion, flatten each part into 1/2" thickness and about three to four inches in diameter (like a pita bread)]. Fry each in a hot, greased skillet or griddle until golden brown, turning once; drain on paper toweling. Keep these covered with a kitchen towel to keep warm. Holding the tortilla in your hand, fold in half and stuff it half full with the meat mixture, lettuce, tomatoes, and cheese. Serve with your favorite chili or taco sauce.

Gorditas Shells – Corn Tortillas
MAKE YOUR OWN - Recipe can be doubled for 12 – (Ingredients not on grocery list)
2 cups Masa Harina (Mexican Corn Flour)   2 tsp Salt
1 tsp Double-Acting Baking Powder   1 cup Water
2 slices fried Bacon, crumbled   2 cups Shredded Longhorn Cheddar Cheese
Aluminum Foil

Note: You can use flour tortillas if you do not like the corn type mixture made from the above recipe. You can stack four tortillas together and wrap with aluminum foil. Warm these in a preheated 325°F oven for 10-15 minutes –**OR**- You can microwave these in a microwave in a safe cooking bag (or unwrapped) on high speed for 30 seconds to one minute – **OR**- as shown if making these from scratch they can be cooked on a greased hot griddle on both sides until slightly browned, drain on paper toweling and kept hot in a tortilla warmer or between a kitchen towel.

Makes 6 – 8 servings
MENU WEEK#40

Decided for You Cookbook – 365 Dinners

BF – (Beef Green Chiles Taco Cheese Pie)

1 Pound Ground Beef
1 Pkg (1-1/4 oz) dry Taco Seasoning Mix (or mix together 1 tsp Cumin, and 1 tsp Chili Powder)
1/4 cup Water
1 Pkg Piecrust Mix (which makes two crusts or they can be frozen, but defrosted)
1 cup (4 oz) shredded Monterey Jack Cheese or Cheddar Cheese
1 can (4 oz) Green Chiles, seeded and diced

Brown the beef in a medium size saucepan; drain off the fats. Stir in the taco seasoning mix and 1/4 cup water. Cover, and simmer following the label directions. Cool 10 minutes. Add 1/2 cup of the shredded cheese to the "two" crust piecrust mix following the package direction (or use your own recipe) and roll out on a floured board. One should be an 11" round pie shell, and one a 10" pie shell. If using frozen/defrosted shells, mix the cheese into the piecrust and re-roll them. Place the 11" pie shell in an 8" pie pan to form the bottom crust. **Drape it over the pie pan, and trim the overhang off. It's easy to trim the piecrust edge by pressing a dinner knife flat against the crust and the edge of the pan in firm downward motion. This will cause the excess dough to fall away from the edge of the pan.** Pierce the center of the piecrust with a fork several times to make steam vents before filling. This will allow the crust to cook and not swell up or shrink too much. Place on top of the bottom crust the meat mixture and the chopped, drained green Chiles. Cover the meat mixture and bottom crust with the top 10" crust. Flour your fingers and flute the top edge of the crust with a fork or pinch a design between your fingers around the edge to seal the two crusts together. Bake in a hot oven (425°F) 25 minutes or until the pastry top is golden brown. Remove from the oven and let the pie stand 5 minutes before serving. Serves 4-6

MENU WEEK#48

BF – (Beef Ground Skillet)

1-1/2 Pounds Ground Beef	1 cup Chopped Onions
1/2 cup Chopped Celery with Leaves	2 Tbsp Vegetable Oil
1 (8 oz) can Tomato Sauce	1 tsp Salt
1-1/4 cups Sour Cream	4 tsp Paprika

Sauté onions and celery in oil for 5 minutes. Add in the beef, and the salt; cook and stir until browned. Drain off excess fats. Add the tomato sauce and half of the paprika. Cook and stir for another 5 minutes. Stir in the sour cream. Heat thoroughly, serve over cooked noodles or steamed rice, as desired. Servings 6

MENU WEEK#45

SPECIAL NOTES:

BF – (Beef Hamburgers)

Basic:
1 to 2 Pounds Ground Lean Beef
(optional) 1/2 Pound Ground Veal or 1/2 Pound Ground Pork Sausage - Bread or Saltine Cracker crumbs binds meats together and increases the volume of the meat if you need to stretch)
1 slightly beaten Egg – binds the meat and crumbs together
Salt and Pepper to taste
Hamburger Buns

Mix all ingredients except the buns and form patties. Broil, pan fry, grill outdoors, **or if it's winter, cook over briquettes in your fireplace.** Serve with condiments (mustard, ketchup, pickle relish, onions or pickle slices) on toasted/warmed Hamburger Buns
Serves 4-6
MENU WEEK#6

HINT: **Adding a little egg yolk or ice water to the ground beef before forming patties will make for juicer burgers.**

OPTIONAL OTHER COMBINATIONS FOR HAMBURGERS:

Bar-B-Q Burgers
Add in 1/2 cup Barbecue Sauce to Ground Beef

Chili Cheese Burger
Warm one can of chili with beans. Add onion to two hamburger patties and cook on both sides. Place toasted Hamburger Buns cut side up on a plate (open faced) and top with the cooked Hamburger patties, add to the top of these patties the shredded Cheddar Cheese. Ladle over the chili beans and serve.

Cordon Bleu Burger
Pat out two thin patties and place one patty on the bottom topped with 1 slice of Ham (can be Deli sliced), and 1 slice Swiss Cheese. Top with the other patty and cooked on both sides until done.

Creole Sausage Burgers
Cut 6 oz of Andoulle sausage in 1-inch pieces and chop this in a food processor (or you can remove the outer skin) and mix into your Ground Beef. Add also 1 slightly beaten egg, 3/4 cup grated sharp Cheddar Cheese, Add 2 Tbsp Garlic Powder, 1 Tbsp Cayenne Pepper, 1 Tbsp Oregano, 2-1/2 Tbsp Paprika, 1/2 chopped Jalapeno Pepper (optional) salt and pepper to taste. Form into patties and cook.

French Onion Burgers
Can mix dry onion soup into Ground Beef and serve on toasted French Steak Sandwich Buns.

Guacamole Burger Topping

1 Avocado	2-1/2 tsp Lemon Juice
1/3 cup finely diced, seeded Tomato	3 tsp minced Green Onion
1/4 tsp Ground Cumin	2 Tbsp chopped Cilantro

Peel, halve and remove the pit by striking it with the edge of a large knife and it will come out cleanly. Place the avocado into a medium sized bowl and mash with either a potato masher or a fork. Stir in the rest of the ingredients and mix well. Salt and pepper to taste and chill until ready to serve.

Mushroom Cheese Burgers
Dice mushrooms and sauté in vegetable or olive oil and cook till the liquid from the mushrooms has evaporated. Mix chopped onion, drained mushrooms and grated cheese of choice into Ground Beef and make patties and cook as above.

Pineapple Burgers
After making patties and grilling on one side, add a drained pineapple slice to steam while the patties complete cooking. Serve on a toasted bun.

(BF)-74

BF – (Beef Hamburger Acapulco)

2 Pounds Ground Beef
1/2 cup minced Onion
Salt and Pepper to Taste
Guacamole Dip (Make Your Own Topping below recipe)

1 cup grated Monterey Jack Cheese
Chili Powder
Buns, Hamburger

Add the onion to the Ground Beef, and shape into patties. Salt and Pepper to taste. Sprinkle chili powder on top of each patty and broil at (500°F) on both sides. After grilling patties on both sides, top with large spoon of Guacamole Topping and serve on Hamburger buns, Flour Tortillas or English Muffins – **OR** - Place on a platter and top with the avocado mixture and serve with refried beans, tortillas, and Spanish Rice if desired.

Guacamole Topping

MAKE YOUR OWN – (Ingredients are not included in grocery list)
1 Avocado
1/3 cup finely diced, seeded Tomato
1/4 tsp Ground Cumin
4 tsp (2 ea) finely chopped, seeded, canned or fresh,
Jalapeno Chiles

2-1/2 tsp Lemon Juice
3 tsp minced Green Onion
2 Tbsp chopped Cilantro
1 Tbsp Olive Oil
1 tsp Vinegar

Halve the avocado and remove the pit by striking it with the edge of a large knife and it will come out cleanly. Scrape out the avocado pulp and place it into a medium sized bowl and mash with either a potato masher or a fork. Stir in the rest of the ingredients mixing well. Salt and pepper to taste and chill until ready to serve   Serves 4-6
MENU WEEK#36

BF – (Beef Hamburgers – Blue Cheese Stuffed)

1-2 Pounds Ground Beef
1/2 cup chopped Onion
Salt and Pepper to Taste

2 Triangle Pkgs of Blue Cheese
1/2 tsp minced Garlic
Hamburger Buns

Add minced garlic, chopped onion, salt & pepper to ground beef and make into thin patties. On top of a patty place a blob of crumbled blue cheese. Then top with another thin patty and pinch the edges of these two patties together sealing inside the blue cheese. Broil, grill etc., and serve on toasted Hamburger Buns or on a platter with topping of the Green peppercorn mayonnaise, add on some type of potato and/or broccoli, if desired.

Green Peppercorn Mayonnaise Topping

MAKE YOUR OWN - (Ingredients not on grocery list)

1 Egg
2 tsp Dijon Mustard
1 Tbsp Olive Oil

1 Tbsp White Wine Vinegar
1/2 tsp Salt
4 tsp drained, Green Crushed Peppercorns

In a bowl or food processor, combine the egg, White Wine Vinegar, Dijon Mustard, 1/2 tsp salt and beat or process for 30 seconds. Add the oil in slowly through the feed tube of the processor or whip in with a mixer and it will form a thick mayonnaise emulsion, add in crushed peppercorns and mix until blended. Serves 4-6
MENU WEEK#34

Decided for You Cookbook – 365 Dinners

BF – (Beef Hamburger Casserole with Potatoes)

1 Pound Ground Beef
5 medium Potatoes
American Processed Cheese

1/2 cup Milk
Margarine
Salt and Pepper to Taste

Peel the potatoes, boil until fork tender and drain. Mash potatoes with salt and pepper, and the margarine. Salt and pepper the meat and fry the meat in a pan till done; drain fat. Mix the meat and potatoes together. Place a layer of this potato/meat mixture in a buttered casserole dish. On that layer, place cuts of the processed cheese followed by another layer of the potato/meat mixture. Continue this until all the ingredients have been used. Pour over the casserole the milk and place it in a 350°F oven and cook until the cheese is thoroughly melted ~ 20 minutes.

Serves 4-6
MENU WEEK #7

BF – (Beef Hamburger Continental)

1-1/2 Pounds of Ground Beef
1/2 Pound Lobster, crabmeat or shrimp
Salt and Pepper to taste

Hot, cooked Asparagus Spears
Lemon and Cucumber slices
Hollandaise Sauce (see below recipe)

Shape the ground beef into thick patties. Sprinkle both sides with salt and pepper and broil to desired doneness (500°F). Place the hamburger patties in a buttered casserole dish topped with the cooked asparagus spears. Top with the Hollandaise Sauce and garnish with cooked seafood of choice and the cucumber slices.

Hollandaise Sauce
MAKE YOUR OWN
In the top of a small double boiler, over simmering water, add 4 beaten egg yolks and 3 Tbsp Hot Water. Stir together with a wire whisk and cook till slightly thickened. Add in 1/2 cup soft butter or margarine, stirring constantly until it's smooth and thickened. Add salt, pepper and 1 to 2 Tbsp of Lemon Juice.
Pour over the ground beef patties and asparagus, and top with the cucumber slices; serve immediately.

HINT: If your sauce curdles, add a small piece of ice and beat vigorously to smooth out the sauce.

Serves 4-6
MENU WEEK#40

BF – (Beef Hamburger Dressing Bake)

1 Pound Ground Beef
1/2 cup Quick-Cooking Oats
1 tsp Salt
2 Tbsp Butter or Margarine
1/3 cup chopped Celery
1 Egg, 1 cup Water

1/2 cup Thousand Island Salad Dressing
1/4 tsp Pepper
1 medium Onion, finely chopped (about 1/2 cup)
6 cups Stuffing Mix (prepared per package directions)
1 can (10-3/4 oz) condensed Cheddar Cheese Soup
1 tsp dried Sage (do not add if using stuffing mix)

Mix the ground beef, oats, salad dressing, egg, salt and pepper together. Heat the oven to 350°F. Mix stuffing mix with water per pkg directions ending up with 6 cups. In a skillet melt the butter and cook the onion and celery until clear and tender about 3 minutes. Remove from the heat and stir in about enough of the water to absorb the butter. Add in the remaining dressing then add in the Sage and toss together. Then mix the dressing into the meat. Add 1/2 cup of water to the soup (if too thick warm on the stove for a few minutes) and mix it into the beef and stuffing mixture. Form into a loaf and bake, uncovered, until the top is golden brown and bubbly; about 40 minutes, drain the fats. Serve with mashed potatoes, vegetable of choice and salad.

4 Servings
MENU WEEK#45

Decided for You Cookbook – 365 Dinners

BF – (Beef Hamburger Meatball Stroganoff)

1 Pkg pre-made Frozen Meatballs defrosted
1 Tbsp Butter or Margarine
1 cup Beef Bouillon Consommé
1 Pkg Stroganoff Sauce, mixed with 1/2 cup water
Salt, Pepper and Paprika
Broiled Tomatoes (Optional)

1/2 cup Tomato Sauce
1 cup Sour Cream
Buttered Green Spinach Noodles (Opt)
2 cans (4 oz) drained Mushrooms sliced
   or bits and pieces or fresh

Sprinkle tops of the meatballs with Paprika. Pan fry or Broil till done; drain fats. In the meantime, melt the butter over low heat and sauté the drained mushrooms. Add in the bouillon, tomato sauce, and stroganoff mix. Simmer uncovered, until slightly thickened. Stir in the sour cream; bring it back to a boil. Remove from heat, stir and pour sauce over meatballs and serve on top of Spinach Noodles with broiled tomatoes. -OR-

Meatballs

MAKE YOUR OWN – (Ingredients not on grocery list)
2 Pounds Ground Beef with 1/4 cup minced Onion. Salt to taste. Shape the meat into medium sized meatballs. **HINT: Use an ice cream dipper to shape balls, dip in warm water if becomes sticky.**

Serves 6
MENU WEEK#38

BF – (Beef Hamburger Mushroom and Potato Casserole)

5 Medium Potatoes, peeled and sliced into thin potato round coins
1 can (10-3/4 oz) Condensed Cream of Mushroom Soup
1 Pound Ground Beef
Sliced Mushrooms
Salt and Pepper to Taste

1 soup can full of Milk
1/4 cup chopped Onion

Peel and slice the potatoes. Place these in a greased casserole dish. Brown the meat in a skillet with the onions and salt to taste; drain the fats. Add to the hamburger the soup and milk and then heat till melted together. Pour this over the potatoes. Cook the casserole covered for 35-45 minutes in a 325°F oven or until the potatoes are fork tender.

Servings 4-6
MENU WEEK#4

BF – (Beef Hamburger Patties with Onions)

1 – 2 Pounds of Ground Beef
1 Pkg Dry Onion Soup or chopped Onion
1 slightly beaten Egg
Vegetable Oil as needed

Salt and Pepper to Taste
1/2 cup Cracker Meal
Sliced Onions

Mix all together and form into patties. Place patties in a skillet with the sliced onion and brown on both sides approximately 10 minutes) - or – you can broil the patties at (500°F) for 10 minutes on each side and sauté the onions separately.

4-6 Servings
MENU WEEK#17

Dry Onion Soup

MAKE YOUR OWN –(Ingredients not on grocery list)
3/4 cup Dried Onions
1/4 tsp Celery Seed
4 tsp Onion Powder

1/3 cup Beef Broth Granules (not cubes)
1/4 tsp Sugar

Mix all ingredients and store in an airtight container. Five Tablespoons equals 1 package of Onion Soup mix.

(BF)-77

BF – (Beef Hamburger Peas and Carrots Over Rice)

1 Pound Ground Beef
1/4 cup chopped Onion
1 (15 oz) can Peas and Carrots - drained
1 (15 oz) can Tomato Sauce
1 tsp Garlic Powder
2 cups cooked Long Grain Rice (leftover cold rice is great)

Brown the beef with chopped onion, and garlic powder. Drain off the fats. Add in the drained peas and carrots, and the tomato sauce. Simmer covered for 10 minutes. Meanwhile cook the rice (or can be leftover and cold). Serve the cooked mixture over the rice. Add Ketchup to the top if desired.   Serves 4-6
MENU WEEK#16

BF – (Beef Hamburger Peas and Corn Casserole)

1 Pound Ground Beef	1 (15 oz) can Green Peas (drained)
1 (15 oz) can Cream Style Corn	1/4 cup chopped Onion
3 tsp Garlic Powder	Evaporated Milk
4 cups Mashed Potatoes - 8 small Potatoes	2 Tbsp Margarine

Peel and boil the potatoes and drain. Add in salt, pepper, margarine, and 1/4 can of evaporated milk and mash to a smooth consistency. In a skillet, brown the hamburger, onion and garlic powder; drain fats. In a 2-quart casserole, put in the drained green peas (salt/pepper and sprinkle a little garlic powder over the top of the peas). Next layer is the Cream style corn (salt/pepper the corn). Next layer is the cooked and drained ground beef (if you are crazy about garlic, sprinkle some additional garlic powder on top of the cooked meat). Top these 3 ingredients with the mashed potatoes. Dot the top of the potatoes with some butter and place into a 350°F oven for 20 – 25 minutes or until the peas on the bottom of the casserole is heated thoroughly; insert a spoon down to bottom layer and test doneness. (Or in the microwave covered with plastic wrap cook for 12 minutes). Remove the hot casserole and allow to cool off a little bit, improves the flavor if served not "too" hot.   Serves 5-6
MENU WEEK#3

HINT: Casseroles - Dried Out - Cover top of casserole with plastic wrap and pierce some holes in it so excessive steam can be removed and re-warm in a Microwave Oven. If you don't have a microwave, you can also put it on the top of a vegetable steamer tray or metal colander, covered with a lid over boiling water to refresh and re-steam.

BF – (Beef Hamburger Pie with Green Beans and Potatoes)

1 Pound Ground Beef	1 medium Onion, chopped
3/4 tsp Salt	Dash of Pepper
1 (15 oz) cut Green Beans, drained	1 (10-3/4 oz) can Tomato Soup
1/2 cup Evaporated Milk	5 medium Potatoes, boiled till done, and drained
1 beaten Egg	1/2 cup shredded Cheddar Cheese (Optional)

Lightly brown the meat; add in the onion and cook until just tender. Add in the seasonings, beans, and soup; pour it into a greased 1-1/2 Quart Casserole. Mash the drained potatoes with margarine, salt and pepper, milk and the egg. Drop the potatoes in mounds on top of the meat in the casserole dish. Sprinkle the mounds with 1/2 cup shredded cheese.

Bake at 350°F for 25-30 minutes   Serves 6
MENU WEEK#10

Decided for You Cookbook – 365 Dinners

BF – (Beef Hamburger Polynesian)

1-1/2 Pounds Ground Beef
1/2 Green Bell Pepper cut into 1/2" chunks
Vegetable Oil
2 tsp Cornstarch
Salt
Maraschino Cherries
Spinach – cooked (can be frozen or fresh, see recipe **VEG (Spinach - Creamed**)

1 can (14-1/2 oz) sliced Pineapple in syrup
1/2 Red Bell Pepper cut into 1/2" chunks
1/4 tsp Dry Mustard (can be Chinese Spicy or Dijon)
1 Tbsp Lemon Juice
Ground Ginger
Hot Cooked Rice

Drain the pineapple, reserving 1/2 cup of the juice. Cut 2 slices in half and the balance into small chunks. Sauté the bell peppers in 1 Tbsp of the oil over low heat until they are soft, clear and shiny. Add in the chunks of pineapple, the juice, and mustard. Blend the cornstarch with a little cold water and add to the mixture. Cook, stirring until thickened. Remove from the heat and add in the lemon juice. Reserve the sauce for serving time. Shape the meat into 4 round patties. Season with the salt and the ginger. Sauté, in a small amount of the hot oil until browned on both sides and desired doneness. Remove the patties and sauté the sliced pineapple halves in the drippings remaining in the skillet, add back in the reserved sauce. Garnish the hamburgers with the pineapple halves and top with the maraschino cherries for color and serve with the sweet and sour sauce, cooked spinach and hot cooked rice.

Serves 4
MENU WEEK#27

BF – (Beef Hamburger Tater Tot Casserole)

1 Pound Ground Beef
1 Pkg dry Onion Soup Mix (or make your own recipe)

3 cups frozen Tater Tots Potatoes
1 can (10-3/4 oz) Cream of Celery Soup

Brown the ground beef in a skillet, cutting it into small chunks and drain off any fats. Put the ground beef in a casserole dish. Mix in the tater tots, the cream of celery soup that has been mixed together with the dry onion soup.

Bake in 400°F oven for 30-45 minutes.

Serves 4-6
MENU WEEK#15

Dry Onion Soup

MAKE YOUR OWN – (Ingredients not on grocery list)
3/4 cup Dried Onions
1/4 tsp Celery Seed
4 tsp Onion Powder

1/3 cup Beef Broth Granules (not cubes)
1/4 tsp Sugar

Mix all ingredients and store in an airtight container. Five Tablespoons equals 1 package of Onion Soup mix.

BF – (Beef Hamburger Teriyaki with Rice)

1-1/2 Pounds Ground Beef
Sesame Seeds
White Steamed Rice or Cooked Curried Rice
2 cans Water Chestnuts drained, sliced and cut into halves

1 Bottle Teriyaki Sauce of choice
Chinese Snow Peas
Vegetable Oil

Salt the meat and shape into 4 oblong Hamburger Steaks. Mix the Soy Sauce, Water, Honey. Ginger and the garlic clove together. Brush the Teriyaki Sauce onto all sides of the hamburger steaks. Broil at (500°F) until done on both sides. Quickly stir fry in a small amount of vegetable oil in a skillet the water chestnuts, Chinese snow peas, sesame seeds and any remaining marinade sauce. Pour over the hamburger steaks and serve with a hot Curried Rice or White Rice as preferred.

Teriyaki Sauce - MAKE YOUR OWN - (Ingredients not on grocery list)

1 Tbsp Soy Sauce
1 Tbsp Water
1 Tbsp Honey

1 crushed Clove Garlic
1/4 tsp Ground Ginger
1 tsp Salt

Curried Rice - (Optional) **– Ingredients not on grocery list**

1 Tbsp Margarine or Butter
1 cup chopped Onion
1/4 cup chopped Celery
1 tsp Curry Powder
1 tsp chopped Garlic
1 cup Long Grain Rice

1/2 cup golden Raisins (optional)
1/8 tsp White Pepper
2 cups Chicken Stock
2 Tbsp chopped Green Onions
Salt and Pepper

In a medium saucepan, heat butter and cook onion, celery, curry powder, and garlic until tender. Add rice, pepper, and chicken stock. Stir well. Bring to a boil, cover and reduce the heat. Simmer for 15 minutes or until the rice is tender. Fold in the green onions and season, to taste, with salt and pepper.   Serves 4-6
MENU WEEK#41

BF – (Beef Hamburgers with Cheese Sauce in a Vegetable Wreath)

2 Pounds Ground Beef
Pepper
Processed American Cheese melted into a sauce
Tiny frozen Vegetables (Baby Peas, White Onions, Brussels Sprouts, or others as desired)

Onion Salt
Monosodium Glutamate
Margarine

Cook the frozen vegetables per package directions, drain and add salt and pepper to taste. Stir in margarine, cover and keep warm. Season the ground beef with the onion salt, pepper, and monosodium glutamate and shape meat into 6 hamburger steaks. Broil until desired doneness and transfer to a warmed serving platter. Pour cooked vegetables over the meat and top with the warmed cheese sauce. **(Can use melted processed cheese) –OR-**   6 Servings
MENU WEEK#30

Cheese Sauce

MAKE YOUR OWN – (Ingredients not on grocery list)
4 Tbsp melted Margarine
1 cup grated (medium or sharp) Cheddar Cheese
1/2 cup Chicken Broth or 1 tsp Chicken Bouillon
1 cup Evaporated Milk or Half-and-Half Milk

4 Tbsp Flour
1/2 tsp Salt
Dash of Cayenne Pepper

In a saucepan melt margarine, salt, stir in flour until blended, add chicken broth (if using a bouillon cube, dilute with 1/2 cup water or milk); when it comes to a rolling boil and looks blended, add in 1/2 of the grated cheddar cheese stir until melted. Pour mixture over desired food. Can be topped with Bread- crumbs that have been mixed into an additional 2 Tbsp of melted margarine.   4-6 Servings

(BF)-80

Decided for You Cookbook – 365 Dinners

BF – (Beef Hamburgers with Onions and Bell Peppers, the Swedish Style)

1-1/2 Pounds of Ground Beef
2-4 Yellow Onions, sliced
1/2 cup boiling Water

3 Tbsp Margarine or Butter
1 or 2 Green Bell Peppers, cut into rings
Salt and Pepper

Melt half of the margarine/butter in a skillet, add in the sliced onion and sauté over low heat until golden brown. Add in the pepper rings and the boiling water; season, stir well and turn the heat off. Add a lid to cover the onions and pepper rings to keep them warm. Salt the meat and shape it into 4 patties. Sauté the meat on both sides in the remaining butter in another the skillet until it's of desired doneness. Top each hamburger steak with the onion mixture. Serve with parsley potatoes (see recipe under **VEG – Potatoes – Parsley**) and (below recipe) pickled cucumbers and onions.

CUCUMBERS AND ONIONS ITALIAN PICKLED – Peel cucumbers and slice in coin shapes, thinly. Slice onion of choice and add half a bottle of tart Italian Dressing and marinate together in the refrigerator until needed. **HINT: If desired you can leave green peel on the cucumbers, but you should cut about a 1/2" piece from the end of the cucumber that had the vine attached. Rotate this piece in a circle against the end of the cucumber where it was removed until extra white moisture is observed. This is the bitterness of the skin being removed from the entire cucumber. Then slice as directed.**   Serves 4

MENU WEEK#32

BF – (Beef Hash and Mashed Potato Casserole)

1 Pound Beef Stew Meat
1 Tbsp Oil/Fat
1/2 tsp Pepper Corns – cracked
1 tsp Baking Powder
1/2 cup Red Wine
4 Large Potatoes, cooked and mashed per that recipe

1 large Onion sliced
1 Bay Leaf
Pinch of dried Thyme, Parsley, and Basil
1 cup Water as needed
Salt and Pepper to taste

Brown the beef and onion in the oil; add the bay leaf, and other seasonings and Baking Powder which should be dissolved in a little bit of water. Add the wine and cook on low in a Crock pot for 4-6 hours until meat readily comes apart (**OR-** can be placed in a heavy covered pot and put on low burner, check to be sure it doesn't boil dry adding more water or wine as needed). Shred the meat with a fork and add to the mashed potatoes with the juices from the meat to keep it moist not soupy. Bake in a buttered dish at 350°F for 40 minutes. **You can use leftover Beef and Leftover Mashed Potatoes for this casserole.**   Serves 4

MENU WEEK#30

BF – (Beef Hash – Ranch Style with Rice)

1 Pound Ground Beef *
1 cup chopped Green Bell Peppers
1/2 cup chopped uncooked Long Grain Rice
1/4 tsp Basil
Dash of Pepper

3-1/2 cups canned chopped Tomatoes
1/2 cup chopped Onion
1/2 cup Ketchup
1/2 tsp Salt
Processed Cheese, sliced

Brown the Ground Beef in a large skillet; add in the canned tomatoes, ketchup and the chopped bell pepper, onion and the uncooked rice. Cover with a tight fitting lid and cook for approximately 20 minutes or until the rice is done. Top with slices of cheese, cover again and heat until the cheese has melted about five minutes.
*CAN USE LEFTOVER SLICED STEAK IN PLACE OF GROUND BEEF IF AVAILABLE.

Serves 4-6

MENU WEEK#29

BF – (Beef Italian Chop Suey with Macaroni and Cabbage)

1-1/2 Pounds Ground Beef
2 Green Bell Peppers sliced
1 Pound Small Shell-Shaped Macaroni
1 cup Soy Sauce

2 medium sliced Onions
5 Stalks of Celery, cut up in round coin fashion
1 can Tomato Paste
1/2 head sliced Cabbage

Sauté the Ground Beef. Add in the sliced peppers, onions, and celery and continued to cook for an additional 5 – 10 minutes or until these are soft. Drain fats. Add in the tomato paste, plus 2 or 3 cans of water and the soy sauce. Stir together, cover and simmer 20 to 30 minutes. In the meantime, boil the macaroni per the package direction, drain, salt and add to the sauce mixture. Stir well and serve.

Serving 4-6
MENU WEEK#7

BF – (Beef Italian Skillet Dinner with Potatoes and Italian Green Beans)

1 Pound Ground Beef
2 tsp Bouquet Browning & Seasoning Sauce
1 tsp Italian Seasonings
3 Tbsp All-Purpose Flour
Salt and Pepper
2 cans (1 Pound each) Whole Potatoes – Rinsed with cold water and drained

1 Pound Mild Italian Sausage
2 cans (1 Pound each) Stewed Tomatoes
1 Pkg (10 oz) frozen Italian Green Beans*
3 Tbsp Water
Parmesan Cheese

Slice the sausage into 1" thick pieces. Brown sausages in an electric skillet or in a heavy fry pan and remove to a bowl to cool. Mix the ground beef together with the Bouquet Sauce and shape into meatballs. Brown the meatballs in the skillet with the sausage drippings. Skim off the fat with a spoon from the skillet. Add in the tomatoes, Italian seasoning, potatoes, and green beans. Cover and simmer 10 minutes. Blend the flour and water together and simmer for 10 minutes or until thickened and pour into the vegetables. Return the sausage and meatballs to the skillet and re-warm. Add salt and pepper to taste and sprinkle the top with the grated Parmesan Cheese and serve.

4-6 Servings
MENU WEEK#27

*If Italian Beans are not available use cut Green Beans

BF – (Beef Italian Steak and Rice)

1 Beef Round Steak, cut in cubes
Long Grain Rice – Steamed
All-Purpose Flour
Vegetable Oil

<u>**Mix Together:**</u>
1-1/2 cups Ketchup
1 Pkg Dry Onion Soup Mix
Salt & Pepper to taste

2 cups Water
1 Tbsp Italian Dressing

Flour meat and brown it in a small amount of Vegetable Oil in a skillet. Mix the sauce together and pour over the steak and bake at 275°F for 2 hours, or until meat is very tender. Serve with cooked rice or mashed potatoes.

4 Servings
MENU WEEK#25

Decided for You Cookbook – 365 Dinners

BF – (Beef Kabobs)

Beef Marinade
1/2 cup Vegetable Oil
2 Tbsp Dijon-Style Mustard
1/4 tsp Pepper

1 Tbsp Red-Wine Vinegar
1/4 tsp Salt

Mix your Marinade ingredients and place the beef in it for at least 1-1/2 to 2 hours. **HINT:** **If meat is not totally covered with the marinade put it in a sealed bowl or ziplock bag so you can flip it occasionally in the frig so all pieces are marinated. Soak your skewers in water before using so they won't catch on fire when broiled.**

2 Pounds Beef Stew Meat, cut in 1-1/2 inch cubes
12 medium whole Mushrooms
4 large Zucchini, each cut in 4 chunks
Wooden Skewers soaked in water
Cherry Tomatoes and canned whole Onions, or fresh boiling Onions
Canned Potatoes – Drain these and sprinkle with salt and garlic powder. Allow the potatoes to rest.
Bell Peppers – Cut into sections so they will fit onto the skewers

1 cup Beef Broth
(Optional) 4 thick slices Bacon, each cut into 4 pieces

Heat the beef broth in a small saucepan to boiling. Place mushrooms in mixture for 2-3 minutes. Alternate on the wooden skewers beef, bacon, mushrooms, zucchini, tomato, green pepper, potatoes, and onions. Grill or broil 500°F 10 to 15 minutes in your oven or out-of-doors on the grill. Baste occasionally with the beef broth.

Alternate Sweet Marinade - (Ingredients not on grocery list)
1/4 cup minced Onions
1/4 cup Brown Sugar
1 clove minced Garlic
1/4 tsp Ground Cloves

3/4 cup Soy Sauce
2 tsp Curry Powder
1/2 tsp Salt
1/2 tsp Ginger (Optional)

4-6 Servings
MENU WEEK#12

HINT: **Tannin in strong, brewed tea works as a tenderizer in a marinate for tougher cuts of meat.**

SPECIAL RECIPES OR NOTES:

BF – (Beef Lasagna)

1 (6 oz) Creamed Cottage Cheese, small curds
1 cup grated Parmesan Cheese
1 Tbsp dried Parsley Flakes
1-1/2 tsp dried Oregano Leaves
1-2 Lbs Ground Hamburger

1 carton (12 oz) Ricotta Cheese
3 cups shredded Mozzarella Cheese
2 tsp Salt
8 oz Lasagna Noodles

Use 1 (26.5 oz) can of Spaghetti Sauce for Lasagna Sauce with 1 Pound of Ground Beef **–OR–** below **MAKE YOUR OWN** recipe.

Mix together the cottage and Ricotta cheeses, 1/2 cup of the Parmesan cheese, parsley, salt and Oregano and put aside. Cook the noodles per package directions, drain. Heat the oven to 350°F. Cut up the meat and cook in a skillet with salt and pepper until done. Drain excessive fats. Mix together with the spaghetti sauce and then place the sauce in the bottom of a 9 x 13" baking dish. Layer the lightly salted cooked noodles. Spoon in your cottage cheese mixture followed by a layer of sauce. Sprinkle some Mozzarella Cheese over the sauce and repeat the layers until all are used. Last layer should be the meat sauce then covered with the balance of any cheeses. Bake uncovered 45 minutes and let stand 15 minutes before serving. **VARIATION:** Make individual servings, coat 12 muffin tins w/nonstick cooking spray. Spoon 1 Tbsp sauce into bottom, layer in same ingredients and cook 350°F for 30 minutes. Serves 8-10

MENU WEEK#1

Lasagna Sauce

MAKE YOUR OWN (Ingredients not on grocery list)
3 Tbsp Vegetable Oil
1/3 cup chopped Onion
1 clove Garlic, minced
1 (8 oz) can Tomato Paste or Puree
1-1/2 tsp Basil 1 tsp Parsley
1/2 cup grated Parmesan Cheese

1 – 2 Pounds Ground Beef
1/2 cup chopped Celery or Celery Salt (Optional)
1 (14.5 oz) large can Tomatoes, chopped
1 (8 oz) can cold water
1 tsp Oregano (or use Italian Seasoning instead of
   Basil and Oregano)

Heat the oil in a skillet and brown the onions until clear and tender. Add in the garlic and brown for 1 – 2 minutes. Add in the ground beef and stir to be sure it's cooked thoroughly. Add all of the other ingredients except the cheese. Cover and simmer for about 1 hour. Turn off the heat and add in the cheese. Layer it in between your Lasagna noodles and top with additional cheese if desired. Makes 1 Quart of Sauce.

BF – (Beef Liver and Onions)

1 – 2 Pounds Beef Liver
All-Purpose Flour
1 – 2 cups Onions sliced

1/4 cup Shortening or Vegetable Oil
Salt and Pepper to Taste

Salt and pepper the Liver and place in flour and cover with the flour on all sides. Melt the shortening and fry the Liver quickly, about 5 minutes on both sides. Add in the onions and sauté until clear and cooked. Cover and simmer an additional 10 minutes or until the liver and onions are fork tender. 4-6 Servings

MENU WEEK#28

BF – (Beef Meat and Cheese Casserole)

1-1/2 Pounds Ground Beef
1 cup chopped Onion
2 cups uncooked Elbow Macaroni
1 tsp Salt
1 tsp Oregano

1-1/2 cups Processed American Cheese, cubed
2 (8 oz each) cans Tomato Sauce
1 cup Water
1/4 tsp Pepper
1 (4 oz) can chopped Green Chiles

Mix all of the ingredients together in a large mixing bowl; place ingredients into a 9" x 13" baking dish, making sure all the macaroni is covered with liquid.   Bake 350°F for about 30 minutes.

6 Servings
MENU WEEK#21

BF – (Beef Meatballs and Gravy)

1 large (40 oz) Pkg frozen meatballs, defrosted
2 (14.5 oz) cans Beef Gravy

Brown the meatballs in a skillet covered for 15 minutes over medium heat. Drain off fats. Add in the gravy and warm for an additional 5 minutes   **-OR-**

MAKE YOUR OWN – (Ingredients not on grocery list)
2 Pounds Ground Beef
2 tsp Garlic Powder
1 cup Breadcrumbs or crushed saltine crackers

2 tsp Onion Salt (or chopped onions)
2 Eggs

Mix the above ingredients and form into 1" meatballs.

Beef Gravy Alternate Recipe

(Ingredients not on grocery list)
Placed drained beef fats into a saucepan, add 1-1/2 cans of water. Mix in two tsp Beef Bouillon. In a sealed container or self-closing bag thoroughly shake 1 Tbsp Cornstarch and 1/2 cup of milk. Stir this thickening mixture into bouillon and bring to a bubble and cook till desired thickness. To darken the color of the gravy add a tsp of Bouquet Browning & Seasoning Sauce and stir.

4-6 Servings
MENU WEEK#1

HINT: Browning Meat - Avoid pot watching on large quantities of meatballs, stew meat or pot roast by spreading in a shallow pan and broil or bake at 450° until browned.

BF – (Beef Meatballs Español with Rice and Zucchini)

1 Pound Ground Beef
3 medium Zucchini, sliced thinly
1 Large Tomato, sliced thinly
1 tsp Oregano
Chopped Green Onions
Salt and Pepper to taste
1 cup either grated Cheddar or Monterey Jack Cheese

1 cup uncooked Rice
1 (7-1/2 oz) can chopped Green Chiles
2 cups (16 oz) Sour Cream
1 tsp Garlic Salt
Chopped Green Bell Pepper

Salt the ground beef and make into meatballs. Brown these on all sides and drain the fats. Set aside. Cook the rice per package directions. Butter a casserole dish, place in the cooked rice, cover with the green Chiles, and add in the meatballs. Sprinkle 1/2 of the cheese over this mixture. Add the tomato slices to the top, add in the Zucchini, and sprinkle with salt and pepper to taste. Combine the sour cream, oregano, garlic, onion and spoon over the top. Scatter on the remaining cheese. Bake 45-50 minutes at 350°F   Serves 6-8
MENU WEEK#14

BF – (Beef Meatballs My New Way)

1 Pound Ground Beef
1/4 cup minced Onion
2 Tbsp chopped Parsley
1/2 cup Water
1 can (10-3/4 oz) Cream of Vegetable Soup **OR** any other kind of soup variety

1/3 cup fine dry Breadcrumbs
1 slightly beaten Egg
1/4 tsp Salt

Mix the beef, Breadcrumbs, onion, egg, and salt. Shape this into 15 meatballs. In a skillet, brown the meatballs; drain off the fats. Stir in the soup, water and the parsley. Cover; cook over low heat 15 minutes; stirring occasionally. Garnish with carrot curls if desired. Serve with a potato or rice.   4 Servings
MENU WEEK#47

BF – (Beef Meatballs Zucchini and Rice Casserole)

1 Pound Ground Beef
1-1/2 tsp Worcestershire Sauce
1 Tbsp Pepper
12 oz Zucchini, thinly sliced (about 2-1/2 cups)
1 Tbsp Cornstarch
3 cups hot cooked steamed Long Grain Rice

1/4 cup each of finely chopped Onion and Celery
1 Egg
1 can (16 oz) stewed Tomatoes
1/2 tsp crushed Oregano, Basil and Sugar
1 cup Beef Broth (canned or made with bouillon)
1/2 Tsp Garlic Powder

Combine the beef, breadcrumbs, onion, celery, Worcestershire sauce, egg, 1-1/2 tsp garlic powder, salt and pepper. Mix thoroughly. Form into 12 large meatballs. Place these in a greased shallow baking pan. Bake at 375°F for 20 minutes. Meanwhile combine the tomatoes and zucchini with the remaining seasonings and simmer in a saucepan for 5 minutes. Blend the cornstarch and broth together and stir into the tomato mixture to thicken. Pour this thickened sauce over the meatballs and continue baking an additional 10 minutes.
6 Servings
MENU WEEK#40

Decided for You Cookbook – 365 Dinners

BF – (Beef Meat Loaf)

2 Pounds Ground Beef	1/2 tsp Garlic Powder
1 Pound of Ground Pork Sausage	1 tsp Salt
1/4 cup Chopped Onion	1/2 tsp Pepper
2 Eggs slightly beaten	
2/3 cups dry Breadcrumbs, cracker meal or torn-up pieces of Bread	

Mix all of the above ingredients and form into a basic loaf 9" x 5" and bake at 375°F for 45-60 minutes until brown. <u>Cool before slicing or it will fall apart.</u>

<u>JAZZED UP VARIATIONS (each numbered item is a standalone idea}:</u> (Ingredients not on grocery list)
1. Add in 1 can Tomato Sauce or mix in 1/2 can of Tomato Soup with the balance of the soup poured over cooked meat loaf before serving.
2. Add chopped celery and 1/2 can of Condensed Cream of Celery Soup mixed into meat loaf with the balance poured over the cooked meat loaf before serving.
3. Add Red Bell Peppers and Spinach to the meat loaf.
4. Use garlic-flavored Croutons (instead of breadcrumbs), 1 tsp Chili Powder, 1/2 tsp Cayenne Pepper, Andouille Sausage for the Cajun flavor (Glaze top 15 minutes after beginning the bake with 1/2 cup Ketchup, 1 tsp Cumin, dash Worcestershire Sauce, 1 Tbsp Honey).
5. Instead of using breadcrumbs soak 1 cup Oatmeal in 1 cup Beef Broth.
6. Hard boil 4 – 6 eggs, peel, slice. Pat half of the meat into a bottom rectangle, Place the hardboiled eggs end-to-end down the center of the meat loaf. Top eggs with salami and slices of Parmesan Cheese or cheese of choice. Cover with another layer of meat and form into the loaf and bake per directions.
7. Prepare meat as in Item #6 in two sections and fill the center with green beans, zucchini, broccoli, or any other vegetable desired with or without the cheese of choice.
8. After forming your loaf, brush it with this glaze: 1/4 cup Ketchup or Chili Sauce, 2 Tbsp brown sugar, 2 tsp white vinegar. Then arrange bacon slices, crosswise, over loaf, overlapping each slightly and tucking them under to prevent curling.
9. Asian Spices, Thai Peanut Sauce, Soy Sauce and Ground Ginger adds another new flair.
10. Dry soup mix – Onion, Tomato or Vegetable flavors.
11. Pesto can be stirred into meatloaf.
12. A jar of chunky style Salsa for a Fiesta taste.
13.

HINT: <u>Meatloaf can be cooked in a Bundt Pan, Angel Food Cake Pan (with potatoes or vegetables served in the center), or in greased individual muffin/cupcake pans, for a quicker meal, or see Meat Loaf – Stove Top Mini's.</u>

Serves 4-6
MENU WEEK #3

BF – (Beef Meat Loaf – Bar-B-Q)

2 Pounds Ground Beef	1/2 cup Bar-B-Q Sauce
2/3 cups dry Breadcrumbs	1/4 cup chopped Onions
2 Eggs	1 tsp Salt
1/2 tsp Garlic Salt	1/4 tsp Pepper

Heat oven to 350°F. Mix all ingredients and shape into a loaf form; place in baking dish. Bake 40-60 minutes. Spoon off the fat/drippings, cool for 10 minutes before slicing. You can add additional sauce to the top of the meat loaf if desired or pour over Ketchup before serving to add color.

4-6 Servings
MENU WEEK#41

BF – (Beef Meat Loaf – Biscuit Wrapped)

2 Pounds Ground Beef	1 cup Milk
2/3 cup Dry Breadcrumbs	1/4 cup chopped Onion
2 Eggs	1 tsp Salt
2 tsp Worcestershire Sauce	1/2 tsp Garlic Powder
1/2 tsp Dry Mustard	1/4 tsp Pepper
1 cup Biscuit Mix	1/4 cup Water
4 – 8 slices (3/4 oz each) processed American Cheese	

Heat oven to 375°F. Mix together the beef, milk, breadcrumbs, onion, eggs, salt, Worcestershire sauce, garlic salt, mustard and pepper. Shape firmly into a loaf 5 x 8 inches; place in a shallow baking dish. Bake one hour; spoon off fat and cool.

Mix the Biscuit Mix and 1/4 cup of water until a soft dough forms; beat vigorously 20 strokes; gently smooth the dough into a ball on a floured cloth-covered or floured hard board surface. Knead 5 times. Roll out a 12-inch circle; place cheese slices on dough and then place cooked loaf in the center and fold the dough around it. Pinch seams together and place in a buttered baking dish. Prick the covered loaf with a fork for steam escape holes and bake at 375°F for about 15 minutes or until dough is lightly browned. Serve with the below Tomato-Bouillon sauce.

Serves 4-6

MENU WEEK#42

Tomato-Bouillon Sauce

Heat 1 cup **Ketchup** and 1 tsp **instant beef bouillon** to a boil over low heat, stirring frequently. Reduce heat, and simmer uncovered, until bouillon is dissolved.

BF – (Beef Meat Loaf – Stove Top Mini's)

2 Pounds of Ground Beef	1 can (10-3/4 oz) Tomato Soup
1/4 cup fine Dry Breadcrumbs	1 Egg, slightly beaten
1/4 cup finely chopped Onion	1 tsp Salt
1/4 tsp each Pepper, Sage, crushed Thyme	2 Tbsp Shortening
2 to 4 Tbsp Water	

Mix thoroughly 1/4 cup of the soup, ground beef, breadcrumbs, egg, onion, salt, and 1/8 tsp each of the pepper, sage, and thyme. Shape these into 6 firm mini loaves. In a skillet brown the loaves in the hot shortening; pour off the fat. Leaving the loaves in the skillet, pour in the remaining soup, seasoning, and water. Cover; cook over low heat 20 minutes or until done. Stir occasionally and lift the loaves from the bottom of the skillet with a pancake turner to make sure they don't stick. Cool for 3 minutes and serve.

6 Servings

MENU WEEK#38

BF – (Beef Meat Loaf with Cheese-Topped Potatoes)

2 Pounds of Ground Beef
1 Tbsp Parsley Flakes
1/2 Pound Grated Cheddar Cheese
Aluminum Foil
1 can (8 oz) Tomato Sauce
2 medium Potatoes, peeled and sliced
1 Pkg of dry Onion Soup Mix or 1 tsp Onion Salt (see Make Your Own recipe) – **OR -** 1/2 chopped Onion (if you do not use the onion soup)
1 cup soft Breadcrumbs (or crushed Saltine Crackers)

1/2 Pound of Ground Pork Sausage with 2
    Eggs slightly beaten
Garlic Powder to taste

Mix the beef, pork, eggs, breadcrumbs, onion soup together and form into a loaf and place in a baking dish. Peel the potatoes and cut into thin sliced rounds. Place these potato rounds on top of the meat loaf. Sprinkle the top layer of the potatoes with salt and the grated cheese. **Tent** (not touching cheese) **with Aluminum foil** and bake at 350°F for 40 minutes. Cool and slice.   Serves 4-6
MENU WEEK#37

Dry Onion Soup Mix

MAKE YOUR OWN – (Ingredients not on grocery list)
3/4 cup Dried Onions
1/4 tsp Celery Seed
4 tsp Onion Powder

1/3 cup Beef Broth Granules (not cubes)
1/4 tsp Sugar

Mix all ingredients and store in an airtight container. Five Tablespoons equals 1 package of Dry Onion Soup mix.

BF – (Beef Meat Pie)

1 (24 oz) canned Beef Stew
2 Tbsp Worcestershire Sauce
1 Tbsp Instant Dry Onion Soup Mix per can of Beef Stew or leftover stew
1 Pkg (9-1/2 oz) Pie Crust frozen (and thawed) or purchase a mix

1 cup frozen Green Peas

Mix together the canned stew, green peas, Worcestershire sauce, and the onion soup mix. Prepare 1 package of piecrust mix according to the directions on the package. Roll half of it to 1/8" thickness and line a 9" pie pan. Add the filling and roll out the balance of the piecrust and cover the filling (making it a two-crusted meat pie). Pinch the edge of the two crusts together to seal, flute if desired. Cut some small slits in the top crust for steam to escape. Bake at 425°F for 30 minutes or until the top crust is browned.   Serves 6
MENU WEEK#42

See **MAKE YOUR OWN RECIPE (BRD) Pie Crust**

Dry Onion Soup Mix

MAKE YOUR OWN – (Ingredients not on grocery list)
3/4 cup Dried Onions
1/4 tsp Celery Seed
4 tsp Onion Powder

1/3 cup Beef Broth Granules (not cubes)
1/4 tsp Sugar

Mix all ingredients and store in an airtight container. Five Tablespoons equals 1 package of Onion Soup mix.

BF – (Beef Meat Turnovers)

Can purchase a box of Refrigerator Roll mix –OR- Make Your Own

Turnover Dough

1 Pkg active Dry Yeast	1 cup warm Water (105°F to 115°F)
1 Tbsp Sugar	1 Tbsp Vegetable Oil
1/2 tsp Salt	2 to 2-1/2 cups All-Purpose Flour, sifted

Dissolve the yeast in the warm water and stir in the sugar, oil, and the salt into a large bowl. It will begin to activate by bubbling. Add in the flour a little at a time and stir well. When the flour has been added, turn the dough out on to a floured bread-board and knead until smooth and elastic; about 5 minutes. Place the dough into a large, greased bowl and then roll the dough forward turning the greased side up; cover the bowl with plastic wrap, and place bowl in a warm spot on the kitchen counter. **(If you are pressed for time, you can place the bowl on top of an electric heating pad turned on low to encourage it to rise quicker).** Allow the dough to rise to double its original size, about 1 hour. Punch down your dough and divide it into 10 parts. On a floured board, roll each of these into a 5" circle. Fill each circle with the filling (don't overfill you won't be able to seal the edges together) and fold in half, pinching the two sides together with your fingers or with the tines of a fork. Place these turnovers on a "greased" baking sheet. Cover with a damp towel and allow to double in size again, another 1 hour. Heat your oven to 375°F and bake until lightly browned, approximately 20-25 minutes. (If you would like a shiny cooked surface, then brush outsides of the turnover before cooking with a mix of a slightly beaten egg with a Tbsp of water.)

Turnover Hamburger Filling

1 Pound Ground Beef	5 oz chopped Mushrooms
1 small Onion, chopped (about 1/4 cup)	1 clove Garlic, crushed
1 Tbsp snipped Parsley	1 tsp Salt
1/2 tsp dried Dill Weed	1/8 tsp Pepper
1/2 can (4 oz) Tomato Sauce	
1 Pkg frozen Peas & Carrots (Optional) defrosted	

Cook the beef in a skillet with the onions and garlic. Drain off the fats. Stir in the other seasonings, the tomato sauce, the mushrooms, the defrosted peas and carrots and stir all ingredients together well.

Serves 5 hungry or more individuals
MENU WEEK#26

BF – (Beef Mexican Stew)

3 Tbsp Bacon Drippings (if don't have drippings cook three pieces of bacon)

3 Pounds of Beef Stew Meat, cubed	1-1/2 cups diced Onions
1 can (28 oz) Tomatoes non-drained	1-1/2 cups Green Chile Strips
1/2 cup Beef Broth	1/2 cup Chicken Broth
1 Tbsp Salt	2 tsp Garlic Salt
2 tsp Cumin	2 Pounds Potatoes

Peel and cube the potatoes and place them in a pan of water **(Potatoes can remain submerged underwater in a large bowl or pot while waiting for the beef/meat to cook to tender, by submerging them they will not turn dark from air exposure).** In a large saucepot or Dutch oven, heat bacon drippings to hot (or cook three pieces of bacon and cut up the meat; leave in the stew). Add in the beef and onions. Sauté the meat until the beef is browned on all sides. Add the tomatoes, Chile strips, broths and seasonings. Bring to a rolling boil and cook over low heat until the meat is tender, about 2 hours; add additional water or broths as needed during the cooking. Add in the cubed potatoes the last 30 minutes of the cooking time.

4 Quarts (Leftovers can be frozen)
MENU WEEK#44

Decided for You Cookbook – 365 Dinners

BF – (Beef Mooligan's Meat)

2 Pounds Beef Round Steak, diced
All-Purpose Flour
2 Green Bell Peppers, finely chopped
2 Celery stalks chopped
1/4 cup Sugar
Vegetable Oil

2 Pounds boneless Pork Steak, diced
Salt to Taste
2 medium Onions, finely chopped
1 (14 oz) bottle Ketchup
1/2 cup Vinegar

Salt the meats and roll in the flour. Sauté the peppers, onions, and celery in hot Vegetable Oil; add in the meat and brown. Add in the sugar, ketchup and the vinegar. Cover and simmer 1 to 2 hours. Can be served over potatoes, rice or noodles or other choice.   6-10 Servings
MENU WEEK#29

BF – (Beef Mother's Baked Steak and Potatoes)

1 to 1-1/2 Pounds Beef Round Steak
1 chopped Onion
2 Tbsp Vegetable Oil or Shortening

4 medium Potatoes, peeled and sliced in thin rounds
Approximately 1/2 cup All-Purpose Flour
1-1/2 cups Water

Trim fat from the steak; cut steak into serving pieces. If the meat has not been tenderized at the Butcher's then pound a little with a meat mallet. Salt the steak and potatoes and place these in a rectangular baking dish. Sprinkle the chopped onion over the top of the steak and potatoes. Sift flour over the top of the steak and potatoes; add in the water and drop the shortening in each corner. Bake 1 hour at 350°F.   Serves 4
MENU WEEK#43

BF – (Beef Oven Porcupine Balls with Rice)

1 Pound Ground Beef
1 tsp Salt
1 can Tomato Sauce
1/2 cup uncooked Long Grain Rice
1/2 tsp Celery Salt
1 cup additional Water

1/2 cup Water
1/8 tsp Garlic Powder
2 tsp Worcestershire Sauce
1/3 cup chopped Onion
1/8 tsp Pepper

Heat oven to 350°F. Mix together the meat, rice, 1/2 cup water, onion, salt, garlic powder and pepper. Using a tablespoon, shape the mixture into meatballs. Place the meatballs into a non-greased baking dish. Stir together the tomato sauce, the 1 cup of water, and Worcestershire sauce and pour over the meatballs. Cover the casserole dish with foil and bake 35 minutes and then uncover and bake another 10-15 minutes.
Serves 4-6
MENU WEEK#7

Decided for You Cookbook – 365 Dinners

BF – (Beef Parmegiana)

1-1/2 Pounds Beef Round Steak (can substitute Veal if desired)

1 Egg beaten	1/3 cup grated Parmesan Cheese
1/3 cup Breadcrumbs	1/3 cup Vegetable Oil
1 Onion – minced	2 cups hot Water
1/2 tsp Salt	1/4 tsp Pepper
1/2 tsp Sugar granulated	1/2 tsp Marjoram
1 (6 oz) can Tomato Paste	1/2 Pound shredded Mozzarella Cheese
Flour for Dipping	Waxed Paper (Optional)

Cut meat into 6 to 8 serving sizes. Beat your egg in a small flat bowl, you can add another egg or water if you run out. Mix together your Parmesan Cheese and Breadcrumbs in another flat container. Dip meat in the flour, then in the egg, and roll on both sides in a mixture of the Parmesan Cheese and Breadcrumbs. Lay aside on a sheet of wax paper or a plate, not stacked one on top of the other. Heat the oil in your skillet and brown the steak on both sides and remove to a shallow baking dish. Then cook the onions in the meat drippings over low heat until they are soft. Add the tomato paste and water, stirring to mix these. Add the salt, pepper, sugar, and marjoram and bring to a boil for 5 minutes. Pour this sauce over your meat in the baking dish, reserving a small amount. Top the casserole with the Mozzarella Cheese and then spoon over the reserved liquid. Bake 1 hour uncovered at 350°F.

Servings 4-6
MENU WEEK#31

BF – (Beef Patty Melt on Rye)

1–1/2 Pounds of lean Ground Beef or Ground Chuck	8 slices Rye Bread
3 medium Yellow Onions – sliced in rings	Margarine
Salt and Pepper to taste	4 slices of Swiss Cheese
Vegetable or Olive Oil	

Salt and Pepper meat to taste, and divide the meat into about 4 portions, (about 6 oz each). Using your hands, form each portion into a ball-shape by gently tossing it from one hand to the other. Press each portion into a (1/4" to 1/2" thick) patty a little larger than the size of the bread as the patty will shrink when cooked. Heat 2 Tbsp of oil in a large skillet over medium-heat. Add in the sliced onions and season with salt and pepper and cook, stirring occasionally, until caramelized (darkened in color), about 7 minutes. Transfer the onion to a bowl and cover with a kitchen towel to remain warm. Return the skillet to the heat, and add in another Tablespoon of oil if needed. Sauté the patties until well browned, turning once, and cook to medium (2 minutes each side) or well done as desired. Arrange the cooked onions on a bread slice, place 1 cheese slice over the onions and top with a patty. Top the patty with another slice of cheese and cover with a bread slice that has been buttered on the outside. Wipe out your skillet or change to a griddle and reheat to medium putting the top buttered bread of your patty melt down to brown, spread margarine on the other slice of bread. Cook the sandwich on both sides until lightly browned and the cheese has melted, about 5 minutes per side. Transfer to a plate or cutting board and slice diagonally and serve.

Serves 4
MENU WEEK#23

BF – (Beef Pepper Steak Sandwiches)

4 Sirloin Beef Steaks or Tenderized Beef Round Steaks cut into strips

4 Green Bell Peppers – sliced	1 Yellow or Red Onion – chopped
Garlic Powder	1/4 cup Water
Steak Sandwich Rolls	Salt and Pepper to taste
Vegetable Oil	

Salt and Pepper the steak. Sprinkle on garlic powder and brown meat and onions in a skillet. Add in the sliced Bell Peppers and 1/4 cup water, cover and simmer 10-15 minutes until the peppers are soft. Serve on toasted Steak Sandwich Buns.

Serves 3-6
MENU WEEK#24

Decided for You Cookbook – 365 Dinners

BF – (Beef Peruvian)

2 Pounds Beef Tenderized Round Steak cut into small pieces
Cayenne Pepper
Vegetable Oil
2 (15 oz ea) cans Peas
Long Grain Rice - Steamed
1/4 cup chopped Onions
1 cup Soy Sauce
1 tsp Worcestershire Sauce   } Marinade
1 tsp Garlic Powder
1 tsp Tabasco Sauce

Marinate the Steak in the above marinade sauce overnight or at least 4 hours. Lightly grease a skillet with oil, sprinkle meat with cayenne pepper and brown the meat. (If not tender, then cover and simmer in the juices for 10-15 minutes). Baste with the excess marinade if necessary during cooking. Cook the rice and Creamed peas per instructions under VEG section.   Place the cooked rice in a circle (like a lifesaver) on a platter leaving a hole in the center where you would place your cooked meat and around the outside with a ring of your creamed peas for color. Warmed marinade can also be used as a sauce for the rice.   Serves 4-6
MENU WEEK#12

BF – (Beef Pot Roast with Carrots and Potatoes)

4 Pounds Beef Pot Roast	2 Tbsp All-Purpose Flour
2 tsp Salt	1/2 tsp Sugar
1/4 tsp Pepper	1 to 2 Tbsp Vegetable Oil
3 medium Onions, quartered	3/4 to 1 cup Beef Broth (or diluted beef bouillon)
2 cups Turnips (Optional) cut in 1" cubes	4 Large Carrots cut into 2" pieces
4 ribs of Celery cut into 2" pieces	

4 medium Potatoes quartered (use New Red or Gold's Potatoes unpeeled if desired)

Mix the flour, sugar, salt and pepper. Roll and coat the pot roast in the mixture (reserve any left-over flour). In a heavy pan or Dutch oven, heat the oil and brown the beef on all sides. Remove the beef and set aside. Add in the onions and brown until clear and tender. Add 3/4 cup of the beef broth and bring it to a boil. Stir in the reserved flour and stir well until blended. Add the beef back in and cover with a tight fitting lid. Simmer 2 hours. Add in additional broth and/or water if needed and re-seasoned if juices lack proper taste. Add in the vegetables and simmer covered for an additional hour. Remove the beef and let stand a few minutes before slicing (the juices will drain if cut too quickly). Remove the vegetables to a warmed bowl, and cover to keep warm.

To thicken pan juices blend in 1 Tbsp of flour with 2 Tbsp of cold water. Bring it to a boil while stirring and cook till smooth and thickened. The juice color can be darkened with a tsp of Bouquet Browning & Seasoning Sauce. Pour over meat and vegetables.   Serves 6-8
MENU WEEK#51

BF – (Beef Potato-Hamburger Meat Pie) - Brazilian - Pastel de Papas

Purchase pre-made Gnocchi's or use the basic potato recipe from MISC (Gnocchi's Potato) **without the sauce** and do not roll into a rope. **You will be using this dough to form a turnover shaped holder** for the below Meat Pie Filling.

GROUND BEEF MEAT PIE FILLING

1-1/2 to 2 Pounds of Ground Beef	1 Large Chopped Onion
1/2 cup chopped Green Bell Peppers	1/2 tsp Paprika
1/2 cup Raisins	2-4 Hard Boiled Eggs cut into pieces
1/2 tsp Cumin	Olives – Stuffed or Black Sliced Pitted
Salt and Pepper to Taste	

Brown the meat, onions, and green bell peppers in a large skillet; drain excessive fats. When the ingredients are tender, add salt, pepper, paprika, raisins, and olives. Blend well and remove from the heat to cool. With floured hands, using the Gnocchi potato dough, form this into 1/4" thick turnover shaped patty in your hand, or on a floured surface. (Pastelitos de Papas). Spoon some of the meat pie in the center of one potato turnover, place a slice of hardboiled egg on top and place another potato turnover on top of this and pinch the edges around the mixture together. (If they become sticky, re-dip in flour before frying) and brown on both sides in hot vegetable oil or melted margarine until golden brown. **–OR–** Place the stuffed turnovers on a greased baking sheet pan. Brush with either melted margarine or vegetable oil. Bake 400°F oven for 20 minutes until outside potato crust is browned **–OR–** Press half of your potato dough mixture into a greased casserole dish being sure to come up the sides. Cut up the eggs and place on top of the crust, pour in the meat pie mixture. Smooth the rest of the dough over the top. Draw lines on the top with a fork, if desired for decorating the top crust. Bake 400°F oven for 20 – 30 minutes until crust is golden brown.   Serves 6-8

MENU WEEK#33

BF – (Beef Prime Rib)

6-Pound Prime Rib Roast (Purchase 1-1/2 Pounds of prime rib per adult)
Meat Thermometer
Rock Salt and Water (Optional step)

Preheat the oven to 475°F. Lightly salt the meat on all sides. Pierce the thickest point of the roast with a meat thermometer Place the roast, rib side down, on a wire rack. Place the wire rack inside a baking pan to catch the drippings. These drippings can be diluted with hot water for Au Jus Dip. The pan should be placed on the center rack. After the first 40 minutes reduce the heat to 325°F. Bake for **RARE:** 16-18 min/ Pound internal temp 140°F, **MEDIUM:** 20-22 min/Pound internal temp 160°F, **WELL DONE:** 25-35 min/Pound 170°F. Let the roast rest at least 10 minutes. **The following is an optional step used at some Restaurants:** Cover the entire roast with a paste of Rock Salt mixed with a small amount of water which will seal in the juices while cooking. Let it set for a half of an hour before cooking so the rock salt creates a hard crust over the roast. Bake at 275°F (20-24 hours). If using this Prime Rib recipe crusted with salt, then remove the meat from the cooking pan and remove the crust by hitting with a meat mallet breaking it into pieces, **if not removed, all this rock salt debri will fall into your Au Jus Sauce.**   Serves 4

MENU WEEK#43

Beef Meat Dipping Sauce

MAKE YOUR OWN - (Ingredients not on grocery list)

3 Tbsp margarine or butter	3 Tbsp All-Purpose Flour
3 cups milk	1-1/2 cups crumbled Blue Cheese
Dash of Cayenne Pepper	Salt to taste

Heat the margarine in a medium saucepan over medium heat until melted. Whisk in the flour and cook for 2-3 minutes. Whisk in the milk and cook until the sauce has thickened. Stir in the blue cheese and cook until the cheese has melted. Season with the cayenne and salt. Whisk again till smooth and pour into individual ramekins and serve along with beef juices (Au Jus).

(BF)-94

BF – (Beef Ravioli Casserole with Green Beans)

1/2 Pound Beef Round Steak cut in strips	2 Tbsp Butter or Margarine
1 tsp instant Beef Bouillon Granules	3/4 & 1/4 cup Water
1 (10 oz) Pkg frozen Cut Green Beans	1 tsp All-Purpose Flour
2 cans (15 oz each) Beef Ravioli in sauce	1 (6 oz) can sliced Mushrooms, drained
1/4 cup Grated Parmesan Cheese	

In a medium skillet, brown the beef strips in melted margarine. Add in the bouillon and 3/4 cup of water. Bring to a boil, reduce the heat to a simmer and cover and cook for 10 minutes. Add in the green beans and simmer an additional 5-10 minutes covered. Combine the flour and 1/4 cup warm water; stir well and cook till bubbly. Remove all from the heat and fold in the ravioli and mushrooms. Place into a large greased casserole dish, sprinkle top with Parmesan cheese. Bake 350°F for an additional 30 minutes.   6 Servings

MENU WEEK#25

BF – (Beef Ravioli's – Stuffed with Meat Loaf)

Commercially prepared Sheets of Ravioli Pasta Sheets – **OR-** Make Your Own Pasta
Use the Beef - Meat Loaf recipe of choice to stuff the Ravioli's
1 (1 Lb) Jar – Roasted Garlic and Parmesan Sauce

Fresh Ravioli Pasta

MAKE YOUR OWN – (Ingredients not on grocery List)

3 cups All-Purpose Flour	2 Large Eggs
3 Tbsp Water	1 tsp Olive Oil
1/2 tsp Salt	Chicken Bouillon/Broth

In a bowl, sift in your flour and make a well in the flour. In a measuring cup mix with a fork the eggs, water, oil and the salt. Slowly with your fingers mix the wet ingredients into the well until all the wet ingredients have been mixed together into a dough. If you are using a pasta machine let the dough rest inside plastic wrap for one hour in the refrigerator. If you are not using a machine, then on a floured work surface, knead the dough for 8 to 10 minutes and **roll out into two flat sheets, place filling into areas, spread hot water around the edge and top with the second sheet. Press the pasta around each filling and cut into squares, making sure the edges are well sealed.** (see PASTA Raviolis).

COOKING RAVIOLIS: Add two chicken bouillon cubes or a large can of Chicken Broth to a large saucepan of water. Bring to a boil; drop in a few raviolis at a time and cook for 3 – 5 minutes, when they float, they are done, drain. Top with a warmed Roasted Garlic & Parmesan Sauce **-OR-** place 2 Tbsp melted margarine or butter in a skillet and just before it turns brown, put in 10 raviolis at a time and toss **-OR-** serve with a Béchamel Sauce

Serves 4-6

MENU WEEK#51

Béchamel Sauce

MAKE YOUR OWN - (Ingredients not on grocery list)

2 cups Milk	Pinch Nutmeg
1 Tbsp Margarine or Butter	1/2 cup Parmesan Cheese
2 Tbsp All-Purpose Flour	

Scald the milk in a heavy saucepan over medium heat (bring it to a boil and remove the heat). Melt the butter in a separate saucepan over low heat. When it's bubbling, add the flour and whisk until it forms a paste, about 3 to 4 minutes. Whisking constantly, add the hot milk in a steady stream. Bring the milk to a gentle simmer and continue to whisk until the sauce thickens to your liking, or about 10 minutes. Whisk in the nutmeg and the cheese. In a serving dish layer the Raviolis and the sauce and serve.

BF – (Beef Roast – Barbecued)

2 – 3 cups of Bar-B-Q Sauce
3-1/2 to 4 Pound Chuck Roast
Non-Seasonized Meat Tenderizer

Apply tenderizer to the meat. Pour bar-b-q sauce over the roast, cover and refrigerate overnight. Place meat about 6" from coals on Bar-B-Q-Grill **or cook on an inside fireplace grate (if you don't have a small bar-b-q grill grate to move on top of your grate in the fireplace, use a wire shelf out of your oven; especially if you have a self-cleaning oven to clean it in afterwards, along with an old pan to hold the briquettes on top of the grate)** and cook one hour over hot coals for rare, turning every 10 minutes. Baste with sauce and be sure to slice across the meat grain when cutting.   This can be cooked in your home oven at 350°F covered, and 325°F if uncovered for 2 hours, otherwise use the Outside Barbecue Grill or Fireplace.

Barbecue Sauce/Marinade
MAKE YOUR OWN - (Ingredients not on grocery list)

1 Tbsp Brown Sugar	1 Tbsp Mustard Seed
1 tsp Oregano	1 tsp Chili Powder
1/2 tsp Salt	1/2 tsp Ground Cloves
1/4 cup Red Wine Vinegar	1 cup Ketchup
1/2 cup Water	2 Tbsp Worcestershire Sauce
1 Bay Leaf	

Combine in a saucepan – brown sugar, mustard seed, oregano, chili powder, salt, cloves, vinegar, ketchup, water Worcestershire sauce, and bay leaf. Simmer uncovered all these ingredients for about (~) 10 minutes, stirring occasionally. Remove from the heat and discard the bay leaf. Cool.

Serves 4-6 with some leftovers
MENU WEEK#14

HINT: Plan-overs should be intentional. If you are having your roast de-boned, ask the butcher for the bones and use these for making a base beef stock for gravies and soups.

BF – (Beef Roast – Chuck)

4-5 Pound Chuck Beef Roast or Rolled Beef Roast	Garlic Powder
1 medium Onion sliced	Prepared Yellow Mustard
4 or 5 Carrots, peeled and cut into 1" coins	Salt and Pepper
5 – 8 medium Potatoes, peeled and quartered	10 oz Water

Salt and pepper the roast. With a dinner knife, coat the outside of the roast with mustard (this will tenderize it). Place the roast in an oversized roasting pan. Add in the potatoes, onion and carrots. Salt, pepper and sprinkle garlic powder on all of these ingredients. Add in the water. Cover with lid or aluminum foil and cook at 275-300°F for 4-6 hours for fall apart roast. (Otherwise cook 350°F 12-18 minutes/Pound if you are planning on slicing the roast). You can also cook this in a Crock Pot, but place vegetables in the bottom, followed by the roast and add 3-5 oz of water.

Serves 6-8
MENU WEEK#26

HINT: If you don't have a microwave for defrosting you can leave your meats out all day, but you must first snugly wrap it in 4 or 5 newspaper sheets. This will insulate it and it will defrost slowly without spoiling (unless your kitchen is very overheated).

Decided for You Cookbook – 365 Dinners

BF – (Beef Roast Hash) – (Leftover Roast)

1 – 2 cups shredded or cubed Leftover Beef Roast or cooked Deli Beef
1 chopped Onion
1/2 tsp Salt and Pepper to taste
2-3 cups Water (reserve after boiling)

1/2 cup Milk
3 Tbsp All-Purpose Flour
1 tsp Bouquet Browning & Seasoning Sauce

Bring 3 cups of water to a boil and add in the beef and chopped onion. Boil until the meat and onion are soft. Remove the beef to a warm area. *Mix together in a sealed container (jar or sealable bowl) 3 Tbsp of the flour with 1/2 cup of milk. Shake the flour and milk until there are no visible lumps. Bring your water back to a boil and stirring constantly put in the flour and milk and as soon as it has thickened; remove it from the heat. If it doesn't get thick enough mix in more of flour and milk combination. Add in the Bouquet Browning & Seasoning Sauce if gravy is not dark enough, stir and add in the warmed beef. Serve over mashed potatoes, rice or Fried Bread.
Serves 6
MENU WEEK#26

*If you don't want to make gravy sauce from scratch, purchase 2 (14.5 oz each) cans of Beef Gravy

BF – (Beef Rollups with Carrots)

1-1/2 Pounds thinly sliced Beef Round Steak or small Cube Steaks
3 slices Bacon cut into 1/2" strips
1/3 cup finely chopped Onion
1/2 cup chopped Celery
3 medium Dill Pickles cut into quarters lengthwise
6 medium Carrots cut into quarters lengthwise

2 Tbsp Dijon Mustard
1 can "Beefy" Mushroom Soup*
2 Tbsp chopped Parsley
Toothpicks

In a skillet cook the bacon until crisp, remove and crumble it. Cut the Round steak into 6" x 4" pieces if not using cube steaks, use these as they come. Spread each steak strip with 1 tsp of mustard. Place two pieces of the pickle and four of the carrots across the narrow end, and sprinkle with chopped onion. Roll up and secure with toothpicks. Brown meat rolls in the bacon drippings, reduce burner to low, cover, and continue to cook for 30 – 45 minutes, stirring occasionally. Place on serving plate and sprinkle on the crumbled bacon.

*If "Beefy" not available, add granulated beef bouillon to Beef Mushroom Soup.
6 Servings
MENU WEEK#31

BF – (Beef Salisbury Steak)

1-1/2 Pounds of Ground Beef
1 Egg, slightly beaten
1/3 cup Water
1 can (10-3/4 oz) Golden Cream of Mushroom Soup

1/2 cup finely dry Breadcrumbs
1/4 cup finely chopped Onion

Mix 1/4 cup of the soup and all the rest of the ingredients, except the water. Mix thoroughly. Shape this into 6 patties and place in a shallow baking dish. Bake at 350°F for 30 minutes, drain off fat. Mix the remaining soup with the water, stir and pour over the meat. Bake an additional 10 minutes.
4 Servings
MENU WEEK#13

BF – (Beef Savory Pie with Potato Topping)

1 Pound Ground Beef
3 Eggs
1 tsp Sugar
1-1/3 cups Water
2 Tbsp Margarine or Butter
1/2 tsp Salt
1 small Green Bell Pepper, chopped (about 1/2 - 3/4 cup)
1-1/3 cups Instant Mashed Potato Puffs (these are not made in flakes, but puffs)

1 medium Onion, chopped (about 1/2 cup)
1 tsp Salt
4 oz Cheddar Cheese cubes (about 1 cup)
1/3 cup Milk
1/2 cup buttered Breadcrumbs (melt 1 Tbsp
       of butter and mix together

Heat the oven to 350°F. Cook and stir the ground beef in a 10" skillet until lightly browned; stir in the onion and green pepper. Cook until the beef is browned; and the onion is clear. Drain the fats. Stir in the eggs, salt, sugar and 1/3 of the cheese. Spoon the mixture into a non-greased 2-quart casserole dish.

Heat the water, milk, butter and salt to a boil and remove from the heat. With either a whisk or a fork stir this hot liquid into the instant potato puffs and whip until the potatoes look like mashed potatoes. Place the mashed potatoes on top of the meat mixture. Sprinkle the remaining cheese and the breadcrumbs over the top of the potatoes. Bake uncovered, until the potatoes tops are golden brown about 25 minutes.

4-6 Servings
MENU WEEK#24

BF – (Beef Short Ribs – Bar-B-Q)

3 Pounds Short Ribs
1/3 cup Vinegar
1 cup Water
1 tsp Prepared Mustard
1/2 Bottle of Bar-B-Q Sauce

1 chopped Onion
2 Tbsp Sugar (granulated)
3 Tbsp Worcestershire Sauce
1/2 cup Chopped Celery
2 tsp Salt

Brown Short Ribs slowly in a heavy skillet, turning frequently. Pour off excess fat as it accumulates. Combine all the rest of the ingredients and pour over the Short Ribs. Cover and cook slowly for 1-1/2 to 2 hrs or until fork tender. Add additional Bar-B-Q sauce over the top before serving.

Can be cooked in your inside oven at 325°F after the browning step **– OR –** can be cooked all day on Low in a Crock pot after the browning step.

Serves 4- 5
MENU WEEK#13

Decided for You Cookbook – 365 Dinners

BF – (Beef Short Ribs – Saucy Onion)

3 Pounds Beef Short Ribs
2-3 cans of Beef Gravy
1 Tbsp Brown Sugar
1 Pkg dry Onion Soup or Make Your Own
1 cup of Water
        Optional Vegetables
4-6 medium Carrots cut in rounds*

All-Purpose Flour
2 Tbsp Vinegar
1 tsp Salt and Pepper

4-6 Yukon Gold Potatoes, quartered*

Trim excess fat from the beef short ribs. Salt and pepper and dust these with flour. Brown the floured beef in a skillet or Dutch oven; drain off fats.   Add in the water, onion soup, and brown sugar. vinegar and the salt and pepper. Heat to boiling and then reduce the heat to a simmer. Cover, stirring occasionally (approximately 1-1/2 hrs) until the meat is very tender, if adding optional vegetables add when meat is almost done, adding additional water if needed to cook the vegetables. Half of an hour before serving, add in the cans of gravy to warm. *If using a Crock Pot, add in everything together and any carrots should be place on the bottom, then the potatoes, then the meat on top, pouring water and spices over the top.   Cook 8-10 hours on low.

4-6 Servings
MENU WEEK#50

Dry Onion Soup Mix

MAKE YOUR OWN – (Ingredients not on grocery list)
3/4 cup Dried Onions
1/4 tsp Celery Seed
4 tsp Onion Powder

1/3 cup Beef Broth Granules (not cubes)
1/4 tsp Sugar

Mix all ingredients and store in an airtight container. Five Tablespoons equals 1 package of Onion Soup mix.

Short Ribs Without Canned Gravy

MAKE YOUR OWN – (Ingredients not on grocery list)
3 Pounds Beef Short Ribs
1 Bay Leaf, crumbled
1 tsp instant Beef Bouillon
1 Pkg dry Onion Soup or Make Your Own
Vegetable Oil
1 Tbsp Brown Sugar

2 cups Water
1 tsp Salt
1/8 tsp Pepper
All-Purpose Flour
2 Tbsp Vinegar

Trim excess fat from the beef short ribs. Salt and pepper and dust these with flour. Brown the floured beef in a skillet or Dutch oven; drain off fats.   Add the water, bouillon, onion soup, vinegar, brown sugar and the bay leaf. Heat to boiling and then reduce the heat to a simmer. Cover, stirring occasionally (approximately 1-1/2 hrs) until the meat is tender. *If using a Crock Pot, only add 1 cup of the water. Cook 8-10 hours on low. Remove the bay leaf.

4-6 Servings

Beef Brown Gravy

MAKE YOUR OWN – (Ingredients not on grocery list)
1 can Beef Broth
3 Tbsp All-Purpose Flour

1/2 cup Cold Water

Shake the water and flour together in a sealed container (jar or bowl) until thoroughly mixed and not lumpy. Add enough of the Beef Broth to the skillet juices to make 1-1/2 cups of liquid. Bring to a boil and stirring constantly mix in the flour mixture. Lower the heat and cook until thickened ~2-3 minutes. Salt to taste. If color of the gravy is not dark enough add in a tsp of Bouquet Browning & Seasoning Sauce. Pour the gravy over the meat and vegetables or serve separately.

BF – (Beef Skillet Patties with Smothered Onions)

1 Pound Ground Beef
1 Tbsp Margarine
Salt and Pepper to taste
1/3 cup ice Water
1/4 cup hot Water

2 large Onions, sliced
1/2 tsp Sugar
1/3 cup Breadcrumbs
1 Tbsp Mustard - Yellow

In a large skillet, sauté onions in margarine until golden, stirring occasionally. Season with sugar, 1/4 tsp salt, and 1/8 tsp pepper. Reduce the heat and simmer until onions are very tender, stirring occasionally. Meanwhile – mix the beef with the breadcrumbs, ice water, and mustard. Salt and pepper to taste. Shape into 4 patties, 1/2" thick. Remove the onions from the skillet and set aside. Heat the skillet until hot, then brown the patties on both sides. Drain off excess fats. Add in the hot water and stir to loosen the pan drippings. Return the onions and patties to the skillet and simmer 2 minutes or until the patties are done to your taste.
4 Servings
MENU WEEK#44

HINT: <u>Copper bottom skillets can be kept sparkling clean by sprinkling the wet bottom with table salt, then rub with a paper towel dipped in Vinegar.</u>

BF – (Beef Sloppy Joe Pie with Green Beans)

1 Pound Ground Beef
1/2 cup Ketchup
1 – 2 Tbsp Molasses (Optional)
1 Tbsp Worcestershire Sauce
1/4 tsp Pepper

1 medium Onion, chopped
2 Tbsp Dijon Mustard or Yellow Mustard
1 Tbsp Garlic Powder
1 tsp Salt
1 can (14-1/2 oz) cut Green Beans drained

3 cups hot Mashed Potatoes (boil and drain) then add the following and mash:
1 Tbsp Margarine
1/4 can Evaporated Milk
Salt and Pepper to taste

In large skillet with ovenproof handles (Cassoulet*), sauté beef and onion until the beef is browned and the onion is clear and tender. Stir in the ketchup, mustard, molasses, Worcestershire, and salt/pepper. Simmer 5 minutes, stirring occasionally. Layer the drained green beans on top of the beef, salt them, and sprinkle the garlic powder on top. Spread a layer of the mashed potatoes, swirling into an attractive pattern. Bake in a 350°F for 15 minutes or heated until heated thoroughly.
Serves 4-6
MENU WEEK#21

*HINT: <u>Most recipes require cooking on top of a stove. If a dish requires to be put under the broiler to brown, it ought to be cooked in a suitable pot or container, without burnable handles, instead of transferring from pot to another pot. Less to clean.</u>

BF – (Beef Sloppy Joes)

1 Pound Ground Beef
1/3 cup chopped Onion
1 (8 oz) can of Tomato Sauce or Ketchup

Salt & Pepper to taste
1-1/2 Tbsp Chili Powder
Hamburger Buns

Brown the beef and onion, and drain off excessive fats. Sprinkle on the beef the chili powder and stir in well, add in the tomato sauce. Cover and simmer 5 minutes. Serve on warmed Hamburger Buns (can use a warmed can of Sloppy Joe or Homo Sapien-wich commercially prepared sauce).
Serves 4-6
MENU WEEK#5

Decided for You Cookbook – 365 Dinners

BF – (Beef S.O.B. or S.O.S.)

(Army's Sh-- on a Shingle, or Sh-- on a Biscuit)

1 Pound Ground Beef	1 chopped Onion
4 Tbsp All-Purpose Flour	1 Quart Milk
Salt and Pepper to taste	Biscuit Mix or Toast

Prepare two biscuits per package directions or two pieces of toast per person. Brown the Ground Beef with onions. Remove the meat with a slotted spoon. Stir the flour into the fats until blended well, add in the milk and stirring constantly, bring this to a rolling boil. Lower to a simmer and cook until the gravy thickens. Add back in the meat and onions then stir. Spoon meat and gravy over the biscuits for SOB and toast for SOS.

Serves 4-6
MENU WEEK#22

BF – (Beef Spanish Steak and Potato Casserole)

2-1/2 Pounds Beef Round Steak, cut into 1" pieces
1-1/2 Pounds New Potatoes (or Yukon Gold potatoes), quartered

1 Large chopped Onion	1 cup Pimiento Stuffed Olives
1 cup bottled Chili Sauce	2 Beef Bouillon Cubes
1/4 tsp Hot Pepper Sauce	1/2 cup of Water
Aluminum Foil	

Preheat oven to 375°F. Place the meat in a casserole dish and top with the potatoes, onion, and olives. In a saucepan over medium heat, place the chili sauce, and bouillon cubes and the water. Bring to a boil, making sure the bouillon has dissolved. Pour this over the meat, potatoes, onion and the olives. Bake 1 hour covered with aluminum foil or until the meat is tender.

Serves 6
MENU WEEK#33

BF – (Beef Spinach and Ricotta Manicotti)

1 Pkg (10 oz) frozen Chopped Spinach, thawed and squeezed dry

1 Pound Ground Beef	1 Egg
1/2 cup grated Parmesan Cheese	1 tsp Garlic Salt
1 can (6 oz) Tomato Paste	1/2 tsp Garlic Powder
1 cup shredded Mozzarella Cheese	1 carton (15 oz) Ricotta Cheese
8 Manicotti Shells, Noodles should be cooked per pkg directions	1 tsp Basil Leaves, crushed

In a skillet cook the ground beef with salt, pepper and garlic powder, drain the fats. Combine the cooked hamburger with the spinach, ricotta cheese, egg, Parmesan cheese and garlic salt. Spoon into cooked shells and place in an 8 x 12 baking dish. Combine the non-drained tomatoes, tomato paste, and basil plus 1 cup water. Pour over the stuffed shells. Sprinkle with the Mozzarella cheese. Bake uncovered in a preheated 350°F oven 30 minutes.

Serves 4-6
MENU WEEK #24

BF – (Beef Steak and Gravy)

1 Large Beef Round Steak, cut in 1" pieces	Garlic Powder
Salt and Pepper	Onion, Sliced
2 Tbsp Margarine or Butter	1/2 cup Water
2 (14.5 oz) cans of Beef Gravy	

Sprinkle garlic powder and pepper on all sides of the steak. Melt the butter in a skillet and brown the onion and meat on all sides ~6–8 minutes. Add in 1/2 cup water, cover and simmer for 30 minutes or until meat is tender. Add in the 2 cans of gravy and warm to a simmer. Remove from the heat. Can be served over Fried Bread, Noodles or Mashed Potatoes.
Serves 4
MENU WEEK#16

HINT: **1/8 tsp Garlic Powder equals 1 fresh Clove of Garlic.**

BF – (Beef Steak and Lobster)

4 Steaks (any cut of steak desired – Sirloin, New York, Rib Eye, etc)	
Salt and Pepper	Garlic Powder

Sprinkle garlic powder and pepper on all sides of the **steak (Do not salt before cooking, this slows down the browning process)**. Place on a broiler pan at (500°F) on the top rack and cook 5-8 minutes on each side or until browned enough to suit you, salt to taste.

4 Lobster Tails	Margarine or Butter
Lemon Juice	Garlic Powder

Rinse the Lobster in cold water and pat dry. With kitchen shears cut both sides of shell on the underside of the tail; remove the shell covering the meat. Loosen around the edges with a knife and pierce through the meatiest part of the tail with a fork and pull the tail out. Lightly salt it and lay it back inside the shell as a reservoir for the seasonings. Mix together 1/2 tsp garlic powder into a 1/2 cube of softened margarine or butter. Spread this over the tail's meat and **broil** at (500°F) 4-6 minutes on each side until its slightly pink. Serve with clarified butter and lemon slices.   **-OR-**   Place about 2 inches of water in the bottom of a large pan and also put inside a metal colander on which you place your washed lobsters (with or without the tails). Bring the water to a boil and cover to **steam** the lobster for approximately 15 minutes or until they turn bright red. **-OR-** the lobsters can be boil in the shell in the water for 15 minutes if you don't have a metal colander.
Serves 4
MENU WEEK#13

Clarified Butter (Drawn Butter)

Cut sticks of margarine or butter in pieces and heat very slowly in a small saucepan. As the butter melts, it separates. The fats rise to the top. Remove this with a spoon just leaving the clear oils of the butter, pour into a small container leaving any impurities in the bottom of the pan. The yellow milky fats can be stored and used for other dishes if desired. Place the heated clarified butter in a small relish dish to be served along with the Lobster meat.

Decided for You Cookbook – 365 Dinners

BF – (Beef Steak – Broiled)

4 Steaks (any cut of steak desired – Sirloin, New York, Rib Eye etc., 1-1/2" thick for broiling)
Salt and Pepper
Garlic Powder

Sprinkle garlic powder and pepper on all sides of the steak **(Do not salt meat before cooking, this slows down the browning process).** Place on a broiler pan on the top rack and cook at (500°F) 5-8 minutes on each side for rare or until browned enough to suit you, salt to taste.   Serves 4
MENU WEEK#6

HINT: To prevent steak curling, cut slits every 1-inch interval around the edges of the steaks or chops before cooking.

BF – (Beef Steak – Chuck and Pan Fried Potatoes)

1 Pound Beef Chuck Steak, partially frozen and sliced thin diagonally
4 medium Potatoes – peeled if desired and sliced thin lengthwise

1 Tbsp Soy Sauce	1 tsp Dry Mustard
1 Large crushed Garlic Clove	4 or 5 Tbsp Oil, used half at a time
All-Purpose Flour	Salt and Pepper to taste

In a bowl, mix the soy sauce, mustard and garlic; add the steak and stir to coat well. Marinate at room temperature while preparing the potatoes. When ready to cook, lightly flour the meat. Heat 3 Tbsp of the oil in a large heavy skillet. Add in the potatoes in to a single layer and fry until fork tender, about 2 minutes on each side. Remove with a slotted spoon, drain on paper toweling and keep warm in a heated plate covered by a towel or tight fitting lid. Add the remaining oil to the skillet; sauté the steak strips a few at a time in hot oil and quickly, about 1 minute. Season the meat with salt and pepper and serve with the potatoes.   Serves 4
MENU WEEK#36

VARIATION: For just plain pan fried steak you can: Salt and pepper the whole steaks. Dust with flour and brown in hot oil on both sides. Cover and simmer for 15 – 20 minutes.

BF – (Beef Steak – Chuck, Marinated)

About 1-1/2 Pounds boneless Chuck Steak 1/2" thick
1 can (4 oz) Mushrooms, drained or 1 Pound fresh button mushrooms

3 Tbsp Vegetable Oil	1/2 tsp Onion Salt
2 medium whole Cloves	1 or 2 cans (16 oz) whole Potatoes drained
3 Tbsp melted Margarine	Paprika
1 crushed Garlic or 1 tsp Garlic Powder	1 Tbsp minced Parsley
Salt and Pepper to taste	

With a fork or skewer, pierce the steak surface every half of an inch. Place it in a shallow baking dish. In a small skillet heat the oil until hot. Add in the halved garlic, and the onion salt. Then pour this hot garlic oil over the steak and allowed to marinate at room temperature at least 1 hour. Arrange the canned potatoes around the steak turning them to coat in the garlic oil evenly. Discard the excess oil and garlic. Sprinkle the salt, pepper, paprika, and garlic powder on the potatoes. Broil these 3-4 inches from the heat source for 7-10 minutes on each side, turning the steak and potatoes once. Meanwhile, sauté the mushrooms in butter and a little garlic powder. Salt and pepper to taste. Stir in the parsley. Slice the steak into 1/2" slices crosswise and top with the mushrooms and serve.

4 Servings
MENU WEEK#46

(BF)-103

BF – (Beef Steak – London Broil)

2-3 Pounds of London Broil or Top Sirloin Round Steak (2-3" thick)
1 tsp Garlic Powder
1 cube Margarine
Salt and Pepper to taste*

Melt the margarine, add in the garlic powder, and spoon this on one side of the steak. Place under the broiler on top rack and broil at (500°F) on both sides for 10 minutes until outside is browned. If you want well done, remove the meat and slice into 1/2" strips. Place these strips back under the broiler for an additional 5 minutes. Place strips on a warmed platter and pour the drippings from the broiled meat back over the top of the strips. *Salt and pepper to taste.
*HINT: Salting the meat before broiling will slow down the browning process.

1-1/2" Thick - **Rare (feels soft to touch),** 14-16 minutes/Lb, **Medium** 18-20 minutes/Lb, **Well Done (feels hard to touch)** 25-30 minutes/Lb
4-6 Servings
MENU WEEK#3

BF – (Beef Steak – Mustard)

6 Beef Sirloin Steaks   4 Tbsp Whole Grain Mustard
2 Tbsp All-Purpose Flour   2 Tbsp chopped Parsley
2 Tbsp Thyme, chopped

Mix together the mustard and the flour, spread it on top of each steak. Line a broiler pan with foil, sprinkle the bottom of the pan with the herbs and put the steaks on top of spices. Broil at (500°F) 8-15 minutes on each side until browned, depends on the thickness of your steaks.

Serves 6
MENU WEEK#14

BF – (Beef Steak – Oriental)

(1/2 to 1 Pound each) Steak of choice Sirloin, New York, Rib Eye, etc
1 (8 oz) Bottle Italian Salad Dressing   1/4 cup Soy Sauce
2 Tbsp Brown Sugar   2 Green Bell Pepper, cut into slices
1 Onion, sliced   1 tsp Sesame Oil
Aluminum Foil

In a shallow baking dish, combine the Italian dressing, soy sauce, sesame oil and brown sugar; add in the steak, pepper and onion. Cover with aluminum foil and marinate in the refrigerator for 4 hours or overnight if convenient, turning occasionally.

Place the drained steak on a broiling pan at (500°F) on the top rack of the oven. Baste as needed with the marinade. Cook approximately 10 minutes on both sides, or until done. In a small covered skillet bring the marinade to a simmer for about 10 minutes until the pepper is tender it has reduced the liquid by half.

If you prefer this steak can pan fried in a covered skillet for approximately 20 minutes. During the last 10 minutes add in the marinade and cook till pepper and onion are tender.
Serves 2
MENU WEEK#52

Decided for You Cookbook – 365 Dinners

BF – (Beef Steak – Rollups and Peas)

4 Cubed (means tenderized) Beef Steaks
2 Tbsp Vegetable Oil or leftover bacon grease
1/2 tsp Salt
1/4 tsp Poultry Seasoning
1 can (16 oz) Peas, drained

2 cups Herb Seasoned Stuffing Mix
1 can (15 oz) Tomato Sauce
1/4 tsp Thyme and Rosemary
8 small White Onions, canned
Toothpicks

Combine the stuffing mix per package directions. Spread each beef steak with a portion of the moist stuffing mix. Jelly-roll the steak and fasten together with a toothpick as needed to secure. Brown the rollup in hot vegetable oil in a skillet. Drain excess fats. Mix the tomato sauce, salt, thyme, rosemary and poultry seasoning. Add this mixture and the onions to the skillet. Heat to a boil, and reduce the heat. Cover the skillet and simmer until the steaks are tender 25-45 minutes. Add in the drained peas, salt to taste, cover and allow these to become heated thoroughly ~8 minutes.   Serves 4
MENU WEEK#27

BF – (Beef Steak – Salami Rolls)

1 – 1-1/2 Pounds of Beef Round Steak
1 Tbsp Oregano
2 Tbsp Olive Oil
All-Purpose Flour
Salt and Pepper to taste
4 hard-boiled Eggs, sliced; or you can use whole ones

2 ribs of chopped Celery
4 Slices of Salami
3/4 cup Burgundy, Sherry or Marsala Wine*
1 cup Water
Toothpicks or Butcher's String

Sprinkle the steak with oregano and salt & pepper, lightly flour on both sides. Place the salami on top of the steak, place the egg slices on top of the salami.   Jelly-roll the steak and tie it every 2" with string. Brown the rolled steak in hot Olive Oil. Add in 1/2 cup of wine and the water. Cover and simmer for about 30 minutes. Turn off the heat; remove the lid and pour the remaining wine over the meat roll. Cover and let set 3 or 4 minutes. Cut into serving size rolls.   *If wine is not used, increase the amount of water to compensate for liquid loss.   4 Servings
MENU WEEK#30

BF – (Beef Steak – San Marco)

2 Pounds Chuck Steak
1 tsp Oregano
4 Tbsp Vegetable Oil
Garlic Powder to taste ~1 to 2 tsp

1 Pkg Dry Onion Soup
Salt and Pepper to taste
2 Tbsp Wine Vinegar
1 can (1 Pound) whole Tomatoes with juice

Heat 2 Tbsp oil and brown the meat on each side. Add in the onion soup mix, tomatoes, oregano, salt, pepper, and balance of the oil, vinegar and garlic powder. Cover with a tight fitting lid, simmer 1-1/2 hours or until tender.   Serves 4
MENU WEEK#7

BF – (Beef Steak Sandwiches)

4-6 Cubed Steaks (tenderized style) or frozen 3 Pkgs of Minute Steaks
4-6 Steak Sandwich Rolls   1/2 tsp Salt and Pepper   2 Tbsp Vegetable Oil
1/2 tsp Garlic Powder   Margarine, softened

Heat 2 Tbsp of the oil into a skillet. Sprinkle the garlic, salt and pepper to both sides of the steak. Pan fry or broil for 10 minutes on each side. (if using the minute steaks, melt the 2 Tbsp margarine and simmer on both sides for 1-2 minutes). Spread the softened margarine on each side of the rolls and brown on a griddle or broil at (500°F) on the top rack of the oven. **VARIATION:** Spread rolls with mayonnaise and browned on a grill and garnished with lettuce, onions, tomatoes, pickles etc., of your choice **–OR- they "are great"** when **toasted buns are** spread with only Mayonnaise and Bar-Q-Sauce.

4-6 Servings
MENU WEEK#1

BF – (Beef Steak Skillet – Saucy with Potatoes and Green Beans)

1 Pound Beef Round Steak, cut into serving size
1 Tbsp Vegetable Oil
1 can (16 oz) Whole Potatoes, drained
  (reserve the liquid)
1 tsp Salt
1/4 tsp Pepper
1 jar (2 oz) sliced Pimiento, drained
1 tsp Instant Beef Bouillon

1/4 cup All-Purpose Flour
1 Large Onion, chopped (about 1 cup)
1/4 cup Ketchup
1 small Green Bell Pepper, chopped finely
1 Pkg (10 oz) frozen Green Beans
1 Tbsp Worcestershire Sauce
1/2 tsp Marjoram

Coat the beef steak pieces with flour; pound the flour into the meat with the edge of a saucer. Brown the beef in hot oil in a skillet; push the beef aside. Cook and stir onion in the oil and cook until tender, drain off excessive fats. Add enough water to the potato liquid to measure 1 cup. Mix the liquids with the ketchup, Worcestershire sauce, pepper, salt, marjoram, bouillon and pour over the beef and onion. Cover and simmer the beef until tender 345 minutes.

Rinse the frozen beans under running water to separate. Add the potatoes, beans and pimiento to the skillet with the other cooked ingredients. Heat to a boil and reduce to a simmer. Cover and cook until the beans and potatoes are fork tender, about 15 minutes.

4 Servings
MENU WEEK#26

BF – (Beef Steaks with Blue Cheese)

4 Beef New York or Top Sirloin Steaks
1 cup Blue Cheese
1/2 to 3/4 cup chopped Walnut Pieces

Garlic Powder
2 Tbsp Softened Margarine/Butter

Mash the Blue Cheese with a fork, add in the margarine or butter and mix together. Add in the walnut pieces and stir together; set aside. Place your steaks on a broiler pan and sprinkle both sides with garlic and **pepper (Do not salt until they are cooked, salt slows down the browning process).** Broil the steaks at (500°F) on the top rack for 8-10 minutes on each side until browned to your liking. Remove the steaks from under the broiler, spread the cheese and nut mixture evenly over them and press it down so the hot meat will absorb it, salt the meat. Return the steaks to the broiler for a further minute or until the topping is melted and bubbling. Serve hot.

Serves 4
MENU WEEK#34

BF – (Beef Steak with Mushrooms)

6 – 8 Beef Cubed Steaks (about 2 Pounds)
1/2 cup dry White or Red Wine or you can use water
2 cans (4 oz each) sliced Mushrooms **–OR–** 2 Pounds Fresh Mushrooms
1 medium Green Bell Pepper, chopped (1/2 cup) - Optional
1 small Onion, chopped (about 1/4 cup)

2 tsp Salt
1/4 tsp Lemon Pepper

Sprinkle the steaks with the salt and Lemon pepper. Brown a few of the steaks at a time in a 10-inch skillet over medium heat, 5 to 10 minutes on each side. Stir in the mushrooms (with the liquid) wine, (optional green pepper) and onion. Heat over low heat until the vegetables are hot, about 5 – 10 minutes. Serves 6-8
MENU WEEK#29

Decided for You Cookbook – 365 Dinners

BF – (Beef Stew – Red)

3 – 4 Pounds Beef Stew Meat   2 Large Onions
1 (8 oz) Tomato Sauce   1 (15 oz) Tomato Sauce
8 medium Potatoes, peeled and quartered or cut in big chunks
1 can Carrots (or 4-6 fresh carrots, peeled, cut in 1-2" thick rounds)
Salt and Pepper to taste

Fill a large stewing pot half full of water and bring to a boil. Add in 1Tbsp salt, the onions, meat, the 8 oz can of tomato sauce and boil for approximately 45 minutes. (If using fresh carrots add these; boil another 10 minutes before adding the potatoes.)   If using the canned carrots just add in the potatoes, the 15 oz Tomato sauce and boil until the potatoes are fork tender. Add in the canned, drained carrots return the stew to a boil until they are warmed. Salt and Pepper to taste.   Serve medium warm. Great with Corn Bread mixed into the stew.   Serves 6-8
MENU WEEK#4

HINT: <u>A leaf of lettuce dropped into the pot absorbs the excessive grease from the top of stew or soup. Remove the lettuce and throw it away.</u>

BF – (Beef Stroganoff)

1 – 2 Pounds Round Steak or Beef Steak of choice, cut into 2" strips
1 Pkg dry Beef Stroganoff Mix cooked per directions
3 Tbsp Margarine/Butter or Vegetable Oil   1 Pint (16 oz) Sour Cream
Water per package directions   1 Pound sliced Mushrooms
1 small chopped Onion (Optional)   Rice, Long Grain or Noodles

Cut the steak into thin strips and sauté with the onion in margarine for 3-4 minutes. Combine the dry stroganoff mix with the water. Stir into the beef. Cover and simmer 10-15 minutes. Stir in the sliced mushrooms, cover and cook until they are tender (~8 minutes).   Remove from the heat and stir in the sour cream. Serve over cooked steamed rice or cooked noodles.   Serves 4-8
MENU WEEK#19

   -OR –

Beef Stroganoff with Sauce
MAKE YOUR OWN - (Ingredients not on grocery list)

1 – 2 Pounds Round Steak or Beef Steak of choice, cut into 2" strips
1/2 cup Beef Broth (can use bouillon with 1/2 cup Water)
All-Purpose Flour   3 Tbsp Butter
1 small Onion, finely chopped   1 Pound sliced Mushrooms
Salt and Pepper to taste   1 Tbsp Dijon Mustard
1 pint (16 oz) Sour Cream   1/4 cup Heavy Cream (Whipping)

Salt and pepper the meat and flour on all sides. Melt the 3 Tbsp butter in an electric skillet and cook the onion till clear. Add in the coated meat and sear on all sides for 2-3 minutes. Add in the beef broth and mustard. Cover and simmer over low for about 35 minutes, stirring occasionally and loosening the browned flour from the bottom of the pan. Add in the mushrooms and cook for another 8-10 minutes. Mix the heavy cream and the sour cream together and stir into the ingredients and cook another 5 minutes or until the sauce is thickened. If you prefer a darker colored sauce you can add in 1 tsp Bouquet Browning & Seasoning Sauce. Serve over cooked rice or an 8 oz Pkg of cooked Egg Noodles.   Serves 4-8

BF – (Beef Stuff-a-Roni)

1 Pkg Stuff-a-Roni Large Hollow Noodles
1 (26 oz) Jar Marinara Sauce (reserve a little to use in the filling)
Aluminum Foil

FILLING:

1/2 Pound Ground Beef	**1 medium, minced Onion**
2 Tbsp Vegetable or Olive Oil	1 cup soft Breadcrumbs
2 Tbsp grated Parmesan Cheese	3 Eggs, slightly beaten
1-1/2 tsp Salt	1/4 tsp Pepper
1/2 cup Water	1 (10 oz) Pkg frozen chopped Spinach, thawed

Cover the bottom of a 9 x 13 baking dish with a cup of the Marinara Sauce. Brown the beef and onion in the hot oil. Mix the remaining ingredients in with the beef and onions and stuff the uncooked Stuff-a-Roni Noodles laying each in a single layer on top of the sauce in the baking dish. Mix the remaining sauce with 1/2 cup water and pour over the top. Cover the dish with aluminum foil and bake at 375°F for 45 minutes to 1 hour (test the noodles to be sure they are very tender). If desired, you can add additional cheese to the top after baking is finished.

Serves 6-8
MENU WEEK#31

BF – (Beef Stuffed Bell Peppers)

1/2 Pound Ground Beef	1/2 Pound Ground Pork Sausage
1 cup chopped Onions	1/2 cup chopped Green Bell Peppers
1/2 cup chopped Celery	Salt and Pepper to taste
1-1/2 cups cooked Long-Grain Rice	1/2 cup (4 oz) Ketchup
1 can Tomato Soup diluted with 2/3 cups water	

4 – 6 Bell Peppers, sliced in half lengthwise, seed removed* (**see Hint** if just cutting the top off the peppers instead of cutting lengthwise in half)

5 Tbsp dry Breadcrumbs
4 Tbsp grated Parmesan Reggiano or Romano Cheese } Topping

Preheat the oven to 350°F. Bring a large pot of water to a boil and drop in the bell pepper halves to parboil for 5 minutes. Remove with kitchen tongs and drain on paper toweling. Lightly salt the inside of the bell pepper halves. In a large skillet, over medium heat, brown the sausage and ground beef together for about 4 minutes. Add in the onions, chopped bell peppers, and the celery. Season with salt and pepper and sauté for 4-5 minutes or until the vegetables are soft. (If there is excessive fats/grease remove some. Remove from the heat, stir in the Ketchup. Add in the rice and mix well. Spoon the mixture into the bell pepper halves. Pour the diluted soup into the bottom of the baking dish*. Place all of the peppers in the dish. Mix together the breadcrumbs, and cheese and spoon on to the tops of each bell pepper half. Bake for 30 minutes or until the tops are crusty and browned.

Serves 4-8
MENU WEEK#15

*HINT: You can use greased muffin tins as support holders when baking, standing upright the stuffed green bell peppers that have the just the tops removed, instead of being cut lengthwise in half and laid down in a regular baking dish.

Decided for You Cookbook – 365 Dinners

BF – (Beef Stuffed Eggplant Parmigiana)

1 Pound Ground Beef
1 Tbsp Vegetable or Olive Oil
1 (15 oz) Spaghetti Sauce
1/4 cup Parmesan Cheese
1 Pkg (8 oz) Mozzarella Cheese cut into strips
1 cup (1/2 Pint) Ricotta or Small-Curd Cottage Cheese
4 oz Angel Hair Pasta (broken into 2-3" pieces)
1 Tbsp Margarine or Butter

2 small Eggplants about 3/4 to 1 Pound each
1/2 cup chopped Onion
Salt and Pepper to taste
Oregano

Cut the eggplant in half and then lengthwise. With a paring knife, or grapefruit knife, carefully remove some of the pulp, leaving a 1/4" thick skin covered shell. Cut the removed eggplant into small cubes. Sprinkle the shells and the cubes with salt. Let it stand for 15 minutes. Preheat the oven to 350°F. Drain the eggplant and drizzle olive oil over both the cubes and the shell. Place the cubes in a small baking dish. Place the dish and the shells on a baking sheet and cook for 15 minutes or until fork tender.

Prepare the pasta per package directions; drain and salt and let stand for 10 minutes. Meanwhile, cook the ground beef with onion and drain off excess fats. Add the spaghetti sauce to the skillet with the ground beef and onion and bring to a simmer for 5 minutes. Add in the eggplant cubes, ricotta cheese and mix thoroughly. Spoon this mixture into the shells. Sprinkle with Parmesan Cheese, add strips of Mozzarella Cheese and sprinkle the tops with Oregano. Bake for 10 to 15 minutes. Top with more cheese if desired.

4-6 Servings
MENU WEEK#37

SPECIAL RECIPES OR NOTES:

BF – (Beef Stuffed Pocket Bread – Pita Bread)

1 Pound London Broil or Flank Steak (Freezing the meat and then partially thawing before slicing
        makes it possible to slice very thinly)

2 Tbsp Olive Oil or Vegetable	1/2 cup Onion Rings
2 Tbsp chopped Parsley	1/2 tsp Salt
1/8 tsp Pepper	1/4 tsp Garlic Powder
Aluminum Foil	Shreds of Lettuce

Mayonnaise Mix (or Salad Dressing of Choice - Ranch, Thousand, Italian etc)

Sprinkle the meat with garlic powder, salt and pepper on all sides. Heat the olive oil in a skillet and cook the onion rings until clear, add in the meat strips and the parsley. Brown on all sides and remove from the skillet and put into a warmed, covered baking dish. Mix together 1 cup mayonnaise (or salad dressing), 1/4 cup milk, and 1/2 cup chopped Tomatoes. **PITA:** Wrap Pita Bread in aluminum foil and warm it in the oven for 5 minutes. Remove it and cut the bread in half; open, spread inside with choice of salad dressing. Fill with sliced, cooked meat, the mayonnaise mix, and top with shreds of lettuce. (If you'd like you can sprinkle in some Hot Red Pepper Sauce, Tabasco, or Falafel's Tahini Sauce).

Pita Bread Mayonnaise Mix

Mix together: 1/4 cup Milk, and 4 Tbsp Mayonnaise

Tabasco or Tahini Sauce (optional)	1/2 cup chopped Tomatoes
Hot Pepper Sauce (optional)	6 Pita Bread (Syrian-Type)*

NOTE: If you <u>can't find Pita Bread*</u> you can <u>use an uncut Steak Sandwich Roll</u>. Slice a cut in the top and hollow out some of the bread and fill.

OPTIONAL FILLING: Fill with Boiled Ham Luncheon Meat slices, shredded Monterey Jack and Swiss Cheese and dill pickles. Wrap in foil and bake at 350°F for 10 minutes. In a saucepan combine 3/4 cup of either Mayonnaise or favorite Salad Dressing with 2 Tbsp Mustard and 1/4 cup Milk. Stir slowly over low heat until warm and spoon into each sandwich.

Pocket Bread*
<u>MAKE YOUR OWN</u> - (Ingredients not on grocery list) - Good Experience to try!

1 Pkg Active Dry Yeast	1 tsp Salt
1 Tbsp Vegetable or Olive Oil	1-1/2 cups Whole Wheat Flour
1/4 tsp Sugar	1-1/2 cups All-Purpose White Flour
1-1/2 cups warm Water (105°F to 115°F)	

In a large bowl, dissolve yeast in warm water. With heavy-duty electric mixer with a dough hook stir in the oil, salt, sugar and whole wheat flour. Beat together until smooth. Mix in enough of the All-Purpose flour to make the dough easy to handle. Knead on a lightly floured surface until smooth and elastic, about 10 minutes. Place the dough in a greased bowl; and then turn the greased side of dough up, cover with plastic wrap or a kitchen towel and let rise in a warm location (**if you are pressed for time you can place the bowl on top of a electric heating pad turned on low**) until doubled, about 1 hour. Punch the dough down and divide into 6-8 parts. Shape each part into a ball on a greased surface and let rise an additional 15 minutes. Sprinkle three non-greased baking sheets with some cornmeal. On a lightly floured surface roll out each section into a flat 6" circle, no bubbles. Place 2 circles on each pan, cover. Bake 8-12 minutes at 450°F, they'll bubble up; cool on a rack for 5 minutes, they'll deflate, tear in half and fill with your choices. **SEE VARIATION TOPPING: BRD Pita Bread**
    Serves 6

MENU WEEK#12

BF – (Beef Stuffed Zucchini Boats)

4 – 6 medium Zucchini's
1 Pkg frozen Chopped Spinach
1/4 cup Ketchup
1 tsp Italian Salad Dressing
2 tsp Onion Salt
Salt and Pepper to taste

1-1/2 Pounds Ground Beef
1 cup Breadcrumbs
1/2 cup grated Romano or Parmesan Cheese
4 Eggs, slightly beaten
1 tsp Garlic Powder

Cut off the ends of the Zucchini. In a large saucepan, bring to a boil a half-filled with water pan. Cook the Zucchini until fork can pierce through them. Drain and run cold water over them to cool and drain again. Slice them in half lengthwise and scoop out most of the pulp so they resemble boats. Put the zucchini's into the refrigerator to chill. Cook your spinach according package directions and squeeze out all liquid. In a skillet cook the ground beef, when partially cooked add in the spinach, stir together and remove from the heat. Place your breadcrumbs, grated cheese and ketchup into a bowl, add in the hamburger and spinach. Add in your eggs, the Italian Salad Dressing, onion salt and garlic powder and mix together (like a meatloaf). Spoon this mixture into your zucchini boats and place them upright in a shallow greased baking dish. Bake at 350°F for 35 minutes. Baste the boats with the excess juices occasionally. Top with additional cheese 5 minutes before the end of the cooking time and return to the oven to finish the time or until the cheese topping is bubbly. Can be served hot or cold. **OPTIONAL: For a child's serving, make a sail** by cutting the crust off of white bread and toast these lightly brown. Stick a wooden skewer through the toast and push the other end down into the Zucchini Boat.   Serves 4-6

MENU WEEK#17

BF – (Beef Swiss Hamburger on Onion Rolls)

1 to 2 Pounds Ground Lean Beef
1/2 Pound Ground Pork Sausage (optional)
1 Pkg dry Onion Soup (this is salty so wait and taste before re-salting)
4 slices of Swiss Cheese
Salt and Pepper to taste
Onion Hamburger Rolls

Follow the procedure for the regular cheeseburger recipe except you use Swiss Cheese. After broiling, grilling, cooking the meat patty be sure that the Swiss cheese (whether placed on top or in between two meat patties) is warm and bubbly, as it will have better flavor. Serve on warmed onion rolls.   Serves 4

MENU WEEK#35

BF – (Beef Swiss Steak – Pepper Steak)

4 – 8 Beef Cube Steaks or tenderized Beef Round Steak
2 tsp Garlic Powder   All-Purpose Flour
Salt and Pepper to Taste   2 or 4 Green Bell Peppers, sliced in strips
2 medium Onions, sliced in half rounds   Mushrooms, fresh and sliced (Optional)
6 Tbsp Melted Margarine or Vegetable Oil   16 oz Water

Salt and pepper both sides of your steaks, sprinkle on a tsp of garlic powder. Dip the steaks in flour on both sides; remove and place on a sheet of waxed paper. **Spoon some extra flour over the steak and take the corner of a saucer and push the excess flour into the tenderized cuts in the meat (this will give you a better gravy at the end)**. Using an electric skillet, if you have one, melt the butter in the skillet and cook the steaks about three minutes on both sides on medium heat, until they are browned. With a pancake turner or spatula, scrape the flour that has stuck to the bottom of the skillet until it's loosened. Spread the onions over the top of the meat. Add half of the water to the skillet and put on the cover and cook on low for about 10 minutes. Remove the cover and turn the onions and meat over. Again, use a pancake turner or spatula, to scrape the flour that has stuck to the bottom of the skillet. Spread on the top of the meat and onions, all of the sliced bell peppers, add in the balance of the water. Salt and pepper all ingredients and cover to cook on low for another 10 – 15 minutes. Remove the cover and add in the mushrooms and stir as much as possible. Taste for flavor and add additional seasoning as needed. Cover and cook on low until the mushrooms are tender another 8-10 minutes.

Serves 4-8
MENU WEEK#4

SPECIAL NOTES:

BF – (Beef Taco's)

1 Pound Ground Beef	1 envelope Taco Seasoning or (1 tsp Cumin, and 1 tsp Chili Powder)	
1 small Onion, chopped	1 cup shredded Iceberg Lettuce	1 cup Water
1 Tbsp Vegetable Oil	Salt and Pepper to taste	Sliced Olives
6 Taco Shells	1 cup shredded Cheddar Cheese	1 small chopped Tomato

Heat the oil in a skillet, adding in the beef and onion, salt and pepper. Sauté till the meat is browned. Drain off any excess fats. Stir in the Taco Seasoning Mix and the water. Simmer uncovered 15 minutes or until the liquid has nearly evaporated. Hang the taco shells over the individual oven rack grates to warm and heat for 3-5 minutes (250°F). Remove the warmed shells and fill them with a spoonful of the meat into each shell, followed by the cheese (being next to the hot meat it will melt) then the lettuce, tomatoes, and more cheese. Add Taco Sauce or Salsa as desired.

Serves 4-6
MENU WEEK#3

OTHER OPTIONAL TACO IDEAS – (Ingredients not on grocery list)

Chipotle Turkey Taco Filling

1 Tbsp Olive Oil	1-1/3 Pounds Ground Turkey Breast
1 small Onion, chopped	2 cloves Garlic, chopped
2 Chipotle Chile's, chopped	1 cup Tomato Sauce or Ketchup w/1/2 cup Water
1 heaping Tsp Chili Powder	Salt to taste

In a skillet heat the oil and brown the meat for 2 or 3 minutes, add in the onions, and the garlic to cook another 3 – 5 minutes with the turkey meat. Stir in the Chile's, chili powder and the tomato sauce. Season with salt, stir in 1/2 cup of water and reduce the heat to medium low, cover and simmer until you are ready to serve.

Pork and Bell Pepper Taco Filling - (Ingredients not on grocery list)

1 Tbsp Olive Oil	1-1/3 Pounds Ground Pork Sausage
1/2 Red Bell Pepper, chopped	Couple pinches of Cayenne Pepper
1/2 small Green Bell Pepper, chopped	1 Tbsp Cumin
1/2 Yellow Bell Pepper, chopped	1/2 tsp Allspice
Salt and Pepper	1/2 cup Water

In a skillet heat the oil and brown the meat for 2 or 3 minutes, add in the peppers and season with cumin, cayenne pepper, allspice, salt and pepper. Reduce the heat and cook for 5 minutes longer. Add in the water and reduce to low to keep until ready to serve. **OTHER TOPPINGS AND SIDES:** Use smoked cheeses, or Monterey Jack, Chopped Scallions instead of onions, Add in diced tomatoes, spoonful of Sour Cream.

Baked Tacos with Enchilada Sauce - MAKE YOUR OWN – (Ingredients not on grocery list)

1 Pound Ground Pork Sausage	4 Tbsp Chili Powder
1 Pound Ground Hamburger	2 tsp Garlic Powder
1 large can Enchilada Sauce	1 cup diced Tomatoes
1/2 cup diced Green Chiles	1/2 cup diced Onion
1/2 cup Green Chile Hot Sauce	1 (16 oz) can Refried Beans
Salt to taste	8 Flour Tortillas
1 Pound shredded Cheddar Cheese	1/2 head chopped Lettuce

In a skillet brown the sausage and ground hamburger with the chopped onion, drain excess fats, add in the refried beans, chili powder, green chile sauce, garlic powder and green chiles. Place half of the Enchilada Sauce in a 9x13 baking dish. Dip each tortilla in the sauce and spread meat filling across the center, top with shredded cheese and lettuce. Roll up the tortilla with the seam side down, fill the dish with rolled Baked Tacos. Pour balance of sauce over the top and top with the balance of the shredded cheese. Bake at 350°F 10-15 minutes or until cheese is melted. Top with diced fresh Tomatoes and additional sliced lettuce.

(Extra Recipe)

BF – (Beef Taco Salad)

2 cups Chili w/Beans, or kidney beans, or cooked pinto beans
1 Pound Ground Beef
1 Onion chopped
1 Tbsp chopped Green Chiles
Salt and Pepper to taste
1 oz Pkg Taco Dry Seasoning
1-2 heads of shredded Lettuce
4 Tomatoes, quartered or sliced in chunks
2 cups broken Taco-Flavored Tortilla Chips
1 (6 oz) can sliced Olives
1/2 cup Salsa (medium to hot)
2 Avocados, pitted, peeled, and cut up
1-1/2 cups grated Cheddar Cheese
Sour Cream

Brown the beef with the chopped onion, chopped chiles, salt and Taco Seasoning. Drain off the fat. Add in the beans to warm and mix well, allow slight cooling. Thoroughly toss the cooled meat mixture and beans with the lettuce, avocado, tomatoes, small pieces of tortilla chips, olives, and cheese. Serve with a Russian Dressing or dressing of choice. Top with Sour Cream and salsa or other items of choice. (Can be made without beans, or chips for less Carbs **–OR-** just cook the hamburger alone with the Taco Seasoning.) **-OR – Use MAKE YOUR OWN – see SAUCE – (Salsa Red or Green)**   Serves 6
MENU WEEK#42

Pico de Gallo
MAKE YOUR OWN – (Ingredients not on grocery List)
Chop 3 tomatoes, 2 small Jalapeno Peppers, seeded and chopped, 1 small onion, chopped, and
3 Tbsp chopped fresh Cilantro Leaves. Salt to taste.

BF – (Beef Tamales)

1 Large (28 oz) can (8 ea) Beef Tamales

Open these and carefully place in a single layer on the paper-wrapped tamales into a 7 x 9" baking dish, include the juice. Cover the top of the dish with a paper towel. Warm in a microwave oven for 8-9 minutes.
–OR-
You can place the canned tamales with their juice into a saucepan and simmer for 5-10 minutes, or until cooked thoroughly. Be sure to watch the tamales and remove from the heat when hot or they will fall apart inside the pan. Remove with a wide spatula.
–OR-
If you purchase "Large, Masa Harina wrapped Mexican tamales" from the frozen food section. Let them thaw. Place a half of a pot of water on the stove and bring to a boil. Insert a metal colander, or vegetable steamer inside the pot to hold the tamales. Cover and steam according to package directions ~10 minutes, add more hot water if needed.   Serves 2 – 4
MENU WEEK#43

BF – (Beef Tamale and Corn Casserole)

2 Pounds Ground Beef
2 (28 oz ea) cans of Beef Tamales
1 can (15 oz) Whole Kernel Corn, drained
1-1/2 Tbsp Chili Powder
1 Large chopped Onion
1 Large (15 oz) can Tomato Sauce
1 can (6 oz) chopped Olives
2 cups (8 oz) grated Cheddar Cheese

Brown the ground beef and onions, drain off excessive fats. Unwrap the tamales and put these in the bottom of a 9 x 13" baking dish. Break these up with a fork so they become a layer. Add the meat and onions to the top of the tamales. Combine the tomato sauce, drained corn, olives and the chili powder. Pour this mixture over the other two layers. Top with the grated cheese and Bake 375°F for 30-45 minutes.   Serves 6-8
MENU WEEK#47

Decided for You Cookbook – 365 Dinners

BF – (Beef Tamale Pie – Skillet)

1 Pound Ground Beef
1 medium Onion, chopped
1 can Whole Kernel Corn, drained
1 (6 oz) can sliced Black Olives (Optional)
1/2 cup Corn Meal

1 Tbsp Garlic Powder
1 (15 oz) can Tomato Sauce
2 Tbsp Chili Powder
Pepper to taste

Brown the ground beef, onion, garlic and salt to taste. Drain excess fats. Spread the chili powder over all of the meat. Add the drained corn and tomato sauce; stir well. Stir in the corn meal. Cover and simmer until all of it is warmed ~5 - 10 minutes, or until bubbly. Remove from heat and stir in the olives then serve when it's cooled down just a little bit, better flavor.   4-6 Servings
MENU WEEK#4

BF – (Beef Tetrazzini with Noodles)

1-1/2 Pounds Ground Beef
1 tsp Salt
1 Pkg (8 oz) Cream Cheese, softened
1 cup Cottage Cheese
1/4 cup chopped Green Bell Peppers
1/4 cup Parmesan Cheese

1 Onion, chopped
1 tsp Italian Seasoning
1 (15 oz) can Tomato Sauce
1/4 cup Sour Cream
1/4 cup chopped Green Onion
8 oz Spaghetti Noodles

Break noodles into small pieces and cook in water and drain. Brown the beef and onion in a large skillet until crumbly. Drain off fat. Add salt, Italian Seasoning and the Tomato Sauce. Beat together the cream cheese, cottage cheese, and sour cream. Add green pepper, green onion and cooked, drained Spaghetti. Spread all of this in the bottom of a buttered 3- quart shallow casserole. Pour the meat sauce over the top. Sprinkle with balance of the cheese. Bake in a 325°F oven for 30 minutes.   8 Servings
MENU WEEK#4

BF – (Beef Tomato Steak)

2 Pounds Beef Round Steak (can be cut into small pieces)
1 can (10-3/4 oz) Tomato Soup, diluted with 1/2 can of Water
1 cup All-Purpose Flour   1 medium Onion, sliced
1/2 tsp Bouquet Garni (Thyme, Bay Leaf, Parsley)   2-4 Tbsp Vegetable Oil

Salt and pepper the meat and dredge it in flour. In a skillet or medium heat place in the vegetable oil and add in the meat. Brown it slowly on all sides. Pour in the tomato soup, diluted with 1/2 can of water and heat slowly scrapping all the browned flour from the bottom of the skillet. Add in the sliced onions and seasonings, cover and cook on low heat for 1 hour on until the meat is very tender. Add additional "hot" water if needed. If desired, you can add in potatoes and carrots.   Serves 4-6
MENU WEEK#11

BF – (Beef Tomato Swiss Steak)

2 Pounds of Beef Round Steak or 6 Cube Steaks
1/2 cup All-Purpose Flour
1/4 tsp Pepper
1 stalk Celery, cut into small pieces
1 can (6 oz) Tomato Paste

1 (20 oz) can Tomatoes, chopped (about 2-1/2 cups)
2 tsp Salt
2 medium Onions, sliced
3-4 Green Bell Peppers, sliced
2 – 4 Tbsp Vegetable Oil

Salt and pepper the meat and dredge in the flour, covering well. Add the vegetable oil to a skillet and brown the onions, till clear and tender. Add in the meat and brown it on all sides. Add in the remaining ingredients, cover and simmer on low heat for about 40 minutes to 1 hour or until the meat is very tender. Be sure to stir it occasionally to keep the flour from burning on the bottom.   Serves 4-6
MENU WEEK#8

BF – (Beef Tostadas)

1 Pound Ground Beef
2 tsp Cumin
1 (16 oz) can Refried Beans
1/2 head of Lettuce, shredded
Vegetable Oil for frying

1 medium Onion, minced
1 tsp Chili Powder
Corn Tortillas
Taco Sauce (med or hot)
6 oz or more of sharp, shredded Cheddar Cheese

In a skillet cook the ground beef, the minced onion, the cumin and chili powder together; drain excessive fats; cover and set aside. Warm the refried beans in a saucepan or in the microwave oven (~5 minutes). Top with grated Cheddar Cheese, and stir cheese in when melted. On a hot griddle place about 2 Tbsp of the Vegetable Oil and fry the corn tortillas on both sides until hot. Place it on a plate, then place a scoop of the refried beans on the top of the tortilla, then a layer of the ground beef mixture, next a layer of shredded lettuce, and then a layer of grated cheese. Sprinkle on Taco Sauce or Salsa, your choice.   Serves 6-8

MENU WEEK#12

BF – (Beef Wellington)

("Time Consuming" Recipe – **GOOD HOLIDAY DISH**)
3 Pound Beef Roast and assorted Mushrooms and Onions
Pastry Shell – from store freezer department (frozen and defrosted) **-OR- Make Your Own**

(1) Cut roast flat (Butterflied), then stuff with chopped mushrooms and onions. Jelly Roll up (Looks great when sliced for serving: Pastry, beef, mushrooms & onion swirl.

(2) Roast your meat in a buttered pan at 475°F for seven minutes, remove, drain juices and cool.

(3) Place stuffed, rolled meat on the center of your newly rolled out pastry, cover the meat with balance of the mushroom mixture. Wrap the meat carefully inside the pastry sheet and seal it by pressing at the seams with your fingers.

(4) Place this wrapped meat in a greased pan, seam side down. Add any cutout dough decals i.e., leaves, flowers etc. Then brush the outside pastry with either oil for even browning, or a beaten egg with 1 Tbsp water for a high gloss. Let it stand in the refrigerator for an hour. Then bake in 375°F oven for 1-1/2 hours or until meat is fork tender and the pastry is browned. (**Great Meal for the Holidays**)

PASTRY SHELL

One Large Pastry Shell made of:
    4 cups sifted Flour
    1/2 tsp Salt
    1/2 Pound Butter softened   **MAKE YOUR OWN** Pastry - (Ingredients not on grocery list)
    3 Egg Yolks, beaten
    3/4 cup cold Water

1. Sift flour and salt onto a pastry board. Make a small hole in the center of the flour, add in the half of the butter, egg yolks, and the water; mix together with a fork or with your hands to make a dough. Chill the dough 1/2 to one hour in frig.

2. Remove dough from the frig and sprinkle flour on a hard surface, roll dough into a large square and put balance of butter in the center of the square.
    i. BUTTER

3. Fold all four corners of the dough over the butter to enclose it completely inside the dough. Then roll the dough out three more times into other rectangles. Each time fold it as follows - Fold the left hand third over the middle and the right third over the middle, thus making a three layer piece. This is called a turn. Roll out again and make 2 more turns and chill dough for 20 minutes.

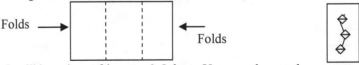

Folds ⟶   ⟵ Folds   Decorate with Designs on Top of enclosed beef

This dough will keep in a refrigerator 3-5 days. You can also purchase a patty shell from the grocery store if you don't want to make it fresh.   Serves 6-8

MENU WEEK#15

Decided for You Cookbook – 365 Dinners

BF – (Beef with Broccoli and Green Bell Peppers Stir-Fry)

1 Pound London Broil Beef Steak cut very thin into 1-1/2" strips*
1 Pkg (10 oz) frozen Broccoli cuts, partially thawed
3 – 4 Tbsp Olives, Vegetable or Peanut Oil
1 Large Onion, sliced thinly
2 chopped or sliced Green Bell Pepper
1 large Clove Garlic, crushed

Stir-Fry Thickening Sauce

1/4 cup Water	3 Tbsp Soy Sauce
1 tsp Cornstarch	1/2 tsp Ginger

In a deep skillet or Wok, heat the oil. Add in one ingredient at a time and stir-fry for 1-3 minutes each & move to the side or remove and hold in a warmed baking bowl. Blend together with a whisk or a fork a mixture of the water, soy sauce, cornstarch and ginger. Add to the skillet the sliced onions, cook till clear and remove. Add in the garlic and cook for only 1 minute, don't burn it. Add in the meat, cook and remove. Add in the bell pepper, cook and remove. Add in the broccoli cuts, cook and remove. Pour off the oil and fats. Pour in your thickening sauce and bring to a boil and cook for 1 minute. Add back in all of the ingredients and stir these in the sauce, then serve over rice.

*HINT: <u>Freeze your beef and slightly thaw, it's easier to slice thinly when partially frozen</u>.

4-6 Servings
MENU WEEK#17

BF – (Beef Wrap–Ups)

1/2 Pound of Ground Beef	1 small Onion, chopped (about 1/4 cup)
2 Tbsp Grated American or Parmesan Cheese	1/4 tsp Salt
1/4 tsp Garlic Salt	

1 Egg White, separated (crack egg and drain yolk by moving yolk from one-half of the egg shell's to the other, dripping the whites into the dish, place yolk in a different dish. Cover yolk with water and save to use later.)

Mix the Ground Beef, onion, cheese, and 1/4 tsp salt, the garlic salt and the egg white; place aside.

Fried Wrap-Up Dough

1 cup All-Purpose Flour (Do not use self-rising flour) ⎫
1/3 cup Water   ⎪
1/2 tsp Salt   ⎬ **DOUGH**
1/4 tsp Paprika   ⎪
1 Egg Yolk   ⎪
Vegetable Oil or Shortening for frying   ⎭

Mix flour, egg yolk, water, 1/2 tsp salt and the paprika until a dough is formed. Knead on a floured surface until dough is elastic, about two minutes. Divide the dough in half. Roll this half into 12-inch squares, about 1/16 inch thick; then cut these into 2 inch squares. Fill each square with scant teaspoon of the beef mixture. Moisten edges of the squares; fold into triangles and pinch edges together. Repeat with remaining dough and meat. Heat 1 inch of the oil in a skillet and fry the wrap-ups until golden, about 45 seconds on each side. Drain – salt to taste. Serve Hot or Cold.

Yields ~72
MENU WEEK#29

Decided for You Cookbook – 365 Dinners

BF – (Beef Zucchini Casserole)

1 Pound Ground Beef
2 Tbsp Olive Oil
1/2 cup diced Celery (1 large rib)
1 cup sliced Mushrooms (4-6)
1/2 tsp Salt
1/4 tsp Pepper

3 medium Zucchini, sliced into 1/4" rounds
1 medium Onion, chopped
1 can (8 oz) Tomato Sauce
1/4 cup Red Wine
1/2 tsp Basil or Oregano
8 oz shredded Mozzarella Cheese

Trim the zucchini, slice in rounds and spread evenly in a baking dish; set aside. In a large skillet heat the oil and brown the beef, onion and the celery. Stir in the tomato sauce, mushrooms, wine and seasonings. Pour over the zucchini. Sprinkle on a layer of cheese and Bake in a 350°F oven for 20 – 25 minutes or until the cheese is lightly browned, the zucchini is fork tender.
Serves 6
MENU WEEK#32

BF – (Beef Zucchini Scramble)

1 Pound Ground Beef
1 tsp Salt
1/4 tsp Garlic granulated or powdered
1/4 cup Ketchup
6 Eggs

1 medium Onion, chopped
1 tsp Worcestershire Sauce
1/8 tsp Red Hot Pepper Sauce
4 medium Zucchini, coarsely shredded
3 Tbsp grated Parmesan Cheese

Slightly beat the eggs with salt and pepper and set aside. Salt the meat and brown it in a skillet, breaking it up as it cooks. Add in the onion, Worcestershire sauce, hot pepper sauce, ketchup, and garlic. Mix it well. Add in the zucchini and cook until tender. Push ingredients to the side. Pour in the eggs and scramble. Mix all ingredients together, sprinkle on the cheese and cover. Let it simmer 5 minutes until the cheese is melted.
Serves 4-6
MENU WEEK#20

BF–PK – (Bow Ties)

1 Pound Ground Beef
1/4 tsp Garlic Powder
1/2 tsp Dry Mustard
1/4 tsp Pepper
1/2 cup finely minced Green Onions

1/2 Pound Ground Pork Sausage
1 tsp Ground Dill
1 tsp Salt
1 Pkg (8 oz) Cream Cheese, softened
Peanut Oil or Vegetable Oil

1 can (8 oz) Water Chestnuts, drained and finely minced
1 Pkg (16 oz) Won Ton Wrappers (sometimes referred to as egg roll skins)
Optional: Bottle of Chili Sauce or Sweet & Sour Sauce

Cook meats until crumbled but not browned. Drain off fats. Mix in the remaining ingredients, except the Won Ton Wrappers. Place a scant tsp of the mixture in the center a Won Ton Wrapper. With your finger dipped into water, run it along the edges of the wrapper (this will allow it to seal edges together). Fold the wrapper in half, pressing the edges together. Then twist the center by moving your hands in opposite directions causing the mixture to move out to both sides and it will resemble a bow tie.

Deep fry in hot oil on both sides. Stuffed Won Tons will float when inside ingredient is done, but cook till golden brown. Drain on paper towels. <u>SERVE WITH OTHER ASIAN DISHES, AND WARM A 12 OZ BOTTLE OF CHILI SAUCE, OR SWEET AND SOUR SAUCE FOR DIPPING</u>
Serves 8-10
MENU WEEK#36

BF – (Braised Beef Rolls)

2 Pounds Beef Round Steak, cut in 3" wide strips or 2 Pounds cube steaks
1 Pkg (8 oz) Pork Link Sausage   Toothpicks
1 Jar (14 oz) Spaghetti Sauce

1. Bring sausages to boil in a small quantity of water. Drain, pat dry with paper towels. (**this renders/removes any bad tastes absorbed from refrigerator storage**). Brown sausages in a large skillet, and remove. Leave drippings in the skillet.
2. Trim all fat from the Round Steak; cut meat into 3" wide x 8" even size pieces. Pound each slice of beef with a mallet or edge of a saucer to 1/4" thickness.
3. Roll each steak around a link sausage; fasten with wooden toothpick.
4. Brown these rolled up steaks a few at a time in the drippings. Drain on paper toweling, and pour off all fat from the skillet.
5. Pour Spaghetti Sauce and 3/4 cup water into skillet; bring to a boil, scraping up browned bits from bottom of the skillet; lower the heat. Return the beef rolls again to the skillet, turn and coat with the sauce. Cover; simmer 30 minutes or until meat is tender. Remove wooden toothpicks from the steak before serving.

Serves 8
MENU WEEK#49

BF–PK – (Cabbage Rolls Stuffed)

Filling:
1 Pound Ground Beef	1 Pound Ground Pork
1 Tbsp Butter or Margarine	1/2 cup chopped Onion
1 Garlic clove, crushed	1 cup Brown Rice/or White
2-3/4 cups Water	1 tsp Salt
1/2 tsp Cinnamon	Dash Cayenne Pepper

2 packets of instant Vegetable Broth or 2 bouillon cubes
In a large skillet cook the hamburger, pork, eggs, onion, garlic until almost done, drain the fats. Add the butter, and stir in the rice; and sauté together. Add the instant vegetable broth, water, salt, cinnamon and cayenne pepper. Bring to a boil; cover and simmer on low heat for 45 minutes until liquid is absorbed into the rice and is cooked thoroughly. Set aside to cool.

Sauce:
3 Tbsp Butter or Margarine	1 cup Chopped Onion
1 Garlic Clove, minced	3 Tbsp Flour
2 cans (16 oz ea) Tomatoes in thick puree sauce	1/2 tsp Salt
1/4 tsp Pepper	2 eggs, slightly beaten

Melt butter or margarine in a large saucepan. Add onion and garlic and sauté until soft. Stir in the flour and cook for one minute. Gradually stir in the tomatoes and their liquid, salt and pepper. Bring to a boil; reduce the heat and simmer 12 to 15 minutes, stirring often.

Head of Cabbage (1)
Remove the center core from the cabbage, cut in half. (Remove smaller leaves and save for Cole Slaw). Place cabbage core side down into a large saucepan in about 1-1/2 inches of boiling water. Cover and steam on medium for 15 minutes until the leaves are soft and pliable. Pour off hot water and rinse in cold water and drain again. Carefully peel off 18 or so of the leaves. Stir another egg and one cup of the sauce into the filling until well mixed. Preheat the oven to 350°F. Spread a cup of the sauce in your baking dish. Remove any hard veins from the leaves and place 1/4 cup of filling in each, roll up and place seam down in a baking dish, stacking if necessary. Bake 20 minutes. Spoon the remaining sauce over the cabbage rolls and bake an additional 20 minutes.

6 Servings
MENU WEEK#5

INFORMATION: 4 cups shredded cabbage = 2 cups cooked

(BF)-119

BF – (Cabbage – Whole Stuffed)

1 Large Head of Cabbage
1 medium Onion, chopped (about 1/2 cup)
1-1/4 tsp Salt
1 can (15 oz) Tomato Sauce
1 can (16 oz) Tomatoes, chopped with the juice
1 cup Herb-Seasoned Stuffing Mix (prepared to package directions)

1-1/2 Pounds Ground Beef
2 Garlic cloves, crushed
1/2 cup Water
1/4 to 1/2 Pound Grated Parmesan Cheese

Preheat your oven to 350°F. Cut the center core out of the cabbage leaving a 2-3" hollow tube. In a skillet cook the ground beef, onion, garlic and salt. Drain excessive fats. Stir in a 1/2 cup of the tomato sauce, the tomatoes, and stuffing mix. Place these ingredients into the hollowed out section of the cabbage. Place the filled cabbage into a large deep baking casserole dish. Mix the tomato sauce with the water and pour around the outside of the cabbage. Cover with foil or a lid and bake until the cabbage is tender about 40 minutes. Remove the cabbage and place on a shallow serving dish and cut into wedges. Sprinkle the grated Parmesan cheese over the top and serve.

Serves 6
MENU WEEK#26

BF – (Chicken Fried Steak)

1-1/2 to 2 Pounds of thick Beef Round Steak (can be tenderized)
1 cup fine cracker meal or cracker crumbs (**can smash 22-23 saltine crackers inside a bag = 1 cup**)
1/4 cup Vegetable Oil   Salt and Pepper
Flour for dipping
Egg Wash = 2 beaten Eggs and 4 Tbsp Milk

Pound steak if not tenderized (Place steaks on to a waxed paper lined work surface and cover with another piece of waxed paper. Pound steaks to 1/4-inch thickness with a meat mallet or rolling pin). Mix the egg and milk and put in a pie plate or shallow, wide saucer. Salt the meat then dip it in the flour on both sides and then dip in egg wash, then in roll on both side into the cracker meal. By flouring meat it will cause the egg wash to coat better. Heat oil in a skillet and brown on both sides for approximately 2-3 minutes per side, or until cooked and remove from the pan, turn burner down
to medium. Season to taste. Cover and cook over very low heat for another 5 minutes on each side.

White and Brown Gravy – (Optional)

Add 2 Tbsp of oil back into the skillet and heat. Add 2 Tbsp of flour to the drippings and stir for 1-2 minutes scraping the meat from the bottom of the skillet. Mix in 1-1/4 cups of beef broth or beef stock (if you don't have this ingredient you can use 1-1/4 cups more of milk. Deleting the beef broth and replacing it with additional milk makes it a "white" gravy). Add salt and pepper. Add in 1/4 cup of half and half milk (or can use Evaporated Milk). When the gravy bubbles, stir together and remove from the heat.   6 Servings
MENU WEEK#7

HINT: Dredging Meats - You can also combine the flour or cracker meal, seasonings, salt and pepper and put the mixture in a sturdy paper or plastic bag. Put the chicken or beef in the bag and shake until coated. If you find that more coating is required. Remove from the bag and dip in a beaten egg and then return to the bag for another dredging.

Decided for You Cookbook – 365 Dinners

BF–PK–VEAL – Creamed Mock Chicken in Pastry Shells)

1/2 pound Veal, cubed	1/2 pound Pork, cubed
1/2 small Onion, chopped	2 Tbsp All-Purpose Flour
1 Tbsp Margarine or Butter	1-1/2 cup Milk
2 Tbsp Green Bell Peppers	1 Pimiento – sliced or chopped
Salt & Pepper to taste	1 (10-3/4 oz) can Cream of Chicken Soup

Pastry Shells (from freezer, defrosted or prepare your own)
1 (10-3/4 oz) Cream of Mushroom Soup – Optional)

Simmer the meat and onion slowly, add in the green peppers and pimiento. In another pan, prepare a white sauce of melted butter, mix in the flour and milk. Bring to a boil and reduce the heat and stir until thickened. Add into the sauce the cooked green bell pepper and pimiento along with the cooked meat and onions. Season with the salt and pepper. Add into the ingredients about 1/4 of the Cream of Chicken soup undiluted. Heat the rest of the soup to use as a gravy. (Variation: add a can of mushroom soup if desired). Prepare pastry shells per package directions. Fill half of the shell with the cooked ingredients and fold over and crimp the edges with a fork tin. Bake 400°F for 15 minutes or until brown on the outside, and serve with the warmed gravy. 4 Servings
MENU WEEK#28

Pastry Shell

MAKE YOUR OWN - (Ingredients not on grocery list)

1-1/2 cups sifted All-Purpose Flour	1/4 tsp Baking Powder
1/2 tsp Salt	1/2 cup Shortening
1/4 cup or less of Ice Water	

Handle pastry dough as little as possible for flakiness. Sift the dry ingredients together. With a fork, or pastry blender, mix in the shortening until dough is made. (For flakier rich crust, add 2 or 3 more tablespoons of melted butter). Roll the dough on a floured board to desired diameter and very thin. Bake at 400°F for 15 – 20 minutes, or per other recipe directions.

BF – (Filet Mignon with Mushrooms and Pinot Noir Sauce)

4 (8 oz) Filet Mignon Steak	Kosher salt and freshly ground Black Pepper
4 – 6 Bacon Strips	4 Tbsp Olive Oil
2 Tbsp Chopped Garlic	4 sprigs Fresh Rosemary
4 cups Pinot Noir Wine	4 Tbsp prepared Demi-Glace
4 Tbsp Margarine/Butter	Butcher's String/Twine

1-3 Pounds assorted mushrooms, such as Shitake, Crimini and Chanterelle, stemmed and halved

Season both sides of the meat generously with the salt and pepper. Wrap a piece of bacon around the sides of each steak and secure with butcher's twine. Heat the Olive Oil over medium high heat and place the steaks in the hot pan and cook until well seared on 1 side, about 3minutes. Turn the steaks over, there should be a nice crust on top. Add in the mushrooms, garlic, and rosemary; give everything a good stir. Transfer the pan to the oven. Roast for 10-12 minutes or until the steaks are cooked to medium-rare. Remove and keep warm. Return the pan to the stove over medium-high heat. Deglaze with the wine, scraping up all the yummy bits in the bottom of the pan. Mix in the 2 Tbsp of Demi-glace (heavy brown veal or beef stock), stirring to combine. Place the steaks and mushrooms back into the pan and coat in the pan sauce. Finish with a couple tablespoons of butter to make it a richer sauce. Cut off your twine, and top with the wine sauce. Serves 4
MENU WEEK#22

DEMI-GLACE: In a saucepan over medium high heat, reduce 1 cup Port Wine to 1 Tbsp liquid. Add in 1 Tbsp of the following reduced Veal Stock: (Combine veal bones, 1 large onion, quartered, 3 small carrots, quartered, 2 celery, 1/2 tsp Thyme, 2 Bay Leaves, 1 Tbsp Salt, 1/2 cup Flour, 2 quarts Water, 4 Tbsp Butter, 1-1/4 cup Tomato Paste, Optional 1 bottle dry White Wine, slow boil and reduce by two-thirds. Season with salt and pepper and strain.)

(BF)-121

BF – (Ginger Beef)

1 to 2 Pounds of Thinly sliced Beef (Round Steak, London Broil, Sirloin, Flank or even Chuck Roast)
HINT: If meat is slightly frozen it's easier to slice thinly.

Ginger Beef Seasoning

1 cup Sugar	1 tsp Salt
1/4 tsp Pepper	1-1/2 tsp Ground Ginger
1/2 tsp Monosodium Glutamate	1 tsp Onion Powder
Dash of Garlic Powder	3 Tbsp Soy Sauce
3 tsp Cornstarch	Beef Broth (optional)

Cooking Ingredients

2 Tbsp Margarine	2 Tbsp Vegetable or Peanut Oil
Sliced Onions (choice of quantity)	Green Bell Peppers, sliced (choice of quantity)

Combine the sugar, seasonings and soy sauce. Coat the beef with this and marinate it in the refrigerator several hours prior to cooking (at least 3 hrs).   In the melted margarine and vegetable oil; quickly brown the beef and onions. Cover and cook the meat over low heat for 10-15 minutes (if using a cheaper cut of meat) until the meat is tender, stirring occasionally. Add in the sliced bell peppers and cook an additional 8-10 minutes until peppers are done but a little crisp. If ingredients are too dry, add in a little beef broth.   Serve with cooked hot rice and other Asian dishes of choice.

4-6 Servings
MENU WEEK#28

BF – (Hot Beef Sandwiches)

1 Pound (thinly sliced) Deli Roast Beef
    (or leftover roast shredded or sliced thinly)
2 (14.5 oz each) cans Beef Gravy Margarine (1 cube softened)
4-8 slices White Bread

Warm the Beef Gravy in a saucepan or in the microwave. Spread the margarine on one side of the slices of bread. Place the Deli Roast Beef in a Microwave to warm for 1-1/2 minutes. Spray a griddle with a Vegetable Oil and heat to medium hot. Brown the bread, on one side only, margarine side down (called Fried Bread). Place two pieces of the Fried Bread, buttered side down. Layer slices of the hot Roast Beef on top of the bread and ladle brown beef gravy over the top.

-OR-

Brown Gravy

Bring 1-1/2 cups of water to a boil in a saucepan. Add in 2 cubes or 2 tsp of beef bouillon. Place 2 Tbsp flour and 1/2 cup milk in a sealed container (bowl or jar) and shake till thoroughly mixed, no lumps. Add this flour mixture slowly to the boiling liquid, stirring constantly. When slightly thickened, add the leftover beef to re-warm in the thickened gravy. Salt and pepper to taste. If the gravy is not dark enough in color, add a tsp of Bouquet Browning & Seasoning Sauce to darken it.   Serve over the fried bread.

Serves 4
MENU WEEK#33

Decided for You Cookbook – 365 Dinners

BF – (Indian Taco's - Pueblo)

1-1/2 Pounds Ground Beef

1/2 Pound grated Cheddar Cheese

2 Tomatoes, chopped

Salsa – Medium to Hot

6 round Indian Fried Bread (recipe follows)

1/2 Head Lettuce, shredded

1 Onion, chopped

Green or Jalapeno Chile, sliced

Brown the ground beef in a skillet, drain excessive fats. Divide the meat on top of the fry bread rounds. Top with cheese, lettuce, tomatoes, salsa, green peppers of choice and onions. **VARIATION: Add 1 can Refried Beans to cooked ground beef.**

Indian Fried Bread

2 cups All-Purpose Flour

2 tsp Baking Powder

2 Tbsp Shortening /Lard, cut into 1/2-inch bits, plus 1 Pound for deep frying

1/2 cup dry milk solids

1/2 tsp Salt

Combine the flour, dry milk solids, baking powder and salt, and sift into a deep bowl. Add in the lard bits and with your fingertips, rub the flour and fat together until the mixture resembles flakes of coarse meal. Pour in the water and toss the ingredients together until the dough can be gathered into a ball. Drape the bowl with a kitchen towel and then let the dough rest at room temperature for about 2 hours. After resting, tear the dough into 6 equal pieces. Then, on a lightly floured surface, roll each dough ball into a circle about 4 inches to 8 inches in diameter, and 1/4" thick. With a small knife, cut one - three (4-5 inch) long parallel slits completely through the dough, down the center of each rolled piece, spacing the slits about 1-inch apart.

In a heavy, 10-inch cast iron skillet, melt the remaining pound of lard over moderate heat until it is very hot, but not smoking. The melted shortening should be about 1-inch deep, add more if necessary. Fry the rolled dough, 1 at a time, for about 2 minutes on each side, turning them once with tongs. The bread will puff slightly and become crisp and brown. Drain on paper towels and serve warm.

Serves 6

MENU WEEK#45

BF – (Joe's Favorite)

1 Pound Ground Beef

1 (1# 11 oz) can of Spinach (drained well)

Soy Sauce

1 chopped Onion

6 Eggs

Salt and Pepper

Fry the ground beef with the onion until meat is browned. Drain off the fats. Stir in slightly beaten eggs, and mix. Add in the spinach; stir well. Add enough salt, pepper and the soy sauce to taste. Cook till eggs are scrambled well. (Can be a great breakfast omelet). Place additional soy sauce at the table in case.

Serves 4

MENU WEEK#10

BF – (Mongolian Beef)

1/2 to 1 Pound Flank Steak or Top Round Lean
2 Tbsp Rice Wine or Dry Sherry
6 Tbsp Corn Oil
~6 Tbsp White Onion, Julienne
1 tsp Sugar
2 Tbsp Soy Sauce

1 tsp Cornstarch
2 Tbsp Green Onion, Large Chop
2 Tbsp Mushrooms, sliced
2 tsp Oyster Sauce
1-1/4 tsp Chili Sauce

Slice beef against grain into 1 x 1-1/2" pieces (easier to slice thinner if it's slightly frozen when you slice). Mix soy sauce, dry sherry and cornstarch in a bowl, add in the beef and marinate for at least 30 minutes. Heat a wok or skillet with oil to hot then swirl to coat sides. Add in the green and white onions, with the mushrooms and sauté about 10 seconds moving the pan back and forth to mix the onions together. Add in the beef and stir-fry about 2 minutes. Add all remaining ingredients and sauté about 10 seconds. Serve with steamed or fried rice.

Serves 4
MENU WEEK#44

BF – (Spaghetti Ring with Beef and Spinach)

1 Pound Ground Beef
8 oz Spaghetti Noodles
1/2 cup chopped Onion
1 (4 oz) jar chopped Pimiento
3 cups sliced fresh Mushrooms

1 (26.5 oz) Spaghetti Sauce
2 – 10 oz Pkgs frozen chopped Spinach
1/2 cup Grated Parmesan Cheese
2 slightly beaten Eggs
1 tsp Olive or Vegetable Oil

HINT: **Place 1 tsp of salt per quart of water into a large pan (causes water to boil quicker) and bring to a boil; add in the tsp of olive or vegetable oil to prevent the spaghetti from sticking together when cooking.** Place in the spaghetti noodles and cook per package directions or until you can cut it and there is no dryness in the center (you will be able to see the difference if not cooked thoroughly) drain and salt. Meanwhile, adding in the chopped onion; cook the frozen spinach according to package directions, drain. In a skillet, brown the ground beef and drain the fats. Combine this with the spaghetti noodles, sauce (reserve a half of a cup to drizzle on top of finished ring), cheese, pimiento, and eggs tossing together well. Turn the ingredients into a 6-inch greased, Bundt pan or angel food cake pan. Cover with aluminum foil and bake in 375°F oven for 25 minutes, remove the foil. Cool in the ring for 5 minutes; unmold by placing a serving platter on top of the pan and turn over carefully holding both the platter and the pan. Remove the pan and drizzle reserved sauce over the top. Add additional grated cheese to the top, if desired. If you want you can place a small bowl in the center of the ring and display your Olives, chopped tomatoes, miniature cooked meatballs, or other condiments of choice – **Be Imaginative!**

Serves 8
MENU WEEK#13

Decided for You Cookbook – 365 Dinners

BF – (Spaghetti with Ground Beef Sauce)

1 (26.5 oz) can Spaghetti Sauce
Garlic Powder
1 cup grated Parmesan Cheese
1/3 pound (~1-/2" circle) of Spaghetti, or
　　Spaghettini Noodles

1-2 Pounds Ground Beef
1 medium chopped Onion
Vegetable Oil

Heat the oil in a skillet and brown the onions until clear and tender. Add in the ground beef , and sprinkle the top with garlic powder. Stir and brown it and cook thoroughly. Drain off excess fats. Add in the spaghetti sauce and heat it to warm. Turn off and add in the cheese. Pour over your cooked, drained salted spaghetti and top with additional cheese if desired. **Cooking the Noodles:** Break up your noodles in half or you can also cook whole if the children like to slurp them into their mouth. Bring water to a boil and place in spaghetti noodles and cook per package directions or until you can cut it and there is no dryness in the center (you will be able to see the difference if not cooked thoroughly) drain and salt. **HINT: Place 1 tsp of salt per quart of water into a large pan of water (causes water to boil quicker), adding in the tsp of olive or vegetable oil will prevent the spaghetti from sticking together when cooking.**

　　　　　　　　-OR –

Spaghetti Sauce with Ground Beef
MAKE YOUR OWN - (Ingredients not on grocery list)

3 Tbsp Vegetable Oil
1/3 cup chopped Onion
1 clove Garlic, minced
1 (8 oz) can Tomato Paste or Puree
1-1/2 tsp Basil
 1 tsp Parsley
1/2 cup grated Parmesan Cheese

1 – 2 Pounds Ground Beef
1/2 cup chopped Celery or Celery Salt (Optional)
1 (14.5 oz) large can Tomatoes, chopped
1 (8 oz) can cold Water
1 tsp Oregano (or use Italian Seasoning instead
　　of Basil and Oregano)

Heat the oil in a skillet and brown the onions until clear and tender. Add in the garlic and brown for 1 – 2 minutes. Add in the ground beef and stir to be sure it's cooked thoroughly. Add all of the other ingredients except the cheese. Cover and simmer for about 1 hour. Turn off and add in the cheese. Pour over your cooked spaghetti and top with additional cheese if desired.

Yields: 1 Quart
MENU WEEK#5

Great extra accompaniment for Spaghetti **is "Fried Cheese, recipe under MISC"**
HINT: 8 oz Dry Spaghetti Noodles = 3-1/2 cups cooked

BF – (Stuffed Beef Cheesie)

6 – 8 Cubed Beef Steaks or 1 Large Beef Round Steak cut into sections
1 Pkg Boiled Ham Luncheon Meat
1 Pkg shredded Monterey Jack Cheese
2 (14.5 oz each) cans Beef Gravy
　　with Mushrooms

1 Pkg shredded Swiss Cheese
1 Pkg shredded Cheddar Cheese
Toothpicks & Waxed Paper

Place the steaks between two pieces of waxed paper or plastic wrap and pound with a meat mallet until thin. Place a small portion of each of the three cheeses in the center topped with slices of the boiled ham luncheon meat. Jelly-roll the steak around the cheese and luncheon meat and fasten the edges together with toothpicks. Either broil at (500°F) on the top rack of the oven on a broiling pan, or you can pan fry on all sides. Serve with the warmed beef gravy and mushrooms over the top.

6 – 8 Servings
MENU WEEK#23

BF–VEAL – (Veal Chops California)

6 Veal Chops or boneless Scaloppini cuts	All-Purpose Flour for dredging
2 Tbsp Margarine/Butter	1 Avocado peeled, pitted, thickly sliced
3/4 cup Heavy Cream (Whipping)	1 Tbsp Lemon Juice
Salt and Pepper to taste	Vegetable or Olive Oil as needed for making the sauce

Use a large **French-type Cassoulet Skillet (no burnable handles so it can go into the oven or broiler, if you don't have, transfer the meat to a baking dish after browning).** Dredge the veal in the flour making sure all of it is covered. Brown the meat for about 7 minutes on each side and remove from the cassoulet. Brown the slices of avocado on both sides, set aside. Gradually stir into the drippings the cream, salt and pepper and simmer stirring constantly the sauce until thickened, (if not enough drippings, then add some vegetable or olive oil and reheat). This sauce is a cream sauce and if you prefer it to be darker brown, you can broil it at (500°F) for a few minutes until you like the color or add in a 1/2 tsp Bouquet Gravy & Seasoning Sauce to the skillet ingredients. Return the chops to the skillet and arrange the avocados on top of the meat and spooning the sauce over the top.

Serves 6
MENU WEEK#16

BF–VEAL – (Veal Cutlets – Breaded)

4 – 6 Veal Cutlets	2 Eggs, slightly beaten mixed with 2 Tbsp Water
Flour	Salt and Pepper
Vegetable Oil	Cracker Meal or crushed Saltine Crackers

Salt the cutlets and flour* on both sides. Dip each in the beaten egg and water mixture then roll them in the cracker meal. Fry quickly on both sides in a small quantity of hot vegetable oil.

*HINT: By flouring meat before it's dipped in egg wash will cause the cracker meal to stick to the meat for a better crust.

4-6 Servings
MENU WEEK#10

BF–VEAL – (Veal in Cream Sauce)

1-1/2 Pounds Veal Scallops (Scaloppini)	2 Tbsp Margarine/Butter
1 Tbsp Oil, Vegetable or Olive	3 Tbsp minced Shallots or Green Onions
1/2 cup Madeira Wine	2/3 cups Beef Stock/Broth
1-1/2 cups Heavy Cream (Whipping)	1/2 Tbsp Cornstarch
1/2 - 1 Pound Margarine/Butter	1 Tbsp Oil, Vegetable or Olive
Salt and Pepper to taste	Parsley
2 cups Fresh, sliced Mushrooms or 2 (6 oz) cans drained, sliced Mushrooms	

Sauté the veal in the margarine/butter and oil. Remove to a dish. Pour off all but 2 Tbsp of drippings. Add in the shallots and cook for one minute and then add in the wine and stock. Boil rapidly until reduced to 1/4 cup. Mix the cornstarch into the milk and add into the skillet. Boil until the cream has thickened. Remove from the heat. In another skillet sauté the mushrooms after salting to taste in the extra margarine/butter for about 5 minutes. Drain and add the mushrooms and veal to the cream sauce. Re-warm for another 4 minutes if not hot enough.

Serves 4
MENU WEEK #17

Decided for You Cookbook – 365 Dinners

BF–VEAL – (Veal Michelle)

8 Veal Cutlets	1/2 Pound shredded Swiss Cheese
1/2 Pound shredded Monterey Jack Cheese	1 can Beef Gravy with Mushrooms
Waxed Paper	Toothpicks
2-3 slices Deli Boiled Ham Luncheon Meat, diced or leftover Ham	

Place the cutlet between 2 pieces of waxed paper or plastic wrap and starting from the center use a meat mallet pounding the meat into a thinner piece. Place the cheeses and the ham in the center of the cutlet. Pull the edges of the meat around these inserts and secure with toothpicks. It the cutlet is not big enough to wrap around then pound a second cutlet and place on top of the other and secure the edges with toothpicks. Broil at (500°F) for 10 minutes on each side. Place in serving plates and pour the warmed gravy over the top.

Serves 4-6
MENU WEEK#18

BF–VEAL – (Veal Parmigana – Betty's)

1 can (26.5 oz) Spaghetti Sauce
6-8 boneless cutlets or Veal Scaloppini Strips or Veal Loin Chops,
1 cup Cracker Crumbs (equals 22-23 saltine crackers)

1 Egg beaten in a flat dish	1/2 tsp Garlic Powder	1/4 cup Parmesan Cheese
1 tsp Salt	1/4 tsp Pepper	Flour
1 cup grated Mozzarella Cheese	Vegetable Oil	

Sprinkle on the meat the garlic powder, salt and pepper. Coat this in flour and then dip in beaten egg and roll in cracker crumbs on both sides. Fry in a small amount of hot oil, 5 minutes on each slide. Place a little of your sauce in a 9 x 13 oblong baking dish. On top of the sauce, place the meat in side-by-side in one layer. Top with 1/4 cup grated Parmesan Cheese, and the grated Mozzarella. Cover with sauce and Bake at 325°F 25-30 minutes or until the Mozzarella Cheese is bubbly and slightly browned.

– OR – MAKE YOUR OWN SAUCE:

2 cans (16 oz ea) Tomato Sauce	1 tsp Oregano
1/2 tsp Garlic Powder	1/2 cup Parmesan Cheese

Place the ingredients in a medium saucepan and bring to a boil, then lower the heat to low, stirring occasionally. Cook on low heat for an hour.

4-6 Servings
MENU WEEK#41

BF–VEAL – (Veal Pot Pie with Carrots, Celery, Peas and Biscuit Topping)

4-6 Boneless Veal Scaloppini Strips in 1/2" diced cuts (about 2 cups cooked)
2 dashes of Hot Pepper Sauce (optional)
2 Chicken Bouillon Cubes or Granulated
Biscuits made from a biscuit mix or canned biscuits

1 cup Carrots (3 medium) diced	1 (10 oz) box frozen Peas
1 cup sliced Celery	1/3 cup Margarine
3 Tbsp All-Purpose Flour	3 cups Milk
1/4 tsp Pepper	Salt to Taste
2 tsp Steak Sauce	

Cook the carrots in a small amount of boiling, salted water until fork tender, adding the peas in during the last 2 to 3 minutes of cooking. Drain if necessary. Salt and pepper your meat and flour it on all sides. In a skillet, sauté in the margarine the onion and celery for 2 to 3 minutes, in the meat and the steak sauce. Cook until browned on all sides. Scrape any flour residue off the bottom of the pan. Mix the bouillon into the milk.

(BF)-127

(Continued - BF - VEAL – Veal Pot Pie with Carrots, Celery, Peas and Biscuit Topping) Then gradually add in the milk and bring to a simmer, stirring constantly until the thickened sauce is made. Salt to taste. Stir in the carrots, peas and pour this into a shallow 2-quart baking dish. Top with the biscuits and place it in the oven at 425°F and bake until the biscuits are browned about 15 minutes. Biscuits can be brushed with a slightly beaten egg mixed with 1 Tbsp of Water for a glossier look.

Biscuits (Heavier Kind) - MAKE YOUR OWN - (Ingredients not on the grocery list)

2 cups sifted All-Purpose Flour	2-1/2 tsp Baking Powder
3/4 tsp Salt	1/3 cup Margarine or Shortening
1/2 cup Milk	1 Egg, slightly beaten (Optional: makes it heavier)

Mix the flour, baking powder, and salt together. Using a pastry blender; cut in the margarine until it forms a granulated effect. Add in the beaten egg into the milk and set aside enough to use to brush over the top of the completed biscuits. Knead this into a soft dough. On a floured work surface pat the dough into a 1/2" thickness and cut out your biscuits with a cutter, or glass with the rim dipped in the flour so it won't stick. Place the biscuits on top of your casserole or put them on top of a greased baking sheet, brush the tops with the egg wash, and bake in a 350°F oven for 12 – 25 minutes or until the tops are golden brown. Serves 4-6

MENU WEEK#37

BF–VEAL – (Veal – Rolled and Stuffed)

2 Pounds Veal Cutlets boneless	1-1/2 tsp Salt
1/2 tsp Pepper	1/2 cup Margarine or Butter
8 slices Monterey Jack Cheese	1 cup Parsley, chopped
2 medium Onions, chopped	Vegetable Oil
1 – 2 cups Water	2/3 cup Whipping Cream
1 Tbsp All-Purpose Flour	2 tsp Sugar (Optional)
2 medium Carrots, chopped or cut up small	1 (10-3/4 oz) can Condensed Cream of Beef Soup

Sprinkle the veal with salt and pepper. Spread softened margarine over the cutlet. Sprinkle with parsley, place onion, carrots, slice of Jack Cheese and Jelly-roll steaks up and tie with string. Heat the oil in a skillet and brown the veal rolls on all sides. Add enough water to the juices to make 2 cups of liquid. Cover with a tight fitting lid and simmer for 1 hour or until the meat is tender. Remove the meat. Place the flour and the whipping cream in a re-sealable container (jar or bowl) and shake to mix until it's smooth and without any lumps. Gradually add into the skillet the beef soup and the flour mixture; stirring constantly and warm until the gravy thickens. Taste the sauce to see if you want to sweeten it. Return the steaks to the sauce to reheat. Remove from the heat and serve. Serves 4-8

MENU WEEK#5

BF–VEAL – (Veal Saltimbocca)

1-1/2 pounds thinly sliced Veal Medallions, or Veal Scaloppini

Salt and Pepper	1/4 pound thinly sliced Prosciutto Ham
Several sprigs of fresh Sage	1/4 cup Olive Oil
4 Tbsp Butter/Margarine	1 cup White Wine
1/2 Lemon juiced	

Season the veal with salt and pepper and layer on top, 1/2 of the medallions, with 1 thin slice of the Prosciutto Ham. The edges of the ham can extend out a bit. Place 1 whole sage leaf on top of the ham, then place another veal medallion on top of the sage (You can pin together with toothpicks to hold in place while cooking). Heat a large, heavy skillet over medium high heat. Add in 2 tbsp of olive oil and 2 tablespoon of the butter and sauté the veal on both sides for 2-3 minutes. Transfer to a warm platter until all has been cooked. Transfer the cooked meat back into the pan and reduce the heat to medium low and add in the wine scraping up the pan drippings. Add in the lemon juice and the remaining 2 tablespoons of butter to the pan and when warmed serve juices over the meat. (Can be thickened with a little flour if desired). 4 Servings

MENU WEEK#39

BF–VEAL – (Veal Scaloppini)

1-1/2 Pounds of Veal Round Steak or Scaloppini cuts
1 tsp Salt
1/2 cup Vegetable Oil
1 Garlic Clove, minced
1/4 tsp Nutmeg
All-Purpose Flour
1 medium Green Bell Pepper, cut into strips
1 (6 oz) can Mushrooms, sliced
1/3 cup grated Parmesan Cheese

1 tsp Paprika
1/4 cup Lime or Lemon Juice
1 tsp Yellow Mustard
1/2 tsp Sugar
1 medium Onion
1/3 cup Chicken Broth or bouillon
1 small jar (9.5 oz) Stuffed Green Olives

Cut the veal round into serving pieces. Combine the salt and paprika, oil, lime juice, garlic, mustard, nutmeg, and the sugar. Arrange the meat in a shallow baking dish and pour sauce over the meat, turning the pieces in the sauce so to coat it on all sides. Let stand 15 minutes, remove the veal from the sauce and roll in flour on both sides. Heat the vegetable oil and place in the onions and peppers and cook until the onions are clear and tender. Push these to the side of the skillet and brown the floured meat on both sides. Pour in the chicken broth and scrape up the cooked flour from the bottom of the pan. Cover and simmer on low for about 15 minutes. Add in the stuffed olives, the mushrooms and sprinkle the top with the Parmesan Cheese. Return it to cooking for an additional 5 minutes.   Serves 4-6
MENU WEEK#11

BF–VEAL – (Veal Tagliarini with Noodles and Corn)

2 Pounds Veal Chuck or Lean Ground Beef
2 cans (6 oz ea) Mushrooms sliced or can use fresh
1 Garlic clove, minced
1 (16 oz) can Tomatoes
1 (15 oz) can Whole Kernel Corn, drained
1 Pound Cheddar Cheese, shredded

1 (12 oz) Pkg Egg Noodles
1 medium Onion, sliced
1 Green Bell Pepper, sliced
2 tsp Vegetable Oil
1 (8 oz) can Olives of choice, drained

Cook the egg noodles in boiling water per package directions; drain – Salt and Pepper these. In a skillet in the vegetable oil, brown the onions and minced garlic. Salt and pepper the meat and brown; drain any excess fats. Add in the corn, tomatoes and simmer for 10 minutes. Stir in the olives and the cooked noodles. Pour all of this into a greased baking dish and top with the cheese. Bake in a 350°F oven for 45 to 60 minutes, or until the cheese is browned and bubbly.   Serves 6-8
MENU WEEK#7

HINT: You can substitute chicken or turkey breast for veal.

REMEMBER TO RESTOCK YOUR STAPLES (Salt, Pepper, Flour, Sugar etc.,) ON YOUR GROCERY/MARKETING LIST AS THEY GET LOW.

Decided for You Cookbook – 365 Dinners

EXTRA SPACE FOR NOTES:

Decided for You Cookbook – 365 Dinners

CHICKEN

HINT: <u>**Under-cooking Poultry will leave it tough and over-cooking it will leave it dried-out.**</u>

CH – (Almond Chicken)

1 envelope Dry Chicken Gravy   1 cup Evaporated Milk or Light Cream
2 cans (5 oz ea) boned Chicken   1/4 cup toasted slivered Almonds
Chopped Parsley

Cook gravy as directed on the package. When gravy begins to thicken, stir in the Chicken and Almonds and warm thoroughly.   Pour above over cooked rice and sprinkle some Almonds and Parsley on top (covers 2 cups of Rice)
Serves 3-4

MENU WEEK #38

CH – (Baked Breaded Chicken)

1 cut-up Chicken (Broiler or Fryer)   Poultry Seasoning
1-2 cans (10-3/4 oz) Cream of Chicken Soup   1/4 cup Milk
Salt and Pepper to taste
1/2 Pkg Herb Seasoned Granulated Stuffing Mix not the cubed

Dilute the Cream of Chicken soup with the milk and stir until blended. Salt and pepper the chicken. Sprinkle it with poultry seasoning. Dip each piece of chicken in the soup and roll it in the dressing mixture.* Place on a greased baking sheet or pan. Bake uncovered at 350°F for 30-45 minutes turning Chicken once on each side. **HINT:** <u>**Leftover soup can be warmed and served as gravy. If you wish your gravy to become darker in color, mix in a little bottled Bouquet Browning & Seasoning Sauce. *If using cubed dressing, place it in a paper sack and smash into crumbs with a rolling pin or the bottom of a pot.**</u>   4-6 Servings
MENU WEEK#27

CH – (Bar-B-Q Chicken)

One Chicken either whole or cut up Fryer
1 (18 oz) Bar-B-Q Sauce

<u>**Pick Your Style:**</u>

Chicken can be placed in a Crock-pot on low for 5-6 hours, and then juices drained. Add Bar-B-Q sauce and cook another half of an hour   **– OR –** **HINT**: <u>**I like to precook my chicken in the microwave before broiling as it makes the chicken, more juicy. Place chicken, which has been salted, in a baking bag or on a microwave-proof plate covered with a paper towel and cook in the microwave at high temperature for 8 minutes.**</u>   Remove the chicken from the microwave and place it on a broiler pan. Salt and pepper it, then spoon on top of the chicken, Bar-BQ Sauce and return to the broiler for an additional 5-8 minutes until bubbling and browned.
– OR – Marinate chicken in Bar-B-Q sauce and cook over Bar-B-Q coals until tender, basting as needed.
 – OR – Place oil or shortening in a skillet. Salt and pepper, then sprinkle tops of the chicken with powdered garlic. Place chicken pieces in the skillet with lid on and cook 20-25 minutes, turning once. Drain off the juices*.   Spoon on Bar-B-Q sauce and return the cover and continue to cook for 10-15 minutes.   Chicken is done when you can pierce it and the juices run out clear.
Serves 4-6

MENU WEEK#23

*HINT: <u>**HOMEMADE BOUILLON: Drained pure chicken or beef juices which can be placed in an ice cube tray. When frozen then removed from the tray and stored in the freezer in a freezer bag up to 6 months. These frozen juices can be added to soups or gravies for additional flavors.**</u>

(CH)-131

CH – (Broiled Chicken)

1 Chicken (Cut into individual pieces or in Quarters)
Salt and Pepper to taste
Garlic Powder (Optional)
Melted Margarine

*Place chicken on a broiler pan and brush with the melted margarine. Salt and pepper (optional sprinkling of garlic powder) to taste. Broil at 500°F 4-6 inches under broiling element 10-15 minutes on each side. Pierce the chicken and if the juice comes out clear, it is done. If juice is pink, cook longer.

4-6 Servings
MENU WEEK#41

* HINT: I like to **precook my chicken** in the microwave **before broiling** as it makes the chicken, much juicier. **Place chicken in a baking bag or on a paper plate covered with a paper towel and cook at high temperature for 8 minutes. Remove and proceed from * above to complete the chicken. ALSO: If you rub the outside skin with soft butter or mayonnaise it will improve the browning.**

CH – (Cashew Chicken)

Dice 2 cups of Boneless Chicken Breasts (Mix together 1 Tbsp Cornstarch and 2 Tbsp Soy Sauce with salt to taste and spoon over the chunks of chicken to marinate for at least 30 minutes).
Dice 1 cup of Smoked Ham
Cut up the following:
1/2 cup Yellow/White Onion, 1/2 cup Bamboo Shoots, 1 to 2 cups tender Celery, 1 small can of button Mushrooms, 1/2 - 1 cup of Bell Peppers, 3/4 cup Cashew Nuts (chop or halve)

In a large skillet (or wok), high heat, sauté the onions with 2 Tbsp oil for one minute. Add the bamboo shoots, celery, and mushrooms and sauté for another minute stirring constantly. Add 2 Tbsp water and cover. Steam these ingredients for two minutes. Remove all the vegetables from the skillet. Add one Tbsp of oil to the skillet and sauté the chicken for 3 minutes. Add in the ham and sauté for another minute then add in the bell peppers; stir. Add back in the rest of the precooked vegetables and mix together. Mix another 1/4 cup of water and 2 Tbsps of cornstarch together and add to the vegetable and chicken mixture. Stir completely until dissolved. This sauce will thicken a little. Finally add the chopped cashews and serve over rice.

Serves 4-6
MENU WEEK#22

CH – (Cheddar Chicken with Broccoli)

2 whole large Boneless, skinned chicken breasts (cut in half)
1 (10 oz Pkg) frozen chopped Broccoli, thawed
2 Tbsp Butter or Margarine   1/2 pound mild Cheddar Cheese, shredded
1/2 cup Beer   2 Tbsp sliced Almonds
Waxed Paper

Pat broccoli dry with paper towels, arrange it into an 8" x 12" baking dish; set aside. On a cutting board or hard surface between two sheets of wax paper, with a meat mallet, pound/flatten each piece of chicken until it's only 1/4" thick. In a 12" skillet over medium high heat, in hot butter or margarine, cook the chicken until its tender and browned on both sides, about 10 minutes. Arrange the chicken on top of the broccoli. In a one-quart saucepan over low heat, melt the cheese and beer together until the cheese is melted thoroughly and the mixture is smooth stirring constantly. Pour this cheesy mixture over the chicken and broccoli. Sprinkle the almonds on top and bake at 350°F 10 – 15 minutes until its heated thoroughly.

Serves 4
MENU WEEK#43

Decided for You Cookbook – 365 Dinners

CH – (Chicken Ala King)

1/2 cup Mushrooms	1/4 cup chopped Green Bell Pepper
1/4 cup Butter or Margarine	3 Tbsp Flour
2 cups Milk	1 beaten Egg Yolk
2-1/2 cups diced cooked Chicken*	Salt and Pepper to taste

Brown the mushrooms and green bell pepper in the butter. Add in flour and stir, add the milk and stir in the egg yolk, bring this to a low bubble and thickened. Add the chicken and warm thoroughly. Serve over rice or fluffy mashed potatoes.   Serves 4

MENU WEEK#10

*Can be canned chicken, leftover Chicken, or you can cook Chicken Breasts in your microwave for about six or seven minutes depending on cut up to small sizes.

CH – (Chicken and Broccoli Casserole)

2 boneless Chicken Breasts cut in small pieces *[1] (White meat can be purchased from Fried Chicken
    Seller or leftover chicken is great)
2 packages (2lbs) frozen or fresh Broccoli chopped or cuts
1/2 package Herb Seasoned Stuffing Mix (a granulated not cubed)

Cook frozen or fresh broccoli until thawed and barely soft, then drain. Cook chicken breasts in the Microwave for 10-14 minutes, if not precooked. Then cut into small pieces. Mix stuffing with proportionate amount of water as directed on package. In a buttered 9 x 13 casserole dish alternate layers of (or mix together) broccoli, chopped chicken and stuffing.

Chicken Cheese Sauce

4 Tbsp melted Margarine	4 Tbsp Flour
1/2 tsp Salt	1 cup Half & Half Milk
1 can Chicken Broth	

1 cup grated (medium or sharp) Cheddar Cheese (Save a little for topping of casserole)

Create the cheese sauce with above ingredients in a saucepan. Melt margarine, stir in flour until blended, add the chicken broth and salt; when warmed, add in grated cheddar cheese stir until melted. Sprinkle any left over grated cheese on top of casserole and then pour white cheese sauce on top of casserole (pierce casserole with fork to make sauce settle to bottom) and it's ready to bake 30 minutes at 350°F uncovered. After baking let stand 10 minutes before serving - taste is better when medium hot. *[1] **Chicken can be optional, Broccoli casserole recipe is good without it. Either of these are a "great" warm-over dish!**
                                                            Serves 4 – 10

MENU WEEK#6

Decided for You Cookbook – 365 Dinners

CH – (Chicken and Dumplings)

1 Cut-up Chicken
Can of Chicken Broth (Optional)
If you are a working mother, cook your chicken all day on low in a Crockpot and drain juices into a larger pot and add additional water as needed. Otherwise, **if not** using a crockpot, you can put the chicken in a large pot and fill with water to 2 inches above the resting meat, add salt and boil this for 20-25 minutes. Remove the chicken to a plate. If the chicken pot is not left half full of water, add a can of chicken broth and some additional water so there will be enough juice to cook all of the dumplings.

Dumpling Dough for Homemade Noodles

2 Eggs slightly beaten	2 cups Flour, sifted (equals 1/2 pound)
2 cups Chicken Broth	2 tsp Salt
Canned Evaporated Milk (Optional)	

Stir these ingredients together with a fork, and it will become a sticky dough. Turn out onto a floured breadboard. Sprinkle dough with flour and flatten out with your hand; dipping your hand in flour again and again to prevent it from sticking to the dough. Pat it down to approximately (~) 1/2" thickness. Cut the dough into 3" x 5" strips with either a large knife or spatula/pancake turner. **Bring your chicken stock to a rolling boil.** Using your spatula (or knife) scoop up your small dumpling trying to keep it flat and drop into the boiling stock. **Drop all the dumplings in one at a time** until you have dumped them all. **HINT: They will float when done, or you can also cut a dumpling in half and if you can still see dry flour in the middle (indicates not done),** then continue to cook until the dry flour disappears. When the dumplings are done, turn off the burner and put your chicken back in with the dumplings to get re-warmed (or you can microwave the chicken for two or three minutes to re-warm). If you would like your dumpling juice to have more of a white color you can add a little bit of evaporated milk to the juices.

Serves 4-6
MENU WEEK #8

NOTE: Another **smaller dumpling** is **called Spaetzle**, which is a fluffier dumpling [2 eggs, slightly beaten, 1-1/2 cups sifted flour, 1/2 cup Milk, 1 tsp Salt, 1/4 tsp Baking Powder – Serves 4]. After mixing all ingredients. Bring the chicken water to a rolling boil. Place about 1/4 of the dough in a colander at a time,(or you can use a metal grater with large holes) and hold it over the boiling water pressing it through the holes with a spatula causing it to drop into the water to cook into small round dumplings. When it floats to the surface it is done. Cover the pan and let sit a few minutes before serving. **Spaetzle Ingredients not on the grocery List.**

CH – (Chicken and Easy Carrot and Biscuit Pie)

1 Jar (14 oz) De-boned Chicken (or you can precook some and shred)

3/4 cup canned Chicken Broth	1 Tbsp chopped Parsley
1/8 tsp Thyme	Dash of Pepper

1 can whole Carrots drained (or cook 1 pound fresh carrots until fork tender)
1 Pkg (9 oz) frozen small Onions with creamed sauce

Biscuit Topping

2 Tbsp Margarine	1 Tbsp chopped Chives
2 tsp chopped Parsley	1 can (8.6 oz) Refrigerator Biscuits

Preheat the oven to 375°F. Pour broth from the chicken into a small saucepan. Add the frozen onions, and cook as per package directions. Remove from the heat. Stir in 1 Tbsp parsley, thyme, and pepper. Turn this into a shallow 1-1/2 quart baking dish. Add the chicken and carrots and mix gently. Butter a baking pan for the biscuits. Remove from their package and place in the pan, sprinkling the chopped chives over the top. Bake both items at the same time in the oven for 15 minutes. Remove the biscuits and arrange them around the top of the chicken casserole and serve. 4 Servings
MENU WEEK#50

CH – (Chicken and Ham Lasagna with Asparagus)

2 cups cubed cooked Chicken (can be leftovers or boneless Chicken Breasts cooked in the microwave)
1 (6 oz) Pkg thinly sliced or shredded Cooked Ham (can be leftovers)
1 (6 oz) Pkg sliced or shredded Mozzarella Cheese
1 cup grated Parmesan or Romano Cheese (use 1/2 cup at a time)
1 (10 oz) Pkg Frozen Cut Asparagus – thawed and drained
1 (8 oz) Lasagna Noodles

1/4 cup Margarine or Butter	1/3 cup Flour
1 Tbsp minced dried Onion Flakes	1/8 tsp Garlic Powder
2 cups Chicken Broth	1 cup Milk
1 (3 oz) can chopped Mushrooms, drained	Salt and Pepper to taste

Cook the noodles per package directions; drain. In a saucepan melt the butter or margarine; blend in the flour, onion, garlic powder and pepper. When blended, add the milk; cook and stir till bubbly. Stir into this sauce the first 1/2 cup grated cheese and the mushrooms. In a 9 x 13 baking dish layer half of the cooked noodles, all of the asparagus, chicken, and mozzarella, and 1/3 of the sauce mixture. Top with the ham, any remaining noodles, the remaining sauce and then sprinkle on top final 1/2 cup grated cheese. Bake in a 350°F oven for 35 minutes or until thoroughly heated. Let this stand for 10 minutes before cutting.

Makes 6-8 Servings
MENU WEEK#44

CH – (Chicken and Links with Green Beans)

Chicken (cut-up)	Vegetable Oil
1 pound Pork Link Sausages	1 pound can of Tomatoes
Worcestershire Sauce	Green Beans
Flour	Salt to taste

Mix 1/2 cup flour with 1 tsp salt. In a large skillet, brown the chicken in a 1/4 cup of hot vegetable oil; remove when cooked. Cut the link sausage into small pieces and brown in the oil and drain. Return the chicken to the skillet with the sausages and add in the tomatoes and Worcestershire sauce. Bring these ingredients to a boil then reduce the heat to a simmer and cover for 30 minutes. Add can of green beans and bring to a boil for an additional five minutes and serve.

Servings 4-6
MENU WEEK#30

CHICKEN - MICROWAVE INFORMATION:

HINT: **To assure that the meat browns, place ingredients in a browning pan or place a pan inside a large brown shopping bag. Fold the bag's opening edge back underneath container, so fats won't escape. Be sure bag doesn't touch ceiling of Microwave Oven might spark unit (check often)**

<u>Pieces</u> – 2-1/2 – 3 min/piece	**Brush with Browning Sauce**
<u>Whole</u> – 18 to 22 min/8 pieces	**Brush with Browning Sauce**

CH – (Chicken and Noodles in Creamy Sauce)

1 cut up 3 Lb Chicken
1 tsp Paprika
1/4 tsp Pepper
1 medium Onion, chopped
1/2 cup Water
1 Bouillon cube (Chicken) *
1 Pkg (8 – 12 oz) cooked and drained Noodles

1/4 cup Flour
1 tsp Salt
1 Tbsp Vegetable Oil
1 clove Garlic, minced
3 Tbsp Lemon Juice
1 cup Sour Cream

1. Add paprika, salt, pepper to the flour. Put the seasoned flour in a bag and drop in a couple pieces of chicken and shake till chicken is covered (or you can roll the chicken in the seasoned flour).
2. Brown the floured chicken in the hot oil. When golden brown, drain on paper toweling.
3. Sauté the onion and garlic in the skillet drippings. Return the chicken to the pan and add water and bouillon to the skillet drippings. Cover and simmer for 30 minutes – scrape the bottom of the pan.
4. Remove from the heat, remove the chicken and stir in 1 tablespoon more of the seasoned flour and gradually blend in the sour cream, add the cooked, drained noodles and toss in the sauce.
5. Place Chicken on top of Noodles and serve.

Serves 4
MENU WEEK#36

HINT: ***Homemade Bouillon – Pour excess meat juices in a bowl and refrigerate. The fats will rise to the top and can be removed easily with a spoon. After fats have been removed, pour the concentrated juices into ice cube trays and freeze. When frozen, remove the cubes from the tray and store in a freezer bag or a sealable container for use later to strengthen soups and stews etc.**

CH – (Chicken and Vegie Dinner with Asparagus, Carrots and Potatoes)

2-1/2 to 3 pound Broiler/Fryer Chicken cut up
1/3 cup Flour (All-Purpose)
1 tsp Paprika
3 Tbsp Vegetable Oil
1-1/2 tsp Salt
1 Pkg (10 oz) frozen Asparagus Spears or cuts
1/4 tsp dried Thyme Leaves 3 medium Carrots, cut into 3 x 1/4" strips
1/2 Pkg (14 oz) frozen crinkle-cut French Fry Potatoes (about 2 cups)

1 tsp Salt
1/8 Tsp Pepper
1-1/2 cups Water
1/2 tsp dried Savory Leaves

Mix the flour, 1 tsp salt, the paprika and pepper; roll the chicken pieces in this. Brown the chicken in hot oil in a 12" skillet or Dutch oven; drain. Add water, savory and thyme. Heat to a boil and reduce the heat, cover and simmer for 30 minutes. Add in the carrots; cover and simmer an additional 10 minutes. Add the frozen fries and asparagus; sprinkle with 1-1/2 tsp of salt. Heat once more to a boil and reduce the heat, cover and simmer until all ingredients are fork tender (when you can stick a fork through them), approximately 10 minutes.

Serves 4-6
MENU WEEK#31

Decided for You Cookbook – 365 Dinners

CH – (Chicken Breast Elisabeth)

6 Boneless, Skinless Chicken Breasts	Salt and White Pepper to Taste
1/2 pound Clarified Margarine/Butter	2 Eggs, slightly beaten
1 Tbsp Vegetable Oil	1 cup Flour
Soft Breadcrumbs	Round Toothpicks
6 slices of Virginia Baked Ham	12 slices of crust-free White Bread
Aluminum Foil	Waxed Paper

Place the chicken breast between two sheets of waxed paper. On a hard surface, pound flat with a meat mallet to a thickness of about 1/4" thick. Be careful not to tear the meat. Lightly salt and pepper all sides. Place a Chicken Peanut Butter Roll in the center of the breast, and roll and fold each breast so that the butter is completely enclosed. Pin the roll together with toothpicks as needed. Wrap the stuffed breast in wax paper or aluminum foil if you feel they need to chill to set the meat. Place in the refrigerator. Mix the egg and the oil together in a small container for dipping the breasts. Roll the breast into the egg-oil mixture and roll on all sides into flour, re-dip into the egg-oil mixture and then generously coat the breast with the soft breadcrumbs completely entombing them to retain the melted butter roll (1 slice Bread = 1/4 cup soft breadcrumbs). Using ~1/4 cup of the clarified butter cook the breast, turning until they are evenly golden brown. Place these browned breasts of chicken in a casserole dish. Oven cook these at 350°F for 10-15 minutes or until the chicken is tender (and when pierced with a fork the juices are no longer pink, but clear). Also at this time warm the ham slices in a casserole dish in the oven along with the chicken or they can also be pan-fried. While these are baking make the Supreme Chicken Sauce, keeping it warm when finished. Cut the white bread into **heart-shaped** pieces and toast. <u>**Plating**</u> – Place 2 heart-shaped toasts on the serving plate; lay ham on top of the toast and top with the baked chicken breast and spoon the Supreme Sauce over each serving or serve it in a warmed gravy boat on the side.

Chicken Peanut Butter Roll

1-1/2 cups of Smooth Peanut Butter
1/2 cup softened Margarine or Butter
Mix together and form into 6 log rolls (3" x 1/2" thick), chill in the refrigerator for 45 minutes or can be prepared and kept in the freezer

Clarified Butter (Drawn Butter)

Cut sticks of margarine or butter into pieces and heat very slowly in a small saucepan. As the butter melts, it separates. The fats rise to the top. Remove this with a spoon just leaving the clear oils of the butter, pour into a small container leaving any impurities in the bottom of the pan. The yellow milky fats can be stored and used for other dishes if desired.

Chicken Supreme Sauce

1 Tbsp Margarine or Butter	2 Tbsp Flour
1/2 cup Heavy Whipping Cream (or Evaporated Milk)	1 cup Chicken Broth

In a small saucepan, melt the butter and stir in the flour. Cook, stirring constantly with a whisk for one minute. Add in the chicken broth gradually and cook for 10-15 minutes on low heat. Add in the cream and whisk smoothly (or can be strained through cheesecloth).

Serves 4-6

MENU WEEK#44

Decided for You Cookbook – 365 Dinners

CH – (Chicken Broccola Supreme)

2 (10 oz) Pkgs or 1 Large Bag Frozen Broccoli Spears
1 Chicken Whole   1 Tbsp Lemon Juice
2 cans (10-3/4 oz ea) Cream of Chicken Soup   1/3 cup Mayonnaise Whipped Salad
1/2 pound grated Cheddar Cheese   Paprika
Dressing   Aluminum Foil

Fill a pan half full of water and boil the chicken until tender (~ 30 minutes). Remove and cool the chicken reserving the boiled liquid. Remove all bones from the chicken. Leave enough of the boiled liquid to cover the broccoli and bring to a boil, add salt to taste. Add the broccoli and cook just a few minutes till it's thawed, drain. Mix the broccoli and chicken meat together and place in a baking dish. Mix together the remaining ingredients except the cheese. Pour this sauce over the chicken and broccoli. Top with the cheese. Bake covered with aluminum foil for 30 minutes at 350°F. Remove the cover; sprinkle with the paprika; bake a few more minutes and serve.

Serves 4-6
MENU WEEK#47

CH – (Chicken Cacciatore with Noodles)

2 Tbsp Vegetable Oil   1 cut up Chicken 3 to 3-1/2 lbs
1 large Onion, sliced   1/4 cup minced Parsley
1 tsp Salt   1/4 tsp Pepper
Cooked Noodles or Rice
1 can (16 oz) Tomatoes, chopped (about 2 cups)

In a large, heavy skillet in hot vegetable oil brown the chicken lightly. Remove and set aside. Cook the onion in the pan drippings until tender. Stir in the tomatoes, parsley, salt and pepper. Add the chicken back to sauce. Simmer uncovered for 30 minutes or until chicken is very tender, turning once. Toss together with hot cooked noodles or rice.

Makes 4 Servings
MENU WEEK#32

Personal Idea:

GREAT WEDDING PRESENT: Staples for the New Bride

Every new Kitchen needs a container of:

Baking Powder	Oils, Vegetable/Spray/Sesame	**SPICES** (Allspice, Anise, Basil
Baking Soda	Pasta (macaroni, noodles etc)	Bay Leaf, Bouquet Garni,
Biscuit Mix	Preserves – Jams/Jellies	Cardamom, Cayenne, Celery
Bouillon Cubes (Beef & Chicken)	Rice	Seed, Chili Powder, Cinnamon,
Chocolate Chips (Semi-Sweet)	Soy Sauce	Cloves, Coriander, Curry, Dill,
Cocoa	Sugar (Brown/Gran./Pwdr)	Garlic Powder, Garlic Salt,
Coconut - Shredded	Syrups (Maple/Berries etc)	Ginger, Horseradish, Marjoram,
Corn Meal	Tabasco Sauce	Mustard Dry, Nutmeg, Onion Salt
Cornstarch	Tomato Sauce	Oregano, Paprika, Parsley,
Cream (Evaporated Milk)	Vinegar	Pepper (Black & White), Sage,
Cream of Tartar	Worcestershire Sauce	Salt, Savory, Tarragon, Thyme,
Flour	Yeast	Tumeric, Vanilla)

CH – (Chicken Company Cakes)

2 Whole Large Boneless Chicken Breasts cut in small pieces, (or have Butcher coarsely grind chicken
   for you at the meat market)

10 Slices of White Bread	1 medium Onion, minced	Butter or Margarine
1/8 tsp Pepper	2 Eggs	Salt to taste
1-1/4 cups Milk	6 large Mushrooms	2 Tbsp All-Purpose Flour
Parsley Sprigs for Garnish	2 Tbsp Processed Cheese Spread or 1/2 cup shredded Cheddar Cheese	

Trim the crust from the bread slices. Cut the removed crusts into cubes. Toast the bread squares and set aside.
Cut the Chicken Breasts into 1" pieces. With either a meat grinder or food processor coarsely grind up the cut
up chicken breasts. In a medium bowl with a fork, beat the eggs until almost smooth and add in the bread
cubes, add in the ground-up chicken and stir. Add in onion, pepper and 1-1/2 tsp of the salt and mix together
well. With wet hands, shape this mixture into 6 patties. Cover and refrigerate.

Flute the edges of the mushrooms with a knife (cut slit from around the edges for decorative use). Remove
the stems and put them in a plastic bag in the refrigerator to be used on another day for salads or other dishes.
In a 12" skillet over medium-low heat, melt 2 Tbsp butter or margarine and cook the mushrooms for 5
minutes, stem-side up, after sprinkling them with the 1/4 tsp of salt. Remove and keep these warm. In the
same skillet over medium-high heat, melt 1/4 cup more of butter and arrange the chicken patties in the skillet,
cook about 20 minutes or until golden brown, turning once. Remove the chicken from the skillet. Add 2
Tbsp margarine/butter and stir in the flour and 1/4 tsp of salt into the drippings, stir well, then add in the milk
(Vermouth if desired). Cook, stirring constantly until sauce is thickened. Stir in the cheese until it melts. To
serve, arrange the toasted bread squares on a warmed platter. Place a chicken patty on each; top each with a
fluted mushroom (cut groves out of the top), and serve with the cheese sauce poured on top, with parsley.
⬦⬦⬦

6 Servings
MENU WEEK #51

CH – (Chicken Eleganté with Green Beans)

1 Pound Sweet Italian Sausage	1/3 cup minced Celery	1 Tbsp Cornstarch
8 Boneless Chicken Breasts	1/2 cup Breadcrumbs	Vegetable Oil
1 Egg, beaten with 1 Tbsp Water	1 small minced Onion	Waxed Paper
1/4 cup of Flour (All-Purpose)	1/2 tsp Paprika	
2 Chicken-flavored Bouillon Cubes or granules	3 (9 oz ea) Pkg frozen Whole Green Beans	
2 Tbsp White Wine	Toothpicks	

Remove the casings from the sausage. In an 8-quart Dutch oven (or heavy pan) over medium-high heat, cook
the sausage meat, celery, and onion in a little vegetable oil. Set aside. Beat the egg with a fork in a flat wide
bowl. On a cutting board place the chicken breast skin side up, place between two sheets of waxed paper and
flatten to 1/4"- 1/2" thickness with a meat mallet or the bottom of a heavy pot. When flattened place a scant
1/2 cup of your cooked sausage meat mixture in the center of the flattened breast. Fold over the edges around
the filling, fasten the edges of the meat together with toothpicks. Repeat to make 8 stuffed breasts. Mix
together your flour and paprika, salt and pepper to taste. Dip your stuffed chicken breast in flour and then dip
both sides in the egg wash and then roll both sides into the flour mixture, dip in egg again and roll in the
breadcrumbs. In your same Dutch oven, over medium heat, adding a little more oil brown the chicken on all
sides. Add the bouillon, green beans and water. Bring to a boil. Then reduce the heat to low, cover and
simmer 30 minutes or until the chicken is fork **tender (when you pierce the chicken with a fork and the
juices run out clear, not bloody).** To serve the chicken, discard the toothpicks. Arrange the chicken and
green beans on a warmed platter. In a cup, mix the cornstarch and wine. Stir into the liquid left in the Dutch
oven/skillet (add water if not enough liquid); cook until the gravy is thickened, stirring constantly. Pour into
a gravy boat and serve.

Serves 8
MENU WEEK#40

Decided for You Cookbook – 365 Dinners

CH – (Chicken Enchiladas - Michelle's)

Cook 2 Boneless Chicken Breasts in a skillet or in the microwave, cool and shred (can also substitute leftover Turkey)
1/2 cup shredded Cheddar Cheese or Monterey Jack Cheese

1 Pkg (8 oz) Cream Cheese	1/4 cup diced Onion or 2 Tbsp minced Onion
1 can chopped Black or Green Olives	1 can (4 oz) diced Green Chiles (Optional)
1/2 cup shredded Cheddar Cheese	1 large can of Mild or Medium Enchilada Sauce
12 Corn Tortillas	Vegetable Oil Spray
Aluminum Foil	

Mix the chicken, 1/2 of the Cheddar Cheese, Cream Cheese, Olives, diced Onion, and chiles in a bowl. Spray your griddle with Vegetable Spray. Soften the corn tortillas by cooking each on both sides on a hot griddle, put them between two kitchen towels to keep warm. Spray your 9 x 13 baking dish with the Vegetable Spray. Place the chicken filling into the center of a warm tortilla and roll up. Place seam side down in the dish until baking dish is filled. Evenly distribute the enchilada sauce over the top of the enchiladas. Cover with foil and bake in a 350°F over for 20-25 minutes. Remove the foil and top with the extra 1/2 cup shredded Cheddar or Monterey Jack Cheese and return the enchiladas to the oven till the top cheese has melted.

Serves 4-6
MENU WEEK#23

CH – (Chicken Enchilada Pie)

1 (2 or 3 lb) Chicken – cooked and deboned	1 medium Onion, chopped
1 (10-3/4 oz) can condensed Cream of Mushroom Soup	1 (10-3/4 oz) can condensed Cream of Chicken Soup
2-3 tsp Margarine or Butter	1/2 can Enchilada Sauce
1 (14 oz) can Chicken Broth	1 (7 oz) can chopped Green Chiles
1 Pkg Flour or Corn Tortillas	1 Pound Longhorn Cheese, grated
Vegetable Oil	

In a large, heavy skillet in hot vegetable oil brown the chicken lightly on both sides. Remove from skillet, cool and remove all bones (**OR**, can be leftover Chicken, or you can cook chopped-up fresh boneless Chicken Breasts in your microwave for about six or seven minutes depending on cut up size). Brown the onion in the pan drippings. Combine in the skillet the soups, broth, and green Chiles. Return the chicken to the pan and mix well. Place a little of this sauce in the bottom of a 9" x 13" or 2 Quart baking dish followed by layers of tortillas, next a layer of the chicken and sauce, sprinkle on each layer the cheese. Repeat layers until casserole dish is filled. Bake uncovered at 350°F for 30 minutes.

Serves 8
MENU WEEK#18

Decided for You Cookbook – 365 Dinners

CH – (Chicken Flautas)

1 cut up Chicken (~2-1/2 lbs) or 2-1/4 cups of diced pork
1/2 cup (4 oz canned, diced, mild) Green Chiles or hot to taste
4 cups Water
1 medium size Onion, chopped (1/2 cup)
1 dozen fresh or frozen but thawed Corn Tortillas
1-1/4 tsp Salt
Vegetable Oil for frying
1 clove Garlic, minced

3 Tbsp Lard or Vegetable Shortening
1 Tbsp Cornstarch
1/4 tsp Pepper
1/2 pint Sour Cream (8 oz or 1 cup)
1/4 cup Milk

Bring chicken and water to a boil in a kettle or heavy skillet; lower the heat. Cover and simmer until fork tender, about 25 minutes. **–OR-,** cook chicken in a Crock pot 4-8 hours on low. Drain; and reserve 1/2 cup broth (can freeze balance in ice cubes for later use). Cool the chicken until it's easy to handle then remove all bones and skin, shred the meat. Heat the lard in a large saucepan until melted. Add onion and garlic; sauté 1 minute. Stir in cornstarch, salt and pepper. Add the reserved 1/2 cup broth, shredded chicken and Chiles. Stir and cook until very thick and bubbly; remove from the heat. Heat 1/8 to 1/4 inch of oil in a small skillet over medium heat until hot. Sauté tortillas one at a time a few seconds on each side until they are limp. They need to be softened so they can be rolled without splitting. After each is warmed, place inside a tortilla holder or wrap between kitchen towels to keep warm. Drain on a paper towel, if needed to absorb the extra oil. Fill each tortilla with three heaping Tbsp of the chicken mixture across the center. Roll the tortilla around the filling, and it now becomes a Flautas Be sure the filling is one inch from the edge to avoid splattering during the next step. Heat oil again in a skillet and place 2 or 3 Flautas, seam side down in the oil and sauté on all sides, until crisp, drain and keep warm in a 9 x 13 baking dish during rest of cooking. Combine the sour cream and milk in a small saucepan. Heat on low and then spoon over the Flautas. Serve with other Mexican dishes. Serves 6-8

MENU WEEK#52

CH – (Chicken in a Coffin)

4 Boneless, Skinless Chicken Breasts (sized to be able to fit inside the potatoes)
4 oz Prosciutto, cut into long, thin slices) or use Bacon strips if Prosciutto is not available
1/2 cup Grated Cheddar Cheese or Parmesan
1-1/2 tsp Sage
1/2 cup Dry White Wine
4 Large Russet or Idaho Baking Potatoes
8 oz sliced Mushrooms – Porcini or Button
Optional Garnish

1/4 cup Olive Oil or Vegetable Oil
2 Tbsp Margarine or Butter
1/4 cup minced Onions
Chopped Parsley
1 Tbsp minced Garlic
Aluminum Foil

Wash the outside of the potatoes and pat dry. Rub each potato with 1/2 tsp of Olive Oil, and lightly season with salt and pepper. Place these on a baking sheet and bake at 350°F until very tender, about
1 hour or 1-1/2 hours. Remove and let them cool enough to handle (these can be baked the day before). Cut the potatoes in half lengthwise and with a melon-baller or a small spoon scoop out the potato pulp and set aside to mash later. Sprinkle the insides of the skins with sage, salt and pepper. Salt and pepper the chicken breasts and wrap them in the Prosciutto (or bacon). Melt the Margarine in a skillet and cook the onions until they are clear and tender. Add in the garlic and brown it. Add in the breast and cover and cook them, on all sides, for an additional 6-7 minutes. Remove the breasts from the pan and add in 1/2 cup of the wine, rosemary and bring to a boil, stirring to deglaze the pan. Cook until the liquid is slightly reduced, about two minutes. Place the bottom halves of the potatoes into a shallow baking dish and put a cooked breast in each, sprinkle the top of chicken with the grated cheese; cover with the top potato half. Pour the sauce mixture over the potato coffins. Salt the mushrooms and place the slices around the edges of the potatoes and cover your dish with aluminum foil and bake these for another 10-15 minutes in a 350°F oven. Remove and garnish with parsley or maybe some additional grated cheese. If you do not feel that the potato coffins are enough of a potato side dish then your pulp can be re-warmed in your microwave oven and used as basis for including a layer of potatoes under the chicken i.e., garlic mashed potatoes for the meal. Serves 4

MENU WEEK#2

CH – (Chicken in Foil)

Slice 3 cooked Boneless Chicken Breasts (cook and de-bone if not boneless)
Chinese Parsley (preferred) or can use Cilantro and Green Onions
Marinate the cut up chicken several hours in:

3 Tbsp Ketchup	1/4 tsp Monosodium Glutamate (Tenderizer)	3 Tbsp Soy Sauce
1 tsp Garlic Powder	1-1/2 tsp Salt	6 Tbsp Vegetable Oil
2 tsp Cornstarch	Aluminum Foil	

Cut foil into 4" squares. Place the chicken, green onions, and Chinese parsley in the center and fold corners over making it into a triangle roll, sealing well to keep in the juices. Bake 15 minutes at 350°F. Yields approximately 70 pieces. Can be served well with any other Asian Foods. Serves 6-8

MENU WEEK#33

CH – (Chicken in Potato Boats with Potato Puffs)

2 cups cut up cooked boneless Chicken*	1 medium stalk Celery, sliced (about 1/2 cup)
1/4 cup Pitted Black Olives	1 Tbsp chopped Pimiento
1/2 tsp Chili Powder	Grated Cheddar Cheese
1 cup Sour Cream (used twice in recipe)	1 can (10-3/4 oz) Cream of Chicken Soup
3 Tbsp Butter or Margarine	1/4 tsp Salt
1/3 cup Instant Mashed Potatoes (puffs preferred if available)	

Heat the oven to 350°F. Mix the chicken, celery, olives, pimiento, chili powder, and 1/2 cup of the sour cream with 1/2 cup of the soup; set aside. *If you don't have leftover chicken you can purchase at the Fried Chicken store –OR- cover sliced boneless chicken breast and cook 6-8 minutes in a microwave then cool and chop.

Potato Boats

Prepare 8 servings of the instant mashed potato puffs per package directions except reducing the water to 2 cups. Stir in 1 slightly beaten egg, and 1/4 cup grated Cheddar Cheese. On a greased baking sheet, spoon this mixture into 8 mounds. Hollow the centers of the mounds with the back of the spoon leaving a sunken depression. Spoon the cooked chicken mixture into the depressions. You can cook additional potato puffs in butter until golden brown and place on top of the chicken. Bake filled boats for 30 minutes. Serves 8

MENU WEEK#36

CH – (Chicken Marsala)

4 large Boneless Chicken Breasts, halved	2 Eggs	Waxed Paper
1 cup Breadcrumbs	Butter or Margarine	1/4 cup Chopped Parsley
2 cloves, sliced Garlic	4 tsp All-Purpose Flour	1/8 tsp Pepper
1 cup Water	1/3 cup Marsala Wine	
1 Chicken-Flavored Bouillon Cube	Other Parsley Sprigs for garnish as needed	

Place the chicken breast between two pieces of waxed paper and with a meat mallet pound each chicken breast half to 1/4 inch thickness. In a small bowl with a fork, beat the eggs slightly and place breadcrumbs and flour in two separate shallow bowls. Dip the chicken pieces into the flour, then into the egg wash, and then into the breadcrumbs coating evenly. In a 12" skillet over medium-low heat, in 2 Tbsp margarine/ butter, cook the garlic and the breaded chicken pieces until the chicken is golden brown on both sides, about 10 minutes. Remove chicken to a warmed platter; keep warm. Discard the garlic cloves. Melt an additional 1/4 cup of butter or margarine and stir in the flour, scraping to loosen brown bits in bottom of skillet. Gradually stir in the water, wine, bouillon, pepper and chopped parsley; cook, stirring until mixture boils and thickens. Pour sauce over warm chicken; garnish with parsley and serve. 8 servings

MENU WEEK#47

CH – (Chicken Olé)

2 Broiler/Fryer Chickens (~3 lbs) – Quartered

1/2 cup sliced Pimiento Stuffed Olives	1/4 cup All-Purpose Flour	1-1/2 tsp Salt
1/3 cup Vegetable Oil	1 medium Onion, diced	1-1/2 tsp Salt
2 medium Tomatoes, diced	2 cups Water	1/4 tsp Pepper
1 cup Raisins	1/2 tsp Sugar	

Coat the chicken quarters with flour. In an 8-quart Dutch oven over medium-high heat, in hot vegetable oil, cook the chicken until browned on all sides. Remove the chicken to a bowl and set aside. In the drippings in the skillet, cook the onion for 5-6 minutes. Return the chicken to the skillet; add the tomatoes and remaining ingredients. Over high heat bring to a boil. Reduce heat to low; cover and simmer 30-35 minutes or until chicken is fork tender.   8 Servings
MENU WEEK #46

CH – (Chicken Paprikash and Noodles)

3 Boneless Chicken Breasts (~ 3 lbs) split in half

2 Tbsp Shortening or Vegetable Oil	1 can (10-3/4 oz) Tomato Soup	1/4 cup Chopped Onion
1/2 cup Sour Cream	Noodles – Flat Egg	2 tsp Paprika
1 medium Bay Leaf	1 can (4 oz) sliced Mushrooms drained	

Cook the noodles per directions on the package. In a skillet, brown the chicken in hot shortening; pour off fats. Add remaining ingredients except the noodles, cover; cook over low heat 40 minutes or until fork tender. Remove the bay leaf. Pour over drained noodles and serve.   6 Servings
MENU WEEK#39

CH – (Chicken Parmesan with Chives)

4 – 6 Boneless Chicken Breasts (can de-bone a regular Chicken Breast, cost is less)

1/4 cup Chopped Chives	1/2 cup Soft Margarine	Waxed Paper
Parmesan Cheese	Salt and Pepper to taste	

Mix together the cheese, chives and margarine. Make several slits in the Chicken Breast with a sharp knife. Insert a small amount of the mixture inside each of the slits. After stuffing, you can fasten the skin together with toothpicks to hold the ingredients inside, (**-OR-** you can pound the breasts flat, skin side up between two sheets of waxed paper. Spread the spiced margarine over the non-skin side of the chicken. Then jelly-roll and fasten with a toothpick and broil on both sides **-OR-** Force the handle of a dinner knife between the skin and meat and stuff mixture in this pocket). Last 3 or 4 minutes brush outside with some melted butter, sprinkle chicken with additional cheese, and return to the broiler until the cheese is browned.   Serves 4 – 6
MENU WEEK#9

CH – (Chicken Potato Oregano Pot)

8 medium Chicken Thighs (about 1-1/2 Pounds)	1 Tbsp chopped Parsley for garnish (Optional)
3 medium Potatoes (about 1-1/2 lbs)	Vegetable Cooking Spray
1 small Onion	1-1/2 tsp Salt, 1/8 tsp Pepper
1/4 cup Butter or Margarine	3/4 tsp Oregano Leaves

Peel the potatoes and cut into small cubes. Mince the onion finely. Spray a 12" skillet with the vegetable cooking spray and place over medium heat. Melt the butter; add the cubed potatoes, onion and chicken thighs; sprinkle with salt and pepper. Cook about 15 minutes, gently turning the potatoes and chicken often with a spatula or pancake turner. Sprinkle with Oregano after the 15 minutes and cook an additional 10 minutes or until the potatoes and thighs are well browned and fork-tender. Sprinkle tops with parsley.
                                          4 Servings
MENU WEEK#34

CH – (Chicken Poulette Parisienne with Artichoke Hearts)

2 Pounds Chicken Pieces
2 Tbsp Vegetable Oil or Shortening
1 can (10-3/4 oz) Cream of Mushroom Soup
1/2 cup chopped canned Tomatoes
1 Pkg (9 oz) frozen Artichoke Hearts, cooked and drained
Generous dash of crushed Basil

In a skillet, brown the chicken in melted shortening; pour off fats. Add in the remaining ingredients except for the artichokes, cover; simmer over low heat 40 minutes or until tender. In a saucepan, cook your Artichokes per package directions, drain and stir into your chicken mixture and serve.

Serves 4
MENU WEEK#42

CH – (Chicken Quick Casserole)

3 (5 oz ea) cans boned Chicken (or two large boneless Chicken Breast cooked in the microwave for 8
   minutes and shredded or cut into chunks, or purchased from commercial Chicken Seller takeout)
1 (10-3/4 oz) can condensed Cream of Chicken Soup undiluted
1/2 cup diced Celery   1/4 cup diced Green Bell Pepper
1/4 cup diced Pimiento   1/4 cup diced Onion
1 (4 oz) can drained, Mushroom pieces and stems   2 hard-cooked Eggs, sliced
4-1/2 cups hot, cooked Noodles or rice (your choice)

Preheat oven to 350°F. In a greased 2-quart casserole, mix together well the first eight ingredients and bake for 30-35 minutes or until hot and bubbly. Remove from the heat and arrange the egg slices in a pattern on top of the casserole. Serve with noodles or hot rice.   Serves 6
MENU WEEK#52

CH – (Chicken Rice Casserole – Joan's)

1 Boneless Chicken Breast per person
2 Chicken Bouillon Cubes, dissolved in 1-3/4 cups water
3/4 cup uncooked Long Grain Rice per person (up to 1-1/2 cups)
Salt and Pepper   3 oz can Mushrooms
1/2 stick Butter or Margarine   1 Tbsp Grated Onion
All-Purpose Flour   Vegetable Oil

Flour and brown chicken breast in a little oil or shortening. While the chicken browns on both sides, put rice, salt and pepper into a greased baking dish and sprinkle grated onion over the rice. Pour the mushrooms with its juice over the top. Arrange the chicken on top and pour bouillon over and dot top with butter. Cover and bake at 350°F for one hour. Serves well with a VEG – (Green Bean Casserole)   Serves 4-6
MENU WEEK#12

Decided for You Cookbook – 365 Dinners

CH – (Chicken Rollups)

1-1/2 cups – cooked boneless Chicken, cut into 1/2" pieces
1/3 cup chopped Black Olives | 1 Tbsp chopped Pimiento | 1/4 tsp Paprika
1/2 tsp minced Onion | 2 Tsp Margarine/Butter | 1/4 tsp Salt
1 Recipe of Biscuit Mix Dough

Combine the chicken, olives, pimiento, onion, salt and paprika. Roll out the biscuit dough into 1/4" thick rectangle. Spread this with butter, then spoon on the chicken mixture. Roll into a jelly roll shape with the chicken inside. Prick top of the roll with a fork to let out the steam. Place in a greased oblong baking dish.   Bake 400°F 25-30 minutes.   8 Servings

MENU WEEK#20

Biscuit Dough - Heavier

Make Your Own
2 cups All-Purpose Flour
1/3 cup Margarine
3/4 tsp Salt

Egg Wash
1 Egg
1/2 cup Milk } Combine
(can reserve a little bit of the egg wash for top brushing)

Mix the first three ingredients (can blend the margarine in with a fork). Beat the egg and milk together and reserve a little bit to brush dough top. Add in the egg and milk and mix into a soft dough with a fork or with your hands. Lightly flour a cutting board and roll out the dough into a rectangle, filling it with the chicken as directed above and place in a lightly greased baking dish and brush with the reserved egg wash. (If using recipe without the chicken ingredients, Bake 15 minutes 425°F for biscuits)

CH – (Chicken Satay with Peanut Sauce)

1 – 2 Pounds Boneless Chicken Breasts, cut into strips
Vegetable oil for broiling | Iceberg or Butter or Lettuce Leaves for Displaying
Fresh chopped Cilantro for Garnish | Water-soaked Wooden Skewers

Chicken Marinade

1 cup Plain Yogurt | 1 tsp grated Ginger or 1/2 tsp powdered
1 Tbsp Curry Powder | 1 clove Garlic, minced

Stir to combine the yogurt, ginger, garlic and curry powder in a shallow square bowl. Place the chicken strips in the marinade and toss until well coated. Cover and let the chicken marinate in the refrigerator for up to 2 hours. Brush vegetable oil on the outside of the water-soaked skewers (soaked so the skewers won't burn up, and oiled to keep the chicken from sticking). Thread the chicken strips onto the skewers working the skewer in and out of the meat down the middle of the piece. Lay side-by-side on a broiling pan. Broil 3 to 5 minutes on each side, until nicely seared and cooked through. Lay the Satay's on lettuce leaves and sprinkle on top the chopped cilantro leaves. Makes ~20 Skewers. Serve with the Peanut Sauce.

Peanut Sauce

1 cup smooth Peanut Butter | 1/3 cup Soy Sauce | 1/2 cup hot Water
2 tsp Red Chili Paste (i.e., Sambal Oelek) | 2 Tbsp dark Brown Sugar | 2 Limes juiced
1/4 cup chopped Peanuts for Garnish

Blend together the peanut butter, soy sauce, red chili paste, brown sugar, and lime juice. If needed, the sauce can be thinned with hot water. Serve in a small, serving bowl on each plate, and garnish with the chopped peanuts. (Yields 3 cups)   Serves 4-6

MENU WEEK#43

CH – (Chicken Sopa Seca)

2 cups Shredded, Boneless Chicken Breast = 4 breasts*
–OR- you can even use canned boneless Chicken

1 Pound grated Cheddar Cheese	1 small Onion, chopped
1 clove Garlic, minced	2/3 cup Water
1 (10-3/4 oz) Cream of Mushroom Soup	1 (10-3/4 oz) Cream of Chicken Soup
1 (14.5 oz) Chicken Broth	2 tsp granulated Chicken Bouillon
1 (4 oz) can Ortega Green Chiles, chopped	8 – 12 Flour Tortillas cut into squares
Aluminum Foil	

*You can cook your chicken breasts in a skillet –OR- you can broil at (500°F) these on both sides for 8-10 minutes on the second rack of the oven until tender –OR- you can stop by an Chicken Outlet and buy white meat pieces and shred.

In a large bowl combine into a sauce the shredded chicken, 1/2 of the cheese and all the remaining ingredients, except the tortillas. Place 1/2 of this sauce in the bottom of a greased 2-3 quart shallow baking dish. Arrange 1/2 of the tortilla squares over the first layer of the sauce. Repeat the layers ending with sauce on the top. Sprinkle on the remaining cheese and cover with aluminum foil. Bake in a 350°F oven for 30 – 40 minutes removing the foil during the last 10 minutes so the cheese can brown.   Serves 6-8
MENU WEEK#17

CH – (Chicken Stroganoff)

4-8 Boneless Chicken Breast/1 per person (can be cut into small pieces and placed in a casserole dish
     with the gravy placed on top, then garnished with the sour cream and served)
2 Pkg instant dry Turkey Gravy **not diluted** per package directions, added dry*
2 Pkg instant dry Chicken Gravy **not diluted** per package directions, added dry*
2 Pkg Stroganoff Mix **not diluted** per package directions, added dry
4 cups Water
1 Pint (16 oz) Sour Cream
Mashed Potatoes, Rice or Noodles

Cook your rice or noodles and keep warm. Broil chicken breast on both sides for 8 minutes each until fork tender. In a saucepan mix together 4 cups of water with the gravies, and the stroganoff mix. Bring to a low boil, stirring/whisking constantly to avoid lumps until thickened. Remove from heat and stir in 3-5 "heaping" Tablespoons of sour cream.

Spoon the rice onto your serving plate. Top with the chicken breast, ladle on the gravy and place a large spoon of sour cream on top. Yum, Yum!

You can substitute 3 cans diluted cream of chicken soup if you don't have the dry gravies.

Serves 4-6
MENU WEEK#16

CH – (Chicken Supreme with Rice and Green Beans)

2 to 3 lbs of cut up Chicken
1/4 cup chopped Onion
Dash Pepper
1 (16 oz) can cut Green Beans, drained
1/4 cup Mayonnaise
2 Tbsp chopped Pimiento
Paprika
1 (10-3/4 oz) can Condensed Cream of Mushroom Soup

1 cup Water
1 tsp Celery Salt
1 cup Long-Grain Rice
1/2 cup Milk
1/2 cup grated Parmesan Cheese
1/4 tsp Worcestershire Sauce

In a skillet (electric preferred) place chicken pieces. Add water, onion, celery salt and pepper. Cover and simmer with the vent closed 20 to 30 minutes or until the chicken is almost tender. Remove the chicken. Measure the broth from the skillet; add enough water to the broth to make 2 cups of liquid, return this to the skillet. Stir in uncooked rice, green beans, soup, milk, mayonnaise, cheese, pimiento and Worcestershire into this broth. Add back in the chicken. Cover and simmer another 30 minutes or till the rice is done. Sprinkle with paprika.

4-6 Servings
MENU WEEK#13

CH – (Chicken Teriyaki)

4 Boneless Chicken Breasts or one cut up Chicken, cut in small pieces
1 (18 oz) bottle Teriyaki Sauce – **OR** – Marinate the Chicken in Teriyaki Sauce for at least one hour (overnight is better). Broil (500°F) on both sides. Brush on additional sauce as needed.

Teriyaki Sauce

MAKE YOUR OWN - (Ingredients not on grocery list)
2 Tbsp grated Ginger Root (can be in dried spice form)
2 cloves Garlic, minced (approximately 2 tsp)
1 Tbsp Worcestershire Sauce
2 tsp dark Sesame Oil
2 Tbsp Brown Sugar
1/2 tsp Hot Pepper Sauce

1/2 cup chopped Green Onions or Scallions
2 Lemons or Oranges (juiced)
2 tsp Sesame Seeds, toasted
1/2 cup Soy Sauce

Mix all of the above ingredients and marinate the cut-up chicken a minimum of one hour in the refrigerator in the sauce (overnight is better). Broil in the oven or Bar-B-Q, spooning the extra sauce over the chicken as it cooks.

Sauce is good with Shrimp or Beef also.

Serves 4
MENU WEEK#25

Decided for You Cookbook – 365 Dinners

CH – (Chicken Turnovers)

8 medium Chicken Thighs (1-1/2 Pounds) or 4 Boneless Chicken Breasts

1 Pkg (8 oz) Pork Sausage Links

Toothpicks

2 Tbsp All-Purpose Flour

1/8 tsp Pepper

1 Egg, slightly beaten + 1 Tbsp Water

2 Tbsp Vegetable Oil

1 Chicken-Flavored Bouillon cubes +1/2 cup Water

3/4 tsp Salt

1-1/2 cups Milk

2 cans (8 oz ea) Crescent Dinner Rolls or Make
     Your Own Rolls

After salt and peppering the chicken thighs place these in a large skillet over medium-high heat in the vegetable oil and cook them until browned on all sides. Add in the water and bouillon; and heat to boiling. Reduce the heat to low; cover and simmer 15 minutes or until the chicken is fork tender. Remove the chicken to a medium bowl; cool until easier to handle. Cook the pork link sausages until browned on all sides and remove, draining on paper towels. Into the pan drippings over medium heat stir in the flour, salt and pepper, until blended; gradually stir in the milk, and cook stirring until thickened. Remove skillet from the heat; and set the gravy aside. Carefully slit the chicken thigh and remove all bones from each chicken thigh, try to leave the meat in one large piece if possible (Or cut the chicken breast into large chunks). Stuff one of the sausages in the middle of the de-boned thigh or you can pull the chicken around the sausage and pin together with toothpicks, if needed). On a lightly floured surface separate the crescent dinner rolls into 4 rectangles. With a floured rolling pin, roll these rectangles out to a larger 6" x 8" rectangle. Place a stuffed chicken thigh in the center, and place a tablespoon of the gravy mixture on top of the chicken. Then fold the edges of the dough over the chicken and press the seams together with a floured fork to seal around the stuffed thighs. Place the turnovers, seam side down onto a large baking sheet. Mix the egg and water together and beat slightly. Brush this egg wash on the top of turnover with a pastry brush. Bake in a 375°F oven for 15-20 minutes or until lightly browned. Meanwhile heat the leftover gravy to be served with the meal. Serves 8

MENU WEEK#45

Author's Special Thoughts

Blender Clean Up

Place a drop of liquid detergent in the blender with warm water, put on the lid and turn it on for self-cleaning action, rinse well.

Broiler Pan Clean Up

When you remove meat from the broiler pan, while it's still hot sprinkle the top with dry laundry detergent and then cover with dampened paper towels and Wo-Lah, it's much easier to clean up without a lot of scrubbing.

Cleaning a Meat Grinder

When finished run a slice of bread through the meat grinder to clean it out of all the meat. If any bread is left inside it will dry out and you can shake out the next day.

Preventing Animals from Getting into the Garbage

Spraying around the base, lid of garbage cans and/or sacks of garbage with Ammonia will prevent dogs from tearing the bags or turning the container over before the garbage is picked up.

Refresh Aluminum Pans

To brighten up aluminum pans that have stains or dullness from cooking acid foods such as tomatoes, apples or rhubarb, add water and stir in 1-1/2 Tsp Cream of Tartar, bring to a boil and the pan should look better, rinse well.

CH – (Chicken Wing Party with Asian Cherry, Classic Buffalo & Soy/Dijon with Ancho Chiles)

Cut the wings in half at the elbow joint and place these in a very large bowl. These can be par-boiled for 2-3 minutes and drained on paper toweling for juicer wings. Use Peanut or Canola Oil for frying, less 'smokin'. **Not a small family recipe will have to reduce for individual family**.

Asian Cherry Chicken Wings

2 tsp grated Ginger-root or 1/2 tsp Ground Ginger
1/4 cup packed Brown Sugar   2 Tbsp Lemon Juice   1 (16 oz) can Pitted Dark Sweet Cherries
3 pounds Chicken Wings   1/2 cup Soy Sauce

Pour the cherries and the syrup into a blender and blend until smooth. Add in remaining ingredients and blend together. Pour the mixture over the wings and marinate 2-3 hours, turning occasionally. Drain, but reserve the marinade for basting. Place marinated wings in a single layer into a greased 9" x 13" baking dish, cover with foil, and cook at 450°F for 10 minutes. Remove the covering and turn the wings over and bake these for another 10 minutes. Then reduce the heat down to 350°F and bake the final 20 minutes. Coat the wings with the reserved marinade.

Serves 10-20
MENU WEEK#39

Classic BuffaloWings

4 Pounds Chicken Wings   Salt and Pepper   1 Tbsp White Vinegar
Canola Oil for frying   1/4 cup Hot Pepper Sauce   1/4 cup Margarine or Butter

Sprinkle the wings with salt and pepper and fry in 370°F oil. Drain on paper toweling, then place in a serving platter. In a small saucepan melt the margarine; stir in the hot sauce and the vinegar. Remove from the heat and pour over the wings and toss to coat them thoroughly. **VARIATION: Use a spaghetti sauce instead of the hot pepper and Vinegar Sauce.**

Serves 8-10
MENU WEEK#39

Soy-Dijon Chicken Wings w/Ancho Chiles

2 – 4 pounds of Chicken Wings   1-1/2 cups Chicken Broth/Stock
1/4 cup Black Pepper   1 cup Red Wine   1/2 tsp Ground Cloves
1-1/2 Tbsp Dijon Mustard   3 Tsp Vinegar   1 Tbsp Oregano
1/2 cup Soy Sauce   2 Tbsp Dried Thyme   1/2 cup minced Garlic
4-6 dry Ancho Chiles, stemmed and seeded (**rinse your hands**)

Mix together all of the above ingredients and mix in the wings and refrigerate over night, turning occasionally. Place the wings in a single layer in a greased 9" x 13" baking dish, tented with foil. Cook at 450°F for 10 minutes. Remove the covering and turn the wings over and bake these for another 10 minutes. Then reduce the heat down to 350°F and bake the final 20 minutes.

Serves 10-20
MENU WEEK#39

Blue Cheese Buffalo Wing Dip

3/4 cup Mayonnaise   1 clove minced Garlic   Salt and Pepper to taste
2 Tbsp finely chopped Parsley   1/2 cup Sour Cream   1/2 cup crumbled Blue Cheese
1 Tbsp fresh Lemon Juice   1 Tbsp White Vinegar
Combine all the ingredients; chill for at least an hour. Adjust wing quantities per needs.

Yields 1-1/2 cups
MENU WEEK#39

Spicy Chicken Wings

1 Pkg **Hot Taco Spices & Seasoning.** Broil Drumettes 5 inches from broiler for 10-12 minutes, turning once. Combine the Taco Seasoning and 1/2 cup Ketchup and 2 Tbsp Hot Water. Brush the wingettes with the sauce and continue to broil 2-3 minutes longer.

MENU WEEK#30

(CH)-149

CH – (Chicken with Mustard Sauce)

1 cut up Chicken (about 3 Pounds)
2 Tbsp All-Purpose Flour
1/8 Tsp Pepper
1 tsp Tarragon
2 Chicken Bouillon cubes dissolved in 1-1/4 cup water

2 Tbsp Vegetable Oil
1/2 tsp Salt
2 Tbsp Dijon-style Mustard
1/2 Lemon, sliced thinly

Brown the chicken in the hot oil in a large skillet and move to a plate. Stir the flour, salt and pepper into the drippings then adding the diluted bouillon, mustard and tarragon until it is blended. After stirring completely return the chicken to the skillet and cover and simmer for 30 minutes. Add the lemon slices and cook an additional 5 minutes until the chicken is very tender.   Serves 4-6
MENU WEEK#37

CH – (Creamed Chicken)

Fry or broil 2 boneless Chicken Breasts – or – cook it in a microwave for 10 minutes. Cut into small strips or pieces. Heat 1 can of Cream of Chicken Soup with 1 can of milk (or water) and 1/2 tsp Poultry Seasoning. Add in the pieces of warmed chicken and serve over mashed potatoes, rice, noodles or toast.

MAKE YOUR OWN – (Ingredients not on grocery list)
2 cups diced cooked Boneless Chicken Breasts
3 Tbsp All-Purpose Flour
2 oz canned Mushrooms, sliced (1/2 cup)
1/8 tsp Pepper, or to taste
1/2 tsp Poultry Seasoning
1 Chicken Bouillon Cube (dissolved in 1 cup boiling water)

2 Tbsp Margarine
1/3 cup Milk
1/2 tsp Salt, or to taste
Long Grain Rice

Melt the margarine in a 1-1/2 quart saucepan over low heat. Blend in the flour until dissolved and smooth, gradually stir in the diluted bouillon. Cook and stir until thickened and smooth. Stirring in the milk, chicken, mushrooms, salt and pepper. Cover and simmer 15 minutes, stirring occasionally. Serve on Hot cooked Rice, Noodles, or Fried Bread.   4 Servings
MENU WEEK#5

Author's Special Thoughts

No Baking Sheet Available

A substitute for "no baking sheet available". Remove your oven rack and cover three quarters of it with Aluminum Foil. Return the rack to its place and bake you recipe on top of the foil, avoid anything with excessive sauces.

Measuring Cup Clean Up from Sticky Stuff

Measuring Cups for sticky stuff. Spray your measuring cup with vegetable oil or smear a little mayonnaise or vegetable oil inside prior to measuring molasses helps ease the clean up job.

Recipe Is Too Salty

If your food is too salty, make another batch and mix them together then separate them into equal parts and freeze one for another day.

CH – (Enchilada Chicken Casserole)

12 Corn Tortillas
1 cup Half and Half Milk
1/2 can Green Chiles
1 can (10-3/4 oz) condensed Mushroom Soup
1 can (10-3/4 oz) condensed Cream of Chicken Soup

6 Boneless Chicken Breasts
2 (7 oz ea) cans Salsa or Picanté Sauce
4 cups grated Cheddar Cheese
Aluminum Foil

Either cook the chicken in a microwave covered for 12 – 15 minutes or wrap inside aluminum foil and bake for about 45 minutes, until fork tender. In a large bowl, shred the chicken. Add in the soups, salsa and green chiles. Mix well. Cut the tortillas into strips. Layer the tortillas in the bottom of a 9" x 13" casserole dish. Top with a layer of chicken, then the soup mixture; ending with a layer of Cheddar Cheese. Try to make two groups of these layers. Cover with foil and refrigerate over night. Remove from the refrigerator and cook at 400°F for 60 minutes. Serve with Spanish Rice.

Spanish Rice

Place 1 or 2 Chicken Bouillon cubes into 1 cup of water and put into a medium bowl. Lightly oil your skillet with 2 Tbsp Vegetable Oil. Brown 1 small chopped onion until browned and clear. Add in 1 cup (or 2) Long Grain Rice and fry until slightly browned. Stir 1 tsp Cumin and 1 cup of Tomato Sauce into the bowl with the chicken bouillon and add to the skillet. Sprinkle all of this with Garlic Powder, Onion Salt and stir. Cover your skillet with a tight fitting lid (or put on top a large dinner plate which will keep the steam inside). Turn the heat down to low and cook for 20-25 minutes not lifting the lid and allowing the steam to escape. Take some rice from the center and taste. See if it needs additional seasoning and is soft and flaky.

Serves 6-8
MENU WEEK #26

CH – (Fried Chicken)

1 (2-1/2 lbs) Chicken Fryer, cut up
1/2 cup All-Purpose Flour
1/2 cup Shortening, melted

1/2 tsp Salt and Pepper
1/2 tsp Baking Powder
Regular Milk or Buttermilk

Soak the chicken in milk in the refrigerator for at least one-half hour. Mix the flour, salt, and baking powder together. Roll the moist chicken into these dry ingredients and place it on waxed paper in a single layer with the pieces not touching each other. **Let** these **floured pieces set until they feel sticky** (15 minutes to one-half hour). Melt the shortening in the skillet and fry the chicken 10 minutes on each side until golden brown. Begin with the dark meat (legs/thighs) as it will take a little longer to cook than the white meat. To be sure that the chicken is done, pierce a thigh or breast with a fork and if the juices run out and are pink, the chicken needs to continue cooking longer. If the juices are clear, it is done. A meat thermometer should show a temperature of 170 degrees when chicken is done. Drain on paper toweling and salt again to taste. **HINT: When frying chicken, shrimp or fish, add several drops of Tabasco Sauce to the cold oil to prevent splattering.**

Chicken Gravy

After cooking your chicken, leave about 1/4 cup of the hot drippings and stir in 2 or 3 Tbsps of flour. Over medium heat, stir or whisk until all lumps have disappeared. Add to this, 1-1/2 cups of milk and stir till consistency desired is attained. Salt and pepper to taste. **– OR-** See Creamed Chicken for using Cream of Chicken Soup.

4-6 Servings
MENU WEEK #5

Decided for You Cookbook – 365 Dinners

How to Cut Up a Whole Chicken

Remember to remove the giblets (neck, gizzard, liver and heart) packaged **inside the chicken cavity**. Can be saved in the freezer for dumpling recipe or Chicken Stock. Firm up your Chicken by first placing in the freezer until slightly frozen which will make it easier to cut up.

1) **Remove the Legs and Thighs**. Place the chicken breast side up and pull one leg away from the body and cut through the skin between the body and both sides of the thigh. Bend the whole leg (thigh and leg) down and away from the body until the ball of the thighbone pops from the hip socket. Cut between the ball and the socket to separate the leg. Repeat with the other leg. 2) Place the leg and thigh skin side down and cut down firmly through the joint between the drumstick and the thigh, cutting into two pieces. 3) **Remove the Wings**. With the chicken on it's back, remove the wing by cutting inside of the wing just over the joint connection. Pull the wing away from the body and cut through the skin and the joint. Repeat with the other wing. 4) **Cut the Carcass in half**. Cut through the cavity of the bird from the tail end and slice through the thin area around the shoulder joint. Cut parallel to the backbone and slice the bones of the rib cage. Repeat on both sides of the backbone. 5) **Remove the Breast** by pulling apart the breast **and the back**. Cut down through the shoulder bones to detach the breast from the back. Cut off the tail and discard. **Cut the Breast in half** or you may leave it whole. To cut in half, use a strong, steady pressure and cut downward along the length of the center breastbone to separate the breast into two pieces. **Another simple idea** is to split the chicken in half or even quarter it by cutting down the center of the breast bone with poultry shears and a sharp boning knife. Then divide each half again at the point where the thigh meets the body of the chicken.

I hope you made it, it is not an easy first time task without pictures, but it'll get easier the more times you do it. Whole chickens cost much less per pound. But, if easier is the word then, of course, buy the chicken already cut up.

CH – (Lemon Chicken)

3-4 Boneless Breasts or medium size Chicken (cut up)

Marinade: Mix together and marinade at least 20 minutes

1 tsp Sherry Wine	1 Tbsp Cornstarch	1-1/2 tsp Sugar
1 tsp Soy Sauce	1 Egg, beaten	1 Tbsp Vinegar
1/4 tsp Salt	1 tsp Pepper (White Pepper is preferred)	
1 small clove Garlic, mashed	1 Tbsp finely chopped Onion	

Coating for Chicken:
3/4 cup All-Purpose Flour   Paper Sack

Place Flour in a paper sack and then drop in the chicken to be Coated/Dredge. Lay out on waxed paper until ready to fry.

Frying of Chicken:

1/4 cup Peanut Oil	1 Tbsp Asian Rice Wine
1 small clove chopped Garlic	Several Lemon Rind Curls
2 slices Fresh Ginger, or 3/4 tsp ground Ginger	2 tsp Cornstarch mixed with 2 Tbsp Water

Heat **Peanut Oil** in a hot Wok or Skillet and fry the chicken on both sides until golden brown. Add in the **Rice Wine** and cover briefly to steam the flavors into the chicken. Remove the chicken from the pan. Add into the drippings: the chopped **Garlic** clove, and simmer for a few seconds stirring so it doesn't burn. Add in the **Lemon Rind** and **Ginger**. (continued)

(continued Lemon Chicken)
Lemon Sauce:

2 tsp Cornstarch	2 Tbsp Water

When mixture comes to a boil, thicken with a mixture of the **Cornstarch** mixed with **Water** to form the sauce. Remove the Rind and the fresh Ginger. Add back in the chicken and **Asian Hot Pepper Oil**. Mix well the **Lemon Juice** with the **instant custard/pie filling** and add.

1/2 tsp Asian Hot Pepper Oil	1/2 cup Lemon Juice
1 tsp instant Lemon Custard Powder/Pie Filling	

Cook until chicken is reheated and sauce has thickened. Place chicken on a platter and cover with any available Lemon Sauce. **NOTE:** If you do not want to fry this Lemon Chicken. You can place the floured chicken in a single layer in a large, greased baking dish. Mix the Hot Pepper Oil and Lemon Sauce, then pour over the chicken and bake at 400°F for 30 minutes. Turn and baste the chicken again for an additional 20 minutes. If you have enough sauce, baste more often. If more tartness is desired, remove chicken from the oven and you can squeeze fresh lemon juice over the top before serving sauce until done). Serves 4-6

MENU WEEK#21

CH – (Peanut Crusted Chicken Fingers with Dipping Sauce)

2 Pounds Boneless Chicken Breasts – cut lengthwise into strips

1 Tbsp Cayenne Pepper in a shaker	1 Tbsp Onion Powder in a shaker
Salt and Pepper to taste	2 Large Eggs, slightly beaten
1/4 cup Milk	1 cup All-Purpose Flour
1/2 cup Breadcrumbs	1 cup crushed salted Peanuts

Preheat the oven to 375°F. Lightly grease a baking sheet. Mix together the peanuts and the breadcrumbs. In a bowl, beat together the eggs, and the milk. Sprinkle the chicken strips with the Cayenne Pepper, Onion Powder, Salt and Pepper. Dredge the strips in the flour, then dip them in the egg mixture and coat these with the crushed peanuts and breadcrumbs. Place these on the baking sheet and bake, turning once, until the chicken is cooked through and the crust is golden ~15 to 20 minutes. Remove the chicken from the oven and transfer to a hot platter.

Chicken Dipping Sauce

1/2 cup Mayonnaise	1/4 cup Sour Cream
2 Tbsp Creole Mustard	2 tsp Cayenne Pepper
2 dashes of Tabasco Sauce	Chopped Green Onions

Mix together and store extra in refrigerator in a sealed container for up to one week. Serves 4-6

MENU WEEK#41

CH – (Stuffed Chicken)

1 (3-1/2 or 4 Pound) Whole Chicken	Stuffing Mix – Herb Seasoned
(Optional) Roasted Potatoes	

Remove the giblets from inside the chicken neck cavity, which consists of the liver, gizzard, and heart, plus the neck, which are usually in a package inside the body of the chicken between the legs. Remove them, discard or freeze in a new container as these can be used later for chicken stock or dumplings. Hold the chicken under running water and rinse it inside and out. Shake off the excess water and pat dry with paper toweling. Sprinkle 1-1/2 tsp salt and 1/2 tsp of pepper over the outside of the chicken, rubbing it all over the skin. Set the chicken, the breast side facing up, in the baking dish and stuff the cavity full of moist herb seasoned dressing mix or use the homemade cornbread dressing shown with the Roast Turkey recipe. **If using a meat thermometer be sure that the rod does not touch a bone while cooking, or reading will be incorrect.** Preheat the oven to 325°F, and bake the chicken and dressing in the center of your oven for 30 minutes. Stick a fork or paring knife into the meat of the thigh where it attaches to the body. If the juices that run out is pink, the chicken needs to continue cooking for another 10 to 15 minutes. If the juices are clear, it is done. Meat Thermometer should show a temperature of 185°F. Pan juices can be used to make a gravy as directed in the Roast Turkey recipe. If you roast potatoes with the chicken, salt and pepper to (continued)

(continued Stuffed Chicken) taste and spread these around the outside of the chicken on the serving platter.

Serves 4-8

MENU WEEK#48

NOTE: Another Alternate: Mix together 1/4 Lb Ground Pork, 1/4 Lb Chorizo Sausage finely ground or chopped, 1 cup chopped Onions, 1/2 cup chopped Celery, Cayenne Pepper to taste and add to your stuffing recipe. Stuff a 4-5 pound chicken and bake per above.

CH – (Stuffed Chicken Breasts)

4 Boneless Chicken Breasts	Grated Parmesan Cheese
Round double pointed Toothpicks	1/2 pound shredded Monterey Jack Cheese
3 – 6 slices Breast of Turkey Luncheon Meat*	2 cans White Sauce or make your own
3 – 6 slices Boiled Ham or 1/2 cup leftover Ham*	1/2 pound shredded Swiss Cheese

Place the chicken breast between two sheets of waxed paper or plastic wrap, skin side down, and pound with a mallet (or cloth covered hammer) until 1/2" thick. In the center of breast place boiled ham, total quantity is your choice.   On top of the ham place desired quantity of both the Jack and Swiss Cheese followed by the slices of Turkey luncheon meat, which makes a pocket of cheese between the meat. Pull the chicken skin and/or meat around the enclosed ingredients and fasten the edges together with tooth-picks. Place on a broiling pan and broil at (500°F) on the top rack of the oven for 10 minutes on each side, remove and reset the oven to Bake 325°F. Warm the **canned white sauce** adding in about 1/4 cup of the Parmesan Cheese or use the **MAKE YOUR OWN Béchamel Sauce** leaving out the Nutmeg, see SAUCE recipe. Place the stuffed chicken into a shallow baking dish and spoon the sauce over the top, sprinkling additional Parmesan Cheese on the top.   Bake in a 325°F oven for about 10 minutes, or until thoroughly warmed. *Hint: Recipe can be tasty without using the luncheon meat, if desired.

Creamy Cheese Sauce

MAKE YOUR OWN - (Ingredients not on grocery list)
See Recipe in SAUCES - Pour the sauce over the stuffed broiled chicken breasts. Sprinkle on another 1/2 cup Parmesan Cheese, sprinkle on the Paprika. Bake at 325°F for an additional 10 minutes, or until thoroughly warmed.

Serves 4

MENU WEEK#1

CH – (Tandori Chicken with Yogurt)

1 (3 Pound) Broiler/Fryer, quartered or cut into pieces, your choice
1/4 cup Plain Yogurt (warmed)   Lemon Wedges for Garnish
Fresh Sliced Onion Rings

Prepare the below marinade the day before and marinate the chicken marinating in it over night in the refrigerator. The next day, about one hour before cooking, remove the chicken from the refrigerator. Preheat the broiler (500°F). Place the chicken skin side down on a broiling pan and brush with some of the marinade. Broil 7 to 9 inches from the source of heat for 20 minutes, turn over; baste again and broil for an additional 25 minutes or until browned and fork-tender. **HINT:** Pierce the chicken with a knife or fork and if the juice comes out clear you will know it is done, if it's pink cook a little longer. Place on a serving platter. Pour the warmed Yogurt over the chicken, and garnish will additional onion rings and the Lemon Wedges (continued)

(continued Tandori Chicken with Yogurt)
Chicken Marinade

1 Tbsp Ginger Root (peeled, minced) or 3/4 tsp ground Ginger	2 medium Onions, diced	1/4 tsp ground Cardamom
	1/4 tsp Cayenne Pepper	1/2 tsp Turmeric
1 clove of Garlic, chopped	2 Tbsp Vegetable Oil	1/2 tsp ground Cumin
2 tsp Salt	1-1/2 tsp ground Coriander	1 tsp Sugar

Place ingredients in a blender, **EXCEPT YOGURT, CHICKEN, LEMON WEDGES**. Place cover on the blender and blend at high speed until the mixture is pureed. Pour this mixture into a large zip lock bag. You can pierce the meat with a small knife to help it to marinate thoroughly, then place it in the marinade. **HINT: <u>Seal the bag and lay it inside of a shallow pan or baking dish in case the bag accidentally comes open.</u>** Turn this over occasionally so all meat parts absorbs the marinade.

Serves 4
MENU WEEK#49

CH – (Tso's Favorite Chicken)

1 Pound boneless, skinless Chicken Thighs and/or Breasts cut into 1-inch cubes
Peanut Oil (doesn't smoke as much) or Vegetable Oil for frying
Steamed Long Grain Rice
Green Onions sliced on the bias for garnish

Marinade:

1 Large Egg White	2 Tbsp Cornstarch
2 Tbsp Soy Sauce	1/4 cup Chicken Stock
3 Tbsp Chinese White Cooking Wine, or dry Sherry	1 Tbsp minced Ginger
1 tsp minced Garlic	

Chicken Broth Sauce:

1 Tbsp Cornstarch	2 tsp White Vinegar
1 + 3 Tbsp Chicken Stock	2 tsp Sugar
1 Tbsp Chinese White Cooking Wine, or dry Sherry	1 Tbsp Soy Sauce

Stir Fry:

1/2 cup chopped, lightly toasted Cashews	1 tsp minced Garlic
1/2 cup additional sliced Green Onions	1/2 tsp Red Hot Pepper Flakes
12 dry Red Hot Chile Peppers	

Use Marinade: In a bowl, whisk together the Egg White, 2 Tbsp Cornstarch, 3 Tbsps Wine, 1 tsp minced Garlic, 1 Tbsp minced Ginger, 1/4 cup Chicken Stock, and 2 Tbsp Soy Sauce. Slit the thighs and remove the bones and/or cut up the breasts and add the chicken to the sauce and toss it to coat. Cover and marinate in the refrigerator 1-2 hours. **Use Chicken Broth Sauce**: Mix in a different bowl 1 Tbsp Cornstarch with 1 Tbsp of Chicken Broth and whisk until smooth. Add in the remaining 3 Tbsp Chicken Broth, 1 Tbsp Wine, 1 Tbsp Soy Sauce, the Vinegar and Sugar and whisk to combine then set aside. **Begin Stir Fry:** In a large hot wok heat enough oil to fill 2 inches inside the wok; splash it up the sides, raise the temperature to 350°F. Remove the chicken from the marinade and carefully slide it into the hot oil. Fry, turning, until golden brown (~ 2 minutes). Remove and drain on paper toweling. Discard all but about 2 Tbsp of the oil from the wok. Reheat the wok and add in the Red Hot Chile Peppers and stir-fry until nearly black. Add in the additional garlic, red pepper flakes and 1/2 cup green onions. Stir-fry about 15-30 seconds. Add in the chicken broth sauce, bring it to a boil and stirring, and cook until the sauce thickens, about 1-2 minutes. Remove from the heat and arrange the chicken on a platter (can be served on top of steamed rice or other steamed vegetables, your choice) and pour the hot Chicken Broth Sauce over it garnishing with the cashews and additional green onions.

Serves 4-6
MENU WEEK#29

CH – (Tuscan Chicken Rollatini with Stuffing)

6 Boneless, Skinless Chicken Breasts
1/2 pound Ground Pork Sausage
1 small finely chopped Onion
1 minced clove Garlic
1/4 Pkg Herb Seasoned Stuffing Mix + Water

1/4 tsp Salt and Pepper
1/2 cup dry White Wine (Optional)
Fresh Chopped Parsley for Garnish
Waxed Paper & Toothpicks
1 beaten Egg

Place a breast between waxed paper on a hard surface. Flatten to 1/4 - 1/2" thickness using a meat mallet or rolling pin (try not to tear holes in the meat), salt and pepper on each side. Mix the stuffing mix with water per package directions. In a skillet combine and cook the ground pork, onion, and garlic stirring to crumble the sausage as it cooks. Pour this mixture into the dressing mix, add in the beaten egg and mix together. Place a ball of the stuffing mix in the center of each chicken breast. Roll up the chicken in a jelly-roll fashion, starting with the short end; secure mid-ends with two round, wooden toothpicks.

Toothpicks   Cut in Half

Cut these rolls in half and arrange them dressing end up, side by side inside a greased shallow baking dish. You can pour the wine over the tops if desired. Bake, uncovered at 400°F for 25 minutes or until chicken rings are lightly browned. Either pour the gravy over the cooked chicken-rolls and the steamed rice, or serve in a side Gravy Boat.

Instant Chicken Gravy

1 (2.5 oz) Pouch/Pkg of Dry Turkey Gravy mixed with 1 cup Water
1 (2.5 oz) Pouch/Pkg of Dry Chicken Gravy mixed with 1 cup Water
Mix together with the water and bring to a rolling boil, will thicken a little more when it begins to cool down.

Serves 6-8
MENU WEEK#11

CH – (Waikiki Chicken)

1 Whole Chicken, cooked or can be a cut-up Fryer

1 Box Shake and Bake Coating

Chicken Sweet Sauce

1 can (14.5 oz) sliced Pineapple
2 Tbsp Cornstarch
1 Tbsp Soy Sauce
1 Chicken Bouillon cube or 1 tsp granulated
1/2 tsp Ginger or minced fresh Ginger

1 cup Sugar or Honey
Milk for Dipping
2 Large Bell Peppers, diced
3/4 cup Cider Vinegar

Drain the pineapple, reserving the juice inside a 2-cup measuring cup. Add enough water to make 1-1/4 cups of liquid. In a medium saucepan combine the sugar, cornstarch, juice, vinegar, soy sauce, ginger and bouillon. Bring this mixture to a boil for two minutes. Dip the chicken into milk and then coat with Shake and Bake Coating. Place the chicken in a greased casserole dish and pour the sauce over the top and bake at 350°F for 30 minutes. Place the pineapple slices and the sliced bell peppers on top. Cook another 30 minutes or until the peppers and chicken are fork tender. Serve with steamed Rice.

Shake and Bake Coating for Chicken

MAKE YOUR OWN – (Ingredients not on grocery list)

1 cup Flour
1 tsp Pepper
Milk or Water

1 tsp each Thyme, Oregano, Basil
1/2 cup Cracker Meal/Breadcrumbs or crushed
Saltine Crackers

2 tsp Salt

Combine the dry ingredients, stirring to mix. Use 1/2 of the mixture for 3 pounds of Chicken. Moisten the meat in the milk or water before you coat with the dry ingredients. **HINT:** Dip the meat in a **Bar-B-Q-Sauce** before coating in the dry ingredients. Store balance of the dry ingredients in a tightly covered container.

Serves 5
MENU WEEK #33

(CH)-156

CRNBF – (Corned Beef Casserole with Sauerkraut and Potatoes)

1 bag (16 oz) frozen shredded Hash Browns   1 cup Sauerkraut, drained
Crushed Cornflakes for Topping   1/2 cup Thousand Island Salad Dressing
1 can Corned Beef or 2 cups shredded cooked Corned Beef
6 oz (1-1/2 cups) shredded Swiss Cheese (keep the 1/2 cup for topping)
1 can (10-3/4 oz) Cream of Mushroom Soup diluted w/1 cup Milk

Heat oven to 350 degrees and combine all ingredients until blended except 1/2 cup of the Swiss Cheese and Corn Flake Topping. Coat a 9" baking dish with nonstick cooking spray. Spoon mixed ingredients into it. Sprinkle top with a mixture of the cornflakes and remaining cheese. Bake 30 minutes. Change heat to broil and broil 2 inches from the heat source for 5-8 minutes or until casserole is golden brown.

Makes 4-6 servings
MENU WEEK#24

CRNBF – (Corned Beef, Potatoes, Carrots and Cabbage Dinner)

2 –3 Pound Corned-Beef Brisket   4 medium Carrots, cut into 2-inch chunks
New Red Potatoes cut in quarters   1 small Onion, studded with 3 cloves
1 medium Bay Leaf   1/4 tsp Pepper Corns and Water
1 medium head Cabbage (about 1 pound) cored and cut into wedges

Place the brisket in a large pot or Dutch Oven covered with cold water. Add in the carrots, onion and spices; bring to a boil. Cover, then simmer for approximately 2-1/2 hours or until slightly fork tender. (allow at least half an hour to each pound, if meat is solid, and thick. If salty, discard half of the water and replace it and return to a slow boil). **Remove the brisket, the onion and carrots, then bring the juice to a boil, add in the *cabbage quarters, the red potatoes and simmer 20 minutes (add additional water if needed) until the vegetables are tender. Slice the brisket diagonally across the grain and arrange it with the vegetables on a large platter. If desired, sprinkle top with finely chopped parsley for color. If you are **using a Crock pot**, place in one cup of water, then the carrots, the onion, the cabbage, the spices and the brisket on top and cook on low all day –**OR**- you can cook the brisket in the Crock pot **by itself** and finish the rest on the top of the stove. Continue from ** above.

6 Servings with Leftovers
MENU WEEK #9

HINT: If your pot is large enough to hold a metal colander or vegetable steamer tray above the boiling liquid in the pot, then place the colander in the pot. Inside the colander place the cabbage with two heels of bread, crust down, on top of the cabbage to absorb the cabbage steam. –OR- you can set a small can containing vinegar on the counter next to the boiling pot. This will help your kitchen to not smell like cabbage –OR- Burn a candle on the counter while it's cooking. ALSO: 1 Pound of Cabbage = 4 cups shredded raw, or 2 cups cooked.

(continued next page)

(continued – Corned Beef, Potatoes, Carrots and Cabbage Dinner

Corned Beef – (Ingredients not on grocery list)

MAKE YOUR OWN – Corned Beef is a fermented Beef Brisket. If you'd like to try:

5 pound Beef Brisket	3-4 Quarts of Water	6 Garlic Cloves, peeled
2 cups Salt	2 cups Brown Sugar	2 Bay Leaves
1 Tbsp Juniper Berries	2 tsp Allspice Berries	

Mix all the liquid ingredients together and stir until the sugar is dissolved. Pierce the beef brisket with a meat fork or a thin knife. Place the brisket in a clean, extra wide mouth gallon pickle jar, if necessary cut in half. Pour the brine over the meat, cover and refrigerate for 10 days. Remove the meat from the brine and rinse thoroughly. Place the meta in a stock pot and cover with fresh water. Bring the liquid up to a boil and then reduce the heat. Simmer for 1 hour. Pour off the water and cook the meat. Slice the meat for Sandwiches using Rye Bread covered with a Russian dressing. Cheese and drained Sauerkraut. Butter the outside of the bread and grill for 2 minutes on each side until the cheese melts **–OR–** Serve with other recipe of choice.

Yields: 4 pounds of Corned Beef

CRNBF – (Corned Beef Tamale Loaf)

2 cans (12 oz) Corned Beef, flaked	2 cups boiling Water
2 Beef Bouillon cubes or 2 tsp granulated	3/8 tsp Pepper
2 cups finely crushed Corn Chips	3 Eggs
1/4 cup chopped Onion	1 Tbsp Chili Powder
1 can (8 oz) Tomato Sauce	

Dissolve the bouillon cubes into the boiling water. Mix together the bouillon water, corn chips, onions, pepper, and 2 of the 3 eggs slightly beaten. Pour half of this mixture into a greased 8" square pan. Mix together the corned beef with the chili powder, tomato sauce, and the last egg. Spoon this mixture into the casserole pan and top with the remaining corn chip mixture. Bake in a 350°F oven for one hour.

Serves 6-8 servings
MENU WEEK #18

CRNBF – (Tacquitos)

1 or 2 cans Corned Beef, shredded	12 Corn Tortillas
Vegetable Oil for frying	1/2 Pint Sour Cream
Guacamole Dip – Commercially made	

On a hot griddle spoon on 1 Tbsp of oil and lay tortillas on one side for 1-2 minutes then turn over and do again to soften and warm the tortillas. When the tortilla is very flexible, spoon a small portion of the corned beef in the center and roll up the tortilla. Place this in a warmed 7 x 9" baking dish with the seam side down, cover with a kitchen towel to keep warm. When you have completed all twelve tortillas, you can rewarm these in the oven or microwave, the entire amount, if needed. Pick up three of the Tacquitos with a pancake turner and place these on a warmed dinner plate. Top with a couple Tablespoons of Sour Cream and Guacamole Dip.

Serves 4
MENU WEEK#2

Guacamole Dip MAKE YOUR OWN – (Ingredients not on grocery list)

2 ripe Avocadoes	1/2 small Onion, minced
2 Tbsp chopped Cilantro, if desired	4 tsp Lime Juice
1/2 tsp Ground Cumin	
1 fresh or picked Jalapeno Chile (wearing gloves, seed and mince)	
1 Garlic clove, minced and mashed to a paste with 1/2 tsp Salt	

Halve and pit the avocadoes and scoop the flesh into a bowl. Mash the avocado pulp with a fork and stir in the onion, garlic paste, lime juice, cumin, chile, and cilantro. The guacamole should be made 2 hours in advance of serving, and then chilled in the refrigerator.

(CRNBF)-158

LAMB

LAMB – (Deviled Lamb Chops)

4-6 oz Lamb Shoulder Chops	4 Tbsp Vegetable Oil
8 Tbsp Water	8 tsp Mustard - Yellow
1/8 tsp Dried Thyme	Dash Garlic Salt
4 Onion slices	4-1/2 inch thick green Bell Pepper Rings
Lemon Juice	

Sprinkle the chops lightly with salt and pepper, <u>being sure that all the fat has been trimmed</u> from the chops. In a small skillet brown the Lamb Chops on both sides in hot vegetable oil. Sprinkle lemon juice on both the top and bottom of the chops. Blend together the water, mustard, thyme, and garlic salt and spread this mixture over the chops. Top with an onion slice. Cover and simmer 15 minutes. Spoon the pan juices over the meat; top with green bell pepper rings. Cover and simmer an additional 5-8 minutes until bell pepper rings are softened.

4 Servings

MENU WEEK#44

LAMB – (Viennese Leg of Lamb)

1 (4 Pound) Leg of Lamb – boned, rolled and tied with Butcher's Twine	
1 tsp Salt	1 tsp Pepper
1/2 cup Olive Oil	1 Large Stalk of Celery – Diced
2 Large Carrots shredded or small coin cuts	1 cup White Wine
1 medium Onion	1 small Bay Leaf
1 Tbsp chopped Parsley	1/2 tsp Garlic Salt
1/2 tsp Thyme	1/4 tsp Nutmeg
1/4 cup Soft Breadcrumbs	1 Tbsp Mustard - Dijon
2 cups boiling Water	1 cup (8 oz) Sour Cream
Butcher's Twine	Aluminum Foil

Be sure that "all" the fat from the lamb has been trimmed off. Sprinkle on salt and pepper. Brown it on all sides in hot olive oil with the onion, the celery and carrots in a large roasting pan. Add in the wine and bring to a boil. Turn down the heat and add in the bay leaf, garlic salt, parsley, thyme, nutmeg, breadcrumbs, and mustard. Mix thoroughly. Cover the bottom of the pan with the boiling water. Cover, or put aluminum foil cover on it and place in an oven (325°F) for approximately 2 hours or until roast is tender. Remove the roast and add to the juices the sour cream and stir well. Place sliced roast on a serving platter. Serve with potatoes or dumplings topped with the sour cream sauce.

Serves 4 – 8

MENU WEEK#15

<u>LAMB</u> - MICROWAVE INFORMATION:

<u>HINT:</u> To assure that the meat browns, place ingredients in a browning pan or place a pan inside a large brown shopping bag. Fold the bag's opening edge back underneath container, so fats won't escape. Be sure bag doesn't touch ceiling of Microwave Oven, might spark unit (check often)

<u>Chops</u> – 4 chops= 5 to 7 min (Brush lightly with oil – Turn at ½ Time)

<u>Roast (Leg or Shoulder)</u> 18-21 min/Lb (Let stand 10 minutes before cutting)

NOTES AND REMINDERS:

MISC – (Cheese Soufflé)

5 slices Bread cut into 1" cubes
1/2 lb shredded medium sharp Cheddar Cheese
Place this into a buttered casserole, alternating the layers of bread and cheese

Beat 3 or 4 eggs together with:
2 cups Milk
1 tsp Salt
1 tsp dry Mustard

Pour the egg batter over the bread and cheese. Bake at 350°F for 1 hour (or longer if not puffed up and browned). This can be made the night before and stored in the refrigerator for a morning cooking.

Serves 4
MENU WEEK#18

MISC – (Chile Relleno)

6 cans whole mild Green Chiles (check how many to a can and adjust quantity to your needs)
6 Strips of Monterey Jack Cheese, Longhorn or mild Cheddar Cheese (1/2" x 1/2" x 3")
Stewed Tomatoes or Seasoned Tomato Sauce or canned green chile salsa; or enchilada sauce
    (your preference)

Green Onions - chopped	3 Tbsp All-Purpose Flour
3 large Eggs, separated	1 Tbsp Water
1/4 tsp Salt	Vegetable Oil for frying

Rinse the Chiles; pat dry with paper toweling. Carefully remove any seeds found inside (makes Chiles too hot if left intact). Insert cheese strip inside the Chile. Roll each Chile in flour to coat all sides and set aside. Beat the separated egg whites until they form a peak with an electric mixer. Place the egg yolks and water into another bowl and mix together until well mixed, add the flour, the salt and mix together (~3 minutes). Gently fold the beaten egg whites into the yolk and flour mixture making an egg batter for coating the Chiles. Heat 1/2 to 1 inch of the oil into a small skillet and heat to medium hot (~370°F). Place an oblong mound of the egg batter 1/2" thick and 2" long on a saucer. Place the floured chile in the center and place additional batter on top to encase the Chile. Slide the batter-coated Chile from the saucer into the hot oil; sauté 3 or 4 minutes until golden brown. Turn the Chile over with two slotted spoons or spatulas, being careful not to splatter the hot oil. After browned, remove to paper toweling to drain. Keep these warm in a low heat oven until all are cooked. Serve hot with warmed, seasoned tomato sauce, stewed tomatoes, canned green Chile Salsa or Enchilada Sauce. Sprinkle tops with chopped green onions before serving.   6 Servings
MENU WEEK#42

MISC – (Chile Relleno Casserole with Salsa)

Dice and mix together:
2 cans (7 oz ea) Green Chiles, diced
1/2 Pound shredded Sharp Cheddar Cheese
1 chopped Bell Pepper

Mix in a blender:
1 cup Evaporated Milk
1/4 cup All-Purpose Flour
3 Eggs

Topping:
1 (8 oz) can Tomato Sauce OR drained stewed tomatoes mixed with 1/2 tsp Cumin
1/4 Pound Monterey Jack Cheese – Grated

In a buttered 9-inch pan or casserole dish, mix in a layer of 1/2 of the cheddar cheese, chopped bell pepper and Chiles mixture. Pour on top, the blender mixture and then the rest of the cheddar cheese. Bake at 375°F 40-45 minutes.   Add to the top of the casserole the Monterey Jack Cheese and the Tomato Sauce and return to the oven to bake an additional 15 minutes. Serve with Salsa and other Mexican dishes i.e., Spanish Rice etc. To double this recipe use a 9 x 13-inch pan and bake 1 hour before adding the tomato sauce and Monterey Jack Cheese. **See recipe - SAUCE - (Salsa) - Red or Green Salsa**   Serves 4-6

MISC – (Chinese Egg Rolls – see PK Egg Rolls)
See Page 199

MISC – (Chow-Chow Relish)

This Relish is "GREAT SERVED WITH BREAKFAST EGGS"
Mix together and refrigerate so it can be used with your Bacon and Eggs or cooked Pinto Beans.
1 jar (8 oz) Picanté Sauce and 1 jar (12 oz) Sweet Pickle Relish

MENU WEEK#46

MISC – (Cinnamon Toast)

4 – 6 Slices of White Bread
Old Salt Shaker full of 1 part Cinnamon to 3 parts Granulated Sugar
Soften Margarine or Butter

Spread your margarine on one side of the bread and sprinkle the top with the cinnamon mixture. Place the bread sugar side up under a broiler placed on the first rack of your oven (500°F) and broil until bubbly and browned. (See Author's Thoughts PK "Cooking at the Beach, Mountains, or Desert" (see page 184).

MISC – (Crackers - Saltine) – Make Your Own

2 cups sifted Flour
1/4 cup Margarine or Butter
1 Egg, slightly beaten

1 tsp Salt, 1/2 tsp Baking Soda
1/2 cup Buttermilk or soured Milk

In a large bowl sift the flour, salt and baking soda. Cut in the margarine (with a hand blender or a fork) until becomes granulated. Stir in the buttermilk and egg; mix to make a firm dough. Knead thoroughly. Place inside an oversized plastic ziplock bag and flatten with your hand. Cut away 1/4" of all side seams and remove the top zipper leaving the dough between plastic sheeting. Roll out into a very thin layer. Peel back the top plastic sheeting. Cut into squares or rounds and place these on lightly greased baking/cookie sheet. Prick the cracker dough with a fork. Sprinkle with coarse salt before baking. Bake 10 minutes at 400°F or until lightly browned.

MENU WEEK#40

MISC – (Crepes - Colossal)

1-1/2 cups Milk
3 eggs
1/8 tsp Salt

1 Tbsp Vegetable Oil
1-1/2 cups All-Purpose Flour
1 Tbsp melted Butter

In a large bowl beat eggs on medium speed. Gradually add in the dry ingredients alternately with the milk and oil. Beat until smooth, add in the melted butter – Batter should have the consistency of heavy cream. Let batter rest for one hour before using. Always stir before using. Lightly grease a 7" Teflon coated Round Crepe Pan (or you can use a griddle but the crepes will not be perfectly round) and ladle about 3 Tablespoons of batter on the griddle. Immediately tilt the pan in all directions so the batter is thinly applied and covers the entire area. Check to view the browning by lifting the outside edge of the crepe with a spatula. When lightly browned, quickly turn the crepe over and grill on the other side for about 15 seconds (may have to be greased again before cooking others). After cooking a crepe, store it in a heated tortilla warming pan or between two towels to keep warm. **Fill with the following; include topping of sour cream in all crepes + garnish**:

Combinations for Inside Crepes: *Be sure to top each combination with Sour Cream before closing crepe.*

"Beef Bourguignon – Glenn's" – see recipe under BF
"Beef Betty" – see recipe under BF

The rest of these are just cooked and pre-warmed ingredient's combinations as listed:
"Glenn's"- cooked Ham, Mushrooms, Tomatoes, Green Onion & Cheeses
"Betty's Ratatouille" Sautéed Onion, Garlic, Bell Pepper, and Zucchini
"Virginia's Americana" cooked Ground Beef, Lettuce, Tomato, Onion, Cheese and Thousand Island Salad Dressing"
"Schell's" cooked diced Chicken Breast, Broccoli, Mushrooms & Cheese or warmed Cream of Chicken Soup used as a Gravy
"Michelle's" cooked Flank Steak, Bell Peppers, Cabbage, Onion & Spices
"Matthew's" cooked Italian Sausage, Cheese, Olives, Onion, Mushrooms & Spaghetti Sauce.
Yields 10 extra large and 20-24 smaller ones

MENU WEEK#31

HINT: Batter not to be used immediately can be put covered, and put into the refrigerator until ready to use - stores up to three days. -OR- You can tightly wrap these cooked, cooled crepes in plastic wrap in the refrigerator (up to one week). They also can be cooked, cooled and stored in a freezer wrap or freezer bags. Place a small square of wax paper between crepes to avoid them sticking together before freezing. Re-warm in an oven or microwave. (continued next page for extra recipe Sweeter Crepe for Dessert sample)

(continued Extra Sweeter Crepe for Dessert sample)

Extra Optional Recipe for a "SWEETER" CREPE FOR DESSERTS

3 Eggs   1/2 cup All-Purpose Flour

1/2 tsp Vanilla   1 tsp Ground Cinnamon (Optional)

1/2 cup Milk

Stuff with: "Justin's Black Cow - Vanilla Ice Cream, chopped Brownies, Marshmallow Whip and Chocolate Syrup, Schell's Vanilla or Strawberry Ice Cream, Bananas, and fresh Strawberry Syrup or Preserves, Glenn's Cinnamon Spiced Apples, sliced Bananas, chopped nuts, warm Gruyere Cheese and Vanilla Ice Cream, Mush's Deluxe Ice Cream of choice, nuts, chocolate syrup, and Sour Cream, Breanne's fresh Boysenberry (or Preserves) with sliced Bananas, Powdered Sugar and Sprinkles." **Great Topping Sauce by melting Vanilla Ice Cream, adding a Liqueur and then top with Whipped Cream on all Choices.**

(Extra Recipe)

MISC – (Croutons – for Soups or Salads)

Sautéed Croutons – Cut slices of bread into even cubes, removing the crust if desired. Sauté these in melted margarine, turning to brown on all sides. Drain on paper toweling.

Baked Croutons – Lightly butter slices of bread on both sides, then cut into cubes, or cube the bread and sauté in melted margarine; removing the crusts if desired. Bake cubes on a baking sheet in a preheated 350°F oven, turning a few times until they are evenly browned.

Garlic or Herb Croutons – Add a minced clove of garlic to your melted margarine/butter and bring it to a medium heat, stirring it constantly drop in the cubes of bread and coat in the margarine and garlic; or sprinkle garlic powder and/or fresh Herbs to the buttered bread then sauté or bake the coated bread cubes.

MISC – (Eggs - Deviled)

Place six eggs into a saucepan and fill the water until it is two inches above the eggs. Boil the eggs for 10 minutes. Drain off the hot water and run cold water*¹ over the eggs for about 3-4 minutes. Peel*² the eggs, and set aside. Cut the eggs in half (very easy to cut if you use a cheese cutter strung with a cutting wire) and place the cooked yolks in a small bowl and smash*³ them together with a fork or a potato masher. Mix in a small amount of **minced onion, 1 to 2 Tbsp Mustard** (depending on the quantity of eggs being used, might have to adjust), pour in a **capful or two of vinegar**, and **2 tsp of Mayonnaise** and mix together. **Salt and pepper** to taste. You can spoon the yolk mixture back into the center of the whites with a teaspoon **–OR–** you can cut the corner out of a ziplock bag, insert a cake decorating tip if desired, then put in the yolk mixture and squeeze the mixture into the center of the whites; or if you don't have a decorating tip just use the small hole you cut out of the bag and fill through this opening. Sprinkle the tops of the finished eggs with paprika or pepper and place a slice of a stuffed olive on it for color. Cover your plate with plastic wrap and chill in the refrigerator if not serving within an hour.

MENU WEEK #5

EGG HINTS:

Eggs Fried – The secret of a good fried egg is to cook it slowly on medium heat. Pan should be greased with oil or butter and then break your egg close to the pan. To turn eggs over, use a pancake turner or wide spatula.

Eggs Hard Boiled – Place eggs in a saucepan and cover with water 2 inches above the eggs, **add 1 tsp salt so the shell won't crack**, and boil for 10 minutes. Drain off the hot water and run cold water over the eggs for about 3-4 minutes. **HINT:** Cooling the eggs quickly will make them easier to peel and will **prevent any darkening around the egg yolks**. Run under faucet until water is cold, drain the (Continued EGG HINTS) water leaving just the eggs and shake and rotate the pan around in a circle, this circular **movement will crack all of the shells at one time**).

Eggs Poached - A Tbsp of **Vinegar added** to the poaching water for eggs will help set the whites so they will not spread. With a spoon make a **whirlpool in the pan**, then slide in the egg off of a saucer.

(MISC)-164

Decided for You Cookbook – 365 Dinners

Eggs Scrambled – Mix together 6 eggs, 1/4 cup Milk, salt and pepper to taste and melt some butter or oil and pour on the greased griddle or skillet, and stir as soon as the bubbles stop popping.

MORE EGG HINTS: AVOID DISCOLORATION AROUND EGG YOLKS

MORE EGG HINTS: **AVOID DISCOLORATION AROUND EGG YOLKS** – Plunge hot, hard-cooked eggs into cold water after cooking before removing shells to prevent a dark ring forming around the yolks. This also makes them easier to peel. **PEEL EGGS EASILY** – After plunging your hard-cooked eggs in cold water, pour off the water. Rotate your saucepan in a circular motion, with a little bit of force. All the shells will practically fall off in one piece. Rinse any small shell particles off the eggs before using. **CUTTING UP EGGS EASIER** – Use a potato masher to cut up eggs for deviling or egg salad. **EGG YOLK STORAGE** – You can place leftover egg yolks in a sealed container and use later if you **cover them with 2 Tbsp of water on their top** and store in the refrigerator. **EGGS FOR A LARGE CROWD COOKING** – For a large crowd, **cook eggs in buttered muffin tins in the oven.** –OR- mix all the eggs in a large greased pan. Place these in a 300°F oven and stir occasionally after the cooking process begins. Be sure and keep a close eye on these. Breadcrumbs can be added for more volume. **SEPARATING YOLKS/WHITES** – If when separating eggs, a bit of yolk gets into the egg whites, it can be easily **lifted out with** a piece of the **egg shell**. Eggs will also separate easier if they are cold. **CLEANING UP DROPPED EGGS** – When you drop an egg, the easiest way to clean it up off the surface, **pour a large quantity of salt on it** and let it set for awhile. Using a pancake turner you can slip it under all of the broken egg at one time to remove it. **STIFFER EGG WHITES (MERINGUE)** – To stiffen egg whites, **add 1 tsp of Cream of Tartar to each cup** (~7 egg whites). **Volume will be added** to your egg whites if they are **at room temperature** before beating. **EGG STORAGE -** Store eggs **in the original carton**. If you do transfer to refrigerator door, store these with the large end up and covered which will prevent the eggs from absorbing moisture causing them to spatter/pop grease when cooking. **PURCHASING EGGS -** If there is only a few cents difference between Large and Extra Large Eggs, **buy the smaller size** for a better value. By the way there is "no" difference inside a Brown or White-shelled Egg. **OMITTING AN EGG IN A RECIPE -** If omitting, **increase the liquid by 3-4 Tablespoons** for each egg. It is a risky switch, however, especially in a delicately balance cake or cookie recipe. **AGE OF AN EGG** – Determining age by **placing it in the bottom of a bowl of cold water.** If it lays on its side, it is fresh. If it stands at an angle, it is at least three days old, and if it standing on its end it is ten days old.

SPECIAL NOTES:

MISC – (Falafel with Tahini Sauce)

Packaged Falafel Mix can be purchased, Tahini Sauce (purchased or **MAKE YOUR OWN** as below recipe), 4 Warmed Pita/Pocket Bread, split in half

Heat the oil to 380°F (hot) over medium-high heat, cook Falafel balls per package directions. Place 4 pita bread's inside aluminum foil, folding into a packet. Warm these in a 325°F oven for 10-15 minutes. If the pitas are very dry to begin with, pat each bread between dampened hands before stacking them. Or, you can microwave by wrapping each stack in microwave-safe bags on high power for 30 seconds to 1 minute. When warmed, open the Pita Bead packet by cutting these in half and fill with 3-5 crisp Falafel Patty Balls and drizzle with the Tahini Sauce, adding in a layer of chopped tomatoes and lettuce on top and if desired the below optional Persian Yogurt & Cucumber Sauce. Serve immediately. **–OR-**

Falafel
MAKE YOUR OWN AS FOLLOWS - (Ingredients not on grocery List)
1-1/2 to 2 cups drained Garbanzo Beans or dried Chickpeas soaked in water and covered overnight, drained

1 Tbsp Lemon Juice	2 tsp chopped Garlic = to 3 cloves
1 tsp Ground Coriander	2 tsp Ground Cumin
1 tsp Salt	1/2 tsp Turmeric
1/4 tsp Cayenne Pepper	1/2 cup Sesame Seeds
6 Tbsp All-Purpose Flour	1/2 tsp Baking Powder
4 cups Vegetable oil, for frying	Shredded Lettuce
2 Tbsp chopped Parsley	Sour Cream, serve with Persian Sauce below
Lettuce, Tomatoes, & Green Onions	Chopped fresh Tomatoes
1/2 cup chopped Yellow Onions	Aluminum Foil

Combine in a food processor the drained chickpeas/garbanzos, onions, parsley, lemon juice, garlic, coriander, sesame seeds, cumin, salt, turmeric, and cayenne in the bowl of a food processor. Process on high speed until it forms a smooth paste, scraping the sides as needed. Transfer to a bowl and mix in the baking powder and the flour. Refrigerate until dough is firm, about 20 minutes. With damp hands, shape the dough into balls a little smaller than a golf ball and then flatten these into patties or balls. Heat the oil to 380°F (hot) over medium-high heat, cook Falafel balls and fry in batches until golden brown, about 3 minutes. Try to serve immediately but you can place under a warmed covered container to drain on paper towels and to stay warm.

Tahini Sauce - MAKE YOUR OWN – (Ingredients not on grocery list)

1/3 cup Tahini Paste (sesame seed paste)	1 to 2 Tbsp Lemon Juice
Pinch of Paprika	1/2 tsp Salt
1-1/2 tsp minced Garlic	Pinch of Cayenne Pepper
1/2 cup Plain Yogurt or Sour Cream or just water (or more as needed)	

Combine in a blender all ingredients into a creamy sauce. **Great as a dip or sauce for Pita Bread sandwiches.** Yields 1/2 cup.

Persian Yogurt & Cucumber Sauce – Optional - (Ingredients not on grocery list)

1 Pound Yogurt	2-3 tsp dried Mint
2 Large Cucumbers, grated	Salt & Pepper to taste
Dash of garlic powder or 1 minced clove	2 oz chopped Walnuts

Mix all ingredients, refrigerate for at least 1 hour before serving.

Serves 8
MENU WEEK#1

Decided for You Cookbook – 365 Dinners

MISC – (Fondue Party)

Hot Oil Cooking Fondue - Meat/Vegetable/Seafood

Beef Steak cut into chunks and marinated	**Chicken Breasts** – Diced	Pork Roast or Steak
Bell Peppers	Chicken Teriyaki	**Potato Balls**-use melon baller
Bratwurst Sausage	Italian Sausage - cut up	**Prawns** – Breaded Frozen
Broccoli	Linguica - cut up	**Scallops**
Brussels Sprouts	**Meatballs**	**Smokie Links** – Miniatures
Cauliflower	**Mushrooms**	**Wooden Skewers**
	Oysters – Frozen	Yams

Clarify 1 cube of butter (melt in a pan over low heat and all the fats will rise to the top, spoon these off (fats can be saved for use later, leaving only the clarified butter). One half-of-an-hour before the party in an electric fondue pot, put 1/2 of a pot of vegetable oil in your fondue pot over medium heat, add in the butter. Keep temperature under the boiling point until you begin to serve, then turn up a little so the meats etc., will fry quickly. Put out your frozen breaded items. Then mix together a **Pancake Mix** Batter leaving out some of the milk or water to keep the mix a little thicker. All foods that are not pre-coated can be skewered and dipped into the batter and then cooked until the outside is brown.
BOLD = Items appear on grocery list. Not on the grocery list are the Optional Fondue dipping sauces. **Please make your choice and add to this week's shopping list.**

Onion – Cheese Fondue – (Excellent Choice)

2 cans (10-3/4 oz each) Cheddar Cheese Soup
1 tsp Yellow Mustard (prepared)
1 or 2 French Bread Loaves cut into cubes
1 container "commercially prepared" French Onion Chip Dip

1 cup shredded Cheddar Cheese
Dash of Tabasco

Warm all of the ingredients in an electric Fondue pot and serve the bread with wooden skewers or (to avoid double dipping) spoon the cheese fondue over the bread cubes on a plate. **WOW GREAT!**

Serves 6-8
MENU WEEK#31

Fondue Sauces for Dipping Tray (Optional)

(Ingredients are not on grocery list) - **Recipe should be increased according to guest quantity.** (Serves 2).
Set out 6 small bowls and in each place 1 heaping Tablespoon of Mayonnaise the mix in choice:
1. 2 tsp Sweet Chopped Gherkins and 2 tsp Capers
2. 1/2 tsp Parsley and 1 tsp Powdered Garlic (or 1 minced clove of Garlic)
3. Pinch of Tarragon and Pinch of Chervil
4. 1/2 tsp Curry Powder
5. 1/2 tsp Tomato Paste and 1/2 tsp Brandy
6. 3 Anchovy Fillets, small dice
7. Hot Mustard, Bar-B-Q Sauce, Hickory Smoked Molasses BBQ Sauce
8. 2 tsp Sweet Chopped Gherkins and 2 tsp Capers
9. 1/2 tsp Parsley and 1 tsp Powdered Garlic (or 1 minced clove of Garlic)
10. Pinch of Tarragon and Pinch of Chervil
11. 1/2 tsp Curry Powder
12. 1/2 tsp Tomato Paste and 1/2 tsp Brandy
13. 3 Anchovy Fillets, small dice
14. Hot Mustard, Bar-B-Q Sauce, Hickory Smoked Molasses BBQ Sauce

FONDUE PARTY (continued)

Chipotle Cheese Fondue (Optional)
(Ingredients not on grocery list)

1/2 pound finely diced Gruyere Cheese (about 2 cups)
1/2 pound finely diced Danish Emmenthal Cheese (about 2 cups) or other strong nutty Swiss Cheese

1-1/2 Tbsp Cornstarch	2 large halved, minced Garlic Cloves
1-1/3 cups Dry White Wine	1 Tbsp Lemon Juice
2 to 3 Tbsp Kirsch	Freshly Ground Nutmeg, if desired
3 canned whole minced Chipotle Chiles	Pepper to taste

Make the fondue by tossing together the cheeses and the cornstarch. Rub the inside of your electric fondue pot or heavy 3 quart saucepan with the garlic halves, leaving the garlic in the pot. Add in the wine and lemon juice and bring the liquid to a boil. Stir in the cheese mixture a little at a time. Bring the mixture to a simmer and stir in the kirsch, nutmeg, Chiles, and pepper to taste, leave in fondue pot and reduce the fondue pot's temperature to low. (Fondue can also be flavored with cooked Shallots, or sliced Green Onions, or crumbled cooked Smoked Bacon).

Pizza Fondue (Optional)
(Ingredients not on grocery list)

2 Tbsp Cornstarch	2 cans (10-1/2 oz) Pizza Sauce or Spaghetti Sauce
1/4 pound finely chopped Pepperoni	1 Tbsp minced Onion
1 tsp dried Oregano	1 Pkg (16 oz) shredded Cheddar Cheese
3 or 4 drops of Hot Pepper Sauce	1 Tbsp Parsley

Mix the cornstarch into the Pizza sauce in a saucepan. Brown lightly in a skillet the pepperoni, onion, oregano and drain fats. Add the spaghetti sauce to the pan. Boil sauce 1-2 minutes, stirring constantly. Remove from direct heat and pour into an electric fondue pot. Stir in the pepper sauce and parsley, then add 1/2 cup of the cheese at a time until melted, be sure and continue to stir well. Can dip fresh vegetables (mushrooms, broccoli, cauliflower, cooked Meatballs, Bread Sticks or French Bread cubes into the fondue).

MISC – (French Toast)

4 – 6 Slices of White Bread or French	3 or 4 Eggs
1 cup Milk	3 – 4 tsp Margarine for Frying

Beat your eggs and milk together. Add a small shake of salt and pepper. Using a griddle, melt your margarine. Dip your bread on both sides into the egg mixture and place on a medium hot griddle and cook on both sides until egg mixture is lightly brown. Serve with jam, sprinkling of powdered sugar, maple syrup or cinnamon cream syrup see recipe (MISC – Pancakes). Serves 4

See Author's Notes (PK)
"Cooking Breakfast at the Beach, Mountains or Desert"

Decided for You Cookbook – 365 Dinners

MISC – (French Toast – Stuffed)

24 slices (1 oz/slice) Cinnamon-Raisin Bread or sliced French Bread
Cooking Spray   3 cups Milk
4 or 5 beaten Eggs   1 cup Egg Substitute
1 cup Half and Half Milk   1/4 cup Sugar granulated
1 Tbsp Vanilla Extract   2 (8 oz ea) Cream Cheese, softened
Aluminum Foil

Spray a 9" x 13" baking dish with Vegetable Oil. Trim the crusts from the bread and arrange a layer in the bottom of the baking dish. Mix all ingredients except the cream cheese together. Either spread the cream cheese on top of the two layers layer of bread – **OR** – you can pour half of the liquid into a blender and place in the cream cheese and blend together. Then pour half of this blended mixture over the first layer of bread. Top with a second layer of bread and pour the balance of the liquid egg ingredients over the second layer of the bread. Cover with aluminum foil and let it rest in the refrigerator for at least eight hours or over night. Cook at 350°F for 55 minutes. Let stand for 5-10 minutes before serving. Sprinkle the top with either an equal combination of sugar and cinnamon or use with a recipe of the **Cinnamon Cream Syrup under MISC – Pancakes. VARIATION:** Melt margarine in the bottom of a baking dish. Sprinkle on a layer of the cinnamon and sugar, then a layer of chopped pecans. Top with the soaked bread slices and a layer of the cream cheese and balance of the liquids per the recipe. Bake as directed.   (Extra Recipe)

MISC – (Fried Cheese)

Frozen Mozzarella Cheese fried or baked per package directions – **OR** -

MAKE YOUR OWN – Ingredients Not on grocery List
4 Tbsp Butter/Margarine   1-1/4 cups Flour
1-1/2 cups Milk   2 Egg Yolks
1 tsp Salt   1/8 tsp White Pepper
2 Eggs beaten together with 1/3 cup Milk   1 cup dry Breadcrumbs
Vegetable Oil for frying
1 cup (1/4 Pound) grated Swiss Gruyere Cheese
1 cup (1/4 Pound) grated Nutty Swiss Emmentaler Cheese or Mozzarella Cheese*

Melt butter over moderate heat. Stir in 3/4 cup of the flour and mix until dissolved. Add the milk in as your whisk constantly. Cook over medium heat until the sauce comes to a boil and thickens. Turn the heat down to low and simmer 10 minutes longer. Remove the skillet from the heat and beat in the egg yolks, one at a time, and season with salt and pepper. Add in the grated cheeses and mix well. Pour this into a 6' x 8" greased baking pan 1/2" thick, smooth the top.   Cool to room temperature and then cover with plastic wrap and refrigerate for 8 hours or overnight making sure it is set firm. Cut the mixture into 2" squares and place them onto a sheet of waxed paper or a Silpat sheet. Coat each square completely by dipping into flour, shaking off any excess. Mix the eggs and milk for the egg wash. Dip the floured cheese squares into the egg wash, followed by rolling them into the breadcrumbs. Place back onto your baking sheet and refrigerate for at least 1 hour or until the coating is firm. Fry for ~5 minutes in a heavy saucepan or fryer in 2-3" of hot oil (375°F). Place some paper towels into a shallow pan and turn oven on warm. As you complete these squares store them in the oven to keep them warm while you finish the entire group. Serve with your drinks, great first course to any evening with friends. **VARIATION: Mix 1 Lb Ricotta Cheese and 2 eggs together. Shape into balls and dip in an additional beaten egg then breadcrumbs and fry in melted butter until golden – drain on paper towels.** *The harder the cheese, the better, look for a block instead of the soft balls of fresh Mozzarella. Try freezing your sticks for ~30 minutes before frying.   Serves 12

MENU WEEK #5

Decided for You Cookbook – 365 Dinners

MISC – (Game Hens - Baked)

6 Rock Cornish Hens (1 to 1-1/2 lbs each)
1/2 cup sliced Green or Black Olives
1/4 cup Vinegar
1 clove Garlic, crushed
1/4 to 1/2 tsp Salt

2 cups Herb Seasoned Croutons or Stuffing Mix
1/4 cup Lemon Juice
1/4 cup Vegetable Oil
1/2 tsp Thyme
Butcher's String

Heat the oven to 350°F. Dry the cavities of the hens with paper toweling (do not rub cavities with salt). Mix water per package directions into the stuffing mix or croutons, mix wet stuffing with the drained olives. Stuff each hen loosely with 1/3 cup stuffing. After stuffing, fasten the cavity sides together with either a skewer or lace it closed with butchers string. Place each hen with its breast side up in a non-greased shallow baking pan.

Mix together the lemon juice, vinegar, oil, garlic, thyme and salt; and pour over the hens. Bake uncovered for two hours, spooning the lemon mixture over the hens basting every 20 minutes. Remove the skewers or lacing and serve on a warmed platter

6 Servings

MENU WEEK#32

MISC – (Gnocchi's – Potato Noodles with Meat Sauce)

pronounced Nay-No-Keys

1 Package Commercially Made Gnocchi's (Available in most Deli's)
Meat Sauce (see below Recipe)

Gnocchi's

MAKE YOUR OWN - Ingredients Not on grocery List
8 to 10 medium Baking-type potatoes like Russets   1-cup All-Purpose Flour
2 Eggs, slightly beaten   Salt and Water
1 (10-3/4 oz) can Chicken Broth

Add 2 Tbsp salt into 6 Quarts of Water and Chicken Broth, bring to a boil. Boil the potatoes in their skin and then while hot, peel the skin off. Place in a large bowl and mash while still hot. Add in the beaten eggs and salt. Working with your hands blend together well, mix in the flour in small quantities until it forms a soft, smooth dough. On a floured or oiled bread board roll a portion of this dough with the palm of your hand back and forth forming a long 1/2" thick rope. With scissors, cut this rope into 3/4" pieces. (Or you can make into small balls or cut the dough out into designs i.e., moons, stars or place the dough in a pastry bag and squeeze through a star tip out into desired lengths). Bring salted chicken water to a boil and drop in a few of the gnocchi's. When they rise to the surface this means they are cooked. Remove with a slotted spoon or cooking spider, drain, and place these in the center of a warmed platter. Cover with the meat sauce and/or cheese of choice and serve.   **(Continue next page Meat Sauce)**

Gnocchi's Meat Sauce

1/2 cup grated Parmesan Cheese, Swiss or Monterey Jack
1/2 pound Beef Stew Meat (chunks) or 1 pound cooked Ground Hamburger

1 Large Minced Onion	1-2 cloves minced garlic
1 can Tomatoes	1 (8 oz) can Tomato Sauce
Bay Leaf, Parsley, Basil	Salt and Pepper to taste
1 tsp Sugar + 1/2 tsp Cumin	3-4 Tbsp Vegetable Oil

Sauté the meat in hot oil till brown, add in the onions, and cook till clear and tender, add in the garlic along with the rest of the ingredients. When it comes to a boil, lower the heat, cover and simmer for 30-45 minutes. This is also good cooked in a crock pot all day on low. Serve over the top of the warm gnocchi's and topped with the grated Parmesan Cheese. (**Other toppings can be**: Ribbons of cooked Prosciutto w/Parmesan Cheese, Cook shallots, onions, mushrooms in 2 Tbsp Margarine and 2 Tbsp of Marsala and 2 Tbsp Madeira Wine, or with a Mornay and Gruyere Swiss Cheese Sauce. **–OR–** any white or creamy cheese sauce desired (See also Potato-Hamburger Meat Pie Recipe Week #33).

Serves 8+
MENU WEEK#25

Gnocchi/Dumpling – Spinach

Optional – (Ingredients not on grocery List)
Defrost 1 (10 oz) frozen Spinach and blanch, drain thoroughly, and chop fine. Add in 1 Lb Ricotta Cheese, 1 large Egg, 1/2 tsp Nutmeg, 1 tsp Salt, 4 Tbsp Parmesan Cheese and 3/8 of a cup of Flour. Mix and roll into small balls ~1/2", lightly again, roll in another 3/8 cup of flour. Bring 1 can Chicken Broth mixed with enough water to cover the dumplings for cooking. Bring to a boil, drop in gnocchi and they will rise to the top when done. Place in serving dish, add melted butter, sprinkle with Parmesan Cheese, serve.

(Extra Recipe)

MISC – (Gravy - Brown) - From pan drippings such as a Roast

2 cups hot Water	4 Tbsp drippings from the roasting pan
3 Tbsp Flour	Salt and Pepper to taste

Bottled Bouquet Browning and Seasoning Sauce (used for darkening gravy color use per package directions)
1. Transfer the drippings from the roasting pan to a skillet,
2. Add the 2 cups of hot water to the roasting pan and dislodge or scrape any baked on juices from the bottom; pour back into your measuring cup
3. Heat the drippings in the skillet and blend in the flour with a whisk
4. Cook over medium heat, stirring until the mixture is lightly browned
5. Slowly stir in the hot water removed from the roasting pan. Stir constantly until the gravy boils and thickens; remove from heat
6. Season with salt and pepper to taste
7. For browner gravy, add bottled Bouquet Browning and Seasoning Sauce to gravy per package directions until you reach desired color

VARIATION: <u>CREAMIER GRAVY</u> – Follow the basic recipe for above gravy instead of using water use 2 cups of milk, or 1-1/2 cups evaporated milk plus 1/2 cup water for the required liquid. **NOTE: <u>Strain lumpy gravy through a fine sieve, and then return to the heat. If sauce is too thin, then mix 2 tsp Flour with cold water and stir into the gravy and when it returns to a boil, it will thicken.</u>**

MISC – (Gravy – Brown) - Without Juice or Drippings

1 can Beef Broth   1/2 cup Cold Water
3 Tbsp All-Purpose Flour   Salt and Pepper to Taste

Shake the water and flour together in a sealed container (jar or bowl) until thoroughly mixed and not lumpy (or whisk together). Add enough of the Beef Broth to the skillet juices to make 1-1/2 cups of liquid. Bring to a boil and stirring constantly mix in the flour mixture. Lower the heat and cook until thickened ~ 2-3 minutes. Salt to taste. If color of the gravy is not dark enough add in a tsp of Bouquet Browning and Seasoning Sauce. Pour the gravy over the ribs and vegetables or serve separately.

GRAVY – BROWN ALTERNATE RECIPE - Placed drained beef fats into a saucepan, add 1-1/2 cans of water. Mix in two tsp Beef Bouillon. In a sealed container thoroughly shake 1 Tbsp Cornstarch (thickener) and 1/2 cup of milk. Stir this mixture into bouillon and bring to a boil and cook till desired thickness. To darken the color of the gravy add a tsp of Gravy Bouquet Browning and Seasoning Sauce and stir.

MISC – (Gravy – Chicken or Turkey)

As indicated within the Turkey and Stuffing recipe you will have a better flavor if you boil the giblets (neck, gizzard etc) from a chicken or turkey and then use these juices for the required liquid when making gravy. **HINT: To save excess juices, after you have cooked a baked chicken and have leftover juices, you can spoon off the fats that will rise to the surface as it cools. Then you can pour these juices into ice cube trays or clean orange juice cans and freeze inside. After the juice is frozen then remove it and store in a freezer bag for when you need the juice; then remove, defrost and dilute with water. This will improve the intensity of your flavor instead of just using plain water to make your gravies.** Follow the directions for making the gravy as indicated on the **Turkey and Stuffing recipe.** If you don't have the available juices follow the recipe shown on **TUR (Hot Turkey Sandwiches)** using instant dry gravy packages of 1 Chicken and 1 Turkey Gravy.

MENU WEEK #12&47

MISC – (Gravy – Pork Chops, Bacon, or Ham Pan Drippings)

4 Tbsp fats left in pan after frying meat
4 Tbsp Flour
1-1/2 cups Milk + 1/2 cup Water **–OR-** 1 cup Evaporated Milk and 1 cup Water
Salt and Pepper to taste
1. Heat the fats in the skillet
2. Stir in the flour and blend until lumps disappear
3. Lightly brown
4. Add salt and pepper to taste
5. Add in the milk and continue to stir until gravy thickens as desired

MENU WEEK #38

MISC – (Grilled Cheese Sandwiches)

8 Slices of White (or of choice) Bread – makes four sandwiches
Soft Margarine/Butter
8 slices of American Cheese (2 slices each for real cheesy)

Spread soft butter on one side of each slice of the bread. Heat your griddle to medium-hot and place the buttered side of 4 pieces of bread onto the hot griddle. Put a slice of American cheese on each piece of bread,

(continued Grilled Cheese Sandwiches) which will make your sandwiches "real cheesy" (if you don't like the cheese to be so gooey only put one slice of cheese per two pieces of bread). When the cheese has begun to melt, with a pancake turner place one half of the cheese sandwich on top on the other cheesy side that will give you a two-sided, browned grilled cheese sandwich. Check the color of the grilled side of the bread and remove when browned on both sides. Cut diagonally into triangle-shaped sandwiches. Make another set, which will give you 4 grilled cheese sandwiches. Serve immediately with chips or a salad.   Serves 4

Ironing a Melted Cheese Sandwich:

When you don't have a stove or a broiler (College Student), lightly butter two pieces of bread and then place in between the two non-buttered sides, 2 American Cheese Slices. Wrap the sandwich inside aluminum foil, tucking in the ends of the foil. Place the sandwich inside of a brown paper bag to protect your iron. Then set your iron at the high setting on each side for 30 seconds to 45 seconds. The cheese will melt and the bread will be slightly toasted.

MISC – (Hi-Roller Sandwiches)

2 Large 14" Round Soft Armenian Cracker Meal Hi-Roller Sheet (looks like an extra-large Tortilla)

2 Pkgs Cream Cheese	Mayonnaise
Yellow or Dijon Mustard	Lettuce – chopped
Sliced Red Onion Rings	Bologna, Chopped Ham, sliced Salami
American Cheese Slices	Plastic Wrap

With a spatula or knife, smear cream cheese about 1/4" thick all over the top of the roller sandwich sheet. Add on a layer of Mayonnaise and then the mustard. Place on top a layer of the luncheon meats, then a layer of the American or processed Cheese. Cover with the onion rings and lettuce. Roll into a jelly-roll fashion and encase in plastic wrap and leave to set in the refrigerator for about 1/2 hour. This will allow it to set in the roll so when you cut the sandwich it won't come unrolled. Remove the large sandwich from the plastic wrap and cut in 1-1/2" thick rounds. Serve the pinwheel-rolled sandwiches with chips and condiments and serve cold.
VARIATION: Can include Peanut Butter and Jelly combination, Ham and scrambled eggs with mushrooms for breakfast, Deviled Egg and Tuna combination or any other Hors d' Oeuvres mixture.

One (Serves 4-6) Two (Serves 8-12)

MISC – (Italian Calzone)

Store-Bought Pizza Crust (frozen or fresh)
1 (10.5 oz – 26.5 oz) can Spaghetti or Pizza Sauce of Choice
1 Egg beaten with 2 Tbsp of Water (Egg-Wash) or Olive Oil
Selection of bolded items on grocery list: Sliced Salami, **Ground Pork Sausage, Thin-Sliced Ham, Shredded Mozzarella Cheese, Grated Parmigiano-Reggiano Cheese, shredded Monterey Jack Cheese**
Optional Choices: Sliced Pepperoni, Sliced Black Olives, **Chopped Onions**, Chopped Bell Peppers, **Sliced Button Mushrooms**

Preheat the oven to 500°F. Roll the dough out into two 8" circles or one 12" circle onto a floured surface. Spread on one half of the dough a spaghetti sauce then in layers, choice of meats (ground Pork Sausage, sliced Pepperoni, Salami, thinly sliced Ham, layer of Mozzarella Cheese, layer of grated Parmigiano-Reggiano Cheese, and a layer of Monterey Jack Cheese, top with a sprinkle of sliced black olives, chopped onions, chopped bell peppers, and sliced button mushrooms). **Fold the top half of the pizza dough down** and over the ingredients.

Fill, fold down ↓ ⬭ ← cut

Decided for You Cookbook – 365 Dinners

(continued from Italian Calzone) Fold the edges of the Pizza Dough together and pinch. Cut in half and re-seal the raw edges after that cut, ending up with two large triangle Calzone(s). Place a couple small slashes through the top layer of the dough for steam escape vents. Place the Calzone(s) on a lightly greased baking sheet or sprinkle some cornmeal on a pizza pan. Brush the top with Olive Oil or the egg wash. Reduce the heat and bake at 475°F for 20-25 minutes or until golden brown. Slice the Calzone in half and place in the center of a plate on top of warmed sauce. Garnish with grated cheese.

Pizza/Calzone Crust

MAKE YOUR OWN - (Ingredients not on grocery list)
1 cup warm Water (~110°F)
Stir into the water:

1 tsp Sugar	1 tsp Salt	2 Tbsp Salad Oil or Olive Oil

Sprinkle on top of the warm water 1 Pkg Yeast – wait five minutes
3-1/2 cups sifted All-Purpose Flour

Sift only 2-1/2 cups of the flour and add in the yeast liquid and mix together forming a ball. On a floured bread board, using the heel of your hand, push, punch and roll over for about five minutes (add as much flour as it takes to keep the dough from sticking to your hands, etc) then place it in a lightly greased bowl, cover with plastic wrap and place in a warm spot in the kitchen for ~45 minutes (sit the covered bowl on top of a heating pad turned on low to cut down on rising time). When the dough has doubled in size work, return it to the floured breadboard and add in the other 1/2 cup of flour or by adding enough additional flour as necessary to form a smooth and elastic dough. Dough should no longer be sticky. When smooth, place on a lightly greased baking sheet or pizza pan, then form into desired size. Cover the crust with a towel and let it rest for 15 minutes.

Yields 2 each 8-inch Calzones

Pizza Sauce – MAKE YOUR OWN – see Recipes under **(MISC) - Pizza or Spaghetti Sauce**
MENU WEEK#17

VARIATIONS:

MISC – (Justin's Stromboli)

MAKE YOUR OWN – (Ingredients not on grocery list)
Inside your crust put in only: 1/4 cup each of **sliced Salami, sliced Canadian Bacon, shredded Mozzarella and American Cheese, and sliced Button Mushrooms**. Seal together and bake as directed above. Add over the top, a ladle of warmed spaghetti/pizza sauce and garnish with additional Mozzarella Cheese. Eat with a knife and fork.

MISC – (Tony's Stromboli)

MAKE YOUR OWN – (Ingredients not on grocery list)
Inside your crust put in only: 1/4 cup each of **sliced Ham, Italian Sausage, American and Mozzarella Cheese, smear the top layer with 2 Tbsp Yellow Mustard**. Seal together and bake as directed above. Add over the top, a ladle of warmed spaghetti/pizza sauce and garnish with additional Mozzarella Cheese. Eat with a knife and fork.

MISC – (Italian Cheese Boats)

4 oz slivered (or sliced) Salami or Bologna Luncheon Meat   1/4 tsp Oregano
4 oz shredded Mozzarella Cheese   1/3 cup Mayonnaise
2 (6") French Style Steak Sandwich Rolls, split in half or Italian Baguettes
4 Tomatoes cut in Wedges (for boat sails)
2 – 4 Stuffed Olives per boat (for sail dividers)
4 Wooden Skewers (for boat masts)

Slice the rolls in half and place on a layer of the sliced meat. Mix the mayonnaise and cheese together, spread this on top of the rolls. (If you would like you can remove some of the bread and mound this in the cavity of the bread.) Place on a non-greased baking sheet and broil 500°F for 3-5 minutes until the cheesy mixtures is bubbly.   To serve, slide a tomato wedge down a skewer followed by an olive then another tomato and another olive, etc until you have used all of them. Leave enough space on the end of the skewer available so it can be pushed into the sandwich roll and stands like a mast on a ship.   Serves 4

MENU WEEK#45

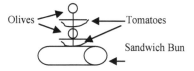

MISC – (Mozzarella Sticks)
Cook frozen Mozzarella sticks per package directions or **MAKE YOUR OWN** see MISC - Fried Cheese

MISC – (Pancakes)

Biscuit Mix or Pancake Flour Mix prepared to package directions (add egg/water) **-OR-**
MAKE YOUR OWN - (Ingredients are not on the grocery list)
Sift all dry ingredients together:
2 cups All-Purpose Flour   2 Tsp Baking Powder
1 tsp Baking Soda sifted   1/2 tsp Salt
2 Large Eggs, lightly beaten   3 Tbsp Sugar
3 cups Buttermilk, or regular milk – can also use a mix of 1/2 Evaporated Milk & 1/2 water
4 Tbsp melted Margarine/Butter + 1 tsp or more for the griddle**. (HINT: Using vegetable oil in waffles or pancakes in place of shortening**. **No extra pan or bowl to melt the shortening and no waiting for the oil to get hot.**

Sift together all your dry ingredients. Heat your griddle **(Test the heat of the griddle by sprinkling a few drops of water on it. If the water sizzles and spatters off the griddle it's hot)** place some margarine on the griddle to melt (my family likes the buttery taste). Using a 4 oz (1/2 cup) ladle; pour on the batter. If you are going to add blueberries, banana slices, strawberries, apple slices w/cinnamon, peaches, pears, coconut, cherries, raisins, chocolate chips, walnuts, pecans, or pineapple sprinkle these over the pool of batter right after it is poured which will help evenly distribute them before turning. Flip the pancake just as the surface bubbles begin to burst. Flipping them after all the bubbles are gone makes a flatter pancake. Cook on both sides and place in a covered, warmed pie plate, or, in a heat-proof plate in a low heat oven – **OR**, in a tortilla warmer to keep hot until the quantity for your meal is ready.   Yields nine or ten 6-inch pancakes. You can also make these in Silver Dollar size or pour inside animal design templates for children. Leftover pancakes can be rewarmed in either a toaster or a microwave.

Serve with Bacon (see recipe PK - Bacon and Eggs). **HINT: Did you know that when camping and you forgot your coffee pot, you can put your ground coffee in a pot and bring it to boil, remove from the heat (campfire or cook stove) pour in a quick dash of cold water and all of the grounds will sink to the bottom of the pot so you can pour out just your coffee. The very last cup from the bottom of the**
(continued next page)

Decided for You Cookbook – 365 Dinners

(continued from Pancakes, etc.) coffee pot has to be poured through a strainer or you get all of the grounds in your cup. Wet coffee grounds make good plant mulch.   Serves 4-5

MENU WEEK#46

Maple Syrup
MAKE YOUR OWN – (Ingredients not on grocery list)

Many times we cook Pancakes and find that we don't have enough Maple Syrup. Here's a solution: **Pour 3-1/2 cups Brown Sugar into 2 cups boiling water. Add 1 tsp Maple Flavoring** (from Spice Section in the store). Stir well, and allow it to stand 24 hours it has a more intense flavor which is preferred, but you can use freshly made in a bind. You can also use Granulated Sugar if you don't have Brown, it will just change the color a little. **– OR-**

Cinnamon Cream Syrup
MAKE YOUR OWN - (Ingredients not on grocery list)

1 cup Sugar   3/4 tsp Ground Cinnamon
1/4 cup Water   1/2 cup Evaporated Milk
1/2 cup Light Corn Syrup

Boil first 4 ingredients for 2 minutes, stirring constantly. Remove and cool 5 minutes then stir in the milk. Serve w/apple pie, ice cream, waffles, and pancakes. Yield 1-2/3 cups.

MISC – (Pizza – English Muffin)

1 can (10.5 oz) Spaghetti Sauce, Marinara or Tomato Sauce with 1/2 tsp dried Oregano
4 – 6 English Muffins, split   1 cup shredded Mozzarella Cheese (about 4 oz)
1 Pkg (4 oz) sliced Salami or Pepperoni   Vegetable Oil
Grated Parmesan Cheese

If muffins are not split, then cut in half. Brush each slice with vegetable oil. Toast them cut sides down in a 10-inch skillet over medium heat or grill, or even a camp stove. Remove from the skillet. Spread the sauce over the toasted sides of the muffin halves. Arrange the salami or pepperoni slices on top of the sauce and top with the Mozzarella Cheese, and sprinkle with the grated Parmesan cheese. You can cover them in a skillet until the cheese melts; if cooking outdoors around 3 to 4 minutes. If indoors place these slices onto a flat pan and broil under the broiler until the cheese melts. See recipe for **MAKE YOUR OWN (BRD) English Muffins.**   4 - 6 Servings

MENU WEEK#19

VARIATION: You can also use a package of canned high-rise (16 oz) biscuits instead of English Muffins to make Pizza. Separate each biscuit into two or three layers. Pat them out and spread evenly, with edges touching, on to a lightly greased 12-pizza pan or baking sheet. Bake 375°F for ~8 minutes or until lightly browned Remove from the oven and cover with sauce, grated cheese of choice, Sprinkle on a Tablespoon of Oregano, then mushrooms, olives, bell peppers, onions and/or sliced meats. Sprinkle on the remaining cheese and bake for another 8-10 minutes of until the cheese has melted.

Decided for You Cookbook – 365 Dinners

MISC – (Pizza – Linguica, Pepperoni, Salami etc)

2 (26.5 oz each) cans of Spaghetti Sauce
Pizza Crust frozen or fresh cook per package directions
Shredded Mozzarella, Parmesan and Monterey Jack Cheeses

Pizza Crust

MAKE YOUR OWN – (Ingredients not on grocery list)
1 cup warm Water (~110°F)
Stir into the water:
1 Pkg Yeast – Sprinkle on top of the warm water; wait five minutes, then add 1 tsp Sugar, 2 Tbsp Salad Oil or Olive Oil, and 1 tsp Salt
Follow this with:
2-1/2 cups sifted All-Purpose Flour, then **add** 1/2 cup sifted All-Purpose Flour, Additional Board Flour as needed

Sift only 2-1/2 cups of the flour and add in the yeast liquid and mix together forming a ball. On a floured bread board, using the heel of your hand, push, punch and roll over for about five minutes (add as much flour as it takes to keep the dough from sticking to your hands, etc) then place it in a lightly greased bowl, cover with plastic wrap and place in a warm spot in the kitchen for ~45 **minutes (sit the covered bowl on top of a heating pad turned on low to cut down on rising time).** When the dough has doubled in size work, return it to the floured breadboard and add in another 1/2 cup of flour or by adding enough additional flour as necessary to form a smooth and elastic dough. Dough should no longer be sticky. When smooth, place on a lightly greased baking sheet or pizza pan; then form into desired pizza pie round size. Cover the crust with a towel and let it rest for 15 minutes. Cover with sauce, and toppings of choice and bake on middle rack at 425°F for 25 minutes or until the crust is brown and the cheeses are melted. Serve hot. (Yields 2 each 12-inch Crusts) **NOTE: You can place all of these ingredients on open-faced French Bread Sandwich Rolls and broil until bubbly – "A Fast and Great impromptu Pizza".** The following PIZZA TOPPINGS WHICH ARE **BOLDED** ARE ON THE GROCERY LIST – **Sliced Salami, Sliced Boiled Ham, Ground Pork Sausage, Linguica, Pepperoni,** Canadian Bacon, Shrimp, cooked Chicken, chopped Bell Peppers, sliced Mushrooms, sliced Olives, drained canned Artichoke Hearts, Pineapple chunks. Bake 425°F for 20 – 30 minutes or until bottom of crust is browned.

Pizza Sauce

MAKE YOUR OWN - (Ingredients not on grocery list)

1 can (16 oz) Tomato Sauce or 1 Large (20 oz) can chopped Tomatoes
1 chopped Onion
3 to 4 Basil Leaves
Optional: Parmesan, Mozzarella Cheese

1 clove Garlic, peeled and minced
1 tsp Oregano
Pinch of Salt and Pepper
3 Tbsp Olive oil for Sauté

In a 2-Quart saucepot, add in the olive oil over a medium high flame brown your onion and garlic, add in the tomatoes, oregano, basil, salt and pepper and bring to a bubbling. Reduce the heat and simmer for 15 – 30 minutes, stirring often until thick. Spoon or ladle the sauce on to the top of your crust and spread out evenly, leaving a 1/2-inch border along the edges of the dough. (Extra sauce can be kept in the refrigerator in an airtight container up to one week). Sprinkle on 1/4 - 1/2 cup each of shredded Mozzarella Cheese, grated Parmesan (Parmigiano-Reggiano) Cheese and/or Jack or Provolone Cheese (can be store-bought sauce, if desired).

Serves 4-8
MENU WEEK#1

MISC – (Pizza – Mini Shrimp)

2 cans store-bought Refrigerator Biscuits
1 (10.5 oz) jar or can Spaghetti or Marinara Sauce
Shredded Cheddar and Mozzarella Cheese
1 cup chopped cooked Shrimp (can be canned, if drained)

Roll a biscuit or pat it flat, spread on the sauce and top with the cheeses. Add to the top the shrimp. (If desired, can add chopped green onion, or chopped olives for color). Place these on a baking sheet and bake at 375°F for 10-15 minutes or until the crust is browned underneath.   Serves 6-9
MENU WEEK#3

MISC – (Pizza – Versatile Style)

1 (26.5 oz) can of Spaghetti Sauce –OR- **MAKE YOUR OWN**
1 large Pizza Crust frozen or fresh
Toppings on grocery list, are bolded: 2/3 cups of Julienne-cut Cooked **Ham** + crisp cooked **Bacon** + 6 – 8 cooked, **scrambled Eggs** + with **Onions**, and **Mushrooms**. Choices of Cheese: 1/4 - 1/2 cup each of shredded **Mozzarella Cheese**, grated **Parmesan**(Parmigiano -Reggiano) **Cheese** and/or Jack or Provolone Cheese

OTHER VERSATILE TOPPINGS CHOICES - (Ingredients not on grocery list)
Spread in layers on top of sauce: Drained Tuna or cooked shredded Chicken + 4-6 sliced Hard-boiled eggs + Olives. –OR-

Mushrooms, Bell Peppers, Onions, Tomatoes, Olives, Pineapple (drained chunks), chopped Artichoke Hearts creamy garlic salad dressing.

<u>White Pizza with Spinach</u>: Using a Roasted Garlic (see PAS – Raviolis – Cheese with Roasted Garlic and Parmesan Sauce). Smash the roasted garlic into 1 Tablespoon of Extra-Virgin Olive Oil. Then spread this over a pizza crust. Mix together 1-1/2 cups Ricotta Cheese with 1 (10 oz) package of frozen chopped Spinach (thawed and squeezed dry in paper toweling). Spread this creamed mixture over the crust and top with 2-1/2 cups of grated Mozzarella and 1 cup shredded Parmesan Cheese. Bake per below crust directions.

Pizza Sauce
MAKE YOUR OWN - (Ingredients not on grocery list)

1 can (15 oz) Tomato Sauce or 1 Large (20 oz) can chopped Tomatoes	1 clove Garlic, peeled and minced
1 chopped Onion	1 tsp Oregano
3 to 4 Basil Leaves	Pinch of Salt and Pepper
	3 Tbsp Olive Oil for Sauté

Optional: 1/4 to 1/2 cup Parmesan Cheese cooked in sauce

In a 2-Quart saucepot, add in the olive oil over a medium high flame brown your onion and garlic, add in the tomatoes, oregano, basil, salt and pepper and bring to a bubbling. Reduce the heat and simmer for 15 – 30 minutes, stirring often until thick. Spoon or ladle the sauce on to the top of your crust and spread out evenly, leaving a 1/2-inch border along the edges of the dough. (Extra sauce can be kept in the refrigerator in an airtight container up to one week). **(continued next page)**

Decided for You Cookbook – 365 Dinners

Pizza Crust
MAKE YOUR OWN – (Ingredients not on grocery list)
1 cup warm Water (~110°F)
Stir into the water:

1 tsp Sugar	1 tsp Salt

2 Tbsp Salad Oil or Olive Oil
Sprinkle in 1 Pkg Yeast on top of the warm water; wait five minutes
Add in 3-1/2 cups sifted All-Purpose Flour as follows

Sift only 2-1/2 cups of the flour and add in the yeast liquid and mix together forming a ball. On a floured bread board, using the heel of your hand, push, punch and roll over for about five minutes (add as much flour as it takes to keep the dough from sticking to your hands, etc) then place it in a lightly greased bowl, cover with plastic wrap and place in a warm spot in the kitchen for ~45 minutes (sit the covered bowl on top of a heating pad turned on low to cut down on rising time). When the dough has doubled in size work, return it to the floured bread board and add in the other 1/2 cup of flour or by adding enough additional flour as necessary to form a smooth and elastic dough. Dough should no longer be sticky. Cover the crust with a towel and let it rest for 15 minutes. When smooth and elastic, place on a lightly greased baking sheet or pizza pan; then form into desired pizza pie round size. **Spread layers on top of sauce and crust:** 2/3 cups of Julienne-cut Cooked Ham + crisp bacon + 6 – 8 cooked, scrambled Eggs + Onions, Mushrooms. Top with shredded Mozzarella and Parmesan Cheeses and bake on middle rack at 425°F for 25 minutes or until the crust is brown and the cheeses are melted. Serve hot. Yields (2) 12-inch Crusts
MENU WEEK#38

Pizza Crust – Cheese Stuffed
After making your pizza crust, or you can use defrosted, frozen style. Approximately 1-1/2 inches in from the edge of the crust, sprinkle evenly 1 cup of grated cheese of choice. Fold the outer 2 inches of the crust over the cheese toward the center and press down to seal in place. Add on your sauce and toppings per choice and cook per baking directions. (Extra Recipe)

MISC – (Poor Boy Sandwiches)

French Bread or 4 Steak Sandwich Rolls
Mayonnaise or Dijon Mustard, your choice to spread on Rolls
Luncheon Meats – Turkey, Bologna, Salami, Roast Beef, Ham etc
Sliced Cheeses of Choice: American, Cheddar, **-OR -** Chipotle, Monterey Jack, Swiss
Lettuce (cut into thin slices)
Sliced Tomatoes
Green Bell Peppers slices (Optional: these have an overpowering flavor)
Sliced Pickles (sweet, bread and buttered, dill, dill/sweet)
Sliced Red Onion Rings
Sliced Jalapeno Chiles (Optional: these have an overpowering flavor)
Salt & Pepper to taste
Tart Italian Salad Dressing (use in a shaker and sprinkle over completed stack of ingredients before placing on top piece of bread)

Spread condiment of choice on Roll slices. Layer on the ingredients, salt and pepper to taste and sprinkle on the Italian Dressing and serve.

Serves 4
MENU WEEK#27

Decided for You Cookbook – 365 Dinners

MISC – (Shake and Bake Coating for Meat)

1 cup Flour
1 tsp Pepper
Milk or Water
2 tsp Salt

1 tsp each Thyme, Oregano, Basil
1/2 cup Cracker Meal/Breadcrumbs or
    crushed Saltine Crackers

Combine the dry ingredients, stirring to mix. Use 1/2 of the mixture for 3 pounds of Chicken or boneless Pork Chops. Moisten the meat in the milk or water before you coat with the dry ingredients. Bake the meat at 350°F in a greased baking dish for 45 minutes to one hour. **VARIATION/HINT: Dip the meat in a Bar-B-Q Sauce before coating in the dry ingredients. Store balance of the dry ingredients in a tightly covered container.**

MENU WEEK #33

MORE SPACE FOR YOUR IDEAS:

Decided for You Cookbook – 365 Dinners

Author's Special Thoughts

"Dishwashing Cooking"

Have you heard about **Dishwasher Cooking. Weird but it Works.** Salmon can be poached, vegetables can be cooked in the dishwasher (i.e., broccoli, cauliflower or any vegetable that takes well to steaming). **Sweet Carrots with Butter:** Mix together and place ingredients into a large cooking bag or make a foil packet by crimping and folding it together making it air tight: 1 pound of thinly sliced carrots cut either in rounds or matchstick size, along with 2 Tbsp of Butter cut into small pieces. Sprinkle carrots with 2 Tbsp Brown Sugar and salt and pepper to taste. Seal and place the bag on the top rack with your dish-washer set on the hottest setting (Sanitize cycle is 150 degrees –avoid cool temperatures) and start your wash cycle that can include yesterday's dirty dishes and soap which is not a deterrent with airtight enclosures.   Transfer the carrots back into a bowl and toss again (4-6 servings).

How about

Cooking Dinner While on a Long "4-6 Hour Automobile Trip"

2-1/2 Pounds Beef Chuck Roast
2 medium quartered Onions
1 Oven Cooking Bag

3 or 5 Carrots, cleaned and cut into 1" coins
Salt ad Pepper
Garlic Powder

Sprinkle roast generously with garlic powder, salt and pepper. Place it inside the cooking bag. Add in the carrots and onions on top of the meat and pour in 1 cup of water. Secure the bag so it is tied tightly with a metal closer provided with the bag. Wedge the bag above the passenger-side exhaust manifold of a rear-wheeled car. The roast will be cooking all during your trip and ready to eat when you arrive at your destination.

COMPLIMENTARY DRINKS ON ME

Ice Cream Soda - Chocolate
Blend 2 Tbsp Chocolate Syrup with 2 Tbsp Milk in a tall glass. Add a scoop of Chocolate Ice Cream and fill with carbonated water.

Ice Cream Soda - Pineapple
Blend 2 Tbsp crushed Pineapple with 1 Tbsp Sugar in a tall glass. Add in a scoop of ice cream and fill with carbonated water.

Ice Cream Soda - Strawberry
1 cup cold Milk, 2 Tbsp Strawberry Preserves, add in 1 scoop Strawberry ice cream and fill with carbonated water.

Lemonade
1 cup Sugar   7 cups Water
1 cup Lemon Juice (5-6 Lemons)
Combine the sugar and 1 cup water in a saucepan. Simmer 5 minutes, or until the sugar is dissolved. Cool. Add in the remaining water and lemon juice. Sweeten to taste with additional sugar. Pour over ice. Yields 8 cups

Limeade
3/4 cup Sugar   6 cups Water
1 cup Lime Juice (6-8 Limes)
Follow directions from the Lemonade recipe

Orangeade
3/4 cup Sugar   4 cups Water
3 cups Orange Juice   1/3 cup Lemon Juice
Follow directions from the Lemonade recipe

Orange Julie's
Place ice cubes into a blender until 1/2 full, dump these into an alternate bowl. In the empty blender, place in 1/2 can frozen concentrated Orange Juice. Add in 2 cups Milk and 1 tsp Sugar. Lightly mix these items together. Add three or four ice cubes at a time, then blend until ice cubes are finely crushed and the Julie's are thick, but pourable. Pour into chilled Champagne Glasses and top with a piece of mint inside or hang orange slices on the outside of the glass. **GREAT** ON A HOT SUMMER DAY!

Punch - Big Red
2-3 small cans of crushed Pineapple   1 large can (46 oz) Pineapple Juice
2 large cans (46 oz ea) of Red Punch or diluted concentrate
Float Ice Ring made of same ingredients in a punch bowl.

Punch - Wedding Ring
1 can sweetened Condensed Milk   1 large frozen Orange Juice
1 large frozen Pineapple Juice   2 Liter Bottle of 7 Up
Mix together. Should float a 1/2 gallon of Orange Sherbet for extra coldness.

Decided for You Cookbook – 365 Dinners

PK – (Bacon and Cheese Frittata)

6 Eggs	1 cup Milk
1 Green Onion, minced	2 Tbsp Butter or Margarine, melted
1/2 tsp Salt	1/8 tsp Pepper
14 oz Pkg shredded Cheddar Cheese	Crumbled cooked Bacon can be fresh or canned

Preheat oven to 400°F, grease a 10-1/2 round, 3" deep, pan or a 9 x 9 baking pan. In a medium bowl with a wire whisk or hand beater, beat the eggs, milk, green onion, butter or margarine, salt and pepper until well blended; pour this mixture into baking pan. Sprinkle the cheese and bacon evenly over the top and Bake 20 minutes or until set and lightly brown.

Makes 4 Servings
MENU WEEK#41

OPTIONAL: Great to mix in some fried rice and green bell peppers for variation

PK – (Bacon and Eggs)

Bacon

1 Pound of Bacon can be cooked in the following ways and drained on paper toweling under a covered, warm plate or dish: **1)** In a cold skillet and place one layer of bacon and cook on both sides, drain on paper toweling under a lid to keep warm; save the drippings in a clean sealable jar for gravies or other recipes. Cook another layer until enough has been completed. **–OR- 2)** Place entire pound of bacon on a broiler pan and place on the middle rack of oven set to Bake at (400°F) until slices begin to separate (approximately 10 minutes), then re-spread the bacon out in one layer on the pan REDUCE THE HEAT TO 325°F to continue to bake until crisp, usually total time of 20-30 minutes. Watch these carefully as they will brown quickly after they have been separated and the fats rendered out of the bacon. **–OR- 3)** You can cook the bacon on a broiler pan in one layer at (Broil 500°F) and brown on both sides, about 10 minutes. **HINT:** If you are **cooking Salt Pork with this instead of Bacon, you should slice and then parboil the pork in boiling water for 3 minutes. Drain on paper toweling, slice and then fry in hot oil until brown. Dipping bacon in water before cooking will help it to cook flat instead of curled. If you are using frozen bacon, heat a metal spatula to assist in separating it easier or roll it into a tube and secure with a rubber band before freezing.**

MENU WEEK#46

Eggs

Fried – The secret of a good fried egg is to cook it slowly on medium heat. Pan should be greased with oil or butter and then break your egg close to the pan. To turn eggs over, use a pancake turner or wide spatula.

Scrambled – Mix together 6 eggs, 1/4 cup Milk, salt and pepper to taste and turn out onto a greased, with butter or oil, griddle or skillet and stir as soon as the bubbles stop popping. **HINT: Can microwave several eggs quickly by placing the individual eggs into a buttered muffin pan (3-4 minutes). Be sure to puncture yolks or scramble with a little milk.**

French Toast (see MISC – French Toast

Hard Boiled – Place eggs in a saucepan and cover with water 2 inches above the eggs, **add 1 tsp salt so the shell won't crack**, and boil for 10 minutes. Drain off the hot water and run cold water over the eggs for about 3-4 minutes. **HINT: Cooling the eggs quickly** will make them easier to peel and will **prevent any darkening around the egg yolks**. Run under faucet until water is cold, drain the water leaving just the eggs and shake and rotate the pan around in a circle, this circular **movement will crack all of the shells at one time**). To determine whether an egg is hard-boiled, spin it. If it spins, it is hard-boiled, if it wobbles and won't spin, it is raw.

Decided for You Cookbook – 365 Dinners

<u>Poached Eggs</u> - A Tbsp of **Vinegar added** to the poaching water for eggs will help set the whites so they will not spread. Remove the egg from the shell and place it on top of a saucer. With a spoon make a **whirlpool in the pan with the vinegar water**, then slide in the egg off of a saucer and cook to your liking – **OR** – use cleaned Tuna cans for the perfect mold for poaching eggs.

<u>REMINDERS:</u> **EGG YOLK STORAGE** – <u>You can place leftover egg yolks in a sealed container and use later if you</u> **cover them with 2 Tbsp of water on their top** <u>and store in the refrigerator.</u> **EGGS FOR A LARGE CROWD COOKING** – <u>For a large crowd,</u> **cook eggs in buttered muffin tins in the oven.** –OR– <u>mix all the eggs in a large greased pan. Place these in a 300°F oven and stir occasionally after the cooking process begins. Be sure and keep a close eye on these. Breadcrumbs can be added for more volume.</u> **SEPARATING YOLKS/WHITES** – <u>If when separating eggs, a bit of yolk gets into the egg whites, it can be easily lifted out with a piece of the</u> **egg shell.** <u>Eggs will also separate easier if they are cold.</u> **CLEANING UP DROPPED EGGS** – <u>When you drop an egg, the easiest way to clean it up off the surface,</u> **pour a large quantity of salt on it** <u>and let it set for awhile. Using a pancake turner you can slip it under all of the broken egg at one time to remove it.</u> **STIFFER EGG WHITES (MERINGUE)** – <u>To stiffen egg whites,</u> **add 1 tsp of Cream of Tartar to each cup** <u>(~7 egg whites).</u> **Volume will be added** <u>to your egg whites if they are</u> **at room temperature** <u>before beating.</u> **EGG STORAGE** - <u>Store eggs</u> **in the original carton.** <u>If you do transfer to refrigerator door, store these with the large end up and covered which will prevent the eggs from absorbing moisture causing them to spatter/pop grease when cooking.</u> **PURCHASING EGGS** - <u>If there is only a few cents difference between Large and Extra Large Eggs,</u> **buy the smaller size** <u>for a better value. By the way there is "no" difference inside a Brown or White-shelled Egg.</u> **OMITTING AN EGG IN A RECIPE** - <u>If omitting,</u> **increase the liquid by 3-4 Tablespoons** <u>for each egg. It is a risky switch, however, especially in a delicately balance cake or cookie recipe.</u> **AGE OF AN EGG** – <u>Determining age by</u> **place it in the bottom of a bowl of cold water.** <u>If it lays on its side, it is fresh. If it stands at an angle, it is at least three days old, and if it standing on its end it is ten days old.</u> **CUTTING UP EGGS EASIER** – <u>Use a potato masher to cut up eggs for deviling or egg salad.</u> **SLICING MADE EASIER** – <u>Wet your knife before each cutting in half will prevent the egg yolks from crumbling.</u>

Author's Special Thoughts

Breakfast at the Beach/Mountains or Desert

Take with you either a metal shelf/rack from your self-cleaning oven or a Barbecue Top Grill. You'll need Barbecue Briquettes and (a few small pieces of wood, if desired and wood burning is allowed) of course, a liquid Barbecue starter with matches. Dig a 1 to 1-1/2 foot hole in the sand/dirt (Ecologically-Minded - Line the bottom of the hole with aluminum foil so you can retract the leftover coals and dispose of them easily). Place on the bottom of the hole, on top of the foil, your wood, briquettes and ignite.

When the flames have died down, cooking in a cast iron skillet, fry your bacon (which greases your pan, saves you from carrying along). Then cook the eggs of choice. And, with a thermos of Hot Chocolate and/or coffee (which also can be cooked there if you do not want to carry the hot liquids with you). **[HINT: To freshen, and sweeten a thermos, put in 1 tsp Baking Soda and fill with warm water and soak 10 minutes. Rinse well before using.]** See **VEG (Potatoes – Mud Cooked Baked Potatoes)** for interesting experiment for the children. (continued next page)

Hot Cocoa Mix

2 cups Coffee Powdered Creamer   1 cup granulated Sugar
1/4 cup Cocoa   1/2 cup non-fat powdered Milk

Combine all ingredients and store in an airtight container. Add 2 Tbsp of mix to 1 cup of hot water for a quick cup of hot chocolate. Yields 34 servings -AND -

You can butter bread on one side and place it in one layer on a shallow baking sheet and tilt this pan up against a stick facing the flames to make toast. (In a large saltshaker you can also mix equal amounts of sugar and cinnamon to sprinkle onto one side of the buttered toast for quick Cinnamon Toast).

Cinnamon Toast

Buttered and sprinkle bread with equal amounts of sugar and cinnamon then you can prop the pan up on its side and toast with your fire heat – this toast can also broiled at home on top of a broiling pan –OR- another way is (Fried Bread Toast)

Daddy's Special

Special Quesadilla – Spread a tortilla with Peanut Butter. Top with a layer of American Cheese and place on a buttered grill or skillet.   When it begins to melt fold in half and brown on both sides.

Fried Bread Toast

Butter one side of the bread, and fry that buttered side down in a hot skillet.

Other Camping Staples

PK - Link Sausage, Ham, PK - Bacon and Eggs, Biscuits and Gravy, Orange Juice and MISC - French Toast

When breakfast is over, cover the hot coals with about 6 – 12 inches (depending on the amount of coals remaining) of clean sand/dirt. **This is a great place for small children to take a warm blanket and be seated on the top of this heated spot to keep warm while the weather warms up for them to play in the water at the beach/mountains/ desert. The top of the sand and/or dirt area should stay warm for another 2-3 hours, or longer.**

If you didn't pre-spray your grill, spread out the already "read" morning newspaper. Place it on top of that used newspaper, sprinkle the moist top of the grill with some scouring cleanser or dry detergent and fold the newspaper around the grill which will soften any cooking residue and make for an easier clean up. If you are using your oven rack then when you return home you can put it in place and turn on the self-cleaning feature.   All other utensils can be dumped into a large sealed container of soapy water and by the time you get home, the dishes are washed. Rinse, and let them air-dry.

AND NOW, "TAKE A NAP".

Decided for You Cookbook – 365 Dinners

PK – (Chile Verde)

3 pound boneless Pork Roast
1/2 chopped Onion (1/4 cup)
Vegetable Oil for frying

2 large cans diced Green Chiles not Jalapenos
Salt and Pepper to taste

Cook the pork roast and one can of diced Green Chiles in a Crock pot, on low all day or until Roast is fork tender.   **-OR –** at 325°F covered in the oven for 3 or 4 hours until you can tear apart with a fork. Remove roast and with a fork, pull the roast into small pieces. Heat oil in a skillet and brown the onion. Add the other can of green Chiles and return the pork to the skillet, cover and simmer for an additional 30 minutes. Serve with Spanish Rice, and Refried Beans.

Serves 4-6
MENU WEEK#6

PK – (Chorizo Casserole)

Cook together and drain fats:
1/2 pound Chorizo (remove from casing)
Chopped Onions

1/2 pound Ground Beef

Add in layers to a casserole dish:
1 can Refried Beans
1 can diced Green Chiles
2 cups grated Longhorn Cheddar Cheese

The cooked Chorizo, Beef mixture
1 cup grated Monterey Jack Cheese

Bake this casserole at 400°F for 30 minutes. Remove from the oven, and
Sprinkle on top of casserole:
1 cup Avocado – smashed
1 cup Sour Cream

Crushed Tortilla Chips
Chopped Green Onions

Topped with 1 can drained, sliced or chopped Black Olives

Serves 6-8
MENU WEEK#20

PK – (Glazed Smoked Sausage - Kielbasa)

1/4 cup packed Brown Sugar
1 Pound cooked smoked Kielbasa Sausage

2 Tbsp Cider Vinegar
1/4 cup Bar-B-Q Sauce

Combine the barbecue sauce, sugar and vinegar. Score the outside of the sausage diagonally with a knife (this will prevent the skin from exploding) . Broil 500°F 4 inches from the heat for 10-15 minutes turning over once. Brush glaze on outside as needed to enhance the flavor and to prevent burning.

Serves 4
MENU WEEK #40

PK – (Ham and Asparagus Rolls)

8 thin slices fully cook Ham (can be Boiled
1 Pkg (10 oz) frozen Asparagus Spears
Toothpicks (Optional)

Ham Luncheon Meat) 1 can (10-3/4 oz) condensed
Cream of Shrimp Soup
1/4 cup Dry White Wine or water

Heat the oven to 350°F. Cook the asparagus spears as directed on the package. Wrap each ham slice around 2 or 3 asparagus spears. (Optional: can pin together with Toothpicks). Place these rolls in a non-greased baking dish. Mix the soup and the wine together and pour over the Ham Rolls. Bake uncovered until bubbly 20–25 minutes.

Serves 4
MENU WEEK#34

PK – (Ham and Cheese Scallop with Potatoes and Carrots)

2 or 3 cups of diced leftover Ham or 1 (12 oz) can Luncheon Meat cut into 1" cubes is also good
1 cup Carrot coins (cut carrots in rounds 1/4" thick)

1-1/2 lbs cubed Potatoes	3 Tbsp Margarine/Butter
3 Tbsp finely chopped Parsley	3 Tbsp Flour
1/2 tsp Salt	Dash of Pepper
Milk and boiling liquid totaling 1-1/2 cups	1 cup shredded Cheddar Cheese

TOPPING: 2 Tbsp Margarine/Butter, melted   1/2 cup coarse Breadcrumbs

Cook potatoes and carrots together in a small amount of salted water until tender. Drain, saving combination of liquids; set aside. In a saucepan melt the butter, stir in the parsley, flour, salt and pepper to form a smooth paste. Remove the sauce from the heat and gradually add the 1-1/2 cup of vegetable liquid/milk while stirring constantly. Return sauce to the heat and warm again adding in the cheese until sauce is thickened. In a 1-1/2 Quart Baking Dish, with oven set at 350°F, add the Ham luncheon meat to the potatoes and carrots and pour the sauce over the top. Melt the margarine and pour over top. Sprinkle on the breadcrumbs on the top; mix lightly and sprinkle extra cheese on top, if desired. Bake 25 – 30 minutes   Serves 4-6
MENU WEEK#14

PK – (Ham and Cheese with Asparagus Casserole

3 or 4 cups cubed Cooked Ham	4 Tbsp Margarine/Butter	1 tsp Paprika
1/8 tsp Tarragon	1/2 tsp Salt	1/4 tsp Garlic Salt
3 cups Milk	2 cups grated Cheddar Cheese	Pepper to taste
2 – 10 oz pkgs frozen Asparagus, cut	1 Onion, peeled and minced	1 Tbsp All-Purpose Flour
1/2 Pkg dry Poultry Seasoned Stuffing Mix or Herb Seasoned		

Cook the asparagus per package directions; drain. Mix the stuffing mix per package directions and spoon into a buttered 9 x 13 casserole dish. Layer in the ham and asparagus. Sauté onion until tender in 2 Tbsp butter, blend in the seasoning and the flour. Add the milk slowly; heat, stirring constantly to avoid lumps until thickened. Stir in the cheese until melted. Add this sauce over the layered ham and asparagus, repeating layers until all has been used. Stop with the last layer of stuffing mix and dot top of casserole with butter and bake in 375°F for 45 minutes or until sauce is bubbly and top is browned.   Serves 6
MENU WEEK#21

PK – (Ham and Fettuccine Noodles with Peas)

2 cups Julienne-cut cooked Ham (cuts are short and lengthwise)
1 Pkg (10 oz) frozen Green Peas (or chopped Broccoli, partially thawed)

1 (12 oz) Pkg Fettuccini Noodles	6 Tbsp Butter or Margarine
1 small Onion, chopped (1/4 cup)	2 – 3 Tbsp All-Purpose Flour
1 cup Heavy Whipping Cream	Salt and Pepper to taste
1/2 cup grated Parmesan Cheese	

Cook the fettuccini in boiling water, following the label directions, or to just barely tender and drained but kept warm. Heat the butter in a large skillet; sauté the onion in the butter until its tender and clear. Stir in the flour until dissolved and smooth, gradually add in the cream. Add in the ham and the defrosted vegetable and cook for about three minutes and as the sauce begins to thicken, keep stirring. Bring to a medium boil. Add salt and pepper to the noodles to taste, stir the noodles back into the sauce in the pan; making sure all pasta has been covered with the sauce. Pour all these ingredients onto a large warmed serving platter, sprinkle on the fresh grated Parmesan cheese and toss lightly. Serve immediately.   Serves 4-6
MENU WEEK #16

Decided for You Cookbook – 365 Dinners

PK – (Ham and Green Bean Potato Bake Casserole)

8 medium Potatoes, peeled and cubed
1/4 cup finely chopped Onion
1 (11 oz) can Cheddar Cheese Soup
3/4 cup Milk
2 Tbsp Butter or Margarine, melted
1 cup soft Breadcrumbs (1-1/2 slices of bread, crumbed with a fork)

3 cups cubed Fully Cooked Ham
2 Tbsp snipped Parsley
1 (10-3/4 oz) can Cream of Celery Soup
1 (9 oz) Pkg frozen cut Green Beans, thawed

In a greased 9 x 13" baking dish, layer half of the potatoes and half of the ham; sprinkle with the onion and parsley. Top with the remaining potato cubes and ham. Mix the soups with the milk and 1/4 tsp pepper and pour this over the ham and potato casserole. Cover; bake at 350°F for one hour. Remove from the oven and melt the butter in a saucepan. Mix in the Breadcrumbs absorbing the butter. Top the casserole with the green beans. Sprinkle the buttered Breadcrumbs* on top of the green beans and return casserole to the oven for an additional 25 minutes more, or until crumbs are nice and brown.

*Breadcrumbs can be separated easier by using a fork to spread.

Serves 6-8
MENU WEEK#22

PK – (Ham and Leek Quiche)

2 Leeks* or 5 Green Onions cut up (1 cup)
1/4 pound (1 cup) cooked diced Ham
1/2 cup grated Monterey Jack Cheese
1 unbaked Pie Shell (frozen, can be defrosted)
1 Large Onion, sliced thinly (not needed if using onions already)

2-3 Tbsp Margarine
4 Eggs, slightly beaten
1 cup Milk
1/8 tsp Nutmeg

1/2 tsp Salt
1/8 tsp Fresh Ground Pepper
1 Tbsp All-Purpose Flour

In a large skillet sauté the chopped leeks and onion in the melted margarine until tender. Over low heat stir in the flour, salt, nutmeg and pepper. Gradually stir in the milk and cook until thickens and begins to boil. Remove from the heat. Crack the eggs into a small bowl and beat with a fork. Remove some of the sauce mixture and stir into the beaten eggs and mix. **(If you add the eggs into all your hot mixture they will scramble and you don't want that to happen).** Return this egg and milk mixture to your sauce and stir in. Stir in the chopped ham and the cheese, then pour all ingredients into your pastry shell. Bake in a preheated 400°F oven for 30 minutes or until a knife can be inserted into the center of the pie and it comes out clean.

Serves 4
MENU WEEK#32

*HINT: <u>CLEANING LEEKS - Cut the stringy root ends off, cut off about 1/2 of the green stems. Slit lengthwise several times, rinse under cold water to remove any garden dirt or sand. Pat dry and slice into small cuts.</u>

PK – (Ham and Noodles)

(Easy recipe for leftovers, GREAT for Outdoor Camping Meal)
2 fresh Ham Steaks chopped into small pieces and cooked (1 - 2 cups) or leftover Ham
1 (12 oz) Pkg Flat Egg Noodles
Salt and Pepper to taste
1/4 to 1/2 can Evaporated Milk

2-3 Tbsp All-Purpose Flour
1/4 lb Butter or Margarine

Cut up the Ham Steaks. Brown in a skillet (Or, if using precooked leftovers, boil meat with the noodles during the last three minutes of the boiling time to reheat). Boil the noodles per package direction and drain. Drain the noodles in a colander. Salt and pepper to taste. Place noodles and ham pieces into a warmed serving dish. Melt the butter in a saucepan and add in 2-3 Tbsp of flour and stir until all the lumps are blended. Add in the 1/4 to 1/2 can of evaporated milk. Stir until the sauce has thickened. Pour sauce over the noodles and stir together. Serve immediately.

Servings 4-6
MENU WEEK#9

Decided for You Cookbook – 365 Dinners

PK – (Ham and Swiss Cheese Sandwiches)

8 Slices of Boiled Ham Luncheon Meat, or Leftover Ham
8 Slices of Swiss Cheese
4 Steak Sandwich French Rolls, split open
Mayonnaise

Spread mayonnaise on each of the Steak Sandwich Rolls. Place the open-faced rolls on a broiling pan or baking sheet. Put ham on top 1/2 of the rolls, followed on top with a layer of Swiss Cheese. On the other 1/2 of the French Roll place another slice of Swiss Cheese. Turn on the Broiler Unit in your oven on at (500°F) and place pan on the top rack under the Broiler. Cook 3-4 minutes till bubbly, put the sandwich sides together and serve warm with chips or other items of choice.   Serves 4-6

MENU WEEK#2

Note: Left-over Ham Ideas: 1) Pan fried with Eggs, 2) Cover with a toasted, English Muffin with a pan fried, thick slice of Ham, with a poached Egg and a Hollandaise Sauce, 3) Dip a Ham and Cheese Sandwich into a French Toast Batter and grill for a "Monte Cristo" Sandwich, 4) Add chunks of Ham to Potato Salad, 5) add Ham to scalloped Potato Casserole, and 6) Add Ham and croutons to Split Pea Soup.

PORK – MICROWAVE INFORMATION:

HINT: To assure that the meat browns, place ingredients in a browning pan or place a pan inside a large brown shopping bag. Fold the bag's opening edge back underneath container, so fats won't escape. Be sure bag doesn't touch ceiling of Microwave Oven might spark unit (check often)

    Bacon = 3/4 to 1 min/slice (1 Lb = 15 to 17 min)
    Canadian Bacon 2 slices = 1-1/4 min Arrange in a single layer
    Ground Pork Sausage 1/2 Lb = 4 Patties 1-1/2 to 2-1/2 min
    Ham Slices – 18 to 27 min/Lb - Let stand 5 minutes before cutting
    Link Sausage - 1/2 to 3/4 min/Link - Arrange in a single layer.
    Pork Chops - (2 ea) 14 – 18 min - Brush w/Bar-B-Q Sauce
    Roast - 15 – 19 min/Lb - Add 1/2 cup Water
    Spare Ribs – 25 to 30 min/Lb - Add 2/3 cups Water turn over at 1/2 time

VERY SPECIAL NOTE AREA:

PK – (Ham – Baked or Canned)

1 Baked Spiral or 5 Pound Canned Ham
Cheese Garlic Dropped Biscuits
1-1/2 cups grated Cheddar Cheese
Garlic Salt

The cooking times for this item have been lessened over the years. The spiral hams are now pre-cooked, pre-cut and only need reheating. For the convenience of the working mother, use one of these or a canned ham, reheated per package directions.

Ham Sweet and Hot Sauce – Side Dish

1 (20 oz) can Crushed Pineapple	1 (10 oz) jar Apricot All Fruit Preserves
2 Tbsp Chinese Dry Mustard	1/2 cup Horseradish
1 tsp Black Pepper	1 Tbsp Brown Sugar

Combine all ingredients and warm, serving with ham and hot biscuits.   Serves 6-8

BRD – (Biscuits – Cheese Garlic Dropped)

Blend together **2 cups Biscuit Mix** with **2/3 cup Milk**. Mix in **1-1/2 cups grated Cheddar Cheese**. Drop dough in 12 equal mounds with their edges barely touching onto a buttered large baking sheet. Bake 425°F in middle of oven until golden, 10 to 15 minutes, or until tops are browned. When removing from the oven sprinkle tops with Garlic Salt and serve – **OR-** Mix together 1/4 cup Margarine/ Butter melted, and 1/4 tsp Garlic Powder then brush over the warmed biscuits before serving.

MENU WEEK#2

Baked, Smoked Ham – Fresh

MAKE YOUR OWN – (Ingredients not on grocery list)

1 Smoked Ham	2 slices Onion	1 stalk Celery; diced
2 – 6 Carrots, peeled and sliced	1 Bay Leaf	1 tsp Thyme
1 cup Sugar, brown or substitute Molasses	Whole Cloves	1 cup Vinegar

Cook the celery, bay leaf, thyme, sugar and the vinegar to a rolling boil and set aside. Cut the Heavy skin off the outside of the ham and place in a baking dish. Pour the mixture over the ham and arrange the carrots, and the onions along side of the ham. Score (cut deep gashes in a square design) along the sides of the ham. Break toothpicks in half and push one through the center of a clove. Then push that toothpick into the meat leaving the clove exposed in the center of each scored square. (Extra Recipe)

Bake uncovered at the following:
3-4 Pounds 325°F 40-45 minutes per Pound – Ham Butt
5-7 Pounds 325°F 22-25 minutes per Pound – Half of a Ham
6-8 Pounds 325°F 25-27 minutes per Pound – Half of a Ham
10-14 Pounds 325°F 18-20 minutes per Pound - Whole Ham
14-16 Pounds 325°F 16-18 minutes per Pound – Whole Ham
All of the above should reach an internal thermometer temperature 150-155°F

Ham Glaze Alternates – Optional – (Ingredients not on grocery list)

Mix together: 1 cup Brown Sugar, 1 Tbsp Dry Mustard, enough Cider Vinegar to make a paste (1-2 Tbsp) – Apply this paste evenly over the outside of the ham. Bake 325°F for a half of an hour. **-OR-** Can baste ham with the following: Mix together 3 Tbsp Sugar, 1 Tbsp Cornstarch, 1-1/2 cups Orange Juice **-OR-** Mix 1 cup Pineapple preserves, 1/4 cup dill pickle juice, 1 tsp curry powder. (Extra Recipe)

PK – (Ham Hocks and White Navy Beans)

1 Pound White Navy Beans or small Whites
4 – 6 pieces of Bacon
Hot Water

4 Ham Hocks (or more if desired)
Salt and Pepper

Place dry beans in a pan of water and wash, removing any rocks or debris. Run clear water up over the top of the beans and soak in the pan over night. Beans will puff up. Next day, pour this soaking water off and replace with clean water about 2 inches above the top of the beans. Salt the water, add in the ham hocks and bacon strips and bring to a boil. Boil over medium heat for 1 – 2 hours. You will have to add water to the beans occasionally to prevent them from burning. **HINT:** <u>**Add "hot" water, "cold" water makes the skin of the bean tough.**</u> Cook until beans are fork tender. Taste to see if they need more salt or pepper. Great served with Corn Bread, Pork Chops, Salisbury Steaks and/or Fried Potatoes.   4-8 Servings
MENU WEEK#6

PK – (Ham Loaf Swirl with Green Beans)

1 Pound Ground Ham – fully cooked
2 Eggs, beaten
3/4 cup Tomato Juice
1/2 tsp Salt
1 Pkg (10 oz) frozen Cut Green Beans
Aluminum Foil

1 Pound Ground Pork Sausage
1 cup Quick-Cooking Oats
1 medium Onion, chopped (about 1/2 cup)
1/4 tsp Pepper
1/4 tsp additional Salt

3 slices of your choice - Mozzarella, American or Swiss Cheese, cut diagonally into triangles

Heat the oven to 350°F. Mix the ground, cooked ham, ground pork sausage, eggs, oats, tomato juice, onion, 1/2 tsp salt and pepper. Pat the meat mixture into a 10 x 12" piece of aluminum foil. Rinse the frozen green beans under running cold water to separate, drain. Arrange the beans evenly on the meat mixture leaving 1" margin on all sides. Sprinkle the top with 1/4 tsp salt. Jelly Roll the meat and green beans up to make a loaf, using the foil to lift the meat as you roll. Press the end edges of the loaf to seal together so it won't unroll. Place the loaf, wrapped inside the foil onto a baking sheet or inside a 9 x 13 casserole dish, in case fats drip out of the foil. Bake the loaf for one hour at 350°F. Just before serving, open the foil and place the triangles of cheese of choice on top and return loaf to the oven until the cheese has melted (about 2-3 minutes). Remove the loaf with a pancake turner from the foil and place on serving platter. When you cut the loaf it will display a center swirl of green beans per serving.   Serves 8
MENU WEEK#33

PK – (Ham with Rice)

About 1/2 pound cooked Ham, cut in Julienne Strips or chunks
1/4 cup chopped Onion
1/2 cup frozen Peas, thawed or canned drained Peas
2 cans (14.5 oz each) Chicken Broth, heated
1/2 cup Dry White Wine

1/4 cup Margarine or Butter
1 – 2 cups Long Grain Rice
3/4 cup fresh grated Parmesan Cheese

In a saucepan sauté the onion in margarine/butter until tender. Stir in the ham and peas, then put in the rice. Stir over medium heat for 5 minutes. Add in the wine and cook another three minutes until almost all the liquid is absorbed. Mix in the chicken broth, cover with a dinner plate or tight fitting lid, and reduce the heat to very low and cook covered until almost all liquid is absorbed and the rice is tender and fluffy. Remove the covering and stir in the Parmesan Cheese and serve.

     Serves 2-4
MENU WEEK#46

Decided for You Cookbook – 365 Dinners

PK – (Italian Sausage and Spanish Rice)

1 Pound Sweet Italian Sausage, sliced
2 Tbsp Vegetable Oil
1 Green Bell Pepper, diced
1 can (28 oz) Tomatoes with the liquid
1 Tbsp Sugar

1/2 Pound Hot Italian Sausage, sliced
1 medium Onion, diced
1 cup Long Grain Rice, uncooked
1 Bay Leaf
1 tsp Salt

In a medium saucepan over medium-high heat, cook onion until clear and almost tender. Add in the sausages and cook until well browned on all sides, about 15 minutes. With a slotted spoon remove the sausages. Drain off all but 2 Tbsp of fat in the saucepan and sauté the bell pepper about 3 – 4 minutes. Return the sausage to the pan and add in the remaining ingredients (rice, tomatoes, bay leaf, sugar, and salt). Heat to boiling; then reduce to a simmer. Cover with a tight fitting lid or place an oversized dinner plate on top and simmer 20 – 25 minutes or until the liquid has been absorbed and the rice is tender. Discard the bay leaf.   4-6 Servings
MENU WEEK#19

PK – (Linguica Sandwiches)

4 Linguica Sausages
Condiments of Choice (i.e., Mustard)

4 Steak Sandwich Rolls
Lettuce, chopped Onions

Split 4 Linguica Sausages in half lengthwise. Place on a broiler pan and broil at (500°F) on the top rack for 4 – 6 minutes. Remove and place on warmed Steak Sandwich rolls with mustard, lettuce, and other condiments of your choice.   Serves 4
MENU WEEK#15

PK – (Link Sausages)

HINT: If you have had your sausage in a casing in the refrigerator for a while and you are afraid that they will taste too strong you can place 1/4 cup of water in the skillet and bring to a boil. Place the sausage patties and/or link sausages into the boiling water for 30 seconds – 1 minute on each side and this will render/remove the strong taste. Drain on paper toweling and then wipe the skillet clean, add in a small amount of vegetable oil and fry.   (Extra Recipe)

PK – (Mozzarella Cristo Sandwich)

16 thin slices firm White Bread
Sliced, Thin Deli Ham, Turkey or Luncheon Meats
Generous dash of Salt
Pepper to taste
Melted Margarine/Butter or Olive Oil

16 oz or 12 slices Mozzarella Cheese
3 Eggs
4 Tbsp Milk
Dry Breadcrumbs or Wheat Germ

Be sure your bread does not have holes in it. Stack 6 slices of bread at a time and trim off the crusts evenly (save the crusts for making Breadcrumbs or croutons). Keep 3 slices in a set. Cut 3 slices per sandwich of the Mozzarella Cheese to fit the bread (should be about 1/4 inch from each edge). Add thin Deli ham slices or other Luncheon Meats of Choice. Center the cheese on top of the ham and bread slices ending up with a top slice of bread.   Slightly pinch the edges together around the cheese and meat to slightly seal it. Continue until you have made four stacked sandwiches. Beat the eggs slightly; stir in the milk, salt and pepper (may have to increase this quantity if bread is very porous and absorbs a lot of the egg mixture). Dip the sandwiches, one at a time, in the egg mixture. Turn to coat all sides and edges well. Roll the sandwich into the breadcrumbs or wheat germ. Cook in margarine/butter hot oil or in a large skillet on both sides until nicely browned. Drain on paper towels. Serve with olives and other condiments of choice (i.e., Strawberry or Blackberry Jam).   4 Servings
MENU WEEK#37

Decided for You Cookbook – 365 Dinners

PK – (Peking Pork Spareribs - King-Tu Style)

1 - 2 lbs cubed boneless Pork Roast or Pork Spareribs (Have the butcher cut the boned ribs into small pieces)
2 cups Peanut Oil (doesn't smoke as much) for Frying or 1" high of oil in your skillet
1 (20 oz) can Pineapple Slices
2 Green Onions or Scallions

Marinate for Spareribs

1/2 tsp Salt	2 Tbsp Vegetable or Olive Oil
1 tsp Baking Soda	1 Tbsp Soy Sauce
1 Tbsp Flour	1 Tbsp Cornstarch
2 Tbsp Cold Water	(Opt) Meat Tenderizer

If using a cheaper cut of pork, 1 tsp Tenderizer (I omit because this makes it too salty)*

Seasoning Sauce for Spareribs

1 Tbsp A-1 Steak Sauce	1 Tbsp Sugar
1 Tbsp Worcestershire Sauce	1 Tbsp Ketchup
2 Tbsp Cold Water	

PROCEDURE: 1) Chop the pork into 1" wide by 2" long pieces. 2) In a bowl combine the salt, (optional meat tenderizer*), baking soda, soy sauce, flour, cornstarch and cold water. Add the cubes of pork and mix them thoroughly. Soak in marinate for 2 to 4 hours. 3) Heat the 2 cups of oil in the frying pan until it is very hot. Put all of the pork in it and deep fry about three minutes over high heat until they are lightly browned and crispy. Remove and keep warm. Drain oil from pan. 4) Heat another 2 tablespoon of oil in the frying pan. Pour in the seasoning sauce. Cook until boiling. Turn off the heat. Add the pork cuts or spareribs and mix well. Pour on to a platter. Decorate with a flower shaped scallion or pineapple slices.

Serves 6
MENU WEEK #50

HINT: <u>**A paste of non-flavored meat tenderizer and water applied to a bee sting area will remove most of the swelling, redness and pain.**</u>

PK – (Pork and Potato Stacks)

6 Boneless Pork Steaks, cubed or tenderized (about 1-1/2 pounds)
1 Pkg (5.5 oz) frozen Hash Brown Potatoes with Onions - thawed

1-3/4 cups hot Water	2 Tbsp Shortening or Vegetable Oil
1/2 tsp Salt	1 cup shredded Cheddar Cheese (about 4 oz)
1 pint (16 oz) Sour Cream	1/4 cup Milk
1-1/4 tsp Salt	1/4 tsp Pepper

Sprinkle the pork steaks with half of the salt and 1/4 tsp pepper on both sides and fry in shortening, about 7 minutes on each side. Place these on a non-greased baking sheet. Heat the milk and cheese in a saucepan over medium heat, stirring constantly until the cheese is melted. Stir in the sour cream, the balance of the salt, and dill. Stir the thawed potatoes into the mixture. Top each steak with 1/2 cup of the potato mixture. Broil at (500°F) with the tops a few inches from the broiler until the potatoes are lightly browned (3-4 minutes).

Serves 6
MENU WEEK #19

PK – (Pork Broccoli Stir Fry)

1 Pound very thinly sliced pork cuts (boneless pork chops, pork roast)
1 Pkg (10 oz) frozen Broccoli Spears, partially thawed and cut into 1" chunks)

3 Tbsp Vegetable Oil   1 Large sliced thinly Onion
1 Large clove crushed Garlic   1/4 cup Water
3 Tbsp Soy Sauce   1 tsp Cornstarch
1/2 tsp Ginger

In a deep skillet or wok, heat oil to hot. Add in the onion and garlic and stir-fry for 2-3 minutes. Add in the broccoli; stir-fry 1-minute. Cover and cook over low heat for an additional 5-minutes. Mix together the water, soy sauce, cornstarch and ginger. Add to skillet and bring to a boil. Cook another 1-minute. Remove from heat and serve over rice. (Optional: can use Boneless Chicken Breast or 1 pound of Ground Beef meatballs as meat).   Serves 4-6
MENU WEEK#32

PK – (Pork Chops and Mushroom Gravy)

4-6 Pork Chops   1 tsp Sage/Poultry Seasoning
1 can (4 oz) sliced Mushrooms (drained) Vegetable Oil
1 (10-3/4 oz) can Cream of Mushroom Soup + 1/2 can Milk

Salt and Pepper the pork chops and brown in a little Vegetable Oil on both sides. Cover and simmer for 15 minutes. Mix the mushroom soup with 1/2 can of milk and the sage seasoning. Pour over the pork chops, cover and warm over low heat until the "mushroom gravy" is hot ~5-10 minutes.   Serves 4-6
MENU WEEK#8

PK – (Pork Chops and Rice Casserole)

4 Pork Loin Chops (~1-1/2 Pounds)   1/2 cup chopped Onions
1-1/2 cups canned Beef Broth – undiluted 1/2 tsp Paprika
1-1/2 tsp Salt   1/8 tsp Pepper
1-1/2 cup regular uncooked Long Grain Rice 2 Pimientos cut into strips
2 Tbsp Vegetable Oil

Preheat oven to 350°F. Salt and pepper the chops. Brown these on both sides in vegetable oil in a large skillet for about 10 minutes. Remove and place into a 2-quart casserole dish. Drain off all of the fat except for 1 Tbsp from the skillet. Sauté the onion until tender and clear in color ~ 5 minutes. Add in the broth, 1-cup water, paprika, salt and pepper and mix well. Sprinkle in the uncooked rice. Pour all of these ingredients over the chops and bake 350°F covered for approximately 30-40 minutes. Add the pimientos during the last 10 minutes of baking.   Serves 4
MENU WEEK#10

Decided for You Cookbook – 365 Dinners

PK – (Pork Chops Creole with Rice)

4 Thick Pork Chops
3 cups Boiling Water

6 Chicken Bouillon Cubes

Brown the pork chops on both sides; remove from the pan and let it cool down a little. Pour in the boiling water and dissolve the bouillon cubes.

Add into the skillet:
1 cup uncooked Long Grain Rice
1/4 tsp Marjoram
1/2 tsp Pepper

1/2 cup diced Onion
2 tsp Salt

Stir these ingredients well and bring them to a simmer, then pour the ingredients into a 9 x 13 casserole dish.

Topping:
1 sliced Onion
1 Sliced Tomato

1 Green Bell Pepper, sliced in rings

Return the cooked pork chops on top of the above ingredients in the casserole dish. Place an onion slice, bell pepper ring and a sliced tomato on top each pork chop. Cover the casserole dish with aluminum foil and bake in a 350°F oven for 40 minutes or until the meat and rice are tender. Add more boiling water if needed.

Serves 4
MENU WEEK#30

PK – (Pork Chops Marengo)

8 Pork Chops, 3/4" thick about 2-1/2 Pounds
1 Jar (14 oz) or can Meatless Spaghetti Sauce
1 Green Bell Pepper, sliced
Aluminum Foil

1 envelope Shake-and-Bake for Pork
1 can (4 oz) sliced Mushrooms
1 medium Onion, sliced

Coat pork chops with seasoned shake-n-bake mix as directed on the package. Combine the spaghetti sauce and mushrooms. Place this in a shallow baking dish and scatter on the top the onion and sliced peppers over the top of the sauce. Arrange the coated pork chops on top and bake covered with aluminum foil at 350°F for 45 minutes or until chops are tender, remove the covering during the last 10 minutes.   Serves 8
MENU WEEK#42

Shake and Bake Coating Mix (Homemade)

Optional – MAKE YOUR OWN – (Ingredients not on grocery List)
1 cup All-Purpose Flour
1 tsp Pepper
Milk or Water
1/2 cup Cracker Crumbs (or crushed 12 saltine crackers)

2 tsp Salt
1 tsp each Thyme, Oregano, Basil

Combine all dry ingredients, stirring to mix. Use 1/2 of the mixture for 3 pounds of pork chops or chicken. Moisten the meat in milk or water to make the coating stick better. Let the dry ingredients set out for a while and stir occasionally so the moisture will escape. Leftovers can be stored in a tightly covered container. Bake the pork chops or chicken at 350°F in a greased baking dish for 45 minutes to 1 hour.

ANOTHER VARIATION: Roll pork in Bar-B-Q sauce, then in the Shake and Bake mix – Add to Shake & Bake 1 tsp of choice: Garlic Powder, Sage, and/or Grated Parmesan Cheese.

PK – (Pork Chops – Pan Fried)

4 – 8 Pork Chops   Salt and Pepper to taste
Vegetable Oil or Shortening

Salt and pepper the pork chops and fry on both sides in a covered skillet in the melted shortening/oil until browned. Simmer 15 – 20 minutes if they are thick. **-OR-** Salt and pepper both sides, place in a broiler pan and broil at 500°F on first rack for 10-15 minutes on each side depending on their thickness.   Serves 4-8
MENU WEEK#38

ADD Pork Chop Gravy from MISC – (Gravy – Pork Chops, Bacon, or Ham Pan Drippings.

PK – (Pork Chops, Rice and Gravy)

5 Pork Chops   Salt and Pepper to taste
1/2 cup Long Grain Rice uncooked   1/4 cup Water
1 can Beef Gravy   1 or 2 Onions – Sliced
2 Tbsp Vegetable Oil   Aluminum Foil

Preheat the oven to 350°F. Trim the excessive fat off the pork chops, if desired, salt and pepper these. Brown in hot vegetable oil, then place these chops in a flat casserole dish. Return the skillet to the heat and add to the drippings the rice. Stir it until it changes to a brown color. Add in 1 can beef gravy and 1/4 cup water. Place the sliced onions on top of the pork chops and pour the rice mixture over the top and bake covered with aluminum foil for 35 minutes, remove the foil and cook another 20 minutes at 350°F.
     Serves 5
MENU WEEK#50

PK – (Pork Chops – Smoked)

4 – 6 Smoked Pork Chops (Ask the Butcher for already smoked)
2 Tbsp Vegetable Oil

Heat oil and fry in a skillet on both sides until browned, cover with a lid for 5-8 minutes. **-OR-**
Can use thick cuts of Ham   **-OR-**
Can marinate pork chops in 1/4 cup Soy Sauce, 2 Tbsp Sugar, 1 Tbsp Liquid Smoke.   Serves 4
MENU WEEK#20

PK – (Pork Chops – Stuffed)

4-6 Extra Thick Pork Chops or you can cut up a boneless Pork Roast
Vegetable Oil   Salt and Pepper to taste
1/4 to 1/2 Pkg Stuffing Mix – Herb Seasoned   Poultry Seasoning or Sage

Mix the stuffing mix per package directions. Make a cutting slit from the outside edge of the pork chop to the edge of the bone. Sprinkle the Poultry Seasoning, salt and pepper to taste on all sides and in the cut slot. Spoon the moist dressing into the slot and seal together with toothpicks.   Brown meat in hot oil on both sides. Place in a baking dish and cook 350°F for 30 minutes (or the chops can be simmered while covered in a skillet).
     Serves 4-6
MENU WEEK#31

Decided for You Cookbook – 365 Dinners

PK – (Pork Chow Mein)

1 Tbsp Margarine or Vegetable Oil	1 cup sliced or chopped Onions	1/8 tsp Pepper
1-1/2 cups chopped Celery	1 tsp Sesame Oil	
1 (8 oz) can Bean Sprouts or 1 Pkg of fresh	2 tsp Sugar	
1 (4 oz) can sliced, drained Mushrooms	1/2 cup Julienne Strips of Carrots	
2 cups Chicken Broth (or diluted bouillon)	3 Tbsp Soy Sauce & 1/2 tsp Cornstarch	
1 (8 oz) can Bamboo Shoots or fresh	2 cups thinly sliced cooked Pork, Beef or Chicken	

2 cups cooked Vermicelli Noodles or soft Chinese Noodles (Chukka Soba).

Melt the margarine, add in the onion, celery, carrots, pepper*. Sauté for 2 or 3 minutes. Fix noodles per package directions. Drain all juices (might have to re-oil the skillet or wok). Add the vegetables (bean sprouts, mushrooms, bamboo shoots and add in the sugar and broth), and sesame oil. Cover and cook for 10 minutes over medium heat. Add in the cooked meat of choice. Blend the cornstarch and soy sauce, stir and add to skillet. Cook an additional 3 or 4 minutes. Place the soft noodles onto a serving platter and top with the chow mein. 4-6 Servings

*Optional Vegetables: 1/2 to 1 cup sliced thinly Cabbage, cooked 1) with other vegetables until wilted –**OR**– 2) Red Pepper Flakes to taste –**OR**– 3) Sliced Shitake Mushrooms –**OR**– 4) all of these.

MENU WEEK #5, #50

PK – (Pork Crown Roast with Apple Stuffing)

1 (7 – 10 pound) Crown Roast of Pork (12-16 chops/roast)	
1 tsp Salt 1/4 tsp Pepper	1/4 tsp Leaf Sage, crumbled or powdered
Apple – Herb-Seasoned Dressing (below)	2 Tbsp Light Molasses (Optional)
2 Tbsp Apple or Orange Juice (Optional)	3 Tbsp All-Purpose Flour
Aluminum Foil	

Place the roast, rib bone toward the outside with their bone ends up forming a circle, in a shallow roasting pan rubbing it well with a mixture of salt, pepper and sage. Then tie a string around the roast to hold it in an upright circle. Insert a meat thermometer into the meat-e-st portion without touching the bone or any of the fat. **(If you don't have a meat thermometer then its the base weight x 35 minutes should be a sufficient time of cooking ratio)** Cover with foil and roast in a slow oven for 1 hour at 325°F. Remove the roast from the oven and drain the juices into a measuring cup or container letting the fat rise to the top, then skim off the fat. Partially cut down half ways between the roast chops and place the dressing inside the created cuts. Then place the rest of the stuffing in the middle of the roast. Place the balance of the stuffing in the center being sure to pack it in firmly. Leaving the roast uncovered, return it to the oven for another 45 minutes of cooking.

Fill with dressing

Cut between chops

i.e. Tie with

HINT: Working Mother – Just mix store-bought Herb-Seasoned Stuffing Mix with celery, apples, onion, nutmeg, sage and thyme instead of making your own to save your time.

HOMEMADE APPLE STUFFING/DRESSING

3 medium size Onions, chopped (1-1/2 cups)	6 Tbsp Butter or Margarine
1/2 cup sliced Celery	3 cups Whole Wheat Bread cubes/or Corn Bread
3 cups finely diced, cored, baking Apples (Green Pippin)	1/2 cup Hot Water
1/4 cup chopped Parsley	1/2 tsp Sage and Thyme
2 Envelopes or tsps of instant Chicken Bouillon/Broth	
1/4 tsp Nutmeg	

In a skillet, sauté onion & celery in butter (~5 minutes). Stir in the apples and cook 3-5 minutes. Remove from the heat and mix in the other ingredients to finish stuffing. **(see gravy next page)**

(PK)-197

(continued Pork Crown Roast with Apple Stuffing) GRAVY: Pour the juices into a small saucepan and bring to a boil. Blend in the 3 Tbsp of Flour (**or shake flour and some warm water in a sealed container until smooth** then add this mixture to the juices and heat until bubbly and thickened. Add enough water to the drippings to make 1-3/4 cups of liquid, stir and cook till thickened. (If you would like a richer gravy **you can substitute milk for the water**. If the gravy is not dark enough in color, add in some bouquet browning and seasoning sauce).

Serves 6-10

MENU WEEK#52

PK – (Pork Cutlets with Apples)

6 Boneless Pork Chops, cut thick
1/2 cup dry Vermouth (Opt: Use equal Water)
1 medium thinly sliced Onion

2 Tbsp Margarine or Butter
1/2 - 1 tsp Ground Cinnamon

2-3 medium-size tart (green-skinned) Apples pared, and thinly sliced

1) Place the pork between two pieces of waxed paper and pound flat with a meat mallet into a 1/4" thickness.
2) Melt the margarine in a large skillet; brown the cutlets on both sides and remove them, but keep them warm.
3) Stir in the Vermouth (can use water if you prefer), scraping up the browned bits that stick to the pan; stir in the Cinnamon.
4) Add in the onion and the apple slices and cook for 2-3 minutes stirring them around to absorb the pan juices.
5) Move the apples and onions to the side and return the pork to the pan. Place the fruit and onions on top of the meat. Cover and cook on low for 25 minutes or until tender. Add salt and pepper to taste.

Serves 6

MENU WEEK#10

PK – (Pork Dinner with Cauliflower, Brussels Sprouts and Carrots)

2-1/2 Pounds Boneless Boston Pork Shoulder Roast
4 medium Carrots, peeled, halved lengthwise and cut into 2" pieces, or frozen and thawed
1 Pkg (10 oz) frozen Brussels Sprouts, slightly thawed and separated
1 Pkg (10 oz) frozen Cauliflower, slightly thawed and separated
1-1/3 cups hot Water
1 tsp dried Dill Seed
1/4 tsp Pepper
Waxed Paper

2 tsp instant Chicken Bouillon
1 tsp Onion Salt
1/2 tsp Salt

Trim any excess fat from the pork and cut into 1" pieces. Rub a 10-inch skillet with some of the fat that you've cut from the pork or lightly grease the pan. Brown the pork pieces in the skillet. Stir in the carrots, water, instant bouillon, dill, onion salt and pepper. Heat to boiling; reduce heat. Cover and simmer 45 minutes. Rinse the frozen Brussels Sprouts and Cauliflower under running cold water to separate. Stir the Brussels Sprouts and Cauliflower into the pork mixture; sprinkle with salt and pepper. Bring back to a boil; reduce to a simmer. Cover and cook until the vegetables are tender ~15 – 20 minutes more.

Serves 6

MENU WEEK#24

Decided for You Cookbook – 365 Dinners

PK – (Pork Egg Rolls – Chinese)

1 Pound Ground Pork Sausage or boneless Pork Steak or Pork Roast cut into 1" squares
1 can (8-1/2 oz) Bamboo Shoots, drained and chopped
1 can (4-1/2 oz) Mushroom Stems and pieces, drained
1 Pound of Egg Roll Wrapper Skins or 16 to 18 Won Ton Wrappers

3 Tbsp Soy Sauce	2 Tbsp Dry Sherry (Optional)
1 tsp Salt	1 tsp Sugar
1/4 tsp Pepper	Vegetable Oil
3 cups finely shredded Cabbage	6 medium Green Onions, sliced
1/4 tsp Salt	1 Tbsp Cornstarch

Mix the soy sauce, sherry, 1 tsp salt, the sugar and pepper; and pour this onto the pork pieces and marinate for at least 5 minutes; stirring occasionally. Drain well, reserving the marinade. If you are using ground pork sausage or cubed pork, cook the meat in 1 Tbsp of the oil in a 10" skillet until pork is light brown, about 4 minutes. Remove the pork to a large bowl. Stir-fry the shredded cabbage, bamboo shoots, mushrooms and onions in 1 Tbsp oil in the same skillet for approximately 2-3 minutes. Sprinkle with the 1/4 tsp salt. Add to the bowl of pork. Heat the cornstarch and marinade to boiling in the skillet, stirring constantly for about 1-2 minutes. Return the pork and vegetables to the skillet and stir and boil an additional 2 minutes then cool for 5 minutes. Place the cabbage and pork filling across the center of an egg roll skin and roll up like a burrito. Dip your finger into water and run it across the end of the egg roll skin, fold the ends inside then roll and seal the edges together. Roll up all the available egg rolls.

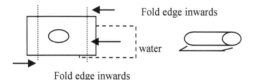

In a clean skillet (can be an electric), heat oil (1-1/2 to 1-3/4 inches deep) fry several at one time turning them as they brown (~2 minutes on each side; drain on paper toweling and keep them under a towel to keep warm or put them in a warming container).

16-18 Egg Rolls
MENU WEEK#13 & 22

PK – (Pork Patties and Pea Pods, Chinese Style)

2 Pounds Ground Pork Sausage, or cut up Pork Boneless Chops or Roast
1 (16 oz) can mixed Chinese Vegetables or frozen mix of choice
1 (6 oz) Pkg frozen Snow Pea Pods (Sugar Peas)
1 Pkg Chow Mein soft Noodles, Cup of Noodles or cooked Vermicelli Noodles

2 Tbsp Soy Sauce	1 Tbsp Sherry
1/2 cup All Purpose Flour	1/2 tsp Salt
1/2 tsp Ground Ginger	2 Tbsp Vegetable Oil
Waxed Paper	

Form the meat into 8 equal patty portions as needed; if using chops or roast, place them between two pieces of waxed paper or plastic wrap and flatten to 1/4 thick with a meat mallet and cut into small pieces. Drain the liquid from the vegetables into a small bowl. Mix into the juice the sherry and soy sauce. Dip each pork patty or meat used into this mixture. Mix together the flour, salt and ginger and coat the meat by dipping and turning it over and over a few times. Brown the patties in hot oil in a large skillet over medium high heat for 5 minutes. Add in the vegetables, soy mixture, the pea pods and the chow mein soft noodles. Cover and warm to taste and serve.

Serves 8
MENU WEEK #13

Decided for You Cookbook – 365 Dinners

PK – (Pork Quicki Casserole with Cream Style Corn)

1 – 2 Pounds Pork Sausage Links*
1 cup thinly sliced Onions
1/2 cup Milk
6-8 Green Bell Pepper Rings

3 cups thinly sliced Potatoes in rounds
1/2 tsp Salt
2 (15 oz ea) cans Cream Style Corn

Preheat oven to 375°F. Place the potatoes in a 9 x 13 baking dish; cover them with a layer of the onions. Sprinkle with salt. Pour the milk over all. Spread the corn over the top of the casserole; top with the pepper rings and sausages. Cover, bake 45 minutes. *** HINT: If you have had your sausage in the refrigerator for a while and you are afraid that it will taste too strong you can place 1/4 cup of water in the skillet and bring to a boil. Place the sausage patties and/or link sausages inside of a casing into the boiling water for 30 seconds – 1 minute on each side and this will render/remove the strong taste. Drain on paper toweling and then wipe the skillet clean, add in a small amount of vegetable oil and fry as directed above.**

Serves 4-6
MENU WEEK#21

PK – (Pork Roast Polynesian)

1 Pork Loin Roast, Center Cut (~4 Pounds) or boneless roast
1 can (6 oz) frozen Pineapple-Orange Juice concentrate
1/3 cup Soy Sauce
Minced Garlic clove
1/4 cup Liquid Smoke

1/3 cup chopped Green Onions
1 Orange cut into small pieces

Place the roast in a shallow baking dish. Combine the juice, soy sauce and liquid smoke. Pour over the pork and marinate for at least 2 hours at room temperature or several hours in the refrigerator turning often if marinade sauce does not reach the top of the roast (Roast and marinade can also be placed in a large zip lock bag, resting in a dish for support, in the refrigerator and turned over occasionally to marinate all sides. Remove the roast from the marinade sauce and reserve the liquid for basting. Make deep cuts, about 2-inches) with the tip of a knife into the meat between each chop. Fill each cut with onion and garlic pieces. Roast covered at 325°F for 1-1/2 hours brushing the outsides from time to time with the reserved marinade sauce to produce a glaze. (I prefer cooking it longer so it falls apart when touched with a fork, my choice. Reminds me of a Hawaiian Luau's Pig Meat). Meat should reach an internal temperature of 170°F to be considered done, when using a meat thermometer.

Serves 4-8
MENU WEEK#49

PK – (Pork Roast, Potatoes and Carrots)

2 – 3-1/2 pounds Boneless Pork Roast
1/2 tsp Ground Sage or Poultry Seasoning
4 medium Potatoes, cut in quarters
1- 2 medium sliced Onion

1 tsp Salt
1/2 tsp each Pepper and Garlic Powder
1-1/2 cups Water
4-6 Carrots cut into 2" long rounds

Mix salt, sage, pepper and garlic powder and rub it on all sides of the roast. Place the roast in a pan and add in the water. Place peeled potatoes, onions and carrots around the edge of the roast. Salt and pepper to taste and sprinkle with the other seasonings. Cook at 275°F (3 – 4 hours). Let stand 10 minutes before slicing. 4-6 Servings

MENU WEEK#35

PK – (Pork Sandwiches – Bar-B-Q)

Leftover Pork Roast, boneless Pork Chops
1 (16 oz) bottle Bar-B-Q Sauce –OR- **MAKE YOUR OWN**
Hamburger Buns

Slice or tear up with a fork leftover pork roast or cut up pork chops into small, thin pieces.   Warm leftover meat in a microwave for 3-5 minutes – **OR -** place cooked meat in a small saucepan with a little bit of water, cover, and bring to a boil – **OR -** fry in a skillet in 2 Tbsp of vegetable oil. Add store-bought Bar-B-Q sauce *and heat till sauce is warmed (~5 minutes).   Spoon ingredients on to warmed Hamburger or Steak Sandwich Buns.

Serves 4
MENU WEEK#43

*HINT: Bread can be warmed in a Microwave Oven but serve quickly as it will become tough -OR - if your buns are a little stale or hard, you can refresh them in the following way. If you have a metal colander, place a little water in a saucepan; place colander inside the pot and place your rolls, buns etc., inside the colander, cover, and bring the water to a boil. This will steam and soften your stale bread products very quickly. – OR – dip your hands in warm water and rub the outside of the stale bread and seal inside aluminum foil and warm in a 325°F over for 8-10 minutes.

Bar–B–Q Sauce

MAKE YOUR OWN - (Ingredients not on grocery list)

1 tsp Salt	1/8 tsp Pepper
1 Lemon juiced	1/2 cup minced Onions (cooked)
1 tsp Chili Powder	1 tsp Celery Salt
1/4 cup Vinegar	1/3 cup Worcestershire Sauce
1 cup Ketchup	2 cups Hot Water
1/4 cup Brown Sugar	Dash of Tabasco Sauce
1 Tbsp Liquid Smoke	

PK – (Pork Sausage Patties)

1-2 Pounds Ground Pork Sausages
2 Tbsp Vegetable Oil
Form into patties* Place in a skillet and fry in a small amount of vegetable oil on both sides until golden brown.

4-6 Servings
MENU WEEK#35

Great served with Pancakes and Eggs (see MISC and PK recipes) –OR- (VEG) Baked Beans and (SALAD) Cole Slaw Salad.

HINT: If you have had your sausage in the refrigerator for a while and you are afraid that it will taste too strong you can place 1/4 cup of water in the skillet and bring to a boil. Place the sausage patties and/or link sausages inside of a casing into the boiling water for 30 seconds – 1 minute on each side and this will render/remove the strong taste. Drain on paper toweling and then wipe the skillet clean, add in a small amount of vegetable oil and fry as directed above.

PK – (Sliced Pork – Leftover Roast)

There should be leftover from the pork roast cooked during the week. Slice the pork and either warm in a microwave or you can place 1/4 cup of water in a saucepan and bring to a boil. Drop in the pork, cover and let simmer for 3-4 minutes. Can add in a mix of one can each of chicken and beef gravy, if desired. You can also de-bone pork steaks or boneless pork if you don't have leftover pork roast. Cut into cubes and brown on all sides.

Serves 4

MENU WEEK#35

PK – (Spaghetti Carbonara)

1/2 pound of Ham Slices or Leftover Ham	3 or 6 slices Bacon
1 Tbsp Olive Oil	3 Eggs
1 Pound Spaghettini or Angel Hair Noodles	1/2 tsp Pepper
Salt	1/2 cup grated Romano Cheese

Fry the bacon and remove to drain on paper towels. Cut up the Ham slices into chunks and cook in the bacon drippings until crisp about 7 minutes; drain the fat. In a large bowl, beat the eggs and pepper together with a fork until blended. **Place 1 tsp salt per quart of water into a large pan and bring to a boil (this cause the water to boil quicker); add in the Tbsp of olive oil to prevent the spaghetti from sticking together when cooking.** Cook the spaghetti per package directions or until you can cut it and there is no dryness in the center (you will be able to see the difference if not cooked thoroughly). Remove 1/4 cup of the hot water and add into it the eggs and stir together. Drain the pasta in a colander, salt it and immediately add the spaghetti to the ham in the pan, tossing well to the mix. Pour the egg mixture over the spaghetti and toss well (the heat from the spaghetti will cook the egg mixture). Cover with a tight fitting lid or set a plate on top of the hot spaghetti to keep it warm until you get your vegetable and salad on the table. Toss spaghetti again after adding in the Romano Cheese* and the crumbled bacon.

White Sauce*

Sauce can be added if a more creamy texture to the Carbonara is desired

4 Tbsp Butter	2 cups Milk
4 Tbsp All-Purpose Flour	1/2 tsp Salt
½ cup grated Romano Cheese	1/8 tsp each White, Black and Cayenne Pepper

Melt butter in saucepan over low heat. Blend in flour, salt, and peppers. Stir in milk. Increase heat to medium, stirring constantly until mixture thickens and bubbles about 3 minutes. Pour sauce over Carbonara and sprinkle on the cheese.

Serves 4-6

MENU WEEK#18

Decided for You Cookbook – 365 Dinners

PK – (Spareribs in Bar-B-Q Sauce)

3 – 5 Pounds of Pork Spareribs   Salt and Pepper
Water   3 Tbsp Vegetable Oil
1 (15 oz) bottle Bar-B-Q Sauce of flavor choice

Cut your spareribs into individual ribs. Fill a large saucepan half full of water and bring to a boil. Drop the spareribs into the boiling water for 5 – 8 minutes. Remove and drain on paper toweling. Place these ribs on top of a broiling pan and brush them on both sides with vegetable oil and sprinkle on salt and pepper. Broil at (500°F) on the first shelf of the oven until both sides are browned. Turn the oven to Bake 325°F. Remove the broiling top pan, pour off excess fats and place the ribs uniformly into the bottom of the pan. Pour the Bar-B-Q sauce over the ribs. Cover the pan with aluminum foil and bake for 25 – 45 minutes, or until fork tender. - **OR** – The ribs can be placed in a crock pot and cook 6-8 hours on low. Remove these and place them on a broiling pan and coat them with Bar-B-Q sauce. Broil at (500°F) for 10 minutes on each side, recoating with sauce as needed.

Serves 4-6
MENU WEEK#16

Bar–B–Q Sauce

MAKE YOUR OWN – (Ingredients not on grocery list)
1 tsp Salt   1/8 tsp Pepper
1 Lemon juiced   1/2 cup minced Onions (cooked)
1 tsp Chili Powder   1 tsp Celery Salt
1/4 cup Vinegar   1/3 cup Worcestershire Sauce
1 cup Ketchup   2 cups Hot Water
1/4 cup Brown Sugar   Dash of Tabasco Sauce
1 Tbsp Liquid Smoke

PK – (Stuffed Pork Roast)

3 Pound to 5 Pound Boneless Pork Roast
1 Pkg Herb Seasoned Stuffing Mix or make your own stuffing from TUR Roast Turkey Recipe
Vegetable Oil   1 chopped Onion
3 stalks of chopped Celery   Salt and Pepper
Poultry Seasoning   String and Aluminum Foil

Make a 2"cut across the length of the roast. Then turn the knife sideways in the cut so you can cut the roast in a jelly-roll fashion; ending up with a flat 2" slab of meat. Mix the stuffing mix with water per package direction. Sprinkle poultry seasoning, salt and pepper on all sides of the roast. Lay it flat and spread a 1-1/2" layer of the stuffing mix over the seasoned surface. Top this with the chopped onion and celery. Roll this up in a Jellyroll fashion and tie every 4 inches with butcher's cotton string.

Brown the outside in the hot oil. Bake, covered with an aluminum foil tent in a 350°F oven for 35-40 minutes per pound. If using a meat thermometer it should reach a 185°F internal temperature. Let it rest for 8-10 minutes before cutting.

Serves 4-6
MENU WEEK#8

(PK)-203

PK – (Sweet and Sour Pork)

1 Pound or more of Boneless Pork Roast, cut into 1" chunks

1 Tbsp Soy Sauce	1/2 tsp Salt
1 can Pineapple Chunks, drained	1 Green Bell Pepper, cut into 1" chunks
2 medium Onions, each cut into eighths	2 medium Carrots, peeled and slice diagonally
1 Garlic Clove, chopped	2 cups + 2 Tbsp Vegetable Oil

Batter for Sweet and Sour Pork

3/4 cup All-Purpose Flour	2 Tbsp Cornstarch
1/4 tsp Baking Powder	1/4 tsp Baking Soda
1/4 tsp Salt	3/4 cup Water

Sauce for Sweet and Sour Pork

1 cup (combine pineapple juice + water)	1/3 cup Dark Brown Sugar or can be
Dash of Tabasco Sauce (Optional)	1/2 cup Sugar (1/4 Gran. 1/4 Brown)
2 Tbsp Cornstarch	1/4 cup Cider Vinegar
2 Tbsp Ketchup	3 Tbsp Soy Sauce

In a bowl, combine the pork, soy sauce, the garlic and the salt; set aside. Combine in a medium bowl the batter ingredients. Blend with a whisk or fork until smooth; set aside. Dip into the batter the onions, carrots, green pepper cook in a skillet or wok in 2 Tbsp hot oil for about 2 minutes stirring quickly and frequently. Remove vegetables with a slotted spoon and drain them on paper toweling and keep warm in a 200°F oven. Add the pork to the batter and toss until pieces are coated. Cook all of the meat, a few at a time into the hot oil, cook for 4 to 5 minutes until the pork is crisp and browned. Remove the pork with a slotted spoon and drain on paper toweling. Keep these in the warmed oven with the cooked vegetables. In a saucepan combine the sauce and cook to boiling, stirring constantly until slightly thickened, add the pineapple chunks to the sauce and stir well. Add back the pork and vegetables into the sauce, and toss all ingredients together and heat thoroughly if needed.

Serves 4-6

MENU WEEK #5

PK – (Sweet and Sour Spareribs with Tomatoes)

Cracker Meal (store bought or use crushed saltine crackers)
Vegetable Oil for frying
2 Pounds of Pork Spareribs, sliced into individual servings (You will get more meat per serving if the first rib is cut right at the edge of the second rib bone, this means you end up with one bone at the end of your rack with very little meat, but you will enjoy the overall difference)

Pork Egg Wash

2 Tbsp Cornstarch	1 Egg, slightly beaten
1/4 tsp Salt	1 Tbsp Soy Sauce
1/4 tsp Monosodium Glutamate	

Prepare the egg wash of the salt, glutamate, soy sauce, egg, and cornstarch. Dip your spareribs in this egg wash, roll in the cracker meal. Set aside in one layer on waxed paper or a baking sheet until they are dry approximately 25 minutes. Cook the spareribs on all sides in a skillet in hot oil for about 10 minutes and keep warm in the oven (200°F).

Sweet & Sour Sauce

1 cup (combine pineapple juice + water)	2 Tbsp Ketchup
Dash of Tabasco Sauce (Optional)	1/3 cup Dark Brown Sugar or can be
1/2 cup Sugar (1/4 Gran. 1/4 Brown)	4 Tbsp Cider Vinegar
2 Tbsp Cornstarch	3 Tbsp Soy Sauce

(**continued Sweet and Sour Spareribs w/Tomatoes**) With a fork or whisk, mix 1 Tbsp Cornstarch with some of the pineapple juice. In a saucepan combine all of the ingredients for the sauce including this cornstarch & juice mixture. Bring it to a slow boil and simmer for one minute. Add in the following:

1 Green Bell Pepper, cut in half strips   12 Tomato Wedges or slices
1 (20 oz) can Pineapple Chunks, drained and cut into thinner chunks

Simmer the sauce until bell peppers and tomatoes are fork tender, about 4 minutes. (Add water if sauce becomes too thick). Place the cooked rice on a serving platter, top with the spareribs, and pour the sauce and vegetables over the top.   Serves 6 -8
MENU WEEK#11

PK – (Tenderloin Pork Rounds)

2 Pounds Boneless Pork Chops (**It's cheaper to use a roast** cut to individual sizes)
12 slices Bacon   12 or more Large Mushrooms, stemmed
1 (10-1/2 oz) can Beef Broth, condensed   1 clove Garlic, crushed
1/4 cup Water   2 Tbsp All-Purpose Flour
Toothpicks   Waxed Paper

Fry the bacon until limp; drain and set aside. Cut the pork into 12 pieces 3" square. Place it between two pieces of waxed paper or plastic wrap and with a meat mallet pound it flat to 1/2" thickness. Place a mushroom cap and chopped stems in the middle of the pork square and bring the edges around the mushrooms, wrap with a piece of the bacon and fasten with toothpicks. Place these meat rounds in a
9 x 9" baking dish. Mix the garlic into the beef broth and pour over the pork rounds. Bake uncovered 40-45 minutes, spooning the broth mixture over the pork occasionally. During the last 8-10 minutes add in your extra mushrooms, salt these and cook for the remaining time. Pour your juices into a saucepan. Place the dish of pork rounds into a warmed oven. Shake in a sealed container (jar or sealed bowl) the flour and water until there is no longer any lumps, or whisk to dissolve the flour. You will need 1 cup to 1-1/2 cups of liquid between the juices and the flour mixture, add more water if needed to the juices. Bring the juices to a simmer and pour in the flour mixture while stirring constantly with either a whisk, slotted spoon or fork make sure no lumps are created and cook till smooth, taste to see if you need additional salt or pepper. If you would like a darker gravy add in a tsp of Bouquet Brown Gravy & Seasoning Sauce. Place the pork and mushrooms in a serving dish and pour the gravy back over it before your serve.   Serves 6
MENU WEEK#28

Replacement for one clove of Garlic is 1 tsp of Garlic Salt

HINTS: Removing Excess Fats – To remove fat from a skillet, tip the pan and use a bulb baster or a paper towel folded several layers to absorb the fats. If "all" fat needs to be removed, pour fats through a flour sifter over a bowl and the fats will remain in the sifter making it possible for you to use the juices. Discard the fats into the garbage. To remove fats from soups, run an ice cube wrapped in cheesecloth or paper towel over the surface to pick it up. You will find that you can remove all the fat after any items has been refrigerated. Coldness causes the fat to rise to the top and then it can be removed with a spoon. –OR- You can place waxed paper touching the surface of the soup. When cooled, the fats will have stuck to the paper. Remove and throw it all away at one time.

PK – (Won Ton – Stuffed & Fried)

Won Ton Stuffing

1 Pound Ground Pork Sausage	2 or 3 Green Onions, cut finely
1/2 Pound cooked Shrimp (chopped)	2 Tbsp Soy Sauce
1 (8 oz) can Water Chestnuts, drained and minced	Vegetable Oil for frying
1 Pkg Won Ton Wrappers (Won Ton Skins)*	

*See Make Your Own Wrapper recipe under SOUP – (Won Ton Soup - Chinese)

1. Mix all of the first group of ingredients. Place a tsp of the mixture into the center of a won ton wrapper:
2. Dip your finger in warm water and run your finger around two edges of the wrapper.
3. Fold the top edge down and press together forming a triangle.
4. Then re-dip your finger and moisten the areas on each side of the inserted mixture.
5. Fold the tips of the triangle down, sealing the mixture in the center.
6. Fry in hot oil on both sides, until they float, and are golden brown. **(Floating means**
7. **they are done inside).**
8. Drain on paper toweling and keep warm by covering with a lid or put these in a tortilla warmer pan and cover.

 When you turn these over they look like this

Optional Filling: Crab Meat and Cream Cheese mix – **OR** – Monterey Jack Cheese, chopped Cilantro – **OR** – Cooked Ground Chorizo and Scrambled Eggs – **OR** – 1 tsp Cream Cheese

Won Ton Dipping Sauce

Use one 12 oz Bottle of Chili Sauce or Cocktail Sauce with 1/4 to 1/2 tsp Cayenne Pepper, and 1/2 tsp Lemon Juice added.   – **OR MAKE YOUR OWN SAUCE** –

2 (8 oz ea) cans of Tomato Sauce
2/3 cups Brown Sugar
1 tsp Celery Salt or Fresh minced Celery
1/4 cup White Vinegar
1 tsp Soy Sauce
1/4 to 1/2 tsp Cayenne Pepper (your choice)

Warm these ingredients together and use as dipping sauce with fried Won Tons **-OR** – Serve with a Hot Mustard Sauce **-OR** –1/2 cup Soy Sauce, 3 Tbsp Rice Wine Vinegar, 2 Tbsp Water   Serves 4-8
MENU WEEK#5

Hot Mustard Sauce

MAKE YOUR OWN – (Ingredients not on grocery list)

1/2 cup Dry Mustard or Chinese Mustard	1/2 cup Vinegar
1/2 cup Sugar	1 Egg Yolk slightly beaten

Combine the dry mustard and vinegar in a very small saucepan, cook together and allow to stand overnight in the refrigerator. Next day combine the mixture with the sugar and the beaten egg yolk. Simmer over medium heat until slightly thickened; stirring constantly.   Makes 1 cup
(Extra Recipe)

HINT: If you would like these to become a moist Pot Sticker. Using less hot oil, brown on both sides. Leaving the Won Tons in the skillet, place your hands into warm water forming a bowl and with your palms together, scoop the water up. Splash, let go of the water over, the cooked Won Tons. Cover the skillet with a tight-fitting lid. Steam the Won Tons for an additional 2-3 minutes or until hot and puffy.

SEAFOOD – (Captain's Tuna Casserole with Rice)

1 (10-3/4 oz) can Condensed Mushroom Soup or Cream of Vegetable Soup
1/2 cup Milk   2/3 cup grated Cheddar Cheese
2 cans (16 oz each) Tuna (drain liquid to water)   Dash of Pepper
1 cup Water (includes oils from tuna can)   1-1/3 cups of Minute Rice (instant)
1/2 tsp Oregano, Optional   1 (1 lb) can of Whole Tomatoes
1/2 Onion sliced thinly   1/4 cup Stuffed Olives
1/2 cup crushed Potato Chips or dry Breadcrumb Topping

Heat the soup, and milk with the cheese until melted stirring occasionally. Combine the rice, oregano and pepper in a greased 1-1/2 quart shallow baking dish. Drain tomatoes, saving 1/2 cup of the tomato juice. Stir the tomato juice and blended water into the rice. Slice the tomatoes; arrange most of these on top of the rice. Add the onion, tuna and olives. Pour on the cheesy soup (sauce) and sprinkle the top of the casserole with the crushed Potato Chips. Bake in a 375°F oven for 20-25 minutes.   6 Servings
                                                                              MENU WEEK#11

SEAFOOD – (Codfish – Baked with Broth Topping and Potatoes)

2 Pounds Codfish, cut into 1" pieces   2 Tbsp Butter or Margarine
2 medium Onions, thinly sliced   1/4 cup snipped Parsley
2 Tbsp Olive or Vegetable Oil   1/2 tsp Salt
1/2 tsp Lemon Pepper or Black Pepper if desired   6 hard-boiled Eggs, sliced
2 Pounds of small new Red Potatoes, cooked, and cut into 1/4" slices

Melt Butter/Margarine in a 12" skillet. Stir and cook onion slices in the butter and oil until tender. Stir in pieces of Codfish, cook uncovered over low heat 30 minutes. Prepare broth topping as shown below. Heat oven to 350°. Layer half of each of the codfish and onions, potatoes, eggs, and broth topping in an non-greased (9 x 13) baking dish. Sprinkle with half of the parsley, salt and lemon pepper. Repeat until all ingredients are used. Bake uncovered until lightly brown and bubbly, about 45 minutes.

Codfish Broth Topping
1/4 cup Butter or Margarine   1/4 cup All-Purpose Flour   1 cup Chicken Broth
1/2 tsp Salt   1/8 tsp Pepper
VARIATION: Use an Aioli Sauce with this food type.   Serves 8-10
                                                                              MENU WEEK #26

SEAFOOD – (Crab Buffet Mornay)
1 – 8 oz can Crabmeat, flaked -   2 – 5 oz cans Mushroom Crowns, drained
2 tsp Lemon Juice   3 Tbsp Butter or Margarine
3 Tbsp Flour   1-1/2 cups Milk
2 Egg Yolks   1-1/4 cups Shredded Swiss or Cheddar Cheese

Arrange mushroom crowns hollow side up in an 8" baking dish. Cover with the crabmeat; sprinkle all with Lemon Juice. Melt butter in a small pan, blend in the flour and add the milk (making a White Sauce); cook stirring constantly until thickened. Add a small amount of the sauce to the egg yolks and mix (this prevents the eggs from being scrambled if you just put directly into a hot mixture), return this egg mixture to your pan. Cook all an additional couple minutes while stirring, and remove from the heat. Stir in 1 cup shredded cheese. Serve over rice.   6 Servings
                                                                              MENU WEEK#10

Decided for You Cookbook – 365 Dinners

SEAFOOD – (Crab Louie Salad)

Iceberg or Romaine Lettuce cut up
Hard Boiled Eggs – Quartered
Cold, drained Asparagus
Black Olives – pitted

Shredded or chunks of cleaned Crab
Chopped Green Onions
Tomato Chunks

Toss all ingredients in Salad Bowl, **use Thousand Island Dressing** or the following:

Crab Louie Dressing
<u>Equal Parts of</u>
Mayonnaise, Ketchup & Sweet Pickle Relish
-OR-
<u>Equal Parts of</u> Mayonnaise & Plain Yogurt
Grated Onion
Cayenne Pepper to taste
1 tsp Worcestershire Sauce
1 tsp Horseradish

1 Lemon Juiced

1/2 pt Chili Sauce (similar to Cocktail Sauce)
Chopped Parsley
1 Lemon Juiced
2 Tbsp chopped Chives

Serves 4
MENU WEEK#8

SEAFOOD – (Crabmeat and Cheese Casserole with Rice)

1 cup Long Grain White Rice
1/2 cup Milk
1/2 tsp Worcestershire Sauce
1 Tbsp Lemon Juice

1 (10-3/4 oz) Mushroom Soup
1 (6-1/2 oz) can Crabmeat
1 cup Shredded Cheddar Cheese

You may substitute canned for fresh crab or shrimp. Cook the rice per package directions. Place the soup into a saucepan and stir in the milk, Worcestershire sauce, and lemon juice and heat to a simmer. Stir in 1/2 of the cheese and the crabmeat. Mix with the hot rice. Turn into a shallow dish (1-1/2 quarts) and top with the remaining cheese. Bake 350°F for 15 minutes.

4-6 Servings
MENU WEEK#14

SEAFOOD – (Crab Newburg on English Muffins)

2 cups Crab Meat or 2 (6-1/2 oz cans of crab)
2 Tbsp All-Purpose Flour
2 cups Thin Cream (Evaporated Milk or other)
Salt and Pepper to taste
1/3 cup Sherry or Water or 1/4 cup Chili Sauce or Ketchup

6 Tbsp Margarine or Butter
4 Egg Yolks
Dash of Nutmeg
English Muffins

Warm the crab in a skillet in a little bit of margarine/butter for about 2 minutes. Sprinkle this with flour and stir well. Add slowly the Sherry/water and cook 2-3 minutes longer. Combine the egg yolks and the cream and beat slightly. Add this egg mixture slowly to the crab, stirring constantly. Reduce the heat; stirring until the mixture thickens. Add the salt, pepper and nutmeg. Serve over warmed English Muffins. (See **MAKE YOUR OWN** recipe **BRD (English Muffins)**

6 Servings
MENU WEEK#35

VARIATIONS – Shrimp – Use 2 cans (7 oz ea) or 2-1/2 cups cleaned cooked fresh shrimp.
Lobster – Use 2 cans (6-1/2 oz) or 2-1/2 cups cleaned cooked Lobster.

Decided for You Cookbook – 365 Dinners

SEAFOOD – (Crab Seafood Thermidor)

2 Pkgs (8 oz ea) frozen but thawed or fresh King Crabmeat well drained
1 can (4 oz) sliced Mushrooms, drained (reserve the liquid)
1 can (10-3/4 oz) condensed Cream of Shrimp Soup

1 Tbsp Margarine or Butter	1/4 tsp Dry Mustard Paprika
Dash of Cayenne Pepper	1/2 cup Parmesan Cheese

Drain the mushroom liquid and reserve. Sauté the mushrooms in the Margarine for 2 minutes. Stir in the soup, the mushroom liquid, dry mustard and cayenne pepper. Heat slowly, stirring often, add in the fresh or thawed crabmeat. Spoon this into 4 individual baking dishes, sprinkle tops with Parmesan Cheese. Place these dishes on a baking sheet and bake in a hot oven 400°F for 15 minutes.   Serves 4
MENU WEEK#39

SEAFOOD – (Crab Seafood Turnovers)

1 (10-3/4 oz) can condensed Cream of Mushroom Soup
1 (6-1/2 oz) flaked Crab Meat or 1 (7-3/4 oz) can Lobster

1/4 cup Mayonnaise or Salad Dressing of choice	1 Pkg Pastry Mix or frozen Pastry Shells, defrosted
1/2 tsp Worcestershire Sauce	1/4 tsp Meat Tenderizer

Combine 1/2 cup of the soup (reserving the balance) with the crabmeat/lobster, mayo and seasonings. Prepare the pastry according to package directions, and roll out to four 6-inch circles. Place 1/4 of the filling on half of each circle; fold to form a turnover, sealing the edges by pressing a fork tine around the edge. Place on a non-greased baking sheet for 15-20 minutes at 400°F, or until golden brown. Dilute the reserved soup with 2 Tbsp of milk and warm; use as a topping sauce.   Serves 4
MENU WEEK#7

SEAFOOD – (Fish and Chips)

2 Pkgs of fresh (1-1/2 lbs) or frozen Fish Fillets/steaks*

BATTER:	Flour for dusting
1/2 cup Beer	1/4 cup Milk
1 cup All-Purpose Flour	1/2 tsp Salt
1/4 tsp Pepper	2 Eggsseparated
Vinegar	Newspaper Cones
French Fries or Potato Rounds	

(HINT: <u>Let raw Potatoes stand in cold water for at least half an hour before frying to improve the crispness of the French Fries). If frozen fish is used, thaw in a bowl of milk which draws out any frozen taste and provides a fresh caught flavor</u>, cook per package directions. Beat the egg yolks until light. Blend in the milk, beer, flour, and seasonings until smooth. (Some say it sticks better if the batter is cold when you begin.) Beat the egg whites until stiff, not dry and fold into the mixture. Dip the fish on both sides into flour then into this batter and fry in 375°F vegetable oil until golden brown on both sides. <u>Salt and pepper to taste and place in rolled newspaper cones with the French Fries, serve with a shaker of vinegar.</u> *Cod, Sole, Flounder or Haddock Fish Fillets/ Steaks are all good choices.   Serves 4
MENU WEEK#34

Decided for You Cookbook – 365 Dinners

SEAFOOD – (Fish Fillets – Pan Fried)

2 Pounds fresh Fish Fillets (Sole, Haddock or your choice)
1-1/4 cups fine dry Breadcrumbs   1 tsp Salt
1/4 tsp Pepper   1 Egg beaten + 1 Tbsp Water
1/2 cup or 2 cubes Margarine   Juice of 1 Lemon
2 Tbsp finely chopped Parsley

Cut the fish into serving pieces. Mix the seasonings, except for the Parsley, into the breadcrumbs. Dip the fish fillets in the seasoned breadcrumbs; then dip in the beaten egg and again in the breadcrumbs. Sauté in a melted 1/4 Pound margarine until browned on both sides and flakes easily when lifted. Remove the fish to a hot platter. Melt the remaining butter and add in the lemon juice; pour over the fish. Sprinkle with the parsley and serve immediately.   Serves 6
MENU WEEK#36

SEAFOOD – (Fish Lemon Rollups)

8 Fish Fillets with skin on one side (about 2 Pounds) fresh or frozen but thawed
2 tsp Chicken-Flavored Instant Bouillon or 2 cubes of bouillon with juice added
2/3 cup Margarine or Butter   1/2 cup Lemon Juice
1 tsp Tabasco Pepper Sauce   Paprika
1 (10 oz) Pkg frozen chopped Broccoli, thawed 1 cup (4 oz) shredded sharp Cheddar Cheese
1 cup cooked Rice   Toothpicks
Optional (Waxed Paper)

Preheat oven to 375°F. In a small saucepan, melt 1/3 cup of the butter; add 1/4 cup of the lemon juice, bouillon, and Tabasco sauce. Heat slowly until bouillon dissolves; set aside. In a medium bowl, combine the cooked rice, thawed broccoli, Cheddar cheese, 1/4 cup softened butter, and 1/4 cup lemon juice; mix well. If the fish fillets are thick then place the skin side up and pound flatter with a meat mallet between 2 sheets of waxed paper. Turn over, skin side down. Divide the broccoli-rice mixture equally into 4 even amounts and place in the center of your fish and jelly-roll these, fastening with toothpicks. Place them with seam side down into a shallow casserole dish. Pour your set aside warmed sauce over the fillets. Bake 25 minutes or until the fish flakes when touched with a fork. Spoon cooked sauce over the individual servings; garnish by sprinkling tops with Paprika.   4 Servings
MENU WEEK#12

SEAFOOD – (Fish Sticks)

Cook any frozen fish sticks per package directions.

Serves 4-6
MENU WEEK#4

Decided for You Cookbook – 365 Dinners

SEAFOOD – (Lobster - Broiled or Steamed)

4 Lobster Tails
Margarine or Butter
Lemon Juice
Garlic Powder

Rinse the Lobster in cold water and pat dry. With kitchen shears cut both sides of shell on the underside of the tail; remove the shell covering the meat. Loosen around the edges with a knife and pierce through the meatiest part of the tail with a fork and pull the tail out. Lightly salt it and lay it back inside the shell as a reservoir for the seasonings. Mix together 1/2 tsp garlic powder into a 1/2 cube of softened butter. Spread this over the tail's meat and **broil** at (500°F) 4-6 minutes on each side until its slightly pink. Serve with clarified butter and lemon slices. **–OR –**

Place about 2 inches of water in the bottom of a large pan and also put inside a metal colander on which you place your washed lobsters (with or without the tails). Bring the water to a boil and cover to **steam** the Lobster for approximately 15 minutes or until they turn bright red.

–OR –
the Lobsters in the shell can be boil in the water for 15 minutes if you don't have a metal colander.

Serves 4
MENU WEEK#41

Clarified Butter – (Drawn Butter)

Cut sticks of butter in pieces and heat very slowly in a small saucepan. As the butter melts, it separates. The fats rise to the top. Remove this with a spoon just leaving the clear oils of the butter. The yellow milky fats can be stored and used for other dishes if desired. Place the heated clarified butter in a small relish dish to be served along with the Lobster meat.

If you'd like to try something different, use the following optional dip for your Lobster and/or Shrimp meat into:

Lemon–Chive Mayonnaise Dip

(Optional) - Ingredients not on grocery list
3 cups Mayonnaise
Juice of 2 Lemons
Chopped Chives

4 Garlic cloves, coarsely chopped
3 handfuls of chopped Parsley
1/2 tsp Tabasco Sauce

Mix all ingredients in a mixing bowl and set aside to allow the flavors to marry.   (Extra Recipe)

SEAFOOD - MICROWAVE INFORMATION:

HINT: To assure that the meat browns, place ingredients in a browning pan or place a pan inside a large brown shopping bag. Fold the bag's opening edge back underneath container, so fats won't escape. Be sure bag doesn't touch ceiling of Microwave Oven might spark unit (check often)
     Fish Fillets/Steaks 1 Lb = 6 to 8 min/Lb (Cook till fish flakes easily)
     Shrimp 1 Lb Peeled – 3 to 6 min/Lb (Stir after 2 minutes)
     Shrimp 2 Lbs Unpeeled – 6 to 10 min/Lb (Stir after 5 minutes)

SEAFOOD – (Lobster Thermidor)

2 cups cooked Lobster Meat	4 Tbsp Margarine or Butter	1 Egg Yolk beaten
1 can (5 oz) Mushrooms, drained	2 Tbsp Chopped Onions	1/4 cup Chicken Broth
2 Tbsp All-Purpose Flour	1/4 tsp Salt	1/2 cup Half and Half Milk
1/8 tsp Pepper	1/8 tsp Paprika	

In a 1-1/2 Quart saucepan place 2 Tbsp of the margarine, mushrooms, and onions. Sauté till onions are tender. Stir in the flour, salt, pepper and paprika. Slowly stir in the chicken broth and the half-n-half milk. Stir constantly until white sauce is thickened. In a separate cup place a little bit of the white sauce and stir in the egg yolk **(if the sauce is too hot the egg will become scrambled, avoid this).** Once the egg is mixed into the small amount of sauce, return it to the saucepan. Add in the lobster and stir well. Remove from the heat and pour into a buttered casserole dish. Bake 325°F for 15 minutes. **TOPPING:** 2 Tbsp margarine, 1/4 cup Breadcrumbs, 3 Tbsp Parmesan Cheese. In a small bowl, place the melted margarine, stir in the dry Breadcrumbs and the Parmesan Cheese. Cover the top of the casserole with this and return it to the oven until it's lightly browned. Serve with cooked rice.   Serves 4

MENU WEEK#23

SEAFOOD – (Prawns Tempura)

2 Pound bag Prawns (cleaned, de-veined, with the tails left on)   Vegetable Oil
   You can also use the tempura batter on **bolded** grocery listed items**: raw vegetables** (whole **green beans,** onions, **broccoli, yam slices, carrots, bell pepper slices, zucchini strips**, etc).
Cocktail Sauce with 1 tsp Lemon Juice, Tartar Sauce, Dipping Sauce, or Ketchup

3 cups sifted All-Purpose Flour
3 tsp Baking Powder
2 Egg Yolks slightly beaten   } **Tempura Batter**
2 cups "cold" Water
Salt & Pepper to taste

Mix the flour, baking powder together. Beat the egg yolks and blend together with "icy cold" water. Stir in the dry ingredients and beat until smooth. Place 2" of oil in your skillet or wok and heat to hot (`370°F) or until sprinkled flour in it sizzles. Dip the prawns and vegetables in the **COLD** batter **(Batter will puff more when fried, if cold)** and fry for 1-1/2 minutes on either side or until light brown. Drain on paper towels covered by a heated lid to keep them warm. Serve hot with the below sauce or commercially made sauce of choice.   Serves 4-6

MENU WEEK #32

Prawns Dipping Sauce

1-2 (12 oz) Bottle Chili Sauce, or Cocktail Sauce. Mix 1 cup Ketchup,
1/4 cup Lemon Juice, dash of Tabasco together **-OR-**
MAKE YOUR OWN - (Ingredients not on grocery List)
Mix ingredients together

1/2 cup Consume	1/4 cup Soy Sauce
2 Tsp Sugar	Dash of Monosodium Glutamate

-OR-

Hot Mustard Sauce

1/2 cup Dry Mustard or Chinese Mustard	1/2 cup Rice WineVinegar
1/2 cup Sugar	1 Egg Yolk slightly beaten + 1 Tbsp Water

Combine the dry mustard and vinegar in a very small saucepan, cook together and allow to stand overnight in the refrigerator. Next day combine the mixture with the sugar and the beaten egg yolk. Simmer over medium heat until slightly thickened; stirring constantly.   Makes 1 cup

MENU WEEK#32

Decided for You Cookbook – 365 Dinners

SEAFOOD – (Raviolis – Cheese with Salmon Pesto Cream Sauce)

2 (7.1 oz) Pouches of Premium Albacore Salmon or Tuna
1 (9 oz) Pkg Frozen Spinach or Cheese Ravioli's
1/3 cup each of Sour Cream and Heavy
   Whipping Cream
2 Tomatoes (prefer Roma Style) cut into 1-inch pcs
Shredded or grated fresh Parmesan Cheese

1/2 cup commercially prepared Basil Pesto*
1/8 tsp fresh Lemon Zest (scrapings of outside skin)
1-1/2 Tbsp Toasted Pine Nuts or sliced Almonds
Fresh Basil Leaves for Garnish
Optional (Red Pepper Flakes)

Cook the ravioli's according to the package directions, and drain in a colander. In a saucepan whisk together the pesto, sour cream, whipping cream and the lemon zest. Heat slowly on low heat until heated thoroughly; stir constantly. Add in the tomatoes and gently flake in the Salmon or Tuna. Salt and pepper to taste. Fold the drained ravioli's into creamy seafood sauce and evenly divide onto 2 plates or in a serving dish. Top with nuts and additional Parmesan Cheese garnishing with a sprig of basil leaves. **VARIATION:** Any bottled Alfredo, Roasted Garlic Parmesan, Béchamel, or Cheese Sauce can be substituted. Serves 2-4

MENU WEEK#50

Pesto Sauce*

MAKE YOUR OWN - (Ingredients not on grocery list)
6 cloves Garlic, crushed
1 cup chopped Parsley (Optional)
2 cups coarsely chopped packed Basil Leaves
1/4 cup Pine Nuts (chopped very finely) – Optional

Salt and Pepper to taste
1-1/2 cups Parmesan/Romano Cheese
1 Tbsp Lemon Juice

1/2 cup Olive Oil
1/2 cup melted Butter

In a food processor, blend with an on/off pulse the garlic, basil, salt, pepper, pine nuts, lemon juice and cheese into a coarse puree. Gradually blend in the olive oil till smooth. Adjust seasonings to taste. Store in sealed Glass container in refrigerator up to a week or freeze in small portions (surface will darken when exposed to air, so stir the pesto before serving) Yields 1-1/2 cups. Can add 1 cup of the sauce over freshly cooked spaghetti; mix well. **EXTRA:** 1 Pound Salmon, cut into 1-inch cubes, 4 cups Bell Pepper, Red Onion and Zucchini cubes, Salt and pepper to taste, 1-1/2 Tbsp Olive Oil, 1-1/2 Tbsp Pesto, 1-1/2 Tbsp Balsamic Vinegar. Thread the Salmon & vegetables onto skewers and season. Place on a grill over medium heat & cook 10-15 minutes, turning once or twice, until Salmon is cooked thoroughly. Stir together remaining ingredients and pour over skewer ingredients. **See Grilling in your Fireplace below**.

SEAFOOD – (Salmon – Broiled)

4 – 6 Salmon Steak Fillets   Melted Margarine   Salt & Pepper to taste

Optional Brush On:
2 Tbsp Lemon Juice   2 tsp Dijon Mustard   1 Tbsp Chopped Parsley

Salmon can be placed in an oven/broiler and broiled, turning once, or on a Bar-B-Q Grill after brushing with melted margarine – **OR** – Brush with French Dressing or Mayonnaise before broiling. **VARIATION: Fish can be poached which means to cook in a liquid (stock) which is about 180 degrees where the liquid is just barely moving but not yet bubbling.** See also **SAUCE – (Lemon Sauce)** for added flavor.

Author's Special Thoughts

If It's Wintertime You Can Grill/Cook in Your Fireplace.

Take an old metal pan (buy one at the second-hand store if you don't have one) or use a small barbeque grill base. Line it with aluminum foil and put your briquettes in it on top of your fireplace grate and light the briquettes, when coals are hot, gray ash in color, place one of your wire shelves from your oven on top, if you don't have a small grill grate, and cook your Salmon turning once until salmon flakes easily when fork is inserted. **(Great Ambience and Bar-B-Q Taste in the midst of Winter).** 4-6 Servings

MENU WEEK#15

Decided for You Cookbook – 365 Dinners

SEAFOOD – (Salmon Loaf)

1 (14-3/4 oz) can of Salmon, de-boned and drained
1 Tbsp Parsley
2 Tbsp melted Margarine or Butter

1-1/2 cups soft Breadcrumbs (3 slices of Bread)
1/2 tsp Red Hot Pepper Sauce (i.e., Tabasco)
1 Egg, beaten

Drain the Salmon, and remove all bones. Mix the breadcrumbs, egg, milk, parsley flakes, melted margarine and pepper sauce in with the Salmon. Form into a loaf pan. Bake at 350°F for 50 minutes.   4 Servings
MENU WEEK#22

SEAFOOD – (Salmon Patties)

1 or 2 (14-3/4 oz) cans *Salmon, de-boned and drained
1 Tbsp Parsley
1/2 tsp Baking Powder
1 tsp Worcestershire Sauce
Melted Butter or Margarine for frying
1-1/2 cups soft Breadcrumbs (3 slices of Bread) or commercial Breadcrumbs

2 Large Eggs, slightly beaten
1/2 cup chopped Onions
Salt and Pepper to taste
1 tsp Dry Mustard

Remove the center bones from the Salmon. Set aside and cook the onions in a little melted margarine or Vegetable oil till clear and tender. Mix together the Salmon, onions, 1/2 cup bread-crumbs, eggs, Worcestershire sauce, baking powder, and mustard with the salt and pepper. Form into 6-8 patties and roll the patties in the leftover breadcrumbs. Fry 3-5 minutes on each side in the melted margarine until golden brown. Optional: Serve a Tartar Sauce containing a couple dashes of Tabasco.   6-8 Servings
MENU WEEK #3

*Can substitute 1 Pound of fresh Crabmeat (or 2-3 cans) for Crab Cakes – **OR**- Add 1/2 tsp Old Bay Seasoning and 1/2 cup Mayonnaise **OTHER SPICY ALTERNATE**: Add in Cayenne Pepper, 1 Tbsp chopped Garlic, 1/4 cup chopped Onions, 3 Tbsp Creole Mustard, and Hot Pepper Sauce,

SEAFOOD – (Salmon Quiche)

1 (11 oz) Pkg Pie Crust Mix, or frozen but defrosted
4 chopped Green Onions (about 6 Tbsps)
4 cups Whipping Cream
1/2 tsp Cayenne Red Pepper

1 – 2 cans (~16 oz ea) Salmon deboned, drained
    and flaked
8 Eggs, beaten
1-1/2 tsp Sugar

Preheat the oven to 425°F. Prepare the pastry for two one-crust pies as directed on the package. Divide the Salmon and onions between pastry lined pie plates and scatter on the bottom. Beat together the eggs and whipping cream, salt, sugar, and Cayenne Pepper. Pour half of this mixture into both of the piecrust shells. Bake 15 minutes. Then reduce the temperature to 300°F and bake until when a knife is inserted one inch from the edge comes out clean or approximately 45 minutes. Let stand a few minutes before cutting into wedges.
8-11 servings
MENU WEEK#30

NOTE: <u>Fish and shellfish are both good sources of Iodine and should be eaten once a week.</u>

Decided for You Cookbook – 365 Dinners

SEAFOOD – (Salmon Spinach Fluff)

1 (14-3/4 oz) can of Salmon
Tartar Sauce commercially prepared
Lemon Wedges

1 Pkg frozen Spinach, Thawed and drained
2 - Egg Whites

Remove any bones and arrange the Salmon un-drained in the bottom of a shallow baking pie plate. Top with a package of the drained Spinach. Beat the egg whites until stiff and combine with 1/2 cup of the Tartar Sauce. Spread over the top of the Spinach. Bake at 375°F for 20-25 minutes. Remove and garnish with Lemon Wedges (Optional: Capers and Parsley for extra garnish).   4 Servings
MENU WEEK#38

SEAFOOD – (Salmon with Scalloped Potatoes and Peas)

1 (14-3/4 oz) can Salmon
1 (14 oz) can Garden Peas
1/4 tsp Pepper
1 tsp Salt
1 (5 oz) Jar Pasteurized Neufchatel Cheese Spread w/Pimento

3 – 4 medium Potatoes, peeled, sliced in rounds
1/2 cup chopped Onion
1 cup Sour Cream
Aluminum Foil

Drain the salmon, reserving the liquid. Layer in a 1-1/2 Quart baking dish, 1/2 of the potatoes (salt/ peppered), the onions, the drained peas, the Salmon. Combine the reserved salmon liquid, the cheese spread, and the sour cream and pour half of it over these ingredients. Add the remaining potatoes in the top layer (salt/peppered), and pour the remaining sauce over the top. Cover with aluminum foil or a lid and bake at 350°F for 35-40 minutes or until the potatoes are fork tender.   Serves 4-6
MENU WEEK#47

VARIATION: Salmon fillets (4-5 oz ea) can be enclosed inside folded aluminum foil and baked at 400°F for 25 minutes. Sprinkle on each fillet 2 tsp Olive oil, salt, and pepper. Place an oiled side down on the foil. Top with either chopped shallots or chopped green onions and 2 or 3 chopped tomatoes (can substitute drained, canned tomatoes), lemon juice, oregano, thyme. When cooked, top with 1 cup sour cream.

SEAFOOD – (Shrimp and Onion Seafood Pie)

3/4 cup Shrimp and Crabmeat or Salmon drained if canned
2 cups (1/2 Pound) shredded Sharp Cheddar Cheese
1 Tbsp Margarine or Butter
1/3 cup (7-1/2 oz) flaked, drained Tuna
3 Eggs
1 tsp Salt
1 medium Tomato, sliced

2 cups thinly sliced Onion Rings
1/4 tsp Pepper
2/3 cup Half and Half Milk
1/3 cup chopped Celery
9-inch unbaked Pastry Shell/Piecrust

In 1 Tbsp margarine/butter sauté 2 cups thinly sliced onion rings and 1/3 cup finely chopped celery until the onion is clear, soft, and golden. Place the **uncooked** pastry shell in a 9-inch pie plate. Add in layers, half of the drained fish of choice (or can use all of the fish or in any combination) half of the onion, and half of the 2 cups of cheddar cheese. Layer until all has been used. Combine the eggs, milk, salt, pepper, and beat slightly. Pour the mixture inside the pie crust shell. Bake in a hot oven at 400°F until firm about 30 minutes. **("Done" is when a dinner knife can be inserted into the center of the pie and the blade comes out clean.)** Five minutes before end of the baking time, top the pie with wedges of the sliced tomato. Can also use additional onion rings and some of the fish. Return to the oven and finish the baking time. Remove and cool on a rack before cutting.   Serves 6-8
MENU WEEK#37

SEAFOOD – (Shrimp and Sesame Asparagus)

1-2 Pounds cleaned, de-veined, large Shrimp/Prawns
1-1/2 to 2 Pounds of Asparagus Spears
1/3 cup Vegetable Oil
4 Tsp Soy Sauce

1 Tbsp Sesame Seed
2 small Onions, sliced
1-1/4 tsp Salt

Prepare Asparagus: Grasp a few of the spears and begin bending them over and the asparagus stalk will break at the point that it is tough. You can discard the bottom of the stalk or you can trim off the outer area of the stalks with a potato peeler and cut up the tender centers. Wash thoroughly and remove any bad discolored areas. Cut the asparagus into 2-3" pieces and set aside. Place 2 Tbsp of the vegetable oil in a skillet over medium heat; stir in the sesame seeds being careful not to burn the seeds and cook to a golden brown. Remove the seeds to a small bowl and set aside, add more oil if needed. In the same skillet, over medium-high heat for about 5 minutes, toss in the onions, soy sauce, asparagus, and shrimp; stirring constantly and cook until the shrimp turn pink and the vegetables are tender-crisp. Salt the ingredients and drop the sesame seeds over the top. Cover, let stand covered for 2 or 4 minutes and let the flavors come together.   6 Servings
MENU WEEK#42

SEAFOOD – (Shrimp Au Gratin – Garlic)

2 Pounds Shrimp (Medium/Large)
2 cups dry Breadcrumbs
4 cloves Garlic, minced
1 cup dry Sherry (optional) or use Water

1-1/2 sticks Margarine or Butter (3/4 cup)
1/2 cup chopped Parsley
Salt and Pepper to taste

Remove the shell, de-vein the shrimp and remove the tail. Toss the shrimp into boiling water and cook for about 3 minutes or until the shrimp turn all **pink (signal that it's done),** drain. In a large skillet melt one stick of the margarine/butter over low heat. Add in the breadcrumbs, parsley, garlic and salt and pepper. Stir a few minutes over low heat; pour in the sherry and cook an additional minute more. Place alternate layers of the shrimp and the breadcrumb mixture into a well-buttered gratin dish ending with a layer of the breadcrumbs. Dot with the remaining margarine/butter. Bake at 350°F for 10-15 minutes. Serve with egg noodles and a white sauce [**see SAUCE – White Sauce**)]   Serves 4
MENU WEEK#10

HINT: 1 Pound small Shrimp = about 50, 1 Pound Medium = about 20

SEAFOOD – (Shrimp Creole)

1 (16 oz) Pkg fresh or frozen Large Grey Prawns/Shrimp
1/2 cup sliced Green Bell Peppers
1 small can (4 oz) sliced Mushrooms
1/4 cup Margarine
Salt & Pepper to taste

1/2 cup sliced Onions
1 large can (28 oz) whole Tomatoes
1/2 tsp Worcestershire Sauce

Clean, de-vein the Shrimp, set aside. In a large skillet, sauté the onions and peppers in melted margarine until tender. Add in the mushrooms, tomatoes and shrimp, simmer until the shrimp turns **pink (action when they are done).** Stir in the Worcestershire sauce. This recipe can be expanded or reduced according to your desire by using bigger cans of tomatoes and increasing the vegetables. Serve over cooked, buttered rice.   Serves 4-6
MENU WEEK#25

NOTE: Store fresh shrimp/prawns on a bed/plastic bag of ice in the refrigerator. Cooked shrimp should be sealed in an airtight container and refrigerated.

SEAFOOD – (Shrimp in Crab Boil)

4 – 5 Pounds Prawns/Shrimp, in the shell – just washed well
1 tsp Red Hot Pepper Sauce
1 box Commercially prepared Crab Boil
2 Lemons
1 (12 oz) Bottle Chili Sauce

Place rinsed prawns in a very large pot and cover with water about 1-inch above the shrimp/ prawns. Bring the water to a boil and drop in the crab boil along with the squeezed lemons. **NOTE: The crab boil should be placed** in a small clean white cloth (dish towel), or a piece of muslin material or better still **inside of a commercial metal large tea ball** – anything to keep the seasonings together, so you can remove them easily when the prawns/shrimp are pink and cooked. At the table, grab the tail and head and snap and pull the body from the shell, make sure that the black vein down the tail came off with the shell. Dip in a commercial bottle of Chili Sauce or Cocktail Sauce.

Serves 6-10
MENU WEEK#24

Seafood Spice Crab Ball

2 Tbsp Mustard Seed	3 Tbsp Coriander Seed
2 - 3 tsp Cayenne Pepper	3 Tbsp Dill Seed
3 Tbsp Allspice	2 tsp Cloves

2 Bay Leaves (if too big they can float in the boil and removed separately)

SEAFOOD – (Shrimp in Puff Pastry Shells)

1 (24 oz) Pkg frozen Shrimp (peeled and cleaned)
1 (9 oz) refrigerated commercially prepared Alfredo Sauce (or make your own)

4 frozen Puff Pastry Shells	1 Tbsp Margarine or Butter
2 Tbsp Lemon Juice	1/2 tsp chopped Dill

Preheat the oven to 400°F. Place puff pastry shells on a large baking sheet and cook for 20-25 minutes or until golden brown. In the meantime, melt margarine in a large skillet. Cook the shrimp until they are fully "Pink" and all the liquid has evaporated, cover and keep warm. Remove the cooked pastry shells from the oven and set aside covered by a kitchen towel to keep warm. Add in the Alfredo Sauce, lemon juice and dill to your shrimp; simmer for 5 additional minutes, stirring frequently. Fill each puff pastry with the shrimp filling and roll like a tortilla and place in a serving dish. Top with left-over sauce. **(Optional topping: Cook together for about 5 minutes in melted butter, sliced mushrooms and coarsely chopped Prosciutto, drain any juices before using as a topping).**

Serves 4
MENU WEEK#52

Alfredo Sauce

MAKE YOUR OWN – (Ingredients not on grocery list)

4 Tbsp Margarine or Butter	2 Tbsp All-Purpose Flour
1 cup grated Romano Cheese	1 Large Egg Yolk, lightly beaten

1 cup Heavy Cream (whipping) or Half and Half Milk

Melt margarine in a saucepan. Stir in the flour until smooth. Add in the heavy cream and cheese. When the cheese has melted, remove the saucepan from the heat so when you now add in the beaten egg yolk, so it won't become scrambled eggs. Return the saucepan to low heat and stir until mixture thickens, and coats the back of a spoon. Remove from the heat, and pour over other ingredients being used.

SEAFOOD – (Shrimp New Orleans with Rice and Artichoke Hearts)

1 (16 oz) Pkg frozen cooked Shrimp
1 cup uncooked Long Grain Rice
2 cups sliced Celery
1 (8 oz) Pkg of Dry Spaghetti Sauce
1 (14 oz) can Artichoke Hearts, drained and cut into halves

1 medium Onion, chopped
1 (28 oz) can Tomatoes, chopped
2 Tbsp Margarine or Butter

In a skillet melt the margarine, stir and cook the onion, celery, rice until the onion is clear and tender. Stir in the tomatoes, and the spaghetti sauce. Reduce the heat to a simmer and cover with a tight fitting lid or an oversized dinner plate. Simmer about 25 minutes or until the rice is done. Stir in the artichoke hearts and the shrimp. Cover and cook another 5 minutes or until the shrimp are hot, being careful that the rice doesn't burn.
4-6 Servings
MENU WEEK#17

SEAFOOD – (Shrimp or Prawns Deep Fried)

2 Pounds frozen breaded Shrimp/Prawns cooked per Pkg Directions in the oven or fried in Vegetable Oil on both sides, drain on paper toweling
    -OR-
Use the Shrimp Boil recipe for non-breaded Prawns, if you don't like fried

Serves 4-6
MENU WEEK #9

SEAFOOD – (Shrimp Scampi and Fettuccini Noodles)

1 – 2 Pounds Large Shrimp/Prawns – cleaned and de-veined
1/2 cup White Wine or Triple Sec (Optional: but increase milk by 1/2 cup if not used)
1/2 cup Margarine or (1 Stick) Butter
1 small Onion, chopped
2 Tbsp chopped Parsley
1/2 cup Whipping Cream
Salt and Pepper to taste

1/4 cup Olive or Vegetable Oil
5 cloves finely chopped Garlic
1/8 tsp each Sweet Basil and Oregano
1 Lemon, juiced
Cooked, drained Fettuccini Noodles

Cleaning Shrimp/Prawns

Cut the shrimp down the back of the shell lengthwise with kitchen shears, remove the shell. With a sharp knife slightly cut open the shrimp body and remove the black vein, tail can be left on if you desired. Rinse with clear water and pat dry between paper towels.

Melt margarine and oil in a skillet. Add in the onion and cook till clear and tender, add in the chopped garlic and cook until the garlic just begins to brown. Add in the basil and oregano. Add in the shrimp, sauté, shaking the skillet to dislodge the shrimp from the pan for 3 – 4 minutes or until the shrimp has turned pink **(bright pink color indicates it's done)**, remove and set aside in a covered warmed bowl. Add into the skillet the whipping cream, the lemon juice and the white wine and cook till the sauce reduces, by about 1/3 around 5 minutes of cooking, and the sauce thickens. Add the shrimp back into the sauce. Pour over the drained noodles, sprinkle on the parsley. Garnish with lemon wedges if you wish.
Serves 4-6
MENU WEEK#49

Decided for You Cookbook – 365 Dinners

SEAFOOD – (Sole in Wine Sauce with Mushrooms)

4 Fish Fillets – Sole   1 small Onion, chopped
6 Tbsp Dry White Wine + 2 Tbsp Water   Salt and Pepper to Taste
1 Bay Leaf   6 Tbsp Margarine or Butter
4 Tbsp All-Purpose Flour   1-1/3 cups Milk
6 Tbsp Whipping or other Heavy Cream   Aluminum Foil
1/2 - 1 Pound of Button Mushrooms (wash and separate stems from tops, finely chop the stems)

Pre-heat the oven to 350°F. Scatter the chopped onions and stems of the mushrooms in the bottom of a baking dish. Cover these with your fish fillets. Pour the wine & water over the fish, salt and pepper to taste and drop in the bay leaf. Cover the dish with aluminum foil and bake for about 15 minutes or until tender. Strain off the cooking liquid, reserving it for the sauce; and place the fish in a warm serving platter making sure that the fish is kept warm while you cook the sauce.

Melt half of the butter in a skillet, add in the buttons of the mushrooms and sauté until they begin to soften, then drain well and sprinkle them with a little salt. Add these around the fish in the serving platter. Melt the remaining butter. Using either a whisk or a fork, stir in the flour until it is smooth. Add in the reserved fish cooking liquid and the milk. Bring this to a simmer, stirring until the sauce thickens, then remove it from the heat and stir in the heavy cream. Pour this sauce over the fish and the mushroom button caps.   Serves 4

MENU WEEK#19

SEAFOOD – (Spaghetti with White Clam Sauce)

(Spaghetti con Vongole)

3/4 Pound Spaghetti Noodles or Angel Hair Pasta   1 can (10-1/2 oz) minced Clams with its liquid
1/2 cup chopped Parsley   1/2 cup Margarine or Butter
1 tsp Salt and Pepper to taste   1/2 cup chopped Onions
2 cloves minced Garlic   2 heaping Tbsp All-Purpose Flour
2/3 cup Whipping Cream or Evaporated Milk
1/2 cup grated Parmesan Cheese* -OR- Myzithra Greek Goat Cheese

HINT: __Add 1 tsp of vegetable oil to your water to prevent the noodles from sticking together when cooking.__ Boil the noodles per package directions, drain and salt. **HINT:** __The noodles are done when you can cut one and there is no dryness in the center (it will appear whiter if not done).__ Melt the margarine in a large skillet and cook the onions till they are clear and tender, add in the parsley, and the garlic. Sauté these until the garlic is lightly browned. Add in the clams and liquid, stir and warm thoroughly for one minute. Stir in the flour until smooth and add in the whipping cream. Bring clam sauce to a rolling boil. Cook till thickened. Add back into the sauce, the salted spaghetti noodles and mix in the Parmesan Cheese. Place a cover on the skillet and turn off the heat, letting it set for 5 minutes. Salt and pepper to taste.

Serves 4-8

MENU WEEK#27

*Can use dry Myzithra Greek Goat Cheese if available in place of the Parmesan or can use both if desired. The Myzithra is a "great" cheese, but not always available.

HINT: __You can completely change the above flavor by mixing in 1/4 cup of Pesto Sauce - See Sauce Section.__

Decided for You Cookbook – 365 Dinners

SEAFOOD – (Sweet and Sour Fish)

1 Pound fresh or frozen Fish Fillets of choice
2 Tbsp Cornstarch
1 (15-1/4 oz) can Pineapple Chunks
Dash of Pepper
1/4 cup Honey
3 Tbsp Vinegar

1 medium Red or Green Bell Pepper
1 Tbsp additional Cornstarch
1/4 cup Soy Sauce
1/4 cup Ketchup
3 Tbsp Peanut Oil or Vegetable Oil

Thaw the fish fillets, if frozen. Cut the fillets into 1" pieces; coat with the cornstarch and set aside.
Cut the bell peppers into 3/4" pieces and set aside. Drain the pineapple, reserving the juice and set the
pineapple aside. In a small bowl, blend the reserved pineapple juice, the additional 1 Tbsp Cornstarch and
pepper. Stir in the soy sauce, honey, ketchup, vinegar, and set all aside. In a skillet or wok, cook the fish
pieces in hot oil for about 2 minutes on all sides; remove from the skillet. Add in the bell pepper cuts and
stir-fry for 2 minutes, remove from the skillet. Return the pineapple juice mixture to the skillet and cook until
it thickens and is bubbly. Return the pineapple, peppers, and the fish to the pan and stir until it is all re-
warmed.   Serves 4
MENU WEEK#44

SEAFOOD – (Sweet and Sour Shrimp)

1 Pound cleaned, de-veined with tails on Shrimp/Prawns
6 Tbsp Chicken Broth or Water
3 Tbsp Granulated Sugar
2 Tbsp Vinegar
3/4 tsp crushed Red Pepper Flakes
2 tsp minced Ginger
2 Tbsp Peanut or Vegetable Oil
1 cup Pineapple Chunks
Steamed Long Grain Rice

3 Tbsp Ketchup
3 Tbsp Pineapple or Orange Juice
2 tsp Soy Sauce
2 tsp Cornstarch
2 tsp minced Garlic
1 cup 1" pieces Bell Peppers
1 bunch thinly sliced Green Onions

In a bowl, combine 1/4 cup of broth, ketchup, sugar, juice, vinegar, soy and 1/2 tsp of the pepper flakes for a
sauce; set aside. In a small bowl, combine the cornstarch with the remaining 2 Tbsp of the stock and stir to
dissolve; set aside. Make a marinade in a bowl of the ginger, garlic and remaining pepper flakes. Add in the
shrimp and stir to cover; let set for 10-20 minutes. When marinating is completed, heat a large wok over high
heat. Add in the oil of choice and coat the sides and the bottom of the pan. Add in the shrimp, garlic and
ginger and stir-fry until the shrimp are pink, about 2 minutes. Remove the shrimp and add in the onions, and
peppers and stir-fry until crisp-tender about 2 minutes. Add in the sauce and stir until the sugar dissolves.
Add in the cornstarch mixture and bring to a boil. Return the shrimp to the pan and add in the pineapple
chunks and green onions. Cook until the sauce thickens about 1 minute. Serve over rice.   Serves 4
MENU WEEK#45

Decided for You Cookbook – 365 Dinners

SEAFOOD – (Teriyaki Fish)

2-3 Pounds Fish Fillets (your choice) can be cubed if you desire
1/2 cup Ketchup   1/4 cup Dry White Wine or Water
1/4 cup Soy Sauce   2 Tbsp Sugar
1 tsp Salt   1/2 tsp Ground Ginger
1 clove Garlic, crushed

Place the fish inside a large zip lock bag. Mix all ingredients and pour over the fish in the bag, seal and place the bag on a plate or in a shallow dish to marinate at least one hour in the refrigerator or over night.   Turn the bag occasionally so all of the fish receives the marinade juices. Remove from the refrigerator and place on a broiler pan on the second shelf of your oven (or place on your outside bar-b-q grill), broil on both sides **until you touch it with a fork and it flakes**. (If you don't want to broil, you can bake it in the oven for 30 minutes at 325°F or you can pan fry in a little melted butter/margarine or olive oil). Baste occasionally with the marinade as needed.
Serves 4-6
MENU WEEK#16

SEAFOOD – (Tuna and Broccoli Rice Casserole)

2 (16 oz ea) cans Tuna, drained and flaked
2 (8 oz) Pkgs or 1 Large (16 oz) Bag frozen Chopped Broccoli
1 cup+ extra for topping, grated sharp Cheddar or American Cheese
1 cup Water   1 tsp Salt
1/4 tsp Pepper   1 cup Quick Cooking Minute Rice

Cook the broccoli per package directions; drain. In a 2-Quart Casserole Baking Dish combine the tuna, broccoli, water, uncooked rice and the cheese. Salt and pepper to taste. Bake at 350°F for 25 minutes (until the rice is thoroughly cooked). Remove the casserole and place additional grated cheese on top and return to the oven for an addition 3-4 minutes until the cheese melts.
Serves 4
MENU WEEK#40

SEAFOOD – (Tuna and Swiss Quiche Pie)

1 unbaked 9" Pastry Shell or frozen shell, thawed   1 can (16 oz) Tuna, drained
1 cup shredded (4 oz) Swiss Cheese   1/2 cup chopped Green Onion
3 Eggs   1 cup Mayonnaise
1/2 cup Milk

Pierce pastry shell with a fork so steam can escape. Bake 375°F for 10 minutes and cool. Mix together Tuna, cheese, onion & pour into the cooked shell. Stir together the Mayonnaise, milk and eggs. Pour over the tuna mixture. Bake 50 minutes or until knife removed comes out clean.
Serves 8
(Extra Recipe)

SEAFOOD – (Tuna Buffet Macaroni Casserole)

2 (7-1/4 oz ea) Box of Macaroni and Cheese Dinner   1-1/2 cups Milk
2 Tbsp Margarine   1/2 cup chopped Onion
1/4 cup chopped Green Bell Pepper   2 (16 oz) cans Tuna, drained
1 (10-3/4 oz) can Cream of Celery Soup   1 (3 oz) can drained Mushrooms
1/4 cup chopped Pimiento

Prepare the macaroni dinners as directed on the package except increasing the milk to 3/4 of a cup per box. Sauté onion and pepper in margarine until tender. Add to the dinner with all remaining ingredients; mixing well. Pour into a 1-1/2 quart casserole dish and bake at 250°F for 30 minutes.
4-6 Servings
MENU WEEK#13

Decided for You Cookbook – 365 Dinners

SEAFOOD – (Tuna Burgers)

2 (16 oz each) cans Tuna, drained and flaked
1/2 cup chopped Celery   2 Tbsp minced Onion
1/3 cup Mayonnaise   1 tsp Lemon Juice
2 Tbsp Bottled Chili Sauce   2 Tbsp softened Margarine/Butter
4 Hamburger Buns, split and toasted   Lettuce, shredded
1/2 cup Breadcrumbs (2 slices bread finely ground)   Tomatoes, sliced

Combine the tuna, breadcrumbs, celery and the onion. Blend in the Mayonnaise, lemon juice and the Chili Sauce (add more breadcrumbs if not firm). Form into patties and lightly brown in 2 Tbsp Margarine/Butter on each side. Spread the margarine or butter on the Hamburger Buns and toast in the broiler, or brown on a griddle until lightly browned. Place shredded lettuce and tomatoes on the buns topped with your tuna patties and the mayonnaise mixture.

Serves 4
(Extra Recipe)

SEAFOOD – (Tuna, Carrots, Peas and Macaroni Casserole)

2 (6 oz ea) cans Tuna, drained and flaked   1 (15 oz) can Garden Peas
1 (1 pound) can Julienne Carrots, drained   2 Hard-Cooked Eggs, sliced
1 (15 oz) can Macaroni & Cheese   1/2 tsp Dried Rosemary
1/4 tsp Pepper   1 (3-1/2 oz) can French Fried Onion Rings
1 (10-1/2 oz) can condensed Cheddar Cheese Soup

Preheat the oven to 350°F. Lightly grease a 2-Quart casserole dish. Drain the peas, reserving 1/3 cup of liquid. In a small saucepan, combine the reserved liquid from the peas with the cheese soup; mix well. Bring to a boil over medium heat, stirring constantly. In the prepared casserole, layer half of the tuna, carrots, peas, egg slices and the macaroni and cheese on the top. Sprinkle the top with the rosemary and the pepper. Drizzle the warmed soup mixture over the tuna and vegetables. Repeat the layers if you have enough, topping it off with the soup mixture. Bake 25 minutes, uncovered or until hot and bubbly. Remove from the heat and top with the fried onion rings. Return it to the oven for an additional 5 minutes longer until the rings are warmed.

Serves 6
MENU WEEK#2

SEAFOOD – (Tuna Casserole with Cheese Biscuit Swirls and Peas)

2 (16 oz ea) cans Tuna, drained   1/3 cup chopped Green Bell Peppers   3 Tbsp Shortening
2 Tbsp Margarine/Butter   Waxed Paper   1-1/2 cups Milk
1/3 cup chopped Onion   1/2 cup Cold Water   1 Tbsp Lemon Juice
2 cups plus 1/4 cup Baking Biscuit Mix   1 (15 oz) can Peas   All Purpose Flour
1 can (10-3/4 oz) condensed Cream of Mushroom Soup
3/4 cup (3 oz) chopped American Processed or Cheddar Cheese

Heat the oven to 425°F. In a skillet melt the shortening and cook the green pepper and onion till the onions are clear and tender. Mix in the soup and the milk together and stir well. Add in the 1/4 cup of biscuit mix and stir. Heat this to a boiling point for 1 minute, stirring constantly. Add in the tuna, peas, and lemon juice. Pour into a 9 x 13"rectangle baking dish. Stir the 2 cups of biscuit mix and the cold water together and form a dough. Knead about 5 or 6 times on lightly floured wax paper. Pat this dough into a rectangle about the size of your baking dish; sprinkle the top with the cheese. Brush the excess flour off your waxed paper and pick up the edges of the longest side and begin to jelly-roll the dough, creating a cheese spiral biscuit roll. Pinch and seal the end of the roll edge with your fingers. Cut this roll into 1-1/4"slices and place the swirled biscuits on top of your casserole side by side covering the entire top. Bake 20-25 minutes or until the biscuit top is golden brown.

Serves 4-6
MENU WEEK #48

SEAFOOD – (Tuna Cheese Toasties with Green Beans)

3 or 4 Hamburger Buns, split buttered
1 (3 oz) Pkg Cream Cheese, softened
2 tsp Lemon Juice
1 tsp creamy Horseradish
4 Tbsp softened Margarine or Butter

2 (16 oz ea) cans Tuna, drained and flaked
2 Tbsp Mayonnaise
1 tsp Dried Onion Flakes
1 (15 oz) can cut Green Beans, drained
1 cup Processed Cheese cut in 1/4" slices (4 oz)

Set the oven to broil 500°F. Mix the tuna, cream cheese, mayonnaise, lemon juice, onion flakes, horseradish; stir in the green beans. Broil 500°F the buttered buns on the top rack in the oven until lightly browned about 2-1/2 minutes. Remove and spoon on top of the buns, the tuna mixture then with the cheese. Return to broil till all are bubbly.   Serves 4-6
MENU WEEK#28

SEAFOOD – (Tuna Colcannon with Cabbage and Mashed Potatoes)

2 cans (16 oz ea) Tuna, drained and broken into chunks
6 medium size Potatoes, peeled and quartered
4 cups shredded Cabbage, steamed until tender
3/4 cup Milk (can be canned Evaporated Milk)

1/2 cup chopped Green Onions
4 Tbsp (1/2 stick) Margarine or Butter
2 tsp Salt and 1/4 tsp Pepper

Peel and quarter the potatoes and put these in a half filled pot of water. *Place inside the pot, above the water line, a vegetable steamer tray or metal colander. Place the shredded cabbage on top of the steamer tray. Bring the potatoes in the bottom to a rolling boil and cover the pan. By the time the potatoes are fork tender, the cabbage will also be done. **This way you cook two vegetables at the same time.** *If you don't cook together, boil separately. Remove from the heat, salt the cabbage to taste. Drain the potatoes well and mix in the milk, the margarine, green onions, salt and pepper and mash or whip with an electric mixer until smooth, no lumps. Mix the tuna and cabbage into the potatoes. Garnish with additional green onions or additional dots of margarine.   Serves 6
MENU WEEK#27

If you are using the colander inside the pot then place two heels of bread, crust down, on top of the cabbage to absorb the cabbage steam. –OR– you can set a small can containing vinegar on the counter next to the boiling pot. This will help your kitchen in not smelling like cooked cabbage.

SEAFOOD – (Tuna Crunchy Bake with Green Beans)

2 (16 oz ea) cans Tuna, drained and flaked
3 Tbsp Mayonnaise or Salad Dressing of Choice
2 (8 oz each) cans French Fried Onions
Aluminum Foil
1 (8 oz) can sliced Water Chestnuts – drained and cut into thirds
1 (10-3/4 oz) can Condensed Cream of Mushroom Soup (**VARIATION:** Cream of Chicken Soup)

1 (16 oz) can cut Green Beans – drained
1/4 cup Milk
1/2 tsp Curry Powder

Heat the oven to 350°F. Mix the onions, reserving 1/4 cup of the Onions, the Green Beans, Tuna and Water Chestnuts. Mix the soup with the milk, mayonnaise, and curry powder and stir into the previous ingredients. Pour all this into a non-greased 2-quart casserole. Cover with aluminum foil and bake for 30 minutes. Remove the foil. Sprinkle the reserved onions and bake uncovered an additional 5 minutes.   6 Servings
MENU WEEK#29

SEAFOOD – (Tuna Noodle Skillet with Peas)

2 (16 oz ea) cans Tuna
1 (15 oz) can Peas, drained
2 – 3 Tbsp All-Purpose Flour
Parmesan Cheese (Optional Topping)
1-1/2 cups Milk (or use 1/2 can of evaporated milk)

1/4 Pound Butter or Margarine
Salt and Pepper to taste
1 (12 oz) Pkg Egg Noodles

Cook the noodles per package directions, drain. Salt and Pepper to taste. Bring the peas to a boil and drain, Salt and Pepper to taste. Mix the peas and tuna into the white sauce and pour over the noodles and mix.

White Sauce

Melt the butter or margarine in a saucepan and add in the flour and stir until all the lumps are blended. Add in the milk. Stir until the sauce has thickened. Pour sauce over the top of the noodles, tuna and peas and stir together. You can sprinkle on some Parmesan Cheese and stir if desired. Serve immediately.

Serves 4-6
MENU WEEK#1

SEAFOOD – (Tuna Panella with Peas and Rice)

2 (6 oz ea) cans Tuna, drained and broken into chunks
1 Large Onion, chopped (1 cup)
3 Tbsp Vegetable Oil
1 Large Green Bell Pepper, sliced
2 tsp Instant Chicken Bouillon or Broth
1-1/2 cups Water
1 (4 oz) jar Pimientos, diced

1 Garlic clove, minced
1 cup uncooked Long Grain Rice
1 bottle (8 oz) Clam Juice
2 tsp Salt
1 Pkg (10 oz) frozen Peas
Aluminum Foil

Sauté onion and garlic in hot oil in a 8-cup baking dish. Push the onion and garlic to the side and place in the rice. Stirring it constantly brown the rice until golden. Add in the tuna, green bell pepper, clam juice, chicken broth, salt and water. Bring to a boil, cover with aluminum foil and bake in a moderate oven (350°F) for 40 minutes; uncover, spoon on top the frozen peas and the diced pimiento around the to edge of the casserole for color. Cover again and bake an additional 10 minutes long or until the liquid is absorbed and the peas and rice are tender.

Serves 6
MENU WEEK#43

SEAFOOD – (Tuna Patties)

2 (6 oz ea) cans Tuna (drain juices and save) or 1 Pound can Salmon
1/3 cup Dry Breadcrumbs (place bread in toaster, then crush inside a plastic bag)
1/2 cup Chopped Onion
1/3 cup Fish Liquid (reserved from can)
1 tsp Mustard (prepared)
Additional 1/2 cup Dry Breadcrumbs

1/4 cup melted Vegetable Oil
2 Eggs, beaten
1/2 tsp Salt

Drain the fish, saving the liquid. Cook the onion until tender in the hot vegetable oil. Remove from the skillet and mix together with the fish, 1/3 cup Breadcrumbs fish liquid, beaten eggs, mustard, salt and pepper. Shape this into (6) patties, roll each patty in the 1/2 cup of the dry Breadcrumbs. Cook in the hot oil for 4 minutes on each side.

Serves 6
MENU WEEK#33

Decided for You Cookbook – 365 Dinners

SEAFOOD – (Tuna Potato Patties with Fine Herbs)

4 Medium Potatoes (3 cups mashed)
3 Eggs, slightly beaten
1/2 tsp each Salt and Pepper
1/2 tsp Thyme or Marjoram
Cracker or Breadcrumbs

2 cans (16 oz ea) Tuna
1 clove Garlic minced or 1/2 tsp Garlic Powder
2 Tbsp Parsley
2 Tbsp minced Chives
Olive Oil, Butter or Margarine

Peel and cook the potatoes in boiling water until fork tender; drain and mash, add in salt and pepper (do not add milk). Cool and combine the potatoes with the tuna and eggs. Mix in the minced clove of garlic with all other seasonings. Form this into patties, and roll them in the breadcrumbs. Sauté these patties in the melted margarine or olive oil until golden browned on both sides. These patties are good served on broiled Parmesan cheese topped tomato slices.

Serves 6
MENU WEEK#18

SEAFOOD – (Tuna Quickie Time with Rice)

2 – 3 (16 oz each) cans Tuna packed in oil, undrained
Salt and pepper to taste
1-2 small Tomatoes, cubed
1 Tbsp Butter or Margarine
1-1/3 cups Minute Rice (prepared per Pkg directions)

1/3 cup Ketchup

Soy Sauce to taste

Cube the tomatoes and mix with the tuna, Ketchup, salt and pepper. As soon as your rice is cooked, sprinkle with Soy Sauce, if desired (be careful may become too salty, maybe each individual person would like to do this process). Mix all of the ingredients together and serve immediately as it cools down quickly.

4-6 Servings
MENU WEEK#20

SEAFOOD – (Tuna Rice Rolls)

1 Pkg (6 oz) Chicken-Flavored Rice Mix
1 (10-3/4 oz) can condensed Cream of Celery Soup
1 Egg beatened with 1 Tbsp Water **(Egg Wash)**

2 cans (16 oz ea) Tuna
1 Pkg Piecrust Mix or defrosted frozen Pie Shells
1/2 cup Sour Cream

Prepare the rice mix per package directions. Add the tuna to the rice, followed by 1/3 of your soup. Mix together. Prepare your piecrust and roll out to 14" x 11" rectangle. Spoon the tuna mixture down the center third of the pastry; bring the sides up and over the filling pinching the seams tightly together into a roll. Fold the ends of the roll tightly together like a Burrito, completely covering the tuna and rice into a roll. Place on a baking sheet; brush the outside of the roll with the egg wash. Bake in a hot oven (400°F) for 30 minutes or until golden brown. Mix together the balance of the soup and add in the sour cream, bringing this mixture to a boil on the stove. Slice the roll into sections and top with the sauce and garnish with lemon wedges or items of your choice.

Fold edges inwards and roll, sealing ingredients inside.

Serves 6
MENU WEEK#51

Decided for You Cookbook – 365 Dinners

SPECIAL PLACE FOR MY NOTES:

TUR – (Turkey and Stuffing)

15-20 Pound **defrosted**/fresh Turkey	Gravy
Salt & Pepper to taste	Stuffing

Defrost turkey under refrigeration one day/for every 4 Pounds - Preheat your oven to 325°F. Lift up the skin at the neck cavity and remove the package of giblets (heart/kidneys/ gizzard) from inside. Remove the neck from inside the body cavity, between the legs, of the turkey. Before you start on the turkey preparation, bring to a boil 4 – 6 cups of water, some chopped celery leaves, 1 Tbsp salt, 1 Tbsp Poultry Seasoning, giblets and the neck of the turkey. Lower the heat and cook these ingredients for about 30 minutes. Remove the giblets and neck and you can cut them up for the dressing, reserving the liquid. This liquid will be used to make gravy later.

TURKEY PREPARATION: Brush it with melted butter, or take some margarine on your fingers and spread all over the outside of the bird, especially on the drumsticks. Salt the inside of the cavities and the outside of the turkey. Add into the pan 1-1/2 cups of water or chicken broth (keeps it from sticking to the bottom of the pan, keeps it moist, and adds more liquid to turkey for gravy). Place the turkey, breast side up inside the pan. Fill the body cavity with dressing as per below directions. You can tie the legs together at bone area to prevent the dressing from flowing out from the bird during cooking, if desired. (If using a meat thermometer, run it through the thigh not touching the bone (180°F for doneness, if no dressing). If with dressing, dressing should be cooked to 165°F). Tent the turkey with large pieces of aluminum foil folded together to keep the steam inside the tent, and tighten around edge of pan. Cook 20 minutes per pound (20 Pounds x 20 minutes=400 minutes ÷ 60 minutes=4 hrs). [If you are not using a meat thermometer you will know the turkey is done when you pierce it through the breast or thigh with a fork and the juices run out "clear" not pink]. I like to drain the juices once half way through the baking process to use for gravies or dressing. Remove the foil during the last twenty minutes of baking so the turkey can brown. [Refrigerate leftovers within 2-hours after coming out of the oven. Remove stuffing and meat from the bones before refrigerating.] See also recipe **SAUCE – (Cranberry Sauce)** if you need it.

Turkey Dressing/Stuffing

4 cups Corn Bread (See Corn Bread Recipe) or purchase ready made mix*
1 Pkg Smokie Links (can use miniatures or cut up the large ones)

1 chopped Onion	1/2 tsp Salt and Pepper
3 Eggs, slightly beaten	1 – 2 Tbsp Poultry Seasoning
1 cup chopped Celery	

1 – 2 cups Turkey Broth (removed from boiling giblets or canned chicken broth)

*If you like the dressing to be a little lighter add in 1/2 to whole package of cubed bread seasoned stuffing mix, moistened per package directions. **OPTIONAL:** You can also cut up the cooked, giblets in the dressing. Mix all ingredients in a very large bowl (cake taker). Stuff the turkey and place any leftovers into a separate 9 x 13 baking dish (if you have any turkey liquid or can use canned chicken broth and pour a cup over top of dressing for extra moisture) and cook covered with aluminum foil at 325°F for ~one hour.

Turkey Giblet Gravy

Pour juices from the turkey baking pan into a large pot (be careful when you do this that the entire turkey doesn't slip forward and cause the juices to splatter and burn you). If this liquid is "too greasy from Turkey fats" spoon some off the top before proceeding (can be frozen for use later). Use 2 cups of turkey juices and 2 cups of giblet water. Shake together (in a sealable container – jar, bowl) 4 Tbsp of flour (or 3 Tbsp Cornstarch) and 1/2 cup milk until smooth, no lumps. Stirring constantly pour into the juice/water and bring the gravy to a boil to thicken. Salt and Pepper to taste. If the gravy color is not dark enough, add in a tsp or less of Bouquet Browning and Seasoning Sauce.

Serves 6-8

MENU WEEK#47

Decided for You Cookbook – 365 Dinners

TUR – (Turkey Broccoli Casserole)

2 (10 oz ea) Pkgs of frozen chopped Broccoli or 1 Large Bag
2 cups cooked Turkey   1 Tbsp Lemon Juice
2 tsp Butter or Margarine   2 Tbsp All-Purpose Flour
1/2 tsp Salt   2 cups Milk
1/2 cup Breadcrumbs   1/2 cup grated Parmesan Cheese
1/2 cup Swiss Cheese, shredded   1 Tbsp melted Margarine

Prepare the broccoli per package directions. Drain well; mix with the lemon juice. Mix the Turkey and the broccoli then spread into a 9" round baking pan or dish. In a saucepan, melt the margarine and blend into it the flour, add in the salt, add in the milk all at once and continue stirring constantly. Cook, until the mixture thickens and bubbles into a white sauce. Remove from the heat and stir in the Swiss cheese until it is melted. Spread the sauce over the broccoli and the turkey. Melt the margarine, stir in the breadcrumbs and the parmesan cheese. Spoon this topping over the casserole. Bake in a 350°F oven for 20-25 minutes or until heated thoroughly.

Serves 5-6
MENU WEEK#47

TUR – (Hot Turkey Sandwiches)

1 Pound thinly sliced Deli Turkey (or Leftover Turkey, shredded)
1 Pouch/Pkg of Dry Turkey Gravy mixed with 1 cup Water
1 Pouch/Pkg of Dry Chicken Gravy mixed with 1 cup Water
4-8 slices White Bread
Margarine (1 cube softened)

Mix the leftover Turkey and Chicken Gravy with the water in a saucepan and bring to a boil until its thickened; keep warm. Place the Deli Turkey (or Leftover Turkey pieces after a big Turkey Dinner; frozen but defrosted) in a Microwave to warm for 1-1/2 minutes. . Spread the margarine on one side of the slices of bread. Using a griddle or skillet, heat to medium hot. Brown the bread, on one side only, margarine side down **(called Fried Bread)**. Place two pieces of the Fried Bread, buttered and browned side down. Layer pieces of the hot Turkey on top of the bread and ladle/spoon Turkey/ Chicken gravy over the top. **-OR-**

Serves 4-6
MENU WEEK#2

Turkey/Chicken Gravy

MAKE YOUR OWN – (Ingredients not on grocery list)

Bring 1-1/2 cups of water to a boil in a saucepan. Add in 2 cubes or 2 tsp of Chicken bouillon. Place 2 Tbsp flour and ½ cup milk in a sealed container (bowl or jar) and shake till thoroughly mixed, no lumps. Add this flour mixture slowly to the boiling liquid, stirring constantly. When slightly thickened, add the leftover Turkey to re-warm in the thickened gravy **(This is an example of a great left-over becoming a great plan-over meal).** Salt and pepper to taste. If the gravy is not dark enough in color, add a tsp of Bouquet Gravy & Seasoning mix to darken it. Serve over the fried bread.

Decided for You Cookbook – 365 Dinners

TUR – (Turkey in Puff Pastry)

1 frozen white/dark meat Turkey Roast (comes in a pan with giblet gravy)
1 can (4-3/4 oz) Liver Pâté (optional)
1 Pkg (10 oz) frozen but defrosted Patty Shells or Piecrust
1 Egg mixed with 1 Tbsp Water (Egg Wash)

Remove the patty shells from the package and let these soften at room temperature for at least 20 minutes. In the meantime, roast the turkey per package directions for approximately 1-1/2 hrs. Remove it from the oven to cool on a rack for 30 minutes (or set it on top of an unused burner on your stove so the bottom will cool). Raise the oven temperature to 450°F. Place the patty shells on a floured work surface, one on top of the other and roll out to a 14" x 16" rectangle, try to not tear the surface, if you do, patch and re-roll that area. Spread the Liver Pate over the roast. Place the pastry over the top of the roast and fold it around and underneath, pinching together the edge to seal in the roast. Place it on a baking sheet with the sealed seam to the bottom. You can use the trimmings to cut out flower or leaf designs and place on the side or top, as you desire. Brush the outside with the egg wash this will make it shiny after it's baked. Bake at 400°F for 20 minutes or until the pastry is golden brown. Let it stand 10 minutes before cutting which will become easier by waiting. Prepare the enclosed giblet gravy per the package directions **–OR–** make instant gravy as directed in the previous Hot Turkey Sandwich Recipe. Place the roast on a serving platter and garnish around it with drained cling peach slices or a cranberry orange relish if you'd like.

Serves 6
MENU WEEK#50

TUR – (Turkey Mushroom Quiche)

1 cup finely chopped Turkey, cooked (legs/breasts)   1 (3 oz) can sliced mushrooms drained
1 (9" or 10") frozen Pastry shell, baked and cooled   3/4 cup shredded American Processed Cheese
1 can condensed Cream of Shrimp Soup   1/4 cup Milk
4 slightly beaten Eggs in an oven proof bowl or a saucepan

Arrange the turkey and mushrooms in a pie shell; distribute the cheese over the top of the turkey and mushrooms. In a small saucepan combine the soup and milk; heat to boiling stirring constantly. **Pour a little hot milk at a time into the eggs and whisk at the same time making sure the eggs don't become "scrambled eggs". If you put the eggs into the hot mixture all at one time they will cook too quickly into scrambled eggs from the intense heat.** Pour the soup/egg mixture over the casserole. Bake in a 350°F oven for 40-45 minutes or until a dinner knife can be inserted in the center of the casserole and it comes out clean. Cool for 10 minutes before serving.

Serves 4-8
MENU WEEK#11

TUR – (Turkey Roast)

1 frozen Turkey Roast (white and dark meat is the juiciest) or small Boneless Breast.   Cook per package directions reserving the juices to mix into the instant gravy mixes for extra flavor. Cook 1 Pkg instant Turkey Gravy made per package directions and 1 Pkg instant Chicken Gravy made per package directions **-OR-**

Turkey Gravy

MAKE YOUR OWN - (Ingredients are not on the grocery list)
Pour juices from the turkey baking pan into a large pot (be careful when you do this that the turkey roast doesn't slip forward and cause the juices to splatter and burn you). Scrape out all the juices from the baking pan and add the juices to 1 cup of water and 2 cups of chicken broth; put into a saucepan and warm to a boil. Shake together (in a re-sealable container – jar, bowl) 4 Tbsp of flour and 1/2 cup milk until smooth, no lumps. Stirring constantly pour into the saucepan containing the juice/water and bring the gravy to a boil to thicken. Salt and Pepper to taste. If the gravy color is not dark enough, add in a tsp or less of Bouquet Browning & Seasoning Sauce.

Serves 4-6
MENU WEEK#12

Decided for You Cookbook – 365 Dinners

TUR – (Turkey Tetrazinni)

MAKE YOUR OWN – (Ingredients not on grocery List)

4 Tbsp Butter/Margarine	1 to 1-1/2 cups Mushrooms, thinly sliced
4 Tbsp Flour	2 cups Chicken Broth
1 cup Heavy Cream (Whipping)	Salt and Pepper to taste
1 Tbsp Parsley, chopped	2 Tbsp Sherry Wine
3 cups **cooked** Turkey or Chicken, cubed	1/2 cup slivered Almonds (Optional)
1/2 cup dry Breadcrumbs	6 Tbsp grated Parmesan Cheese

8 oz Fettuccine Noodles, broken in small pieces, cooked and drained

Grease a shallow baking dish with margarine/butter. Melt additional butter in a saucepan and sauté the mushrooms until cooked but not browned, remove from pan. Stir in the flour and mix until smooth. Add in the broth and cream, and whisk until boiling and thick. Simmer about 10 minutes. Stir in the salt and pepper and parsley. Add in the Sherry, stirring constantly. Add in the diced meat and almonds and mix well. Place the cooked fettuccine noodles in the baking dish, salt and pepper to taste. Top with the poultry and cream sauce, mix. Sprinkle the top with the breadcrumbs and cheese. Brown under a broiler and serve. If you have sun-dried tomatoes on hand, dice them and sprinkle a bit on top of each serving.   Serves 4
(Extra Recipe)

TURKEY - MICROWAVE INFORMATION:

HINT: To assure that the meat browns, place ingredients in a browning pan or place a pan inside a large brown shopping bag. Fold the bag's opening edge back underneath container, so fats won't escape. Be sure bag doesn't touch ceiling of Microwave Oven might spark unit (check often)
Whole – 11 to 13 min/Lb - (Cook in baking bag, brush with browning sauce)

ADDITIONAL SPACE FOR YOUR NOTES:

WIENERS/FRANKFURTERS

WNR – (Chili Dogs)

Wieners (Frankfurters)
Can of Chili without beans or canned Chili Sauce if available
Hot Dog Buns
Chopped Onion

You can microwave the wieners for about 3 minutes, **-OR-** pan fry your wieners covered, **-OR-** steam them by placing a metal colander inside a covered pan of small amount of boiling water, **-OR-** boil them in a small amount of water and drain. Warm the can of Chili and place the hot wiener inside a warmed bun topped with a few chopped onions. Spoon the chili on top and serve. Great made with leftover chili.

Serves 4-6
MENU WEEK#6

WNR – (Circle Hot Dogs)

8 Wieners/Frankfurters)
8 slices processed American Cheese
4 Hamburger Buns, split and toasted

2 small Tomatoes, each cut into 4 slices
8 Pickle Slices – Sweet or Kosher

Make cuts (Cuts to be across the wiener, almost cut through to the bottom) of each wiener and place them in an non-greased baking pan. Set the oven control to Broil at (500°F) about 4 or 5 inches from the burner and heat until lightly brown. They will curl into a circle with the heat (2-3 minutes). Place the wiener circles on top of your toasted buns. Place cheese on top of the wieners and broil until melted. Garnish with the pickle and tomato slices.

4 – 6 Servings
MENU WEEK#19

WNR – (Corn Dogs)
1-2 Packages of Frozen Corn Dogs **–OR-**

Corn Dogs with a Little Help
MAKE YOUR OWN – (Ingredients not on grocery List)
1 pound of Wieners (~8)   1 Tbsp Sugar
1 cup Pancake Mix   2/3 cup Water

Mix together and then follow directions from ** below Make Your Own recipe

4-6 Servings
MENU WEEK#9

Corn Dog Batter Made from Scratch
MAKE YOUR OWN - (Ingredients not on the grocery list)**
1/2 cup All-Purpose Flour   1/2 cup Corn Meal
1 Tbsp Sugar   2 tsp Dry Mustard
1/2 tsp Salt   1 tsp Baking Powder
1 tsp Vegetable Oil   1/2 cup Milk
1 Egg – beaten

Beat egg and milk together, add in rest of dry ingredients stirring well. **Place the batter into a tall drinking glass. Skewer the wiener with Popsicle sticks, fondue sticks. Dip wiener in flour (this makes the coating stick better) and then push in down into the glass of batter until it's entirely covered. Remove carefully and brown on all sides in hot Vegetable Oil 2-3 minutes at 375°F. Drain on paper toweling.

(WNR)-231

(Corn Dogs continued)

Corn Dogs Made in the Oven with Cheese

MAKE YOUR OWN - (Ingredients not on the grocery list)

2 Tbsp Vegetable Oil
1/2 cup All-Purpose Flour
1/4 tsp Salt
1 egg
7 Wieners cut in half

1/2 cup Yellow Cornmeal
1 tsp Baking Powder
1/2 cup Buttermilk
1/2 cup (2 oz) grated Cheddar Cheese

Using a lightly greased Corn-shaped cast iron pan, place the pan in the oven to preheat for about 15 minutes. Combine the other ingredients in a mixing bowl stirring till smooth. Remove the hot pan from the oven and spoon in approximately 3 Tbsp of batter into each well. Lay one half of a wiener in the center of this batter. Spoon the remaining batter covering each wiener. Bake 400°F for 18 minutes. Turn cooked corn dog out onto a serving platter, corn patterned side up. (Extra Recipe)

WNR – (Frankfurter Goulash)

1 pound Wieners/Franks, sliced diagonally
2 Bell Peppers, cut in chunks
1 tsp Caraway Seed
1 can (8 oz) Tomato Sauce
Mashed Potatoes, Hot cooked Noodles, or Rice (Optional)

2 Tbsp Butter or Margarine
1/2 cup diced Celery
1 Tbsp Sweet Paprika
1-1/2 cups thinly sliced Onion

Cook the onion in melted butter in a skillet until golden. Add in the peppers, and celery stirring for another three to four minutes. Add in the caraway seed, paprika, and tomato sauce. Cover and simmer, stirring often, for approximately 10 minutes or until sauce is fairly thick and celery is fork tender. Serve over mashed potatoes or noodles.   Servings 4

MENU WEEK#36

WNR – (Frankfurter Hot Dog Macaroni)

2 – 6 Wieners/Frankfurters, cut into thin slices
3-1/2 oz uncooked macaroni rings (about 1 cup)
1/2 cup Creamed Cottage Cheese, small curd or Ricotta Cheese
1/2 cup shredded Sharp Cheddar Cheese (about 2 oz)
1 Egg slightly beaten
Dash of Pepper

3/4 tsp Salt
2 medium Tomatoes, sliced

1 Egg
2 Tbsp grated Parmesan Cheese   } Topping
1/8 tsp dried, crushed Oregano Leaves

Cook the macaroni per package directions; drain. Heat the oven to 350°F. In a greased 9" pie plate, mix the cooked macaroni, cottage cheese, beaten egg, salt, pepper, cheddar cheese and wiener slices – pat down into the pan. Arrange the tomato slices on top. Mix the other egg with the Parmesan Cheese and Oregano; pour over the top of the tomatoes. Bake uncovered until bubbly 25 to 30 minutes.   Servings 5

MENU WEEK#23

WNR – (Frankfurters in Bar-B-Q Sauce)

Hot Dog Buns
1 Pkg Wieners
Bar-B-Q Sauce (use commercial product of choice or recipe to make your own below)

Cut the wieners into small rounds. Pan fry until warmed. Add enough Bar-B-Q sauce to cover, simmer for an additional 5 minutes. Serve on toasted Hamburger Buns, Toast, or even over mashed or parsley potatoes or rice.

Serves 4-6
MENU WEEK#38

Bar-B-Q Sauce
MAKE YOUR OWN - (Ingredients not on the grocery list)

1 tsp Salt	1/8 tsp Pepper
1/2 cup minced Onions – cooked	1 tsp Chili Powder
1 tsp Celery Salt	1/4 cup Worcestershire Sauce
1 cup Ketchup	2 cups hot Water
1/4 cup Brown Sugar	Dash of Tabasco Sauce
1 Tbsp Liquid Smoke	

Juice of a small Lemon (cut Lemon in half and pierce inside with a fork and squeeze till drained)

Mix together and bring to a boil. Cool and keep leftover in a sealed, sterile container in the refrigerator.

WNR – (Frankfurters Mardi Gras with Grilled Cheese Sandwiches)

8 Wieners/Frankfurters cut lengthwise in half
1 small green Bell Pepper, chopped (about 1/2 cup)

1 medium Onion, sliced	2 Tbsp Margarine
1 can (16 oz) whole Tomatoes	1 tsp Seasoned Salt
1 tsp Sugar	1 can (4 oz) sliced Mushrooms, drained
1/4 cup Water	2 Tbsp Cornstarch

Grilled Cheese Sandwiches (below)

Cook in melted margarine the onion, and green bell peppers in a 3-Quart saucepan over medium heat until the onion is clear and tender. Stir in the tomatoes including the liquid, season with salt and sugar. Heat to boiling; then reduce heat and simmer uncovered for 6 minutes. Stir in the frankfurters and mushrooms. Simmer uncovered for an additional 10 minutes. Mix together the water and cornstarch and add to the tomato-frankfurter mixture and stir until it thickens. Pour the thickened sauce over the Grilled Cheese Sandwiches.

Grilled Cheese Sandwiches

Spread soft butter on one side of each of the 8 slices of the bread. Heat your griddle to medium-hot and place the buttered side of 4 pieces of bread onto the hot griddle. Put a slice of American cheese on each piece of bread that will make your sandwiches "real cheesy" (if you don't like the cheese to be so gooey just put one slice of cheese per two pieces of bread). When the cheese has begun to melt, with a pancake turner place one half of the cheese sandwich on top on the other which will give you a two-sided browned grilled cheese sandwich. Check the color of the grilled side of the bread and remove when browned on both sides. Make another set, which will give you 4 grilled cheese sandwiches. Servings depends on how many sandwiches you make.

Serves 4-8
MENU WEEK#24

See Ironing Melted Cheese Sandwiches page 173

Decided for You Cookbook – 365 Dinners

WNR – (Frankfurter Pronto Pups)

(Frankfurters in a Blanket)

2 Pkgs of Crescent Dinner Rolls or Biscuit Baking Mix (or from the Make-It-All Mix under Breads)
8 – 10 Wieners

Roll the wieners inside Crescent Dinner Rolls and pinch one end of the covering together around the wiener. Leave about 1/2" of the wiener exposed so fats can drain from this end while cooking.   Bake on a non-greased baking sheet per package direction.   Serves 4-5
– OR-
Mix one Biscuit Recipe from directions on the Biscuit Baking Mix Box. On a greased or floured breadboard pat the dough to a 1-inch thickness. Cut into 8 – 10 pieces 4" x 6" rectangles. Place a wiener in the center of the dough and roll up smooth the seam together, allow 1/2" of the wiener to be exposed on one end to drain fats during cooking. Lay these on a lightly greased baking sheet with spaces left between them for swelling while cooking. In a oven at 350°F temperature bake for 15 to 20 minutes or until the crust is browned.   Serve with Mustard or Ketchup.

MENU WEEK#25

WNR – (Frankfurter Skillet and Scalloped Potatoes with Ham)

1 pound Frankfurters/Wieners, sliced diagonally
1-1/2 cups Julienne Cut Cooked Ham
1 medium Onion, sliced
3/4 tsp Salt
1-1/2 cups Milk
1 cup grated Cheddar Cheese

2 Tbsp Margarine or Butter
4 medium Potatoes, sliced in rounds
1/4 tsp Pepper
1/2 cup minced Parsley

Melt the margarine in a large heavy skillet over low heat; add in the onion and sauté until tender (do not brown), stirring occasionally. Add in the potatoes; sauté about 2 minutes stirring them so they don't stick. Season with salt and pepper to taste. Add in the milk and bring to a boil. Cover, and simmer until the potatoes are almost tender, about 8 minutes, stirring occasionally. Add in the frankfurters, grated Cheddar Cheese, ham, parsley and cover again and simmer another 3 minutes until the potatoes are tender and the frankfurters are plump and hot.   Serves 4-6

MENU WEEK#39

WNR – (Hot Dogs)

1 Pound Wieners/Frankfurters
8 Hot Dog Buns

Several different ways to cook wieners: 1) Place a metal colander inside a larger pot, which has boiling water underneath. Drop the wieners into the colander, cover with a lid and steam the wieners. Can also warm your buns this way. 2) Place a small amount of water in a saucepan and drop in the wieners and bring to a boil, drain. 3) Grill in a covered skillet till plump or on an outside Bar-B-Q grill. 4) Broil at 500°F on top shelf of oven. 5) Or, warm in a microwave on a paper plate for two minutes.

Serve these with condiments: Ketchup, mustard, sliced onions, pickle relish, and/or cheese of choice.

Serves 4-6
MENU WEEK#8

WIENERS - MICROWAVE INFORMATION:

Franks/Wieners 4 – 5 min/Lb – (Can cook entire package unopened)

(WNR)-234

Decided for You Cookbook – 365 Dinners

WNR – (Hot Dog Casserole with Potatoes)

1 Pound Wieners, sliced in 2" pieces
1-1/2 Tbsp All-Purpose Flour
4 oz (1 cup) shredded Cheddar Cheese or cheese
   of choice
1 Tbsp chopped Parsley

1-1/3 cups Milk
1 Tbsp minced Onions
4 Medium Potatoes, peeled and sliced in
   thin, round coins

In a saucepan, stir the flour into the milk until smooth (or Place the flour and milk in a sealed container [bowl or jar] and shake till thoroughly mixed, no lumps) then warm in the saucepan until thickened and smooth. Layer the potatoes slices and wieners in a 9 x 13 casserole dish. Pour this cheese sauce over the potatoes and sliced wieners and bake uncovered for 30 minutes (350°F) or until the potatoes are fork tender.   Serves 4-8
MENU WEEK#22

WNR – (Hot Dogs with Bacon and Cheese Wraps)

1 Pound Wieners/Frankfurters
6-8 slices of Bacon
Cheddar Cheese or American Cheese cut in Strips
Toothpicks

Split each wiener lengthwise, but do not cut all the way through. In the center slit of the wiener, stuff in strips of cheese. Wrap a piece of bacon in a spiral fashion around the outside of the wiener and cheese. Fasten the bacon with toothpicks, if necessary. Place on a broiler pan on a lower shelf so wiener doesn't burn and Broil at 500°F until the bacon is crisp ~4 to 5 minutes. Can be served as a hot dog or as a meat course with other vegetables of choice.   Serves 4–6
MENU WEEK#3

WNR – (Wieners and Pork-n-Beans)

1 (16 oz) Pkg Wieners/Frankfurters, diced into round cuts
1 Large (31 oz) can of Pork-n-Beans
1/3 cup Brown Sugar
Vegetable Oil

1 medium chopped Onion
2 tsp Cinnamon

Heat the vegetable oil in a skillet, and cook the onions until they are clear and tender. Add in the wieners and lightly brown. Mix together the balance of the items and stir in the onions and wieners and pour into a small baking dish. Bake in a 325°F oven for 10-15 minutes –OR- you can warm in a covered skillet over low heat until the wieners and beans have been thoroughly warmed.   Serves 4-6
MENU WEEK#4

WNR – (Wieners and Sauerkraut)

1 Pkg Wieners, cut in coins about 1" thick
1 Sml Diced Onion

1 (2#) can Sauerkraut
Vegetable Oil

Place a small amount of oil in a pan, heat and brown the onions. Add in 1 can of sauerkraut without the juice and lightly brown. Add in the wieners and sauerkraut juice. Cover, and simmer on low until the wieners are plump approximately 10 minutes. **VARIATION:** Place 2 Lbs Pork Spareribs in a pan and sprinkle with 1 pkg dry Onion Soup, top with Sauerkraut. Cover with foil and bake 325°F 30-45 minutes or until ribs are tender. Uncover last 10 minutes to brown.   Serves 4-6
MENU WEEK#35

MY SPECIAL NOTES:

BREADS

HINT: <u>Mix all dry ingredients before adding in any liquids will make sure all ingredients are thoroughly distributed . Don't substitute Shortening for Oil in a recipe. Shortening normally needs to be cut into dry ingredients. Substituting oil will make batters too sticky. Don't over mix quick breads, batters, biscuits etc., they will become tough. Buy good quality Yeast, when it has been opened, store in the refrigerator in an Air Tight container. (Last ~6 months)</u>

BRD – (Biscuits – Biscuit Mix Commercially Made, or Make It All Mix

Baking Mix recipe which you should follow according to package directions and bake accordingly. You can also purchase canned Biscuits or Make Your Own (see Make It All Mix recipe)

BRD – (Biscuits – Buttermilk)

2 cups All-Purpose Flour	3 tsp Baking Powder
1/4 tsp Baking Soda	3/4 tsp Salt
4 Tbsp Shortening or Softened Butter/Margarine	1 cup Buttermilk, chilled

NOTE: can substitute regular milk for the Buttermilk

Preheat oven to 400°F. In a large mixing bowl, sift the flour, baking powder, baking soda and salt. Using your fingertips, make a well in the center and drop in your shortening. Cut the shortening into the flour with a pastry blender or two knives until the mixture looks granulated. **(Mix together the faster the better, the more you work the dough after adding in the liquid, the biscuits might become tougher and not as light).** Make another well and pour in the buttermilk. Stir with a fork just until the dough comes together.
 It will be sticky, so flour the top and work it with your hands into a smooth dough. Turn the dough onto a floured surface, re-dusting the dough top with flour and gently fold it over on itself 4 or 5 times. Press this into a 1/2 to 1" thickness. Cut out the biscuits with a cutter being sure to push straight down through the dough. Flour the edge of your cutter between biscuits. (**-OR**, you can use a drinking glass edge after dipping it into flour to keep it from sticking to your biscuits). Melt a little of the shortening in your pan. Pick up the biscuit and rub the top in the melted shortening and then place the biscuits on top of a greased baking sheet with their edges just barely touching. Any scrap dough can be reshaped for other biscuit cuttings. If you don't want to use melted shortening you can brush the tops with melted butter. Bake 10 – 20 minutes until tops are lightly golden brown. **HINT: <u>If butter is too cold to slice easily. Heat a small saucepan and then invert over the butter dish for a while. ALSO: 1 Pound unsifted flour = 4 cups.</u>** (Extra Recipe)

BRD – (Biscuits – Cheese Garlic Dropped)

Blend together **2 cups Biscuit Mix** with **2/3 cup Milk**. Mix in **1-1/2 cups grated Cheddar Cheese**. Drop dough in 12 equal mounds with their edges barely touching onto a buttered large baking sheet. Bake 425°F in middle of oven until golden, 10 to 15 minutes, or until tops are browned. <u>When removing from the oven sprinkle tops with Garlic Salt and serve</u> – **OR-** Mix together 1/4 cup Margarine/Butter melted, and 1/4 tsp Garlic Powder then brush over the warmed biscuits before serving.

ANOTHER VARIETY: Mix together 1/3 cup Green Goddess Salad Dressing and 1/2 cup of shredded Mozzarella Cheese. After cooking the dropped cheese biscuits, cut them in half and spoon or spread the mixture on the cut sides and broil until topping bubbles.

BRD – (Biscuits – Heavier)

Good with Stews

2 cups All-Purpose Flour
3/4 tsp Salt
1/2 cup Milk (about)

2-1/2 tsp Baking Powder
1/3 cup Margarine or Shortening
1 Egg

Preheat the oven to 400°F. Sift the flour, salt and baking powder together and then cut in the margarine with a pastry blender until granulated looking. Slightly beat the egg into the milk; setting aside enough of the egg mixture to brush the top of the biscuits before baking (1/2 oz). Add the remaining milk and egg to the sifted ingredients and form it into a soft dough either with a fork or your fingers. Form the dough into a 1/2" thickness on a lightly floured board and cut into biscuits with either a cutter or drinking glass rim which has been dunked into flour to avoid sticking to the dough. Place these biscuits on top of a greased baking sheet or into a shallow greased baking dish (9" x 13"). Brush the tops with the egg wash. Bake for 10 – 15 minutes or until the biscuit tops are golden browned. Yields: 8-12 depending on diameter size.   (Extra Recipe)
NOTE: Save cutting time by rolling biscuit dough out into a rectangle to fit a baking pan; place in a greased pan and cut into squares.
Butter = 8 Tablespoons = 1/2 cup = 4 oz.

BRD – (Biscuits – Yeast)

This recipe **can be kept for one week in the refrigerator** and you can use as needed.

1 Pkg Dry Yeast
1 Tbsp Sugar
1 tsp Salt

1/2 cup Warm Water
1 Tbsp Baking Powder
3/4 cup plus 2 Tbsp Shortening

5 cups All-Purpose Flour
1 tsp Baking Soda
2 cups Buttermilk

Place warm water in a small bowl and sprinkle (dissolve) the yeast in it. Let it stand for 10 minutes undisturbed (will get bubbly). Sift the flour, sugar, baking powder, baking soda, and the salt into a large bowl. With a hand pastry blender cut the shortening into the flour mixture until becomes somewhat granulated in its look. Stir in the buttermilk and the dissolved yeast and work together only until well moistened. Place this dough into a greased bowl, turning it over with a greased side up. Cover with plastic wrap and refrigerate until needed. When needed remove portion and carefully roll out on a well-floured surface into 1/2" to 3/4" thickness and cut into 2-1/2" round biscuits (can use a flour biscuit cutter, or dip a glass in flour and use this as a cutter). Smear a little shortening or butter on the top of a saucer. Rub the top of the biscuit in the shortening/butter and place in a greased baking dish or baking sheet, side by side until pan is full. Bake in a 400°F oven for 15 minutes.   Yields: 4 doz Biscuits
(Extra Recipe)

HINT: Anchoring Bowls/Flour Boards: Use a crumpled wet towel or a wet sponge under a bowl/ board and it will prevent it from sliding around when you are mixing ingredients or kneading and rolling out dough. It also cuts down on the noise factor.

Decided for You Cookbook – 365 Dinners

BREADS – MICROWAVE INFORMATION:

Some people don't like to re-warm in a microwave as they say the bread products become tough, use you own judgment. Remove any metal ties before cooking.

Bread, Buns or Muffins (1 Lb Pkg) 3 or 4 minutes Turning over after 2 minutes
Dinner Rolls (1 – 3) – 1/4 to 1-1/2 minutes
Dinner Rolls (4 – 6) – 1-1/2 to 2-1/2 minutes
Coffee Cakes, Sweet Rolls, Pull Aparts (6.5 – 12 oz) 2 – 3 minutes
Doughnuts (4 – 6) – 2-1/2 minutes

BRD – (Breadcrumbs – How to Make)

Toast a piece of bread in your toaster, then roll it between your hands like rolling a ball.

–OR- Hold a slice of bread flat on a breadboard or hard surface and tear away the edges with a fork. Using a funnel, pour leftover breadcrumbs into an empty salt container for storage – 1 slice Bread = 1/4 cup dry breadcrumbs.
–OR- Keep day old bread in the freezer and this will grate easier giving you fine breadcrumbs.
–OR- Keep your breadcrumbs stored in the freezer if you are afraid they will mold store in the cupboard.
–OR- You can also toast bread in the oven or toaster and then put it into a plastic bag and roll over the bread with a rolling pin breaking it into crumbs or you can pound with a meat mallet. If your crumbs are not crisp enough spread them on a cookie sheet and bake at 250°F for 5-8 minutes or just leave them on the counter over night to dry out.
–OR- If you don'thave any breadcrumbs, you can top a casserole or coat meat with finely crushed cornflakes, wheat flakes that can be used plain or mixed with grated cheeses or melted butter. **Seasoned Breadcrumbs** = 1/2 cup of Breadcrumbs and adding 1/2 cup Parmesan Cheese with 1 Tbsp Basil or Oregano. If using with chicken, add in 2 tsp of Sage. For fish add 2 tsp grated Lemon Rind.
Buttered Breadcrumbs = 1/2 to 1 cup Breadcrumbs can be mixed with 2 Tbsp melted margarine/ butter. Add additional margarine as needed.

BRD – (Bread – French, Easy)

Two Loaves

1 Pkg Yeast (1 Tbsp Dry)	1-1/2 tsp Salt
1 Tbsp Sugar	1-1/4 cups Warm Water
1 Tbsp Shortening, melted	2-1/2 – 3 cups All Purpose Flour

Mix in 1/2 cup of warm water the yeast, salt, sugar and shortening and stir with a fork. Allow liquid to rest. In a large container, sift your flour. Grease the inside of another large bowl. Removing 1/2 cup of the sifted flour at a time begin mixing or kneading together the liquid and flour until all of the flour has been incorporated and the dough comes away from the sides of the bowl. Cover the bowl with plastic wrap and topped with a kitchen towel and place in a warm, draft-free area to rise for 30 – 60 minutes, or until it has doubled. Remove from the bowl and knead again. Cut it into two long loaves. Place a little white corn meal on the top of a baking sheet pan. Place the loaves on top and slit the dough tops diagonally down the middle with a sharp knife. Let them rise another 30 minutes. Place a cup of water in a baking dish on one of your oven racks, this will cause the crust to become harder. Bake at 400°F for 25 minutes. Remove and brush with beaten egg whites and return to the oven for 5 minutes longer to brown. (Extra Recipe)

BRD – (Bread – Fried)

Spread margarine/butter on one side of the bread and grill until browned. **See BF – Hot Beef Sandwiches or Author's Thoughts PK – Breakfast at the Beach.**

BRD – (Bread – Garlic French Bread)

1 Loaf precooked Sweet/Sour Dough French Bread (sliced lengthwise making two halves)
4 cloves Garlic, minced (or you can use 1 Tbsp granulated Garlic Powder)
Sprinkling of Italian Seasoning (or) 2 sprigs of chopped Parsley & 1 tsp Oregano
4 oz Margarine/Butter, melted
1/2 tsp Paprika
Aluminum Foil

Melt the butter in a skillet add in the garlic and cook 1-2 minutes and remove from the heat. Slice the bread lengthwise so you have two halves. Brush or spoon on the melted butter and minced/ powdered garlic. Sprinkle with the Italian seasoning and/or parsley and the Paprika over the top of both halves. Set this bread into an aluminum foil boat (this will keep the crust of the bread, not to get too hard). Place the boats with the bread in them on the top shelf of your oven and broil at (500°F) until brown ~4 minutes. Avoid burning. Remove from the aluminum foil and cut into serving portions. Optional: Sprinkle on buttered, garlic tops 1-1/2 cups grated Cheddar Cheese and broil until cheese is melted.

BRD – (Bread – Garlic French Bread Another Way) – Large Crowd Servings

1 Loaf precooked Sweet/Sour Dough French Bread cut in half lengthwise
1/2 tsp Pepper
1/4 tsp Oregano
1/4 cup each Margarine and Butter   1/4 cup White Wine (Optional)
1/4 cup Olive or Vegetable Oil   2 Tbsp fresh Parsley, chopped
2 cloves fresh Garlic, minced

Melt the butter, margarine, and oil in a saucepan. Add in the garlic and simmer over low heat for one minute. Add in the pepper, oregano and wine and bring again to a boil. Remove from the heat and pour into the bottom of a broiling pan or into a shallow baking pan. Place the sliced lengthwise two halves of the sweet French bread under the broiler at (500°F) and toast until golden brown. **Remove and dip the toasted halves, cut side down into the margarine/butter mixture and serve immediately**.

BRD – (Bread in a Bag) – <u>Good Project for Children</u>

2-1/2 cups All-Purpose Flour (reserve a little for flouring your work surface)
1 envelope Rapid Rise Yeast   3 Tbsp Powdered Milk
1 cup Water   3 Tbsp Sugar
1 tsp Salt   3 Tbsp Vegetable Oil

Combine <u>one cup</u> of the <u>flour</u> with the yeast, sugar, dry milk, and salt into a 1-gallon heavy-duty plastic freezer zip-lock bag. To make sure there is no air in the bag, loosen the edge and squeeze the upper part of the bag to force out the air. Shake and press on the ingredients to mix well. Heat the water and the vegetable oil until very warm (120°F to 130°F), pour into the bag and reseal the bag allowing the air to escape again. Mix thoroughly by working the bag with your fingers. Gradually add enough of the remaining (1-1/4 cups) flour to make a stiff batter that pulls away from the bag. Remove the dough from the bag; knead on a lightly floured surface (1/4 cup flour) until smooth and elastic, about 8 – 10 minutes. Cover; let rest 10 minutes. Beginning at the short end, roll up tightly into a jelly roll. Pinch the seams and ends to seal. Roll the dough into an approximate 7"x12" loaf. Place into a greased loaf pan, rolling the dough over inside the pan to grease the top of the loaf. Cover; let rise in a warm, draft-free place until doubled in size, about 1 hour **(or you can set on top of an electric heating pad on the counter to hurry up the doubling process).** Bake at 375°F for 30 to 35 minutes or until crust is lightly browned. Remove from the pan and cool on a wire rack.
(Extra Recipe)

BRD – (Bread – Cinnamon Raisin Bread)

1 Batch White Bread	1-1/2 tsp Cinnamon
3 Tbsp Sugar	1-1/2 cups (7.5 oz) Raisins
2 – 4 Tbsp Flour for Board Dusting	

During the period of the bread rising, place the raisins in a bowl ad fill with warm water to just cover. Don't overfill as you will drain off the sweetness of the raisins. Place the dough on a lightly floured surface (~2 Tbsp) and pat into a rectangle that is about 3/4" thick, by 6" by 12" in size. Mix the cinnamon and the sugar and sprinkle it evenly over the dough. Drain the raisins and toss them with the remaining flour and spread over the dough and gently press these into the dough. Starting at a short side, roll the dough into a log. And tuck in any raisins that fall out. Seal the seam of the log gently but tightly, or pinch it shut with your fingers. Place the loaf on a buttered 9" x 5", cover with plastic wrap. Let the dough rise for another 1-1/2 hours at room temperature or until the loaf has risen about 1" above the sides of the pan(s). Bake 450°F on the center rack. Mist the loaf 8 to 10 squirts over the outside. Place a small Pyrex bowl of water in the oven and bake 15 minutes, then reduce the oven to 375°F for 20-30 minutes or until the crust is browned and the loaf sounds hollow when tapped on the bottom. Let cool 5 minutes in the pan before removing. Cool, then slice. (See **MISC Stuffed French Toast**).

BRD – (Bread – Indian Fried Bread)

2 cups All-Purpose Flour	1/2 cup dry milk solids
2 tsp Baking Powder	1/2 tsp Salt
2 Tbsp Lard/Shortening, cut into 1/2-inch bits, plus 1 Pound Lard for deep frying	

Combine the flour, dry milk solids, baking powder and salt, and sift into a deep bowl. Add in the lard bits and with your fingertips, rub the flour and fat together until the mixture resembles flakes of coarse meal. Pour in the water and toss the ingredients together until the dough can be gathered into a ball. Drape the bowl with a kitchen towel and then let the dough rest at room temperature for about 2 hours. After resting, tear the dough into 6 equal pieces. Then, on a lightly floured surface, roll each dough ball into a circle about 4 inches to 8 inches in diameter, and 1/4" thick. With a small knife, cut 1 (4-5 inch) long parallel slits completely through the dough, down the center of each rolled piece, spacing the slits about 1-inch apart.

In a heavy, 10-inch cast iron skillet, melt the remaining pound of lard over moderate heat until it is very hot, but not smoking. The melted shortening should be about 1-inch deep, add more if necessary. Fry the rolled dough, 1 at a time, for about 2 minutes on each side, turning them once with tongs. The bread will puff slightly and become crisp and brown. Drain on paper towels and serve warm.

Serves 6

BRD – (Bread – Pita/Pocket)

1 Pkg Active Dry Yeast
1 Tbsp Vegetable or Olive Oil
1/4 tsp Sugar
1-1/2 cups warm Water (105°F to 115°F)

1 tsp Salt
1-1/2 cups Whole Wheat Flour
1-1/2 cups All-Purpose White Flour

In a large bowl, dissolve yeast in warm water. With heavy-duty electric mixer with a dough hook stir in the oil, salt, sugar and whole wheat flour. Beat together until smooth. Mix in enough of the All-Purpose flour to make the dough easy to handle. Knead on a lightly floured surface until smooth and elastic, about 10 minutes. Place the dough in a greased bowl; and then turn the greased side of dough up, cover with plastic wrap or a kitchen towel and let rise in a warm location **(if you are pressed for time you can place the bowl on top of a electric heating pad turned on low)** until doubled, about 1 hour. Punch the dough down and divide into 6-8 parts. Shape each part into a ball on a greased surface and let rise an additional 15 minutes. Sprinkle three non-greased baking sheets with some cornmeal. On a lightly floured surface roll out each section into a flat 6" circle, no bubbles. Place 2 circles on each pan, cover. Bake 8-12 minutes at 450°F, they'll bubble up; cool on a rack for 5 minutes, they'll deflate, tear in half and fill with your choices.

Serves 6

VARIATION – Topping: (Ingredients not on grocery List). Heat 1/2 Olive Oil, and sauté 2 cloves cracked Garlic. Brush the breads with the garlic oils and reserve rest. Cut breads into wedges. Sprinkle with 1 cup grated Parmesan, 1 tsp ea Poppy Seeds & Red Pepper Flakes. Bake bread about 5 minutes 400°F. Remove and sprinkle with salt. Mix 1-1/2 cups grated Cheddar cheese into reserved garlic oil and spoon over the top of the breads, broil until cheese is melted.

BRD – (Bread – Salt Rising Bread)

Salt Rising Bread Starter:
1-1/2 cups Hot Water
2 Tbsp Cornmeal
1 tsp Salt

1 medium Potato, peeled and sliced thinly
1 tsp Sugar

Bread Dough:
1/2 cup Warm Water (100-115°F)
1/2 cup lukewarm Whole Milk (90-110°F)
1 tsp Salt

1/4 tsp Baking Soda
2 Tbsp Butter, melted
5 cups Flour + extra for board dusting

PREPARE YOUR SALT STARTER in a warm glass bowl by mixing together all ingredients as shown. Cover with a dinner plate for a good seal. Place the bowl in a roasting pan and fill the pan with boiling water to surround the bowl. Cover it all with a cover or dishtowel to keep ingredients warm. In a slightly preheated warmed 250°F oven that has now been turned off, let this stand covered for at least 10-12 hours or until the top is covered with 1/2 to 1" of foam (the pilot light in a gas stove is sufficient heat to keep it warm). **MAKE THE BREAD:** Strain the liquid from the salt starter through a sieve over a large mixing bowl. Place the sliced potato in the bottom of a small bowl and pour 1/2 cup of the warm water over the potato. Press the potato to extract as much liquid as possible; discard the potato. Add this liquid to the bigger bowl and stir in the baking soda, milk, butter and salt into the liquid. Add 2 cups of flour and beat until smooth. Add an additional 2-1/2 cups of flour, stirring until the dough is smooth. Divide this dough into two loaves. Place the loaves into well-buttered loaf pans, cover and set aside in a warm place to double (4-5 hours). Cook in a preheated oven 375°F for 35-45 minutes or until the bottom of the loaves sound hollow when tapped. Turn out and cool completely before slicing. [If you want a harder crust, place a small bowl of water in the oven during baking or mist the loaves prior to cooking]. (Extra Recipe)

Decided for You Cookbook – 365 Dinners

BRD – (Bread – White)

1 Pkgs Dry Yeast	2-3/4 cups Water (105°F-115°F)
6-1/2 cups Sifted All –Purpose Flour*	3 Tbsp Sugar
3 tsp Salt	2 Tbsp soft Shortening

In a large bowl for an electric mixer, sprinkle the dry yeast into the water; let stand for a few minutes, then stir until dissolved. Add 3-1/4 cups Flour, sugar, salt and shortening. Blend with an electric mixer at low speed; then beat for 2 minutes at medium speed.   Add in the remaining flour by hand and beat together again. Cover and let rise until doubled, about 45 minutes. Stir the batter beating it hard for half minute with your fists and rolling forward after each mixing. Spread the dough into two greased loaf pans (9" x 5" x 3"). Let rise until doubled, about 20 minutes. Bake in a preheated oven (375°F for 40-50 minutes. ***-OR- use 2 cups Whole Wheat Flour and 4-1/2 cups white flour for wheat tasting bread.**   (Extra Recipe)

BRD – (Bread – Whole Wheat Honey)

2 Pkgs Active Dry Yeast (2 Tbsp)	1/2 cup Warm Water
7-1/3 cups Whole Wheat Flour	5 cups Hot Water
2 Tbsp Salt	2/3 cup Honey
2/3 cup Vegetable Oil	7 cups All Purpose White or Wheat Flour

Dissolve the yeast in the 1/2 cup warm water.   Sift all of the first 7-1/3 cups of wheat flour and add in the additional 5 cups of "hot" water. Add in the honey, vegetable oil, salt and yeast. Mix well. Add in the other 7 cups of sifted white flour and knead for 10 minutes or until the dough is elastic and smooth. Divide into 4 parts. Place these in greased pans and let them rest for 5-10 minutes, then reshape into loaves by pressing them flat and then jelly-roll into a loaf. Cover with a kitchen towel and allow to rest and double for another hour. Bake at 350°F for 45 minutes.   Yield: 4 Loaves

(Extra Recipe)

HINT: <u>Day old bread is best for sandwiches, because it is firmer.</u>

BRD – (Buns, Hamburger/Hot Dog)

MAKE YOUR OWN – (Ingredients not on grocery List)

4-3/4 to 6-3/4 cups Flour	1/3 cup Powdered Milk
1/2 cup Sugar	1 Tbsp Salt
2 Pkgs Yeast	1/3 cup Soft Margarine
2 cups Very Warm Water	

Place all ingredients except the flour in a bowl and gradually add in 2 cups very warm water. Add in 3/4 cup of flour and beat 2 minutes. Add in the rest of the flour to make a stiff dough. Knead about 10 minutes, bringing sides to the center top to the middle, bottom to the middle and knead with your hands, turn over and stretch and knead again. Place in a shortening greased extra large bowl, turning the dough over so the it grease all sides. Cover with a towel and sit in a warm, draft -free area to rise and double in size. In 20 minutes, punch it down into the bottom of the bowl. Grease a cookie sheet with the shortening or non-stick spray. Pinch off a small portion of the dough and form into desired sizes (roll into a smooth ball by first making it round with your hands. Then pull the dough up, pinching at the top of the dough ball. Keep pulling and pinching up at the top until you have a tight ball. Turn the ball on its side on the lightly greased surface. With a floured pastry cutter, cut the ball of dough directly in half through the waist of the ball (not through the pinched end). Take one half and place it on top of the other, meeting the cut sides in the middle. Pinch around the circumference of the circle of dough to seal. Flatten the circle gently, but firmly. Make sure that the pinched seam is under the bun as you flatten it, and place these on the baking sheet separated by about 2 inches apart. –OR- for larger buns you can cut them out with a wide-mouthed canning jar screw band.   Place a piece of wax paper on top of your buns. Then place another cookie sheet on top to keep the buns from rising too high and let rise again for about 45 minutes to 1 hour. You can brush the tops with an egg wash (1 beaten egg and 1 Tbsp Water or with melted margarine). Bake at 375°F for 15 – 20 minutes,

Decided for You Cookbook – 365 Dinners

(continued Buns-Hamburger/Hot Dogs) cool on a rack . Makes about 20 buns. Store cooled buns in a large heavy, duty plastic bag. If you want to freeze them, squeeze out all the air you can out of the bag after placing the buns inside. Place the bagged buns inside another bag before placing these in the freezer. This will help prevent freezer burn. To thaw, let them sit on the counter in their original bag until soft.
TOPPING VARIATIONS: 1 egg white beaten with a teaspoon of water and then sprinkle on Sesame or Poppy Seeds – **OR -** 1 cup minced yellow onions which have been sautéed in a little vegetable oil with 2 tsps of poppy seeds and a little black pepper **- OR** – egg wash and sprinkle on toasted dehydrated onions that have been soaked in hot water for fifteen minutes to swell and soften.

BRD – (Corn Bread – Made from Scratch)

1-1/2 cups Corn Meal (white or yellow)	1 cup Hot Water
3 Tbsp Melted Butter or Margarine	1 tsp Salt
1 cup Sifted Flour	1 cup Milk
4 tsp Baking Powder	1 Tbsp Sugar
3 eggs, well beaten	

Slowly add the corn meal to the hot water, stirring constantly. When smooth, cool if very hot. Add in the eggs, butter, salt and sugar. Sift the flour and baking powder together. Alternating add in milk then flour/baking powder. When totally mixed together bake in a square 9"x 9" greased pan at 400°F for about 30 minutes or until top is golden brown.   Serves 6-8

(Extra Recipe)

HINT: What size should your pan be? To know how much a container holds, fill a pan with water and then empty the water into a measuring cup for the quantity size it will hold

BRD – (Corn Bread – Tex-Mex Style)

2 cups Yellow Corn Meal	1 Tbsp Baking Powder
1 cup (4 oz) shredded Cheddar Cheese	2 eggs, slightly beaten
1/2 cup Vegetable Oil	1 cup Sour Cream
1 can (8 oz) Cream Style Corn	1 can (4 oz) chopped Green Chiles

Preheat oven to 400°F. Grease a Bundt Pan (12-cup) or a 9" x 13" baking dish and set aside. In a large bowl combine the corn meal, baking powder and cheese. In another medium bowl mix the eggs, vegetable oil, sour cream, corn and chiles until well combined. Add the wet ingredients to the dry ingredients and stir just until moistened. Spoon or pour into the greased baking dish. Bake for 40 – 50 minutes or until golden brown.

Makes 12 servings

BRD – (Corn Bread with a Little Help)
Using Commercially Store-Bought Biscuit Mix)

1 cup White Corn Meal	1/2 cup Biscuit Mix
1 tsp Baking Powder	1 tsp Salt
1 Egg, slightly beaten	

Mix all the ingredients together along with enough water to make a medium batter. Pour this into a greased, 9" x 9"square pan. Bake 400°F about 30 minutes or until golden brown. **NOTE: Double this recipe for making corn bread dressing for Thanksgiving.**
Serves 6-8

Decided for You Cookbook – 365 Dinners

BRD – (Crackers – Saltine)

2 cups sifted Flour
1/4 cup Margarine or Butter
1 Egg, slightly beaten

1 tsp Salt, 1/2 tsp Baking Soda
1/2 cup Buttermilk or soured Milk

In a large bowl sift the flour, salt and baking soda. Cut in the margarine (with a hand blender) until becomes granulated. Stir in the buttermilk and egg; mix to make a firm dough. Knead thoroughly. Roll out on some waxed paper into a very thin layer. Cut into squares or rounds and place these on lightly greased cookie/ baking sheet. Prick the cracker dough with a fork. Sprinkle with coarse salt before baking. Bake 10 minutes at 400°F or until lightly browned.

BRD – (Crepes)
See recipe **MISC – (Crepes)**

BRD – (Croutons)

Place a little vegetable oil or melted butter in a plastic bowl that has a lid (or you can use a plastic bag which seals). Dice up left over breads into small cubes. Place the bread inside the container, put on the lid and shake until the bread is lightly coated. Remove the bread and place it in a single layer on a shallow baking sheet and sprinkle garlic powder (not garlic salt) over the bread. Place the garlic croutons in a warm oven (approximately 200°F) for an hour or two or until the croutons are at the desired crispness (remember they will continue to dry a little more after removing from the oven). **VARIATIONS: Sprinkle with Romano and Parmesan Cheese, or Italian Seasonings in addition to the Garlic Powder.**

*HINT: <u>**Soggy croutons can be refreshed by placing them in a single layer in a shallow pan and bake at 350°F for 5 minutes. They can also be popped into a microwave**</u>.

BRD – (English Muffins)

1 cup Milk
1 Tbsp Sugar
1 Pkg Dry Yeast
1/2 cup Water + 1/4 cup

2 tsps Salt
1 Tbsp Shortening
3 cups White Flour + dusting

Bring the 1/2 cup water to a boil, mix it in with the milk, salt, sugar and shortening in a large bow. Let this cool to lukewarm. Stir the yeast into another 1/4 cup warm water and let it stand for 5 minutes to dissolve. Add the bubbly yeast and the 2 cups of flour to the first mixture and beat vigorously. Cover with plastic wrap and let rise in a warm non-drafty place until the dough doubles in bulk (Can cover with a kitchen towel). Stir, add the remaining flour, and beat well. Cover, and let the dough double in bulk once again. Turn out onto a lightly floured surface and pat the dough until it is 1/2 inch thick. Cut it into 3-inch rounds, cover, and let rise. Cook these on a well-greased, fairly hot griddle or in a heavy skillet for about 15 minutes on each side, turning and adjusting the heat if they are getting browned too quickly. Cool a little, then split in half with two forks and toast in the toaster. Serve with butter and jam.   Yields 15 Muffins

BRD – (Gorditas Shells – Corn Tortillas)

See Recipe BEEF – (Beef Gorditas)
2 cups Masa Harina (Mexican Corn Flour)   2 tsp Salt
1 tsp Double-Acting Baking Powder   1 cup Water
2 slices fried Bacon, crumbled   2 cups Shredded Longhorn Cheddar Cheese
Aluminum Foil

Mix all of the ingredients for the shells, divide the dough into 6 equal parts. With a patting motion, flatten each part into 1/2" thickness and about three to four inches in diameter (like a pita bread). Fry each in a hot, greased skillet or griddle until golden brown, turning once; drain on paper toweling. Keep these covered with a kitchen towel to keep warm. To reheat, you can stack Gorditas shells together and wrap with aluminum foil. Warm these in a preheated 325°F oven for 10-15 minutes **–OR-** You can microwave these in a microwave in a safe cooking bag (or unwrapped) on high speed for 30 seconds to one minute   Makes 6 – 8 servings

MORE WRITING ROOM:

BRD – (Make It All Mix)

Master Baking Mix for - Cookies, Muffins, Cakes, Waffles, Biscuits, Gingerbread etc (STORES 2-6 MTHS, if sealed)

5 Pounds of All Purpose Flour	2-½ cups Dry Milk Solid	2 Pounds Vegetable Shortening
3/4 cups Baking Powder	3 Tablespoons Salt	
2 Tbsps Cream of Tartar	½ cup Sugar	

Stir in the baking powder, salt, cream of tartar, dry milk solids and sugar into non-sifted flour. Then sift all together and cut the shortening into the dry ingredients until it looks like Cornmeal. Place in two Econo-Canisters or one Giant Canister. Store at room temperature. This quantity will yield 29 cups of mix and is enough to make one batch of every item given below. **Combine ingredients in the order given across the chart:**

Product Baking Time And Temp	Amount of Mix	Sugar	Eggs	Water	Other Ingredients Needed or Information	Method
Biscuits (12 ea) 450°F – 10 Min.	3 cups	-	-	3/4 cup	Bake on Greased Pan	Blend, Knead 10 strokes, ½" thick
Cake, Coffee – (8"x 8") - 400°F for 25 minutes	3 cups	½ cup	1	2/3 cup	½ cup Brown Sugar, 3 Tbsp Butter, ½ Tbsp Cinnamon Nuts and Raisins	Mix all ingredients except top the cake with the Brown Sugar before baking
Cake (Yellow or Chocolate) 2 – 8" pans – Bake 325°F – 25 min.	3 cups	1-½ cups	2	1 cup	1 tsp Vanilla ½ cup cocoa	Add sugar to dry ingredients beat eggs+water. Add ½ of the dry ingredients & beat – then add in balance of dry ingred. and beat again.
Cookies - Drop (4 dozen) – 375°F – 10 to 12 minutes Bake 10 min.	3 cups	1 cup	1	1/3 cup	1 tsp Vanilla, ½ cup nuts or chocolate chips	Blend all ingredients and drop cookies on a baking sheet. Smash tops with a fork
Cookies – Peanut Butter 375°F	2 cups	½ cup ea Brown & Wh.Sugar	1	1/3 cup	1 cup Peanut Butter, 1 tsp Vanilla, ½ tsp Baking Soda	Blend all ingredients And roll out and cut into Cookies
Corn Bread or 12 Individuals-425°F 20-25 minutes	1 cup ea Mix/Corn Meal	½ cup Optional	1 Beaten	1 cup Milk	1 cup Vegetable Oil	Mix all ingredients and Bake.
Gingerbread (1 Layer 2"x8"x8") – 350°F, 40 minutes	2 cups	1/4 cup	1	½ cup	½ cup Molasses, 1 tsp Cinnamon, ½ tsp Ginger, ½ tsp Cloves	Mix molasses, into beaten egg & water, add in spices and mix.
Muffins (12 ea) 450°F – 25 Minutes	3 cups	2 Tbsp to ½ cup	1	1 cup	1 tsp Vanilla	Mix water & egg, blend with dry ingred. (can add 3/4 cup fruit or ½ cup Brand Flakes)
Pancakes (18 medium)	3 cups	-	1	1-½ cups or Milk	-	Blend
Waffles (6 ea)	3 cups	-	2	1-½ cups	1 tsp Baking Soda & 2 tsp Vegetable Oil	Blend well. Cook on Greased Waffle Iron

(Extra Recipes)

BRD – (Pastry Shell)

4 cups sifted Flour
1/2 Pound Butter or Margarine softened
3/4 cup cold Water

1/2 tsp Salt
3 Egg Yolks, beaten

(1) Sift flour and salt onto a pastry board. Make a small hole in the center of the flour, add in the half of the butter, egg yolks, and the water; mix together with a fork or with your hands to make a dough. Chill the dough 1/2 to one hour in frig.
(2) Remove dough from the frig and sprinkle flour on a hard surface, roll dough into a large square and put balance of butter in the center of the square.

(3) Fold all four corners of the dough over the butter to enclose it completely inside the dough. Then roll the dough out three more times into other rectangles. Each time fold it as follows - Fold the left hand third over the middle and the right third over the middle, thus making a three layer piece. This is called a turn. Roll out again and make 2 more turns and chill dough for 20 minutes.

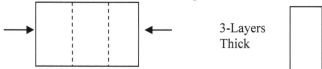

This dough will keep in a refrigerator 3-5 days. You can also purchase a patty shell from the grocery store if you don't want to make it fresh. Yield: One Large

BRD – (Pie Crust)

6 oz (12 Tbsp) Butter, chilled
1 Tsp Salt
12 oz (2 cups) All Purpose Flour + extra for dusting surface
~32 – 64 oz of dried Beans, for weighting crust during baking

2 oz (4 Tbsp) Shortening or Lard, chilled
1/2 cup Ice Water, in a Spritz Bottle

Yields two (9-inch) crusts

Cut butter and shortening into small pieces. Chill in the freezer for 15 minutes. You can do this in a large bowl using a handle blender or a fork, but most prefer doing this in a food processor. Combine the flour and salt by pulsing 3 to 4 times. Add in the butter and pulse 5 to 6 more times until the texture looks granulated. Replace the lid and pulse around 5 times, then, add more water and pulse again until the mixture holds together and becomes doughy when squeezed. Divide the dough into two pieces and place the mixture into 2 large ziplock bags. Squeeze the granulated mixture together until it forms a ball (great job for the kids to help you do). Then press this dough into a rounded shape and refrigerate for about 30 minutes. Preheat the oven to 425°F. Remove the dough from the refrigerator and turn out on a hard floured surface and roll out into a circular pie crust. Place a pie pan face down on the counter, pick up your pie crust and drape over the bottom of it. Place another pie pan on top of the dough. And flip both pans right side up. Trim the edges of the pie crust and then remove the first pan. Poke holes in the dough with a fork and place it in the refrigerator for 15 minutes while you roll out the other pie crust, then let this one rest in the frig when finished. Place a piece of parchment paper inside your piecrust and then fill with dry beans (this will keep them from shrinking too much). Bake for approximately 10 minutes and remove the beans and parchment paper and continue baking until the crust is golden in color (~10-15 minutes). Let cool before adding pie filling.

BRD – (Pizza Crust)

1 cup warm Water (~110°F)	Stir into the water:
1 tsp Sugar	1 tsp Salt
2 Tbsp Salad Oil or Olive Oil	2-1/2 cups + 1 cup sifted White Flour
1 Pkg Yeast – Sprinkle on top of the warm water; wait five minutes	

Sift 2-1/2 cups of the flour and add in the yeast liquid and mix together forming a ball. On a floured bread board, using the heel of your hand, push, punch and roll over for about five minutes (add as much flour as it takes to keep the dough from sticking to your hands, etc) then place it in a lightly greased bowl, cover with plastic wrap and place in a warm spot in the kitchen for ~45 minutes **(If desired, sit the covered bowl on top of a heating pad turned on low to cut down on rising time).** When the dough has doubled in size work, return it to the floured breadboard and add in another 1/2 cup of flour or by adding enough additional flour as necessary to form a smooth and elastic dough. Dough should no longer be sticky. When smooth, place on a lightly greased cookie sheet or pizza pan; then form into desired pizza pie size. Cover the pizza crust with a towel and let it rest for 15 minutes. Cover with sauce, and **toppings shown in recipe (MISC – Pizza – Linguica, Pepperoni**, etc) and bake on middle rack at 425°F for 25 minutes or until the pizza crust is brown and the cheeses are melted. Serve hot.   Yields (2) 12-inch crusts

BRD – (Rolls – Crescent)

For the **Working Mother or Beginner Cook, purchase** Crescent Rolls already prepared. – **OR -**

1/2 cup Milk	1/2 cup (1 stick) Butter, softened
1/3 cup Granulated Sugar	1/2 tsp Salt
1 Pkg Active Dry Yeast	1/2 cup warm Water (105°F-115°F)
1 Large Egg, lightly beaten + 1 for Egg Wash	Topping 3-1/2 to 4 cups All Purpose Flour

In a saucepan, heat the milk until bubbles appear round the edge of the pan. Combine the butter, sugar, and salt. Add in the hot milk and stir well. Cool to a lukewarm (95-100°F). In a small bowl, dissolve the yeast in warm water and let it stand until it is foamy (~5 to 10 minutes). Beat the yeast mixture and the egg into the milk mixture at a low speed. Add in 2 cups of flour slowly until smooth. Continue beating until dough is thick. Mix in enough extra flour until the dough pulls away from the sides of the bowl. On a floured surface, knead the dough very gently until smooth and elastic (2-3 minutes). Place the dough into a large greased bowl, turning the dough to cover outside areas. Let this dough rise in a warm place until it has doubled (~1 hour). Punch down the dough and place on a floured surface dividing the dough in half. Cover with a damp cloth and let rise again for 10 minutes. Grease 2 baking sheets. Using a floured rolling pin, roll 1 dough half into a 12" circle. Cut the circle into 6 wedges. Starting at the largest end, roll up each crescent roll. Slightly curve the rolls into a crescent shape and place on the greased baking sheet (Leave space between each for expansion). Cover loosely with a damp cloth; let these rise in a warm place until almost doubled (~30 minutes). Lightly beat an egg and brush the tops of the rolls. Bake in a preheated 400°F oven for 15 minutes or until golden in color. Transfer to a warmed serving dish.   Yields 12 rolls

BRD – (Rolls – Easy)

Softened Margarine for greasing muffin pans

2 cups **Self-Rising Flour**	1 cup Milk
2 Tbsp Sugar	4 Tbsp Mayonnaise

Preheat the oven to 350°F and lightly grease twelve individual cup muffin tins with the softened margarine. Combine in a large bowl the flour and milk, blending it well. Add in the sugar and the mayonnaise and stir until combined. Spoon the batter into the muffin tins half way to the top. Bake 12-15 minutes or until golden brown. (Extra Recipe)

BRD – (Rolls – Parker House)

2 Pkgs Active Yeast	1-1/2 cups Warm Water
3/4 cup Evaporated Milk	1/2 cup melted Shortening
1 Tbsp Salt	1 cup Sugar
9-10 cups All Purpose Flour	

Dissolve the yeast in the warm water. Add in the milk and stir in the melted shortening, salt and sugar. Add the flour a little at a time. Mix with an electric mixer or knead the dough until it is smooth. Grease the bottom of a large bowl with either softened margarine or shortening. Rub the dough around the bottom of the bowl and turn the greased side up toward the top, cover with plastic wrap topped with a kitchen towel, and set in a warm, draft-free spot in the kitchen (85°F) to double in size. Remove and roll to 1/2-inch thickness. Pinch or cut into 2-inch rounds. Place these on a greased baking sheet, cover with a towel and let the dough rise again. Bake at 425°F for 15-20 minutes. Yield: 44 rolls

(Extra Recipe)

BRD – (Rolls – Refrigerator)

Can purchase ready made rolls, canned or fresh – **OR-**
MAKE YOUR OWN
6 cups of All Purpose Flour (White, Whole Wheat or 1/2 & 1/2 this includes 1/2 cup flour for surface work)
Vegetable Oil, as needed to grease a bowl

1-1/4 cups Water	3 Tbsp Sugar
1 cup Milk (fresh, canned or powdered)	2 tsp Salt
1/4 cup Margarine or Butter	1 Envelope Active Dry Yeast

Pre-heat the oven to 400°F. In a saucepan heat the water, milk and margarine until very warm (120-130°F), butter doesn't completely dissolve. In a very large bowl, sift 2 cups of the flour and the salt. Add in the sugar, and yeast. Add in the melted margarine and the warm water. Beat with an electric mixer or food processor on low speed, then beat at high speed for 3 minutes. Add an additional cup of sifted flour to the dough, beat another 5 minutes. Stir in 2-1/2 cups of sifted flour or enough so it comes away from the sides of the bowl. Sprinkle flour on to your work surface. Turn out your dough and knead on the floured surface; re-dusting the dough top with flour, and gently folding it over on itself 6 or 10 times (~10 minutes); punching it down well. Grease the bottom of a large bowl with either softened margarine or shortening. Rub the dough around the bottom of the bowl and turn the greased side up toward the top, cover with plastic wrap topped with a kitchen towel and set in a warm, draft-free spot in the kitchen (85°F). **HINT: Bread bowl can be placed on top of an electric heating pad if you need to "speed up" this process).** Let it rest for 20 to 60 minutes while it doubles. Take this time to get your mess cleaned up. After it has risen, punch it down again and cut into 2 pieces if making two loaves of bread which should be jelly-rolled to about an 8" x 12" loaf. Cinnamon Bread can be made easily right now by smearing soft butter over the flat, rolled bread and then sprinkle with equal parts of ground cinnamon and granulated sugar (and/or chopped nuts) before it is rolled into a loaf for baking **–OR-** If making rolls, punch down the doubled batch and roll into a log, this will make it easier to handle. **–OR-** To make into rolls, pinch off some dough and roll in the palm of your greased hand into a ball and place in your greased baking pan (Yields 48 rolls). Brush the tops with vegetable (continued)

(BRD)-250

(continued Rolls – Refrigerator) oil or melted margarine, cover again with plastic wrap and allow it to rest another 15 minutes. You can make this the day before and let the dough rise in the refrigerator (can be kept there for two days to be used as needed). Bake 30-40 minutes for the loaves, and 350°F for 20-35 minutes for the rolls until the tops are golden brown. **–OR-)** You can cut dough into wedges and shape into crescent rolls. Brush with mixture of 1 egg yolk and 1 Tbsp Water and Bake 400°F for 15-20 minutes. Recipe can easily be doubled if desired.

BRD – (Rolls – Yeast)

2 Eggs	1/4 cup Margarine/Butter
2 cups Warm Water	2 Tbsp Yeast
2 Tbsp Sugar (sprinkled over yeast and water)	1/2 cup Powdered Milk
5 cups+ of All-Purpose Flour	1 Tbsp Salt

Mix the water, margarine, yeast and sugar together. Let it stand 10 minutes. Mix the other ingredients (eggs, powdered milk, flour and salt). Knead together and place into a greased bowl, turning the greased side from the bottom to the top, cover with plastic wrap, set in a warm spot in the kitchen and allow this to double in size. (Is wrap for Beef Burgers Stuffed by Jean Menu Week #2)   Serves 8 –10

BRD – (Tortillas – Corn)

Recipe can be doubled for 12

2 cups Masa Harina (Mexican Corn Flour)	2 tsp Salt
1 tsp Double-Acting Baking Powder	1 cup Water
2 slices fried Bacon, crumbled	2 cups Shredded Longhorn Cheddar Cheese
Aluminum Foil	

You can stack tortillas together and wrap with aluminum foil. Warm these in a preheated 325°F oven for 10-15 minutes **–OR-** You can microwave these in a microwave in a safe cooking bag (or unwrapped) on high speed for 30 seconds to one minute **– OR-** if making these from scratch they can be cooked on a greased hot griddle on both sides until slightly browned, drain on paper toweling and kept hot in a tortilla warmer or between a kitchen towel.   Makes 6 – 8 Servings
MENU WEEKS #40, #12

BRD – (Tortillas – Flour)

3 cups All-Purpose Flour
1/3 cup Shortening or Lard
1 tsp Salt
3/4 - 7/8 cup lukewarm Water (test it on your wrist like you do a baby's milk)

Sift the flour and salt together. Work in the shortening with a fork (or a pastry blender). Add in the water until the dough forms a ball that comes away cleanly from the side of the bowl. Knead dough in a floured bowl until smooth. Cover with a moist cloth and let it rest 15 minutes at room temperature. Divide the dough into 12 equal parts. On a floured board roll out the dough to a 7" thin circle. Place between two towels to keep moist. When you have rolled out all of the dough, cook each tortilla on a lightly greased griddle over medium heat for two minutes on each side, slightly browned.   Makes a Dozen
MENU WEEKS#36, #25

BRD – (Turnover Dough)

1 Pkg active Dry Yeast
1 Tbsp Sugar   1 cup warm Water (105°F to 115°F)
1 Tbsp Vegetable Oil
1/2 tsp Salt
2 to 2-1/2 cups All-Purpose Flour

Dissolve the yeast in the warm water and stir in the sugar, oil, and the salt into a large bowl. It will begin to activate by bubbling. Add in the flour a little at a time and stir well. When the flour has been added, turn the dough out on to a floured bread-board and knead until smooth and elastic; about 5 minutes. Place the dough into a large, greased bowl and then roll the dough forward turning the greased side up; cover the bowl with plastic wrap, and place bowl in a warm spot on the kitchen counter. **(If you are pressed for time, you can place the bowl on top of an electric heating pad turned on low to encourage it to rise quicker).** Allow the dough to rise to double its original size, about 1 hour. Punch down your dough and divide it into 10 parts. On a floured board, roll each of these into a 5" circle. Fill each circle with the filling (don't overfill you won't be able to seal the edges together) and fold in half, pinching the two sides together with your fingers or with the tines of a fork. Place these turnovers on a "greased" baking sheet. Cover with a damp towel and allow to double in size again, another 1 hour. Heat your oven to 375°F and bake until lightly browned, approximately 20-25 minutes. (If you would like a shiny cooked surface, then brush outsides of the turnover before cooking with a mix of a slightly beaten egg with a Tbsp of water.)

BRD – (Wrap-Up Dough)

1 cup All-Purpose Flour (Do not use self-rising flour)⎫
1/3 cup Water
1/2 tsp Salt
1/4 tsp Paprika   ⎬   DOUGH
1 Egg Yolk
Vegetable oil or Shortening for frying   ⎭

Mix flour, egg yolk, water, 1/2 tsp salt and the paprika until a dough is formed. Knead on a floured surface until dough is elastic, about two minutes. Divide the dough in half. Roll this half into 12-inch squares, about 1/16 inch thick; then cut these into 2 inch squares. Fill each square with scant teaspoon of the beef mixture. Moisten edges of the squares; fold into triangles and pinch edges together. Repeat with remaining dough and meat. Heat 1 inch of the oil in a skillet and fry the wrap-ups until golden, about 45 seconds on each side. Drain – salt to taste. Serve Hot or Cold.   Yields ~72
(Extra Recipe)

BRD – (Won Ton Wrappers)

1-1/2 cups Flour + dusting Cornstarch   1 tsp Salt
1 Egg, slightly beaten   1/2 cup lukewarm Water

Mix the flour and salt. Make a well in the center. Add in the egg and water and mix well. Turn this ball of dough out on to a surface floured with cornstarch.   Knead to make it into a soft smooth dough. Cover with a clean towel and let set for 15 minutes.   Roll the dough out to paper thin sheets (8" x 12" x 1/8" thick). Sprinkle with more cornstarch as needed to prevent dough from sticking. Cut sheets into 24 (2 to 3-inch) squares. Cover with a moist kitchen towel, be careful, **they will dry out if left too long exposed to the air.**

PASTA

HINT: <u>The most important requirement for cooking pasta properly is to use a very large pot.</u>

PAS – (Baked Macaroni with Two–Cheeses)

1 Pound Elbow Macaroni
1/2 cup Margarine or Butter
3 cups 1/2 & 1/2 Milk or Evaporated Milk
1/3 cup chopped Onions
Aluminum Foil

1 tsp granulated Chicken Bouillon
1/2 cup All-Purpose Flour
1/4 tsp Pepper and Salt to taste
Breadcrumbs mixed with melted 2 Tbsp Butter
Aluminum Foil

3 cups grated Sharp Cheddar Cheese (reserve a little for topping if desired), and 8 oz of shredded Gruyere Swiss **–OR-**
1/2 cup grated fresh Parmesan Cheese (reserve a little for topping if desired), and 1-1/4 cups (5 oz) grated Romano Cheese

In a large saucepan, boil the macaroni until fork tender (6-8 minutes), drain in a colander and salt. Place the macaroni back into the pan and add in the cheeses and stir together. In a small saucepan melt the margarine and cook the onions until they are clear and tender. Stir in the flour until smooth (add more margarine if needed). With a whisk or a fork stir the milk into the flour mixture, and the chicken bouillon (if using a bouillon cube, dilute with 1 cup water) and bring this sauce to a simmer, stirring constantly to avoid lumps. When slightly thickened, pour the sauce over the macaroni and cheeses and mix well. Spoon this into a 9" x 13" greased baking dish. Top with the Breadcrumbs, cover with aluminum foil, and bake at 350°F for 20 minutes or until topping is browned. Remove the foil and sprinkle on additional cheese and bake another 5 – 8 minutes or until cheese is melted.   Serves 6-8
MENU WEEK#6

NOTE: 2 cups uncooked Macaroni = 8 oz uncooked = 4 to 4-1/2 cups cooked Pasta.

PAS – (Fettuccini Alfredo)

1 (8-12 oz) Pkg of Fettuccini Noodles   2/3 cup shredded Parmesan Cheese
1 Pound Jar Roasted Garlic and Parmesan Sauce, warmed
Optional: Sliced Mushrooms or 1/4 Pound Proscuitto

Cook the Fettuccini noodles in boiling salted water for 8 to 10 minutes and drain. Salt freely. Toss the noodles and sauce together and serve immediately. Sprinkle in the Parmesan Cheese (save a little for a topping, if desired), and stir until it's melted.   Serves 4-6
MENU WEEK#8

Fettuccini Sauce

MAKE YOUR OWN – (Ingredients not on grocery list)

1/2 cup Margarine or Butter
1/8 tsp Pepper
2 Tbsp Flour
Dash of Nutmeg
1 slightly beaten Egg (Optional)

1 cup Half and Half Milk or Evaporated Milk
2/3 cup Parmesan Romano Cheese (fresh or grated)

Melt the margarine and stir/whisk in the flour making sure there are no lumps. Add in the milk, pepper, nutmeg, and stir until sauce begins to thicken. (Optional: Add the egg into the sauce and mix well. Toss the noodles and sauce together and serve immediately. Sprinkle in the Parmesan Cheese (save a little for a topping, if desired), and stir until it's melted.

Decided for You Cookbook – 365 Dinners

HINT: Thickening Agents – **Both flour and cornstarch are used to thicken sauces. One and one-half Tablespoons of flour per one cup of liquid. Cornstarch has twice the thickening properties so reduce the recipe accordingly. Mix flour and water or juices in a bowl with a whisk, or put it in a small jar or sealable bowl and shake this together until all lumps are gone before adding this slurry into other ingredients.**

PAS – (Fresh Made Pasta – Optional – Egg Noodles, Raviolis, etc)

MAKE YOUR OWN - (Ingredients not on grocery list)

3-1/2 cups All-Purpose Flour	4 Large Eggs
3 Tbsp Water	1 tsp Olive Oil
1/2 tsp Salt	2 cubes Chicken Bouillon

In a bowl, sift in your flour into a mound, make a well in the middle flour. In a measuring cup mix with a fork the eggs, water, oil and the salt. Slowly with your fingers mix the wet ingredients into the well until all the wet ingredients have been mixed together into a smooth and elastic dough; takes about 10 minutes. You should lightly flour your hands to avoid sticking. If you are using a pasta machine cover the dough with an inverted greased bowl or plastic wrap; allow it to rest for an hour in the refrigerator, or chill overnight. Divide the dough into large sized pieces. Quickly knead and flatten each portion of dough into a disc; very lightly dust with flour. Feed these through the pasta machine at the widest setting, (If the pasta tears just simply sprinkle on a little more flour over the dough and redo). You can run all of the discs through the machine several times on a finer setting each time (may take as many and 5 - 10 times. When finished, dry brush excess flour from the discs. On the final pass-through, set noodle size to last choice for cooking. If you are not using a machine, then on a floured work surface, knead the dough for 8 to 10 minutes and roll out flat to desired thickness, cut into thin noodles (or squares for a ravioli and add any filling as required). Add two chicken bouillon cubes to a large saucepan of water. Bring to a boil; drop in a few noodles/raviolis at a time and cook for 3 – 5 minutes, when they float they are done. Place 2 Tbsp melted margarine or butter in a skillet and just before it turns brown, put in noodles or 10 stuffed raviolis at a time and toss **-OR-** Serve with a Béchamel sauce or other sauce of choice.   Serves 4-6

NOTE: Add 1 (10 oz) frozen, thawed, pureed, drained Spinach and 1/8 tsp Nutmeg to the basic pasta recipe for MAKE YOUR OWN Spinach Noodles.

PAS – (Macaroni and Cheese)

Salad or Elbow Macaroni (1/2 pound)	1 can Evaporated Milk
1/4 Pound Margarine	1 cup (5 oz) grated medium Cheddar Cheese
3 – 4 Tbsp of All-Purpose Flour	1 tsp granulated Chicken Bouillon
	or 1 cup Chicken Broth

Cook macaroni per package directions, drain and salt. In a saucepan melt margarine, salt, stir in flour until blended, add chicken bouillon or broth and the milk. Bring to a slight boil, stirring constantly to avoid burning. Add in 1/2 of the grated cheddar cheese stir until melted. Pour cheese mixture over the cooked and drained macaroni, top with the balance of the cheese and mix thoroughly to re-coat all macaroni. Salt and pepper to taste.   4-6 Servings
MENU WEEK#52

HINT: Adding 1 tsp of vegetable oil to your water will prevent the macaroni from sticking together when cooking. Boil the macaroni per package directions (6-8 minutes), or until tender, drain and salt.
HINT: The macaroni is done when you can cut one and there is no dryness in the center (it will appear whiter than the outside edge if not done).

ALTERNATE IDEAS: Add in leftover, diced cooked Ham to the Mac and Cheese **–OR-** Add in a 2-pound package of thawed Tater Tots (Bake for 40 minutes) **–OR-** Use 8 oz of shredded Gruyere Swiss and 1-1/4 cups (5 oz) Pecorino Romano Cheese and/or 1/2 pint Sour Cream.

PAS – (Noodles – Cashew Sesame)

Cashew Sesame Sauce

2 large Garlic Cloves, chopped	3 Tbsp Soy Sauce
1-1/2 Tbsp Rice Vinegar	1/4 cup Asian Sesame Oil
3/4 tsp dried Hot Red Pepper Flakes, or to taste	1 tsp Sugar
1/2 cup salted roasted Cashews	1/3 cup Water

In a blender, blend all sauce ingredients with salt and pepper to taste until smooth. (Sauce can be made 3 days in advance and chilled, covered. If made early, bring the sauce to room temperature and then stir before using).

Cashew Sesame Noodles

1-Pound Thin Spaghettini or Angel Hair Pasta
1-1/2 cups loosely packed fresh Coriander Springs, washed well, and dried with paper towels and
   chopped finely
Garnish with chopped Salted Roasted Cashews and fresh Coriander Springs.

Just before serving, bring 5 quarts of salted water to a boil and cook the Spaghettini per package directions. Drain off the water in a colander and place in serving bowl, add salt and pepper to taste and toss with the sauce and chopped coriander. Garnish with cashews and coriander.

Serves 8
(Extra Recipe)

PAS – (Noodles – Green Spinach Noodles with White Sauce)

Use Green Spinach Noodle (<u>**information listed under fresh Pasta Optional**</u>) with **PAS (Noodles with White Sauce).**

PAS – (Noodles – Italian Style)

4 – 8 oz medium Noodles Egg, Flat or Fettuccini Noodles	2 oz Cream Cheese
1/4 cup Evaporated Milk	1/4 cup Milk
1/4 cup grated Parmesan Cheese	1/8 tsp Salt and pepper to taste
Chopped Parsley mixed with a 1/4 tsp Italian Seasoning	

Soften the cream cheese in a medium-size bowl and blend in the cream, the milk, cheese, salt and pepper. Cook the noodles in salted, boiling water and drain. Pour the cheese sauce over the noodles and toss lightly to coat well. Spoon into a serving dish, and garnish with the parsley.

Serves 4 - 6
(Extra Recipe)

Decided for You Cookbook – 365 Dinners

PAS – (Noodles – Noodles and Broccoli Parmesan)

1 Pkg (16 oz) frozen Broccoli (if fresh. ~1-1/2
    pounds)
1/2 cup chopped Onion
1 can (10-3/4 oz) Cream of Mushroom Soup
1/2 tsp Tarragon, crushed
1 cup (4 oz) shredded Cheddar Cheese or
    American

5 cups cooked Fettuccini Noodles (8-12 oz
    uncooked)
1 clove Garlic minced
2 Tbsp Margarine or Butter
1 cup Sour Cream
1/2 cup grated Parmesan Cheese
    Aluminum Foil

Prepare the frozen Broccoli per package directions and drain. (If fresh, cut the broccoli into small chunks and cook over medium heat in 1" of boiling water 6 minutes or until fork tender and drain, and salt). Boil the noodles per package directions, drain and salt a little. In a saucepan, over medium heat, in hot margarine cook the onion and garlic until tender, stirring to be sure it doesn't burn. Stir in the soup, the tarragon and mix well. Add in the cheese, stirring until melted. Stir in the sour cream, broccoli and the cooked noodles. Place all ingredients into a greased 2-Quart casserole dish, cover with foil or a lid and bake at 350°F for 30 minutes or until hot and bubbling.   Serves 6 – 8

NOTE: 3-1/2 cups uncooked Noodles = 8 oz uncooked = 4-1/2 cooked Pasta.

PAS – (Noodles with Cheeses)

8 oz Noodles Egg, Flat or Fettuccini Noodles
1/2 cup Blue Cheese, room temperature
1/4 cup chopped Parsley
3 eggs, well beaten
Salt and Pepper to taste

1 cup Cream-Style Cottage Cheese
1/4 cup melted Butter/Margarine
1/4 cup minced Onion
1 small clove Garlic, crushed

Cook the noodles in salted, boiling water until tender and drain. Combine the remaining ingredients, add the cooked noodles and toss well. Grease a 1-1/2 quart casserole, add the noodle mixture and bake in a preheated oven at 350°F for 30 minutes.   Serves 4
                                                                                    (Extra Recipe)

HINT: Left-over pasta can be reused in casseroles. They can be topped with any number of sauces, and the basis for a Vinaigrette or Ranch "cold" salad.

PAS – (Noodles with Garlic, Oil and Red Pepper Sauce)

1 Pound Fettuccini Noodles
3 cloves cut up Garlic
3 Tbsp chopped Parsley

3 Red Pepper Pods (seeded)
1/3 cup Olive Oil
Grated Parmesan Cheese

Bring to a boil 5 quarts of salted water. Drop in the pasta and stir well, cook until you can easily cut it with a fork. In a skillet sauté the red peppers and garlic in the Olive Oil. Remove both when the garlic is brown. Remove from the heat and drain the pasta. Place drained noodles in a serving dish. Salt and pepper to taste. Toss on the parsley, then top with grated Parmesan Cheese.

PAS – (Noodles with White Sauce)

6 oz (1/2 Pkg) Flat Egg Pasta Noodles, Vermicelli, Angel Hair, Spaghettini, or Green Spinach Noodles

3 Tbsp Margarine or Butter   2 cups Evaporated Milk or Whipping Cream
3 Tbsp All-Purpose Flour   1/2 cup grated Parmesan or
Optional: Greek Myzithra Goat Cheese
    (very good, but difficult to find)

Boil the noodles per package directions, drain and salt.   Melt the butter in a saucepan over low heat otherwise it will burn. When it's medium hot, stir in the flour and whisk until it forms a paste, about 3 minutes. Stirring/whisking constantly, add in the milk/cream in a steady stream. Bring the sauce to a gentle simmer and continue to whisk until it thickens, about 6-8 minutes.   Stir in the Cheese of choice and stir into the noodles.   Serves 4-6

HINT: Add 1 tsp of vegetable oil to your water to prevent the noodles from sticking together when cooking. The noodles are done when you can cut one and there is no dryness in the center (it will appear whiter if not done).   HINT: Thickening Agents – Both flour and cornstarch are used to thicken sauces. One and one-half Tablespoons of flour per one cup of liquid. Cornstarch has twice the thickening properties so reduce the recipe accordingly. Mix flour and water or juices in a bowl with a whisk, or put it in a small jar or sealable bowl and shake this together until all lumps are gone before adding this slurry into other ingredients. VARIATION: Use a Pesto Sauce over any kind of pasta GREAT!

PAS – (Raviolis – Cheese with Roasted Garlic and Parmesan Cheese Sauce)

1 (9 oz) Pkg (frozen) Cheese Raviolis
1 (1 Pound) Jar Roasted Garlic and Parmesan Cheese Sauce
1/2 cup shredded Parmesan Cheese

Boil the raviolis per package direction and drain in a colander. Salt and pepper to taste. Place half of these in a serving dish. Warm the sauce in a microwave, and cover the layer of ravioli's with sauce. Then add additional layers of Ravioli's covering each with the sauce, topping the cooked raviolis with shredded Parmesan Cheese and chopped Chives – **OR-**
MAKE YOUR OWN ROASTED GARLIC SEASONING:
Place two heads of cleaned garlic cloves in aluminum foil along with 1-2 Tablespoon of Virgin Olive Oil. Each head of garlic will yield about 1-1/2 Tablespoons and 2 heads about 3 Tablespoons of garlic butter. Fold the aluminum foil into an envelope so it will not leak and place on a small flat pan into a 325°F oven and bake for approximately 1 hour, or until the garlic is very soft and golden brown. Remove from the oven and let sit until cool enough to handle. Open the package and place it on a saucer or shallow dish and add in 1 heaping Tablespoon of Margarine/Butter and then smash the cooked garlic with the flat edge of a rubber spatula until it blends into the butter and olive oil.   Add these ingredients to a cooked White Sauce with Parmesan. **HINT: You can cook several heads of garlic and store in an airtight container in the refrigerator until you need them**.

Raviolis – Spinach Cheese Filling - MAKE YOUR OWN – (Ingredients not on grocery list)

1 Large carton Ricotta Cheese   2 bunches Spinach
1 handful of chopped Parsley   1/2 to 1 cup grated Parmesan Cheese
2 Egg Whites   Dash of Nutmeg
Salt and Pepper to taste

Place the chopped spinach in a pan with boiling salted water and boil until wilted and tender. Squeeze out the water, place in paper toweling and drain well. Add the parsley to the well drained spinach and add in the balance of the ingredients. Mix well. Seal inside the ravioli pasta **(BF-Beef Raviolis Stuffed with Meat Loaf)** and boil per pasta directions.   (Extra Recipe)

PAS – (Rice – Long Grain) – Wash Rice

Place rice into either a pot or put in a colander and run the water slowly over the rice, rubbing the rice with your fingers. Rice has a vegetable white talcum on it that needs to be removed. Pour off the water until the water stays clear. **HINTS:** **One cup of rice absorbs 2 cups liquid. ONE HALF CUP OF UNCOOKED RICE INCREASES TO 1-1/2 CUPS WHEN COOKED.** **NOTE:** **2 cups uncooked Rice = 1 Pound uncooked Rice = 6 cups cooked Rice.**

Rice – Fried Rice

It's best if you are using cold rice that was steamed the day before, easier to use as it is not so sticky. Place **2 Tbsp vegetable oil** in a skillet and roll the skillet in a circle to coat the bottom with the oil. On a medium setting on your stove heat add in **chopped green onions** and sauté lightly, add in **6-8 cups pre-cooked/ leftover cold rice** and begin to break up by stirring. Add enough **soy sauce (approximately 3-4 Tbsp)** that will change the color of the rice to a light brown. Add in **diced cooked shrimp**. Move the rice and shrimp to the side and put in **a couple eggs** and scramble these. Mix the rice, onion, shrimp and the eggs together. Sprinkle over the top, **1/2 tsp Garlic Powder**. Cover and warm about 5-10 minutes or until all the ingredients are warmed. Add **salt and pepper to taste**. If there is not enough soy flavor add some more and stir, the quantity depends on the amount of rice used).

Rice – Pilaf Rice

2 Tbsp Margarine   1 medium Tomato, chopped
2 Tbsp chopped Parsley   1 cup sliced Mushrooms
1 Pkg Beef Flavored Rice (Plain rice and beef bouillon can be mixed if you don't have)

Sauté the mushrooms in the margarine. Add the contents of the seasoning to the rice and water. Heat to boiling. Stir in the tomatoes into the rice. Cover with a tight fitting lid and simmer for 15 minutes. Let stand covered in a warm place for an additional 5 minutes. Stir in the Parsley with a fork.   Serves 5
(Extra Recipe)

Rice – Rice and Mushrooms

Sprinkle the tops of the mushrooms with garlic powder. Cook them in melted butter until tender. Cook the rice (per Steamed Rice recipe) and combine into one serving dish.

Rice – Spanish Rice

Place **1 or 2 Chicken Bouillon cubes** into 1 cup of water and put into a medium bowl. Lightly oil your skillet with **2 Tbsp Vegetable Oil**. Brown **1 small chopped onion** until browned and clear. Add in **1 cup (or 2) Long Grain Rice** and fry until slightly browned. Stir **1 tsp Cumin** and **1 cup of Tomato Sauce** into the bowl with the chicken bouillon and add to the skillet. Sprinkle all of this with **Garlic Powder, Onion Salt** and stir. Cover your skillet with a tight fitting lid (or put on top a large dinner plate which will keep the steam inside). Turn the heat down to low and cook for 20-25 minutes not lifting the lid and allowing the steam to escape. Taste the rice for additional seasoning when the rice is soft and flaky. **HINT:** **Simple use for left-over rice is to add to Quesadillas (Mexican Grilled Cheese), which are based on flour tortillas, grated cheese, and Salsa. Simply place a flour tortilla on a griddle or baking tray. Sprinkle top with cheese and add on the rice, meats and/or vegetables. Top with a second tortilla, grill on both sides until bubbly and melted together. Serve with a dollop of Sour Cream and Salsa (or can be made in a microwave). QUESADILLAS VARIATION: Use Spinach Wraps with 3/4 Lb Brie with Herbs, 4 Tbsp chopped green onion or chives, dash of Thyme. After grilling, cut into wedges and top with sour cream.**

Rice – Steamed/Boiled Rice

After washing your rice per above instructions, add enough clear water to your saucepan that when you stick your middle finger touching the top of the rice that the water height will rest on your first bend (joint/ knuckle) in the finger which is a sufficient amount of water. Bring the rice to a boil, stir thoroughly. Place a tight fitting lid on top of the saucepan (or put on top a large dinner plate which will keep the steam inside). Lower the heat to very low, and steam the rice for 20-25 minutes or <u>until the center kernels of rice is soft and flaky</u>. **Avoid peeking into the pan allowing the steam to escape. HINT: <u>A few drops of lemon juice added to simmering rice will keep the grains separate. HINT: Children love pastel colored rice. To color, just add a few drops of food coloring to the water in which the rice is cooked. MICROWAVE: 1 cup rice, 2 cups Water, 1/2 twp Soy Sauce, 1 tsp chopped Green Onion or Cilantro. Combine all ingredients in a bowl. Stretch plastic wrap over the top. Microwave on high for 10 minutes, then half power for 10 minutes. Fluff with a fork and serve.</u>**

PAS – (Spaghetti - Baked)

8 oz Angel Hair Pasta or Spaghetti Pasta cooked per package directions
1 cup grated Cheddar Cheese   1 cup grated Mozzarella or Monterey Jack Cheese
1 Large (26.5oz) can of Spaghetti Sauce   **-OR-**

Spaghetti Sauce

MAKE YOUR OWN – (Ingredients not on grocery list)

2 cups diced canned Tomatoes	2 cups Tomato Sauce	1-1/2 Pounds Ground Beef
1 cup water	1/2 cup diced Onion	1-1/2 tsp Sugar
1/2 cup diced green Bell Pepper	2 chopped cloves Garlic	
1/3 cup chopped Parsley Leaves	1-1/2 tsp Italian Seasoning	

Preheat oven to 350°F. If using prepared Spaghetti Sauce, skip to asterisk*. (In a stockpot, combine the tomatoes, tomato sauce, water, onions, peppers, garlic, parsley, seasoning mixtures, sugar and bay leaves. Bring to a boil over high heat, and then reduce to a simmer, cover and cook for one hour.) *Crumble the ground beef in a large skillet. Cook this till brown. Add to the sauce. **HINT: <u>Place 1 tsp of salt per quart of water into a large pan (causes water to boil quicker) and bring to a boil; add in the tsp of olive or vegetable oil to prevent the spaghetti from sticking together when cooking.</u>** Place in about 1/3 of a package of Spaghetti and cook per package directions or until you can cut it and there is no dryness in the center (you will be able to see the difference if not cooked thoroughly) drain and salt. Cover the bottom of a 9 x 13 pan with sauce. Add in a layer of pasta and then a layer of the cheeses. Repeat the layers until all has been used, ending with the cheese. Bake in the oven for 20 minutes while you put your feet up and relax. Remove from the oven and slightly cool and serve.   Serves 8 – 10
MENU WEEK#52

PAS – (Stuffed Pasta Shells)

1 Pound Jumbo Pasta Shells	2 Pounds Ricotta Cheese	1 cup Bechamél Sauce
1/2 Lb Mozzarella Cheese	2 Eggs	1 (8 oz) Tomato Sauce
1/2 cup grated Parmesan Cheese	1 tsp chopped Parsley	Pinch grated Nutmeg

Boil jumbo shells in 5 qts of salted, water for 10 minutes and drain. Mix the Ricotta, Mozzarella, eggs, Parmesan and Parsley together. Season with salt, pepper, and nutmeg. Fill the shells and then cover the bottom of a baking dish with Tomato Sauce. Arrange the stuffed shells over the Tomato Sauce, Salt and Pepper to Taste. Place a large spoonful of the Bechamél Sauce over each shell. Bake in a 350°F oven for 30 minutes. Sprinkle tops with grated Parmesan Cheese.   Serves 4-6
(Extra Recipe)

PAS – (Tortellini in Cream Sauce)

9 oz frozen or fresh Cheese Tortellini (Ravioli's can be used), cooked per package directions and
    drained
1 (1 Pound) jar Roasted Garlic and Parmesan Sauce warmed, and poured over Tortellini/Ravioli's
2/3 cup of shredded Parmesan Cheese or crumbled Feta Cheese

Cream Sauce
MAKE YOUR OWN – (Ingredients not on grocery list)
1 can (10-3/4 oz) Condensed Cream of Mushroom Soup
1/2 cup grated Parmesan Cheese or crumbled Feta
1 tsp Olive or Vegetable Oil   2 cloves minced Garlic
1/2 cup chopped Bell Pepper   1/4 cup chopped Onion
1/2 cup Half and Half Milk   1/4 tsp dried Tarragon crushed
1/4 cup sliced Green Onion - garnish   Optional: 1/2 cup white Wine

In a 2-Quart microwave-safe casserole, combine the oil, garlic, bell pepper and the onion. Cover and cook on High for 2 minutes or until the vegetables are tender. Stir in the soup until smooth. Add in the Half-and-Half Milk, wine (add equal amount of liquid if not using the wine) and Tarragon. Cover and cook 5 minutes or until hot and bubbling, stirring once during the cooking and let it stand, covered for 5 minutes. Toss this sauce over the Hot Tortellini. Sprinkle with the cheese of choice and green onions.   Serves 4

PASTA/RICE – MICROWAVE INFORMATION:

HINT: **Purchase specific Microwave Dish, for Pasta and use about half the amount of water needed for conventional boiling, there is less evaporation in a microwave. Add the regular amount of salt and 1 tsp of oil to prevent sticking. For rice use the same or slightly greater amount of water as with conventional. Cover the pasta and rice tightly with plastic wrap, leaving one corner rolled back to vent. At half cooking time stir or rearrange. Drain the pasta immediately after microwaving. Little changes between microwaving and conventional cooking.**

Macaroni (8 oz)   Add 3 cups water. Cook 15 to 18 min. and stir after
                                                              10 minutes, check for doneness after this time.

Manicotti (5 oz)   Brush with oil, then cover with water, turn over
                                                              every 5 minutes.

Noodles (8-10 oz) – Egg (Angel Hair, Fettuccini,
Lasagna, Spinach, etc)   Add 8 cups water. Stir after 10 minutes.
Rice, Long Grain (1 cup)   Add 2-1/2 cups water. Stir after 10 minutes. Cook
                                                              18 to 21 minutes.

Rice, Minute (1-1/2 cups)   Add 1-1/2 cups Water. Stir after 2 minutes
              REHEATING PASTA
Lasagna – Frozen (21 oz)   13 to 18 minutes
Pasta, Rice – Frozen in a pouch/bag   Puncture bag, cook 6-9 minutes

SALADS AND SALAD DRESSINGS & MARINADES

Salads can be produced by just changing the mixtures of many ingredients or even changing the Lettuce from Iceberg to Romaine, Butter, or Escarole. Combinations of the salad ingredients can be the crowning touch that is needed to make your dinner the very best. Salads can become "Mealtime Magicians".

I **have not included recipes for all the possible types of salads**, but most of them, which are listed in the menus and are made from "combinations of the items in the title" as shown. You can even use the latest pre-bagged salads currently sold in your grocery store without having to think about what ingredients make up a salad. However, for those new cooks which would like to make a **GREEN SALAD** up fresh then you should know that you separate your greens into leaves and rinse them under cold water and shake off as much water as possible. You can also roll the greens in lots of paper toweling until they are thoroughly dry, if desired. Break these into bite-size pieces usually ending up with about 6 cups of greens. **HINT:** __If you cut greens or avocados with a metal knife the oxidation from the blade will cause the edges to turn brown, so be sure that you tear them up or cut with a plastic knife.__ Add in your sliced __radishes, chopped onions, tomato wedges and that completes your basic green salad__. Place all left over in plastic bags or covered plastic containers in your refrigerator to keep crisp. If you store in plastic bags you might want to include a paper towel to absorb any excessive moisture.

Salad – (Apple, Raisin, Walnut Salad)
Combine these ingredients and serve with the Poppy Seed or Waldorf Dressing.

Salad – (Artichoke and Crab Meat Salad)

1 cup diced cooked Artichoke Hearts	1 cup Crab Meat
1/2 cup Heavy Cream, Whipped	1 cup Mayonnaise
1/2 cup Ketchup	1/2 tsp Worcestershire Sauce
Salt and Pepper to taste	

Combine the artichokes and crab meet and chill. Mix the whipped cream with the mayonnaise, ketchup, Worcestershire sauce, salt and pepper and chill.   At serving time, combine the sauce with the crab mixture.

Serves 6
(Extra Recipe)

Salad – (Artichokes – Marinated)
These can be purchased already marinated. But, if not, you can marinate in tart Italian Salad Dressing.

Salad – (Avocado Salad)
Avocados can be peeled, pitted, sliced and placed in a tossed green salad **–OR–** Peeled, and mashed and mixed into a dressing. If you are letting avocadoes set for a while, then sprinkle with lemon juice to keep them from changing color. You can have a delicious treat by adding avocadoes to cooked shrimp, chopped onions, and bell peppers. **HINT:** __If your avocado is not ripe, place it inside a brown paper sack and leave on your kitchen counter near a window and this will cause it to ripen faster.__

Decided for You Cookbook – 365 Dinners

Salad – (Avocado, Tomato and Egg Salad)

Boil your eggs and **HINT:** **(Run cold water over these to make them easier to peel and also prevents dark circles around the yolks).** Place a bed of lettuce on your plate topped with cut up tomatoes. Mix your favorite dressing into the cut up eggs, chopped tomatoes and diced avocado. Place a large scoop of this mixture on top of the lettuce bed. **HINT:** **(If you need to stretch the ingredients to feed more, add chopped lettuce to the mixture).**

Salad – (Beans—Green Beans, Carrots and Beet Salad)

1 Pound Green Beans, ends trimmed, blanched to al dente **–OR–** 2 (14.5 oz) cans of drained French
       Style Green Beans **–OR–** 2 (9 oz) Pkgs frozen French Style Green Beans defrosted
1 (14.5 oz) can Pickled Beets Julienne
4 Large Carrots, peeled and shredded

Mustard Vinaigrette

1 clove Garlic, minced	1 Shallot or Green Onions minced
1 Tbsp Dijon Mustard	4 Tbsp Red Wine Vinegar
3 Tbsp Olive Oil	Salt and Pepper

Whisk together ingredients, taste and adjust seasonings. Marinate the green beans and the carrots in the Mustard Vinaigrette dressing and let stand for at least 1 – 4 hours marinating in the refrigerator. Toss in the pickled beets and serve.   Serves 8
(Extra Recipe)

Salad – (Beans–Green Beans – Dilly Salad)

Using leftover Dill Pickle Juice, pour over drained, canned green beans and let stand in the refrigerator for several days and you will have dilly beans.   (Extra Recipe)

Salad – (Beans–Green Beans – French Style with Onion Salad and Italian Dressing)

Drain 2 cans green beans. Mix with sliced onions and marinate in an tart Italian Salad Dressing
(Extra Recipe)

Salad – (Beans–Green Beans and Onion Salad with Italian Dressing)

Marinate 1 (14.5 oz) can of French Style Green beans overnight in a tart Italian Salad dressing. Toss these beans into shredded Iceberg Lettuce and sliced onions. Add Italian Salad dressing as needed.
(Extra Recipe)

Salad – (Beets and Celery Salad)

Chop the Celery and mix in the Pickled Beets.   (Extra Recipe)

Salad – (Beets Pickled and Sliced Onion Salad)

Marinate these combinations in a tart Italian or Oil and Vinegar dressing. Can be mixed with shredded lettuce of your choice.

Salad – (Bell Pepper and Onion Ring Salad)

Slice Red or Green Bell Peppers and Red Onions into slices. Marinate at least one hour in a tart Italian Salad Dressing.

Salad – (Cabbage, Carrots, Pineapple Slaw Salad)

Shred the cabbage and carrots. Drain either crushed, or chunk Pineapple and mix together. Serve with a sweet dressing, Waldorf Salad or Cole Slaw Dressing.

Salad – (Cabbage – Red Salad)

Discard outside wilted leaves. Cut cabbage into shreds and serve with a Vinaigrette Dressing. If too tart, add in granulated sugar to taste. **HINT: 1 Pound of Sugar = 2 cups**

Salad – (Caesar Salad)

1 clove Garlic, crushed	3/4 cup Vegetable Oil
1/4 cup Olive Oil	2 cups Croutons*
1-1/2 tsp Salt	1/2 tsp dry Mustard
1/2 tsp freshly Ground Pepper	1 Tbsp Worcestershire Sauce
1/4 cup crumbled Blue Cheese	1/2 cup grated Parmesan Cheese
2 Eggs, slightly beaten	1/2 clove Garlic for inside bowl rub
1 medium head of Romaine Lettuce, washed and chilled	1/4 cup Lemon Juice

Combine the crushed clove of garlic with the salad and olive oil. Refrigerate 1 hour. Add salt, mustard, pepper and Worcestershire sauce. Shake dressing vigorously. Rub the inside of a large wood salad bowl with the 1/2 clove of garlic; discard garlic. Tear the lettuce into small size pieces. Shake dressing and pour over the greens. Sprinkle over the lettuce the Parmesan and Blue Cheese. Beat eggs and lemon juice together with a fork; pour over salad and toss thoroughly. Add croutons and serve immediately. *See how to make croutons in the Bread section.

MENU WEEK#1

Salad – (Carrot, Celery, Nut, Pineapple Slaw)

Dice the celery, shred or grate the carrots, add drained pineapple (chunks or crushed) and your choice of walnuts, almonds, or pecans. Serve with a sweet dressing or a Cole Slaw Salad Dressing.

Salad – (Carrot, Radish and Celery Salad)

Grate the carrots, slice the radishes and dice the celery and serve with a Thousand Island Dressing.

(Extra Recipe)

Salad – (Carrot Slaw Salad)

Shred the carrots, with or without Cabbage, and serve with French, Blue Cheese or a Sweet Dressing. Raisins can be added, if desired.

Salad – (Cauliflower Salad – Hot or Cold Marinated)

1 medium head of Cauliflower (~1-1/2 pounds)	3 Tbsp Wine Vinegar
2 Tbsp Butter/Margarine	2 Tbsp diced Pimiento
2 Tbsp chopped Green Bell Pepper	1 tsp Sugar
1/4 tsp Salt	

Break the cauliflower into flowerets; cook these in a small amount of boiling, salted water for about 10 minutes; drain. While cauliflower cooks, combine remaining ingredients in a small saucepan; cook over low heat for about 5 minutes. Pour over the drained, hot cauliflower. This can be served as a cold salad or as a side vegetable. If serving as a cold salad, marinate in dressing of your choice 1-2 hours before serving.

Serves 6

(Extra Recipe)

Salad – (Chef Salad)

This is a "SHOW-OFF" salad. Make the basic green salad and **add all cold items you can find in the refrigerator**. **Bolded items** in grocery list: Add in drained **asparagus spears, sliced hard-boiled eggs, Cheddar cheese strips, and sliced luncheon meats**. Top with croutons. See MAKE YOUR OWN Recipe (**MISC – Croutons**). Arrange this salad in a large, Clam Shell dish, is very pr-e-tty. Salad dressing of choice.

Salad – (Cheese Cubes and Onion Salad)

Basic greens with diced cheeses and onions sliced in rounds.

Salad – (Chicken Salad Stuffed Tomato)

1-2 cups diced/shredded Chicken (2 or 3 Boneless breasts can be cooked in the microwave and shredded, -
OR- purchase some white meat from a commercial chicken seller, or used canned chicken, or use leftover
chicken, your choice)

4 Large Tomatoes	2 Large Carrots – shredded
1 stalk Celery – chopped	1 Onion – chopped
1 cup Mayonnaise or Salad Dressing of Choice (i.e.,	2 Tbsp Lemon Juice
Thousand, Ranch, Blue Cheese)	Dash of Pepper
1 (15 oz) can Asparagus cuts, drained	Sliced Black Olives
Garlic/Onion-Flavored Croutons	3 Hard-Cooked Eggs – Chopped or sliced

Lettuce, shredded and other large leaves used as the base for the stuffed salad

Cut and "X" across the top of the tomato, but not all the way through to the bottom of your tomato.
With a spoon, hollow out most of the pulp, dice it, saving this in a large bowl. If your tomato is not large
enough to hollow out, then cut it almost all the way through and lay the sections flat on top of shredded lettuce
on a bread plate. Mix the diced tomato pulp with all of the other ingredients. Place the mixed ingredients
back into the center of the tomato and drizzle additional dressing and croutons on top of salad.   Serves 4

MENU WEEK #48

Salad – (Chinese Beef Oriental Salad)

1 – 2 Pounds Beef Steak (Sirloin, London Broil or even Flank)

1-1/2 pounds fresh Asparagus Spears	2 cloves crushed Garlic
3/4 cup dry White Wine	1/2 cup Soy Sauce
1/4 cup Honey	3 Tbsp minced Fresh Gingerroot + 1 Tbsp
3/4 pound fresh snow pea pods, trimmed	1/4 pound sliced fresh Mushrooms
1 Tbsp toasted Sesame Seeds	2 Tbsp dark Sesame Oil
1 Pkg fresh Soybean Sprouts	Green Onions chopped finely

Cut the meat into 2" or 3" x 1" thick pieces and marinate in the wine, soy sauce, honey, 3 Tbsp Gingerroot and
garlic for at least three hours, turning occasionally. Remove the meat and cook under a broiler 6 inches from
the heat for 5-7 minutes on each side or until at least medium rare (can be cooked on a Bar-B-Q as well. Let
the meat cool. Cook the juice drippings and the left over marinade in a saucepan for about 15 minutes until it
reduces by one half and reserve. Snap off the tough ends of the asparagus and remove scales from the stalks
with a knife or Vegetable peeler. Cut them diagonally into 1-inch pieces. Blanch the asparagus in boiling
water for 2-4 minutes or until crisp-tender, drain and rinse with cold water. Salt to taste. Blanch the snow
peas in boiling water for one minute or until crisp-tender; drain and rise with cold water. Salt to taste.
Combine the cooked meat, asparagus, snow peas, mushrooms, green onions, soybean sprouts and sesame
seeds in a large bowl. Combine the reserved marinade, sesame oil, and the additional Tbsp of Gingerroot; stir
well. Pour this dressing over the salad mixture tossing gently to combine. **VARIATION:** Can substitute
store-bought Rotisserie Chicken for the Beef.   Serves 8

(Extra Recipe)

Salad – (Chinese Chicken Salad)

1/4 cup Sesame Seeds
1-1/2 cups crispy Chow Mein Noodles
1/2 bunch of Soybean Sprouts
1 head of Iceberg Lettuce
Chinese Salt if available
Chinese Parsley or Cilantro
Dry Mustard – Mix into a paste with a small amount of water
Wonton Skins or Rice Sticks (these should be cut into small strips and fried quickly in hot vegetable and sesame oil)

5 Boneless Chicken Breast
1/2 Pound Sugar Snap Snow Peas
1 bunch chopped Green Onions
1/4 cup Vegetable Oil
Water

Cut the chicken breast into small pieces and fry in some vegetable oil till done. (if you prefer you can cook these whole and then shred them with a fork). Season with salt and pepper. Cut the lettuce into strips, combine all of rest of the ingredients including the chicken and toss in the Dressing. (Optional: Can add peanuts, sliced almonds, or walnuts to salad if desired)

Chinese Chicken Salad Dressing

1/4 cup Vegetable Oil
1 Tbsp Soy Sauce
1 tsp Sugar
1/2 tsp Chili Paste (Optional)

1/2 tsp dry Mustard, dissolved in 1/2 tsp Water
3 Tbsp Rice Wine Vinegar
2 Tbsp Oriental Sesame Oil
1 Tbsp Creamy Peanut Butter (Optional)

Serves 4-6
MENU WEEK#22, #19

Salad – (Chinese Ribbon Vegetable Salad)

1 medium Cucumber
3 large Celery Ribs
2 tsp Seasoned Rice Vinegar or to taste

2 large Carrots
2 Green Onions
1/8 tsp Asian Sesame Oil

Halve the cucumber lengthwise and remove seeds. Peel and trim the carrots. With a vegetable peeler cut both the cucumber and carrots lengthwise into thin ribbons, transferring to a bowl. Cut the Celery and Green Onions into 2" long pieces. Then cut the pieces lengthwise into Julienne Strips, transferring to the bowl. Add in the vinegar and oil and toss to marinate at least 45 minutes.

Serves 2
(Extra Recipe)

Salad – (Cole Slaw Salad – Asian)

1 head Green Cabbage, shredded
1/2 head Red Cabbage, shredded
1 Tbsp Salt
1/4 cup Soy Sauce
1/2 tsp Chile Paste
1 cup Bean Sprouts
1 tsp fresh Ginger, grated
Salt and Pepper, to taste

1/2 cup Rice Wine Vinegar
2 Tbsp Sesame Oil
3 Tbsp Creamy Peanut Butter
2 Carrots, shredded
4 Scallions, or Green Onions – cut
   strips the long way
2 Tbsp Sesame Seeds, for garnish

Toss the cabbage together in a large colander and set in aside. Sprinkle the cabbage with salt and let stand for 15 minutes. The salt will draw out some of its moisture so the slaw will remain crunchy. In a bowl, whisk together the vinegar, soy sauce, oil, chile paste, peanut butter, and ginger. Toss together with the cabbage, carrots, bean sprouts and scallions, season again with salt and pepper and garnish with extra sesame seeds before serving.

Servings 8
(Extra Recipe)

Salad – (Corn - White, Pimento and Peas Marinated Salad)

1 to 3 cans (15 oz ea) drained White Whole Kernel Corn
1 medium chopped Onion   1 to 2 cans (15 oz ea) drained Baby
1 (4 oz) chopped Pimento   Lesuer Peas
Sprinkle Garlic Powder over the top   **VARIATION:** 1 can French Style Green Beans
1 (16 oz) Zesty/Tart Italian Salad Dressing (reduce to half if only using 1 can each of Veggies)

Stir well and marinate over night, or at least two hours. **HINT:** <u>**To remove garlic smell from plastic bowls, place washed, empty bowl upside down on top of your grass and leave all day in the sun. The chlorophyll in the grass will remove the smell.**</u>

Salad – (Crab Louie Salad)

Iceberg or Romaine Lettuce cut up   Shredded or chunks of cleaned Crab
Hard Boiled Eggs – Quartered   Chopped Green Onions
Cold, drained Asparagus   Tomato Chunks
Black Olives – pitted
Toss all ingredients in Salad Bowl, use Thousand Island Dressing **–OR-**

Crab Louie Salad Dressing
<u>MAKE YOUR OWN</u> - Equal Parts of
Mayonnaise, Ketchup & Sweet
Pickle Relish   1 Lemon Juiced
                                                                   -OR-
<u>Equal Parts of</u> Mayonnaise & Plain Yogurt   1/2 pt Chili Sauce (similar to Cocktail Sauce)
Grated Onion   Chopped Parsley & chopped Chives
Cayenne Pepper to taste   1 Lemon Juiced
1 tsp Worcestershire Sauce   1 tsp Horseradish

MENU WEEK #8

Salad – (Cucumber and Onions – Italian Pickled)
HINT: <u>If desired you can **leave green skin on** the cucumbers, **but you must cut about a 1/2" piece from the end of the cucumber that had the vine attached. Rotate this piece in a circle against the end of the cucumber where it was removed until extra white froth moisture is observed. This is the bitterness of the skin being removed from the entire cucumber. Throw away cut off end. Rinse cucumber, then slice as directed.**</u>   Slice in coin shapes, thinly. Salt and let stand for 10 minutes, and then squeeze out excessive liquids. Slice onion of choice and add half a bottle of tart Italian Dressing and marinate together in the refrigerator until needed.

Salad – (Eggplant Garlic Salad)

1 small Eggplant   1 Onion
2 cloves Garlic, crushed   1 Tbsp Extra-Virgin Olive Oil
2 tsp Red Wine Vinegar   1 Tbsp Lemon Juice
1 Tbsp grated Parmesan Cheese   Salt and Pepper
1/4 cup loosely packed, chopped Cilantro

In a preheated 400°F oven, place the cleaned (can be peeled or not) eggplant that has been rubbed with the olive oil. Bake the onion and eggplant until they are fork tender ~15 minutes. Cool until you can handle. Peel the eggplant and the garlic and place these in the bowl of a food processor. Cut up the onion into quarters or large chunks and add to the processor. Add the vinegar, lemon juice, Parmesan Cheese, salt and pepper. Pulse until combined. Add in the cilantro and taste and adjust the seasonings. Refrigerate until ready to eat.
Serves 6   (Extra Recipe)

Decided for You Cookbook – 365 Dinners

Salad – (Green Salad) = Lettuce Salad

Tear up Iceberg Lettuce and chop up 1 medium onion. Cut off the top and bottom ends of radishes and slice into rounds. Cut the core from the center of a tomato and dice it into cubes or slices for tossing in the salad. Salad dressing of your choice.

Salad – (Green Salad with Bell Peppers and Onion Rings)

Tear up Iceberg Lettuce and slice onion rings. Chop or slice Bell Peppers and add to the Salad. Dressing of your choice.

Salad – (Lettuce and Bean Sprouts Salad)

Clean the above ingredients, slice and combine into a salad. Salad dressing of choice

Salad – (Lettuce, Green Pepper Ring Salad)

Clean the above ingredients, slice and combine into a salad. Salad dressing of choice

Salad – (Lettuce, Mayonnaise and Onion Salad)

Break up your Iceberg Lettuce into a green salad. Toss in chopped red onions. Add enough mayonnaise (usually 2-3 heaping Tbsp). Salt and pepper to taste and stir well to coat the lettuce.

Salad – (Lettuce Salad) = Green Salad

This is a standard Green Salad denoted in the grocery list as Iceberg Lettuce, Radishes, Onions and Tomatoes with your choice of salad dressing.

Salad – (Lettuce Wedges)

Wash the outside of your lettuce and then cut in half, rinse again and drain. When drained, then cut into quarters. Drizzle top with Thousand Island or Salad Dressing of Choice.

Salad – (Lettuce with Carrots, Radishes, Celery Salad)

Clean the above ingredients, slice and combine into a salad. Salad dressing of choice.

Salad – (Lettuce with Cucumber Slices)

HINT: If desired you can **leave green skin on** the cucumbers, but you must cut about a 1/2" piece from the end of the cucumber that had the vine attached. Rotate this piece in a circle against the end of the cucumber where it was removed until extra white froth moisture is observed. This is the bitterness of the skin being removed from the entire cucumber. Throw away cut off end. Rinse cucumber, then slice as directed. Slice in coin shapes, thinly. Salt and let stand for 10 minutes, and then squeeze out excessive liquids. Add half a bottle of tart Italian Dressing and marinate together in the refrigerator until tossed into a lettuce salad.

Salad – (Macaroni Salad)

2-3 cups Salad Macaroni (smaller than elbow)	1/2 cup chopped Tomatoes
1/4 cup chopped Onion	1/2 cup chopped Sweet Pickles
1/4 cup chopped or sliced Olives (optional)	2-3 heaping Tbsp Mayonnaise

Boil the **macaroni** per package directions. Drain in a colander and **run cold water over it, which will prevent sticking together, salt and toss.** Place the macaroni into a large bowl. Add in the Tomatoes, Onion, and Sweet Pickles. Stir in the Mayonnaise. Taste and re-season with salt and pepper. **VARIATION: Stir in 1 to 2 cans drained, canned Tuna and diced hard-boiled sliced eggs. HINT: If you have left over mashed potatoes and want to stretch your ingredients for a Mashed Potato salad you can boil the macaroni and drain. Salt and pepper it and coat with 1 Tbsp Mayonnaise and add to your Potato Salad.**

(SALAD)-267

Salad – (Marinara Macaroni Salad)

2-3 cups Salad Macaroni
1/4 cup chopped Onion
1 (20.5 oz) can or Jar Marinara Sauce

1 can chopped or sliced Black Olives
2-4 heaping Tbsp Mayonnaise

Cook Salad Macaroni per package directions. Drain in a colander, rinse with cold water. Salt and toss with the Mayonnaise. Place the macaroni into a large bowl. Add in the olives, onion and the Marinara Sauce; stir well. Let it sit in the refrigerator for at least two hours or more.

Salad – (Onion, and Olive Salad)

4 Sweet Red Onions
3 Tbsp Wine Vinegar
Pitted Ripe Black Olives

6 Tbsp Olive Oil
2 Diced Anchovy Fillets (Optional)

Slice the onions very thin. Soak them for 30 minutes in salted water with ice cubes. Drain and dry in paper towels.   Toss the onions with the diced anchovies and olives in a large salad bowl, add in the oil and vinegar and marinate in the refrigerator until served. Serves 6.   (Extra Recipe)

Salad – (Onion, Tomato, Cucumber Salad)

Slice the cucumbers, salt and let rest 10 minutes. Squeeze out excessive liquid. Marinate slices of all of the ingredients in a tart Italian Dressing and serve cold.

Salad – (Pasta Primavera Salad)

1 cup Broccoli, Zucchini, Green Peas, sliced Mushrooms, halved Cherry Tomatoes
1 cup small Pasta Shells
2 Tbsp chopped Green Onions
1/3 cup Wine Vinegar
2 Tbsp Lemon Juice
Salt and Pepper to Taste

2 Tbsp Dijon Mustard
2 Tbsp chopped Parsley
1/2 cup Heavy Cream (Whipping)
2 heaping Tablespoons of Mayonnaise

Blanch all the vegetables (drop in hot boiling water for one minute then drain). Refresh in cold water, if desired. Boil the pasta shells until done and drain in a colander. Pour cold water over the shells to prevent them from sticking together. In a large bowl, blend together the mustard, onions, parsley, vinegar, cream, mayonnaise, lemon juice and salt and pepper. Fold in the cooked, drained and salted shells. Fold in the vegetables and let sit in the refrigerator for at least 20 minutes (**Best if made the day before**). If not tart enough, add in a little Tart Italian Dressing. **VARIATION: Add a Pesto Sauce instead of the cream and mayonnaise. OTHER: Can add any of the following to a pasta salad: Different cheese (Feta, Goat, Provolone), Pre-cooked Chicken, Turkey, Ham Smoked Sausages, Tuna, Salmon, Canadian Bacon, Chives, Green Onion, Celery, Jicama, Water Chestnuts, Bottled Salad Dressings, Tahi Peanut Sauce, Hot Sauces and/or Salsa.**

Salad – (Potato Salad)

HINT: If you are cooking Baked Potatoes in a different menu this week, bake extra potatoes to be used in this salad.

4-6 Large Baked Potatoes (or boiled with skins on, can then be peeled or leave skins on) cube, or slightly smash these with a potato masher (see next page)

Decided for You Cookbook – 365 Dinners

(continued Potato Salad)

1/4 cup French Salad Dressing or Mayonnaise
1/3 cup chopped Onions
1 tsp Salt and Pepper to Taste
1/2 cup diced Sweet Pickles
1/4 cup Mayonnaise if French dressing used

1 cup chopped Celery
4 Hard-cooked, sliced Eggs
1 tsp Celery Seed
1/2 cup pitted Black Olives chopped or sliced
3 Tbsp Vinegar

Optional: 6 slices cooked, smoked, crumbled Bacon, 1 cup crumbled Blue or Smoked Cheese **–OR–** Leave out French Dressing and replace with 1 container of Hot Dog Mustard Relish.

Salad – (Potato Salad – Hot German Style)

4-6 Large Baked Potatoes (or boiled with skins on, can then be peeled or leave skins on) cube, or slightly smash these with a potato masher place in a buttered baking dish

1 Tbsp Vegetable Oil
1 cup sliced Onion
4 slices of chopped Bacon
2 Tbsp Margarine or Butter
1 Tbsp Flour
1/4 cup Vinegar

1/4 cup Whole Grain Mustard
1/4 tsp Onion Salt
1/2 tsp Sugar
Salt and Pepper to taste
1/4 tsp Paprika

Place the vegetable oil in a skillet and lightly brown the sliced onion. Add in the bacon and cook until crisp. Be careful to not burn the juices. Add in the margarine and as soon as melted, stir in the flour until dissolved, add in the vinegar, and all other ingredients except the Paprika. If not enough liquid to cover the potatoes, add in a little water. Pour this heated mixture over the potatoes and stir. Sprinkle the top with Paprika. Place in a warm oven 250°F for one hour to meld the flavors together. **HINT: Can be made in advance and just warmed.**

Salad – (Potato Salad – Leftover Mashed)

Save your leftover mashed potatoes and when you have a sufficient amount you can make potato salad. You might have to increase these ingredients depending on how many leftover potatoes you have. **HINT:** If you want to **stretch your ingredients** you can boil 1/2 - 1 cup of macaroni and drain. Salt and pepper it and coat with 1 Tbsp mayonnaise then add to your leftover potatoes.

3 or 4 cups of leftover Potatoes or can be made fresh
3 Tbsp Mustard - Yellow
1 Tbsp Mayonnaise
1/4 cup or less Sweet or Sweet Dill Pickle Juice

2 or 3 eggs hardboiled and chopped
2 to 4 capfuls of Vinegar
1 medium chopped Onion
1/2 cup diced Sweet Pickles or Sweet-Dills

HINT: Cooling the eggs quickly will make them easier to peel and will prevent any darkening around the egg yolks. Pour off the cold water leaving just the eggs and shake and rotate the pan around in a circle, that will crack all of the shells at one time). Stir these eggs together with all other ingredients, taste to be sure it is tart, if not add additional vinegar or mustard. Refrigerate for a couple of hours before serving.

Salad – (Potato Salad – New Red Potatoes with Garlic Italian Dressing)

1-1/2 Pounds Red Boiling Potatoes
1 (16 oz) Bottle of Tart Italian Salad Dressing
1 medium Red Onion, chopped
1 can (15 oz) French Style Green Beans

1 Tbsp Rosemary
1 can (8 oz) Pitted Black Olives Chopped
2 tsp Garlic Powder

Drain the green beans, cut up the onion and place these ingredients into a large bowl and sprinkle with the garlic powder and Rosemary. Add in the bottle of Italian Salad Dressing and let marinate. Wash the outside of he potatoes and place them in a medium saucepan and add enough water to cover by 1 -inch. Bring to a boil over high heat and cook until the potatoes are fork tender, about 15 to 20 minutes. Drain, cool, cut the potatoes.

(continued Potato Salad - New Red Potatoes with Garlic Italian Dressing) into quarters or halves and salt them. Add the potatoes to the marinade and toss to coat the potatoes evenly. Let this salad marinate again for at least two hours, until the potatoes are flavorful. Prior to serving, add in the drained, pitted olives and toss again.   Serves 4 – 6

Salad – (Romaine Lettuce and Cucumbers)
Wash Romaine Lettuce and dry in paper towels. Fix cucumbers same as recipe with Lettuce and Cucumbers. Salad Dressing of your choice.

Salad – (Romaine Lettuce and Garlic Croutons)
Wash the Romaine lettuce, dry in paper towels. Tear lettuce into small pieces. Add in garlic croutons and toss with Salad Dressing of choice. Season with salt and pepper to taste.

Salad – (Romaine Lettuce and Red Onion Ring Salad)
Wash Romaine Lettuce and dry in paper towels. Clean and slice the red onions and toss together with a Salad Dressing of your choice.

Salad – (Romaine Lettuce, Mushroom and Avocado Salad)
Rinse the lettuce and mushrooms and dry. Slice and mix all of the ingredients and use Italian Dressing or your choice. **HINT: <u>If you cut greens or avocados with a metal knife the oxidation from the blade will cause the edges to turn brown, so be sure that you tear them up and cut the avocado with a plastic knife or sprinkle with lemon juice to avoid discoloration.</u>**

Salad – (Romaine Lettuce with Pickled Beets)
Wash Romaine Lettuce and dry in paper towels. Add in one can of Julienne sliced pickled Beets and a Salad Dressing of your choice.

Salad – (Spinach, Mushroom and Onion Ring Salad)

Use **8 cups of torn, fresh spinach** of lettuce or you could even mix spinach into your lettuce for a variation. Spinach needs to be wash with "warm" water to loosen any sand or dirt. Then dry it off with paper toweling, making sure there is no sand left between the leaves. Wash **2 cups sliced mushrooms** and dry off with paper toweling. Slice **1 Red Onion** into rings. Just before serving combine the spinach, onions and mushrooms in a large salad bowl. Warm the Spinach Dressing and spoon over salad and toss**. (see SDR Spinach Salad dressing recipe)**

Salad – (Taco Salad)
See recipe in BF Beef Taco Salad, Menu Week #42

Decided for You Cookbook – 365 Dinners

Salad – (Three Bean Salad)

1 can (15 oz) drained Kidney Beans   1 can (15 oz) drained Garbanzo Beans
1 can (15 oz) drained French Style Green Beans 2 tsps Garlic Powder
1 medium chopped Onion
1 (16 oz) bottle of tart Italian Salad Dressing or use the alternate Make Your Own Bean Salad Dressing
  recipe. Mix together and marinate for at least two hours before serving.

Salad – (Tomato, Cucumber, Onion Salad)

Slice each of the ingredients and marinate in a Tart Italian Salad Dressing for at least one hour before serving.
These can be tossed with shredded Iceberg Lettuce if desired.

Salad – (Tomatoes, Peppers, Onion Salad)

Slice and drain excessive juices of all ingredients. Pour in 1/2 cup Tart Italian Salad Dressing and marinate
for at least one half of an hour.

Salad – (Tomato Wedges)

Wash and remove the stem, core and cut off any blemishes. Cut Tomatoes into quarters and drizzle tops with
Thousand Island Salad Dressing.

Salad – (Waldorf Salad)

2 medium stalks Celery, thinly sliced and cut into small pieces (~1 cup)
4 Apples, 2 red, 2 green; peeled, cored and diced
1/2 cup Golden Raisins   1/2 cup Mayonnaise + 2 Tbsp Sour Cream
1-1/2 Tbsp Lemon Juice   or 2 Tbsp Whipped Cream
1/2 cup chopped Walnuts

**HINT: Before beginning, bring a pot of water to a boil and drop in the celery for 1-2 minutes to blanch
it. This will bring out the sweet flavor and extend the salad's shelf life if you have leftovers. After
slicing the apples, sprinkle the lemon juice over them to prevent them from turning dark.** Mix all other
ingredients except the walnuts and let set in the refrigerator at least two hours. Just before serving add in the
chopped walnuts **(they will become tough if left in the salad too long)**. Top with the Sweet Dressing or
Blue Cheese Dressing, and stir to coat the ingredients.

SWEETER WALDORF - HINT: If you **add** in the following optional items to the PREVIOUS Waldorf
recipe **+ 1 cup whipped cream or sour cream**, this **becomes a great Dessert**.
2 cups miniature Marshmallows (optional)   2 sliced Bananas
3 chopped Oranges (optional)   1 cup seedless Grapes (optional)
1 cup Strawberries, sliced (optional)

**HINT: If you are cutting up marshmallows, rub your scissors with margarine making it easier to cut
these up without sticking to the blades.**

Salad – (Wilted Lettuce Salad)

(Very Old-Fashion Recipe). Break up your lettuce into bite-size pieces and sprinkle on salt and pepper.
Mix in a chopped medium onion (optional). Use the Bacon Salad Dressing. **BE VERY CAREFUL** - When
you put in the vinegar mixture into the hot grease it sizzles and it might splatter on you. Immediately pour
this mixture over your lettuce and toss. **MUST BE SERVED IMMEDIATELY BEFORE THE
WILTING DRIPPINGS TURN COLD AND CONGEALS. YUCK!**   (Extra Recipe)

SALAD DRESSINGS

SDR – (Bacon Salad Dressing – Hot)

4 slices Bacon	1/2 small Onion, chopped
1/4 cup Vinegar	1 Tbsp Sugar
1 tsp Salt	

Fry the bacon until crisp; drain on paper toweling and break into very small pieces. In the bacon drippings (approximately 3-4 Tbsp bacon grease) add in the onion and cook until onion is tender, but not browned. Mix the vinegar, sugar and salt together and pour into the hot grease. **BE VERY CAREFUL** - When you put the vinegar into the hot grease **- it sizzles and might splatter on you**.

SDR – (Bean Salad Dressing)

1 cup Vinegar	1/2 cup Sugar
1/2 cup Vegetable Oil	1 tsp Salt
1/2 tsp Dry Mustard	1/2 tsp Garlic Powder

Combine all ingredients. Good for any kind of beans of choice.

SDR – (Blue Cheese Salad Dressing) – "My Very Best Choice"

1 cup Vegetable Oil	1 Tbsp minced, Onion
1 Large (2 oz) Pkg Roquefort Blue Cheese	3 Tbsp Vinegar
(crumbled)	1 cup Sour Cream
Salt and Pepper to Taste	1 Tsp Sugar

Mix together with a fork the vinegar, salt and pepper, sugar and onion. Add in the vegetable oil and the crumbled Blue Cheese. Blend in the sour cream. If this **too thick**, thin with cold water. Will store in a refrigerator in a sealed container for two weeks.

Blue Cheese Salad Dressing – Alternate

1 Pkg (3 oz) Blue Cheese	2 cups Mayonnaise
2 tsp chopped Chives	1 tsp Pepper
1 tsp Garlic Powder	1/2 tsp Worcestershire Sauce
1 cup Sour Cream	1/2 cup Buttermilk
Lemon juice, if desired.	

Blend all ingredients, mixing the sour cream and buttermilk in last. Chill, if the dressing is too thick, thin with additional buttermilk.

Decided for You Cookbook – 365 Dinners

SDR – (Buttermilk Tangy Salad Dressing)

1 cup Mayonnaise
1/4 cup minced Onion
1/2 tsp Paprika

1/2 cup Buttermilk
2 Tbsp chopped Parsley
1 clove minced Garlic

SDR – (Cole Slaw Salad Dressing)

1/4 cup Evaporated Milk or Heavy Cream
2 capfuls Vinegar

1/2 cup Mayonnaise
1 tsp Sugar

Mix all ingredients and pour over the shredded Cabbage. Let the salad rest in the refrigerator for the flavors to blend together and to soften the slaw.

Cole Slaw Salad Dressing – Alternate

1-1/2 cups Sugar
2 tsp Salt
2 cups Vegetable Oil

3/4 cup Vinegar
1 tsp Dry Mustard
1 tsp Celery Seed

Mix all ingredients and warm the dressing **DO NOT BRING TO A BOIL**. Place the dressing on slaw and let the salad rest in the refrigerator for the flavors to blend together. Be sure to store leftover dressing in the refrigerator.

SDR – (Crab Louie Salad Dressing)

Use Thousand Island Salad Dressing
        –OR-

Crab Louie Salad Dressing - Homemade

Equal Parts of
Mayonnaise, Ketchup & Sweet Pickle Relish
        –OR-

1 Lemon Juiced

Equal Parts of Mayonnaise & Plain Yogurt
Grated Onion
Cayenne Pepper to taste
1 tsp Worcestershire Sauce
1 tsp Horseradish

1/2 pt Chili Sauce (similar to Cocktail Sauce)
Chopped Parsley
1 Lemon Juiced
2 Tbsp chopped Chives

SDR – (Cucumber Salad Dressing)

3/4 cup Vegetable Oil
1 tsp Salt
1 tsp Paprika
1 Tbsp Sugar
1/2 small Onion, chopped
1/3 of a Cucumber, peeled and diced

1/4 cup Vinegar
1 tsp Horseradish
1 tsp Dry Mustard
1 small clove garlic, minced
1/4 of an Avocado diced
Pepper to taste

SDR – (Curry Salad Dressing)

1 cup Mayonnaise
1-1/2 Tbsp Curry Powder
1 tsp Dry Mustard

1 Tbsp Vinegar
4 Tbsp Evaporated Milk
1 tsp Poppy Seeds

Mix together and serve. Refrigerate when not in use.

Curry Salad Dressing – Alternate

1 cup Sour Cream
2 Tbsp Lemon Juice
1 tsp Salt
1 tsp Poppy Seeds

1 cup Mayonnaise
1-1/2 Tbsp Curry Powder
1 tsp Dry Mustard

Stir lightly and refrigerate.

SDR – (French Salad Dressing)

1 tsp Lemon Juice
1/2 cup Vegetable Oil
1 tsp Paprika
1 tsp Garlic, minced
1/2 cup Vinegar

1/3 cup Sugar
1 tsp Salt
1 tsp Onion, minced
1/3 cup Ketchup

Beat together the lemon juice, sugar, oil, salt paprika, onion, garlic and ketchup until thickened. Add in the vinegar and stir well.

SDR – (French Salad Dressing – Tart & Creamy)

1 cup Mayonnaise
1/4 cup minced Onion
1/2 tsp Paprika

1/2 cup Buttermilk
2 Tbsp chopped Parsley
1 clove Garlic, minced

SDR – (Garlic Salad Dressing)

2/3 cup Vegetable Oil
3 cloves, crushed Garlic
1 tsp Salt

1/3 cup Red Wine Vinegar
1 tsp Italian Seasonings
1/4 tsp Pepper

SDR – (Green Goddess Salad Dressing)

1 clove Garlic, minced
1 Tbsp Lemon Juice
1/2 cup Sour Cream
1/3 cup finely chopped Parsley

3 Tbsp finely chopped Green Onions
3 Tbsp Tarragon Wine Vinegar
1 cup Mayonnaise
Salt and Pepper

SDR – (Italian Salad Dressing – Creamy)

3/4 cup Mayonnaise
1 Tbsp Lemon Juice
1 Tbsp Water
1/2 tsp Oregano
1 Garlic clove, minced

1 Tbsp Wine Vinegar
1 Tbsp Corn or Vegetable Oil
1 tsp Worcestershire Sauce
1 tsp Sugar

SDR – (Mayonnaise – Dijon)

1 Large Egg
2 tsp Dijon Mustard
1/2 tsp Salt

1 Tbsp White Wine Vinegar
1 cup Vegetable Oil
1 tsp Pepper

(SALAD)-274

(continued – Dijon Mayonnaise) In a blender or food processor combine the egg, vinegar and mustard on high speed for 30 seconds. With the machine running, add oil through the feed tube and process until it forms a thick mayonnaise. Adjust seasoning to taste. Good with Hamburgers.

SDR – (Mayonnaise – Make Your Own)

1 Egg	1 Tbsp Lemon Juice or Vinegar
1/4 tsp Dry Mustard	1/4 tsp Salt
1/2 cup Olive Oil	1/2 cup Vegetable Oil

HINT: Easier if you have an Electric blender with a removable, capped hole in the top. Mix the oils together. Place in the blender the egg, lemon juice, salt, mustard and 1/4 cup of the oil. Cover and blend for 15 seconds at low speed. Remove the capped hole from the top of your blender (If you do not have one, then remove the cover and place a kitchen towel around the top leaving a hole in the center of the opening to keep the mixture from splashing into your eyes). Turn your blender on high speed and pour in the remaining oil in a steady, quick stream. **Behold you now have Mayonnaise.**

SDR – (Mayonnaise – Green Peppercorn)

1 Egg	1 Tbsp White Wine Vinegar
2 tsp Dijon Mustard	1/2 tsp Salt
1 Tbsp Olive Oil	4 tsp drained, Green Crushed Peppercorns

In a bowl or food processor, combine the egg, White Wine Vinegar, Dijon Mustard, 1/2 tsp salt and beat or process for 30 seconds. Add the oil in slowly through the feed tube of the processor or whip in with a mixer and it will form a thick mayonnaise emulsion, add in crushed peppercorns and mix until blended.

SDR – (Mustard Vinaigrette Salad Dressing)

2 cloves Garlic, minced	1 Shallot or Green Onions minced
1 Tbsp Dijon Mustard or 2 Tbsp Dry Mustard	1/3 cup Red Wine Vinegar
2/3 cup Olive Oil/Vegetable Oil	Salt and Pepper

Whisk together ingredients, taste, and adjust seasonings. Pour dressing over the tossed vegetables and let stand for at least 1 – 4 hours marinating in the refrigerator. Pour over lettuce greens just before serving if not marinating vegetables.

Serves 8

SDR – (Oil and Vinegar Salad Dressing)

1/4 cup Olive Oil	1 Tbsp Wine Vinegar
1/2 tsp Salt	Dash of Pepper
1/2 clove Garlic, finely minced	

Combine the oil, vinegar, salt, pepper and garlic in a jar with a tight lid and shake vigorously. Good served over lettuce of choice and 2 hard-cooked chopped eggs with garlic croutons.　　Serves 6

SDR – (Orange or Cranberry Vinaigrette Salad Dressing)

4 Tbsp Olive Oil
Fresh ground Pepper
1 Tbsp Sugar
4 Tbsp Orange Juice or Cranberry Juice or other choices.   Combine and mix well

1 tsp Salt
1 Tbsp Sesame Oil

SDR – (Parmesan Cheese Salad Dressing)

2/3 cup Mayonnaise
1/4 tsp Worcestershire Sauce
1 tsp White Wine Vinegar

1/3 cup grated Parmesan Cheese
1/3 cup Milk

SDR – (Poppy Seed Salad Dressing for Fruit Salads)

1-1/2 cups Sugar
2 cups Vegetable Oil
2 Tbsp Onion Juice
2 tsp Salt

2 tsp Dry Mustard
2/3 cup Vinegar
2 Tbsp Poppy Seeds

Mix the sugar, mustard, salt and vinegar in an Electric Blender. Add in the onion juice and blend together. Slowly add the oil while the blender is in operation, and blend until thick. Add in the poppy seeds and mix lightly together. Chill

SDR – (Ranch Salad Dressing)

1 clove chopped Garlic
3/4 cup Buttermilk
2 Tbsp Lime Juice
1 Tbsp chopped Chives

3 pinches of Salt
1/2 cup Sour Cream
1 Tbsp chopped Parsley
Salt and Pepper to taste

In the bottom of a small bowl mash together the garlic and the pinches of salt to form a paste. Whisk in the buttermilk, sour cream, lime juice, parsley, chives and season to taste with salt and pepper. Refrigerate if not in use.   Yields 1-1/3 cups

SDR – (Roquefort Dressing) - Excellent Choice

1 cup Sour Cream
1 (2 oz) Wedge of Roquefort Cheese, crumbled
1 tsp Horseradish Sauce

1 cup Mayonnaise
2 tsp Lemon Juice
Dash of Tabasco Sauce

Mix all ingredients leaving the Roquefort Cheese crumbled, not blended.

SDR – (Rum Salad Dressing – Fruit Salads)

1 cup unsweetened Pineapple Juice
2/3 cup Vegetable Oil
1/4 cup Light Rum
1 tsp Ground Ginger

1/3 cup Honey
2/3 cup shredded Coconut
2 Tbsp Lemon Juice

Shake all ingredients in tightly covered container. Store in the refrigerator up to 2 weeks.

Decided for You Cookbook – 365 Dinners

SDR – (Russian Salad Dressing)

1/4 cup Sugar	3 Tbsp Water
1-1/2 tsp Celery Seeds	1/2 tsp Salt
1/2 tsp Paprika	2-1/2 tsp Lemon Juice
1 Tbsp Worcestershire Sauce	1 Tbsp Vinegar
1 cup Vegetable Oil	1/2 cup Ketchup
1/4 cup minced Onion	

Cook the sugar and water till mixture spins a thread (232°F), cool. Add the remaining ingredients
Together, and then blend in the syrup and chill.

SDR – (Russian Salad Dressing – Alternate)

1 cup Mayonnaise	1/4 cup Chili Sauce (bottled)
1 Tbsp Evaporated Milk or Milk	1 tsp Lemon Juice
2 Tbsp chopped Sweet Pickle Relish	

SDR – (Seafood Salad Dressing – Pourable)

1 cup Mayonnaise	1/4 cup Tomato Juice
2 Tbsp Chopped Onion	2 Tbsp chopped Parsley
1 Tbsp Sweet Pickle Relish	

SDR – (Spinach Salad Dressing)

3/4 tsp Salt	1/2 tsp Sugar
1/3 tsp each dry Mustard & Pepper	1 clove Garlic, minced
3 Tbsp Lemon Juice	1/4 cup Wine Vinegar
1 Tbsp Water	1/2 cup Corn Oil
1/2 cup Chopped Green Onions	2 Tbsp Soy Sauce

Mix together thoroughly in a Blender: Salt, sugar, dry mustard, pepper, garlic, lemon juice, wine vinegar,
water, corn oil and onion. Warm the dressing slightly before adding to the salad. See alternate dressing
recipes.   Serves 8

SDR – (Strawberry Salad Dressing – Fruit Salads)

3/4 cup sliced Strawberries	2 Tbsp White Corn Syrup
1/2 cup Mayonnaise	

Smash or blend the strawberries and corn syrup together. Add in the mayonnaise and chill for at least one
hour. **VARIATION**: You can exchange out the fruit for any other i.e., cranberry sauce, blackberries,
blueberries orange juice, or lime juice, etc.

SDR – (Sweet Dressing – for Waldorf or Fruit Salads)

1/2 cup Mayonnaise + 2 Tbsp Whipping Cream	Pepper to Taste
1 tsp finely grated Lemon Rind Zest	2 Tbsp Lemon Juice
1 Tbsp Evaporated Milk or 2 Tbsp Sour Cream	1 Tbsp Sugar

In a small bowl, whisk together the mayonnaise, milk/or sour cream, sugar and lemon zest and season with
pepper. Add the mayonnaise mixture to the salad to coat. Refrigerate if not using immediately.

SDR – (Thousand Island Salad Dressing)

1 cup Mayonnaise
3 Tbsp Ketchup
2 Tbsp chopped Green Bell Pepper
1 tsp Paprika
Celery Salt

4 Tbsp Chili Sauce – bottled
1 tsp Vinegar
1 tsp chopped Red Bell Pepper
1/2 tsp chopped Chives
Onion Seasoning (or chopped Onions)

If you don't want to use fresh Bell Peppers, use Sweet Pickle Relish

SDR – (Tomato Vinaigrette Salad Dressing/Vegetable Marinade)

3 Tbsp Vegetable Oil
1 Tbsp minced Parsley
1/2 tsp Sugar
Pepper to Taste

1-1/2 to 2 Tbsp Vinegar
3/4 tsp Garlic Salt
1/8 tsp Oregano
2 medium sliced, diced, and mashed Tomatoes

Chill at least one hour

SDR – (Vinaigrette Salad Dressing)

1/2 tsp Salt
1/2 tsp Sugar
1/4 cup Vegetable Oil
1 Tbsp Parsley
1 Tbsp chopped Green Bell Pepper

1/8 tsp Pepper
1/2 tsp Paprika
2 Tbsp Vinegar
1 Tbsp minced Onion

Mix together, salt, pepper, sugar, and paprika in small saucepan and heat, **DO NOT ALLOW TO BOIL**. Add in the remaining ingredients, serve over beets or spinach salad. –OR- add in 1/4 cup Sour Cream for a Creamy Vinaigrette.

SDR – (Vinegar and Oil Salad Dressing)

1/4 cup Sugar
2 Tbsp Water
8 tsp Yellow Mustard
3 cups Virgin Olive Oil

1 cup Red Wine Vinegar
2 Tbsp Garlic Powder
1 tsp White Pepper
2 tsp Salt

Place all ingredients except the oil into a blender and blend on high speed until the salt and sugar are dissolved (1 to 1-1/2 minutes). Add in the olive oil and run again on high speed until the oil is mixed (~20 seconds). Store in a Mason jar in frig. If it separates, return it to a blender and run on high speed just until re-combined.

SDR – (Waldorf Salad Dressing)

1/2 cup Mayonnaise + 2 Tbsp Sour Cream or
2 Tbsp Whipped Cream
1-1/2 Tbsp Lemon Juice

Use this, the Sweet Dressing, or a Blue Cheese Salad Dressing Mix.

(SALAD)-278

SAUCES

SAUCE – (Aioli Sauce)
Pronounced "I-oh-lee"
Robust Sauce for Artichokes, Asparagus, Cherry Tomatoes, Bell Peppers, Mushrooms, Cauliflower, Hard-cooked Eggs, Green Beans, or New Potatoes. Codfish, Crab, Shrimp, or Lobster

3 Egg Yolks	1 tsp Salt
6 cloves Garlic, minced	1-1/2 cups Olive Oil
1 Tbsp Lemon Juice	3 Tbsp White Vinegar

Place egg yolks in a bowl. Put salt on a cutting board with the garlic on top. Mince the garlic, incorporating the salt as you chop. Turn your knife blade flat and mash the garlic and salt into a paste. Add this to the egg yolks. Blend in the oil, drop by drop whisking or stirring briskly. When the sauce has thickened a little, increase the speed of dropping the oil to a thin slow stream. When all of it is incorporated, add in the lemon juice and blend well. **OPTIONAL: Two Ingredient Dipping Sauce** – Combine Mayonnaise and chopped Garlic.

SAUCE – (Alfredo Sauce)
White creamy sauce for any Ham, Pasta and/or Vegetables

4 Tbsp Margarine or Butter	2 Tbsp All-Purpose Flour
1 cup grated Romano Cheese	1 Large Egg Yolk, lightly beaten
1 cup Heavy Cream (whipping) or Half and Half Milk	

Melt margarine in a saucepan. Stir in the flour until smooth. Add in the heavy cream and cheese. When the cheese has melted, remove the saucepan from the heat so when you now add in the beaten egg yolk it won't become scrambled eggs. Return the saucepan to low heat and stir until mixture thickens, and coats the back of a spoon. Remove from the heat, and pour over other ingredients (noodles/rice etc) being used.

SAUCE – (Bar-B-Q Sauce)
Serves well with any Pork, Beef or Chicken

1 Tsp Salt	1/8 tsp Pepper
1 Lemon juiced	1/2 cup minced Onions (cooked)
1 tsp Chili Powder	1 tsp Celery Salt
1/4 cup Vinegar	1/3 cup Worcestershire Sauce
1 cup Ketchup	2 cups Hot Water
1/4 cup Brown Sugar	Dash of Tabasco Sauce
1 Tbsp Liquid Smoke	

Mix together and bring ingredients to a boil, cool. Store in a sealed, sterile container in the refrigerator.

SAUCE – (Bar-B-Q Sauce) – Alternate Recipe
Serves well with any Salmon and/or Chicken

1/2 small finely chopped Onion	3 Tbsp Red Wine Vinegar
1 cup Maple Syrup, dark	1 Tbsp Tomato Paste
1 Tbsp Worcestershire Sauce	1 tsp Curry Powder
1/8 tsp Liquid Smoke Flavoring	1 tsp Black Pepper

Cook the onion until tender and then add in the vinegar and reduce by half. Add in the syrup, tomato paste. Worcestershire, smoke flavoring, pepper and simmer until thickened. Brush meats or fish and broil or Bar-B-Q.

SAUCE – (Béchamel Sauce)
Serves Well with any Pasta and Vegetables

1 cup milk + 1/2 cup Whipping Cream*	1 Tbsp Margarine or Butter
2 Tbsp All-Purpose Flour	Pinch Nutmeg
1/2 cup Parmesan Cheese	Salt and Pepper to Taste

Scald the milk in a heavy saucepan over medium heat (bring it to a boil and remove the heat). Melt the butter in a separate saucepan over low heat. When it's bubbling, add the flour and whisk until it forms a paste, about 3 to 4 minutes. Whisking constantly, add the hot milk in a steady stream. Bring the milk to a gentle simmer and continue to whisk until the sauce thickens, about 10 minutes. Whisk in the nutmeg and the cheese, and serve at once. *Undiluted Evaporated Milk can be exchanged.

SAUCE – (Béarnaise Cream)
Serves well with Fish or Beef

2 Tbsp minced Onion or Shallots	3 Tbsp Vinegar
1 tsp Dried Tarragon	1/2 Pound (2 sticks) Margarine or Butter
1/4 Pound sliced Mushrooms	1 cup Whipping Cream
3 egg yolks, slightly beaten in a cup	Salt and Pepper to taste

In a small saucepan combine the onions, vinegar, and tarragon. Boil over medium heat until the liquid has evaporated. Add in the margarine and mushrooms, cook until the mushrooms are browned. Add in the cream, and bring to a boil. Stir some of this hot mixture into the egg yolks, (this will avoid them becoming cooked scrambled eggs). Return this diluted egg mixture to the sauce. Cook on simmer, stirring until slightly thickened. Serve in a heated gravy boat over meat or fish.

SAUCE – (Bordelaise Sauce)
Serves well over any Meat

1-1/2 cups Beef Stock or 1-1/2 cups canned Beef Gravy

2 Tbsp Margarine or Butter	2 Tbsp finely minced Onion or Shallots
3/4 cup Dry Red Wine	Salt and Pepper to Taste

Melt the margarine in a saucepan and cook the onions/shallots until they are transparent. Add in the wine and simmer until reduced to one-half original quantity. Add in the broth/gravy and heat thoroughly. Season with salt and pepper. **<u>SERVES WELL OVER ANY MEAT</u>** Yields 2 cups

Decided for You Cookbook – 365 Dinners

SAUCE – (Cheese Sauce)
Serves Well over any Pasta, and Vegetables

4 Tbsp melted Margarine   4 Tbsp Flour
1 cup grated (medium or sharp) Cheddar Cheese   1/2 tsp Salt
1/2 cup Chicken Broth or 1 tsp Chicken Bouillon   Dash of Cayenne Pepper
1 cup Evaporated Milk or Half-and-Half Milk

In a saucepan melt margarine, salt, stir in flour until blended, add chicken broth (if using a bouillon cube, dilute with 1/2 cup water or milk); when it comes to a rolling boil and looks blended, add in 1/2 of the grated cheddar cheese stir until melted. Pour mixture over desired food. Can be topped with Breadcrumbs that have been mixed into an additional 2 Tbsp of melted margarine.   4-6 Servings

VARIATION: Richer Sauce add 1-1/2 cups Sour Cream. **Jalapeno**: add 2 chopped peppers, 1 small can green chiles finely chopped.

HINT: To melt cheese easily, cut into small pies or shred before cooking. It will melt and blend together much quicker. NOTE: One half pound of Cheese makes two cups when shredded.

SAUCE – (Chicken Cheese Sauce)
4 Tbsp melted Margarine   4 Tbsp Flour
1/2 tsp Salt   1 cup Half & Half Milk
1 can Chicken Broth
1 cup grated (medium or sharp) Cheddar Cheese (Save a little for topping of casserole)

Create the cheese sauce with above ingredients in a saucepan. Melt margarine, stir in flour until blended, add the chicken broth and salt; when warmed, add in grated cheddar cheese stir until melted. Sprinkle any left over grated cheese on top of a casserole and then pour this white cheese sauce on top of what you are cooking.

SAUCE – (Chicken Dipping Sauce)
1/2 cup Mayonnaise   1/4 cup Sour Cream
2 Tbsp Creole Mustard   2 tsp Cayenne Pepper
2 dashes of Tabasco Sauce   Chopped Green Onions

Mix together and store extra in refrigerator in a sealed container for up to one week. Serves 4-6

SAUCE – (Chicken Supreme Sauce)
1 Tbsp Margarine or Butter   1/2 cup Heavy Whipping Cream (or
1 cup Chicken Broth
2 Tbsp Flour   Evaporated Milk)

In a small saucepan, melt the butter and stir in the flour. Cook, stirring constantly with a whisk for one minute. Add in the chicken broth gradually and cook for 10-15 minutes on low heat. Add in the cream and whisk smoothly (or can be strained through cheesecloth).

Serves 4-6

SAUCE – (Chicken Sweet Sauce)

1 can (14.5 oz) sliced Pineapple
2 Tbsp Cornstarch
1 Tbsp Soy Sauce
1 Chicken Bouillon cube or 1 tsp granulated
1/2 tsp Ginger or minced fresh Ginger

1 cup Sugar or Honey
Milk for Dipping
2 Large Bell Peppers, diced
3/4 cup Cider Vinegar

Drain the pineapple, reserving the juice inside a 2-cup measuring cup. Add enough water to make 1-1/4 cups of liquid. In a medium saucepan combine the sugar, cornstarch, juice, vinegar, soy sauce, ginger and bouillon. Bring this mixture to a boil for two minutes. Dip the chicken into milk and then coat with Shake and Bake Coating. Place the chicken in a greased casserole dish and pour the sauce over the top and bake at 350°F for 30 minutes. Place the pineapple slices and the sliced bell peppers on top. Cook another 30 minutes or until the peppers and chicken are fork tender. Serve with steamed Rice.

SAUCE – (Clam Sauce)
See SAUCE – White Clam Sauce

SAUCE – (Cranberry Sauce)

1 Quart Cranberries
2 cups Sugar

2 cups Water

Pick over berries, wash, drain and put these through a coarse grinder or pulse in a food processor. Add in the water, and cook to boiling for 10 minutes. Add in the sugar, stir well and let the mixture return to a boil for another 5 minutes. Pour into molds of choice.

SAUCE – (Creamy Cheese Sauce)
Serves well on Cauliflower, Broccoli or other vegetables

3 (8 oz ea) Cream Cheese
1-1/2 tsp Salt
1/2 tsp Garlic Salt

3 cups Milk
1 cup Parmesan Cheese, grated or Cheddar
Paprika

Blend the cream cheese and milk in a blender; add in the salt and 1/2 cup Parmesan or Cheddar Cheese. Cook this in a double boiler until thick, about 20 minutes, stirring occasionally. Pour the sauce over the meat. Sprinkle on another 1/2 cup Parmesan Cheese, sprinkle on the Paprika. Bake as per meat recipe for an additional 10 minutes, or until thoroughly warmed.

SAUCE – (Demi-Glace) – Heavy Beef Stock

In a saucepan over medium high heat, reduce 1 cup Port Wine to 1 Tbsp liquid. Add in 1 Tbsp of the following reduced Veal Stock: (Combine veal bones, 1 large onion, quartered, 3 small carrots, quartered, 2 celery, 1/2 tsp Thyme, 2 Bay Leaves, 1 Tbsp Salt 1/2 cup Flour, 2 quarts Water, 1-1/4 cup Tomato Paste, Optional 1 bottle dry White Wine, slow boil and reduce by two-thirds. Season with salt and pepper and strain.)

SAUCE – (Dipping Sauce for Beef)

3 Tbsp Margarine or Butter   3 Tbsp All-Purpose Flour
3 cups Milk   1-1/2 cups crumbled Blue Cheese
Dash of Cayenne Pepper   Salt to taste

Heat the margarine in a medium saucepan over medium heat until melted. Whisk in the flour and cook for 2-3 minutes. Whisk in the milk and cook until the sauce has thickened. Stir in the blue cheese and cook until the cheese has melted.   Season with cayenne pepper and salt.   Whisk again till smooth and pour into individual ramekins and serve along with beef juices (Au Jus)

SAUCE – (Enchilada Sauce)

3 cans (8 oz ea) Tomato Sauce   1 cup Water
2 to 3 tsp Chili Powder   1/2 tsp Oregano
1/4 tsp Cumin   1 clove Garlic, finely chopped

Blend together in a medium saucepan and cook for about 5 minutes

SAUCE – (Ham Sweet and Hot Sauce)
Serves well over any Ham Products

1 (20 oz) can Crushed Pineapple   1 (10 oz) jar Apricot All Fruit Preserves
2 Tbsp Chinese Mustard   1/2 cup Horseradish
1 Tsp Black Pepper   1 Tbsp Brown Sugar

Combine all ingredients and warm, serve separately with ham and hot biscuits.

Serves 6-8

SAUCE – (Hollandaise Sauce)
Serves well with all Meats, Asparagus and Fish Products

1 Pound Margarine or Butter   4 Egg Yolks
3 Tbsp Boiling Water   2 Tbsp fresh Lemon Juice
1/4 tsp White Pepper

Melt margarine/butter in the top of a double boiler over boiling water. Skim off the clarified fats from the top of the butter clarification process. In a blender place the egg yolks, cover and run on low for about 1 minute. Continuing on low speed, slowly add in the boiling water, melted margarine/ butter, lemon juice and pepper. Turn the blender up to high and blend just until mixed. Serve immediately, pouring sauce over selections. **VARIATION:** Add 3 Tbsp hot dry mustard for **Hot Mustard Sauce -OR-** Add 1/2 cup Heavy Whipping Cream which has been whipped and stirred into the sauce for **Mousseline Sauce**.   **HINT: If your sauce curdles, add a small piece of ice and beat vigorously to smooth out the sauce.**

SAUCE – (Horseradish Cream Sauce)
Serves well with all Steaks

3/4 cup Heavy Cream (whipping)   4 Tbsp prepared Horseradish
1 cup Mayonnaise   Salt to Taste
2 Tbsp Vinegar

Beat the cream until stiff. Gently stir into mayonnaise, the horseradish, vinegar and the salt. Refrigerate until used. If you desire a lighter sauce don't include the mayonnaise. Yield ~3 cups

SAUCE – (Ketchup)

1 cup chopped Onions   1/2 cup chopped Red Bell Peppers   1-1/2 tsp Celery Seed
1 tsp Mustard Seed   1 tsp Whole Allspice   1 stick Cinnamon
1 cup Sugar   1 Tbsp Salt   1-1/2 cups Vinegar
1 Tbsp Paprika   Pint Jars
4 Quarts peeled, cored, chopped Tomatoes (~24)

Cook the tomatoes, onions, and peppers until soft. Press the mixture through a fine sieve or a food mill. Bring this mixture to a boil and reduce in volume by half and thickened (~1 hour). Tie the spices in a cheesecloth bag or inside a metal tea ball. Continue to cook the mixture and spices together slowly (low bubble) for another 25 minutes. Stir frequently. Add in the vinegar & paprika. Discard the spice ball and pour ketchup into clean, hot jars, leaving 1/4" head space. Seal and process in a hot water bath canner for another 10 minutes. Remove from bath and cool jars which yields 3 pints.

SAUCE – (Lasagna Sauce)
Serves well with any Pasta

3 Tbsp Vegetable Oil   1 – 2 Pounds Ground Beef
1/3 cup chopped Onion   1/2 cup chopped Celery or Celery Salt (Optional)
1 clove Garlic, minced   1 (14.5 oz) large can Tomatoes, chopped
1 (8 oz) can Tomato Paste or Puree   1 (8 oz) can cold Water
1-1/2 tsp Basil or Italian Seasoning   1 tsp Oregano Salt
1/2 cup grated Parmesan Cheese   1 tsp Parsley

Heat the oil in a skillet and brown the onions until clear and tender. Add in the garlic and brown for 1 – 2 minutes. Add in the ground beef and stir to be sure it's cooked thoroughly. Add all of the other ingredients except the cheese. Cover and simmer for about 1 hour. Turn off and add in the cheese. Layer in between your Lasagna noodles and top with additional cheese if desired. Makes 1 Quart of Sauce

SAUCE – (Lemon Sauce – Fish)
Serves well with any Seafood

1 tsp granulated Chicken Bouillon
1 cup Water
2 Tbsp Flour
1 cup Heavy Whipping Cream
1/2 tsp Tabasco Sauce

2 Tbsp Margarine or Butter
1/2 tsp Salt and 1/4 tsp Pepper
3 Egg Yolks
1 Tbsp Lemon Juice

Mix bouillon and water together. Blend the cream and the egg yolks together. In a skillet melt the margarine over low heat, stir in the flour until dissolved, stir in the bouillon mix and stir until the sauce begins to simmer and thickens. Stir in the salt and pepper. Lower the heat. Remove a little of the hot, cooking sauce and stir into egg yolks and cream (if you add eggs directly to the hot, cooking sauce they will scramble, don't want that to happen).   Gradually return the mixed sauce, eggs, and cream to the main sauce, whisking constantly.   Stir in the Lemon Juice and the Tabasco Sauce. Turn off the heat but let the sauce simmer in its own heat until thickened (do not boil), but stir constantly.   Yields ~2-1/2 cups. Good with broiled poached or baked fish of any kind.

SAUCE – (Meat Sauce)
Serves well with any Potato or Pasta recipes

1/2 cup grated Parmesan Cheese, Swiss or
    Monterey Jack
1 Large Minced Onion
1 can Tomatoes
Bay Leaf, Parsley, Basil
1 tsp Sugar + 1/2 tsp Cumin

1/2 pound Beef Stew Meat (chunks) or
    1 pound cooked Ground Hamburger
1-2 cloves minced garlic
1 (8 oz) can Tomato Sauce
Salt and Pepper to taste
3-4 Tbsp Vegetable Oil

Sauté the meat in hot oil till brown, add in the onions, and cook till clear and tender, add in the garlic along with the rest of the ingredients. When it comes to a boil, lower the heat, cover and simmer for 30-45 minutes. This is also good cooked in a crock pot all day on low. Serve over the top of ingredients being served and top with the grated Parmesan Cheese. (**Other toppings can be**: Ribbons of cooked Prosciutto w/Parmesan Cheese, Cook shallots, onions, mushrooms in 2 Tbsp Margarine and 2 Tbsp of Marsala and 2 Tbsp Madeira Wine, or with a Morney and Gruyere Swiss Cheese Sauce. **–OR-** any white or creamy cheese sauce desired).

SAUCE – (Mushroom – Creamy Sauce)
Serves well with any Beef, Chicken or Pork

1 cup sliced Mushrooms – fresh or canned
3 Tbsp Margarine or Butter
1-1/2 cups Milk or 3/4 cup Evaporated Milk –
    Dilute the evaporated milk with 3/4 cup Water

2 Tbsp Vegetable Oil
1 Chicken Bouillon Cube
Dash of Pepper and Nutmeg, 1/4 tsp Salt
1 tsp Lemon Juice

Sauté mushrooms in the vegetable oil until tender, about 10 minutes. Blend in the flour and gradually stir in the milk avoiding lumps. Add in bouillon cube and cook over simmer; stirring constantly until the sauce thickens and the bouillon cube has been dissolved. Stir in the lemon juice and seasonings. Makes about 2 cups.

SAUCE – (Mustard – Creole)

1-1/2 tsp Yellow Prepared Mustard	1 tsp Flour	1 tsp Dry Mustard
1 tsp grated Horseradish	1 tsp Pepper	1/2 tsp Sugar
1 dash Celery Salt	1 dash Salt	1/3 cup Boiling Water

Blend all ingredients in a sauce pan then stir in the water. Cook while stirring until smooth and thick.

SAUCE – (Mustard Sauce - Hot)

Serves well with Ham

1/2 cup Dry Mustard or Chinese Mustard	1/2 cup Vinegar
1/2 cup Sugar	1 Egg Yolk slightly beaten
1 tsp Sesame Oil	1 Tbsp Honey
1 Tbsp Ginger	1/4 cup Peanut Oil

Combine the dry mustard and vinegar in a very small saucepan, cook together and allow to stand overnight in the refrigerator. Next day combine the rest of the ingredients with this. Simmer over medium heat until slightly thickened; stirring constantly. Makes 1 cup **HINT: (Mousseline Sauce or Other Mustard Sauce see Hollandaise Sauce Variation)**

SAUCE – (Oriental Sauce)

Serve with Chicken or Pork

3/4 cup Soy Sauce
3 oz Honey
3/4 tsp Ground Ginger
1/8 tsp Garlic Powder

Combine all ingredients and mix well. (Yield: 1 cup)

SAUCE – (Peanut Saté)

Serves well with any Chicken, Beef or Asian Meats

Combine chunky peanut butter and honey-mustard – **OR-**

SAUCE – (Peanut Sauce)

1 cup smooth Peanut Butter	1/3 cup Soy Sauce
2 tsp Red Chili Paste (such as Sambal)	2 Tbsp dark Brown Sugar
2 Limes juiced	1/2 cup hot Water
1/4 cup chopped Peanuts for Garnish	

Blend together the peanut butter, soy sauce, red chili paste, brown sugar, and lime juice. If needed, the sauce can be thinned with hot water. Serve in a small, serving bowl on each plate, and garnish with the chopped peanuts. (Yields 3 cups)   Serves 4-6

SAUCE – (Persian Yogurt and Cucumber)
Serves well with Pocket/Pita Bread (Falafel) ingredients and all Lamb or Beef

1 Pound Yogurt	2 Large Cucumbers, grated
2-3 tsp Dried Mint	2 oz chopped Walnuts
Salt & Pepper to taste	Dash of garlic powder or 1 minced clove

Mix all ingredients, refrigerate for at least 1 hour before serving.   Serve 8

SAUCE – (Pesto Sauce)
Serves great with a Pasta, for Meats or any Seafood

6 cloves Garlic, crushed	Salt and Pepper to taste
1 Tbsp Lemon Juice	1-1/2 cups Parmesan/Romano Cheese
1/2 cup melted Butter or Margarine	1/2 cup Olive Oil
1 cup chopped Parsley (Optional)	1/4 cup Pine Nuts chopped finely) - Optional
2 cups coarsely chopped packed Basil Leaves	

In a food processor, blend with an on/off pulse the garlic, basil, salt, pepper, pine nuts, lemon juice and cheese into a coarse puree. Gradually blend in the olive oil till smooth. Adjust seasonings to taste. Store in sealed Glass container in refrigerator up to a week or freeze in small portions (surface will darken when exposed to air, so stir the pesto before serving) Yields 1-1/2 cups. Can add 1/4 cup of the sauce over freshly cooked pasta; mix well.

SAUCE – (Pizza Sauce)
Serves well with any Pasta or Pizza

1 can (6 oz) Tomato Sauce or 1 (16 oz) can chopped Tomatoes	1 clove Garlic, peeled and minced
1 chopped Onion	1 tsp Oregano
3 to 4 Basil Leaves	Pinch ofSalt and Pepper
Optional: Parmesan, Mozzarella Cheese	3 Tbsp Olive Oil for Sauté

In a 2-Quart saucepot, add in the olive oil over a medium high flame brown your onion and garlic, add in the tomatoes, oregano, basil, salt and pepper and bring to a bubbling. Reduce the heat and simmer for 15 – 30 minutes, stirring often until thick. Spoon or ladle the sauce on to the top of your crust and spread out evenly, leaving a 1/2-inch border along the edges of the dough. (Extra sauce can be kept in the refrigerator in an airtight container up to one week).

SAUCE – (Pork Chop Charcutiere)
Serves well on Pork and Ham Products

1 tsp Butter/Margarine	1 tsp finely chopped shallot or Onion
1 Tbsp White Wine	1 Tbsp Wine Vinegar
1 cup Veal Sauce	Salt and Pepper to taste
1/2 tsp chopped Parsley	2 Tbsps finely chopped Dill Pickles

Melt the butter and cook the shallot/onion for a few minutes, stirring occasionally. Add in the wine and vinegar and simmer until the liquid is reduced to half its original quantity. Add in the Veal Sauce and boil for 1 minute. Salt and pepper to taste and add in the parsley and pickles.   (Yield: 1 cup)

SAUCE – (Prawns Dipping Sauce)

Mix ingredients together

1/2 cup Consume
2 Tsp Sugar

1/4 cup Soy Sauce
Dash of Monosodium Glutamate

-OR- commercial prepared bottled Chili Sauce, or Cocktail Sauce **- OR-** Mix 1 cup Ketchup, 1/4 cup Lemon Juice, dash of Tabasco together.

SAUCE – (Salsa) - Red or Green

Great with Omelets, Burritos, Enchiladas, Beef, Pork or Chicken
Store Bought Item – **OR- MAKE YOUR OWN**

2 fresh Jalapeno Chiles
2 Garlic Cloves
3 Tbsp chopped fresh Cilantro Leaves
1/3 to 1/2 cup Water
1/2 Pound fresh Tomatillos, husks discarded and rinsed

1/2 Pound Plum Tomatoes
1 (1") wedge of a large white Onion
2 tsp Salt

In a heavy cast-iron skillet over moderate heat, roast the tomatoes, tomatillos, Jalapenos, and onion, by turning these over and over with tongs until all sides have been charred (approximately 10-15 minutes. Core the roasted tomatoes, discarding the stems from the Jalapenos. **For Red Salsa**, coarsely puree the tomatoes, 1 Jalapeno, and half of the onion, 1 garlic clove, and 1 tsp of salt in a blender or food processor, then transfer to a bowl. **For the Green Salsa:** Coarsely puree the tomatillos, remaining Jalapeno, half the Onion, remaining garlic clove, remaining tsp of salt, Cilantro, and 1/4 cup of the water (add more if needed for desired consistency, then transfer to a bowl).   Serves 4

SAUCE – (Spaghetti Sauce with Ground Beef)

Serves well with any Noodles

3 Tbsp Vegetable Oil
1/3 cup chopped Onion
1 clove Garlic, minced
1 (8 oz) can Tomato Paste or Puree
1-1/2 tsp Basil
1 tsp Parsley
1/2 cup grated Parmesan Cheese

1 – 2 Pounds Ground Beef
1/2 cup chopped Celery or Celery Salt (Optional)
1 (14.5 oz) large can Tomatoes, chopped
1 (8 oz) can cold Water
1 tsp Oregano (or use Italian Seasoning for Basil
        and Oregano)

Heat the oil in a skillet and brown the onions until clear and tender. Add in the garlic and brown for 1 – 2 minutes. Add in the ground beef and stir to be sure it's cooked thoroughly. Add all of the other ingredients except the cheese. Cover and simmer for 30-45 minutes. Turn off and add in the cheese. Pour over your cooked spaghetti and top with additional cheese if desired. Makes 1 Quart of Sauce.

SAUCE – (Spanish Sauce for Omelets)

2 Tbsp Margarine/Butter
1 chopped Onion
6 Olives, chopped
1/4 tsp Salt and Pepper

1-1/2 cups Tomatoes
1 can sliced Mushrooms
1/2 Green Bell Pepper
1/4 tsp Red Pepper Flakes

Heat the margarine/butter, add in the onion, green pepper, tomatoes, seasoning, olives and mushrooms. Cook until the moisture has nearly evaporated. Before folding the omelet, place a spoonful of sauce in the center. Fold and pour rest of the sauce over and around the omelet.

Decided for You Cookbook – 365 Dinners

SAUCE – (Stir Fry Thickening Sauce)

1/4 cup Water
1 tsp Cornstarch

3 Tbsp Soy Sauce
1/2 tsp Ginger

Mix together well and add to vegetables or meats and cook till thickened.

SAUCE – (Sweet and Sour Pork Sauce)
Serves well with Asian foods, Beef, Chicken and Pork products

1 cup (combine pineapple juice + water)
Dash of Tabasco Sauce (Optional)
2 Tbsp Cornstarch
2 Tbsp Ketchup
1/2 cup chunks of Pineapple

1/3 cup Dark Brown Sugar or can be
  (1/2 cup Sugar (1/4 Gran. and 1/4 Brown)
1/4 cup Tbsp Cider Vinegar
3 Tbsp Soy Sauce

In a saucepan combine the sauce and cook to boiling, stirring constantly until slightly thickened, add the pineapple chunks to the sauce and stir well.

SAUCE – (Taco Sauce)
Serves with Tacos and Burritos

3 cans (8 oz ea) Tomato Sauce
2-3 tsp Chili Powder
1/4 tsp Garlic Powder
1/4 cup grated Cheddar Cheese

1 cup Water
1/2 tsp Oregano
1/4 tsp Paprika

If hot is desired, add in 3/4 tsp Hot Pepper Sauce.

SAUCE – (Tahini Sauce)
Serves great with Falafel, Pita Breads

1/3 cup Tahini Paste (sesame seed paste)
Pinch of Paprika
1 to 2 Tbsp Lemon Juice
1/2 tsp Salt

1/2 cup Plain Yogurt or Sour Cream or just
  water (or more as needed)
1-1/2 tsp minced Garlic
Pinch of Cayenne Pepper

Combine in a blender all ingredients into a creamy sauce. **Great as a dip or sauce for Pita Bread sandwiches**. Yields 1/2 cup.

SAUCE – (Tartar Sauce)
Serves well with any Seafood

1 cup Mayonnaise
1 Tbsp chopped Sour or Sweet Dill Pickle
1 Tbsp chopped Parsley

1 Tbsp Capers, chopped
1 Tbsp finely chopped Onion or Chives
1 tsp chopped Tarragon

-OR-
Add mix Mayonnaise and Sandwich Spread together.

SAUCE – (Teriyaki Sauce)
Serves well with any Beef, Chicken, Pork or Seafood product

1/2 cup Ketchup
1/4 cup Soy Sauce
1 tsp Salt
1 clove Garlic, crushed

1/4 cup Dry Wine or Water
2 Tbsp Sugar
1/2 tsp Ground Ginger

SAUCE – (Tomato Sauce)
Serves well with any sauces for Pasta, Pizza, Soups, Stews and some Vegetables

2 Tbsp Margarine or Butter
1 Tbsp chopped fine Carrot
Chopped Parsley
1/2 tsp Salt & Pepper
1/4 tsp Celery Salt

1 Tbsp Flour
1/2 can (14.5 oz) Tomatoes
2 cloves chopped Garlic
1/4 tsp Onion Seasoning
1/4 tsp Ground Chili Powder

Heat the margarine in a saucepan and add in the onion seasoning, chopped carrot and brown slightly. Add in the flour, stir until smooth. Add all other ingredients and bring to a rolling boil. Lower the heat and cook slowly for 30 minutes, stirring occasionally, and strain ingredients when cooking is completed if desired. Store in a clean jar in the refrigerator.

SAUCE – (Tomato Sauce - Quick)
Empty one 10 oz can Condensed Tomato Soup into a saucepan and stir in 3 Tbsp Water. Heat to the boiling point slowly stirring. Add in 3 Tbsp margarine or butter. Yields 3/4 cup

SAUCE – (Tortellini or Ravioli Cream Sauce)
1 jar Roasted Garlic Parmesan Cheese Sauce stirred over Tortellini **–OR -**
1 can (10-3/4 oz) Condensed Cream of Mushroom Soup
1 tsp Olive or Vegetable Oil
1/2 cup chopped Bell Pepper
1/2 cup Half and Half Milk
1/4 cup sliced Green Onion - garnish
2/3 cups of shredded Parmesan Cheese or crumbled Feta Cheese

2 cloves minced Garlic
1/4 cup chopped Onion
1/4 tsp dried Tarragon crushed
Optional: 1/2 cup white Wine

In a 2-Quart microwave-safe casserole, combine the oil, garlic, bell pepper and the onion. Cover and cook on High for 2 minutes or until the vegetables are tender. Stir in the soup until smooth. Add in the Half-and-Half Milk, wine (add equal amount of liquid if not using the wine) and Tarragon. Cover and cook 5 minutes or until hot and bubbling, stirring once during the cooking and let it stand, covered for 5 minutes. Toss this sauce with the Hot Tortellini/Ravioli's. Sprinkle with the cheese and green onions. **–OR-**

MAKE YOUR OWN ROASTED GARLIC SEASONING:
Place two heads of cleaned garlic cloves in aluminum foil along with 1-2 Tablespoon of Virgin Olive Oil. Each head of garlic will yield about 1-1/2 Tablespoons and 2 heads about 3 Tablespoons of garlic butter. Fold the aluminum foil into an envelope so it will not leak and place on a small flat pan into a 325°F oven and bake for approximately 1 hour, or until the garlic is very soft and golden brown. Remove from the oven and let sit until cool enough to handle. Open the package and place it on a saucer or shallow dish and add in 1 heaping Tablespoon of Margarine/Butter and then smash the cooked garlic with the flat edge of a rubber spatula until it blends into the butter and olive oil. Add these ingredients to a cooked White Sauce with Parmesan. **HINT: <u>You can cook several heads of garlic and store in an airtight container in the refrigerator until you need them</u>.**

Decided for You Cookbook – 365 Dinners

SAUCE – (White Clam Sauce)
Great with Noodles or Pastas

1/2 cup Margarine or Butter
1 (10-1/2 oz) can minced Clams with its liquid
1/2 cup chopped Parsley
2 cloves minced Garlic
2/3 cup Whipping Cream or Evaporated Milk

1/2 cup chopped Onions
1 tsp Salt and Pepper to taste
2 heaping Tbsp All-Purpose Flour
1/2 cup grated Parmesan Cheese* -OR- Myzithra
   Greek Goat Cheese

Melt the margarine in a large skillet and cook the onions till they are clear and tender, add in the parsley, and the garlic. Sauté these until the garlic is lightly browned. Add in the clams and liquid, stir and warm thoroughly for one minute. Stir in the flour until smooth and add in the whipping cream. Bring clam sauce to a rolling boil. Cook till thickened. Mix in the Parmesan or Myzithra Cheese. Salt and pepper to taste.

SAUCE – (White Sauces - Standard)
Serves well with any Pasta, Vegetables or Meats

THIN: 1 Tbsp Margarine or Butter, 1 Tbsp Flour, 1 cup Milk or 1/2 cup Evaporated Milk plus 1/2 cup Water, 1/2 tsp salt and dash of Pepper.

MEDIUM: 2 Tbsp Margarine or Butter, 2 Tbsp Flour, 1 cup Milk or 1/2 cup Evaporated Milk plus 1/2 cup Water, 1/2 tsp Salt and dash of Pepper.

THICK: 3 Tbsp Margarine or Butter, 3 Tbsp Flour, 1 cup Milk or 1/2 cup Evaporated Milk plus 1/2 cup Water, 1/2 tsp Salt, dash of Pepper.

COOKING: Melt the butter or margarine in a saucepan and add in the flour and stir until all the lumps are blended. Add in the milk. **Stir constantly** until the sauce has thickened. Salt and Pepper to taste. Serve immediately. Yields: 1 cup

VARIATIONS: For **richer flavor**, you can use chicken or beef stock or 1 chicken or beef bouillon dissolved in 1/2 cup boiling water for part of the liquid measurement. For a **Cheese Sauce** add in 3/4 cup shredded or finely cut American, Cheddar, Parmesan Cheese while stirring to melt and thicken your sauce.

SAUCE – (Won Ton Dipping Sauce)

Serves well with any fried Asian Side Dishes and Stir Fry Vegetables

Use one 12 oz Bottle of Chili Sauce or Cocktail Sauce with 1/4 to 1/2 tsp Cayenne Pepper added.
– OR -
MAKE YOUR OWN SAUCE
(Ingredients not on grocery list)

2 (8 oz ea) cans of Tomato Sauce	2/3 cup Brown Sugar
1 tsp Celery Salt or Fresh minced Celery	1/4 cup White Vinegar
1 tsp Soy Sauce	1/4 to 1/2 tsp Cayenne Pepper (your choice)

Warm these ingredients together and use as dipping sauce with fried Won Tons
-OR – Serve with a Hot Mustard Sauce **-OR** –1/2 cup Soy Sauce, 3 Tbsp Rice Wine Vinegar, 2 Tbsp Water

SAUCES – MICROWAVE INFORMATION:

Gravies and sauces thickened with flour or cornstarch (1 cup) – 4 to 5 minutes
Melted butter sauces, clarified butter 1/2 cup = 1/2 to 1 minute
Thin Juice (Au Jus, Clam etc) 1 cup – 2 to 3 minutes
Spaghetti, Bar-B-Q, Sweet N Sour (2 cups) – 5 to 7 minutes

MORE SPECIAL NOTE AREA:

SOUPS

SOUP – (Chicken Noodle)

1 Large Can (14.5 oz) Chicken Broth or use pre-frozen juices
1 Pkg Chicken Thighs or Leftover Chicken parts
1 cup sliced Mushrooms (Optional)

1/2 cup chopped Onion   1 stalk Celery cut into small pieces
1 Tbsp Lemon Juice   8 oz Pkg of thinly cut Egg Noodles
2 Carrots, peeled and sliced on a grater or with a potato peeler into small thin slices

Combine the chicken, carrots, onions, celery, lemon juice, chicken broth, and enough water to cover two inches above the chicken and bring to a boil. Reduce the heat and cover partially and simmer about 20 minutes until the chicken is cooked thoroughly. Remove the chicken and cool to touch. Add to the soup the mushrooms and the noodles, cooking the noodles per package directions. Strip the meat from the cooled chicken and chop into small bite-size pieces and return the meat to the soup. Season the soup to taste with salt and pepper.   (Extra Recipe)

Chicken Stock – Homemade Broth/Bouillon

Boil Chicken parts in a large stew pot in salted water two inches about meat, remove – cool and remove meat and bones. Reserve the juice for future use – Freeze in ice cube trays. Or, pour into double plastic bags, squeeze out excessive air and place flat on a cooking sheet and freeze beings they are now flat it will make it easier to store.

SOUP – (Chicken Potsticker Soup)

12 cups Chicken Broth   2 cups Water
1/4 cup Cornstarch   25 - 40 Chicken Potstickers (frozen)*
2 Tbsp minced Ginger   1/4 tsp White Pepper
1 tsp Garlic Powder   1 bunch sliced Green Onions
Salt to taste   2 Tbsp Tomato Paste
2 Tbsp Hot Pepper Sauce or Pepper Flakes
8 cups frozen mixed Vegetables (Chinese preferred with Snow Peas and Carrots)

In a large pot combine the broth and water, ginger, pepper, garlic powder, tomato Paste, hot pepper sauce and the green onions. Bring to a boil. Add in frozen Potstickers and vegetables and return to a boil. Cook 4- 8 minutes, stirring occasionally, until the vegetables are soft. Add 1/4 cup cold water to the cornstarch and whisk or stir until dissolved, add to the soup. Season with the salt and pepper. Taste, stir again when it's returned to a boil. Remove and Serve. **HINT: <u>You can substitute Pork for Chicken if desired.</u> –OR-** Make Your Own see below   8 Servings
(Extra Recipe)

Won Ton Skins/Wrappers

MAKE YOUR OWN – (Ingredients not on grocery list)
1-1/2 cups Flour + dusting Cornstarch   1 tsp Salt
1 Egg, slightly beaten   1/2 cup lukewarm Water

Mix the flour and salt. Make a well in the center. Add in the egg and water and mix well. Turn this ball of dough out on to a surface floured with cornstarch. Knead to make it into a soft smooth dough. Cover with a clean towel and let set for 15 minutes. Roll the dough out to paper thin sheets (8" x 12" x 1/8" thick). Sprinkle with more cornstarch as needed to prevent dough from sticking. Cut sheets into 24 (2 to 3-inch) squares. Cover with a moist, kitchen towel, be careful, <u>they will dry out if left too long exposed to the air.</u>

Decided for You Cookbook – 365 Dinners

Potstickers – (Jiaozi Stuffed Chinese Dumplings)

MAKE YOUR OWN – (Ingredients not on grocery list)

3 cups shredded Chinese (Napa Cabbage)
1 cup Garlic Chives, minced
1 Tbsp Sesame Oil
1/2 Tbsp Cornstarch
1 (14.5 oz) can Chicken Broth
1/2 Tbsp Shiaoxing Rice Wine (or white cooking Wine)
25 Round (or Square but trimmed to a circle) Won Ton Wrappers (Skins) - See **MAKE YOUR OWN recipe**

1/2 Pound Ground Pork Sausage
1-1/4 Tbsp Soy Sauce
1/2 Tbsp minced Ginger
1/2 tsp Salt
2 beaten eggs

In a large bowl, lightly toss the cabbage and salt and let stand 30 minutes. Squeeze excess water from the cabbage and return it to the bowl. Add in the pork, chives, soy sauce, rice wine, sesame oil, ginger and cornstarch and stir until combined. Drain any excess liquid. To make the dumpling, place a tablespoon of the filling in the center of the wrapper. Spread a little of the beaten egg along edge of the wrapper and fold over, sealing the edges to make a half-moon shape. Using your thumb and index finger, form small pleats along the folded edge, squeezing firmly so the pleats do not become undone. As the dumplings are made, place them on a baking sheet that's been lightly dusted with cornstarch. Cover with a moist kitchen towel, be careful <u>they will dry out if left too long exposed to the air</u>. If cooking soup, then boil in the juices. Otherwise, bring a large pot of water to boil, add in the chicken broth. Add in half of the dumplings stirring to prevent them sticking together and boil for about 8 minutes (they will float when done). Repeat with the remaining dumplings. These can be a **standalone meal when drained and dipped into a mixture of: 1/2 cup Soy Sauce, 3 Tbsp Chinese Black Rice Vinegar, and 2 Tbsp Water.**

(Extra Recipe)

SOUP – (Clam Chowder – Manhattan)

2 cans (6 oz ea) minced or whole clams, drained (reserve the liquid)
1/4 cup diced Bacon
2 cups peeled, diced Potatoes
1/3 cup diced Celery
1/4 tsp Thyme
Garnish with snipped Parsley

1/4 cup minced Onion
1 cup Water
1 can (16 oz) Tomatoes
Salt and Pepper to taste

In a large saucepan, cook and stir the bacon with the onion until the bacon is crisp and the onion is tender. Stir in the clam liquid, potatoes, water and celery. Cook uncovered until the potatoes are tender, about 10 minutes. Add in the clams, tomatoes and seasonings. Heat to a boil, stirring occasionally. Serves 6 - **(New England Style:** Decrease the water to 1/2 cup, omit the celery, tomatoes, and thyme and add in 1 cup of milk with the clams). (Extra Recipe)

SOUP – (Egg Drop Soup – American Chinese)

6 cups Chicken Broth/Stock/Bouillon
1 tsp Soy Sauce
2 Large Eggs, lightly beaten

1/2 cup thinly sliced Green Onions
Pinch of finely ground White Pepper
1 cup sliced thinly Mushrooms (Shitake or Button)

In a medium saucepan, bring the stock to a simmer. Add in the green onions, mushrooms, soy and white pepper. Lower the heat to a bare simmer and cook for an additional 3 minutes. Stirring the soup with either a fork or chopstick fast enough to make a Whirlpool, gradually pour in the beaten eggs in a slow steady stream. Cook until the eggs are set and float. Continual stirring creates shreds or ribbons of the eggs (~1 minute). Remove from the heat and ladle into bowls and garnish with additional green onions and serve immediately.

Serves 4-6
(Extra Recipe)

Decided for You Cookbook – 365 Dinners

SOUP – (Enchilada Soup with Tortilla Chips)

1 can Boneless Chicken or shredded leftover Chicken
1 (14.5 oz) can Chicken Broth   1/2 (10 oz) can Enchilada Sauce
1 cup Sour Cream   1 (8 oz) Tomato Sauce
Garnish with Fried Flour/Corn Tortilla Chips (Vegetable Oil for frying) or Taco Chips

Add all ingredients except the chicken and half of the sour cream. Simmer for 10 minutes. Either cut a corn tortilla into strips and fry in hot oil or use Taco Chips as a cracker. Add in the can of boneless chicken and stir. Place soup in individual bowls, topped with a Tbsp Sour Cream and stick into the Sour Cream topping fried Tortilla or Taco chips.   Serves 4

MENU WEEK#21

SOUP – (Garbage Vegetable Beef Soup)

Leftover Beef Meat   Left Over Vegetables
1/2 head of chopped or sliced Cabbage   2 Large chopped Onions
3 – 4 stalks of chopped Celery   1 – 2 Tbsps Garlic Powder
1 Tbsp Oregano   Salt and Pepper to taste
1 Large can (16 oz) chopped Tomatoes or larger if you really like Tomatoes)
3 cans (16 oz) Tomato Sauce or 2 cans of Tomato Paste
4 Beef Bouillon cubes or 1 can (14.5 oz) Beef Broth

At the **end of your regular meals** and you are **cleaning up the table** and have left over meat, or vegetables, **strain off all butters and sauces**. Using an extra large plastic bowl with a sealing cover, place all of the vegetables in the bottom of the bowl, put a piece of waxed paper on top of the vegetables and put the meats on top of the paper. Seal your bowl and place inside your freezer. **Each day** as you begin to **add additional meat or vegetables** remove the cover, **run the lid under some hot water over the seal, or warm in the microwave oven, so it is easy to replace** on top of your bowl after adding new ingredients. **When your freezer bowl is full** or you feel you want to **cook your GARBAGE SOUP** remove the bowl from the freezer. Cut the meats into small pieces or shred. Place the cut up meat into a large cooking kettle of hot water. Add in the chopped tomatoes, tomato sauce, sliced cabbage, onion, celery, beef bouillon cubes or beef broth, garlic powder, Oregano. Cover ingredients by one - two inches of water. Bring to a boil and simmer for 10-15 minutes until the cabbage is tender. Salt and Pepper to taste, add more tomato sauce if needed. **VARIATION**: add cubed potatoes and cook till fork tender. **HINT: You can also have a bowl in your freezer of left over Chicken meats and make Chicken Vegetable Soup instead of Beef or any other favorite meat.**

(Extra Recipe)

SOUP – (Gazpacho – Cold Spanish Tomato Soup)

1-1/2 cups Tomato Juice   1 tsp granulated Beef Bouillon
1/4 cup chopped Cucumber   2 Tbsp chopped Bell Pepper
2 Tbsp chopped Onion   2 Tbsp Wine Vinegar
1 Tbsp Vegetable Oil   1/2 tsp Salt
1/2 tsp Worcestershire Sauce   Dash of Tabasco Sauce
1 (14.5 oz) can Stewed Tomatoes, chopped

Heat the tomato juice to boiling. Add in the bouillon, stir until dissolved. Stir in the remaining ingredients. Chill several hours. Serve with herbed croutons, extra tomatoes, cucumbers, onions and bell peppers of choice.   5 Servings

(Extra Recipe)

SOUP – (Hot and Sour Soup – Chinese)

4 Large Wood Ears (Chinese) or Shitaki Mushrooms sliced thinly
Chopped Green Onions and Cilantro Leaves (Chinese Parsley)
1-inch piece of fresh Ginger, peeled and grated
1 Tbsp Red Chile Paste, such as Sambal Oelek
3 Tbsp Cornstarch mixed with 1/4 cup Water

2 Tbsp Olive or Canola Oil	1/2 cup canned Bamboo shoots, sliced
1/4 Pound Barbecued Pork, shredded	1/4 cup Soy Sauce
1/4 cup Rice Vinegar	1 tsp Salt and White Pepper
Pinch of Sugar	2 quarts of Chicken Stock or Broth
1 Large Egg, lightly beaten	

If mushrooms are dried, place these in a small bowl and cover with boiling water and let stand for 30 minutes. Drain. Heat oil in a wok or large pot over medium-high flame. Add in the ginger, chile paste, mushrooms, bamboo shoots, and pork; cook and stir for 1 minute to melt the flavors. Combine the soy sauce, vinegar, salt, pepper, and sugar in a small bowl and pour this into the wok and toss everything together. Pour in the Chicken Stock and bring the soup to a boil, simmer for 10 minutes. Dissolve the cornstarch in the water and stir until smooth. Mix this slurry into the soup and continue to simmer until the soup thickens. Remove the soup from the heat and stirring in one direction to get a whirlpool effect going. Stop stirring and slowly pour in the beaten eggs in a steady stream and it will feather in the broth and cooks immediately upon contact. Garnish with chopped green onions and cilantro before serving.

4-6 Servings
(Extra Recipe)

SOUP – (Japanese Soba Noodle Soup)

8 oz Fresh or Frozen Shrimp	6 oz dried Soba Noodles or Vermicelli
2 cups Chicken Broth	1/4 cup Mirin (Japanese Sweet Rice Wine)
1/4 cup Soy Sauce	2 tsp Sugar, granulated
2 Green Onions, bias-sliced	
1/2 tsp Instant Dashi granules (dried tuna-and-seaweed-flavored soup stock)	

Thaw, peel and de-vein the shrimp, leaving the tail intact if desired. Rinse and pat dry. Cook the soba noodles or vermicelli in boiling water for about 4 minutes or until tender. In a medium saucepan, combine the broth, Mirin, soy sauce, sugar and Dashi granules. Bring to a boil and then reduce the heat. Add in the shrimp; simmer 2 minutes or until the shrimp turns opaque pink. Drain the noodles; divide the noodles into 2 bowls. Pour the shrimp and broth over the noodles, garnish with the green onions and serve. All products are available in the Asian section of your grocery store.

Yields 2 servings.
(Extra Recipe)

SOUP – (Onion Soup – Dry Mix)

3/4 cup Dried Onions	1/3 cup Beef Broth Granules (not cubes)
1/4 tsp Celery Seed	1/4 tsp Sugar
4 tsp Onion Powder	

Mix all ingredients and store in an airtight container. Five Tablespoons equals 1 package of Onion Soup Mix. To make a soup mix with 4 cups of water with the 5 Tbsps of dry mix and bring to a boil. Simmer uncovered for 8-10 minutes.

SOUP – (Onion Soup – French)

Can purchase ready made **–OR-**

MAKE YOUR OWN – (Ingredients not on grocery List)
6 – 10 Sweet Onions sliced thinly (Vidalia, Stockton Reds, or Maui) can use Yellow Onions

Tie together (**Bouquet Garni**) Sprigs of Thyme, a Bay Leaf and Parsley and drop into soup. **HINT:**
<u>Place spices in a small clean white cloth (dish towel), **-OR-** a piece of muslin material **-OR- inside of a**</u>
<u>**commercial metal large tea ball** – anything to keep the seasonings together, place in case you want to</u>
<u>remove quickly.</u>

1 can (10 oz) Chicken Broth	1 can (10 oz) Beef Broth Consume
1 can (10 oz) full of Burgundy or White Wine	2 Tbsp Margarine or Butter
1 cup Fontina or Gruyere Swiss Cheese, grated	Pepper
Garlic Flavored Croutons	
1 Loaf or Baguette of French Bread, cubed and toasted in the oven or garlic croutons	

Trim the ends off each onion, remove the peel and finely slice into half moon shapes. Set an electric skillet to 300 degrees and add butter. Once the butter has melted, add a layer of onions and sprinkle them with a little salt. (Optional: can cook a couple pieces of bacon in the butter and remove the bacon leaving only the drippings). Repeat layering the onions and salt until all the onions are in the skillet. Do not stir the onions until they have sweated down for 15 to 20 minutes on low heat. After that, stir occasionally until the onions are a dark mahogany in color and they are reduced to approximately 2 cups. This should take 45 minutes to one hour. Cover the onions with the wine and turn the heat to high, reducing the wine to a syrup consistency. Add in the broths, and the Bouquet Garni spices. Reduce the heat and simmer another 15 to 20 minutes. Remove the Bouquet Garni, taste and season again with salt and pepper.

Arrange 4 small, deep soup bowls or crocks on a baking sheet. Preheat the broiler to high (500°F). Once the soup has reached a boil, ladle it into the bowls. Float toasted crusty, bread cubes on top of the soup and cover these with a mound of Swiss Cheese. Place the baking sheet with the soup bowls on it under the hot broiler until the cheese melts and bubbles. Serve hot. (**Optional toppings to croutons**: thinly sliced chopped green onions/scallions, crumbled cooked bacon, bread sticks, toasted county bread rounds, or coat sliced shallots in 3 Tbsp flour and cook in 4 Tbsp Vegetable Oil).   Serves 4
MENU WEEK#48

SOUP – (Potato Soup)

(Great Winter Meal)

2– 6 medium sized Potatoes	1 Large Sliced Onions
3 Tbsp Margarine	1/2 cup Evaporated Milk
1 Tbsp Salt and Pepper	

Peel and cut up the potatoes in medium-sized chunks. Fill a large pan half-full of water, add in the salt and bring to a boil. Place in the potatoes, onions, and cook until the potatoes are fork-tender. Remove from the heat and add in the margarine and the evaporated milk. Cool to a medium heat and serve with saltine crackers.

Serves 4-6
(Extra Recipe)

See recipe **MAKE YOUR OWN**, BRD – (Crackers - Saltine)

SOUP – (Potato Soup – Leftover Baked)

4 Leftover Baked Potatoes, halved, pulp scooped out and put through a sieve, ricer or mashed very well, cut the skins into small strips

3 Tbsp Margarine or Butter
1-1/2 Tbsp minced Garlic
1-1/2 cups Buttermilk
1/2 cup fresh grated Parmesan Cheese
1 tsp Pepper
2-1/2 tsp Salt

1/4 cup minced Chives
1-1/2 cups finely diced Leeks
6 cups Chicken stock or broth, hot
1/2 cup Sour Cream

2 Tbsp Sherry or Wine Vinegar

In a large saucepot, over high heat melt the margarine/butter and add in the leeks and garlic. Cook over medium heat until they are clear/translucent. Add in the hot stock and whisk to combine. In a separate bowl, whisk together the mashed/riced potatoes, a handful or two of the potato skin strips, buttermilk, sour cream and grated Parmesan Cheese. Add this mixture to the soup stirring constantly. Season with salt and pepper. Remove from the heat and add in the vinegar. Ladle into bowls and garnish with chives.   4-6 Servings

MENU WEEK#40

SOUP – (Split Pea Soup)

1 Large chopped Onion
1/2 cup diced Ham
Salt and Pepper
2/3 cup Chicken Stock/Broth
1-1/2 cups Evaporated Milk
Sour Cream to taste

2 ribs chopped Celery
1 Pound Split Peas (dried)
1 Bay Leaf
4 cups Water
Dry Sherry Wine (Optional)
2 Tbsp Olive Oil

Sauté the onions in 2 Tbsp of the Oil add in the Celery and Ham and cook two to three minutes. Add in the split peas and stir well. Add in the salt and pepper to taste, the bay leaf, and the Chicken stock/broth and the water. Simmer slowly for 2-3 hours. Strain the soup discarding any vegetable pulp. Return to a very low heat and add the cream in slowly. Serve in individual bowls and provide the Sherry and Sour Cream to be added according to individual taste.   Serves 4

(Extra Recipe)

SOUP – (Taco Soup)

1 Pound Ground Beef
1 cup Water
1 (15 oz) can Black Beans
1 (1.0 oz) Pkg Taco Seasoning
1 (6 oz) can Black Olives, sliced
1 (14.5 oz) can diced Tomatoes with Green Chile
1 Pkg (1.5 oz) Ranch-Style Salad Dressing Mix
Taco Chips or Fried Corn Tortilla for garnish

1 Onion, chopped
1 (15 oz) can Pinto Beans
1 (15 oz) can Cream Style Corn
Sour Cream

Brown the beef with the onions in a medium size saucepan. Drain excess fats. Add in the remaining ingredients and simmer for 20 minutes before serving. Either cut a corn tortilla into strips and fry in hot oil or use Taco Chips as a cracker. Place soup in individual bowls, top with a Tablespoon of Sour Cream, sliced olives and Taco chips.   Serves 4

(Extra Recipe)

SOUP – (Tomato and Spinach Soup)

2 Tbsp Olive Oil	1 Large Onion, chopped or shallots
2 cloves Garlic, chopped	1 (28 oz) can diced Tomatoes in Juice
1 (28 oz) can crushed Tomatoes	
1 (10 oz) Pkg washed fresh Spinach,	2 cups Vegetable stock (can be commercially made)
Shredded or can be defrosted, frozen	Salt and Pepper to taste

In a large pot, place the olive oil and cook the onions and garlic until slightly browned, 5 minutes. Add in the tomatoes and the vegetable stock. Stir to combine and bring to a boil. Add in the spinach in handfuls to wilt it. Season the soup with salt and pepper to taste. Reduce the heat and simmer 10-15 minutes.

(Extra Recipe)

SOUP – (Turkey Noodle Soup)

Broth:

1 Turkey (10-15 lb Bird) Carcass with some meat left on	1 Large Onion with 4 Whole Cloves
2 Celery Stalks with leaves, halved	1/2 cup Fresh Dill
2 Carrots, Halved	4 Peppercorns and Salt to Taste
1/4 cup Parsley	4 cloves Garlic cut up

Soup:

2 cups Egg Noodles	3 Carrots, peeled and cut into 1/4" rounds
2 Celery Stalks, diced	2 medium sliced Onion
3 Tbsp Parsley	Salt & Pepper to taste
Left-over Turkey cut into small pieces	

Cook on a low simmer all of the ingredients listed in Broth for 1-1/2 hours and strain discarding the carcass and the vegetables. Allow to cool so you can skim off the excessive fats. Add in all of the soup ingredients, except the noodles and the turkey, and bring to a boil. Cook until the carrots are fork tender, add in the noodles, the turkey and cook for an additional 5 –10 minutes. Salt and pepper to taste and garnish with the parsley and serve with a good crusty French Bread. (Extra Recipe)

SOUP – (Won Ton Soup – Chinese)

1 Pkg Won Ton Skins/Wrappers (fresh, frozen)   –OR-

Won Ton Skins/Wrappers

MAKE YOUR OWN – (Ingredients not on grocery list)

1-1/2 cups Flour + dusting Cornstarch	1 tsp Salt
1 Egg, slightly beaten	1/2 cup lukewarm Water

Mix the flour and salt. Make a well in the center. Add in the egg and water and mix well. Turn this ball of dough out on to a surface floured with cornstarch. Knead to make it into a soft smooth dough. Cover with a clean towel and let set for 15 minutes. Roll the dough out to paper thin sheets (8" x 12" x 1/8" thick). Sprinkle with more cornstarch as needed to prevent dough from sticking. Cut sheets into 24 (2 to 3-inch) squares. Cover with a moist, kitchen towel, be careful, they will dry out if left too long exposed to the air.
MIX YOUR MEAT FILLING next page

(Extra Recipe)

Won Ton Meat Filling

1/2 Pound Cooked Ground Pork Sausage, and ¼ Pound small cooked Shrimp
(Optional: 1/2 cup shredded Cooked Chicken or Ham)

2 tsp minced Green Onion	Dash of White Pepper
1 tsp Sesame Oil	1-1/4 tsp Soy Sauce

Optional: 1/2 cup shredded Chinese Napa Cabbage & chopped Water Chestnuts

Mix the ingredients and **start stuffing** the dumplings by placing a tablespoon of the filling in the center of the wrapper. Dip your finger into an additional beaten egg and spread a little of along edge of the wrapper and fold over, sealing the edges to make a half-moon shape. Using your thumb and index finger, form small pleats along the folded edge, squeezing firmly so the pleats do not become undone (this is why you seal with egg instead of just water as in the Fried Won Ton recipe). As the dumplings are made, place them on a baking sheet that's been lightly dusted with cornstarch.

Bring to a **boil the below** amounts of broth, water and celery. Add in half of the dumplings stirring to prevent them from sticking together, then add in the balance and boil for about 8 minutes (they will float when done). After all of the Won Ton are all boiling, drop in the spinach to cook for 3-5 minutes

Won Ton Chicken Vegetable Broth

4 cups Chicken Broth or Bouillon	1 cup lightly packed Sliced Raw Spinach
1/2 cup minced Celery	Leaves with Stems removed)
2 quarts salted boiling Water	

Serves 6 – 8
(Extra Recipe)

SOUPS – MICROWAVE INFORMATION:

Water – Based Soups - One cup takes 2-1/2 – 3-1/2 minutes
Cream Soups heat quickly because of the milk so keep an eye on it, that it doesn't boil over. A can of condensed soup, diluted with water = 5 to 7 minutes.

WOW! MORE SPACE FOR NOTES:

VEGETABLES

NOTE: <u>**CLEAN, CUT AND PREPARE ALL VEGETABLES AND SALAD INGREDIENTS WHEN YOU COME HOME FROM THE STORE**</u>. This will save you precious moments during the week in getting your meals completed in a quicker time. Peel and/or clean vegetables over newspaper or paper towels that will save you washing a bowl. Just throw everything away. To defrost frozen vegetables, place entire package in cold water to defrost or in a microwave inside original packaging. **Also, HINT:** <u>**When large amounts of water are used in boiling the vegetables, add in 1 tsp salt for each quart of water used which will cause it to boil quicker and hotter.**</u>

VEG – (Artichokes)

Wash and cut off the stem end, and any discolored leaves. Trim the bottom end of the stem and shave the stem down to expose the tender, inner part of the artichoke. Snap or cut off the discolored outer petals until you reach the pale green, softer leaves toward the center. Cut off about ½ inch of the tops so it's flat. Soak 30 minutes in cold water. Cook, covered or uncovered in a small amount of boiling, salted water and lemon juice for 30 to 45 minutes. Drain upside down. Avoid the hairy choke and it from the center that should be discarded. If serving hot, then supply melted butter as a dipping sauce. Or, if it is served cooler dip the leaves in either Mayonnaise or Hollandaise Sauce. **MICROWAVE:** After being thoroughly washed and trimmed, re-dip the entire artichoke into water allowing water to remain clinging to the leaves. Surround the entire wet artichoke with either plastic wrap or waxed paper. Place it on a glass pie plate or dish and microwave on High power for 5 to 7 minutes, rotating it through the cooking cycle. Remove it from the microwave and allow it to rest in the paper for 5 minutes before serving. Serve with a Hollandaise Sauce

VEG – (Artichoke Hearts – Canned)

If not marinated, remove the artichokes from the can and rinse in clear water, drain. In a bowl, mix together 1/2 cup vegetable or olive oil, 1/2 cup Vinegar, 1/2 tsp Garlic Powder, 1/2 tsp Onion Salt, with a dash of Sugar, 1/2 tsp Oregano; stir well. Marinate the artichokes hearts at least two hours in this mixture. Better if left overnight in the refrigerator to marinate.

VEG – (Artichoke Hearts – Marinated)

Open the Jar and serve

VEG – (Asparagus and Cauliflower with Cheese Sauce)

Cook Cauliflower and Asparagus per frozen food package directions. Drain and season with Salt and Pepper. Blend together and mix the cheese sauce into your vegetables

4 Tbsp melted Margarine	1 cup shredded Sharp Cheddar Cheese
1/2 cup Chicken Broth	1 cup Half and Half Milk or Evaporated Milk
4 Tbsp Flour	1/2 tsp Salt
Dash of Cayenne Pepper	

Melt the margarine, stir in the flour until smooth. Add in the Chicken Broth, the milk, pepper and the shredded cheese and stir until melted together, thickened and warmed.

VEG – (Asparagus – Buttered)

If using fresh asparagus. Grasp a few of the spears and begin bending them over and the asparagus stalk will break at the point that it is tough. You can discard the bottom of the stalk or you can trim off the outer area of the stalks with a potato peeler and cut up the tender centers. Wash thoroughly and remove any bad discolored areas. Place them into bunches of "standing-up stalks" of 6-8 and tie with string keeping the ends even. Stand them upright in about 1" of boiling, salted water in a covered deep kettle or asparagus cooker and cook for 5-8 minutes. Otherwise you can place them loosely laying down in boiling, salted water in a covered saucepan and cook approximately 10 to 15 minutes or until stalk is fork-tender; drain. Stir butter over the asparagus and salt and pepper to taste. If using frozen asparagus, cook per package directions. **VARIATION:** Can be served with a Béchamel Sauce, Cheese Sauce, Aioli Sauce or even cooled and marinated in a Vinaigrette Sauce for a cold salad. **–OR-** Lay the buttered asparagus in a casserole dish. Cover the top or layer with grated cheeses and Paprika. Bake 350°F for 20 additional minutes. **–OR-** boil in chicken broth, then sauté in garlic butter. Serve with tops covered with chopped almonds or pecans.

VEG – (Asparagus – Cold)

Remove from the can, drain and serve with Mayonnaise, Salad Dressing or a sauce of your choice.

VEG – (Asparagus – Stir-Fried)

1 Pound fresh Asparagus Spears

2 Tbsp Margarine, melted

1/2 tsp Salt

1 Tbsp Sliced Almonds or toasted Sesame Seeds

1 clove Garlic, minced

1/2 cup canned diluted Chicken Broth

1/2 tsp Sugar

Snap off the tough ends of the asparagus. Remove scales from the stalks with a knife and cut asparagus diagonally into 1-inch pieces. Set aside. Sauté the minced garlic in the melted margarine in a large skillet for one minute. Add in the asparagus pieces, stirring well to combine. Add in the chicken broth, salt and sugar, stirring well to combine. Cook over high heat for 3-4 minutes or until the asparagus is crisp-tender, stirring frequently. Transfer drained asparagus to a serving platter and garnish with Sesame Seeds or sliced Almonds. **VARIATION:** Add in 3 tsp Soy Sauce, 1 tsp corn-starch, 1-1/2 cups sliced fresh mushrooms and 2 small tomatoes, cut into thin wedges. Serves 4

VEG – (Asparagus – Supreme Asparagus Casserole)

2 Pounds fresh Asparagus or 1 Large (16 oz) Pkg Frozen Cut Up Spears

1/2 cup buttered Cracker Crumbs or French Fried
  Onion Rings

1 (10-3/4 oz Cream of Mushroom Soup

2 Pkgs (3 oz ea) of Pimento Cream Cheese

2 Tbsp Butter or Margarine

2 Tbsp chopped Onion

1/4 cup Milk

Grasp a few of the spears and begin bending them over and the asparagus stalk will break at the point that it is tough. You can discard the bottom of the stalk or you can trim off the outer area of the stalks with a potato peeler and cut up the tender centers. Wash thoroughly and remove any bad discolored areas. Place them loosely laying down in boiling, salted water in a covered saucepan and cook approximately 10 to 15 minutes or until stalk is fork-tender; drain. Or you can cook the frozen broccoli per package directions and drain. In a saucepan mix the soup, onions, milk, cream cheese and margarine together and stir until blended. Mix the cooked asparagus into the sauce mixture and pour half of it into the bottom of a 1-1/2 quart, buttered casserole dish. Top with 1/4 cup of the cracker crumbs or onion rings followed by another layer of the sauce ending with the cracker crumbs. Bake in a 350°F oven for about 25 minutes. Serves 4-6

VEG – (Avocados)

Avocados are really a tropical fruit. Peeling and slicing avocados with a plastic knife instead of metal will prevent it from turning dark.

VEG – (Beans – Baked – From Scratch Recipe)

MAKE YOUR OWN – (Ingredients not on grocery list)

3 cups <u>cooked</u> Small White (Navy) Beans	1 Tbsp Mustard
1 tsp Ginger	2 Tbsp Molasses
1 Tbsp Brown Sugar	Paprika
Chopped Onions	Salt and Pepper to taste
Bake at 325°F for 25 minutes	(Extra Recipe)

VEG – (Beans – Baked – Simple Recipe)

(Working Mother and Beginner's Quick Recipe)

1 Large (31 oz) can Pork and Beans placed in a 2-Quart Baking Dish, add one chopped onion (or 1 Tbsp dehydrated Onion Flakes), 1 Tbsp Cinnamon, 2 Tbsp Brown Sugar,1 tsp Mustard, 1/4 cup Ketchup and mix together. This can be warmed on top of a stove or in the oven (325°F) for 15 minutes.

VEG – (Beans – Butter/Lima Beans)

Place two cans of the Butter Beans into a saucepan and add 2 Tbsp bacon grease in the beans, along with salt and pepper to taste. Boil until tender or until most of the water has been consumed. If you do not save bacon grease, cook two pieces of bacon separately in a skillet and add bacon drippings/fats to the recipe. – **OR-** Place a couple pieces of diced bacon in the beans and boil until the bacon is tender.

VEG – (Beans – Green Beans – Canned

Salt and pepper to taste. Add margarine/butter (or you can eliminate the margarine and put in 2 Tbsp bacon grease or 2 slices of chopped bacon). Boil for 5 minutes in a saucepan or drain the juices and cook, in a microwavable container, with margarine for 7 minutes. **VARIATION:**
1) Sprinkle the top of the green beans with garlic powder, sprinkle over the beans 2 Tbsp granulated sugar, add 2 Tbsp dehydrated Onion Flakes (or 1/4 of a small, chopped onion) along with 2 Tbsp margarine. Boil for 5 minutes. **–OR-** before cooking **add in 1/4 cup dried bacon bits used in salads <u>for</u> that <u>smoky taste</u>**.

VEG – (Beans – Green Beans – Fresh

Break off the stem where it was attached to the plant. With these stems occasionally there are strings that pull off, remove these as well. Wash the beans and break these into 1-inch lengths or slice lengthwise (for French Style). Cook 10-12 minutes (broken) or 10 to 15 minutes (sliced lengthwise) in a covered pan which has salted water 1-1/2 inches above the beans and brought to a boil. Drain, season with salt, pepper, margarine/butter. **VARIATION:** Serve with a white or Béchamel sauce. Can be served cold with a Vinaigrette Dressing **–OR-** 1 Tbsp Extra-Virgin Olive Oil, 1 Tbsp Butter, 1 small chopped Onion, 1 cup Chicken Broth, 1 - 1-1/4 Lbs fresh green beans. Over medium heat add olive oil and butter with the onion and sauté 3 minutes, add broth and bring to a boil. Add in the beans, season with salt and cover and simmer 8 minutes or until tender.

(Extra Recipe)

VEG – (Beans – Green Bean Casserole)

1 Large Pkg (16 oz) French Style Green Beans
   (frozen), or 2 cans Green Beans
3/4 cup Milk

1 can French Fried Onion Rings
1 can Cream of Mushroom Soup
Salt and Pepper to taste

Cook the frozen beans per package directions or use the canned beans. Drain, salt and pepper to taste and place the beans in a 1 Quart casserole dish. Combine the milk, soup, 1/2 of the onion rings (these can be crumbled if desired) and pour over the beans. Bake 325°F for 20 minutes. Remove and garnish the top of the casserole with the 1/4 cup of Onion Rings and return the casserole to the oven for an additional 5 minutes. Serves 6

VEG – (Beans – Green Bean Cheesy)

10 slices Bacon
1 Pound sliced Mushrooms
3/4 tsp Black Pepper

2 Pkgs (16 oz ea) frozen cut Green Beans
3/4 cup chopped Onion
1 Jar (16 oz) Process Cheese Spread

Cook the bacon until crisp and drain all expect 1/4 cup of the drippings. Crumble the bacon and set aside, separate out ~2 Tbsp for a topping. Microwave the beans as directed on the package and drain well. Heat the drippings and add together the mushrooms, and onions and cook for 10 minutes; drain. Mix in the beans and crumbled bacon, salt and pepper to taste. Spoon into a 2-quart baking dish. Heat the process cheese spread in the microwave per jar directions. Pour over the green bean, mushroom, onion and bacon mixture. Stir together and top with the 2 Tbsp of bacon and serve.

Yields 8+ servings

VEG – (Beans – Green Beans and Baby Carrots Savory)

3/4 lb Green Beans, trimmed cup chopped Shallots   1/2 cup Chicken Broth
8 oz baby Carrots, sliced lengthwise
1/2 tsp Herbes-de-Provence (if not available it consists of: sage, basil, fennel, oregano & optional Lavender)*

In a sauepan, cook green beans and baby carrots in boiling salted water for 5 minutes. Drain, plunge green beans and carrots into cold water. Drain. In a skillet coated with cooking spray over medium-high heat, cook shallots 5 minutes or until soft. Stir in the green beans, carrots, chicken broth and the Herbes-de-Provence.* Cook 5 minutes more or until heated thoroughly. Season with salt and pepper to taste. Serves 4

HINT: <u>Green Beans are loaded with Riboflavin and helps to get rid of headaches</u>

VEG – (Beans – Long Green Szechwan)

1 Pound Long Green Beans, blanched
1 Tbsp Peanut Oil
2 Tbsp minced Garlic
1/4 cup Water
Dash of Chili Powder

4 oz Mild Red Chiles
1/4 cup Oyster Sauce
1 Tbsp chopped Parsley

Heat the peanut oil in a skillet or wok. Sauté the chilies and garlic. Add the blanched (dropped into boiling water for two minutes, and drained). Stir in the oyster sauce and water. Stir fry for 2-3 minutes. Season with black pepper. Mound the green beans in the center of a platter. Drizzle any remaining sauce over the top. (Extra Recipe)

VEG – (Beans – Refried Beans - Canned

Place in a baking dish and top with shredded Cheddar Cheese and warm 15 minutes at 325°F. You can also warm these in a saucepan on top of the stove, be sure to use low heat because they will burn easily.

Decided for You Cookbook – 365 Dinners

VEG – (Beans – Refried Beans – Freshly Made

Cook the day before (per recipe below - see VEG – Beans, White or Pinto Beans). Using these beans, drain all the liquid off and mash with a potato masher. Place a little oil in a skillet and reheat the beans stirring constantly.
(Extra Recipe)

VEG – (Beans – White, Small Navy -OR- Pinto Beans)

1 Pound Dry Beans – washed
4-6 slices Bacon or 3/4 Pound Salted Pork or 4 Ham Hocks
Salt and Pepper

Place beans in a pan of water and wash, removing any rocks or debris. Run clear water up over the top of the beans and soak in the pan over night. Beans will puff up. Next day, pour this soaking water off and replace with clean water in a large kettle, about 2 inches above the top of the beans. Salt the water, add in the bacon or salted pork or ham hocks and bring to a boil. Boil over medium heat for 1 – 2 hours. (If the beans boil down too far, you should add "Hot" water to the beans, "Cold" water will cause the skins to become tough). Beans are done when they become soft enough to mash between your fingers easily.

VEG – (Beets – Pickled)

If you do not have pickled beets but have canned beets you can use this and marinate them in the following marinade per can:

1/2 cup Vegetable Oil	1/2 cup Vinegar
1/4 cup Granulated Sugar	2 tsp Ground Cloves or 1 Tbsp Whole Cloves

VEG – (Bell Peppers)

Use greased muffin tins as molds when baking stuffed green peppers. Bell peppers can be sliced and cooked in shortening with sliced onions as a side dish.

VEG – (Broccoli)

Discard big leaves and tough stalk ends. Wash thoroughly. Slit big end of stalk up 2 – 3 inches follow direction of choice for seasonings etc –OR- can be frozen, but thawed.

VEG – (Broccoli – Broccoli and Mushroom Pilaf)

4 Scallions or Green Onions	1/4 lb Mushrooms
1 cup Long-Grain Rice	1 can (14-1/2 oz) Chicken Broth
1 cup chopped Broccoli Spears	

Slice onions on a bias and cut mushrooms into thin slivers. In a saucepan coated with nonstick cooking spray over medium heat, sauté onions and mushrooms for 3 minutes or until tender. Stir in rice. Add 3/4 cup water and chicken broth to rice mixture. Bring to boil; reduce heat, cover and simmer 10 minutes. Stir in the broccoli florets. Cover and cook an additional 10 minutes or until rice & broccoli are tender. Season with salt and pepper to taste.
Serves 4
(Extra Recipe)

Other substitutes for Rice Pilaf: Replace above ingredients by adding specified amounts of one tablespoon minced garlic, vegetable broth with asparagus -OR- 1/2 cup chopped red onion, white wine and frozen baby peas -OR- 1/2 cup sliced radishes, beef broth and grated carrots -OR- 1/4 cup chopped celery, tomato juice and corn kernels -OR- 1/2 cup chopped Leeks, clam juice and chopped spinach.

VEG – (Broccoli – Broccoli and Noodles Parmesan)

1 Pkg (16 oz) frozen Broccoli cuts (if fresh ~1-1/2 pounds)
1/2 cup chopped Onion
1 can (10-3/4 oz) Cream of Mushroom Soup
1/2 tsp Tarragon, crushed
1 cup (4 oz) shredded Cheddar Cheese or American

5 cups cooked Fettuccini Noodles (8-12 oz uncooked)
1 clove Garlic minced
2 Tbsp Margarine or Butter
1/2 cup grated Parmesan Cheese
1 cup Sour Cream

Prepare the frozen Broccoli per package directions and drain. (If fresh, cut the broccoli into small chunks and cook over medium heat in 1" of boiling water 6 minutes or until fork tender and drain, and salt). Boil the noodles per package directions, drain and salt a little. In a saucepan, over medium heat, in hot margarine cook the onion and garlic until tender, stirring to be sure it doesn't burn. Stir in the soup, the tarragon and mix well. Add in the cheese, stirring until melted. Stir in the sour cream, broccoli and the cooked noodles. Place all ingredients into a greased 2 =quart casserole dish, cover with foil or a lid and bake at 350°F for 30 minutes or until hot and bubbling.   Serves 6-8

VEG – (Broccoli – Broccoli Au Gratin)

1 Large (16 oz) Pkg of frozen Broccoli –OR- 1 bunch fresh Broccoli (cooked fork tender Spears (or cuts) defrosted, blanched and drained
1 Envelope Onion Mushroom or Dry Beef Mushroom Soup
1 cup Water
1 cup Half and Half Milk
3 Tbsp Flour   Buttered Bread Crumbs (mix w/butter)
1 tsp Worcestershire Sauce   1-1/2 cups (4 oz) shredded Cheddar Cheese

Preheat oven to 375°F. In a medium saucepan, bring the water to a boil and stir in the soup mix. Simmer covered for 5 minutes. Add in the Worcestershire sauce, then gradually stir in the flour and blend in the cream avoiding lumps. Simmer, constantly stirring, until sauce is slightly thickened, about 5 minutes. Stir in the shredded cheese and heat until the cheese is melted. Stir the broccoli into the cheese sauce and place it in a shallow baking dish. Top with the breadcrumbs and any remaining cheese. Bake 15 minutes`   Serves 6

VEG – (Broccoli – Broccoli Buttered)

If using fresh broccoli, discard the biggest leaves and the tough stalk ends. Wash thoroughly. Slit the big pieces of the stalk up 2-3 inches. Cook covered in 1/2" of boiling water below the top of the vegetables for 15 to 20 minutes, or per package directions. Drain and add salt and pepper during last 5 minutes of cooking. Stir in butter or margarine and a little Lemon Juice (optional).   If you are using frozen broccoli cook per pkg direction. **VARIATION:** Can be served with a Hollandaise Sauce. **MICROWAVE: Slice fresh broccoli and tightly cover with plastic wrap cook 5 minutes/ Lb on high.   When fork tender, add on butter and/or Parmigiano-Reggiano Cheese and toss.**

VEG – (Broccoli – Broccoli, Cauliflower and Carrots)

If using frozen, cook per package directions and drain.   Add salt, pepper and two Tablespoons of Margarine/Butter and stir to coat vegetables.

VEG – (Broccoli – Broccoli Casserole)

1 Pkg (16 oz) frozen Broccoli Spears Cuts or Chopped or (2 Pounds of fresh Broccoli)
1/4 to 1/2 pkg Seasoned (Herb Seasoned Stuffing Mix)

Cook frozen broccoli until thawed (fresh broccoli should be cleaned, stems peeled and cut into uniformed pieces, cook till barely softened); drain. Mix stuffing mix with proportionate amount of water as directed on package. Place it in a buttered 9 x 13 casserole dish; mix together with the moistened dressing mix*.

Create a **White Sauce** of:
4 Tbsp melted Butter/Margarine
4 Tbsp Flour
1/2 tsp Salt

When blended, add:
1 cup Half and Half Milk
1 cup grated Cheddar Cheese (medium or sharp)
1 can Chicken Broth

Stir until melted. Crumble additional shredded cheese on top of broccoli/ dressing if desired*, pour sauce over casserole. Bake 350 degrees uncovered for 30 minutes. Remove from oven to cool as it will taste better medium hot.

*Cut up leftover chicken, or purchase from the Fried Chicken Store, can be added to casserole for a one-meal casserole. Serve with tossed green salad. **Great Microwave Warm-over.**

VEG – (Brussels Sprouts – Buttered)

Fresh Brussels sprouts, discard any wilted leaves. Wash, separate and cut a small "x" across the bottom core end of the sprout and cook for 10 – 20 minutes in 1" boiling, salted water in a covered saucepan. Drain. Season with salt, pepper, and butter or margarine. Can use frozen sprouts and cook according to package directions. **VARIATION:** Can be served with a Hollandaise Sauce. **–OR-** After cooking sprouts, melt 3 Tbsp Margarine or butter in a saucepan. Add in 1-1/2 cups cut Celery and cook for 2 minutes. Stir in 3 Tbsp flour mixed with 1-1/2 cups milk. Cook together until sauce is thickened. Add back in the sprouts and serve **–OR-** with drained Brussels Sprouts, cook a Bechamél Sauce with 1/2 cup of melted grated Cheddar Cheese added.

Feeds 6-8 people

VEG – (Cabbage – Green)

Discard wilted outside leaves. Cut the cabbage into quarters or sixths, (or shred) removing most of the hard core. Cook the wedges for (15 to 25 minutes) in salted, boiling water about 1" above the top of the cabbage in a covered kettle. If it is shredded, boil for about 8 – 10 minutes. Drain. Add additional salt and pepper to taste after drained (we like to put ketchup on it). **HINT: If your pot is large enough to hold a metal colander or vegetable steamer tray above the boiling liquid in the pot, then place the colander in the pot. Inside the colander place the cabbage with two heels of bread, crust down, on top of the cabbage to absorb the cabbage steam. –OR- you can set a small can containing vinegar on the counter next to the boiling pot. This will help your kitchen to not smell like cabbage.**

VEG – (Cabbage – Red)

Discard wilted outside leaves. Cut the cabbage into quarters or sixths, (or shred) removing most of the hard core. Add 1 Tbsp Vinegar or Lemon juice to preserve the color and cook the wedges (12 to 15 minutes) in salted, boiling water about 1" above the top of the cabbage in a covered kettle. If it is shredded, boil for about 8 – 10 minutes. Drain. **VARIATION:** Can be served cold with a Vinaigrette Dressing. **–OR –** Sweet & Sour: Sauté 1 medium onion in melted butter until tender. Add sliced medium cabbage, 2 diced Granny Smith Apples, 2/3 cup Wine Vinegar, 1/4 cup Brown Sugar, 2 Tbsp Lemon Juice, 1/2 tsp Caraway Seeds with Salt and Pepper to taste. Boil, cover, and simmer for 45 minutes. Serves 10. **HINT:** <u>**1 Pound = 4 cups shredded raw or 2 cups cooked.**</u>

VEG – (Carrots)

<u>**CLEANING:**</u> Slice off skin or scrape with the edge of a knife. Sometimes if cooked with skin on may be bitter.

VEG – (Carrots) – Carrots Buttered, etc.

<u>**Fresh**</u> – Wash; peel (or turn your knife perpendicular to the carrot and scrape the thin skin off of the carrots). You can cook the carrots whole; split large ones lengthwise, or slice **–OR-** you can cut in rounds. Cook these in salted, boiling water about 1" above the top of the carrots for 15 to 20 minutes (halves or smaller wholes 10-15 minutes) in a covered saucepan. Drain and salt and pepper to taste and mix in 2 Tbsp margarine **–OR-** A different effect is to shred the carrots. Then place them in a small amount of water and bake covered 325°F for 20-25 minutes or until carrots are fork tender. Drain and add in margarine, salt and pepper. **–OR-** Boil fresh carrot rounds until fork-tender, drain. Arrange in a baking dish Mix together 1/2 cup Mayonnaise, 2 Tbsp chopped Onion, 2 Tbsp Horseradish and a little of the boiling liquid. Pour over carrots, top with bread- crumbs and bake 375°F for 15 minutes. **VARIATION: Sweet Carrots** Add in 3 Tbsp brown sugar to the buttered carrots, boil 3 minutes, and it totally changes the flavor **–OR –** **Zesty Carrots**: 6-8 carrots cut in Julienne Strips, 1/2 cup Mayonnaise, 2 Tbsp Horseradish, 2 Tbsp Grated Onion, 1/2 tsp Salt, 1/4 tsp Pepper, 1/4 cup breadcrumbs, 1 Tbsp Margarine, Dash of Paprika. Boil carrots in a water for ~8 minutes, drain reserving 1/4 cup the water. Place carrots in an oblong baking dish. Combine the reserved liquid, mayonnaise, horseradish, onion, salt, pepper and pour over carrots. Combine breadcrumbs with the margarine and paprika and sprinkle over the carrots. Bake at 375°F for 15-20 minutes **-OR- Microwave sliced carrots in a plastic wrapped dish 5 min/Lb. When fork tender add 1-2 tsp Real Butter, Juice of half a Lemon, freshly snipped Parsley and Dill for Lemon Buttered Carrots with Dill.**   Serves 6-8

VEG – (Carrots – Carrot Sticks)

Peel the carrots and cut into small sticks. Soak several hours in cold water that has a teaspoon of granulated sugar added to it, this will create additional crispness. If you slice with a vegetable peeler the sticks will curl after being in the water soak. Add curls to radish roses, and celery fans to a vegetable dip. **–OR –** use your cookie cutters or other small vegetable cutters to make carrots into different shapes for your bowl **–OR - To uniquely display** you can <u>disguise wooden skewers by slipping inside a green onion skin</u>. Place the cut out vegetables in a tall glass or stick the base of the skewer into a Cheese Ball for displaying at the table.

Cheeseball

VEG – (Cauliflower)

Cauliflower is generally boiled or steamed and then garnished with butter or elegantly topped with Swiss or Cheddar (4 oz) grated, melted cheese laden Bechamél Sauce, and breadcrumbs with a dash of Cayenne Pepper and sprinkled with Parmesan Cheese on top.

VEG – (Cauliflower and Asparagus with Cheese Sauce)

Cook Cauliflower and Asparagus per frozen food package directions. Drain and season with Salt and Pepper. Blend together 1/4 cup Vinegar, 1/2 cup Water, 1 Tbsp Margarine/Butter, 1/4 tsp Dry Mustard, 1/2 tsp Salt, 1 Tbsp Lemon Juice, 1/4 tsp Paprika, 1 tsp Sugar and bring to a boil. Remove from the heat and cool. Add in 4 beaten Egg Yolks. Pour into a double boiler and return to the heat. Beating constantly until mixture thickens. Serve over the vegetables listed and sprinkle tops with Paprika.

VEG – (Cauliflower and Mushrooms)

1 medium Cauliflower or frozen cooked per Mushrooms	package directions 1-1/2 cups sliced fresh
2 Tbsp Flour	
2 Tbsp Margarine/Butter melted	1 cup (4 oz) shredded sharp Cheddar Cheese
1 cup Milk	1/4 tsp Salt
1 tsp Dijon Mustard	1 Tbsp minced Parsley
White Pepper	

VEG – (Cauliflower, Broccoli and Carrots)

Can use frozen vegetables and cook per package directions, adding in salt, pepper and butter or can cooked per Canned Green Bean's variation or Vegetable Medley recipe.

VEG – (Cauliflower, Broccoli and Carrots – Vegetable Medley Casserole)

1 Pkg (16 oz) frozen Vegetable Blend of the above listed vegetables

8 oz Sour Cream	4 oz (1 cup) shredded Swiss Cheese
4 oz (1 cup) shredded Cheddar Cheese	8 oz can French Fried Onions
1 (10-3/4 oz) can Cream of Mushroom Soup	1 (4 oz) jar chopped Pimentos

Save 1/2 of the French Fried Onions and 1/2 of the cheese for a topping. Mix all ingredients, other than those listed. Place this in a 9"x13" baking dish. Bake 350°F for 30 minutes. Five minutes before it's done sprinkle on the remaining cheese and onion flakes. **VARIATION:** Use celery soup instead of mushroom soup, or chicken soup. **MICROWAVE:** Cook covered with plastic wrap for 8 minutes then top with the remaining cheese and dry onions. Cook uncovered for an additional 2 minutes until the cheese melts.

Serves 6-8
MENU WEEK #11

VEG – (Cauliflower – Buttered)

Discard the leaves; cut out the woody base and any discolored portion. Cook the cauliflower whole or break into flowerets. Cook in 1" boiling, salted water in a covered pan for 10-12 minutes for flowerets and 20-25 minutes for whole. Drain, season with salt, pepper and margarine. **VARIATION:** Can be served with a Béchamel Sauce, Cheese Sauce or Hollandaise Sauce. **–OR- Grandma's Cauliflower Cheese Bake:** 2 Tbsp Margarine, 6 Saltine Crackers, crushed, 1 (10 oz) package frozen cauliflower, cooked and drained, 4 oz American processed cheese rectangle (cut into 1/2" cubes). Melt the margarine over low heat and add in the cracker crumbs and cook until they are lightly browned. Spray a 1-quart casserole dish with a nonstick cooking spray. Arrange the cooked cauliflower in the dish, top with the cheese, and sprinkle with the cracker crumb mixture. Cover with aluminum foil. Bake 350°F for about 20 minutes or until the cheese is melted. (Serves 2) **HINT: Cauliflower Will Look Whiter if a piece of lemon is added when cooking - OR- add a little milk to the water to keep it whiter. Overcooked cauliflower will be dark, so be careful to cook only until tender.**

VEG – (Cauliflower – Marinated)

Wash and remove green stem leaves. Break the cauliflower heads into small spears. Marinate spears for at least 2 hours, turning occasionally to coat in a mixture of:

2/3 cup Vinegar   2/3 cup Vegetable Oil
1/4 cup Chopped Onions   2 minced Cloves of Garlic,
1 tsp each Sugar, Oregano, Salt & Basil   1/4 tsp Black Pepper

-OR – (Working Mother or New Cook easier to - Marinate in a tart Italian Dressing (see also Salad – Cauliflower Salad – Hot or Cold)   (Extra Recipe)

VEG – (Celery – Celery Sticks)

Cut off the tops and ends of the celery stalks. Cut these into small sticks. Soak several hours in cold water that has a tsp of granulated sugar added to it, which will create additional crispness. By cutting small slits half ways down the center of the stalk will cause the tops to fan out and curl.

VEG – (Chinese Vegetables – Stir-Fried)

Use Large Bag of Frozen and/or fresh Vegetables (California Mixed Corn and Green Beans*)
3 firm ripe Tomatoes (or several cherry tomatoes)   3/4 tsp Salt
8 oz can drained Water Chestnuts   1/4 Pound Mushrooms
2 Green Onions cut into 2" pieces   1 Tbsp Soy Sauce
2 cups Broccoli flowerets   3 Tbsp Peanut or Vegetable Oil
1 Tbsp Sesame Oil   Red Pepper Flakes
*1 (9 oz) each Pkg of Frozen defrosted Green Beans & Corn if CA mix not available

Cut the tomatoes into small wedges. Slice the mushrooms and water chestnuts. Snip the ends of the green beans if fresh. In a Wok or skillet on high heat, add in the oil and stir in the soy sauce and salt. Stir-Fry the broccoli and the beans for three minutes, remove and keep warm or just move to the outside of the wok. Add in the mushrooms, water chestnuts, and tomatoes and Stir-Fry for two minutes. Add in the onions, and stir-fry. Then mix everything together making sure it is all hot. **VARIATION:** Add in corn and cauliflower.   Serves 4

If using fresh, remove outer leaves and stalk of cauliflower, and break into florets then wash. Steam the cauliflower for 15 minutes in a vegetable steamer (if you don't have a steamer, place a metal colander inside a large pot with 1/4 full of water, place cauliflower florets in the colander and cover to steam). Sauté the mushrooms in the butter/margarine over medium heat until tender. Reduce heat to low. Add in the flour, stirring constantly. Gradually add in the milk; cook over medium heat, stirring constantly until mixture is thickened and bubbly. Add in the cheese, mustard, salt and pepper, and stir until the cheese melts. Spoon the mushroom cheese sauce over the drained and salted cauliflower. Sprinkle with minced parsley.

(Extra Recipe)

VEG – (Corn – Corn and Jalapeno Casserole)

1 cup Long Grain Rice, uncooked   1 cup chopped Celery
1 medium green Bell Pepper, chopped   1 to 2 Large Jalapeno Peppers seeded, and
1/2 cup Margarine/Butter melted   chopped
2 (14.5 oz) cans Cream-Style Corn   1-1/2 cups (6 oz) shredded mild Cheddar
1 Tbsp Sugar   Cheese
1 medium Onion, chopped
Optional Garnish: Green Pepper Rings, Cherry Tomatoes, and chopped Parsley.

Cook the rice according to package directions, set aside. Sauté the onion, green pepper, and celery in the melted butter/margarine in a large skillet until the vegetables are tender.   Combine reserved rice and sautéed vegetable mixture into a large bowl. Add in the Jalapeno Peppers, corn, cheese, and sugar; stir well. Spoon the corn mixture into a lightly greased, shallow 2-quart casserole. Bake at 350°F for 40 to 5 minutes or until thoroughly heated.   Garnish if desired.   Serves 8-10

Decided for You Cookbook – 365 Dinners

VEG – (Corn – Corn-off-the Cobb)

You can prepare the same way as "on the cob" then remove the kernels with a sharp knife –OR- You can cut the kernels off prior to cooking and then cook as you would any other whole kernel corn. **HINT: An easier way to cut the corn from the cob is to use a Shoe Horn, perfectly shaped for shearing.**   (Extra Recipe)

VEG – (Corn – Corn-on-the Cobb)

Shuck (remove) the outer leaves (Husks). Pull off all of the corn silks. Cut off any discolored kernels. Break the cob in half if it is too long to fit inside your covered kettle of unsalted, boiling water. Cook the corn in batches if you have a large group for which you are cooking: 1 ear per person in each bath, that way everyone can start eating at one time). Boil for 5 minutes. Drain, butter and salt to taste.

VEG – (Corn – Cream Style)

Place the corn in a saucepan and add salt, pepper and 2 Tbsp Margarine. Cook over low heat on the stove or microwave for 7 minutes. (this can be warmed in a double boiler, and even the oven. NOTE: Cream Style corn burns quickly if the heat is too high and if you don't stir it while warming.

VEG – (Corn – Hominy White or Yellow)

Add salt and pepper to taste. Mix in 2 Tbsp of either bacon grease (from 2 pcs of bacon) or margarine and boil until most of the water has been reduced, boil about 5 minutes.

VEG – (Corn – Mexican Style)

You can add chopped green and bell peppers to your corn –OR- you can purchase Mexican Style canned corn. After warmed add in 2 Tbsp margarine/butter and salt and pepper to taste.

VEG – (Corn – Whole Kernel)

Can be fresh or canned. Warm and add 2 Tbsp margarine/butter and salt and pepper to taste. **VARIATION**: You can add a small amount of evaporated milk to change the flavor. –OR- Drain half of 1 (14.5 oz) can of Whole Kernel Corn's liquid. Beat 4 eggs. Add in 1-1/2 Tbsp melted Butter and 2 cups Milk. Salt and Pepper to taste. Add in 1/2 cup grated Cheddar Cheese. Place half of this into a buttered baking dish and cover with 1/2 cup breadcrumbs, add in the remaining corn mixture, then another 1/2 cup breadcrumbs and bake 350°F for 30-40 minutes.

VEG – (Cucumbers)

Is considered a fruit - Marinate over night 2 sliced Cucumbers with 2 sliced red hot Chiles or Pepper Flakes, 2 cups Rice Vinegar, 2 Tbsp Vegetable Oil and 4 tsp Sugar with Salt and Pepper to taste. **HINT: If desired you can leave green peel on the cucumbers, but you should cut about a 1/2" piece from the end of the cucumber that had the vine attached. Rotate this piece in a circle against the other end of the cucumber where it was removed until extra moisture (froth) is observed. This is the bitterness of the skin being removed from the entire cucumber. Then slice as directed. Marinate in Italian Dressing with chopped Onions.**

VEG – (Eggplant – Eggplant Breaded)

Peel and slice this into 1/8" slices. Press the slices between paper toweling to squeeze out excess water. Dip the slices in beaten eggs and then roll in an equal combination of breadcrumbs and Parmesan Cheese. Place 3 Tbsp of vegetable oil, or you can use margarine/butter, in a skillet and fry the slices in single layers until golden brown.

VEG – (Eggplant in Curry-Coconut Sauce – Vegetarian Dish)

1/2 cup Ghee **(see below recipe)**	1 chopped Yellow Onion
1 Tbsp Curry Powder	1 cup unsalted Cashews, coarsely
–OR- MAKE YOUR OWN see below	chopped
1/2 Lemon, juiced	2 cups unsweetened Coconut Milk
1/2 cup shredded Coconut	8 small Eggplants
2 cups Vegetable Broth	1 dried Red Hot Chile and Salt
1/2 Ground Cinnamon (can use 1 fresh stick)	

Heat 1/4 cup of the Ghee in a large pot over medium heat, add in the onions, and sprinkle these with the curry powder. Cook and stir for a few minutes until the onions are soft. Add in the cashews, coconut, coconut milk and vegetable broth. Bring to a simmer and cook for 15 to 20 minutes. Prepare the eggplant by cutting them into large chunks. Heat another 1/4 cup of Ghee in a deep skillet and add in the eggplant. Cook and stir until the eggplant gets browned and sticky to touch. Puree the cooked coconut sauce with a handheld blender until reasonably smooth. Pour the sauce over the cooked eggplant and toss in the cinnamon and chile. Season with salt to taste and simmer for an additional 15 minutes until sauce is thick. **Microwave the lemon for 10 seconds** (will help extract the juices), then top with a squeeze of the lemon juice to brighten the flavor, and serve with steamed rice or flat or Pita bread.   Serves 4

MENU WEEK#46

Ghee – (East Indian Clarified Butter)
Make in advance, if possible.

1 Pound Unsalted Butter - **HINT: <u>If you preheat your pot then place in your butter to melt it will do so quicker.</u>** Place the butter into a heavy saucepan over moderate heat, swirl the pot or the butter with a fork so it melts slowly and doesn't burn or sizzle. Once melted, raise the heat a little and bring the butter to a boil. When the surface is covered with foam, stir the butter gently and reduce the heat to the lowest possible setting. Gently simmer, uncovered, for 45 minutes (do not stir any more) until the milk solids in the bottom of the pan have turned golden brown and the top area is transparent. Place several layers of cheesecloth in a colander and strain the melted butter until it is perfectly clear and smells nutty. Pour into a clean glass jar and seal tightly.   Yields 1-1/2 cups

Curry Powder – (East Indian)
MAKE YOUR OWN – (Ingredients not on grocery list)

2 Tbsp Coriander Seeds	1 Tbsp Cumin Seeds
1 tsp Fennel Seeds	1/2 tsp Whole Cloves
1/2 tsp Mustard Seeds	1 Tbsp Cardamom Seeds
1 Tbsp Whole Black Peppercorns	1 Tbsp Tumeric
2 Dried Red Hot Chiles broken into pieces with seeds discarded	

Place all the spices, except the Tumeric, and the chiles in a small dry skillet over medium-low heat, shaking the pan often to prevent them from burning. Toast them for 2-3 minutes. They will smell great and aromatic. In a clean grinder, grind the toasted spices together into a fine powder. Add in the Tumeric and give it another quick grind to combine. Spice blend is now ready to use, or store in a clean sealed jar for as long as one month.   Yields 1/2 cup

Decided for You Cookbook – 365 Dinners

VEG – (Garlic)

Replacement for one clove of Garlic is 1 tsp of Garlic Salt.

VEG – (Mixed Vegetables)

Boil with salt and pepper per package directions or until fork tender. Salt and Pepper to taste. Stir in 2-3 Tablespoons of Margarine/Butter

VEG – (Mixed Vegetables – Molded)

2 Large fresh Yellow Squash cut in thin rounds and *blanched (dropped in boiling water for a   minute, then removed)
1/4 cup frozen Green Peas (or the whole package if you like)
2 medium Zucchini cut in thin rounds and blanched*)

1 can Green Beans	2 medium Carrots, cut in wide Julienne strips
1 cup Brussels Sprouts, blanched*	6 Cabbage leaves, blanched*
Softened Margarine/Butter	1-1/2 cups cooked mashed Potatoes
1/4 cup Butter melted	Salt and Pepper

All vegetables should be seasoned after they are cooked. Coat a baking mold generously with margarine. Place a row of the green peas around the outside bottom edge of the mold. Place a row of overlapping slices of the yellow squash on the bottom of the mold. Place a row of overlapping zucchini slices next to the squash to form an inner circle. Repeat the squash and zucchini until the bottom of the mold is covered. Alternate a green bean and a carrot strip standing upright against the side of the mold. Cover the sides and bottom with a layer of the mashed potatoes. Cover the potatoes with the cabbage leaves. Place an outer circle of Brussels sprouts over the cabbage. Make an inner circle with the cauliflower. Repeat the circles of squash, zucchini, sprouts and cauliflower until the mold is full. Pour melted butter over the vegetables and cover with cabbage leaves. Add a final layer of mashed potatoes. Bake at 350°F for 20 minutes. Remove from the oven and place a serving dish on top of the mold and reverse the plate and mold which will cause the vegetables to come out of the mold on to the serving plate. Garnish with half slices of cherry tomatoes or other garnish you desire. *Blanched = dropped into boiling water and cooked for ~30 seconds, removed and drained.   (Extra Recipe)

VEG – (Mixed Vegetables – Stir Fry)

1 (10-3/4 oz) can of Beef Broth	1 Tbsp Cornstarch
1 Tbsp Soy Sauce	3 Tbsp Vegetable Oil
1 minced clove Garlic	4 diced Green Onions
1 cup Broccoli cuts (can be defrosted, frozen	1 (8 oz) can Bamboo Shoots, drained
1 cup miniature Carrots cut in rounds	

Combine the broth, cornstarch, and soy sauce. In a hot skillet or work, add 3 Tbsp of the Vegetable Oil and stir in the minced garlic. Stir, add in the onions and the carrots. Stirring for and additional one minute. Add in the Bamboo Shoots and broccoli and cook for another two minutes. Stir well and serve.

HINT: You can easily slice mushrooms evenly with an egg slicer. However - do not peel, do not soak and do not overcook mushrooms. HINT: The quickest way to clean a mushroom is to wipe it with a damp cloth. Don't wash or scrub them. The soil in which mushrooms are grown is sterilized properly so you need not act like they are raised in untreated manure, not so. If you mush wash them, just rinse them and drain or dry them just prior to using, otherwise, the extra moisture will cause them to mold.

VEG – (Mushrooms – Garlic Buttered Mushrooms)

Melt 3-4 Tbsp Margarine in a skillet. Add in the washed, drained mushrooms (whole or sliced). Sprinkle with salt and pepper and garlic powder. Cover and cook 5-10 minutes for sliced, 10-12 minutes if whole; stirring occasionally. **NOTE: 5 cups sliced, fresh mushrooms or 18 to 20 medium-size Whole = 1 Pound of fresh Mushrooms.**

VEG – (Mushrooms – Marinated Mushrooms)

Can be purchased or **MAKE YOUR OWN**

2 cups Button Mushrooms	1 cup Tarragon or Cider Vinegar
1/2 cup finely minced onion	2 Tbsp Olive Oil
1 clove Garlic, minced	1/4 tsp Celery Seed
1/4 tsp granulated Sugar	1/4 tsp Ground Pepper, 1 Tbsp Salt

Sterilize a large glass jar and lid by washing in your dishwasher. Wash and dry the mushrooms; do not peel or slice. Pack the mushrooms into your clean jar. Mix all of the remaining ingredients and pour into the jar. Shake lightly to coat. Refrigerate for at least 24 hours. Serve as a Hors d' Oeuvres with toothpicks or as part of an Antipasto Tray.   Serves 8

   –OR-

VEG – (Mushrooms – Quickie Marinated Recipe)

1 Pound small whole Mushroom caps (remove stems, chop into small pieces)

3/4 cup Vegetable Oil	3/4 cup Red Wine Vinegar
1/4 cup finely chopped Onion	1/4 cup finely chopped Parsley
2 cloves Garlic, crushed and minced	

Wash the mushrooms, dry on paper toweling. Cut up per above directions. Prepare marinade in a large flat bowl or sealable plastic bag. Place in ingredients and coat the mushrooms. Refrigeration, covered for about 1-1/2 hours and serve using a slotted spoon.   Serves 6-8

VEG – (Mushrooms – Stuffed Mushrooms)

1 Pound of Button Mushrooms ~12 each	2 Tbsp Margarine or Butter
1/2 chopped small Onion	4 cloves chopped Garlic
1 cup French Breadcrumbs	1 cup grated Parmesan Cheese or Cheddar
1/2 tsp Lemon Juice	1 small jar (8 oz) Marinated Artichokes*

Drain the artichokes and cut into tiny pieces. Wash and dry the Mushrooms. Remove the stems from the mushrooms and chop up into tiny pieces. Melt the margarine in a skillet and sauté the onions, garlic and the stems. Mix together the breadcrumbs, the cheese, the artichoke hearts, and the lemon juice. Stuff this mixture into the mushroom tops and place them side-by-side, stuffed side up, into a square 9" x 13" baking dish. Cover with aluminum foil and bake in a 350°F oven for 10 minutes. Remove the foil, and if you want them to be browned; then broil (500°F) for an additional 3 minutes. **VARIATION:** Replace half of these with *Chopped Miniature Smokie Links. **OTHER CHOICES:** Vienna Sausage, Salami, Pepperoni, Linguica, choice of cheese, Ketchup or Spaghetti Sauce (mix 1/4 cup Stuffing Mix, water, 1 tsp Oregano, 1 tsp garlic powder (375°F 20 minutes).

   -OR- any other **VARIATION** of the following on the next page.

VEG – (Mushrooms – Stuffed Mushroom <u>Variations</u>)

1 Pound of Button Mushrooms ~12 each

1 can (7 oz) drained Crab Meat	2 Tbsp Mayonnaise
2 Tbsp chopped Onion	1 tsp Lemon Juice
1/2 cup Breadcrumbs	2 Tbsp Margarine or Butter

Wash and dry the Mushrooms. Remove the stems from the mushrooms and chop up into tiny pieces. Melt the margarine in a skillet and sauté the onions, and the stems. Mix together the breadcrumbs, crab meat, mayonnaise, onion and the lemon juice. Stuff this mixture into the mushroom tops and place them side-by-side, stuffed side up, into a square 9" x 13" baking dish. Bake uncovered for 15 minutes at 350°F.

-OR-

Wash and dry the Mushrooms. Remove the stems from the mushrooms and chop up into tiny pieces. Melt the margarine in a skillet and sauté the onions, and the stems with 1/2 pound of "Ground Beef" or "Ground Pork Sausage". Drain off the fats and mix with shredded cheese of your choice. Stuff this mixture inside the mushroom crowns (tops). Place under a broiler (500°F) for 3 minutes or until the cheese bubbles. Serve hot.

-OR-

using the same sequence **use these ingredients to stuff** 1 Pound of Button Mushrooms ~12 each

– Broil or Bake

1/2 cup finely chopped Onion	1 Pkg Cream Cheese
1/4 cup dry Breadcrumbs	1/2 cup cooked Bacon

-OR-

1 Pkg (3 oz) Cream Cheese	1 can (7 oz) drained, minced Clams
1 Tbsp minced Parsley	1/2 tsp Garlic Powder
1/4 cup crushed French Fried Onions	

-OR-

2 Tbsp Butter/Margarine	1/3 cup chopped cooked Onion
1/2 cup chopped Walnuts	1 tsp Lemon Juice
1/8 tsp Salt	1/4 cup chopped Salami

-OR-

1/4 cup chopped Green Bell Peppers	1/4 cup chopped Celery
3 Tbsp Margarine/Butter	1 Pkg (3 oz) Cream Cheese
1 cup Breadcrumbs	1 tsp Lemon Juice

VEG – (Mustard Greens – Braised Mustard Greens)

3 bunches Mustard Greens, remove thick center veins, trim, chop and wash

4 slices Bacon, chopped	2 Tbsp White Vinegar
2 tsp Sugar (granulated)	Salt to Taste
2 cups Chicken Broth	

In a large skillet over medium high heat, brown bacon and render its fat. Add chopped greens to the pan in batches into the rendered fat, and turn until they wilt, then add more greens. When all of the greens are in the pan, add the vinegar and cook a minute (this will remove any bitterness). Season greens with sugar and salt. Add the chicken broth to the pan and cover. Reduce the heat to medium low and simmer greens 15 to 20 minutes before serving.   8 Servings

VEG – (Okra)

Wash thoroughly; cut off stem ends – Prepare per recipes.

Okra – Boiled Okra

Wash thoroughly one pound of Okra; cut off the stems. Cook the whole Okra 10-35 minutes in 1" boiling, salted water in a covered saucepan. Drain well in a colander. Return to serving dish and season with salt, pepper, and 2 Tbsp margarine and a little lemon juice or serve with Hollandaise Sauce.   (Extra Recipe)

Okra – Fried Okra

Wash the Okra and cut off the stems. Then cut the pods into coins. Dip in beaten egg and roll in equal amounts of Flour and Corn Meal or Cracker Meal and Salt and Pepper. Fry for 4-6 minutes in 1/2" hot Vegetable Oil until golden brown, be sure to turn Okra over to cook on all sides. **VARIATION:** Cut the Okra lengthwise, then in half. Sprinkle on Hot Red Pepper Sauce and 1/8 tsp Cayenne Pepper and 1 tsp Garlic Powder. Let the Okra and Pepper Sauce marinate at least 10 minutes.   Beat 2 eggs with 1 Tbsp Water and dip in the Okra and then roll in the cornmeal/flour mixture and fry until golden brown.

VEG – (Onions)

Small boiling onions or sliced onions, 2 Tbsp Butter/Oil, 2 Tbsp Flour, 1/4 tsp Salt, 1/4 tsp White Pepper, 1 cup Milk, 1/4 cup grated Parmigiano-Reggiano Cheese, fresh chopped Parsley, Seasoned Breadcrumbs. Place onions in a microwave bowl and tightly seal with plastic wrap. Cook on high 5 minutes/Lb. Set aside and prepare the batter of butter, flour, salt and pepper. Microwave on high for 30 seconds to melt the butter. Whisk in the milk. Microwave on high for 2 minutes. Whisk well. Microwave another 2-3 minutes to thicken. Stir into the cooked onions, the cheese and parsley. Top with the breadcrumbs and brown the top under the broiler.

HINT: Less tears if you place your onion in the freezer for 5 minutes before cutting. Also, leave the root end on until last then cut it off; helps delay the tears.   One medium Onion = 1 cup chopped.

VEG – (Onions – French Fried)

Yellow Onions – Sliced   Eggs (quantity per batter amount used)
Pancake or Waffle Batter (leave thick by leaving out a little water when mixing in the eggs)

HINT: Peeling onions under running water will keep your eyes from tearing. If your eyes are weepy, go outside and look at something GREEN, which will clear up the problem quickly. Slice the onion into thick slices and separate into rings and cover with salted water. Let stand in the water or milk at least 30 minutes; remove and drain on paper toweling. Prepare a medium thick pancake batter, using a mix or your favorite recipe. Dip the rings into **flour**, into the **batter** and **fry** in hot vegetable oil at 375°F or until golden brown. Drain and season to taste.

VEG – (Onion Rings Texas Style – Variation)

1/2 Pound Onions, 1 Egg White, beaten stiff, 1/3 cup Milk, 1/2 tsp Salt, 1/8 tsp Pepper, 3/4 cup Breadcrumbs – Flour for dipping. Combine the stiff egg whites and milk together. Dip the onion rings into flour then into the breadcrumbs. Place these into a skillet with at least 1/2" hot Vegetable Oil and fry until browned. They will float when cooked inside. Drain on paper toweling, salt and pepper to taste.
                                                                                   (Extra Recipe)

VEG – (Peas)

If fresh, shell and wash – Cook per recipes

VEG – (Peas and Carrots)

I prefer the canned version of these and just bring to a rolling boil. Salt and Pepper to taste and add in 2-3 Tablespoons of Margarine/Butter.

VEG – (Peas – Black-Eyed)

Place the peas into a saucepan. Add salt and pepper to taste. Add in 2 Tbsp Bacon drippings (grease) and boil 2 pieces of Bacon in the beans until the beans are tender for 10 – 20 minutes. Serve medium hot. Salt and Pepper to taste.

VEG – (Peas – Canned Creamed)

Cook in a saucepan with 2 Tbsp Margarine, salt and pepper. After turning off the heat, add in 1/4 cup Evaporated Milk. **VARIATION:** Peas are good with a white or Béchamel Sauce –**OR** – Sauté onions, then add frozen peas allowing their water to evaporate and moisten the peas. When they are heated through, add 1 cup Ricotta Cheese and 1/4 cup chopped parsley and smash these together with a potato masher. Add lemon zest, salt and pepper and serve when warmed.

VEG – (Peas – Fresh)

Wash and shell the peas from the pods. Snap the end off and bring your finger down the lengthwise of the pod causing the peas to come out and fall into a bowl. Cook the peas 10-25 minutes in 1" of boiling, salted water in a covered saucepan. Drain, season with salt, pepper. Mix in 2 Tbsp Margarine.   (Extra Recipe)

VEG – (Peas – Peas and Mushrooms)

Sauté salted and garlic powdered mushrooms and chopped onion in 1/2 stick of margarine. Cook the steamed rice. Pour entire can of peas into the rice and stir until liquid is absorbed. Add in the mushrooms. You can add a "White Sauce (see PAS Noodles with White Sauce recipe), if desired.

VEG – (Potatoes – Au Gratin Potatoes)

Peel and slice cold boiled potatoes (or peeled baked potatoes), mix with salt and pepper to taste. Butter the inside of a 9" x 13" casserole dish. Make a Cheese Sauce (see recipe **SAUCE – (Cheese Sauce) –OR** – (mix the following and use as a sauce)

1 can Cheddar Cheese Soup diluted with 2 cans of Half and Half Milk	1 can Cream of Mushroom Soup 2 Tbsp Onion Flakes
1 cup grated Sharp Cheddar Cheese or mix with Parmesan Cheese	

Place a layer of the **seasoned** potatoes in the dish and then spoon on the cheese sauce followed by another layer of each. Sprinkle additional grated cheddar cheese on top and bake at 300°F for 30 minutes. (If you use raw potatoes, then it must be cooked covered for about 1 hour or until fork tender).

VEG – (Potatoes – Baked Potatoes)

Wash the outside of Russet Baking Potatoes and dry off with a paper towel. Cut off any eyes or discoloration. Lightly oil the outside the potato skin with vegetable oil or melted butter if you want a crisp skin. If you want a softer skin, then wrap each potato in aluminum foil. Place the potatoes on a baking sheet and bake in a 350°F - 400°F oven for one hour for large and 40-45 minutes for medium ones (Microwave uncovered for 6-7 minutes or until fork tender). When you remove these from the oven, put a kitchen towel on top of a work surface. Before you remove the foil, throw the potato down hard against the top of the solid work surface like you would throw a ball against a wall. This causes the inside of the potato to break up and makes for a softer fuller taste to your baked potato when cut. Make a slit down the middle of the potato and squash the two ends back toward the center to make it pop open so you can add any or all of the following: Butter, Sour Cream, Chives, or chopped Green Onions, Salt and Pepper to taste. **VARIATION:** After oiling the outside of the potatoes roll in a recipe of Shake and Bake coating (see recipe) before cooking. –OR- Cut the potatoes into thin slices, but not all the way through. Sprinkle tops with melted butter, salt, parsley, chives. Microwave 10 minutes. Let rest 5 minutes. Sprinkle with grated cheese and microwave another 4-6 minutes. **Note: If you don't own a microwave, a baked potato can be re-warmed in the oven if you first dip it in water, wrap in foil, and bake in a 350°F for 20 minutes.**

VEG – (Potatoes – Boiled)

Wash the outside of Russet, New Red, or Golden Yukon Potatoes and dry off with a paper towel. Cut off any eyes or discoloration. These can be boiled with the skins on (Jacket Potatoes) or they can be peeled and cut into quarters then boiled until fork tender. Follow any other recipe of choice for seasoning and other ingredients. **HINT: <u>One Pound of Potatoes = 3 medium-size Whole or 2 cups cooked and mashed or 3-3/4 cups sliced. You can also peel and cut these up in advance as long as you cover with water while waiting to begin cooking. If not thoroughly covered with water the surface potatoes will turn black.</u>**

VEG – (Potatoes – Canned Potatoes)

2 cans (15 oz) of either whole or sliced Potatoes. Drain off the water and rinse the potatoes in clean water, drain. Place 3 Tbsp Vegetable Oil in a baking dish or a skillet and add in the potatoes and toss to coat with the oil. Sprinkle tops with salt and pepper to taste and a generous sprinkling of Garlic Powder. Cover and cook over medium heat for 10 minutes. Turn the potatoes over and season the other side. Leave skillet uncovered so the potatoes will slightly brown after an additional 10 minutes. If you prefer you can cook these uncovered in a 325°F oven for 20-30 minutes. **VARIATION: Sprinkle on 1 recipe dry Onion Soup Mix before cooking –OR- After browning potatoes, mix in 1/4 cup grated Parmesan Cheese with 1 Tbsp dried Parsley.**

VEG – (Potatoes – Cheddar Mushroom Stuffed Potatoes)

6 Large Russet Potatoes	2/3 cup Whipping Cream
1/4 cup chopped fresh mushrooms	1/2 – 1 tsp Garlic Salt
1/2 tsp Dried Basil	1/2 tsp dried Oregano
4 Bacon strips, cooked and crumbled, divided	
1 cup (4 oz) shredded sharp Cheddar Cheese, divided	

Bake the potatoes at 375°F for 1 hour or until tender. When cool enough to handle, cut a thin slice off the top of each potato and discard. Scoop out the pulp, leaving a 1/4 inch shell set shells aside. Place pulp in a mixing bowl; add cream and mash. Stir in 3/4 cup cheese, mushrooms, garlic salt, basil and oregano. Set aside 2 Tbsp Bacon; stir remaining bacon into the potato mixture. Spoon into the potato shells. Top with the remaining cheese and bacon. Microwave, uncovered on high for 5-8 minutes or bake, uncovered, at 375°F for 25-30 minutes or until potatoes are heated through   (Yield 6 servings)

VEG – (Potatoes – Chili Cheese Fries)

Bake frozen French fries per package directions –OR- fry in hot oil. Warm 1 can Chili with no Beans. Place fries in a small bowl and ladle on the warmed chili sauce and top with grated Cheddar Cheese, serve.

VEG – (Potatoes – Creamed Cheese Potatoes)

Boil the unpeeled potatoes in water until fork tender. Remove and cool so you can grate these. Stir into the grated potatoes 1/4 cup chopped green onions, 1 container (8 oz) Sour Cream. Place the mixture into a baking dish and sprinkle the top of the casserole with 1/2 cup grated Cheddar Cheese. Let this mixture rest for 1/2 hour if possible for the flavors to meld together. Bake uncovered in a 350°F oven for 25 minutes. You can top with additional cheese if available.

VEG – (Potatoes – Fingers Roasted)

Wash your small finger sized potatoes (fingerlings about 3" long x 1-1/2"to 2" thick) and allow them to dry. Spread these on top of your baking pan. Smash with the flat part of your large knife 5 or 6 cloves of garlic, this will crush these allowing the flavor to flow out of them. Scatter the crushed garlic over the top of the potatoes. Cover all lightly with extra-virgin Olive Oil and salt and pepper. Roast these at 500°F for about 20 minutes.   (Extra Recipe)

VEG – (Potatoes – French Fried Potatoes)

Purchase frozen or **MAKE YOUR OWN.** Peel and cut the potatoes into French fry slices. Let soak in cold water for 15 minutes to improve the crispness. Drain on paper toweling. Cook these in a skillet filled about 1/2" to 1 inch of hot vegetable oil until golden brown. Drain on paper toweling and Salt to taste. – **OR** – **Oven Steak Fries** – Scrub potatoes with a scouring pad or stiff brush, leaving skins on, and dry. In a plastic bag mix together 1/4 cup grated Parmesan Cheese, 1/2 tsp Garlic Salt, 1/4 tsp Paprika, 1/8 tsp Onion Powder. Cut each potato into slices and brush the surface with melted margarine and drop these into your seasoning bag and toss to coat on all sides. Place these potatoes on a greased baking sheet (Teflon coated preferred). Bake uncovered at 400°F approximate 30-40 minutes or until golden brown and tender. **HINT:** <u>French Fries will turn a golden brown if you add a pinch of granulated sugar to the frying oils.</u> –**OR**- per Frozen Fries directions on the package.

VEG – (Potatoes – Fried Potatoes)

Peel, dice or cut potatoes in French fries, rounds small chunks. Salt and pepper to taste. Fry in bacon grease or Vegetable Oil until fork tender, stirring occasionally. Drain any fats off before serving.

VEG – (Potatoes – Hash Brown Potatoes)

Peel the potatoes, (use the grater which has large holes in it) grate. You can drop these into cold water if you are grating a lot, cause they will discolor otherwise. Drain and salt. Place 2 or 3 Tbsp of vegetable oil on a griddle or in a skillet. Pile up individual size portions of the potatoes and fry on both sides until golden brown. Or you can fry the whole pan full of the hash brown at one time. **VARIATION**: You can grate or slice cold, boiled potatoes and refry into hash browns if desired. – **OR** – 1 Pkg (32 oz) frozen Hash Browns, 1 can Cream of Potato Soup, 1 can Cream of Onion Soup, 8 oz Sour Cream. Place frozen has browns in a lightly greased 9"x13" baking dish. Mix the sour cream and soups and pour over the potatoes. Bake 350°F for 1 hour. – **OR** – **Cheesy Potatoes**: Place 1 Pkg (32 oz) frozen Hash Browns in a 9"x13" baking dish. Top with 2 cups grated Swiss and Cheddar Cheese or Processed Cheese. Pour over this: 1 pint Whipping Cream and 1/2 cup melted butter/margarine and bake 1 hour at 350°F. **O'Brien** – Add diced bell peppers, onion and/or breadcrumbs.

VEG – (Potatoes – Jacket Potatoes)

Jacket Potatoes means leave the skins on. Wash the potatoes, scrubbing with a stiff brush or scouring pad. Place these in a large kettle of boiling, salted water covering an above the potatoes. Boil until fork tender. Drain. Cut open and smash the inside of the potatoes up a little with your fork. Spoon on the top some heated bacon grease, (if you don't save bacon drippings, cook 2 pieces of bacon in a skillet and then pour off the drippings/fats or melted butter to be used with the potatoes, but butter isn't as tasty Believe Me!) Salt and pepper to taste, mash with your fork and spoon over the drippings or butter. You can eat the entire potato.

VEG – (Potatoes – Make Ahead Potatoes)

6-8 medium Potatoes	1 (8 oz) Sour Cream
4 Tbsp Margarine or Butter	Garlic Salt and Pepper to taste
Aluminum Foil	

Peel and cut potatoes into chunks. Boil these in salted water until fork tender. Drain and mash well. Mix in the remaining ingredients. Cover and refrigerate up to 2 days. When ready to serve, place the potatoes in a buttered baking dish. Cover with foil and bake 45 – 60 minutes. These can also be re-warmed in a microwave for 8-10 minutes. **HINT:** <u>If you have a pot of potatoes that is about to boil over the top, i.e., "drop a large mouthed spoon into the pot and slightly reduce the heat source. This will keep them from bubbling over again.</u>

(Extra Recipe)

VEG – (Potatoes – Mashed Potatoes)

Peel 6 – 8 medium potatoes and cut up into eighths and place in a saucepan with water about 1 inch above the potatoes. Boil until fork tender; drain. Place the potatoes back into the pot, add in salt and pepper to taste, 1/3 cup margarine/ butter, 1/2 can (16 oz) Evaporated Milk and mash until all lumps are gone.
VARIATION: Cook 1/2 lb carrots (3 or 4) and 1/2 lb Potatoes. Mash these together for color variations.
HINT: __Whiter Potatoes – Extra whiteness can be obtained by adding 1 tsp Vinegar to the boiling water. ALSO, You can put mashed potatoes in a pastry bag or a plastic bag with the corner cut and pipe the potatoes around your meat or vegetable dish. You can also peel and cut these up in advance as long as you cover with water while waiting to begin cooking. If not thoroughly covered with water the surface potatoes will turn black.__

VEG – (Potatoes – Mashed Potatoes with Blue Cheese)

2 lbs Large Russet/Idaho Potatoes (about 6)
1 medium Onion, chopped   1/2 cup Sour Cream
1 tsp Dried Thyme   1/2 cup Crumbled Blue Cheese

Peel and cut up the potatoes into large chunks. In a saucepan over medium heat, bring potatoes and onion in enough salted water to cover to a boil. Cook 15 minutes or until potatoes are tender, pierce with fork to test. Drain. Heat broiler in oven. Using a potato masher or hand mixer, mash potatoes and onion until smooth. Stir in remaining ingredients and transfer to a 1-quart oven-proof dish. Broil 5 minutes or until golden brown. Makes 4 servings. (Alternate ways to perk up mashed potatoes: add Buttermilk and chopped Leeks with Cheddar Cheese -or- Crème Fraîche, roasted Garlic and Cream Cheese -or- Ricotta Cheese and Chopped Shallots and Swiss Cheese -or- Yogurt and chopped Chives and Parmesan Cheese – or Blue Cheese and Bacon.

VEG – (Potatoes – Mashed Potatoes with Garlic)

Cutting the top 1/4 off of a **large garlic head** containing multiple cloves (at least 3-5 cloves of Garlic). Place this large garlic group inside a piece of aluminum foil, drizzle tops with **3 Tbsp of Olive Oil**. Fold the foil into a sealed pouch. Place the pouch on a baking pie plate or dish and bake at 450°F for 30-40 minutes or until butter-like tender. Unwrap and squeeze out the cooked cloves into a small bowl. Add in **1/3 cup melted margarine** and mash the garlic with a fork until blended smoothly with the margarine, keep it warm. When you have completed the mashed potatoes, stir this into the hot mashed potatoes **(can (continued Mashed Potatoes w/Garlic) be made in advance and stored in a sealable container).** **HINT:** Substitute 1 tsp Garlic Salt for the Garlic Clove). Peel **6 – 8 medium potatoes** and cut up into eighths and place in a saucepan with water about 1 inch above the potatoes. Boil until fork tender; drain. Place the potatoes back into the pot, add in **salt and pepper to taste, 1/3 cup margarine/ butter, 1/2 can (16 oz) Evaporated Milk or heavy Whipping Cream** and mash until all lumps are gone. Stir in the warmed garlic and **WAH-LAH! Vampire's Look Out!**

     -OR- Add to the mashed potatoes, the roasted garlic cloves with a dash of Nutmeg

VEG – (Potatoes – Mashed Potatoes with Sour Cream and Chives)

3 Pounds Potatoes   3/4 cup Sour Cream
1/4 cup Evaporated Milk   1/4 cup Margarine/Butter softened
1 Tbsp each chopped Chives and Chopped Parsley   1 tsp Salt
1/4 tsp Pepper

Place enough water in a pan to cover the peeled, cut up potatoes. Add a little salt to the water and boil them until fork tender about 12 minutes, drain the water. Return the potatoes to the pot. Using a hand masher or electric mixer mash the potatoes until smooth. Stir in the sour cream, milk, softened butter, chives, parsley, salt and pepper until combined. Leftovers make a great mashed potato salad base.   Serves 8-12

Decided for You Cookbook – 365 Dinners

VEG – (Potatoes – Mashed Potatoes with Sweet Carrots)

Follow each individual recipe and then mix together after draining the carrots.

VEG – (Potatoes – Mud Cooked Baked Potatoes)

When you go camping take along 4 Large Russet Potatoes and when your fire has been reduced to glowing red-hot coals, have the kids dig up enough fresh dirt in a bucket to cover the potatoes well. Add in some water to the dirt and let the kids squish it until it is smooth mud. Pierce each potato a few times with a fork and then prepare to encase them in a thick protective shell of sticky mud. If you are squeamish about packing the dirt around the potatoes then cover with aluminum foil first and re-poke the holes in it, then mud-cover these about half–inch to one inch in thickness. Let the outside dry out a little. Then with tongs drop them inside the coals (mark the area with something that won't burn). In an hour, remove the potatoes with those tongs and as soon as they have cooled enough to handle, tap them gently against a rock or a log and the mud will crack off leaving a clean baked potato.   **See Author's Special Thoughts in PORK Section**

VEG – (Potatoes – New Red Potatoes)

10-12 New Red Potatoes	1 tsp Rosemary
1/2 cup Olive Oil	1/4 tsp Oregano
1/2 tsp Pepper	2 cloves Garlic, minced
Salt to Taste	1/2 cup grated Parmesan Cheese
4 sprigs Parsley	

Cut the potatoes into quarters or like French Fries. Place in a 9" x 13" baking dish and pour in the olive oil and toss the potatoes to coat all sides. Sprinkle in all the seasonings and toss again. Bake at 375°F for 30 to 35 minutes (will take less time if cut like French Fries). Stir occasionally to be sure they are not sticking to the bottom of your dish. Five minutes before done, sprinkle with the Parmesan Cheese and return to the oven until the cheese is melted.   Serves 4-6

VEG – (Potatoes – New Red Potato Casserole)

After cutting up the New Red Potatoes, mix together the following 1/4 cup Margarine, 1 can Cream of Chicken Soup, 1/3 cup chopped Green Onions, 1 Pint Sour Cream. Pour over the potatoes, which are in the baking dish. Top with 1 cup crushed Corn Flakes mixed with 2 Tbsp Margarine. Bake 350°F for 45 minutes (325°F if using Glass). – **OR** – Cook new red potatoes per above recipe upon removing from the oven, stir in a can of drained peas. Make a White or Béchamel Sauce and mix with the potatoes and the peas and return it to the oven for another 5-8 minutes. – **OR – Creole Potatoes** - Sauté chopped onions and 1 chopped Bell Pepper in melted margarine in a skillet, stir into the potatoes, 2 Tbsp Creole Seasoning, 1 Tbsp salt, 1 stick Margarine (1/4 cup), and 1 Tbsp Crab Boil Spice concentrate. Cover and simmer 30 minutes or until potatoes are fork tender, stirring occasionally.

VEG – (Potatoes, Onions and Carrots)

Peel potatoes and slice into thin rounds. Place a 1/4 cup vegetable oil in a skillet and lightly brown sliced onions until they are limp. Add in the sliced potatoes and fry on both sides. Add in a can of drained carrots and salt and pepper to taste. Add in 2 Tablespoons of margarine/butter and heat until all ingredients are hot.

VEG – (Potatoes – Oven Fried Dinner Fries)

Frozen Fries or 4 Large Potatoes (~2 Lbs)   1/4 cup extra Virgin Olive Oil
1 Tbsp chopped fresh Rosemary   1 tsp Salt
1/4 tsp Red Pepper Flakes

Peel, and cut into 1/2" wedges or long dinner fry slices. Heat the oven to 500°F. In a large bowl, toss the potato wedges, olive oil, chopped rosemary, salt and red pepper flakes until evenly coated. Spread coated potato mixture in a single layer on a large greased baking sheet. Roast for 15 minutes turning once, or until the potatoes are tender and golden brown. Season with salt and pepper to taste. Serves 6   – OR - Toss potato wedges with 3 Tbsp Olive Oil, sprinkle on 1 tsp dried Italian Seasoning. Roast in a single layer for 15 minutes, turning once. Add salt and pepper to taste and then sprinkle on top 1/2 to 1 cup grated Parmigano-Romano Cheese or Cheddar Cheese and roast for another 10 minutes.

VEG – (Potatoes – Parisienne Potatoes)

Peel and slice 3 cups of Potatoes and with a Melon Cutter, cut balls out of the potatoes and drop these into cold water until you are ready to use. Drain the balls on paper toweling. Melt 1/4 cup (1 stick) margarine in a skillet. Cook the balls until golden brown. **VARIATION:** Add in 1/2 cup Bacon Bits when frying.

VEG – (Potatoes – Parmesan Au Gratin)

5 Tbsp Butter/Margarine at room temp   4 medium Potatoes
1 clove Garlic, cut in half   Salt and Pepper to taste
1/4 cup Evaporated Milk   1/2 cup Grated Parmesan Cheese
1 Large Onion, chopped
2 eggs, separated

Cook the potatoes boiling, salted water until fork tender, drain. In a skillet melt 1 Tbsp of the butter and cook the onion and garlic until tender. Add garlic, onions and butter, including the balance of the 2 Tbsp of butter to the potatoes. With an electric mixer whip the potatoes. Beat the egg yolks into the potatoes, beat the egg whites until stiff but not dry and fold into the potatoes. Generously grease a casserole, and spoon in the potato mixture. Sprinkle the top with the Parmesan Cheese. Bake, uncovered, for 15 to 20 minutes in a preheated 350°F. Place under a broiler for a few minutes to crisp the tops.   Serves 6-8

VEG – (Potatoes – Parsley Potatoes)

Follow a baked or mashed potato recipe and top or stir in a mixture of parsley and margarine just before serving –OR- Mix 2 cloves minced Garlic, 2 Tbsp chopped Parsley, 4 Tbsp Extra–Virgin Olive Oil and 1 tsp Balsamic Vinegar and drizzle over baked or mix into mashed.

VEG – (Potatoes – Potato Casserole Suprema)

6-8 medium baking Potatoes, peeled and quartered
2/3 cup Milk (can be Evaporated Milk)   1/2 cup softened Margarine or Butter
1 – 2 tsp Salt and 1/4 tsp Pepper   1-1/2 cups (6 oz) shredded Cheddar Cheese
1 cup whipped Whipping Cream

Boil the potatoes until fork-tender. Drain; mash adding in the milk, butter, salt and pepper mix until smooth. Spoon this mixture into a lightly greased 9 x 13" baking dish. Fold the cheese into the whipped cream and spread over the top of the potatoes. Bake 350°F for 25 minutes of until lightly browned.   Serves 8-10

VEG – (Potatoes – Potato Pancakes)

1 cup grated fresh Potatoes
4 Tbsp Flour
1 tsp Baking Powder
1 Egg, lightly beaten
Salt and Pepper to taste

2-1/2 Tbsp grated Onion (or 1/4 cup chopped Leeks)
1/4 cup Milk (or Evaporated Milk)
1/4 cup Vegetable Oil

Grate the potatoes and place in a colander, drain; squeeze out as much water as possible. Place in a bowl and add in all ingredients except the oil. Mix well together. Heat the oil in a skillet and drop batter by the large spoonful into the oil and press down into a circular pancake form. Cook, turning once, until golden brown. Drain on paper towel and salt.

Serves 10

-OR –

VEG – (Potatoes – Potato Pancakes – Leftover Mashed)

Place 2 cups of leftover potatoes into a medium bowl and add in 1 Egg, beaten lightly, 6 Tbsp Flour, 1-1/2 Tbsp grated onion (grated chives if desired). In a lightly oiled skillet or on a griddle (vegetable or melted margarine) place a scoop of the potato batter and down into a circular pancake form. Fry for 1 – 2 minutes on each side removing them to paper towels to drain, cover and keep warm in a preheated oven (250°F).

VEG – (Potatoes – Potato Puffs)

Peel 6 – 8 medium potatoes and cut up into eighths and place in a saucepan with water about 1 inch above the potatoes. Boil until fork tender; drain. Add salt and pepper to taste. Mash the potatoes. (Can use Instant Potatoes if desired). Heat in a double boiler, 1-1/2 cups Half and Half Milk (or a heavy cream) and 1/3 cup of margarine/butter. Fold this into the mashed potatoes, stir well and spoon this into mounds on a buttered casserole dish or greased baking sheet. Bake 350°F until lightly browned.

VEG – (Potatoes – Potato Skins)

5 or 6 Large Potatoes   4 oz grated Colby Cheese   2 oz Sour Cream with Chives

Wash the outside of Russet Baking Potatoes and dry off with a paper towel. Cut off any eyes or discoloration. Place the potatoes on a baking sheet and bake in a 350°F - 400°F oven for one hour for large and 40-45 minutes for medium ones (Microwave uncovered for 6-7 minutes or until fork tender). Cut the potatoes in half and with a spoon remove all except 1/2" thickness of the potato pulp from inside the skin. (Reserve the pulp for other recipes). Arrange the potatoes on a greased baking sheet and sprinkle them evenly with the cheese. Place in the oven and cook until the cheese melts, remove and cut lengthwise into 8 or 9 strips. Serve with a sour cream and chopped chive dipping sauce. **– OR- (Potatoes – Oven Fried Potatoes)**.

VEG – (Potatoes – Rosemary Potatoes)

2 Lbs Red Potatoes, quartered
1/2 cup Olive Oil
1 Tbsp chopped Garlic

2 Tbsp chopped Rosemary (dried or fresh)

In a large pot of boiling, salted water cook the potatoes until just tender; drain well. Place in a bowl and sprinkled on salt and pepper. Then add in the remaining ingredients and coat the outside of the potatoes. Bake the potatoes at 375°F for 25 minutes or until lightly browned.   Serves 6

VEG – (Potatoes – Scalloped Potatoes)

2-1/2 Tbsp Margarine
1 tsp Salt
6 medium-sized Potatoes
1-1/2 cups grated Cheddar Cheese

2-1/2 Tbsp Flour
2 cups Milk
2 Tbsp Minced Onion

Peel and slice thinly the potatoes in rounds. Place a layer of these in a 9"x13" baking dish. Melt the margarine in a saucepan, stir in the flour and salt. Stirring constantly, add in the milk slowly until the sauce comes to a boil and begins to thicken. Add in the cheddar cheese reserving a little for a topping over the casserole. Pour the sauce over the first layer, sprinkle top with cheese and add another layer of potatoes and then more sauce, etc. Complete these layers until you run out, ending up with cheese on top. Place in a moderate oven (350°F) for 30 minutes or until fork tender

VEG – (Potatoes – Shoestring Potato Casserole)

1 Pkg frozen Shoestring Potatoes
1 can Cream of Chicken Soup
Grated Cheddar Cheese

1 can Cream of Mushroom Soup
1/2 Tbsp minced dry Onion Flakes

In a 9" x 13" greased pan, mix the potatoes, soups and onion. Top with cheese. Bake at 350°F for approximately 25 minutes or until soft.

VEG – (Potatoes – Stewed Potatoes)

(This style is not for everyone's taste buds)
Peel and dice 3 or 4 medium potatoes. Add enough water to cover 1-inch above the potatoes and generously salt and pepper. Add in 3 Tbsp Bacon grease and bring to a boil. And cooked until fork tender. If the water has not been reduced to the top of potatoes, drain off some of the water. Remove from the heat and serve.
NOTE: If you do not store left over Bacon Fats, then fry a couple pieces of Bacon and use the drippings.

VEG – (Potatoes – Stuffed Bake–Again Potatoes with Broccoli)

Wash outside of potatoes and dry off with paper toweling. Rub each with a vegetable oil to help them absorb more heat. Pierce each potato and bake microwave on high for 12 minutes, or 425°F for 15 minutes. With oven mitts on, slice the potato in half lengthwise and scoop out the pulp. Mash the pulp adding in salt and pepper to taste. In 2 Tbsp margarine sauté 1 chopped small onion. Add in 1 (10 oz) pkg frozen, thawed, drained, chopped broccoli. Mix the onion, broccoli, potato pulp and 1/2 cup Ranch Salad dressing and 2 tsp dried Parsley together. Mix in either 1cup grated Cheddar or other cheese. Fill the potatoes with the mixture and place on a baking sheet. Bake about 15 minutes until hot. Serve with sour cream. (Extra Recipe)

VEG – (Potatoes – Sweet Potatoes)

Boil or bake the sweet potatoes until quite soft. Peel and mash while hot. (Can use canned sweet potatoes resuming the recipe here), Add in 1/4 pint of Half and Half Milk and 2 mashed ripe Bananas for every 6 potatoes. Mix well, place in a buttered baking dish, cover with miniature marshmallows. Bake 300°F until the marshmallows are browned on the top. **VARIATION: Butterscotch:** For every 2 (16 oz) cans of Yams used combine 1/2 cup firmly packed Brown Sugar, 1/2 cup Corn Syrup, 1/4 cup Whipping Cream, 2 Tbsp Margarine, 1/2 tsp Salt, 1/2 tsp Ground Cinnamon. Pour mixture over canned yams and bake 20 minutes. Serves 6 **HINT: Sweet Potatoes will not turn dark if put in salted water (five teaspoons to one quart of water) immediately after peeling.**

VEG – (Potatoes – Swiss Cheese Potatoes)

Peel and dice potatoes. Salt and pepper to taste. Add 4 Tbsp vegetable oil or melted margarine to a skillet. Place in the potatoes. Cover, and cook until the potatoes are fork tender. Sprinkle over the top 3/4 cup shredded Swiss Cheese and cook until the cheese is melted.

VEG – (Potatoes – Tater Tots)

Prepare and bake Frozen Tater Tots per package direction and serve.

VEG – (Potatoes – Thrice Baked Potatoes)

3 Pounds large firm Baking Potatoes (about 8)
1 (12 oz) container Sour Cream
1/2 cup chopped Green Onions
1 Tbsp Rosemary sprig, chopped
Salt & Pepper to taste

1 Tbsp chopped fresh Basil
12 oz grated Cheddar Cheese
2 Tbsp chopped fresh Parsley
Vegetable Oil

Preheat oven to 350°F and scrub the potatoes and pat dry with paper towels. (Brush outside of potato skin with vegetable oil if you wish these to become crispy). 1) Bake potatoes for 45 minutes. Remove from the oven and place on a cutting board and let cool for 30 minutes. Slice each potato lengthwise in half. Scoop out the potato pulp to form the boat Put the pulp into a large bowl and add sour cream, scallion/onion, basil, rosemary, salt and pepper. 2) Mash and mix together until you have a smooth texture. 3) Fill each potato boat with these mashed potatoes. Sprinkle top with Cheddar Cheese and parsley. Return to oven until cheese has melted - **OR** – place in a covered barbecue and cook for another 15 minutes.   Serves 8

VEG – (Radishes)

Wash well and trim both the top and bottom center of the radish. Radishes will turn into beautiful rose-like flowers if you make four cuts around the center of the radish, almost all the way through to the bottom but not quite.

Place radishes into a bowl of water that has a tsp granulated sugar added to it over night and they will open up. If radishes and other fresh vegetables (i.e., carrots, celery, bell peppers) become wilted and limp. Rinse the vegetables in cool water and wrap inside of paper toweling and place inside of an airtight container in the refrigerator for a couple hours and they will become crispy again.

VEG – (Snow Peas/Sugar – Chinese)

1 Pound Stringed Snow Sugar Peas (Haw-Lon-Dow)
1/2 cup canned Bamboo Shoots, sliced to 1/8" in length
1 cup Mushrooms

1 cup Celery sliced
1 small Diced Onion

Mix together a sauce of **1 Tbsp Soy Sauce, 1 tsp granulated Sugar, and 2 tsp Rice Wine**. Heat 1 Tbsp of vegetable or sesame oil in a Wok or large skillet. Add in 1/3 tsp salt, celery, bamboo shoots, mushrooms, onion, snow peas and Stir-Fry, toss frequently for about 3 minutes. Add in the sauce and cover and let steam a couple minutes or cook till the vegetables are done to your expectations. **Thicken with a paste of 1 Tbsp Cornstarch mixed with 1 Tbsp Water**, stir until warmed and dissolved. **HINT: <u>Always cook these quickly. Can be blanched (put in salted, boiling water for 30 seconds – 1 minute, drain and dump immediately into ice water bath to stop the cooking process and to preserve color. Just toss into salads or stir fry by heating butter and olive oil in your pan, add garlic, salt and pepper and sauté 10-15 seconds because they have already been blanched.</u>**

VEG – (Spinach)

Place the fresh spinach in a pan and cover in "warm" water. This will remove any dirt or sand easier than using cold water. Remove any tough stems. Add 3 Tbsp of bacon grease (If you do not save bacon grease/drippings then fry 2 pieces of bacon in a skillet and use those fats/drippings) or butter in a large skillet and melt. Pick up the wet spinach and place it into the skillet and cook until wilted and tender. Drain excessive water from spinach in a colander and then return it to the skillet and add salt and pepper to taste and more butter/grease if desired.

VEG – (Spinach – Creamed Spinach)

3 Pounds fresh Spinach, stems discarded, coarsely chopped (about 24 packed cups) or frozen and thawed

~ 1 tsp Salt	3 cups heavy Whipping Cream
1/2 cup Margarine/Butter	Pinch of freshly ground (~1/2 tsp) Nutmeg
1-1/2 small Onions, minced (~1 cup)	
Freshly ground Black Pepper	
1 cup Flour	

Wash the spinach and drain in a colander. Don't dry the spinach – leave the water clinging to the leaves. Heat a large, skillet over medium-high heat and melt the margarine/butter (or add 3 Tbsp Bacon Grease) in a large skillet. Add the onion and cook, stirring, until soft, about 4 minutes. Add the wet spinach and cook, stirring occasionally, until wilted and hot (~10 minutes). Transfer the spinach again to a colander and press out as much liquid as possible. Return the spinach and onions to the skillet. Add the flour gradually, stirring constantly. Add the milk, still stirring and cook until evenly blended and hot. Stir in the nutmeg and season with salt and pepper. Cook the spinach, stirring occasionally until most of cream is absorbed into a creamed sauce, about 4 minutes.

VEG – (Spinach – Spinach Balls)

1 Pkg (16 oz) frozen chopped spinach – cooked and drained well	
1 cup Parmesan Cheese	6 Eggs beaten well
3/4 cup Soften Butter/Margarine	Salt and Pepper to taste

2 cups granulated Chicken Flavored Stuffing Mix (easier to handle than the cubed), mixed with water per package directions

Mix all the ingredients and form into balls about golf-ball size (~24, more quantity if made bite-sized). Place these on a baking sheet and freeze. When you need Hors d'Oeuvres, remove from the freezer and cook 350°F for 15 minutes. Serve hot. (**CAN SUBSTITUTE CHOPPED BROCCOLI FOR THE SPINACH**).

VEG – (Squash – Buttered) Any Variety

Wash and slice the squash. Boil it in 1" of salted water above ingredients, until fork tender. Pour off water and stir in 2 Tbsp margarine or butter, coating all the pieces. Salt and Pepper to taste. Can sprinkle top with grated Parmesan Cheese, if desired.

VEG – (Squash and Mushrooms)

Cook squash per above then drain, salt and butter. In a skillet melt 2 Tbsp of butter put in your mushrooms and coat them with the melted butter. Salt and Pepper to taste and sprinkle garlic powder over the tops. Sauté these for 4-5 minutes. Add in the squash and stir together and serve. You can also sprinkle the tops with grated Parmesan Cheese, if desired.

VEG – (Sweet Potatoes or Yams)

Boil or bake the sweet potatoes until quite soft. Peel and mash while hot. (Can use canned sweet potatoes resuming the recipe here), Add in 1/4 pint of Half and Half Milk and 2 mashed ripe Bananas for every 6 potatoes. Mix well, place in a buttered baking dish, cover with miniature marshmallows. Bake 300°F until the marshmallows are browned on the top. **VARIATION**: **Butterscotch:** For every 2 (16 oz) cans of Yams used combine 1/2 cup firmly packed Brown Sugar, 1/2 cup Corn Syrup, 1/4 cup Whipping Cream, 2 Tbsp Margarine, 1/2 tsp Salt, 1/2 tsp Ground Cinnamon. Pour mixture over canned yams and bake 20 minutes.

Serves 6

HINT: 1 cup Marshmallows = 1 cup miniatures or 11-12 Large Marshmallows

VEG – (Tomatoes)

HINT: It's easier to peel a tomato if you dip it into boiling water for one minute, then dip in cold water. Remove the tomato and the skin will be easier to peel. You can ripen tomatoes and fruit by putting these in a paper sack, close and leave at room temperature for a few days. To reduce acidity add 1 tsp Sugar per 8 oz of Tomatoes.

Tomatoes – Broiled

Mix softened butter/margarine into breadcrumbs, add in 1 tsp Oregano. Cut tomatoes in half, spread the cut tops with the breadcrumb mixture. Dip the top into a beaten egg + 1 Tbsp Water and then re-dip in the breadcrumbs. Place these on top of a broiling pan and Broil in a 500°F oven for 5-6 minutes, until mixture is bubbly and browned. **VARIATION: Before broiling sprinkle on Parmesan Cheese.**

Tomatoes – Fried

Wash, peel or not, cut into slices (these are firmer if they are green, but ripe is also ok). Dip into melted butter/margarine and then roll in breadcrumbs and fry in melted butter.   (Extra Recipe)

VEG – (Vegetable Medley Casserole – Cauliflower, Broccoli and Carrots)

1 Pkg (16 oz) frozen Vegetable Blend of Carrots, Broccoli, and Cauliflower
8 oz Sour Cream   4 oz shredded Swiss Cheese
4 oz shredded Cheddar Cheese   8 oz can French Fried Onions
10-3/4 oz Cream of Mushroom Soup

Mix all ingredients together except save 1/2 of the French Fried Onions and 1/2 of the cheese for a topping. Place the mixture of sour cream, cheese, soup, vegetables and onions in a 9"x13" baking dish.   Bake 350°F for 30 minutes. Five minutes before it's done sprinkle on the remaining cheese and onion flakes.
VARIATION: Use celery soup instead of mushroom soup, or chicken soup. **MICROWAVE:** Cook covered with plastic wrap for 8 minutes then top with the remaining cheese and dry onions. Cook uncovered for an additional 2 minutes until the cheese melts.   Serves 6-8

VEG – (Yams)

See recipe for Potatoes (Sweet Potatoes)

VEG – (Zucchini)

Cut both ends off of the Zucchini and wash.. Cut into strips, chunks or grated. Boil it in salted water 1/2" above the vegetables. Drain off the water and salt and pepper to taste. Mix in 2-3 Tbsp of Margarine – **OR**- can be used in Italian Seasoned Sauces.

(Extra Recipe)

Decided for You Cookbook – 365 Dinners

VEG – (Zucchini – Zucchini Bake)

3 cups grated Zucchini
1 cup crushed Saltine Crackers
1/4 cup Parmesan Cheese
3 Tbsp finely chopped Onion

1 cup grated Mozzarella Cheese
2 eggs slightly beaten
Salt and Pepper to taste

Combine all ingredients and place in a 2-quart baking dish. Bake at 350°F for one hour. Serve while very hot.
Serves 4-6

VEG – (Zucchini – Buttered)

Cut both ends off of the Zucchini and wash. Cut into strips, chunks or grated. Boil it in salted water 1/2" above the vegetables. Drain off the water and salt and pepper to taste. Mix in 2-3 Tbsp of Margarine – **OR** – can be used in Italian Seasoned Sauces.

VEG – (Zucchini – Zucchini Fritters)

1-1/2 cups Flour*
3/4 tsp Salt
1 Egg beaten + 1 Tbsp Water
Vegetable Oil for frying

2 tsp Baking Powder
1 cup Milk
1 cup Zucchini, shredded

Mix the flour, baking powder and salt together. Add in the milk, egg, and the zucchini. If more flour is needed, please add and mix again. In hot oil, drop by the tablespoon size and fry 3-4 minutes (golden brown). Serve hot. *After dipping in flour and egg wash can substitute cracker or corn meal, if desired more crispness.

VEGETABLES – MICROWAVE INFORMATION:

HINT: Do not salt before microwaving, sometimes causes brown spots. Most vegetables are cooked while covered tightly. Cook per package direction or general information as follows:
Vegetable Casseroles – 4 to 5 min/Lb
Vegetables in Slices – 11 to 17 min/Lb
Vegetables Watery – Tomatoes, Summer Squash – 4 to 5 min/Lb
Vegetables – Whole, Large or Starchy (i.e., Potato, Squash, Cauliflower etc 12 to 20 min/Lb – Prick before cooking

FINALE SPACE:

Decided for You Cookbook – 365 Dinners

Author's Special Thoughts

Food offers us a wide variety of color, forms and textures. Four of our five senses are employed in the enjoyment of food: Taste, Smell, Touch, and Sight. We eat with our eyes, our nose and our mouth. Garnish your foods with any of the following: Lemon slices, Parsley, fresh Spinach, Tomatoes, Hard-cooked Eggs, Grapes, Red Peppers, Tomatoes, Glazed Onions, Bacon, Fluted Mushrooms, Paprika, Green Onions, Cherries, Grapes, Apple Slice, Orange and Mandarin Slices, Cucumbers, Peaches, Pineapple, Watermelon slices, Radishes, Edible Flowers, Celery Brushes/Fans, Pickle Fans, Chives, Piped Mashed Potatoes into decorative designs, Carrot Curls, and Vegetable Cut-Outs. **If you don't have time to garnish, at least serve your foods in a <u>very attractive</u> dish.**

For every beginner, working mother or stay at home Mom who deserves all the raves they can get! I hope this cookbook teaches you some basics and simple techniques and then you can take the time to experiment with what you have learned.

YOUR REWARDS WILL BE GREAT, AND THEY SHOULD BRING YOU THE PRAISE YOU DESERVE!

If this book is a success, I will follow with others on "Decided For You" <u>Desserts</u> and "Decided For You" <u>Hors d'Oeuvres</u>. Until then, I couldn't resist putting this recipe in here because I know you how rare it is. It is for making Homemade Sweet Condensed Milk at a reasonable expense:

Homemade Sweet Condensed Milk

1 cup Hot Water
2 cups Sugar, granulated
1/4 cup Butter
4 cups Instant Granulated Milk (or 2 cups regular Powdered Milk)

Put sugar and milk into a blender and mix. Heat the water and melt in it the butter. Stir, then pour into the blender and beat until smooth. Divide equally into containers and store indefinitely in a refrigerator. Makes equivalent of two (2) cans of commercially sold Sweet Condensed Milk

Yields 1-1/3 cups

DISCLAIMER: Most of these recipes have been handed down from generation-to-generation or friend-to-friend. Therefore, not personally knowing all of their origin, I am not responsible for any infringement to a second or third party.

STAR RATING INDEX FOR FUTURE MENUS OF CHOICE:
FAVORITES:

1.
2.
3.
4.
5.
6.
7.
8.
9.
10.
11.
12.
13.
14.
15.
16.
17.
18.
19.
20.
21.
22.
23.
24.
25.
26.
27.
28.
29.
30.
31.
32.
33.
34.
35.
36.
37.
38.
39.
40.
41.
42.
43.
44.
45.
46.
47.
48.
49.
50.
51.
52.

Decided for You Cookbook – 365 Dinners

Decided for You Cookbook
Table of Contents

Decided for You Cookbook
Table of Contents

Decided for You Cookbook
Table of Contents

Decided for You Cookbook
Table of Contents

Decided for You Cookbook
Table of Contents

Decided for You Cookbook
Table of Contents

Decided for You Cookbook
Table of Contents

Decided for You Cookbook
Table of Contents

Decided for You Cookbook
Table of Contents

Decided for You Cookbook – 365 Dinners

Decided for You Cookbook
Table of Contents

Decided for You Cookbook
Table of Contents

Decided for You Cookbook
Table of Contents

Decided for You Cookbook
General Index

Decided for You Cookbook
General Index

Decided for You Cookbook – 365 Dinners

Decided for You Cookbook
General Index

Decided for You Cookbook
General Index

Decided for You Cookbook
General Index

Decided for You Cookbook
General Index

Decided for You Cookbook – 365 Dinners